COMPLETE GUIDE TO
CRUISING
& CRUISE SHIPS 2000

by Douglas Ward
President
The Maritime Evaluations Group (MEG)

Berlitz Publishing Company, Inc.

Princeton   Mexico City   Dublin   Eschborn   Singapore

Cover design: Suzanne B. Garfield
Cover photo: *SuperStar Leo*, courtesy of Star Cruises
Layout: Media Content Marketing, Inc.

Although the publisher tries to insure the accuracy of all the information in this book, changes are inevitable and errors may result. The publisher cannot be responsible for any resulting loss, inconvenience, or injury. If you find an error in this guide, please let the editors know by writing to Berlitz Publishing Company, 400 Alexander Park, Princeton, NJ 08540-6306.

ISBN 2-8315-7207-X

Printed in Canada

Publisher's Note: The Maritime Evaluations Group (MEG) has evaluated cruise ships since 1980, issuing annual reports on the world's best cruise fleet. All professional opinions and ratings are strictly those of the author and not of the publisher, Berlitz, which makes this survey available in bookstores.

CONTENTS

STOP PRESS

The very nature of a book such as this, which contains so much factual information, is subject to constant change, just as many parts of the cruise industry itself constantly change. The book is up-to-date and as accurate as possible, until July 1999, when it was completed, although last-minute changes received are noted below.

→ American Cruise Lines, a new company (resurrected from a former company with the same name), has placed an order for a new 49-passenger coastal cruise vessel, to be named *American Eagle*. The ship is scheduled to be in service between Maine and Florida (east coast of the US) in April 2000. The new ship announcement arrived too late to be included in the Ships to Debut Chart on page 520.

→ Carnival Cruise Lines will reposition its *Inspiration* to New Orleans for year-round cruises beginning September 24, 2000. Meanwhile, *Carnival Destiny* will move to San Juan for year-round cruises beginning September 17, 2000.

→ Carnival Cruise Lines announced a program of complete revision of its menus and wine lists when I had completed this edition. This should affect the ratings in a positive way. Also, the company has placed more ships into year-round short-cruise operation: *Fantasy* (3/4 night cruises from Port Canaveral); *Holiday* (three- and four-night cruises from Los Angeles); *Imagination* (four- and five-night cruises from Miami); *Tropicale* (four- and five-night cruises from Tampa).

→ Coastal Cruise Line, a new division of the Delta Queen Steamboat Company, has ordered two 266-passenger ships for delivery in March and June 2001. The announcement arrived too late to be included in the Ships to Debut Chart on page 520.

→ Costa Cruises announced a plan to lengthen the sister ships *CostaClassica* and *CostaRomantica* by 146.9 ft (44.8 m) in order to increase capacity, add an additional deck, as well as to add some balcony cabins. The ship would increase from 55,000-tonnes to approximately 75,000-tonnes, and add an estimated 370 additional cabins.

→ Cunard Line's *Queen Elizabeth 2* will undergo an extensive $31.3 million, one-month-long refit and interior refurbishment in late 1999, which includes replacement of much of the soft furnishings and the addition of three new luxury suites (named *Aquitania, Caledonia*, and *Carinthia*, after former Cunard ships). The Queens Grill will receive new lighting, new upholstery, new etched glass doors, and a complete re-build of the galley. The Princess Grill will receive a redesign and refurbishment. The Britannia Grill will receive a new enhanced table layout for better dining comfort. The Caronia Restaurant will be redesigned to create an English country house feel with rich mahogany paneling. The Mauretania Restaurant will receive chandeliers, glass doors, and new furnishings. Additionally, several public rooms will receive a complete makeover, 106 cabin bathrooms not complete during the 1994 refit will be replaced, and the ship will receive teak "steamer" deck lounge chairs to replace the existing deck furniture.

→ Cunard Line's *Vistafjord* was scheduled to undergo a refit and interior refurbishment in late 1999, with a name change to *Caronia*.

→ Since being taken over by Carnival Corporation, standards aboard Cunard ships have been cut. Passengers are now even asked to pay for their own drinks at Bon Voyage parties.

→ Golden Sun Cruises will take delivery of Mediterranean Shipping cruises' *Symphony* in March 2000. The ship will be renamed *Aegean Odyssey*.

→ Norwegian Cruise Line's recently lengthened *Norwegian Majesty* now features three- and four-night cruises from Miami during the winter season, and seven-night Boston–Bermuda cruises during the summer.

→ Orient Lines will take delivery of its second ship, *Crown Odyssey* (the former *Norwegian Crown*) from Norwegian Cruise Line in June 2000.

→ P&O Cruises and Princess Cruises have jointly placed an order for five new ships (with options for three further ships). Two ships, of 110,000 tonnes, for 2,600 passengers, will be built by Mitsubishi in Japan, and operated by Princess Cruises. Two further ships, of 88,000 tonnes, for 1,950 passengers, will be built by Chantiers de l'Atlantique in France, and operated by Princess

Cruises. The fifth ship, of 110,000 tonnes, for 2,600 passengers, will be built by Fincantieri in Italy, and operated by P&O Cruises. The announcement regarding the new ships arrived too late to be included in the Ships to Debut Chart on page 520.

→ Princess Cruises will move the steam turbine-powered *Sky Princess* to its sister (and parent) company P&O Cruises, whose P&O Holidays division will operate the ship in Australia, replacing the ancient *Fair Princess*, which will be withdrawn. *Sky Princess* will be renamed *Pacific Sky* and is due to take up her new role in November 2000.

→ Royal Caribbean International's new *Voyager of the Seas* (the world's largest cruise ship) even has its own US zip code (postal code): FL 33101-9645.

→ Seabourn Cruise Line's *Royal Viking Sun* will undergo an extensive $15 million refit and interior refurbishment in late 1999, and her name will be changed to *Seabourn Sun*. The company also announced plans to add balcony cabins to *Seabourn Legend*, *Seabourn Pride*, and *Seabourn Spirit*.

FROM THE AUTHOR

Ever since my first transatlantic crossing, in July 1965, aboard Cunard Line's 83,673-tonne ocean liner RMS *Queen Elizabeth* (then the largest passenger ship in the world), I have been captivated by passenger ships and the sea. More than 4,300 days at sea, involving participation in over 820 cruises, 147 transatlantic crossings, and countless Panama Canal transits, shipyard visits, ship christenings, maiden voyages, and ships later, I am even more fascinated by and absorbed in every aspect of cruising and cruise ships.

So don't be land bound when you can be cruise bound! Speak to anyone who has taken a cruise — they'll be enthusiastic in their praise. So will you — that is, *if* **you choose the** *right* **ship, for the** *right* **reasons**. That brings me to the purpose of this book. It is intended to be a comprehensive source of information about cruising and the ships that offer to take you away from the pressures, stresses, and confines of daily life ashore.

When you first look into taking a cruise, you will be confronted by an enormous and bewildering choice. Don't panic. Simply read through this book carefully. At the end you will be nearer to making the right choice and you will leave for your cruise as well informed as most specialists in the industry! In fact, any professional cruise sales agent will find this book a valuable reference source about ships and cruising.

The book is divided into two sections. Part One introduces you to the world of cruising, helps you define what you are looking for in a cruise vacation and what kind of accommodation to choose, and provides valuable advice on what to know before you go. It provides a look at life aboard ship and how to get the best from it; the cuisine; nautical terminology; amusing anecdotes; the ship's hierarchy; and advice about going ashore. Alternative cruises, such as expedition cruises, sail-cruise ships, coastal and river cruises, and freighters, are discussed, too, culminating with that ultimate travel experience: the around-the-world cruise.

Part Two contains profiles of 241 oceangoing cruise vessels. From large to small, from unabashed luxury to ships for the budget-minded, old and new, they are all here. The ratings and evaluations are a painstaking documentation of my personal work. I travel constantly throughout the world; indeed, I am "on the road" for more than nine months each year.

Use the ratings according to your personal tastes and preferences. If cuisine is important to you, or your concern is for entertainment, then these aspects of the ratings will be more significant for you than the overall score or number of stars achieved. The attraction of cruising is in the variety of products and choices available. This book is intended to help you make informed decisions, given the enormous differences between ships, service standards, and cruise lines today.

This book is a tribute to everyone who has made my seafaring experiences possible, and a thank-you to all the cruise lines for their cooperation.

Douglas Ward
July 1999

The evaluations of cruise ships in this book have been made objectively without bias, partiality, or prejudice. In almost all instances, the ships have been visited recently by the author or one of his team in order to update earlier ratings or to assess current status. Passenger comments and feedback are also taken into account in the final evaluations.

Most of the statistical information contained in the profiles in Part Two was supplied and checked by the cruise lines and shipowners. Any errors or updated information should be sent to the author at the address below.

The author's cruise and ship inspection schedule means that he is very seldom on land. He regrets that he will not answer any letters that do not include full return postage, or letters that seek information or telephone/fax numbers of cruise lines. Further, note that absolutely no correspondence will be entered into regarding the ship ratings and evaluations.

Mr. Douglas Ward
Berlitz Guide to Cruising
Canada House
1 Carrick Way
New Milton
Hampshire BH25 6UD
ENGLAND

WHY TAKE A CRUISE?

WHY IS A CRUISE VACATION SO POPULAR?

Well over eight million people cannot be wrong (that's how many people took a cruise last year)! Cruising is popular today because it takes one away from the pressures and strains of contemporary life by offering an escape from reality. Cruise ships are really self-contained resorts, without the crime, which can take you to several destinations in the space of just a few days.

The sea has always been a source of adventure, excitement, romance, and wonder. It is beneficial and therapeutic, and, because you pay in advance, you know what you will spend on your vacation without any hidden surprises. There is no traffic (except when you go ashore in ports of call), and no pollution. The hassles of ordinary travel are almost eliminated in one pleasant little package. It's no wonder that 85 percent of passengers want to go again. And again. And again.

Warning: Cruising Is Addictive!

ISN'T CRUISING EXPENSIVE?

Cruising can be an all-inclusive vacation (or almost all-inclusive). If you compare what it would cost on land to have all your meals and entertainment provided, as well as transportation, fitness and sports facilities, social activities, educational talks, parties, and other functions, you will soon realize the incredible value of a cruise. Further, a ship is a destination in itself, which moves to other destinations. No land-based resort could ever do that! Finally, give yourself a vacation budget, and go to your professional travel agent with it. The rest, as they say, will be taken care of.

JUST WHO TAKES A CRUISE?

Those who are single, couples, families with children of all ages (including single parents and grandparents), honeymooners, second- or third-time honeymooners, groups of friends, and college buddies are all passengers. In fact, today's passengers are probably your next-door neighbors.

WHERE CAN I GO ON A CRUISE?

There are over 30,000 cruises to choose from each year, and 500-plus destinations in the world. A cruise can also take you to places inaccessible by almost any other means, such as Antarctica, the North Cape, the South Sea islands, and so on.

BUT ISN'T CRUISING FOR WRINKLY OLD PEOPLE?

Nothing could be further from the truth. Indeed, the average age of passengers gets younger each year. Although those of silver years have found cruising to be a very safe way to travel the world, the average age of first-time passengers is now well under 40. But do remember that even wrinkly old people can have fun, too, and many of them have more get-up-and-go than many people under the age of 40!

SEVEN-DAY CRUISES ARE OFTEN ADVERTISED FOR $400 PER PERSON. IS THIS TOO GOOD TO BE TRUE?

As a rule, yes! Consider that a decent hotel room in New York costs at least $200 per night (plus taxes) *without meals,* it stands to reason that something is not quite as it seems. Before booking, read the fine print. Look at the additional costs such as tips to cabin and dining room stewards, shore excursions, drinks (plus a 15 percent gratuity), plus getting to and from the ship. That $400 per person could well be for a four-berth cabin adjacent to the ship's laundry or above the disco, but in any event, not in a desirable location (just like a $20 hotel room in New York).

WON'T I GET BORED?

Usually it's men who ask this. But get them aboard, and it is almost guaranteed that there won't be enough time in the day to do all the things they want to do (as long as you choose the right ship, for the right reasons). So, whether you want to lie back and be pampered, or go nonstop, you can do it on a cruise vacation, and you will only have to pack and unpack once.

1

WHY DOES IT COST MORE TO CRUISE IN EUROPE AND THE FAR EAST THAN IN THE CARIBBEAN?

The answer is twofold:

1) Almost all aspects of operations, including fuel costs, port charges, air transportation, supplying food to the ships, are much higher.

2) Cruise companies can make more money (called yield) than in the cut-price Caribbean, where sun, sea, and sand are the principal attractions, whereas sight-seeing, architecture, culture, and other things are part of a more enriching cruise experience.

CAN I LEARN ABOUT COMPUTERS WHILE ON A CRUISE?

Absolutely. Crystal Cruises, Cunard, and Seabourn Cruise Line are just three examples of cruise companies that provide computers and lectures. Indeed, the Computer Learning Center aboard the *Queen Elizabeth 2* is always full. And, unlike learning centers on land, this one serves caviar and smoked salmon to its participants.

IS CRUISING FOR SINGLES?

Yes, indeed. A cruise vacation is ideal for people traveling alone (over 25 percent of all passengers are solo travelers), because it is easy to meet other people in a noncompetitive environment. Many ships also have special cabins for singles as well as special add-on rates for single occupancy of double cabins. Some cruise lines will even find a cabin mate for you to share with, if you so desire.

ARE CRUISES FOR HONEYMOONERS?

Absolutely! In fact, a cruise is the ideal setting for romance, for shipboard weddings (these can be arranged in some ports, depending on local regulations), receptions, and honeymoons. Most decisions are already made for you so all you have to do is show up. Most ships have accommodation in double-, queen-, or king-sized beds, too. And for those on a second honeymoon, many ships now perform a "renewal of vows" ceremony (some ships charge for this, some do not).

ARE CRUISES FOR CHILDREN, TOO?

Oh, yes! In fact, a cruise provides families with more quality time than any other type of vacation (family cruising is the largest growth segment in the cruise industry). Activities are tailored to various age groups (even Disney has special cruise ships). In addition, a cruise is educational, allows children to interact in a safe, crime-free environment, and takes them to destinations in comfortable and familiar surroundings. In fact, kids have such a good time aboard ship and ashore, you will have difficulty getting them home after the cruise (if you choose the right ship). And you as parents (or single parent) will get time to enjoy life, too.

CAN I FIND A QUIET, SERENE CRUISE, AWAY FROM CHILDREN AND NOISE?

Yes, indeed. If you don't like crowds, noise, long lines, there are some beautiful small ships ready to cater to your every whim. Perhaps a sail-cruise vessel or a river or barge cruise could also provide the right antidote. There are so many choices.

IS THERE A CRUISE WITH NO PORTS OF CALL?

Yes, but it is not really a cruise. It is a transatlantic *crossing*, from New York (United States) to Southampton (England) aboard Cunard Line's *QE2*. While I have been advising cruise lines for years that a ship doing occasional three-, four-, or seven-day cruises to nowhere would be most welcome for many repeat passengers, no cruise line has yet taken the initiative. Many passengers are so "allergic" to places that are tourist rip-off destinations that they really want nothing more than to be aboard a ship at sea, with all the creature comforts of home.

ARE THERE DIFFERENT CLASSES ABOARD SHIP?

Not any more. Gone are the class distinctions and the pretensions of formality of the past. Differences are now found mainly in the type of accommodation chosen, in the price you pay for a larger cabin (or suite), and the location of your cabin (or suite).

ISN'T IT DIFFICULT TO FIND ONE'S WAY AROUND LARGE SHIPS?

Well, it can take at least a few hours, or a day or so. However, in general, remember that decks are horizontal, stairs are vertical. The rest comes naturally, with practice.

CAN I GO SHOPPING IN PORTS OF CALL?

Yes, you can. Many passengers engage in "retail therapy" when visiting ports of call such as Hong Kong, Singapore, St. Martin, and St. Thomas, among so many others. Just remember that you will have to carry all those purchases home at the end of your cruise, as the luggage companies know well enough.

AREN'T ALL SHIPS AND CRUISES SIMILAR?

Indeed, no, far from it! Look through this book and you will see that ships range from under 200 feet (60.9 meters) to over 1,000 feet (304.8 meters) in length. They carry from under 100 to almost 4,000 passengers; facilities, food, and service vary according to the size of the ship. Ambience ranges from ultra-casual to very formal (starchy and reserved). Entertainment ranges from amateur dramatics to full-fledged high-tech production shows, from the corner cabaret to a world-famous headliner, and everything in between.

AS A REPEAT PASSENGER WHO LIKES LARGE SHIPS, I FIND IT DIFFICULT TO GET AWAY FROM CONSTANT NOISE. WHAT DO YOU SUGGEST?

I understand your problem. Simply contact the hotel manager and let him (or her) know that the volume level is unacceptable and to please do something about it. If enough people do this, things will have to change for the better. Or take earplugs!

AS A REPEAT PASSENGER, I'VE NOTICED STANDARDS DROPPING. WHY?

Well, prices are the same as ten years ago, but operational and crew costs have risen considerably. Somewhere along the line, something has to give. It is usually in the small details that cruise lines think passengers will not notice, like standards!

WHAT IF I DON'T LIKE IT?

I'm almost certain that you *will* enjoy your cruise vacation. Two companies — Carnival Cruise Lines and Renaissance Cruises — have a *Vacation Guarantee* that states that if you do not like the cruise, the ship, or other aspect of the vacation, you can disembark in the first port of call, and the line will return all your money. Now, that's an excellent guarantee that less than one-tenth of 1 percent of its passengers take up. All other lines should follow these examples.

WHERE TO?

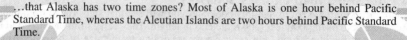

DID YOU KNOW...?

...that Alaska has two time zones? Most of Alaska is one hour behind Pacific Standard Time, whereas the Aleutian Islands are two hours behind Pacific Standard Time.

...that the Pacific Ocean has a tide of 22 feet (6.7 meters) and the Atlantic Ocean has a tide of only 8 inches (20.3 centimeters)?

...that the Wallace Line is not a new cruise company, but the scientific demarcation separating Asia and Oceania?

...that the average time for a ship to pass through the Panama Canal is eight hours? The fastest transit time was set by the uss *Manley* at 4 hours and 38 minutes.

With so many destinations available to cruise ships, there is almost certainly a ship to take you wherever you want to go. Because itineraries vary widely, depending on each ship and cruise, it is wise to make as many comparisons as you can by reading the cruise brochures for descriptions of the ports of call.

Several ships may offer the same or similar itineraries simply because these have been successfully tried and tested. Narrow the choice further by noting the time spent at each port, and whether the ship actually docks in port or lies at anchor. Then, compare the size of each vessel and its facilities.

CARIBBEAN CRUISES

There are over 7,000 islands in the Caribbean Sea, although many are small or uninhabited. Caribbean cruises are usually destination-intensive cruises in a warm, sunny climate that cram between four and eight ports into one week, depending on whether you sail from a Florida port or from a port already in the Caribbean, such as Barbados or San Juan. This means you could be visiting at least one port a day, with little time at sea for relaxation. This kind of "island hopping" leaves little time to explore a destination before you have to be back on board. Although you see a lot of places in a week, by the end of the cruise you may need another week to unwind. *Note*: June to November is hurricane season in the Caribbean.

→ **Eastern Caribbean** cruises typically include ports such as Barbados, Dominica, Martinique, Puerto Rico, St. Croix, St. Kitts, St. Martin, and St. Thomas.

→ **Western Caribbean** cruises typically include ports such as Calica, Cozumel, Grand Cayman, and Playa del Carmen.

→ **Southern Caribbean** cruises typically include ports such as Antigua, Aruba, Barbados, La Guaira (Caracas), and Grenada.

PRIVATE ISLANDS

Several cruise lines featuring Bahamas/Caribbean itineraries have a "private island" (also called an "out-island"). This is a small island in the Bahamas close to Nassau (or the Turks and Caicos Islands) outfitted with all the ingredients to make an all-day beach party a "nice day out." Also available are water sports, scuba, snorkeling, crystal-clear waters, warm sands, even a hammock or two. There are no reservations to make, no tickets to buy, and no hassles with taxis.

Norwegian Cruise Line was the first to feature a private island in 1977. But today, Disney Cruise Line, whose first ship debuted in July 1998, has the most extensive facilities of all on its private island (which is wholly owned, not leased, like most).

Some private islands change names depending on the day of the week, and what ship is in. Beaches that look idyllic for 200 passengers can prove extremely noisy and crowded with 2,000 or more pas-

Courtesy Douglas Ward

Arguably, sun and sea are best enjoyed on a private island.

sengers from a large ship anchored for a "Beach Barbecue." Cruise lines have their own names for these islands, such as *Blue Lagoon Island* (Premier Cruise Lines), *Castaway Cay* (Disney Cruise Line), *Coco Cay* (Royal Caribbean International), *Little Stirrup Cay* (Norwegian Cruise Line), *Half Moon Cay* (Holland America Line), *Princess Cays* (Princess Cruises), and *Serena Cay* (Costa Cruises).

One bonus is that a "private island" will not be cluttered with hawkers and hustlers, as are so many Caribbean beaches. And, because they *are* private, there is security, and no fear of passengers being mugged, as occurs in some islands.

Private island beach days are not all-inclusive, however, and attract high prices for snorkel gear (and mandatory swim vest), pleasure craft, and "banana" boat fun rides; it has become yet another way for cruise lines to increase revenue. However, it costs a lot of money to develop a private island. Examples: Disney Cruise Line spent $25 million developing and outfitting Castaway Cay (formerly known as Gorda Cay), while Holland America Line spent $16 million developing Half Moon Cay.

EUROPE/MEDITERRANEAN CRUISES

Traveling within Europe (including the Baltic, Black Sea, Mediterranean, and Norwegian fjord areas) makes economic sense. European/Mediterranean cruises are popular because:

→ Many of Europe's major cosmopolitan cities — Amsterdam, Barcelona, Copenhagen, Genoa, Helsinki, Lisbon, London, Monte Carlo, Nice, Oslo, St. Petersburg, Stockholm, and Venice — are on the water. It is far less expensive to take a cruise than to fly and stay in decent hotels (and have to pay for food and transport).

→ You will not have to try to speak or understand different languages when you are aboard ship as you would ashore (if you choose the right ship).

→ Aboard ship you use a single currency.

→ A wide variety of shore excursions are available.

→ Lecture programs provide you with insights before stepping ashore. Small ships are arguably better than large ships, as they can obtain berthing space (large ships may have to anchor in more of the smaller ports, so it can take time to get to and from shore — a frustrating inconvenience). Note that many Greek islands are only accessible by shore tender. When looking at itineraries, one company may give you more time ashore than another company, so compare the brochures.

ALASKA CRUISES

For a real cold rush, try an Alaskan cruise. They are popular because:

→ They offer the best way to see Alaska's magnificent shoreline and glaciers.

→ It is a vast, relatively unexplored region.

→ There is a wide range of shore excursions to choose from, including many floatplane and helicopter tours.

→ There is an extensive array of excursions to add to your cruise. These can include "dome car" rail journeys to Denali National Park to see North America's highest peak — Mt. McKinley.

→ Pre- and post-cruise journeys to Banff and Jasper National Parks can be made from Vancouver.

There are two popular cruise routes:

→ **The Inside Passage Route**, which usually includes visits to tidewater glaciers, such as those found in Glacier Bay's Hubbard Glacier or Tracy Arm (just two of the fifteen active glaciers along the 62-mile-long Glacier Bay coastline). Typical ports of call might include Juneau, Ketchikan, Skagway, and Haines.

→ **The Glacier Route**, which usually includes the Gulf of Alaska during a seven-day, one-way cruise between Vancouver and Anchorage. Typical ports of call might include Seward, Sitka, and Valdez.

Two of the major cruise lines, Holland America Line and Princess Cruises, have such comprehensive facilities ashore (hotels, tour buses, and even trains) that they are committed to Alaska for many years. Holland America Line-Westours and Princess Tours (a division of Princess Cruises), have, between them, invested over $300 million in Alaska; Holland America Line-Westours is the state's largest private employer. Other lines depend on what's left of the local transportation for their land tours. In 1998, Holland America Line took 196,000 passengers to Alaska, while Princess Cruises took 165,000.

Some ships anchor rather than dock in some ports of call, due to the limited amount of docking space. Many cruise brochures unfortunately do not indicate which ports are known to be anchor (tender) ports.

Sadly, there is now so much congestion in many of the small Alaska ports (more than 400,000 passengers visited Alaska in 1999), where several large ships may be in port on any given day, that avoiding crowded streets is an unpleasant part of the cruise experience. Even nature is retreating;

with more humans around, wildlife is becoming harder to spot. And some of the same shops can now be found in Alaska as well as in the Caribbean.

For those of a more adventurous nature, consider one of the more unusual Alaska cruises to the far north, around the Pribilof Islands (superb for bird watching) and into the Bering Sea.

TRANSCANAL CRUISES

Transcanal cruises take you through the Panama Canal, constructed by the United States after the failure of a French effort started by Ferdinand de Lesseps. The French labored for twenty years, beginning in 1880, but disease and financial problems defeated them. The United States took over the building effort in 1904 and the waterway opened just ten years later on August 15, 1914. The Panama Canal runs from northwest to southeast, and the best way to experience this engineering wonder is from the deck of a cruise ship. Control of the canal passes from the US government to Panama in 2000.

Cruising from the Caribbean to the Pacific, a ship is lifted 85 feet (26 meters) in a continuous flight of three steps at Gatun Locks to Gatun Lake through which it will travel to Gaillard Cut where the Canal slices through the Continental Divide. It will be lowered at Pedro Miguel Locks 31 feet (9.4 meters) in one step to Miraflores Lake, then the remaining two steps to sea level at Miraflores Locks before passing into the Pacific Ocean. Ships move through the locks under their own power guided by towing locomotives. The 50-mile (80 kilometers) trip across the Isthmus of Panama takes about 9 hours.

Panama Canal cruises typically depart from Ft. Lauderdale or San Juan, calling at one or two Caribbean islands before entering the canal and ending in Acapulco, Los Angeles, or San Francisco.

AUSTRALASIA AND ORIENT CRUISES

If you like the idea of Australasia, Southeast Asia, and the Orient and you live in Europe or North America, be aware that the flying time to get to your port of embarkation and ship will be long. It is advisable to arrive at least two days before the cruise, as time changes and jet lag can be severe. The area has so much to offer that it is worth taking a cruise of at least fourteen days to make the most of it.

Choose an itinerary that appeals to you, and then read about the proposed destinations and their attractions. Your cruise or travel agent will be able to provide some of the essential background on destinations and help you select an itinerary. Australia, New Zealand, the islands of the South Pacific, Hong Kong, China, Japan, Indonesia, Malaysia, Singapore, and Thailand offer superb cruise destinations.

WHERE TO?

Today's cruise ships do indeed roam all over the world. For the sake of simplicity, some of the major cruise areas are grouped together on the following pages, together with the names of the companies and, in most cases, the cruise lines that will take you there.

Cruise lines with several ships tend to switch ships to operate certain itineraries from year to year; thus, the names of ships are not provided. When it was compiled, the list was as accurate as it was possible to make it, given the fact that many companies had not released their full itineraries for 2000.

WHEN IS THE BEST CRUISE SEASON?

MONTH	Alaska	Amazon	Antarctica	Arctic/Greenland	Around Great Britain	Around South America	Australia/New Zealand	Bahamas	Bermuda	Black Sea	Caribbean
January		★	★			★	◎	★			★
February		★	★			★	★	★			★
March		★				★	★	★			★
April								★		★	★
May					★			★	★	★	★
June	★				★			◇	★	★	◇
July	★			★	★			◇	★	★	◇
August	★				★			◇	★	★	◇
September	★				★			◇	★	◇	◇
October						★	★	◇	★		◇
November			★			★	★	◇			◇
December		★	★			★	◎	★			★

Key:

★ = this is the best cruise season

◇ = this is hurricane season, which can mean unpredictable weather patterns in this region

◎ = this is cyclone season, which can mean unpredictable weather patterns in this region

Egypt/Israel	Galapagos Islands	Mediterranean	Mexican Riviera/US West Coast	New England/Canada	North Cape/Norwegian Fjords/Iceland	Northwest Passage	Red Sea/East Africa/Indian Ocean	South Pacific	Southeast Asia	US East Coast	World Cruises
★		★					★	✪	★		★
★		★					★	✪	★		★
★		★					★		★		★
★	★							★			★
	★							★		★	
	★				★			★		★	
	★			★		★		★		★	
	★		★	★	★			★		★	
	★		★					★		★	
★	★		★				★		★	★	
★		★					★		★		
★		★					★	✪	★		★

WHERE TO?

Key:
X = Frequent and infrequent calls
Y = Year-round calls

See NOTES on page 16

	Alaska	Amazon	Antarctica	Arabian Gulf (Red Sea)	Around Africa	Around Britain	Around South America	Around the World	Atlantic Isles (Canary Isles/Madeira)	Australia/New Zealand/South Pacific
Abercrombie & Kent	X		X					X		X
Airtours (Sun Cruises)									X	
Alaska Sightseeing/Cruise West	X									
American Canadian Caribbean Line										
American Hawaii Cruises										
Arcalia Shipping/Classic International Cruises										
Arkona Touristik				X				X		
Canaveral Cruise Line										
Canodros										
Carnival Cruise Lines	X									
Celebrity Cruises	X						X			
Classical Cruises										
Clipper Cruise Line	X	X	X			X		X		
Club Med Cruises									X	
Commodore Cruise Line										
Compagnie des Isles du Ponant			X							
Costa Cruises									X	
Croatia Cruise Lines										
Crown Cruise Lines										
Crystal Cruises	X	X					X	X	X	X
Cunard Line		X					X	X	X	X
Curnow Shipping							X			
Delphin Seereisen		X						X	X	
Direct Cruises										
Disney Cruise Line										
Dolphin Hellas Cruises										
Far East Shipping										Y
Festival Cruises/First European Cruises									X	
Fred Olsen Cruise Lines		X			X				X	
Galapagos Cruises										
Golden Sun Cruises										
Hapag-Lloyd Seetouristik	X	X	X	X	X	X	X	X		X
Hebridean Island Cruises							X			
Holland America Line	X						X	X	X	X
Hyundai Merchant Marine										

Bahamas	Bermuda (summer season contract)	Canada/New England	Caribbean	Chilean Fjords/Patagonia	Europe (Eastern, including Black Sea)	Europe (Mediterranean)	Galapagos Islands	Greek Islands	Hawaii	Indian Ocean	Mexican Riviera (3,4, and 7-day cruises)	North Cape/Baltic Sea	Northwest Passage	South America (east coast)	Southeast Asia	Tahiti and surrounding islands	Transatlantic Crossing	Charter/Roaming Ships
				X	X	X	Y					X						
			X		X	X				X							X	
		X	X												X			
									Y									
			X			X						X	X					
		X	X		X	X											X	
Y																		
							Y											
Y		X	Y						X		Y							
Y	X	Y			X	X		X						X			X	
			X			X												
		X	X	X		X							X	X				
			X													X	X	
			Y															
			X			X		X										
			X		X	X		X						X			X	
					X	X												
	X		X															
		X	X								X	X		X	X	X	X	
		X	X			X					X	X		X	X	X	X	
		X	X											X	X			
			X			X												
Y																		
					X	X		X										
																Y		
		X	X		X	X		X									X	
		X	X			X								X	X		X	
				Y														
					X	X												
		X	X		X	X		X	X	X				X	X	X	X	
Y		X	Y			X		X						X	X	X	X	
																Y		

WHERE TO?

	Alaska	Amazon	Antarctica	Arabian Gulf (Red Sea)	Around Africa	Around Britain	Around South America	Around the World	Atlantic Isles (Canary Isles/Madeira)	Australia/New Zealand/South Pacific
Imperial Majesty Cruise Line										
K&O Cruises										
Kristina Cruises										
Leisure Cruises						X	X	X		
Louis Cruise Lines										
Majestic International Cruises										
Mano Cruises										
Marine Expeditions	X	X	X				X			
Mediterranean Shipping Cruises					X					
Metropolitan Touring										
Mitsui OSK Lines								X		
Nina Cruise Line										
Noble Caledonia				X	X		X			
Norwegian Capricorn Line										Y
Norwegian Cruise Line	X									
NYK Cruise Line								X		X
Orient Lines				X				X		X
P&O Cruises					X				X	X
P&O Holidays										Y
Paquet Cruises										
Paradise Cruises										
Peace Boat								X		
Phoenix Seereisen	X	X		X	X		X	X	X	X
plantours & Partner		X			X	X		X	X	
Premier Cruise Lines										
Primexpress Cruises										
Princess Cruises	X	X					X	X	X	X
Quark Expeditions			X							
Radisson Seven Seas Cruises				X	X		X	X	X	Y
Raymond & Whitcomb							X			
Regal Cruises								X		
Renaissance Cruises										
Royal Caribbean International	X						X			X
Royal Hispania Cruises									X	
Royal Olympic Cruises		X			X			X		

Bahamas	Bermuda (summer season contract)	Canada/New England	Caribbean	Chilean Fjords/Patagonia	Europe (Eastern, including Black Sea)	Europe (Mediterranean)	Galapagos Islands	Greek Islands	Hawaii	Indian Ocean	Mexican Riviera (3,4, and 7-day cruises)	North Cape/Baltic Sea	Northwest Passage	South America (east coast)	Southeast Asia	Tahiti and surrounding islands	Transatlantic Crossing	Charter/Roaming Ships
Y																		Y
												X						
				X		X						X		X			X	
						X	X											
						X												
						X												
				X									X	X				
			X		X	X				X		X				X		
							Y											
																Y		X
			Y															
				X	X	X		X				X				X		
Y	X	X	Y			X			X							X		
											X					Y		
				X		X		X			X		X	X				X
		X	X			X		X			X	X						X
				X		X						X						X
						Y												
																		X
		X	X			X		X			X	X		X				
			X			X		X				X					X	
Y		X	Y			X								X			X	
																		X
Y	X	X	Y			X					X	X	X	X	X		X	
				X									X	X				
			X	X		X		X			X			X	X	Y	X	
								X										
		X	X															
						Y		X								Y		
Y	X	X	Y			X			X	X	Y	X			X		X	
						X												
		X				X								X				

WHERE TO?

	Alaska	Amazon	Antarctica	Arabian Gulf (Red Sea)	Around Africa	Around Britain	Around South America	Around the World	Atlantic Isles (Canary Isles/Madeira)	Australia/New Zealand/South Pacific
Saga Shipping								X		
Sea Cloud Cruises										
Seabourn Cruise Line	X	X					X	X	X	X
Seetours		X						X	X	X
Silversea Cruises		X						X	X	X	X
Society Expeditions	X		X				X	X		
Lindblad Special Expeditions	X									
Star Clippers									X	
Star Cruises										X
Star Line Cruises/African Safari Club										
Sun Cruises										
Swan Hellenic Cruises					X		X			
Tall Ship Adventures										
Thomson Cruises					X				X	
Transocean Tours	X	X					X	X	X	X
Union-Castle Line					X					
Venus Cruise	X									X
Windjammer Barefoot Cruises										
Windstar Cruises										X
World Cruise Company									Y	
World Explorer Cruises	X									

Bahamas	Bermuda (summer season contract)	Canada/New England	Caribbean	Chilean Fjords/Patagonia	Europe (Eastern, including Black Sea)	Europe (Mediterranean)	Galapagos Islands	Greek Islands	Hawaii	Indian Ocean	Mexican Riviera (3,4, and 7-day cruises)	North Cape/Baltic Sea	Northwest Passage	South America (east coast)	Southeast Asia	Tahiti and surrounding islands	Transatlantic Crossing	Charter/Roaming Ships
						X		X		X					X		X	
		X				X											X	
		X	X			X		X	X	X		X		X	X		X	
		X	X			X						X		X	X		X	X
		X	X	X		X		X		X		X		X	X		X	
				X														
					Y		Y											
		X				X									X		X	
																Y		
						X				X								
																Y		
								X		X	X							
		X																
		X				X		X									X	
X	X					X		X		X				X	X		X	
																Y		
	Y																	
	Y					X									X		X	

NOTES FOR WHERE TO? CHART

Bahamas: Only those ships that feature year-round cruises to the Bahamas are included.

Bermuda (summer): Only the five cruise lines (featuring five ships) that have long-term Bermuda government contracts for weekly summer season cruises to Bermuda are listed here, although several other companies operate cruises that include Bermuda infrequently throughout the year.

New England/Canada: These cruises are typically seven-day northbound voyages between New York and Montreal or southbound voyages from Montreal to New York. Of course, these can be combined to make a 14-day round-trip voyage.

Caribbean: Note that there are several more companies than those listed here whose ships visit the Caribbean infrequently, but their schedules are seldom known far enough in advance to be included.

Alaska: These cruises are operated between May and September only.

Mexican Riviera Year-Round (three/four/seven days): Ships based on the US West Coast.

Hawaii: A number of cruise lines have ships that call at Hawaii, but none on a regular basis, due to archaic US cabotage laws. The Jones Act states that only US flag ships (there is only one major oceangoing US-flagged ship at present) can embark and disembark passengers in US ports without first going to a foreign port (a US flag ship is one that is registered in the United States).

Antarctica: The Antarctic is not a place for normal cruise ships. To operate in this region, where ice can easily crush a ship within the hour should the weather deteriorate (as it often does), a ship must have an "ice-strengthened" or "ice-hardened" hull capable of breaking through pack ice in the formative stage. Rubber-inflatable Zodiac landing craft are used for venturing ashore (there are no docks on the Antarctic continent). The austral summer is the only time ships can travel to the Antarctic Peninsula, where many nations have their research stations, because the ice is so dense during the winter months that the continent (which, at its smallest, is the size of North America) swells to twice its summer size.

Roaming Ships: Cruise lines with "roaming" ships constantly roam around the world, mostly on nonrepeating itineraries of varying cruise lengths.

Part One:
THE WORLD OF CRUISING

CostaClassica; courtesy Costa Cruise Lines

YOUR FIRST CRUISE: WHAT TO EXPECT

Make sure you have your passport and any visas required (in some countries, you might go ashore on organized excursions under a group visa). Pack any medication you may need, and advise family members and friends where you are going.

With anticipation and excitement running high, if you've never been on a cruise before, allow me to take you through a typical initial embarkation process.

You already have been sent your cruise tickets and documents by the cruise line or your travel agent. A typical document package might include:

→ Flight ticket

→ Cruise ticket

→ Luggage tags

→ Embarkation card (to fill out before you get to the embarkation point)

→ Discount coupons for the shops on board

→ Bon Voyage gift selection form

→ Shore excursion brochure

→ Onboard credit account form

→ Guide to services on board

→ Ship's telephone and fax contact numbers

→ Coupon for tuxedo rental

Assume that you've arrived at the airport closest to your ship's embarkation point, and retrieved your luggage. It is probable that there will be a representative from the cruise line waiting, holding a sign that says "Condor Cruise Lines" or something similar. You will be asked to place your luggage in a cluster together with those of other passengers on the same flight as you, or with passengers on other flights arriving at roughly the same time.

Alternatively, you could have perhaps driven to the port of embarkation (or taken a limousine, train, or specially chartered bus). Once there, you would hand over your luggage to a representative of the cruise line or to a baggage handler (who would probably expect a tip, even for moving it a few feet).

In any case (no pun intended), the next time you see your luggage should be aboard your ship, where it will be delivered to your cabin. Now, let's proceed to the check-in point.

Go to the registration (check-in) area in the terminal building. For large ships, numerous desks will be set up (with the alphabet split into several parts), probably with lines of people at each of them. Go to the desk that displays the first letter of your surname, wait in line (having filled out all embarkation, registration, and immigration documents), and then check in. If your accommodation is designated as a "suite," there should be a separate check-in facility (sometimes called gold card service).

If you are cruising from a US port and you are a non-US citizen or "Resident Alien," you will go to a separate desk to check in (*Note*: Do not buy duty-free liquor to take on board — it will not be allowed by the cruise line and will be confiscated until the last day of the cruise). You will be asked for your passport, which you leave with the check-in personnel (be sure to ask for a receipt — it is, after all, a valuable document). If you are cruising from any other port in the world that is not a US port, be advised that each country has its own check-in requirements, setups, and procedures (passport control and inspection, for example). In any event, once you've checked in, you will be only a few steps away from your ship and cruise.

Documents in hand, you will probably go through a security-screening device, for both your person and hand luggage (just like at airports). Next, you'll walk a few paces towards the gangway. This may be a covered, airport-type gangway, or an open gangway (hopefully with a net underneath it in case you drop something over the side). The gangway could be flat, or you may have to walk up (or down) an incline, depending on the location of the gangway, the tide, or other local conditions. As you approach the gangway you will probably be greeted by the ship's photographers, a snap-happy team ready to take your photograph, bedraggled as you may appear after having flown or otherwise traveled for hours. If you do not want your photograph taken, say "no" firmly, and proceed.

Once on the gangway, you will feel a heightened sense of anticipation. At the ship end of the gangway, you will find a decorated (hopefully) entrance and the comfortable feel of air-conditioning if the weather is hot. The ship's cruise staff will welcome you aboard. Give them your cabin number, and a steward should magically appear to take your carry-on luggage from you and take you directly to your cabin. At last you've arrived.

Courtesy Douglas Ward

*Celebration and ceremony make a ship-christening event special, this one for **Legend of the Seas** (Royal Caribbean International).*

The door to your cabin should be unlocked and open. If it is locked, ask the steward to obtain the key to open the door. On the newest ships, you will probably be handed an electronically coded key card, which you insert into the door lock. Once inside the cabin, put down your personal effects and take a good look. Is it clean? Is it tidy? Are the beds properly made? Check under them to make sure the floor is clean (on one cruise I found a pair of red women's shoes, but, alas, no one to go with them!). Make sure there is ice in the ice container. Check the bathroom, bath (if there is one), or shower. Make sure there are towels and soap. If all is clean and shipshape, fine.

If there are problems, bring them to the attention of your cabin steward immediately. Or call the purser's office (or reception desk), and explain the problem, then quietly, but firmly request that someone in a supervisory position meet you to resolve it. The housekeeping on cruise ships is generally very good, but sometimes when "turnaround" time is tight, when passengers disembark in the morning and new passengers embark in the afternoon, little things get overlooked. They shouldn't, but they do (just as in any hotel ashore).

One thing you also should do immediately is to remember the telephone number for the ship's hospital, doctor, or for medical emergencies, just so you know how to call for help should any medical emergency arise.

Your luggage probably will not have arrived yet (if it is a ship carrying more than 500 passengers) so don't sit in the cabin waiting for it. Once you've oriented yourself with the cabin and its features, put your hand luggage away somewhere, and, deck plan in hand, take a walk.

Familiarize yourself with the layout of the ship. Learn which way is forward, which way is aft, and how to reach your cabin from the main stairways. This is also a good time to learn how to get from your cabin to the outside decks in an emergency. A Passenger Lifeboat Drill will probably take place *before* the ship sails. This means that the drill will not disturb your cruise (or your sleep) should it be held the next morning. Regulations dictate that a drill *must* take place within 24 hours after the ship sails from the embarkation port.

After the drill (you'll find your lifejacket in the cabin and directions to your assembly station will be posted on the back of the cabin door), you can take off the lifejacket and *relax*. By now, your luggage probably will have arrived.

Unpack, then go out on deck just before the ship sails. It's always a magical moment, and a good time to meet some new faces. Now, enjoy yourself. You're on a wonderful cruise vacation. No cares. No hassle. No hype. Just you (and maybe a loved one) and that bracing sea air. You'll soon be ready for that first night's dinner. It is simply amazing how the sea air gives you an appetite, although there's no truth to the rumor that the sea air seems to shrink your clothes by the end of the cruise.

19

CRUISING FOR FREQUENT PASSENGERS: WHAT'S NEW

The cruise industry is buoyant, and the introduction of new ships continues at a dizzying rate. Approximately 45 new ships are scheduled for delivery between January 2000 and December 2003 alone, at a cost of more than $12 billion, fueled by the increase in demand for high-value cruise vacations.

New ships incorporate the latest in sophisticated high-tech electronic navigation and safety equipment, recent advances in propulsion technology and the best in advanced ship design and construction, offering passengers an unprecedented number of options, choice of facilities, and dining and entertainment experiences.

At press time, the world's largest cruise vessel is scheduled to debut in late 1999 (more are on order): it is the 142,000-tonne *Voyager of the Seas*, a floating resort-hotel playground for Royal Caribbean International, based in Miami and aimed at the standard cruise marketplace. Is bigger better? That's up to the individual, but it is rather like being in a big shopping mall environment as opposed to a small boutique environment.

PROPULSION

New ships are now powered by gas-turbines, diesel-electric or diesel-mechanical propulsion systems that propel them at speeds of up to 28 knots (only Cunard Line's *QE2*, with a service speed of just under 30 knots, is faster).

A new technology is now incorporated into propulsion design, the "pod" system. Briefly, pods, which resemble huge outboard motors, replace internal electric propulsion motors, shaft lines, rudders and their machinery, and are compact, self-contained units that weigh about 170 tonnes each. Pod units *pull*, rather than *push*, a ship through the water. When going ahead, pod units face with the propeller forward (ships can go astern either by rotating the pods 180 degrees or by reversing the thrust). A vessel's turning circle diameter is reduced considerably, as is stern vibration.

EXTERIORS

Indented, cascading after-decks of ships such as *Aurora, Oriana, SuperStar Leo,* and *SuperStar Virgo* are both stunning and practical — overlooking aft pool areas — more dramatic, but no less practical, than the terraces aboard *Norwegian Dream* and *Norwegian Wind*. Other cruise ships take the "block" approach and fill in stern areas with cabins that have an aft-facing view (*Carnival Destiny, Carnival Triumph, Century, Galaxy,* and *Mercury*), or multilevel dining rooms with a huge expanse of glass windows, or other public rooms and facilities.

The most instantly recognizable exterior is that of *Aida* (Arkona Reisen), named after the Verdi opera, where huge bold red lips and brown eyes adorn her prow. And, when she leaves port on the first day of a cruise, the laser light show on deck is dramatic.

INTERIORS

Retro is in, contemporary is out, as interior designers change tack to create luxurious, welcoming interiors reminiscent of Europe's grand hotels, particularly in the small and mid-size ships, where the sense of intimacy can be genuinely established.

Large ship interiors include such things as multideck-high atriums, large theaters complete with revolving stages, hydraulic orchestra pits, huge scenery stowage spaces, Internet cafes, computer learning centers, and interactive television in the cabins. Several ships now feature two atrium lobbies instead of just one (*Carnival Destiny, Carnival Triumph, Galaxy,* and *Mercury*).

As for contemporary, among the most stunning, bold, and graphic interiors are those that are found in the ships of . Somehow, lilac neon, fiber optics, mosaics, and multicolored carpeting go together here although they never would in *any* setting other than a Las Vegas hotel. It is all a feast for the eyes and mind (entertainment architecture, as the interior designer calls it), but for many (especially for European passengers) it could be sensory overload (but a good advertisement for the fiber optic and lighting industries).

Ships have become instant floating art museums (some are better than others), with collections of artwork costing several million dollars per ship. For example: $12 million (*Voyager of the Seas*); $6 million (*Vision of the Seas*); $4 million (*Enchantment of the Seas*); $3.8 million

(*Century*); $3 million (*Galaxy*); $2.5 million (*Sun Princess*); $2 million (*Veendam*); $1 million (*Aida, Inspiration*). However, it is not the money spent that's important; it is the fact that artwork now forms a more important integral part of the physical interior decor than ever before, and particularly so with large ships, with ever larger wall spaces to cover.

COMPUTER-DRIVEN CRUISING

Computer users should note that many cruise lines have web sites on the Internet (see *Appendices* in Part Two). Computers now link almost all departments and functions aboard the latest ships, and interactive television systems let you order wine, arrange shore excursions, play casino games, go shopping, and order pay-per-view movies, all from the comfort of your cabin. Computers cannot yet pour you a drink, although you can order one, accompanied by a light snack. But, order a croissant with your breakfast and the "point and select" system won't bother to ask whether you'd like it warm or cold. Oh, well, that's technology for you; as long as you are a "standard" photofit passenger, it'll work for you. Otherwise, call room service (sort of defeats the purpose, doesn't it?).

FLOATING SPAS

Health and fitness spas are among the hottest passenger facilities in the latest cruise ships, with more space than ever devoted to them. The basic sauna, steam room, and massage facility has evolved into specially designed spas that include the latest in high-tech muscle exercising, aerobic and weight-training machines, and relaxation treatments, such as: hydrotherapy and thalassotherapy baths, jet blitz, rasul (graduated steam and all-over body mud cleansing), and seaweed wraps.

Spas are likely to be located on the uppermost decks of the latest ships, with large floor-to-ceiling ocean-view windows. Treatment rooms are flexible and can be adapted to incorporate the latest trends, gimmicks, and themes. Traditional Japanese design elements, including a rock garden and shoji screens, provide a serene environment in the AquaSpas aboard *Century*, *Galaxy*, and *Mercury*. Or how about a 30-person coed sauna, with a huge glass wall overlooking the port side of *Aida*?

FOR SMOKERS

Cigar smoking is back in vogue, and special rooms have been created aboard several ships, including: *Century, Galaxy, Horizon, Mercury, Mistral, SuperStar Leo, SuperStar Virgo*, and *Zenith*.

FOR NONSMOKERS

' *Paradise* is the first cruise ship to be totally nonsmoking (even the shipyard workers who built the ship were not allowed to smoke). Think you can smoke anyway? Forget it — there's a fine if you do (crew and other passengers can detect cigarette smoke within five miles). You will be fined $250 *and* asked to leave at the next port (at *your* expense). Renaissance Cruises' R-class ships *R One, R Two, R Three, R Four, R Five*, and *R Six* are also totally nonsmoking throughout (including cabins, all public rooms and areas, and open decks, although there is a crew smoking room). Meanwhile, nonsmokers will be pleased that many ships now feature totally nonsmoking dining rooms and show lounges.

DINING AND SERVICE

→ What's hot (no pun intended!)? Several ships now feature 24-hour casual dining, so you can eat what you want, when you want. Although the concept is good, the delivery (it is often serve yourself, more like a freeway/motorway café experience) often is not.

→ Two-deck-high dining rooms are back in vogue: *Century, Dawn Princess, Galaxy, Legend of the Seas, Maasdam, Mercury, Nordic Empress, Rotterdam VI, Ryndam, Splendour of the Seas, Statendam, Sun Princess,* and *Veendam* have them, while *Voyager of the Seas* has a huge three-deck-high dining hall.

→ New ships such as *SuperStar Leo* and *SuperStar Virgo* feature seven different restaurants (four are included in the cruise fare, three are a la carte special dining spots that incur an extra charge — just like going out ashore).

→ Ships operating seven-day cruises repeat menu cycles each week. So, if, for example, you take two back-to-back seven-day Eastern and Western Caribbean cruises, the menu may be

The unique design of Princess Cruises' Grand Princess makes for a grand impression.

repeated for the second week (so will the whole entertainment program and the cruise director's spiel, jokes, and activities).

→ Generally, cruise ship food and service standards have suffered during the past few years due to deep discounting. Ships carrying over 1,000 passengers cannot seem to deliver what is portrayed in the cruise brochures consistently. Also, because of the acute shortage of waiters who speak good English (the majority of passengers being North American), many cruise lines have had to train personnel from Caribbean basin and Central American countries whose command of the language is often less than adequate.

WHAT'S NOT SO HOT

→ Floating resorts that travel by night and are in port during the day provide little connection with the sea and nature. Almost everything is designed to keep passengers *inside* the ship (to spend money, increasing onboard revenue and shareholders' dividends).

→ Entertainment — either production shows or cabaret acts — it's all so much the same no matter what ship you are aboard. It's time for more creative thinking.

→ The latest breed of aggressive, so-called "cruise directors" who insist on interposing themselves into every part of your cruise, day and night. Public address systems are consistently overused by these bouncy youngsters, and are too loud, which hardly makes for a restful cruise. Some of these cruise directors may make excellent cheerleaders, but they seem unable to communicate with anyone over the age of 25!

→ Homogenous accommodation. As identically-sized standard cabins are the same shape and layout (good for incentive planners, but not for individual passengers), they also tend to be the same colors: eggshell white, off-white, or computer-colored beige! Although such colors are welcome after days in the sun, they are tedious on voyages over long stretches of water. Only bold bedspreads or the occasional color prints that adorn a spare wall bring relief. The plain ceilings are also boring. Close to useless are the wall-mounted hairdryers in bathrooms (which have poor directed pressure); they should, instead, be located in the vanity desk or dressing area.

→ Calling passengers "guests" is confusing and nautically incorrect (a guest in one's house is someone that doesn't pay). Passengers pay to be aboard ship. Ships are different from hotels (and should remain so). They provide a nautical experience and move through water; passengers have cabins and suites, and decks, not floors. That's how it should remain, although several cruise lines think they are in the hotel business, as hoteliers and accountants run them, not shipping people.

→ Two things that have almost disappeared: streamers and free champagne, formerly provided at bon voyage parties on deck on sailing day (exception: world cruises and some Japanese ships). Instead, waiters hustle you to buy a "bon voyage" cocktail, or some "Bahamaramamaslammer" in a polystyrene sports cup!

→ One thing that *should* go by the wayside is the amateurish, intrusive "Baked Alaska Parade." Popular with first-time passengers, it is old hat for many. It's time the cruise lines were more creative. The industry should also find a better way to sing "Happy Birthday" than the present waiter-induced chant that always seems to sound like a funeral dirge!

→ In the seven-day cruise market (particularly from US ports) disembarkation is poor. Passengers are unceremoniously dumped ashore, with little help after the trying procedures of locating their luggage and going through customs inspection. An absence of representation once they get to their respective airports for check-in may be an added ordeal. Of particular concern is the fact that the same procedure applies to all passengers, whether they are in the finest penthouse suite or the smallest inside cabin. The final impression of these seven-day cruises, therefore, is poor. Worst disembarkation ports: Ft. Lauderdale, Los Angeles, Miami, and San Juan.

CRUISING: A BACKGROUNDER

DID YOU KNOW...?

...that the first vessel built exclusively for cruising was Hamburg-Amerika Line's two-funnel yacht, the 4,409-tonne *Princessin Victoria Luise*? This luxury ship even included a private suite for the German kaiser.

...that the first ship to be fitted with real stabilizers (not an autogyro device) was the Peninsular & Oriental Steam Navigation Company's 1949-built 24,215-tonne *Chusan*?

...that the first consecrated oceangoing Roman Catholic chapel aboard a passenger ship was in Compagnie Generale Transatlantique's *Ile de France* of 1928?

...that the latest life rafts called Hydrostatic Release Units (HRU), designed in Britain and approved by the Royal Navy, are now compulsory on all British-registered ships? Briefly, an HRU is capable of automatically releasing a life raft from its mountings when a ship sinks (even *after* it sinks) but can also be operated manually at the installation point, saving precious time in an emergency.

Although the first cruises (actually "pleasure voyages") really started in the early 1800s, it was not until around 1960 that the modern-day cruise industry began, following the demise of transatlantic ocean liner crossings.

In June 1958, the first commercial jet aircraft flew across the Atlantic and forever altered the economics of transatlantic travel. It was the last year in which more passengers crossed the North Atlantic by sea than by air. In the early 1960s, passenger-shipping directories listed over 100 passenger lines. Until the mid-1960s, it was cheaper to cross the Atlantic by ship than by plane, but the appearance of the jet aircraft changed that rapidly, particularly with the introduction of jumbo jets in the early 1970s. In 1962, more than one million people crossed the North Atlantic by ship; in 1970, that number was down to 250,000.

The success of the jumbo jets created a fleet of unprofitable and out-of-work passenger liners that appeared doomed for the scrap heap. Even the famous big "Queens," noted for their regular weekly transatlantic service, found themselves at risk. Cunard White Star Line's *Queen Mary* (81,000-tonnes) was withdrawn in September 1967. Sister ship *Queen Elizabeth*, at 83,673-tonnes the largest passenger liner ever built (until 1996), made her final crossing in October 1968 (I sailed the final voyage aboard this great ship).

Transatlantic shipping companies searched for new ways to employ their aging vessels, but few survived the fast growth of the jet aircraft. Ships were sold for a fraction of their value. Many lines went out of business and ships were scrapped. Those that survived attempted to mix transatlantic crossings with voyages south to the sun. The Caribbean (including the Bahamas) became appealing, cruising became an alternative, and an entire new industry was born, with new lines being formed exclusively for cruising.

Then came smaller, more specialized ships, capable of getting into the tiny ports of developing Caribbean islands (there were no commercial airlines taking vacationers to the Caribbean then, and few hotels), which were built to carry a sufficient number of passengers in a single class arrangement.

Instead of cruising long distances south from more northerly ports such as New York, companies established their headquarters in Florida. This not only avoided the cold weather, choppy seas, and expense of the northern ports but also saved fuel costs with shorter runs to the Caribbean. Cruising was reborn. California became the base for cruises to the Mexican Riviera, and Vancouver on Canada's west coast became the focus for summer cruises to Alaska.

Flying passengers to embarkation ports was the next logical step, and soon a working relationship emerged between the cruise lines and the airlines. Air/sea and "sail 'n' stay" packages thrived — joint cruise and hotel vacations with inclusive pricing. Cruising became an integrated part of tourism, with ships and hotels offering comfort and relaxation, and airlines providing quick access.

Some of the old liners came out of mothballs, purchased by emerging cruise lines and refurbished for warm-weather cruising operations, often with their interiors redesigned and refitted. During the late 1970s, the modern cruise industry grew at a rapid rate.

CRUISING TODAY

Today's cruise concept hasn't changed much from that of earlier days, although it has been improved, refined, expanded, and packaged for ease of consumption. No longer the domain of affluent, retired people, the industry today is vibrant and alive with passengers of every age and socio-economic background. Cruising is no longer the shipping business, but the *hospitality* industry.

New ships are generally larger than their counterparts of yesteryear, yet cabin size has decreased to provide more space for entertainment and other public facilities. Today's ships boast air conditioning to keep heat and humidity out; stabilizers to keep the ship on an even keel; a high level of maintenance, safety, and hygiene; and more emphasis on health and fitness facilities.

Cruise ship design has moved from the traditional, classic, rounded profiles of the past to the extremely boxy shapes with squared-off sterns and towering superstructures today. Although ship lovers lament these design changes, they resulted from the need to fit as much as possible in the space provided (you can squeeze more in a square box than you can in a round one, although it may be less aesthetically appealing). Form follows function, and ships have changed from ocean transportation to floating vacation resorts.

Although ships have long been devoted to eating and relaxation in comfort (promulgating the maxim "Traveling slowly unwinds you faster"), ships today offer more activities, and more learning and life-enriching experiences than before. And there are many more places you can visit on a cruise: from Antarctica to Acapulco, Bermuda to Bergen, Dakar to Dominica, Shanghai to St. Thomas, or if you prefer, perhaps *nowhere at all*.

The cruise industry is a $15 billion business worldwide and growing. It provides employment to a growing number, both directly (there are over 60,000 shipboard officers, staff and crew, as well as about 15,000 employees in cruise company offices), and indirectly (suppliers of foodstuffs and mechanical and electrical parts, port agents, transport companies, destinations, airlines, railways, hotels, car rental companies).

In 1998, over eight million people worldwide took a cruise, packaged and sold by cruise lines through tour operators and travel agents. The most recent (1998) breakdown of passengers by

Courtesy Royal Caribbean International

Service with a smile on a Royal Caribbean International cruise.

nationality choosing to take an oceangoing cruise vacation is provided below (taken from figures supplied by the Maritime Evaluations Group):

United States	5,500,000
UK*	635,000
Asia (not including Japan)	800,000
Germany	283,000
Canada	250,000
Italy	250,000
Australasia	200,000
Japan	200,000
France	165,000
Rest of Europe	120,000
Cyprus**	75,000
Freighter Passengers	3,000
TOTAL	**8,481,000**

*This figure includes 130,000 British passengers who took a two- to seven-day cruise from Cyprus in conjunction with a resort/hotel stay.
**Local Cyprus market.
Additional — River Cruise Passengers:
Britain: 145,000; Germany: 117,500; France: 60,000; Japan: 30,000

CONSTRUCTING A MODERN CRUISE SHIP

More than any other type of vessel, a cruise ship has to fulfill fantasies and satisfy exotic imaginations. It is the job of the shipyard to take those fantasies and turn them into a steel ship without unduly straining the laws of naval architecture and safety regulations, not to mention budgets.

Although no perfect cruise ship exists, turning owners' dreams and concepts into ships that embody those ideals is the job of specialized marine architects and shipyards, as well as consultants, interior designers, and a mass of specialist suppliers. Computers have simplified this complex process, although shipboard management and operations personnel often become frustrated with designers who are more idealistic than they are practical. Ships represent a compromise between ideals and restrictions of space and finance, the solution being to design ships for specific areas and conditions of service.

Ships used to be constructed in huge building docks, from the keel (backbone) up. Today, ships are built in huge sections, then joined together in an assembly area (as many as fifty or more sections for a large ship). The sections may not even be constructed in the shipyard, but they will be assembled there.

Formerly, passenger spaces were slotted in wherever there was space within a given hull. Today, computers provide highly targeted ship design, enabling a new ship to be built within two years instead of within the four or five years it took in the 1950s.

The maximum noise and vibration levels allowable in the accommodation spaces and recreational areas are stipulated in any owner's contract with the shipyard. Vibration tests are carried out once a ship is built and launched, using a finite method element of evaluation; this embraces analyses of prime sources of noise and excitation, namely the ship's propellers and main engines.

Prefabricated cabin modules, including *in situ* bathrooms complete with toilets and all plumbing, are used today. When the steel structure of the relevant deck is ready, with main lines and insulation installed, cabin modules are then affixed to the deck, and power lines and sanitary plumbing are swiftly connected. All waste and power connections, together with hot/cold water mixing valves, are arranged in the service area of the bathroom and can be reached from the passageway outside the cabin for maintenance.

CRUISING TOMORROW

Current thinking in ship design follows two distinct paths: large ships or smaller ships.

→ Large ships, where the "economy of scale" helps the operator to keep the cost per passengers down. Three companies (, Princess Cruises, and Royal Caribbean International) have ships measuring over 100,000 tonnes, capable of carrying over 3,000 passengers, with the "bigger is better" principle being pursued for all it's worth. These ships are, however, limited to the Caribbean, being too wide to transit the Panama Canal (non-Panamax).

→ Small ships, where the "small is exclusive" concept has gained a strong foothold, particularly in the luxury category. Cruise lines offer high-quality ships of low capacity, which can provide a highly personalized range of quality services.

Other cruise lines have expanded by "stretching" their ships. This is accomplished literally by cutting a ship in half, and inserting a newly constructed midsection, thus instantly increasing capacity, adding more accommodation and public rooms, while maintaining the same draft. "Stretched" ships include: *Black Watch* (ex-*Royal Viking Star*), *Carousel* (ex-*Nordic Prince*), *Hyundai Kumgang* (ex-*Royal Viking Sky*), *Norwegian Dream* (ex-*Dreamward*), *Norwegian Majesty* (ex-*Royal Majesty*), *Norwegian Star* (ex-*Royal Viking Sea*), *Norwegian Wind* (ex-*Windward*), *Sundream* (ex-*Song of Norway*), and *Westerdam* (ex-*Homeric*).

Whatever direction the design of cruise vessels takes in the future, ships are becoming increasingly environmentally friendly. With growing concern, particularly in eco-sensitive areas such as Alaska and the South Pacific, better safeguards against environmental pollution and damage are being built into the vessels.

The cruise industry is fast approaching "zero discharge," whereby nothing is discharged into the world's oceans at any time. This is an easier objective to attain for the latest batch of ships, while older ships have a more difficult time achieving zero discharge owing to outdated equipment.

Courtesy Princess Cruises

An aerial view of one of the four swimming pools aboard **Grand Princess** *(Princess Cruises).*

CHOOSING YOUR SHIP AND CRUISE

So, you've decided your next vacation will be a cruise. Good choice! But the decisions do not stop there. Bombarded with glossy cruise literature tempting you with every imaginable lure and overly prolific use of the phrases "five-star luxury," "gourmet dining," and "fabulous destinations," selecting the right ship can be a chore.

There are different ships to suit different needs. Despite constant cruise company claims that theirs has been named the "Best Cruise Line" or "Best Cruise Ship," *There really is no such thing*, only what's good, and right, for you.

Most shipowners want to be a "luxury" cruise operator, and most passengers want to sail aboard one of the top-rated "luxury" ships. But *few* operators can really deliver a five-star ship, product, and crew.

WHAT A CRUISE IS

A cruise is a vacation. It is an antidote to (and escape from) the stress and strain of life ashore. It offers you a chance to relax and unwind in comfortable surroundings, with attentive service, good food, and a ship that changes the scenery for you. It is virtually a hassle-free, and, more important-ly, a crime-free vacation. You never have to make blind choices. Everything's close at hand, and there are always polite people to help you.

WHAT A CRUISE IS NOT

Some cruises simply aren't relaxing, despite cruise brochures proclaiming that "you can do as much or as little as you want to." For example, large ships that carry 3,000 or more passengers tend to cram lots of passengers into small cabins and provide nonstop activities that do little but insult the intelligence and assault the wallet.

Price is, of course, the key factor for most people. The cost of a cruise provides a useful guideline to the ambience, type of passengers, and degree of luxury, food, and service that you will likely find on board.

The amount you are prepared to spend will determine the size, location, and style of shipboard accommodation you get. Be wary of cruise lines that offer huge discounts — it either means that the product was unrealistically priced at source or that there will be a reduction in quality somewhere. Ships are as individual as fingerprints: each one can change its "personality" from cruise to cruise, depending on the character of passengers (and crew).

Passengers encompass all types of personalities and lifestyles, from affluent, reserved, and mature to active, athletic, fun-loving, and youthful, or family-oriented, or conservation-minded, or adventurous, or wild fun seekers. They may be well traveled, or honeymooners on their first cruise, or veteran passengers who cruise several times a year.

HOW LONG?

The standard of luxury, comfort, and service is generally in direct proportion to the length of the cruise. To operate long, low-density voyages, cruise lines must charge high rates to cover the extensive preparations, high food and transportation costs, port operations, fuel, and other expenditures. The length of cruise you choose will depend on the time and money at your disposal and the degree of comfort you are seeking.

The popular standard length of a cruise is seven days, although cruises can vary from two-day party cruises to a slow exotic voyage around the world of up to 180 days. If you are new to cruising and want to "get your feet wet," try a short cruise first.

WHICH SHIP?

Because cruise ships (particularly large ones) are self-sufficient resorts, there really is a cruise line, cruise, and ship to suit virtually all tastes, so it is important to take into account your own personality and vacation requirements when selecting a ship.

Ships are measured (not weighed) in gross register tonnes (grt) and come in three principal size categories, as follows:

Small Ships: for up to 500 passengers

(generally 2,000–20,000 tonnes)

Ships in the harbor at St. Thomas, US Virgin Islands.

Mid-Size Ships: for 500–1,000 passengers

(generally 20,000–50,000 tonnes)

Large Ships: for over 1,000 passengers

(generally 50,000–150,000 tonnes)

Whatever the physical dimensions, all cruise ships provide the same basic ingredients: accommodation, activities, entertainment, plenty of food, good service, and ports of call, although some do it much better than others (and charge more, accordingly).

SPACE

To get an idea of the amount of the space around you, look at the Passenger Space Ratio given for each ship in Part Two (tonnage divided by number of passengers).

Passenger Space Ratio:

→ 50 and above — the ultimate

→ 30 to 50 — very spacious

→ 20 to 30 — reasonably spacious

→ 10 to 20 — moderate to high density

→ 10 or below — extremely cramped

SMALL SHIPS (UP TO 500 PASSENGERS)

Choose a small ship for an intimate cruise experience and a small number of passengers. Some of the most exclusive cruise ships in the world belong in this group (but so do most of the coastal vessels with basic, unpretentious amenities, sail-cruise ships, and the expedition-style cruise vessels that take passengers to see nature).

Choose this size ship if you do not need much entertainment, large ship facilities, gambling casinos, several restaurants, and if you do not like to wait in lines. If you want to swim in the late evening, or have champagne in the Jacuzzi at midnight, it is easier aboard small ships than aboard larger ships, where more rigid programs provide the kind of inflexible thinking that passengers detest.

Small Ships: Advantages

→ More like small inns than mega-resorts.

→ Easy to find your way around, and signage is usually clear and concise.

→ At their best in warm weather areas.

→ Capable of truly catering to the highest degree of culinary excellence, with fresh foods cooked individually to order.

→ Most provide an "open seating" in the dining room; this means that you can sit with whomever you wish, whenever you wish, for all meals.

→ Provide a totally unstructured lifestyle, offering a level of service not found aboard most of the larger ships, and no or almost no announcements.

→ Provide an "open bridge" policy, allowing passengers to go to the navigational bridge at almost any time (except during difficult maneuvers and in cases of difficult weather conditions).

→ Some small ships have a hydraulic marina water sports platform located at the stern and carry equipment such as jet skis, Windsurfers, a water ski powerboat, and scuba and snorkeling gear.

→ When the ship is at anchor, going ashore is easy and speedy, with a continuous tender service.

Small Ships: Disadvantages

→ Do not have the bulk, length, or beam to sail well in open seas in inclement weather conditions.

→ Do not have the range of public rooms or open spaces that large ships can provide. Options for entertainment, therefore, are limited.

MID-SIZE SHIPS (500–1,000 PASSENGERS)

Choose a mid-size ship if you want to be among up to 1,000 passengers. They are well suited to the smaller ports of the Aegean and Mediterranean, and are more maneuverable than larger ships. Several of these ships operate around-the-world cruises and other long-distance cruising itineraries to exotic destinations not really feasible aboard many of the ships in the small or large ship categories.

There is a big difference in the amount of space available. Cabins vary from large "penthouse suites" complete with butler service to tiny inside cabins.

These ships will generally be more stable at sea than those in the "small ships" category, due to their increased size and draft. They provide more facilities, more entertainment, and more dining options. There is some entertainment, and more structured activities than small ships, but less than large ships.

Mid-Size Ships: Advantages

→ They are neither too large, nor too small, but often strike a happy balance in terms of size and facilities.

→ It is an easy matter to find one's way around.

→ They generally sail well in areas of inclement weather, being neither high-sided like the large ships, nor of too shallow draft like some of the small ships.

→ Lines seldom form (except for ships that are approaching 1,000 passengers), but if they do, they are likely to be short.

→ They appear more like traditional ships than most of the larger vessels, which tend to be more "boxy" in shape and profile.

Mid-Size Ships: Disadvantages

→ They do not offer as wide a range of public rooms and facilities as do large ships.

→ Few have large show lounges for large-scale production shows; hence entertainment tends to be more of the cabaret variety.

LARGE SHIPS (1,000–2,000 PASSENGERS)

Choose a large ship if you enjoy being with lots of other people, in a large-scale city environment, out to have a good time. If you are sociable, and like to experience plenty of entertainment and dining options, these ships will certainly provide a well-packaged standard or premium cruise vacation experience, usually in a seven-day cruise.

These ships have extensive facilities and programs for families with children of all ages. But if you meet someone on the first day and want to meet them again, make sure you appoint a place and time, or you may not see them again (apart from the size of the ship, they may be at a different meal seating). These ships have a highly structured array of activities and passenger participation events each day, together with large entertainment venues, and the most lavish production shows at sea.

It is in the standard of service, entertainment, lecture programs, level of communication, and finesse in dining services that really can move these ships into high rating categories, but they must be exceptional to do so. Choose higher-priced suite accommodation and you get better service levels than lower-grade accommodation.

Large ships are run on a highly programmed basis. It is difficult, for example, to go swimming in the late evening, or after dinner (decks are cleaned and pools are netted over by 6:00pm — too early). Having champagne delivered to outdoor hot tubs late at night is virtually impossible. Large ships have lost the flexibility for which cruise ships were once known, and have become victims of company "policy" legislation and insurance regulations. So many large ship passengers feel they are participants in "conveyor-belt" cruising.

Large Ships: Advantages

→ Have the widest range of public rooms and facilities, often a wraparound promenade deck outdoors, and more space (but more passengers).

→ Generally better flexibility in dining options.

→ The newest ships have state-of-the-art electronic interactive entertainment facilities and options (good for those into computers and high-tech gadgetry).

→ Generally sail well in open seas in inclement weather conditions.

→ There are more facilities and activities for people of all ages, particularly for families with children.

Large Ships: Disadvantages

→ Trying to find your way around the ship can prove frustrating.

→ Lines to wait in: for embarkation, the purser's office, elevators, informal buffet meals, shore tenders, shore excursions, and disembarkation.

→ They resemble floating hotels, and many items cost extra. Actually, they are more like retail parks surrounded by cabins.

→ Signage is often confusing; there is a lack of elevators at peak times.

→ The larger the ship, the more impersonal the service (unless you have "butler" service in a penthouse suite).

*Windstar Cruises **Wind Surf** in full sail — a beautiful sight to behold.*

→ There are too many announcements (they could be in several languages).

→ Dining room staff is so programmed to provide speedy service, it is almost impossible to sit and dine in leisurely fashion.

→ Food may well be rather bland (cooking for 2,000 is not quite the same as cooking for a little dinner party of twenty).

→ Telephoning room service can be frustrating, particularly in those ships with automatic telephone answering systems that state "your call will be answered by room service personnel in the order it was received."

→ Room service breakfast is not generally available on the day of disembarkation.

→ Swimming pools are often closed at 6:00pm; some even take away the deck chairs.

→ The in-cabin music aboard the latest batch of ships is supplied through the television set, and it is impossible to turn off the picture (so much for quiet, romantic late-night music, and darkened cabins).

→ When the ship is at anchor, you will need to stand in line, or wait in a lounge, with a "tender ticket" — then wait in the lounge until your ticket number is called — to go ashore by ship-to-shore craft. This can take an hour or more! Getting back on board could take some time, too.

→ Some large ships have only two main staircases. In the event of an emergency, the evacuation of more than 2,000 passengers could prove difficult.

THE BIG EIGHT CRUISE LINES

All eight offer one thing: a well-packaged cruise (generally of seven days) that includes interesting itineraries, plenty of food, reasonable service, and a good selection of entertainment and production shows (mostly by the use of technical effects and great lighting). The ships also provide large casinos, shopping malls, and extensive spa and fitness facilities. Most ask you to pay port taxes, insurance, gratuities to staff over and above the cruise fare, and for many additional items.

The lines differ in the facilities, space, food, and service featured, together with subtle differences in the delivery of the cruise product. Here are some of the positive and negative differences among the Big Eight cruise lines. Note that changes, upgrading and downgrading of products and services, may have occurred since this book was completed.

Carnival Cruise Lines

Carried 1,500,000 passengers in 1998. This is the largest and most successful cruise line in the world. It specializes in cruises for the young at heart, with plenty of upbeat music, and passenger participation games typically found in an adult summer camp atmosphere. While some could be taken to be potentially degrading, they are nevertheless well liked by passengers who associate such activities with "fun," the line's theme. All the ships have incredibly imaginative multicolored, very upbeat décor (each ship has its own décor theme).

Carnival *does not* try to sell itself as an "upmarket" cruise line and consistently delivers *exactly* what it says in its brochures, for which there is a huge, growing first-time cruise audience. provides a well-packaged cruise vacation, with smart new ships that have the latest high-tech entertainment facilities and features. Shore excursions are booked via the in-cabin ("Fun Vision") television system (there is no longer a shore excursion desk, and thus no one to answer questions).

With almost identical large ships, the company does a fine job of providing almost nonstop activities. If you do not mind drinks in plastic glasses (on deck) and basic hamburger/hot dog and fast foods in abundance, this line provides them almost round-the-clock (pizzas *are* available 24 hours a day). The company provides excellent "dazzle and sizzle" production shows and a lot of nighttime entertainment options for party people, as well as some excellent children's programming (ideal for young families).

The cabins throughout the fleet are a decent size. Carnival will help you have fun all the way, but do not expect the finesse or small details you might find with some of the lesser-known lines. Major sources of passenger complaints include embarkation and disembarkation (shore-side staff), and the large number of security staff aboard ship (these complaints are also true of Royal Caribbean International).

The company has grown dramatically over the last few years and has improved its product substantially. In 1996, the company introduced a "Vacation Guarantee" program (the first of its kind in the industry) to great success, particularly for first-time passengers who do not know whether they will enjoy cruising (few passengers ever consider leaving the cruise).

Celebrity Cruises

Carried 405,952 passengers in 1998. Celebrity Cruises has established an outstanding reputation for its cuisine, particularly in the dining rooms, with their formal service. All meals *are* made from scratch, and no pre-packaged, boxed, or pre-prepared items are used at all, which is an admirable achievement, and different from all others in the Big Eight group. The sauces accompanying the main dishes, in particular, are excellent. Thus, there is a good degree of *taste* that is often lacking aboard the larger, standard market ships of today. The waiters (many of them from Eastern European countries) are well trained, and it is easy to communicate with them. There are several tables for two in the dining room, although dining room chairs do not have armrests and would be more comfortable with them.

Another reason this line provides a high-quality cruise experience is the fact that each ship simply has much more staff than other ships of comparable size and passenger number carry. This is particularly noticeable in the housekeeping and food and beverage departments, thus providing passengers with a superior product. The artwork in the latest ships in the fleet is also rather stunning, and comprises what is probably the most stunning collection of contemporary art in the cruise industry today.

Two ships in its present five-ship fleet (*Horizon* and *Zenith*) have teak outdoor complete wraparound promenade decks, while *Century, Galaxy,* and *Mercury* do not. The ships are always spotlessly clean, and constant vacuuming and polishing take place around the clock. There are more cleaners and service personnel aboard Celebrity Cruises' ships (per passenger) than in any of the other Big Eight cruise lines. In fact, there are more staff members per passenger than aboard any of the others in the Big Eight group.

Whether the high standards established can be continued under new owner Royal Caribbean International remains to be seen. At present, however, the standard of food and its delivery remain the best of any of the Big Eight, with the exception of Star Cruises.

Costa Cruises

Carried 351,000 passengers in 1998. This company specializes in cruises for Europeans (or passengers with European tastes), particularly Italians. The ships have a definite European "feel" to them, in their decor and manner of product delivery, which is very laid back.

The food is really standard hotel banquet fare, disappointing and nonmemorable, as is the service, which displays little or no finesse (it is hard to find an Italian waiter anywhere — something the company was once known for). The company does, however, present good Italian pasta dishes, which are always popular, and, on formal nights, dining by candlelight. But there are no wine waiters! The buffets are particularly disappointing and arguably the worst of all the Big Eight.

The cabins tend to be on the mean side in size, but the decor is fresh and upbeat, and the bathrooms are very practical units (some ships have sliding doors), an excellent alternative to those that open inward, taking space from the bathroom).

What is good is the variety of public rooms, lounges, and bars, many of which provide fairly intimate spaces. The entertainment and shows are geared toward the international passengers found aboard almost any ship in the fleet. Costa Cruises is the only company to have a chapel aboard each of its ships, with Roman Catholic Mass featured daily. Carnival Corporation, parent company of , purchased the company in 1997.

Holland America Line

Carried 500,000 passengers in 1998. This line features teakwood outdoor promenade decks fleet-wide, whereas most other cruise lines feature artificial grass or some other form of indoor-outdoor carpeting. The ships are very clean.

The food is fairly reasonable, though not memorable, but the food quality, presentation, and service have become very standardized in recent years, and ingredients are mostly from pre-packaged goods, although the menu variety has improved. Dining room service is too fast but provided by friendly, almost always-smiling Indonesian waiters whose communication skills leave much to be desired. The company does, however, offer cappuccino and espresso coffees, and free ice cream during certain hours of the day aboard its ships, as well as hot hors d'oeuvres in all bars — something other major lines seem to have dropped, or charge extra for.

When it comes to buffets, there are more canned fruits (liked by older passengers because they are soft) used by this line than by Celebrity Cruises or Princess Cruises, by comparison, but about the same amount as found aboard the ships of or Costa Cruises.

The company's claim to "five-star" ships in its brochures is misleading. The ships are extremely pleasant and have an elegant "feel" to them, with some fine, eclectic artwork from the Dutch East and West Indies. What is excellent is the fact that social dancing is always on the menu. This is something that older passengers, in particular, enjoy. However, communication with many of the smiling staff *can* prove frustrating, and passenger care (for which Holland America Line used to be well known) has now become quite mediocre.

The suites and cabins are of good proportions, and come nicely equipped. They are quite comfortable, and Holland America Line also provides a good array of personal toiletry amenities. An additional bonus item is a canvas tote bag provided for all passengers, which is a nice extra and useful for shopping or for going to the beach.

Carnival Corporation, the parent company of Carnival Cruise Lines, wholly owns Holland America Line.

Norwegian Cruise Line

Carried 511,015 passengers in 1998. This line provides a good product for a youthful, active, sports-minded audience. Most of the staff is from the Caribbean basin, and, in general, they do not have the finesse of those ships that have a greater percentage of European staff. The cabins are reasonably attractive and functional, although closet and drawer space is somewhat limited in the newest ships.

The dining room cuisine is generally not memorable, but lighter fare is available in a "bistro" setting aboard all ships in the fleet for those that want to "eat and run" and not bother with the more formal dining room setting. Sports fans in particular will see much evidence of sports bars and memorabilia aboard these ships. This is good for those young-at-heart sports fans and devotees, who are well catered to.

As for entertainment, the production shows are of the colorful, well-choreographed, slightly belittling, noisy, high energy type.

Princess Cruises

Carried 500,000 passengers in 1998. Despite billing itself as "The Love Boat," Princess Cruises does not have any tables for two in its dining rooms (exceptions: *Dawn Princess, Grand Princess, Sea Princess,* and *Sun Princess*).

Princess Cruises was once known for its good food but today it is very much run-of-the-mill fare and quite nonmemorable, with the exception of its pasta dishes, which are prepared daily by some talented head waiters, and are very good.

The cabins are of generous proportions (exceptions: *Dawn Princess, Sea Princess,* and *Sun Princess*) and well designed. They are all well equipped and very comfortable, with warm decor and practical, well-designed bathrooms. All ships have Filipino cabin stewardesses and plenty of European staff in front-line service areas, as well as their British bartenders.

The company's Shore Excursion Program is arguably the best run of any of the Big Eight companies noted here. Entertainment tends to be very traditional, with a mix of elegant production shows and the usual cabaret acts, but volume levels are thankfully moderate. The company now charges extra for airport transfers, which is a shame. The UK-based P&O Group, which also owns P&O Cruises, wholly own Princess Cruises.

Royal Caribbean International

Carried 1,421,884 passengers in 1998. *Enchantment of the Seas, Grandeur of the Seas, Legend of the Seas, Rhapsody of the Seas, Splendour of the Seas,* and *Vision of the Seas* have slightly larger cabins than in the earlier ships *Majesty of the Seas, Monarch of the Seas,* and *Sovereign of the Seas.*

The company places more emphasis than most on passenger participation activities, such as a Passenger Talent Show, Masquerade Parade, Country & Western Jamboree, and so on. It is all very predictable, and the same programming is featured aboard all its ships, because it is tried, tested, and proven, if perhaps a little "old hat" by now.

Although Royal Caribbean International's food is of approximately the same standard as that aboard Carnival Cruise Line ships, Carnival's ships have larger cabins, as do the ships of Celebrity Cruises, Holland America Line, and Princess Cruises. French, Italian, Oriental, Caribbean, and American are the main themes for the menus for different nights. Wine lovers should note that there are no vintages on the wine lists (because they are all so young).

The ships are shapely, with well-rounded sterns, and interesting design profiles that make them instantly recognizable. They also feature a trademark Viking Crown Lounge, set around the funnel stack, either in front of it or part way up it. Large, brightly lit casinos are provided, as are shopping galleries that passengers have to walk through in order to get almost anywhere else. It is all cleverly designed to extract maximum revenue from you, in a nice way, of course.

Royal Caribbean International also owns Celebrity Cruises, although the two brands are kept reasonably separate as far as the onboard product is concerned.

Star Cruises

Carried 718,511 passengers in 1998. The company, established only in 1994, has a diverse fleet of ships and caters to many nationalities and types of passengers, but markets principally to Australians, Europeans (particularly British and German passengers), Indians, and Southeast Asians. At present, Star Cruises operates in the Pan-Asia region.

Since its inception as an operator of casino ships, the company has been making the transition into a full-fledged cruise line. Its intention is to have a fleet of twelve ships, one for each sign of the zodiac (at present there are eight ships).

Star Aquarius and *Star Pisces* operate short cruises for serious casino players, while *Megastar Aries* and *Megastar Taurus* are two small and beautifully fitted luxury ships for VIP club members and private charters.

The purpose-built new ships, *SuperStar Leo* and *SuperStar Virgo,* together with *SuperStar Europe* (ex-*Europa*) are, first and foremost, superb cruise ships. *Leo* and *Virgo* feature more entertainment (Asian passengers enjoy activity-oriented vacations rather than relaxing ones), and as many as seven restaurants and dining spots. More ships are on order.

In addition, *SuperStar Capricorn* (presently named *Hyundai Kumgang*) is on a four-year charter to Hyundai Cruises.

Star Cruises is the only cruise line to have its own simulator center, an excellent training facility for its Scandinavian navigation officers. Star Cruises' parent company, Genting Berhad, owns a string of land-based resorts and hotels, huge tracts of land for development, and other interests including entertainment, aviation, power stations, oil and gas units, and rubber and palm oil plantations, among others.

This cruise line is young, but growing rapidly. Although service levels and finesse remain inconsistent, the hospitality aboard the ships is excellent (better than most of the other Big Eight cruise lines), as is the choice of food available.

THE BIG EIGHT CRUISE LINES

A look at this chart shows just what cruise lines do (or do not) provide in your cabin and bathroom

Cruise line	Carnival Cruise Lines		Celebrity Cruises		Costa Cruises	
	Standard Cabins	Suites	Standard Cabins	Suites	Cabins	Suites
Cabin						
Bed Linen: Duvets (not sheets/blankets)	No	No	No	Yes	No	No
Bed Linen: 100% Cotton	No	No	No	No	Yes	Yes
Bed Linen: 50% Cotton/50% Polyester	Yes	Yes	Yes	Yes	No	No
Towels: 100% Cotton	No	No	Yes	Yes	Yes	Yes
Towels: 86% Cotton/14% Polyester	Yes	Yes	No	No	No	No
Nonallergenic Pillows	No	No	No	No	Yes (2)	Yes (2)
Fresh Fruit Bowl	No	No	No	Yes	Yes (2)	Yes (2)
Fresh Flowers	No	No	No	Yes	Yes (2)	Yes (2)
Telephone	Yes	Yes	Yes	Yes	Yes	Yes
Personal Safe	Yes	Yes	Yes	Yes	Yes	Yes
Personalized Stationery	No	No	No	Yes	No	No
Television	Yes	Yes	Yes	Yes	Yes	Yes
VCR Player	No	Yes	No	Yes	No	No
CD Player	No	No	No	Yes (7)	No	No
Shoe Shine	No	No	No	Yes	Yes	Yes
Continental Breakfast	Yes	Yes	Yes	Yes	Yes	Yes
Full In-Cabin Breakfast/Lunch/Dinner Service	No	No	No	Yes	No	Yes
Complimentary Espresso/Cappuccino	Yes	Yes	No	Yes	No	No
Free Local Newspaper in Port (when available)	No	No	No	Yes	No	No
Complimentary Pressing Service (First 24 Hours)	No	No	No	Yes	No	Yes
Cabin Bathroom						
Real Glasses in Bathroom	Yes	Yes	Yes	Yes	Yes	Yes
Plastic Glasses in Bathroom	No	No	No	No	No	No
Soap/Shampoo Dispenser Unit	No	No	No	No	Yes (3)	Yes (3)
Soap	Yes	Yes	Yes	Yes	Yes	Yes
Shampoo	No	No	No	No	Yes	Yes
Conditioner	No	No	No	No	Yes	Yes
Combined Shampoo/Conditioner	No	Yes	Yes	Yes	No	No
Foaming Bath Oil	No	No	No	Yes	No	No
Hand Lotion	No	Yes	Yes	Yes	Yes	Yes
Mouthwash	No	No	No	Yes	No	No
Shower Cap	No	No	No	Yes	Yes	Yes
Loofah Sponge	No	No	No	Yes	No	No
Hairdryer	Yes (8)	Yes (8)	Yes	Yes	Yes	Yes
Weight Scale	No	No	No	Yes	No	No
Bathrobes	Yes (9)	Yes	No	Yes	No	Yes
Shaving/Make-Up Mirror	No	No	No	Yes	No	No

Key

(1) = Selected suites only

(2) = On request only

(3) = In the shower unit only: *Costa Victoria*

(4) = On back-to-back cruises only (turnaround day)

(5) = Deluxe cabins only

(6) = Royal Suite only

(7) = Penthouse Suite only

(8) = *Carnival Destiny* only

(9) = Balcony cabins *Carnival Destiny* only

(10) = *SuperStar Leo* and *SuperStar Virgo* (

Holland America Line		Norwegian Cruise Line		Princess Cruises		Royal Caribbean International		Star Cruises (10)	
Standard Cabins	Suites	Standard Cabins	Suites	Standard Cabins	Suites	Standard Cabins	Suites	Standard Cabins	Suites (Balcony Class)
No	No	No	Yes	No	No	No	No	Yes	No
No	No	Yes (2)	Yes (2)	No	No	No	No	Yes	Yes
Yes	Yes	Yes	Yes	Yes	Yes	Yes	Yes	No	No
No	No	Yes	Yes	Yes	Yes	Yes	Yes	Yes	Yes
Yes	Yes	No	No	No	No	No	No	No	No
No	No	No	No	Yes	Yes	Yes	Yes	No	No
Yes	Yes	Yes (2)	Yes	Yes	Yes	No	No	No	Yes
Yes	Yes	No	Yes	No	Yes	No	No	No	Yes
Yes	Yes	Yes	Yes	Yes	Yes	Yes	Yes	Yes	Yes
No	Yes	No	Yes	Yes	Yes	Yes	Yes	Yes	Yes
No	Yes	No	No	No	No	No	No	No	No
Yes	Yes	Yes	Yes	Yes	Yes	Yes	Yes	Yes	Yes
No	Yes	No	Yes (1)	No	No	No	Yes (6)	No	Yes
No	No	No	Yes (1)	No	No	No	Yes (6)	No	Yes
No	No	No	No	No	Yes	No	No	No	No
Yes	Yes	Yes	Yes	Yes	Yes	Yes	Yes	No	Yes
Yes	Yes	Yes	Yes	Yes	Yes	Yes	Yes	No	No
No	No	No	No	No	No	No	No	No	Yes
No	No	No	No	Yes (4)	Yes (4)	No	No	No	Yes (2)
No	Yes	No	No	No	No	No	No		
Yes	Yes	Yes	Yes	Yes	Yes	Yes	Yes	Yes	Yes
No	No	No	No	No	No	No	No	No	No
No	No	No	No	No	No	No	No	No	No
Yes	Yes	Yes	Yes	Yes	Yes	Yes	Yes	Yes	Yes
No	No	No	Yes	Yes	Yes	Yes	Yes	No	Yes
No	No	No	No	Yes	Yes	No	Yes (5)	No	Yes
Yes	No	Yes	Yes	No	No	No	No	Yes	No
No	Yes	No	Yes (1)	No	No	No	No	No	Yes
Yes	Yes	Yes	Yes	Yes	Yes	No	Yes (5)	No	Yes
No	No	No	No	No	No	No	No	No	Yes
Yes	Yes	Yes	Yes	Yes (2)	Yes (2)	Yes	Yes	Yes	Yes
No	No	No	Yes	No	No	No	No	No	No
No	Yes	Yes	Yes	Yes	Yes	No	No	Yes	Yes
No	No	No	Yes (1)	No	No	No	No	No	Yes
No	Yes	No	Yes	Yes	Yes	No	Yes	No	Yes
No	No	No	No	No	No	No	No	No	Yes

New vs. Old Ships

A ship built before 1970 is considered old. Yet, many passengers like older ships.

Although it is inevitable that some older tonnage cannot match the latest in high-tech ships, it should be noted that ships today are not constructed to the same high standards, or with the same loving care, as in the past.

New Ships: Advantages

↪ Incorporate the latest in high-tech electronic equipment and the best in advanced ship design and construction.

↪ Meet the latest safety and operating standards as laid down by the international maritime conventions.

↪ Feature more public room space, with public rooms and lounges built out to the sides of the hull (enclosed promenade decks are no longer regarded as essential).

↪ Offer more standardized cabin layouts and fewer categories.

↪ Are more fuel-efficient.

↪ Have a shallower draft, which makes it easier for them to enter and leave ports.

↪ Have bow and stern thrusters, so they seldom require tug assistance in many ports, thus reducing operating costs.

↪ Have plumbing and air-conditioning systems that are new and work.

↪ Have diesel engines mounted on rubber to minimize vibration.

↪ Are usually fitted with the latest submersible lifeboats.

New Ships: Disadvantages

↪ Do not "take the weather" as well as older ships (the experience of sailing across the North Atlantic in November on one of the new large ships can be unforgettable). Because of their shallow draft, these ships roll, even when there is the slightest puff of wind.

↪ Tend to have smaller standard cabins, which can mean narrow, short beds.

↪ Have thin hulls and therefore do not withstand the bangs and dents as well as older, more heavily plated vessels.

↪ Have decor made mostly from synthetic materials (due to stringent regulations) and, therefore, could cause problems for those passengers who are sensitive to such materials.

↪ Have toilets of the powerful vacuum suction "barking dog" type.

↪ Are powered mainly by diesel (or diesel-electric) engines, which inevitably cause some vibration; although on the latest vessels, the engines are mounted on pliable, floating rubber cushions and are, therefore, virtually vibration-free.

↪ Have cabin windows that are completely sealed instead of portholes that can be opened.

Older Ships (pre-1970): Advantages

↪ Have strong, plated hulls (often riveted) that can withstand tremendously hard wear and tear; they "take the weather" well.

↪ Have large cabins with long, wide beds/berths, due to the fact that passengers of yesteryear needed more space, given that voyages were much longer.

↪ Have a wide range of cabin sizes, shapes, and grades that are more suited to those families traveling with children.

→ Have toilets that are of the "gentle flush" variety instead of the powerful "barking dog" vacuum toilets found aboard newer ships.

→ Are powered by steam turbines, which are virtually free of vibration or noise and are considerably quieter and smoother in operation than modern vessels.

→ Have portholes that, in many instances, actually open.

→ Have interiors that are built from more traditional materials such as wood and brass, with less use of synthetic fibers (less likely to affect anyone who is allergic to synthetics).

→ Have deep drafts that help them to achieve a smooth ride in the open seas.

Older Ships (pre-1970): Disadvantages

→ Are not so fuel efficient and, therefore, are more expensive to operate than the new ships.

→ Need a larger crew, because of the more awkward, labor-intensive layouts of the ships.

→ Have a deep draft (necessary for a smooth ride) but need tugs to negotiate ports and tight berths.

→ Have increasing difficulty in complying with the current international fire, safety, and environmental regulations.

→ Are usually fitted with older-type open lifeboats.

→ Ten years or older are more likely to have plumbing and air-conditioning problems in cabins and public areas.

THE CREW

You can estimate the standard of service by looking at the crew-to-passenger ratio. The best service levels are aboard ships that have a ratio of one crew member to every two passengers, or higher. The best ships in the world, from the point of view of crew living and working conditions, also tend to be the most expensive ones (the adage "you get what you pay for" tends to be true).

Most ships have a multinational crew (exceptions: some German-, Greek-, Italian-, or Japanese-owned cruise lines). The crew mixture gives the impression of a ship being like a miniature United Nations. If the crew is happy, the ship will be happy, too, and passengers will sense it.

MAIDEN/INAUGURAL VOYAGES

There is an element of excitement in taking the maiden voyage of a new cruise ship, or in joining the inaugural voyage of a recently refurbished, reconstructed, or stretched vessel.

If you have a degree of tolerance and you are not bothered by some inconvenience, slow or nonexistent service in the dining room, fine; otherwise, wait until the ship has been in service for at least three months. Then again, if you book a cruise on the third or fourth voyage, and there is a delay in the ship's introduction, you could find yourself on the maiden voyage! One thing is certain — any maiden voyage is a collector's item, but Murphy's Law prevails: "If anything can go wrong, it will." For example:

→ A strike, fire, or shipyard bankruptcy are possible causes of delay to a new ship.

→ Service aboard new or recently refurbished ships (or a new cruise line) is likely to be uncertain at best and could be a complete disaster. An existing cruise line may use experienced crew from its other vessels to help "bring out" a new ship, but they may be unfamiliar with the ship's layout and may have problems training other staff.

→ Plumbing and electrical items tend to cause the most problems, particularly aboard reconstructed and refurbished vessels. Examples: toilets that do not flush or do not stop flushing; faucets incorrectly marked, where "hot" really means "cold"; room thermostats mistakenly fitted with reverse wiring; televisions, audio channels, lights, and electronic card key locks that do not work; electrical outlets incorrectly indicated; and "automatic" telephones that refuse to function.

39

↪ The galley (kitchen) of a new ship causes perhaps the most consternation. Even if everything works and the executive chef has ordered the right supplies, they could be anywhere other than where they should be. Imagine if they forgot to load the seasoning, or if the eggs arrived shell-shocked!

↪ "Software" items such as menus, postcards, writing paper, or remote control units for television and/or video systems, door keys, towels, pillowcases, glassware, and perhaps even toilet paper may be missing, lost in the bowels of the ship, or simply not ordered.

↪ In the entertainment department, items such as spare spotlight bulbs may not be in stock. Or there may be no hooks in the dressing rooms to hang costumes on (many older ships do not even have dressing rooms). Or what if the pianos arrived damaged, or "flip" charts for the lecturers didn't show up? Manuals for high-tech sound and lighting equipment may be in a foreign language.

THEME CRUISES

If there's a theme, there's probably a cruise to suit. Each year, an ever richer variety of theme cruises is available, with many cultural, ecological, and educational subjects.

Typical theme cruise topics include:

Adventure, Antiques, Archaeological, Art Lovers, Astronomy, Backgammon, Ballroom and Latin Dancing, Big Band, Blues Festival, Bridge, Chess Tournament, Chocoholics, Classical Music, Computer Science, Cosmetology, Country and Western, Diet and Nutrition, Educational, Exploration, Fashion, Film Festival, Food and Wine, Gardening, Holistic Health, Gay/Lesbian, Jazz Festival, Maiden Voyage, Movie Buffs, Murder Mystery, Naturalist/Nude, Octoberfest, Ornithology (Bird Watching), Photography, Scottish Dancing, Sequence Dancing, Singles, Steamboat Race, Superbowl, Theatrical, and Wine Tasting.

SIGNS YOU'VE CHOSEN THE WRONG SHIP

↪ When, just after you've embarked, a waiter hands you a drink in a tall plastic glass from a whole tray of drinks of identical color and froth, then gives you a bill to sign without having the courtesy to say "Welcome Aboard."

↪ When the so-called "luxury" cabin you booked has walls so thin you can hear your neighbors combing their hair.

↪ When what the brochure describes as a "full bathtub" actually means "a large sink" located at floor level.

↪ When you wanted a quiet, restful cruise, but your travel agent booked you aboard a ship with 300 baseball fans and provided them all with signed baseball bats and boom boxes for their use on deck (solution: read this book thoroughly first)!

↪ When you packed your tuxedo, but other passengers take "formal" attire to mean clean cut-off jeans and a less stained T-shirt. Check the brochure carefully.

↪ When the "medical facility" is in fact located in the purser's office and consists of a box of adhesive bandages with directions for their use in a foreign language.

↪ When the gymnasium equipment is kept in the maître d's office.

↪ When you have a cabin with an "obstructed view" (this will usually mean there is a lifeboat hanging outside it!), and it is next to or below the disco. Or the laundry. Or the garbage disposal facility. Or the anchor!

↪ When the "fresh selected greens" on the menu means a sprig of parsley on the entree plate, at every lunch and dinner seating (boring even on a three-day cruise).

↪ When the cruise director tries to sell passengers a watch, or a piece of art, over the ship's public address system.

↪ When front-row seats at a rock concert would be quieter than a poolside deck chair at midday.

→ When you hear *Achy-Breaky Heart*, *Mary Ann*, the *Macarena*, or *Yellow Bird* ten times during the first day.

→ When you have to buy shin pads to prevent injury from the 600 children that try to run you down in the passageways.

→ When the cruise brochure shows your cabin with flowers and champagne, but you get neither. If you want them, you get a bill and the flowers will never be watered anyway.

→ When the bottled water on your dining room table comes with a bill ever so quickly if you dare to open the bottle.

→ When "fresh catch of the day" on the menu means that the fish is so old that it would be best used as a door stop.

→ When the brochure says "Butler Service," but you have to clean your own shoes, get your own ice, and still tip twice the amount you would for a cabin steward.

→ When the Beer Drinking or Hog Calling Contest, Knobby Knees Contest, and Pajama Bingo are listed as "enrichment lectures."

→ When the "fresh-squeezed orange juice" you just ordered means fresh-squeezed, but last week, or the week before that, on land, and then poured into industrial-size containers, before transfer to your polystyrene plastic cup on deck.

→ When the brochure says tipping is not required, but your waiter and cabin steward tell you otherwise and threaten they will break your kneecaps if you do not hand them something that approaches what to you is a large sum of money.

→ When the cruise director thoughtfully telephones you at 2:30am to tell you that the bingo jackpot is up to $1000!

→ When, on the final day, the words "early breakfast" means 5:00am, and "vacate your cabin by 7:30am" means you must spend about three hours sitting in the show lounge waiting for disembarkation, with 500 available seats, your hand luggage, and 2,000 other passengers, probably playing bingo.

→ When the Lifeboat Drill consists of a crew member who hands you a lifejacket and asks you to teach him how to wear it, and what the whistle is for.

→ When you are out on deck, you look up and notice a big hole in the bottom of one or more of the ship's lifeboats.

→ When the cabin steward tries to sell you a time-share in his uncle's coal mine in wherever he is from, at a greatly reduced price, or says you must go without soap and towels for a week.

→ When the proclaimed "five-course gourmet meal" in the dining room turns out to be four courses of salty chicken soup and a potato.

→ When the "Deck Buffet" literally means that there are no tables and chairs, only the deck, to eat off.

→ When the brochure shows photos of smiling young couples, but you and your spouse/partner are the only ones under 80.

→ When the library is located in the engine room.

→ When the captain tells you he is really a concert pianist and his diploma is for the piano, not navigation.

ACCOMMODATION

DID YOU KNOW...?

...that the first "en suite" rooms (with private bathroom in cabin) were on board Cunard Line's *Campania* of 1893?

...that the first liner to offer private terraces with their first-class suites was *Normandie* in 1935?

...that the first single-berth cabins built as such were aboard Cunard Line's *Campania* of 1893?

...that the first ships to feature private balconies were a trio of ships built for the Compagnie des Messageries Maritimes, France? They were the 13,520-tonne *Cambodge*, *Laos*, and *Vietnam*, built in 1953.

...that the first ship to be fitted with interior plumbing was the 6,283-tonne *Normandie* of 1883?

...that the first ship to be fitted with an internal electric lighting system was aboard the Inman liner *City of Berlin* in 1879?

...that cruising today is not the same as it was in the nineteenth century? On the first cruise ships there was little entertainment, and passengers had to clean their own cabins! Orders enforced on all ships sailing from Great Britain in 1849, for example, instructed all passengers to be in their beds by 10:00pm!

You should feel at home when at sea, so it is important to choose the right accommodation for your needs. Like houses ashore, all cabins have good and not-so-good points. Choose wisely, for if you find your cabin (incorrectly called a "stateroom" by some companies) is too small when you get to the ship, it may be impossible to change it or to upgrade, as the ship could very well be completely full.

Cruise lines designate cabins only when deposits have been received (they may, however, guarantee the grade and rate requested). If this is not done automatically, or if you come across a disclaimer such as one spotted recently — "All cabin assignments are confirmed upon embarkation of the vessel" — get a guarantee in writing that your cabin will not be changed upon embarkation.

There are three main types of accommodation, but many variations on each theme:

→ **Suites**: (the largest living spaces, with or without private balcony); and "junior" suites (with or without private balcony)

→ **Outside-view cabins**: a large picture window or one or more portholes (with or without private balcony)

→ **Inside cabins**: so called because there is no window or porthole, although there could be an inner "courtyard" view.

PRIVATE BALCONIES

A private balcony (or "veranda") is just that. It is a balcony adjoining your cabin where you can sit, enjoy the view, dine, or even have a massage. These add another dimension to your home away from home. There's something quite civilized (if slightly antisocial) about sitting on one's balcony eating caviar and sipping champagne, or having breakfast "a la deck" in some exotic place. It is also pleasant to get fresh air and to escape cold (air-conditioned) cabins. The value of a private balcony, for which you pay a premium, comes into its own in warm weather areas. One thing is almost certain: once you have a private balcony, you'll be hooked. Balconies are like cruises.

They are totally addictive! Indeed, some ships have enough private balconies for more than 400 budding Juliets to be wooed by their Romeos.

Some private balconies are not so private. Balconies not separated by full floor-to-ceiling partitions (examples: *Carnival Destiny, Carnival Triumph, Maasdam, Norway, Oriana, Ryndam, Statendam,* and *Veendam*) don't quite cut it. You could get noise or smoke from your neighbor, but when all things are in your favor, a balcony is a wonderful extra. Some ships have balconies with full floor-to-ceiling privacy partitions *and* an outside light (examples: *Century, Galaxy, Mercury,* and *Radisson Diamond*). *Note:* Some partitions in *Century, Galaxy,* and *Mercury* are full, some are partial, depending on deck and location.

Some suites with forward-facing private balconies may not be so good, as the wind speed can make these balconies all but unusable. And when the ship drops anchor in ports of call, the noise can be loud.

All private balconies have railings to lean on, but the balconies in some ships have solid steel plates between railing and deck, so you cannot look out to sea when you are seated (examples: *CostaClassica, CostaRomantica, Dawn Princess,* and *Sun Princess*). Better are those ships with balconies that have clear glass (examples: *Century, Galaxy, Mercury,* and *Nordic Empress*) or horizontal bars.

HOW MUCH?

→ The amount you pay for accommodation is directly related to the size of the cabin, its location, and the facilities.

→ There are no set standards, each line implementing its own system according to ship size, age, construction, and profit potential.

→ Most cruise lines *do not* give cabin sizes in their brochures, but you will find the size range in the ship profiles in Part Two of this book.

→ If this is your first cruise, choose the most expensive cabin you can afford. If it is too small (and most cabins are small), the cruise might fall short of your expectations.

→ It is arguably better to book a low-grade cabin on a good ship than book a high-grade cabin on a poor ship.

→ If you are in a party of three or more and do not mind sharing a cabin, you will achieve a substantial saving per person, so you may be able to book a higher-grade cabin without paying extra.

A private balcony offers a romantic retreat aboard ship.

CABIN SIZES

Cabins are like miniature hotel rooms and provide more or less the same facilities, except space. Ships necessarily have space limitations and utilize space efficiently. Viewed by most owners and designers as little more than a convenient place for passengers to sleep, shower, and change, cabin space is often compromised in favor of large public rooms and open areas. In some of the smaller inside (no-view) and outside cabins, changing clothes is a challenge; and to take a shower, you need to be an acrobat!

The latest ships come with more standardized cabin sizes, because they are made in modular form. They all have integrated bathrooms (mostly made from noncombustible phenolic-glass-reinforced plastics) fitted into the ship during construction.

Older (pre-1970) ships had more spacious cabins (there were more days at sea, fewer ports of call, and fewer entertainment rooms). This encouraged many to spend a great deal of time in their cabins, often entertaining other passengers. Ask your travel agent for the dimensions of the cabin you have selected.

CABIN LOCATION

→ An "outside-view" cabin is recommended for first-time passengers (an "inside" cabin has no portholes or windows, making it more difficult to orient you or to gauge the weather or time).

→ Cabins located in the center of a ship are more stable and tend to be noise- and vibration-free. Ships powered by diesel engines (this applies to most new and modern vessels) create and transmit some vibration, especially at the stern.

→ Take into account personal habits when choosing the location of your cabin. For example, if you like to go to bed early, avoid a cabin close to the disco. If you have trouble walking, choose a cabin close to the elevator.

→ Generally, the higher the deck, the higher the cabin price (and the better the service). This is an inheritance from transoceanic times, when upper-deck cabins and suites were sunnier and warmer.

→ Cabins at the bow (front) of a ship are slightly crescent-shaped, given that the outer wall follows the curvature of the ship's hull. But they can be exposed to early morning noises, such as the anchor being dropped at ports where the ship cannot dock.

→ Cabins with interconnecting doors are fine for families or close friends, but the wall between them is usually thin, so you can plainly hear anything that's being said next door.

→ Many brochures now indicate cabins that have "obstructed-views." Cabins on lower decks are closer to engine noise and heat, especially at the aft of the vessel and around the engine casing. Be aware that in many older ships, elevators will probably not operate to the lowermost decks.

FACILITIES

Cabins provide some, or all, of the following:

→ Private bathroom (generally small and compact) fitted with shower, wash basin, and toilet. Higher-grade cabins and suites may have full-size bathtubs. Some even have a whirlpool bath and/or bidet, a hairdryer, and more space.

→ Electrical outlets for personal appliances, usually 110 and/or 220 volts.

→ Multichannel radio, television (regular satellite channels or closed circuit), and VCR.

→ Two beds or a lower and upper berth (possibly, another one or two upper berths) or a double-, queen-, or king-size bed. In some ships, twin beds can be pushed together to form a double.

→ Telephone, for intercabin or ship-to-shore communication.

→ Depending on cabin size, a chair, or chair and table, or sofa and table, or even a separate lounge/sitting area (higher accommodation grades).

→ Refrigerator and bar (higher accommodation grades).

→ Vanity/desk unit with chair or stool.

*A standard suite aboard Silversea Cruises' **Silver Cloud.***

→ Personal safe.

→ Closet space, some drawer space, plus storage room under beds for suitcases.

→ Bedside night stand/table unit.

→ Towels, soap, shampoo, and conditioner. (Many ships, particularly the "upscale" ones, provide a greater selection of items.)

Many first-time passengers are surprised to find their cabin has twin beds. Double beds are a comparative rarity except in the higher-priced suites. Aboard some ships you will find upper and lower berths. A "berth" is a nautical term for a bed held in a wooden or metal frame. A "Pullman berth" tucks away out of sight during the day, usually into the bulkhead or ceiling. You climb up a short ladder at night to get into an upper berth.

THE SUITE LIFE

Suites are the most luxurious and spacious of all shipboard accommodation. A suite (literally a "suite of rooms") should comprise a lounge or sitting room separated from a bedroom by a solid door (not just a curtain); a bedroom with a large bed; one or more bathrooms, and an abundance of closet, drawer, and other storage space. Be advised, however, that many cruise lines inaccurately describe some accommodation as suites, when in fact they are simply nothing more than larger cabins with a curtain that divides sitting and sleeping areas.

Some ships have whole decks or sections of decks devoted to suites. Cruise lines know that some passengers will pay handsomely to stay in the best and quietest accommodation. They will also expect the best service and preferential treatment throughout the ship.

Suites are best on long voyages with several days at sea. Be aware that in large ships (those carrying more than 1,000 passengers), there may be a whole deck or two devoted to penthouses and suites, but you have to share the rest of the ship with those in lower-priced accommodation. That means there is no preferential seating in the showroom, the dining rooms, or on sunbathing decks. You may, however, get separate check-in facilities and preferential treatment upon disembarkation, but your luggage will be lumped together with that of everyone else (not so "suite"!).

TYPICAL CABIN LAYOUT

The following rates are typical of those you can expect to pay for (a) a seven-day and (b) a ten-day Caribbean cruise aboard a modern cruise ship. The rates are per person and include free roundtrip airfare or low-cost air add-ons from principal North American gateways.

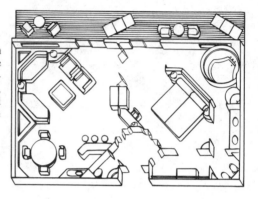

Luxury outside suite with private verandah, separate lounge area, vanity area, extra-large double or queen-sized bed, bathroom with tub, shower, and extensive closet and storage space.
   (a) $2,250 (b) $4,000

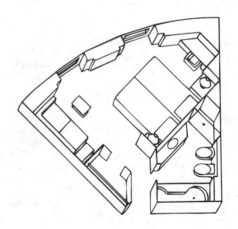

Deluxe outside cabin with lounge area, double or twin beds, bathroom with tub, shower, and ample closet and storage space.
   (a) $2,250 (b) $2,850

Note that in some ships, third- and fourth-person berths are available for families or friends wishing to share. The upper Pullman berths, not shown on these cabin layouts, are recessed into the wall above the lower beds.

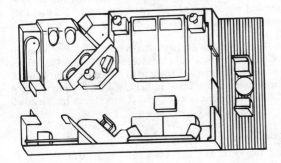

Large outside double with bed and convertible daytime sofabed, bathroom with shower, and good closet space.
(a) $1,750 (b) $2,450

Standard outside double with twin beds (plus a possible upper third/fourth berth), small sitting area, bathroom with shower, and reasonable closet space.
(a) $1,450 (b) $1,975

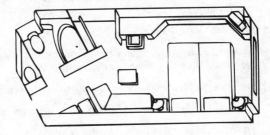

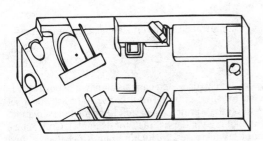

Inside double with two lower beds that may convert into daytime sofabeds (plus a possible upper third/fourth berth), bathroom with shower, and fair closet space.
(a) $1,250 (b) 1,750

BOOKING YOUR CRUISE

TRAVEL AGENTS

Travel agents do not charge for their services, although they earn a commission from cruise lines for booking their clients on a cruise. Consider a travel agent as your business advisor, and not merely as a ticket agent. He/she will handle all matters relevant to your booking and should have the latest information on changes of itinerary, cruise fares, fuel surcharges, discounts, and any other related items, including insurance in case you have to cancel prior to sailing. Most travel agents are linked into cruise line computer systems and have access to most shipboard information.

There is *no* "Best Cruise Line in the World" or "Best Cruise Ship" — only the ship and cruise that's right for *you*. Your travel agent should find exactly the *right ship* for *your needs* and *lifestyle*. Some sell only a limited number of cruises and are known as "preferred suppliers," because they receive special "overrides" on top of their normal commission (they probably know their limited number of ships well, however).

If *you* have chosen a ship and cruise, be firm and book exactly what you want, or change agencies. In the UK, look for a member of the Guild of Professional Cruise Agents. PSARA (Passenger Shipping Association of Retail Agents) provides in-depth agent training in the UK, as well as a full "bonding" scheme to protect passengers from failed cruise lines. In the US, look for a member of NACOA (National Association of Cruise Oriented Agencies), or a CLIA (Cruise Lines International Association) affiliated agency.

Questions to Ask Your Travel Agent

→ Is air transportation included in the cabin rate quoted? If not, what will be the extra cost?

→ What other extra costs will be involved? These can include port charges, insurance, gratuities, shore excursions, laundry, and drinks.

→ What is the cruise line's cancellation policy?

→ If I want to make changes to my air arrangements, routing, dates, and so on, will the insurance policy cover everything in case of missed or canceled flights?

→ Does your agency deal with only one, or several different insurance companies?

→ Does the cruise line offer advance booking discounts or other incentives?

→ Do you have preferred suppliers, or do you book any cruise on any cruise ship?

→ Have you sailed aboard the ship I want to book, or that you are recommending?

→ Is your agency bonded and insured? If so, by whom?

→ If you book the shore excursions offered and recommended by the cruise line, is insurance coverage provided?

RESERVATIONS

Plan ahead and book early. After choosing a ship, cruise, date, and cabin, you pay a deposit that is roughly 10 percent for long cruises, 20 percent for short cruises (most cruise lines ask for a set amount). The balance is normally payable 45 to 60 days prior to departure. For a late reservation, you pay in full when space is confirmed (when booking via the Internet, for example). Cruise lines reserve the right to change prices in the event of tax increases, fluctuating rates of exchange, fuel surcharges, or other costs beyond their control.

When you make your reservation, also make special dining requests known: seating preference, smoking or nonsmoking sections.

After the line has received full payment, your cruise ticket will be issued, along with baggage tags and other items. Check your documents when they arrive. In these days of automation, it is prudent to make sure that the ship, date, and cruise details you paid for are correctly noted. Also verify any connecting flight times.

EXTRA COSTS

Cruise brochures boldly proclaim that "everything's included," but in most cases you will find this is not strictly true. In fact, for some cruises "all-exclusive" would be a more appropriate term.

Your fare covers the ship as transportation, your cabin, meals, entertainment, activities, and service on board; it typically does not include alcoholic beverages, laundry, dry cleaning or valet services, shore excursions, meals ashore, gratuities, port charges, cancellation insurance, optional onboard activities such as skeet shooting, bingo, horse racing or casino gambling.

Expect to spend about $25 per day per person on extras, plus another $10–$12 per day per person in gratuities. Genuine exceptions can be found in some small ships (those carrying fewer than 500 passengers) where just about everything *is* included.

Typical Extra-Cost Items:

Baby-sitting (per hour)	$5.00
Bottled Water	$2.50–$7.00 (per bottle)
Cappuccino/Espresso	$1.50–$2.50
Cartoon Character Bedtime "Tuck-In" Service	$20.00
Wash One Shirt	$1.50–$3.00
Dry-Clean Dress	$3.00–$7.50
Dry-Clean Jacket	$4.00–$8.00
Golf Simulator	$15.00 (30 minutes)
Hair Wash/Set	$17.00–$28.00
Haircut (men)	$20.00
Ice Cream	$1.00–$3.75
In-cabin Movies	$6.95
Laundry Soap	$0.50–1.50
Massage	$1.00-plus per minute (plus tip)
Satellite Phone/Fax	$6.95–15.00 per minute
Sodas (soft drinks)	$1.00–$2.00
Souvenir Photo	$6.00–$8.00
Trapshooting (three or five shots)	$5.00, $8.00
Wine/Cheese Tasting	$5.00
Wine with Dinner	$7.00–$500

Calculate the total cost of your cruise (not including any extra-cost services you might decide you want once on board) with the help of your travel agent. Here are the approximate prices per person for a typical seven-day cruise aboard a well-rated mid-size or large cruise ship, based on an outside-view two-bed cabin:

Cruise fare	$1,200
Port charges	$100 (if not included)
Gratuities	$50
Total per person	**$1,350**

This is under $200 per person per day. For this price, you wouldn't even get a decent hotel room in London, New York, Tokyo, or Venice!

DISCOUNTS AND INCENTIVES

→ Book ahead to get the best discounts (discounts decrease closer to the cruise date).

→ You may be able to reserve a cabin grade, but not a specific cabin — "tba" (to be assigned). Some lines will accept this arrangement and may even upgrade you.

→ It is useful to know that the first cabins to be sold out are usually those at minimum and maximum rates. *Note*: Premium rates apply during Christmas/New Year cruises.

→ Some cruise lines have "frequent passenger" clubs. Members are first to be notified of any special offers being made. Discounts can frequently be high, so it is worth belonging, especially if you like cruising with a particular line.

CANCELLATIONS AND REFUNDS

Do take out full cancellation insurance (if it is not included), as cruises (and air transportation to/from them) must be paid in full before your tickets are issued. Without such insurance, if you cancel at the last minute (even for medical reasons) you could lose the whole fare. Insurance coverage can be obtained from your travel agent.

Cruise lines usually accept cancellations more than 30 days before sailing, but all charge full fare if you do not turn up on sailing day, whatever the reason. Other cancellation fees depend on the cruise and length of trip. Curiously, many lines do not return port taxes, which are *not* part of the cruise fare.

MEDICAL INSURANCE

Whether you intend to travel overseas or cruise down a local river, and your present medical insurance does not cover you, you should look into extra coverage for your cruise. A "passenger protection program" will be offered by the cruise line, and the charge for it will appear on your final invoice unless you decline. It is worth every penny, and it typically covers such things as evacuation by air ambulance, high-limit baggage, baggage transfers, personal liability, and missed departure.

PORT TAXES/HANDLING CHARGES

These are assessed by individual port authorities and are generally shown in the brochure. Port charges form part of the final payment, although they can be changed at any time up to the day of embarkation.

AIR/SEA PACKAGES

When your cruise fare includes "free air" (as in a one-way or round-trip air ticket), note that airline arrangements usually cannot be changed without paying a premium, as cruise lines often book group space on aircraft to obtain the lowest rates.

If you *do* make changes, remember that in the event of the airline canceling your flight, *the cruise line is under no obligation* to help you or return your cruise fare if you do not reach the ship on time. If you are flying to a foreign country you should allow extra time (particularly in the winter) to cover the risk that any airline connections may be delayed or canceled.

Airlines often use a "hub-and-spoke" system, which can prove frustrating. Because of changes to air schedules, cruise and air tickets may not be sent to passengers until a few days before the cruise.

In Europe, air/sea packages generally start at a major metropolitan airport; some include first-class rail travel from outlying districts. In the United States, many cruise lines include connecting flights from small suburban airports as part of the whole package.

Most cruise lines offer the flexibility of jetting out to join a ship in one port and flying home from another. An advantage is that you only have to check your baggage once at the departure airport. The baggage transfer from plane to ship is handled for you.

Note: This does not include intercontinental fly/cruises, where you must claim your baggage at the airport on arrival in order to clear it though customs.

Although the cruise package may state "free air," there is no such thing as a free air ticket. The cost of the airfare is simply hidden in the overall cruise fare. However, air tickets are not always included. Some cruise lines simply do not believe in increasing their rates to cover "free air," or they simply may wish to avoid subsidizing airline tickets. These are, for the most part, the upscale lines that operate long-distance cruises to more exotic destinations.

CRUISE CUISINE

DID YOU KNOW...?

...that there is an unwritten rule called "Ward's Third Law of Gluttony," which states that passengers will eat precisely *twice* as much food as they need from breakfast and luncheon buffets, then add a lettuce leaf or two at dinner to justify the guilt complex brought about by overconsumption?

...that the liner *Amerika* in 1938 was the first ship to have an alternative restaurant open separately from the dining saloons? It was named the Ritz Carlton.

...that the first a la carte restaurant aboard a passenger ship was in the German ship *Amerika* of 1905?

...that the longest bar on any cruise ship is aboard *Aida*? It is 195 feet (59.5 meters) long.

...that a whole county in Iowa raises all its beef cattle for Carnival Cruise Lines?

...that *Legend of the Seas* was christened with the world's largest bottle of champagne? It had to be specially made, and was a "Sovereign-size" bottle (the equivalent of 34 bottles) of Moet & Chandon champagne.

...that the United States Line's *Manhattan* in 1931 was the first ship to have a cocktail named after it — perhaps the *only* ship with that distinction?

...that 2,000 Methuselah-sized bottles (the equivalent of 12 bottles) of *Cristal* champagne will be made specially for Crystal Cruises' passengers to purchase for the eve of the year 2000 (the millennium)? The cost — $2000 each!

Dining is often the single most talked- and written-about aspect of the cruise experience. There is a thrill of anticipation that comes with dining out in a fine restaurant. The same is true aboard ship, where dining in elegant, friendly, and comfortable surroundings stimulates an appetite sharpened by the bracing sea air. Some passengers do carry abundance therapy to the limit, however.

Attention to presentation, quality, and choice of menu in the honored tradition of the transatlantic luxury liners has made cruise ships justly famous. Cruise lines know that you will spend more time eating on board than doing anything else, so their intention is to cater well to your palate, within the confines of a predetermined budget.

The "intelligent standardization" of the food operation and menus translates to cost-effectiveness in the process of food budgeting for any cruise line. Being able to rationalize expenditure *and* provide maximum passenger satisfaction is, therefore, almost a science today. Quite simply, *you get what you pay for*. Aboard low-priced cruises, you will get portion-controlled frozen food that has been reheated. To get fresh food (particularly fresh fish and the best cuts of meats), cruise lines must pay significantly more, adding to the cruise price.

Cruise lines put maximum effort into telling passengers how good their food is, often to the point of being unable to deliver what is shown in the brochures. But not all meals aboard all ships are gourmet affairs by any stretch of the imagination. In general, cruise cuisine compares favorably with the kind of "banquet" food served in a standard hotel or family restaurant, in other words, almost tasteless.

Most ships cannot offer a real "gourmet" experience because the galley (ship's kitchen) may be striving to turn out hundreds of meals at the same time. What you *will* find is a good selection of palatable, pleasing, and complete meals served in comfortable surroundings, in the company of good friends (and *you* do not have to do the cooking!). Maybe you will even dine by candlelight, a pleasant way to spend any evening.

Experienced passengers who "collect" cruises have seen it, smelled it, and tasted it all before aboard ship: real rubber duck-foul (fowl) food, fit only to be stuffed, painted, and used as children's toys in their bathtubs! Talk about rock-hard lobster, leather fish, inedible month-old shrimp, veterinarian-rejected chicken, and grenade-quality meats. Not to mention teary-eyed or hammer-proof cheese, soggy salty crackers, unripe fruits, and coffee that looks (and tastes) like army surplus paint! Or yellow-green leaves that could be either garnish or an excuse for salad! Sadly, it is all there, in the cruise industry's global cafeteria.

Most ships feature self-serve buffets for breakfast and luncheon, one of the effects of discounted fares (and less staff are required). Strangely, passengers do not seem to mind lining up for serve-yourself food. But while buffets look fine when they are fresh, after a few minutes of passengers serving themselves, they do not. And, one learns soon enough that the otherwise sweet little old ladies can become ruthlessly competitive at buffet opening time! Passengers should not have to play guessing games when it comes to food, but many cruise lines forget to put labels on food items, which slows down any buffet line. Labels on salad dressings, sauces, and cheeses would be particularly useful.

Passengers have different preferences and tastes. Some like their food plain, some like it spicy; some like *nouvelle cuisine*, some like meat and potatoes (and lots of it). Some try new things, some stick with the same old stuff. It is all a matter of personal taste. Cruise lines tend to cater to general tastes. The best ships offer food cooked more or less individually to your liking. Some people are accustomed to drinking coffee out of polystyrene plastic cups and eating food off paper plates at home. Others wouldn't dream of doing that and expect fine dining, with food correctly served on fine china, just as they do at home.

If you are *left-handed*, tell your waiter at your first meal exactly how you want your cutlery placed and to make sure that tea or coffee cup handles are turned in the correct direction (this is impossible with a fish knife, of course!). It would be better if right- or left-hand preferences were established when you book, and the cruise lines informed the ship.

Menus are displayed outside the dining room each day so that you can preview each meal. Suite occupants have menus delivered. When looking at the menu, one thing you will never have to do is to consider the price: it is all included.

HEALTHY EATING

With more emphasis placed on low-cholesterol and low-salt diets today, most ships have "spa" menus with calorie-filled sauces replaced by spa cuisine. Some cruise lines include basic nutritional information, such as the calorie count and fat, protein, and carbohydrate content, on their

Courtesy Douglas Ward

*The large selection of teas aboard Arkona Reisen's **Aida**.*

"spa" menus, or for selected "light" items on their regular menus (mostly for dinner, seldom for breakfast or luncheon).

If you are vegetarian, vegan, macrobiotic, counting calories, want a salt-free, sugar-restricted, low-fat, low-cholesterol, or any other diet, advise your travel agent at the time of booking, and get the cruise line to confirm that the ship can actually handle your dietary requirements. *Note*: Cruise ship food does tend to be liberally sprinkled with salt, and vegetables are often cooked with sauces containing dairy products, salt, and sugar.

THE DINING ROOM
Aboard many ships, the running and staffing of dining rooms is contracted to a specialist maritime catering organization. Ships that cruise in waters away from their home country find that professional catering companies do an excellent job. The quality is generally to a good standard. However, ships that control their own catering staff and food are often those that go to great lengths to ensure that their passengers are satisfied.

DINING ROOM STAFF
The maître d' is an experienced host, with shrewd perceptions about compatibility. It is his responsibility to seat you with compatible fellow passengers. If a table reservation has been arranged prior to boarding, you will find a table assignment/seating card in your cabin when you embark. If not, make your reservation with the maître d' or one of his assistants immediately after you embark.

Unless you are with your own family or group of friends, you will be seated next to strangers. Tables for two are a rarity; most tables seat four, six, or eight. It is a good idea to ask to be seated at a larger table, because if you are a couple seated at a table for four and you do not get along with your table partners, there is no one else to talk to. And remember, if the ship is full, it may be difficult to change tables once the cruise has started.

If you are unhappy with any aspect of the dining room operation, the sooner you tell someone the better. Do not wait until the cruise is over to send a scathing letter to the cruise line, for then it is too late to do anything positive.

The best waiters are those trained in European hotels or hotel/catering schools. These qualified individuals excel in fine service. They will learn your likes and dislikes quickly. They normally work aboard the best ships, where dignified professionalism is expected and living conditions are good.

SMOKING/NONSMOKING
Many ships have totally nonsmoking dining rooms, while some provide smoking (cigarettes only, not cigars or pipes) and nonsmoking sections. Nonsmokers who wish to sit in a no-smoking area should tell the maître d' when reserving a table. Note that at open seating breakfasts and luncheons in the dining room (or informal buffet dining area), smokers and nonsmokers may be seated close together.

THE CAPTAIN'S TABLE
The captain usually occupies a large table in or near the center of the dining room on "formal" nights. The table seats eight or more people picked from the passenger or "commend" list by the hotel manager. If you are invited to the captain's table it is gracious to accept, and you will have the chance to ask all the questions you like about shipboard life.

WHICH SEATING?

↪ **Open Seating**: you can sit at *any* available table, with whom *you* wish, at *whatever time* you choose (within dining room hours).

↪ **Single Seating**: you can choose *when* you wish to eat (within dining room hours) but have an assigned table for the cruise.

↪ **Two Seatings**: you are assigned (or choose) one of two seatings, early or late. Typical meal times for two-seating ships are:

a) Breakfast: 6:30am/8:30am
b) Lunch: 12:00noon/1:30pm
c) Dinner: 6:30pm/8:30pm

International Dinner

HEALTHY CHOICE MENU

Our Healthy Choice Menu reflects today's awareness of lighter, more balanced diets. In response to these nutritional needs, Princess Cruises offers dishes that are low in cholesterol, fat, and sodium but high in flavor.

U.S.A.: FRESH FRUIT CUP CALIFORNIA STYLE

CHINA: WOR WON TON AND VEGETABLE SOUP

NEW ZEALAND: JOHN DORY FILLET MAORI STYLE

AUSTRIA: KRANZ CAKE, WARM VANILLA CUSTARD SAUCE

VEGETARIAN MENU

U.S.A.: FRESH FRUIT CUP CALIFORNIA STYLE

GREECE: GREEK SALAD, MEDITERRANEAN DRESSING

ITALY: RISOTTO WITH ASPARAGUS

FRANCE: PUFF PASTRY VEGETABLE ROLL WITH TOMATO SAUCE

SWITZERLAND: VACHERIN SUISSE

ASSORTED INTERNATIONAL CHEESE AND CRACKERS

ALWAYS AVAILABLE

CLASSIC CAESAR SALAD

BROILED NORTH SEA SILVER SALMON FILLET

GRILLED SKINLESS CHICKEN BREAST

GRILLED BLACK ANGUS SIRLOIN STEAK

Baked Potato and French Fries can be requested in addition to the daily vegetable selection.

APPETIZERS

ITALY: COCKTAIL DI GRANSEOLA COSTA ESMERALDA
Crabmeat Served in Half Cantaloupe Melon with Aurora Sauce
FRANCE: SMOKED BREAST OF STRASBOURG DUCKLING
ENGLAND: CURED YORK ROLLS ON A BED OF FRESH BABY LEAVES
U.S.A.: FRESH FRUIT CUP CALIFORNIA STYLE

SOUPS

CHINA: WOR WON TON AND VEGETABLE SOUP
SCOTLAND: MUTTON AND BARLEY SOUP
POLYNESIA: CHILLED TROPICAL FRESH FRUIT CREAM SOUP

SALAD

GREECE: GREEK SALAD, MEDITERRANEAN DRESSING

PRINCESS FAVORITE

ITALY: RISOTTO CON POLLO E ASPARAGI
*A Combination of Italian Carnaroli Rice with Green Asparagus Tips and
Strips of Chicken Finished with Freshly Grated Parmesan Cheese and Herbs*

ENTRÉES

NEW ZEALAND: JOHN DORY FILLET MAORI STYLE

NORWAY: RAINBOW TROUT SEVEN SISTERS FJORD FASHION
Poached and Served with a Delicate Dill Sauce. Potatoes au Gratin
HOLLAND: GLAZED MILK-FED VEAL LEG ANCIENNE
Sliced and Served with a Mushroom Morel Cream Sauce, Hollandaise Potatoes
AUSTRALIA: OVEN-BAKED SPRING LEG OF LAMB AUSSIE STYLE
Coated with Mustard and Aromatic Herbs Flavored with Mint
U.S.A.: SURF AND TURF
*Fillet Mignon and Jumbo Shrimp from the Grill
with Browned Red New Potatoes and Bâtonnet Vegetables*

CELLAR MASTER SUGGESTIONS

	Glass	*Bottle*
FUME BLANC ROBERT MONDAVI, NAPA VALLEY	$5.50	$21.00
CHARDONNAY CUVAISON, NAPA VALLEY		$34.00
CABERNET SAUVIGNON WENTE ESTATE, LIVERMORE VALLEY	$5.50	$22.00
CABERNET SAUVIGNON GUENOC ESTATE, LAKE COUNTY		$24.00

Note: Some ships that operate in Europe (the Mediterranean) or South America will probably have later meal times. Dinner hours may also vary when the ship is in port to allow for the timing of shore excursions.

A TYPICAL DAY

From morning till night (and beyond), food is offered to the point of overkill, even aboard the most modest cruise ship.

→ 6:00am: hot coffee and tea on deck for early risers.

→ Full breakfast: typically with as many as 60 different items, in the main dining room. For a more casual meal, you can serve yourself buffet-style at an indoor/outdoor deck café (the choice may be more restricted than in the main dining room, yet adequate).

→ Lunchtime: with service in the dining room, buffet-style at an informal café, or at a separate grill for hot dogs and hamburgers, and a pizzeria, where everything is cooked right in front of you but usually presented with less style than at a fast food restaurant.

→ 4:00pm: Afternoon tea, in the British tradition, complete with finger sandwiches and cakes. This may be served in one of the main lounges to the accompaniment of live music (it may even be a "tea-dance") or recorded classical music.

→ Dinner: the main event of the evening, and apart from the casualness of the first and last nights, it is formal in style.

→ Midnight Buffet: without a doubt the most famous of all shipboard meals. They are grand spreads, often based around a different theme each night, (seafood, Oriental, tropical fruit fantasy, chocoholic, etc.). There may be a Gala Midnight Buffet (usually on the penultimate evening), for which the chefs pull out all the stops.

PLATE SERVICE VS. SILVER SERVICE

Plate Service: When the food is presented as a complete dish, it is as the chef wants it to look; color combinations, the size of the component parts, and their positioning on the plate. All are important. In most cruise ships, "plate service" is now the norm. It works well and means that most people seated at a table will be served at the same time and can eat together, rather than let their food become cold, as can be the case with silver service.

Silver Service: When the component parts are brought to the table separately, so that the diner, not the chef, can choose what goes on the plate and in what proportion. Silver service is best when there is plenty of time (few cruise ships provide silver service). What some cruise lines class as silver service is actually silver service of vegetables only, with the main item, be it fish, fowl, or meat, already positioned on the plate.

NATIONAL DIFFERENCES

The different nationalities among passengers present their own special needs and requirements. Some examples:

→ Asian, British, German, and other European passengers like boiled eggs served in real china eggcups for breakfast. North Americans rarely eat boiled eggs, and most often put the eggs into a bowl and eat them with a fork.

→ German passengers tend to prefer breads (especially dark breads) and a wide variety of cheeses for breakfast and lunch. They tend to like yellow (not white) potatoes. They also have an obvious liking for German draught or bottled beers rather than American canned beers.

→ French passengers have a liking for soft, not flaky, croissants, and may request brioche and confitures.

→ Japanese passengers like "bento box," breakfasts of salmon and eel, and vegetable pickles, as well as Japanese rice, which is very different from Chinese rice.

*A lovely presentation of breakfast for two from room service aboard **Silver Cloud.***

→ Southern Italians like to have red sauce with just about everything, while northern Italians like less of the red sauces and more white sauces and flavorings, such as garlic, with their pasta.

→ Australian passengers need "vegemite" to spread on bread and toast.

→ North Americans like weak coffee with everything, often before, during, and after a meal. This is why, even on the most upscale ships, sugar is placed on tables (also for iced tea). North Americans tend to eat and run, whereas Europeans, for example, like to dine in a more leisurely fashion, treating mealtimes as a social occasion.

→ Most passengers agree that cruise coffee is appalling, but often it is simply the chlorinated water that gives it a different taste. Europeans prefer strong coffee, usually made from the coffee beans of African countries like Kenya. North Americans usually drink the coffee from Colombia or Jamaica.

→ European tea drinkers like to drink tea out of tea cups, not coffee or sports mugs (very few cruise ships know how to make a decent cup of tea, so British passengers in particular should be aware of this).

THE EXECUTIVE CHEF

The executive chef plans the menus, orders the food, organizes his staff, and arranges all the meals on the menus. He makes sure that menus are not repeated, even on long cruises. On some cruises, he works with guest chefs from restaurants ashore to offer tastes of regional cuisine. He may also purchase fish, seafood, fruit, and various other local produce in "wayside" ports and incorporate them into the menu with a "special of the day" announcement.

THE GALLEY

The galley ("kitchen" for landlubbers) is the heart of all food preparation on board. At any time of the day or night, there is plenty of activity, whether it is baking fresh bread at 2:00am, making meals and snacks for passengers and crew around the clock, or decorating a special birthday cake. The staff, from executive chef to pot-washer, all work together as a team, each designated a specific role, with little room for error.

The galley and preparation areas consist of the following sections (the names in parentheses are the French names given to the person who is the specialist in the area of expertise):

Fish Preparation Area (Poisonnier): This area contains freezers and a fully equipped preparation room, where fish is cleaned and cut to size before it is sent to the galley.

Meat Preparation Area (Butcher/Rotisseur): This area contains separate freezers for meat and poultry. Their temperatures are kept at approximately 10°F. There are also defrosting areas (35°F to 40°F). Meat and poultry are sliced and portioned before being sent to the galley.

Vegetable Preparation Area (Entremetier): Vegetables are cleaned and prepared in this area.

Sauce Preparation Area (Saucier): This is where the sauces are prepared.

Soup Preparation Area (Potagier): Soups are made in huge tureens.

Cold Kitchen (Garde Manger): This is the area where all cold dishes and salads are prepared, from the simplest sandwich (for room service, for example) to the works of art that grace the buffets. The area is well equipped with mixing machines, slicing machines, and refrigeration cabinets where prepared dishes are stored until required.

Bakery and Pastry Shop (Baker): This area provides the raw ingredients for preparing food, and contains dough mixers, refrigerators, proving ovens, ovens, and containers in all manner of shapes and sizes. Dessert items, pastries, sweets, and other confectionery are prepared and made here.

Pantry: This is where cheese and fruits are prepared, and where sandwiches are made.

Dishwashing Area: This area contains huge conveyor-belt dishwashing machines. Wash and rinse temperatures are carefully controlled to comply with public health regulations. This is where all cooking utensils are scrubbed and cleaned, and where the silverware is scrupulously polished.

HYGIENE STANDARDS

Galley equipment is in almost constant use, and regular inspections and maintenance help detect potential problems. There is continual cleaning of equipment, utensils, bulkheads, floors, and hands.

Cruise ships sailing from or visiting US ports are subject to sanitation inspections. These are voluntary, not mandatory inspections, based on forty-two inspection items, undertaken by the United States Public Health (USPH) Department of Health and Human Services, under the auspices of the Centers for Disease Control. The cruise line pays for each ship inspection. A similar process takes place in Britain under the Port Health Authority, which has even more stringent guidelines.

A tour of the galley proves to be a highlight for some passengers, when a ship's insurance company permits. A video of *Behind the Scenes*, for use on in-cabin television, may be provided instead.

In accordance with internationally accepted standards, all potable water brought on board, or produced by distillation on cruise ships, should contain a free chlorine or bromine residual equal to or greater than 0.2 ppm (parts per million). This is why drinking water served in the dining room often tastes of chlorine.

ENVIRONMENTAL CONCERNS

Cruise ships refine oil, treat human waste, and incinerate garbage, but that's not enough today, as pressure continues to mount for clean oceans. Cruise ships and their operating companies have a unique position among all shipping interests. They are not likely to damage the ocean environment as compared with oil tankers, although spillage of any kind is regrettable.

Other environmental concerns involve the condition of the air aboard ships. Of particular note is the fact that a ship's air-conditioning system can provide an ideal site for mold growth such as that found in the aerospora group (including *Cladosporium sp.*). Thus, it is vitally important that cruise lines not skimp on maintenance, and the replacement of filters and other items in air-conditioning systems.

WASTE DISPOSAL

Cruise ships must be capable of efficient handling of garbage and waste materials, as trash generated by passengers and crew must be managed, stored, and disposed of efficiently and economically. The larger the ship, the more waste is created, and the greater the need for reliable disposal systems.

Trash includes bottles, cans, corrugated cartons, fabrics, foodstuffs, paper products, plastic containers, as well as medical waste, sludge oil, wet waste, and so on. The sheer magnitude of waste materials can be highly problematic, especially on long cruises. If solid waste is not burnable, or cannot be disposed of overboard (this must be biodegradable), it must be stored for later off-loading and disposal on land.

Although the latest breed of cruise ships is equipped with "zero-discharge" facilities, many older cruise ships still have a way to go when it comes to garbage handling. One method of dealing with food waste is to send it to a waste-pulping machine that has been partially filled with water. Cutting mechanisms reduce the waste and allow it to pass through a special sizing ring to be pumped directly overboard or into a holding tank or an incinerator when the ship is within three-mile limits.

Whichever method of waste disposal is chosen, it, as well as the ship, must meet the extremely stringent demands of Annex V of MARPOL 73/78 international regulations.

CAVIAR AND CHAMPAGNE

Although it might seem like it from menu descriptions, most ships do not serve Beluga caviar, but the less expensive and more widely available Sevruga and Sevruga Malossol (low-salt) caviar. Even more widely served aboard the standard cruise ships is Norwegian lumpfish caviar. If you are partial to the best caviar, you might want to know that Cunard's *QE2* is reputed to be the world's largest single buyer of Beluga caviar (spending about half a million dollars annually), after the Russian and the Ukrainian governments.

Those who have not tasted good caviar may find it very salty. That's because the eggs are taken fresh from a sleeping female sturgeon (it takes about 20 years for a female beluga sturgeon to mature). The eggs are then passed through a screen to separate them from other fibrous matter, then mixed with salt, which acts as a preservative and also promotes the taste. The more salt added, the better the caviar is preserved; the less salt added the finer the taste.

The process is done by highly skilled labor, which adds to its cost. The two countries that produce most of the world's caviar are Iran and Russia (both countries produce farmed sturgeon stock, which is released into the Caspian Sea continually to replenish dwindling stocks). In general, Russian caviar is more highly salted than caviar from Iran. And just as each vineyard produces different wines, so each fishery will produce different-tasting caviar. Additionally, there are about 400 species of sturgeon, so grades can differ.

The Caspian Sea is the spawning ground for 90 percent of the world's caviar-producing sturgeon. There are three types that are fished for caviar.

→ The giant beluga is hardest to find and the most expensive. It can weigh 1,500 pounds or more. One fish can yield up to 20 pounds of caviar, and its smoky-gray eggs are the largest (they are also the most delicate).

→ The second most desirable caviar fish is the ossetra. This takes about 13 years to mature, and weighs up to about 40 pounds. These are the most durable eggs (they are also smaller) and range in color from a darkish brass to olive green.

→ The third caviar fish is the sevruga, which weighs about six pounds. It also has small eggs, ranging in color from soft gray to dark gray.

→ There is also a fourth type of sturgeon, known as a sterlet, which produces a translucent golden egg, although it is hard to find today (prior to 1917 all the golden caviar was sent to the Tsar in Russia).

There was a time when sturgeon was found in abundance. So much so that caviar was often placed on the bars of London and New York as a snack to promote the sale of beer and ale. Caviar is a natural accompaniment for good champagne, but good champagne (like anything else of high quality) doesn't come cheap. What most ships use as champagne, for the Captain's Welcome Aboard Cocktail Party, for example, just about passes as champagne. Some ships feature a caviar and champagne bar on board, offering several varieties of caviar at extra cost.

Champagne making is a real art (in France itself the production of Champagne is restricted to a very small geographic area). Unlike wine, it is bottled in many sizes, ranging from the minute to the ridiculously huge, and with a variety of names to match:

Quarter bottle:	18.7 centiliters
Half bottle (split):	37.5 centiliters
Bottle:	75 centiliters
Magnum:	2 bottles
Jeroboam:	4 bottles

Rehoboam:	6 bottles
Methuselah:	8 bottles
Salmanazar:	12 bottles
Balthazar:	16 bottles
Nebuchadnezzar:	20 bottles

The three main grape-growing districts in Champagne are: the Montagne de Reims, to the south and east of Reims; the Vallée de la Marne, surrounding the river; and the Côtes des Blancs, south of Epernay. The first two mainly grow the dark pinot-noir and pinot-meunier grapes; the latter grows the white chardonnay variety (all are used in making champagne). Removing the husks before full fermentation prevents the dark grapes from coloring the wine red. If pink champagne is required, the skins are left in the grape mix for a longer time to add color.

Although the Champagne area has been producing wines of renown for a long time, its vintners were unable to keep their bubbles from fizzling out until a monk in the Abbey of Hautvilliers, whose name was Dom Perignon, came up with the solution. The bubbles — escaping carbonic acid gas — had always escaped, until Dom Perignon devised a bottle capable of containing the champagne without it exploding from the bottle, a common occurrence in local cellars. The legacy of this clever monk is that the champagne bottle is the strongest bottle made today. Its thickness is concentrated around the bottle's base and shoulders. Dom Perignon's bottle was aided by the coincidental development of the cork.

Even after his work, champagne was not the perfect elixir enjoyed today. It was rather cloudy due to residual sediment (dead yeast cells). Its bubbles, therefore, could not be truly relished visually until la Veuve Cliquot (the Widow Cliquot) devised the system of *remuage* in the nineteenth century. Rather than laying the bottles down horizontally for their period of aging, she put them in a special rack, called a pupitre, which held them at a 45-degree angle, with the neck of the bottle facing down. Each day, the bottles are given a short, sharp, quarter turn so as to shake the sediment, which gradually settles in the neck of the bottle.

Once this is complete, a process called *dégorgement* freezes the neck of the bottle. It is then uncorked and internal pressure ejects the ice containing the sediment. Obviously, this means that the bottle is a little less than totally full, so the champagne is topped up with what is called the *dosage*, which is a sweet champagne liqueur. The degree of sweetness of this addition depends on the tastes of the market to which the champagne is ultimately destined. After the *dosage* is added, the permanent cork is forced in and wired up. The bottles then remain in the cellar of the winery until they are ordered. Each bottle is then washed and labeled prior to being shipped for sale.

SAMPLE FOOD AND BEVERAGE CONSUMPTION AND STORES

Consumption and stores required for one transatlantic crossing of the *QE2* (six days):

Food Consumption

Beef	9,000 pounds	Cereals	800 pounds
Veal	8,000 pounds	Rice/Other Grains	3,000 pounds
Lamb	2,000 pounds	Flour	5,000 pounds
Pork	2,500 pounds	Cream	250 gallons
Chicken	3,500 pounds	Milk	1,150 gallons
Duck	1,000 pounds	Ice Cream	450 gallons
Turkey	1,000 pounds	Butter	2,500 pounds
Bacon	2,000 pounds	Eggs	43,000
Sausages	2,000 pounds	Juices	3,000 gallons
Ham	8,000 pounds	Jam/Marmalade	300 dozen jars
Caviar	75 pounds	Jam/Marmalade (bulk)	700 pounds
Foie Gras	15 pounds	Pickles/Condiments	200 bottles
Fish	1,000 pounds	Tea Bags	12,800
Lobster	1,500 pounds	Kosher Food	800 pounds
Crab	800 pounds	Biscuits	2,000 pounds
Tinned Fish	1,500 cans	Dog Biscuits	50 pounds
Fresh Vegetables	12,000 pounds	Baby Food	600 jars
Potatoes	3,000 pounds		

Bar Consumption

Champagnes	780 bottles	Liqueurs	260 bottles
Assorted Wines*	1,560 bottles	Port	120 bottles
Whiskey	500 bottles	Sherry	240 bottles
Gin	600 bottles	Beer (passengers)	5,230 bottles
Rum	240 bottles	Beer (crew)	8,530 cans
Vodka	130 bottles	Fruit Juice	25,720 pints
Brandy	240 bottles	*the cellar contains 25,000 bottles	

The Laundry List

Tablecloths	2,932	Bath Mats	1,650
Blankets	4,300	Hand Towels	15,500
Oven Cloths	1,000	Bath/Other Towels	13,000
Sheets	11,600	Aprons	1,500
Pillow Cases	13,100	Deck Rugs	750
Laundry Bags	3,250		

CRUISING FOR THE PHYSICALLY CHALLENGED

The *advantages* of a cruise for the physically challenged are many:

→ Good place for relaxation and self-renewal.

→ Pure air at sea (no smog, no pollen).

→ No packing and unpacking.

→ Spacious public rooms.

→ Excellent medical facilities close by.

→ Specialized dietary requirements can be catered to.

→ The staff will generally be very helpful.

→ Varied entertainment.

→ Gambling (but, as yet, no wheelchair-accessible gaming tables or slot machines).

→ Security (no crime on board).

→ Different ports of call.

The *disadvantages* of a cruise for the physically challenged are:

→ No ships have yet installed access-help lifts into their swimming pools or thalassotherapy pools.

→ Unless cabins are specifically designed for the physically challenged, problem areas include the entrance, furniture configuration, closet hanging rails, and beds.

→ Cabin bathrooms: doors that open inward are useless; the grab bars, wheel-in shower stall, toiletries cabinet should be at an accessible height.

→ Elevator doorways: the width of the door is important for wheelchair passengers; controls are often not at a height suitable for operation from a wheelchair (except in the newer ships).

→ Sometimes having to wait behind hordes of able-bodied passengers who really do not need to use the elevators.

→ Access to outside decks is not often provided through electric-eye doors that open and close automatically. Rather it is provided through doorways that have to be opened manually.

Cruise lines, port authorities, airlines, and various allied services are slowly improving their facilities for the physically challenged. Not all are in wheelchairs, of course, but all have needs that the cruise industry is (slowly) working to accommodate. Few cruise lines show photographs of passengers in wheelchairs.

The design of ships has traditionally worked against the mobility-limited. To keep water out or to prevent water escaping from a flooded cabin or public area, raised edges (known as "coamings" or "lips") are often placed in doorways and across exit pathways. Also, cabin doorways are often not wide enough to accommodate even a standard wheelchair. A "standard" cabin door is about 24 inches (60.9 centimeters) wide.

Cabins designed for the mobility-limited have doors that are about 30 inches (76.2 centimeters) wide. "Standard" bathroom doors are normally only about 22 inches (55.8 centimeters) wide, whereas those designed for wheelchairs are about 28–30 inches (71.1–76.2 centimeters) wide. Ask your travel agent to confirm the width of cabin and bathroom doors. Remember to allow for the fact that your knuckles on either side of a wheelchair can add to the width of your wheelchair. Beds in cabins for the physically challenged aboard *Carnival Destiny* are equipped with a "panic" button, adjacent to a bedside light switch.

Bathroom doors are a particular problem, and the door itself, whether it opens outward into the cabin or inward into the bathroom, only compounds the problems of maneuvering a wheelchair within a cramped space. Four cabins for the physically challenged in the *QE2*, however, have electrically operated sliding doors into the bathroom, a completely level entrance into both cabin and bathroom, and remote-controlled lights, curtains, and doors, as well as a door intercom and alarm.

Bathrooms in many older ships are normally small and full of plumbing fixtures, often at odd angles, awkward when moving about from the confines of a wheelchair. The bathrooms aboard new ships are more accessible, but the plumbing is often located beneath the complete prefabricated module, making the floor higher than that in the cabin, which means a ramp must be fitted in order to wheel in.

Some cruise lines will, if given advance notice, remove a bathroom door and hang a fabric curtain in its place. Many lines will provide ramps for the bathroom doorway, where a sill or "lip" is encountered.

It was once the policy of almost all cruise lines to discourage the mobility-limited from taking a cruise or traveling anywhere by ship for reasons of safety, insurance, and legal liability. But a cruise is the ideal holiday for the physically challenged, as it provides a relaxed environment with plenty of social contact, organized entertainment, and activities. Despite most brochures declaring that they accept wheelchairs, few ships are well fitted to accommodate them. Some cruise lines (such as) openly state that all public restrooms and cabin bathrooms are inaccessible to wheelchair-bound passengers.

The list at the end of this chapter pertains to all the ships presented in Part Two and provides a guide as to their accessibility (the author, or one of his staff, personally wheels around each ship to check).

Once you've decided on your ship and cruise, the next step is to select your accommodation. There are many grades of cabin, depending on size, facilities, and location. Choose a cruise line that permits you to choose a specific cabin, rather than one that merely allows you to select a price category, then assigns you a cabin immediately prior to your departure date or, worse still, actually at embarkation.

Cabins: What They Should Include:

→ No "lip" or threshold at the cabin door, which should be a minimum of 35 inches wide (89.0 centimeters).

→ Bedside "panic" button linked to the navigation bridge (which is manned 24 hours a day).

→ Enough space to maneuver a wheelchair between entrance, bed, closet, and bathroom.

→ Closet with "pull down" clothes rail.

→ Telephone mounted at wheelchair height (not high up on wall).

→ Mirrors that are useable when seated in a wheelchair.

→ Safe or lockable drawer that is reachable at wheelchair height.

Bathrooms: What They Should Include:

→ Outward opening door.

→ No "lip" at bathroom door.

→ No "lip" into shower stall.

→ Shower stall (with detachable showerhead located at head height when seated in a wheelchair).

→ Shower chair that folds up when not in use, and grab rails.

→ Grab rails for toilet.

→ Toilet with electric automatic seat pad cleaner.

→ Sink at low enough height for wheelchair to move up close.

→ Emergency (panic) button in or adjacent to shower (for falls).

The following tips will help you choose wisely:

→ If the ship does not have any specially equipped cabins for the physically challenged, book the best outside cabin in your price range or choose another ship. However, be careful as you may find that even cruise brochures that state that a ship has "wheelchair accessible" cabins fail to say whether the wheelchair will fit through the *bathroom* door, or whether there is a "lip" at the door. Find out whether the wheelchair can fit into the shower area. Get your travel agent to check, and recheck the details. Do not take "I think so" as an answer. Get specific measurements.

→ Choose a cabin that is close to an elevator. Not all elevators go to all decks, so check the deck plan carefully. Example: The cabins for the physically challenged in *Radisson Diamond* are located as far away from the elevators as possible. Smaller and older vessels may not even have elevators, making access to many areas, including the dining room, difficult or almost impossible.

→ Avoid, at all costs, a cabin down a little alleyway shared by several other cabins, even if the price is attractive. The space along these alleyways is extremely limited and entering one of these cabins in a wheelchair is likely to be a frustrating experience.

→ Cabins located amidships are less affected by vessel motion, so choose something in the middle of the ship if you are concerned about rough seas, no matter how infrequently they might occur.

→ The larger (and therefore the more expensive) the cabin, the more room you will have to maneuver in. Nowhere does this assume more importance than in the bathroom.

→ If your budget allows, pick a cabin with a bath rather than just a shower, because there will be considerably more room, especially if you are unable to stand comfortably enough.

→ Meals in some ships may be served in your cabin, on special request. This is a decided advantage should you wish to avoid dressing for every meal. There are, however, few ships that have enough actual space in the cabin for dining tables.

→ If you want to join other passengers in the dining room and your ship offers two fixed-time seatings for meals, choose the second rather than the first. Then you can linger over your dinner, secure in the knowledge that the waiter will not try to rush you.

→ Space at dining room tables can be somewhat limited in many ships. When making table reservations, therefore, tell the maître d' that you would like a table that leaves plenty of room for your wheelchair, so that it doesn't become an obstacle for the waiters and leaves plenty of room for them — or other passengers — to get past.

→ Even if you do find a travel agent who knows your needs and understands your requirements, try to follow up on all aspects of the booking yourself so that there will be no slip-ups when the day arrives for you to travel.

→ Take your own wheelchair with you, as ships carry a very limited number of wheelchairs; in any case these are meant for emergency hospital use only. An alternative is to rent an electric wheelchair, which can be delivered to the ship on your sailing date.

→ Hanging rails in the closets on most ships are positioned too high for someone who is wheelchair-bound to reach (even the latest ships seem to repeat this basic error). There are some cruise ships, however, that do have cabins specially fitted out to suit the mobility-limited, in which this and similar problem areas have been dealt with. Four special cabins in the *QE2* and *Seabourn Sun*, for example, are fitted with walk-in closets and have a pull-down facility to bring your clothes down to any height you want.

→ Elevators are a constant source of difficulty for wheelchair passengers. Often the control buttons are located far too high to reach, especially those for upper decks.

→ Doors on upper decks that open onto a Promenade or Lido Deck are very strong, are difficult to handle, and have high sills. Unless you are ambulatory, or can get out of your wheelchair, these doors can be a source of annoyance, even if there is help at hand, as they open inward or outward (they should ideally be electrically operated sliding doors).

→ Advise any airline you might be traveling with of any special needs well ahead of time so that arrangements can be made to accommodate you without last-minute problems.

→ Advise the cruise line repeatedly of the need for proper transfer facilities, in particular buses or vans with wheelchair ramps.

EMBARKATION

Even if you've alerted the airline and arranged your travel according to your needs, there is still one problem to surmount when you arrive at the cruise embarkation port to join your ship: the actual boarding. If you embark at ground level, the gangway to the ship may be level or inclined. It will depend on the embarkation deck of the ship and/or the tide in the port. Alternatively, you may be required to embark from an upper level of a terminal, in which case the gangway could well be of the floating loading-bridge type, like those used at major airports. Some have flat floors; others may have raised lips spaced every three feet (awkward to negotiate in a wheelchair, especially if the gangway is made steeper by a rising tide).

TENDERING

Cruise lines should provide an anchor emblem in brochures for those ports of call where a ship will be at anchor instead of alongside. If the ship is at anchor, be prepared for an interesting but safe experience. The crew will lower you and your wheelchair into a waiting tender (ship-to-shore launch) and then, after a short boat-ride, lift you out again onto a rigged gangway or integral plat-form. If the sea is calm, this maneuver proceeds uneventfully; if the sea is choppy, your embarka-tion could vary from exciting to harrowing. Fortunately (or not) this type of embarkation is rare unless you are leaving a busy port with several ships all sailing the same day.

WHEELCHAIRS

Wheelchair passengers with limited mobility should use a collapsible wheelchair. By limited mobil-ity, I mean a person able to get out of the wheelchair and step over a sill or walk with a cane, crutch-es, or other walking device.

The chart that follows indicates the best cruise ships for wheelchair accessibility. Remember to ask questions before you make a reservation. Examples:

→ Does the cruise line's travel insurance (with a cancellation/trip interruption) cover you for any injuries while you are aboard ship?

→ Are there any public rooms or public decks on board the ship that are inaccessible to wheelchairs (for instance, it is sometimes difficult to obtain access to the outdoor swimming pool deck)?

→ Will you be guaranteed a good viewing place in the main showroom from where you can see the shows if seated in a wheelchair?

→ Will special transportation be provided to transfer you from airport to ship?

→ If you need a collapsible wheelchair, can this be provided by the cruise line?

→ Are passengers required to sign a medical release?

→ Do passengers need a doctor's note to qualify for a cabin for the physically challenged?

→ Will crew members be on hand to help, or must the passengers rely on their own traveling com-panions for help?

→ Are the ship's tenders accessible to wheelchairs?

→ How do you get from your cabin to the lifeboats (which may be up or down several decks) in an emergency if the elevators are out of action and cannot be used?

WAIVERS

Passengers who do not require wheelchairs but are challenged in other ways, such as those who have impaired sight, hearing, or speech, present their own particular requirements. Many of these can be avoided if the person is accompanied by an able-bodied companion experienced in attending to their special needs. In any event, some cruise lines require physically challenged passengers to sign a waiver.

HEARING IMPAIRED

Many people suffer from hearing loss. Those affected should be aware of problems aboard ship:

→ Hearing the announcements on the public address system.

→ Use of the telephone.

→ Poor acoustics in key areas (for example, boarding shore tenders).

Take a spare battery for your hearing aid. More new ships have cabins specially fitted with colored signs to help those who are hearing impaired. Crystal Cruises' *Crystal Harmony* and *Crystal Symphony*, and Celebrity Cruises' *Century*, *Galaxy,* and *Mercury* are fitted with movie theaters with special headsets for the hearing impaired.

Many ships make life difficult for the hearing impaired, with constant, irritating, and repetitive announcements. It is often difficult for the hearing impaired to distinguish important or useful announcements from those that are of little or no importance.

Finally, when going ashore, particularly on organized excursions, be aware that most destinations are simply not equipped to handle the hearing impaired.

SHIPS RATED FOR WHEELCHAIR ACCESSIBILITY

Ship	Suitability Level	Ship	Suitability Level
Aegean I	D	*Enchanted Capri*	D
Aida	B	*Enchanted Isle*	D
Albatros	D	*Enchantment of the Seas*	B
Ambasador I	D	*Europa*	B
Apollon	C	*Explorer*	D
Arcadia (Golden Sun Cruises)	D	*Fair Princess*	D
Arcadia (P&O Cruises)	B	*Fantasy*	C
Arkona	C	*Fascination*	C
Astor	C	*Flamenco*	D
Astra II	D	*Flying Cloud*	D
Asuka	C	*Fuji Maru*	D
Atalante	D	*Funchal*	D
Aurora	A	*Galapagos Discovery*	D
Ausonia	D	*Galapagos Explorer II*	D
Azur	D	*Galaxy*	B
Black Prince	D	*Grande Caribe*	D
Black Watch	C	*Grande Mariner*	D
Bolero	D	*Grandeur of the Seas*	B
Bremen	D	*Grand Princess*	A
Caledonian Star	D	*Hanseatic*	D
Carnival Destiny	B	*Hebridean Princess*	D
Carnival Triumph	B	*Holiday*	D
Carnival Victory	B	*Hong Kong Dragon Star*	D
Caronia	C	*Horizon*	B
Carousel	D	*Hyundai Bongnae*	C
Celebration	D	*Hyundai Kumgang*	D
Century	B	*Hyundai Pungak*	C
Clelia II	D	*Imagination*	C
Clipper Adventurer	D	*Independence*	D
Clipper Odyssey	C	*Inspiration*	C
Club Med 2	D	*IslandBreeze*	D
Columbus	C	*Italia Prima*	D
CostaAllegra	D	*Jason*	D
CostaAtlantica	B	*Jubilee*	D
CostaClassica	B	*Kapitan Khlebnikov*	D
CostaMarina	D	*Kristina Regina*	D
CostaRiviera	D	*Legacy*	D
CostaRomantica	B	*Legend of the Seas*	B
CostaVictoria	B	*Leisure World*	D
Crown Dynasty	C	*Le Levant*	D
Crown Princess	B	*Le Ponant*	D
Crystal Harmony	A	*Maasdam*	B
Crystal Symphony	A	*Majesty of the Seas*	C
Dalmacija	D	*Mandalay*	D
Dawn Princess	A	*Marco Polo*	C
Delphin	D	*Maxim Gorkiy*	D
Disney Magic	B	*MegaStar Aries*	D
Disney Wonder	B	*MegaStar Taurus*	D
Dolphin IV	D	*Melody*	C
Don Juan	D	*Mercury*	B
Ecstasy	C	*Mermoz*	D
Elation	C	*Millennium*	A
Emerald	D	*Minerva*	C

SHIPS RATED FOR WHEELCHAIR ACCESSIBILITY

Ship	Suitability Level	Ship	Suitability Level
Mistral	C	*Renaissance Seven*	D
Monarch of the Seas	C	*Renaissance Eight*	D
Monet	D	*Rhapsody*	D
Monterey	D	*Rhapsody of the Seas*	B
Nantucket Clipper	D	*Rotterdam*	A
Neptune	D	*Royal Clipper*	D
Niagara Prince	D	*Royal Princess*	B
Nieuw Amsterdam	C	*Royal Star*	D
Nippon Maru	D	*Ryndam*	C
Noordam	C	*Saga Rose*	C
Nordic Empress	C	*St. Helena*	D
Norway	B	*Sapphire*	D
Norwegian Crown	B	*Seabourn Goddess I*	D
Norwegian Dream	C	*Seabourn Goddess II*	D
Norwegian Majesty	D	*Seabourn Legend*	D
Norwegian Sea	D	*Seabourn Pride*	D
Norwegian Sky	B	*Seabourn Spirit*	D
Norwegian Star	C	*Seabourn Sun*	A
Norwegian Wind	C	*SeaBreeze*	D
OceanBreeze	D	*Sea Cloud*	D
Ocean Explorer I	C	*Sea Cloud II*	D
Oceanic	D	*Sea Princess*	A
Ocean Majesty	D	*Seawind Crown*	D
Ocean Princess	A	*Seawing*	D
Odysseus	D	*Sensation*	C
Olvia	D	*Seven Seas Navigator*	B
Olympic Countess	D	*Shota Rustaveli*	D
Olympic Voyager	C	*Silver Cloud*	C
Oriana	B	*Silver Shadow*	A
Orient Venus	D	*Silver Star*	D
Oriental Pearl	D	*Silver Wind*	C
Orpheus	D	*Sir Francis Drake*	D
Pacific Princess	C	*Sky Princess*	C
Pacific Venus	C	*Song of Flower*	D
Paradise	C	*Sovereign of the Seas*	C
Paul Gauguin	C	*Sovetskiy Soyuz*	D
Polaris	D	*Splendour of the Seas*	B
Polynesia	D	*Star Aquarius*	D
Princesa Amorosa	D	*Star Clipper*	D
Princesa Victoria	D	*Star Flyer*	D
Princess Danae	D	*Star Pisces*	D
Professor Khromov	D	*Statendam*	C
Queen Elizabeth 2	B	*Stella Oceanis*	D
R One	B	*Stella Solaris*	D
R Two	B	*Sunbird*	C
R Three	B	*Sundream*	D
R Four	B	*Sun Princess*	A
R Five	B	*Sun Viva*	D
R Six	B	*Sun Viva II*	D
Radisson Diamond	C	*SuperStar Europe*	A
Regal Empress	D	*SuperStar Gemini*	C
Regal Princess	B	*SuperStar Leo*	B
Rembrandt	C	*SuperStar Virgo*	B

SHIPS RATED FOR WHEELCHAIR ACCESSIBILITY

Ship	Suitability Level	Ship	Suitability Level
Switzerland	D	*Voyager of the Seas*	A
Symphony	D	*Westerdam*	C
Taras Shevchenko	D	*Wilderness Adventurer*	D
The Mercury	D	*Wilderness Discoverer*	D
The Neptune	D	*Wind Song*	D
Topaz	D	*Wind Spirit*	D
Triton	D	*Wind Star*	D
Tropicale	D	*Wind Surf*	C
Universe Explorer	D	*World Discoverer*	D
Veendam	C	*World Renaissance*	D
Victoria	C	*Yankee Clipper*	D
Viking Serenade	D	*Yorktown Clipper*	D
Vision of the Seas	B	*Zaandam*	B
Vistamar	D	*Zenith*	B
Volendam	B		

Notes

A) Recommended as most suitable for wheelchair passengers
B) Reasonably accessible for wheelchair passengers
C) Moderately accessible for wheelchair passengers
D) Not suitable for wheelchair passengers

1) The following ships of Carnival Cruise Lines have double-width entertainment deck prome-nades that are good for wheelchair passengers, but the public restrooms are not accessible. In addi-tion, although the cabin bathrooms are equipped with shower stalls and grab rails, the bathrooms have a steel "lip" and are, thus, neither suitable nor accessible when stepping out of a wheelchair: *Celebration, Ecstasy, Elation, Fantasy, Fascination, Holiday, Imagination, Inspiration, Jubilee, Paradise, Sensation.*

2) *Crystal Harmony* and *Crystal Symphony* (Crystal Cruises) are the only ships presently in oper-ation that provide special access ramps from an accommodation deck directly to the ship's lifeboats.

3) *Crown Princess* and *Regal Princess* (Princess Cruises) both have large outside cabins for the physically challenged, but they have lifeboat-obstructed views.

CRUISING FOR ROMANTICS

DID YOU KNOW...?

...that motion picture's most famous on-screen odd couple, Jack Lemmon and Walter Matthau, teamed up to be gentlemen dance hosts aboard a Caribbean cruise ship, in a film released in the US in July 1997? Called *Out to Sea*, the film also stars Gloria DeHaven, Dyan Cannon, Hal Linden, Alexander Powers, and Brent Spinner. The "cruise ship" interior was filmed at Raleigh Studios in Hollywood.

...that Epirotiki Line's *Jupiter* was used to carry the 61 finalists of the Miss Universe contest in 1976 (Epirotiki Line is now part of Royal Olympic Cruises)?

...that on Valentine's Day, 1998, some 5,000 couples renewed their vows aboard the ships of Princess Cruises.

TRAVELING SOLO OR SINGLE

Back in 1932, Warner Bros. released the film *One Way Passage*, a bittersweet story starring Kay Francis and William Powell. Remember the shipboard romance between Bette Davis and Paul Henried in the film *Now, Voyager*? Or Irene Dunne and Charles Boyer in *An Affair to Remember*? All involved oceangoing passenger ships and romance. Then there was *Gentlemen Prefer Blondes*, in which Marilyn Monroe and Jane Russell starred. In the early 1950s, Howard Hughes presented Jane Russell in an RKO movie called *The French Line*, which depicted life on board one of the great ocean liners of the time — the ss *Liberté* — as being exciting, frivolous, promiscuous, and romantic! The movie was, in fact, made on board the great ship. Today that same romantic attraction is still very much in vogue. In 1997, Kate Winslet and Leonardo DiCaprio showed young love and its great adventure aboard a stricken ocean liner on its maiden voyage across the North Atlantic, in the major Hollywood blockbuster *Titanic*.

While you may not believe in mermaids, romance does happen. With more and more people traveling alone, the possibility of a shipboard romance affords a special attraction. More than two million cruise passengers (more than 25 percent of all cruise passengers) traveled as singles in 1999. About 25 percent of all calls to travel agents are made by singles and single parents. Cruise lines are just waking up to this fact and are trying to help by providing special programs for single passengers. Some cruise lines or tour operators advertise special cruises for singles, but remember that the age range could be anything from 7 to 70.

Some singles are turned off to cruising because most cruise lines charge a single occupancy supplement for anyone traveling alone. The most precious commodity aboard any cruise ship is space. Every square foot must be used for essential facilities or revenue-earning areas. Since a single cabin is often as large as a double and uses the same electrical wiring, plumbing, and fixtures — and thus is just as expensive to build — cruise lines naturally feel justified in charging supplements or premiums for those who are occupying single cabins.

Single cabins are often among the most expensive, when compared with the per-person rates for double occupancy cabins. From the point of view of the crew, it takes as much time to clean a single cabin as it does a double. And there is only one tip instead of two.

SINGLE SUPPLEMENTS

If you want to travel alone and not share a cabin you can pay either a flat rate for the cabin or a single "supplement" if you occupy a double cabin. Some lines charge a fixed amount — $250, for instance — as a supplement, no matter what cabin category, ship, itinerary, or length of cruise you require. Single supplements, or solo occupancy rates, vary between lines, and sometimes between ships. Check with your travel agent for the latest rates.

GUARANTEED SINGLE RATES

Although some singles travel with friends or family, many others like to travel alone. For this reason, cruise lines have established several programs to accommodate them. One is the

"Guaranteed Single" rate, which provides a set price without having to be concerned about which cabin to choose. Some cruise lines have guaranteed singles' rates, but the line and *not* the passenger picks the cabin. If the line does not find a roommate, the single passenger may get the cabin to himself/herself at no extra charge.

GUARANTEED SHARE PROGRAMS

A "Guaranteed Share" program allows you to pay the normal double-occupancy rate, but the cruise line will find another passenger of the same sex to share the double cabin with you. Some cruise lines do not advertise a guaranteed-share program in their brochures but will often try to accommodate such bookings, particularly when demand for space is light. You could book a guaranteed share basis cabin only to find that you end up with a cabin to yourself. As cruise lines are apt to change such things at short notice, it is best to check with your travel agent for the latest rates, and read the fine print.

CRUISING FOR SINGLE WOMEN

Any single woman can take a cruise vacation knowing that she is going to be as safe — if not safer — than she would be in any major vacation destination, but that does not mean that a cruise ship is a totally safe, completely hassle-free environment. Common sense should be the rule. Undoubtedly though, cruising is a great way to relax, and if you are seeking that special someone, cruising somehow brings people closer together.

There is always someone to talk to, be they couples or other singles, and cruising is not a "meat market" where you are always under observation. The easiest way to meet other singles, however, is to participate in scheduled activities. Be a little assertive, and get the cruise director or cruise staff to introduce you to other singles.

In the dining room, ask the maître d' to seat you with other singles, or a mix of singles and couples. Single black women should note that there is often a dearth of single black men for dancing or socializing with (they simply have not discovered cruising yet).

If you *are* looking for romance, however, beware of the lure of the uniform, of an easy affair or fling with a ship's officer (or member of the crew). They get to see new faces every week (or every cruise), and thus the possible risk of sexually transmitted diseases should be borne in mind.

GENTLEMEN CRUISE HOSTS

The female-to-male passenger ratio is high (as much as eight-to-one on world cruises and other long voyages), especially for passengers of middle to senior years, so some cruise lines provide male social hosts, specially recruited as dance and bridge partners, and company during social functions. First used to good effect aboard Cunard's *QE2* in the late 1970s, gentlemen hosts are now employed by a number of cruise lines.

They generally host a table in the dining room, appear as dance partners at all cocktail parties and dance classes, and accompany women on shore excursions. These gentlemen, usually over 55 years of age and/or retired, are outgoing, mingle well, are well groomed, and enjoy cruise ships and traveling around the world almost free of charge.

If you think you would like such a job, do remember that you'll have to dance for several hours most nights, and dance just about every kind of dance well! Crystal Cruises, Cunard, Holland America Line, Ivaran Lines, and Silversea Cruises, among others, provide gentlemen hosts, especially on the longer voyages and world cruises.

THE *LOVE BOAT* CONNECTION

Two famous television shows, *The Love Boat* (US) and *Traumschiff* (Germany), have given a tremendous boost to the concept of cruising as the ultimate romantic vacation, although what is shown on the screen does not quite correspond to reality. Indeed, the real captain of one ship, when asked the difference between his job and that of the captain of *The Love Boat*, remarked: "On TV they can do a retake if things are not right the first time around, whereas I have to get it right the first time!"

Ships are indeed romantic places (watching the blockbuster Hollywood movie *Titanic*, released in 1997, should convince you). There is nothing quite like standing on the aft deck of a cruise ship with your love — your hair blowing in the breeze — as you sail over the moonlit waters to yet another discovery. Of course, a full moon only occurs once a month, so check the calendar to make sure the timing of *your* moonlit cruise is perfect.

There is no doubt that cruises provide excellent opportunities for meeting people of similar interests. So if you are looking for romance, and if you choose the right ship, the odds are in your favor.

GETTING MARRIED ABOARD SHIP

As in all those old black-and-white movies, a ship's captain can indeed marry you when at sea (unless the ship's country of registry prohibits, or does not recognize, such marriages), although in practice, this service is rarely offered by cruise lines today. You would need to inquire in your country of domicile (or residence) whether such a marriage is legal, and ascertain what paperwork and blood tests are required. The onus to provide the *validity* of such a marriage is yours. The captain could be sued and perhaps held criminally liable if he marries a couple not legally entitled to be married (for example, an underage male or female who do not have the consent of a parent or guardian, or if one or both parties are not legally divorced).

It is a simple matter to arrange to get married aboard almost any cruise ship when the ship is alongside in port, provided you take along your own registered minister. American Hawaii Cruises, Carnival Cruise Lines, Holland America Line, and Princess Cruises offer complete wedding packages. These include the services of a minister to marry you, wedding cake, champagne, bridal bouquet and matching boutonniere for the bridal party, a band to perform at the ceremony, and an album of wedding photos. Carnival Cruise Lines' program includes a marriage ceremony on a beach in Grand Cayman or St. Thomas. Princess Cruises offers weddings on a beach in St. Thomas (price range $525–$1175 per package). Or you could arrange a romantic wedding Disney-style on its private island, *Castaway Cay.*

Princess Cruises features weddings aboard *Grand Princess*, in what is the first oceangoing wedding chapel aboard a contemporary cruise vessel, performed by the ship's captain (the wedding is legal because of the ship's registry, Liberia, and no medical or blood tests are required). There are three packages, Pearl, Emerald, and Diamond; the cost is $1400, $1800, and $2400, respectively). A Wedding Coordinator at the line handles all the details. And what better way than to be married aboard ship *and* have your honeymoon aboard, too!

Even if you can't get married aboard ship, you could have your wedding reception aboard one. Many cruise lines offer outstanding facilities and provide complete services to help you plan your reception. Contact the Director of Hotel Services at the cruise line of your choice. The cruise line should go out of its way to help, especially if you follow the reception with a honeymoon cruise.

UK-based passengers should know that P&O Cruises has a series of cruises called the "Red-Letter Anniversary Collection" for those celebrating 10, 15, 20, 25, 30, 35, 40, 45, 50, 55, or 60 years of marriage. Gifts you will receive with the compliments of P&O Cruises include a brass carriage clock, leather photograph album, free car parking at Southampton, or free first-class rail travel from anywhere in the UK (check with your travel agent for the latest details).

A cruise also makes a fine, no-worry honeymoon vacation (perhaps that should read a "no *worrymoon*" vacation), and a delightful belated honeymoon getaway if you had no time to spare when you were married. You will feel as if you are in the middle of a movie set as you sail away to fairytale places, though actually, the ship is a destination in itself.

RENEWAL OF VOWS

There has recently been an upsurge in cruise lines performing "renewal of vows" ceremonies. A cruise is a wonderful setting for reaffirming to one's partner the strength of commitment. A handful of ships have a small chapel where this ceremony can take place; otherwise it can be anywhere aboard ship (a most romantic time is at sunrise or sunset on the open deck). The ceremony is conducted by the captain, and a nondenominational text reaffirms the love and trust between "partners, lifetime friends, and companions."

Although some companies, such as Carnival Cruise Lines, Celebrity Cruises, Holland America Line, and Princess Cruises, have complete packages for purchase, which include music, champagne, hors d'oeuvres, certificate, corsages for the women, and so on, other companies do not charge (yet). The ship's photographer usually records the event (it is a revenue-generating photo opportunity) and will have special photo albums embossed with the cruise line's logo.

CRUISING FOR HONEYMOONERS

Cruising is popular as a honeymoon vacation. The advantages are obvious: you pack and unpack only once; it is a hassle-free and crime-free environment; and you get special attention, if you want it. It is also easy to budget in advance, as one price often includes airfare, cruise, food, entertainment, several destinations, shore excursions, and pre- and post-cruise hotel stays. Once you are married, some cruise lines often offer discounts to entice you to book a future (anniversary) cruise. Just think, no cooking meals, everything will be done for you. You can think of the crew as your very own service and kitchen staff.

Although no ship as yet provides bridal suites (hint, hint), many ships do provide cabins with queen-sized or double beds. Some, but by no means all, also provide tables for two in the dining room.

Some cruise ships feature Sunday departures, so couples can plan a Saturday wedding and reception before traveling to their ship. Pre- and post-cruise hotel accommodation can also be arranged.

Most large ships accommodate honeymoon couples well; however, if you want to plan a more private, intimate honeymoon, try one of the smaller, yachtlike cruise vessels such as those of Seabourn Cruise Line, Radisson Seven Seas Cruises, Silversea Cruises, or Windstar Cruises.

And what could be more romantic for honeymooners than to stroll by themselves on deck, to the forward part of the ship, above the ship's bridge. This is the quietest (except perhaps for some wind noise) and most dimly lit part of the ship, and an ideal spot for stargazing and romancing.

Cruise lines offer a variety of honeymoon packages, just as hotels and resorts on land do. Although not all cruise lines provide all services, typically they might include:

→ Private captain's cocktail party for honeymooners.

→ Tables for two in the dining room.

→ Set of crystal champagne or wine glasses.

→ Honeymoon photograph with the captain, and photo album.

→ Complimentary champagne (imported or domestic) or wine.

→ Honeymoon cruise certificate.

→ Champagne and caviar for breakfast.

→ Flowers in your suite or cabin.

→ Complimentary cake.

→ Special T-shirts.

*Enjoy the Jacuzzi aboard Royal Caribbean International's **Monarch of the Seas**.*

Courtesy Windstar Cruises

Share a quiet, relaxing moment with someone special.

Finally:

→ Remember to take a copy of your marriage license or certificate, for immigration (or marriage) purposes, as your passports will not yet have been amended.

→ Remember to allow extra in your budget for things like shipboard gratuities (tips), shore excursions, and spending money ashore.

→ If you want to sleep in a large bed next to your loved one, check with your travel agent and cruise line to make sure the cabin you have booked has such a bed. Better still, book a suite. But check and double-check to avoid disappointment.

→ If you need to take your wedding gown aboard for a planned wedding somewhere along the way — in Hawaii or Bermuda, for example — there is usually space to hang it in the dressing room next to the stage in the main showroom, especially on larger ships.

CRUISING FOR FAMILIES

Yes, you *can* take children on a cruise. In fact, once you get them aboard, you will hardly see them at all, if you choose the right ship and cruise. Families can do different things on a cruise, and parents do not have to be concerned about the whereabouts of their children. Where else can you go out for a night on the town without having to drive, and be home in a moment should the baby-sitter need you?

Dad can sleep in. Mom can go swimming and join an aerobics class. The kids can join in the organized activities that go on all day long. Whether you share a cabin with them or whether they have their own separate but adjoining cabin, there will be plenty to keep them occupied. Aboard several ships that cruise in the Caribbean, you will even find favorite life-sized cartoon characters.

Some cruise lines have token family programs, with limited activities and only a couple of general staff allocated to look after children, even though their brochures might claim otherwise. But cruise lines that are really serious about family cruise programs dedicate complete teams of children's and "tweens and teens" counselors, who run special programs that are off-limits to adults. They also have facilities such as high chairs in the dining room, cots, and real playrooms. Most children's entertainment is designed to run simultaneously with adult programs. For those cruising with very young children, baby-sitting services may also be available. For example, the *QE2* has real children's nurses and even trained English National Nursing Examination Board-qualified nannies. *Arcadia, Aurora,* and *Oriana* have a "night nursery" for children of two to five years of age, so parents can go "out on the town" while the staff takes care of their offspring.

Parents, of course, have long realized that children cost more as they age. For example, children under two years travel free on most cruise lines (and airlines). If they are over two, they cost money.

There is little doubt that families who cruise together stay together! There is no better vacation for families than a ship cruise, especially at holiday time, whether it is at Christmas and New Year, Easter, or during the long summer school vacation. Active parents can have the best of all worlds, family togetherness, social contact, and privacy. Cruise ships provide a very safe, crime-free, encapsulated environment, and give junior passengers a lot of freedom without parents having to be concerned about where their children are at all times. Cruising has never been more child friendly or affordable.

A cruise also allows junior passengers a chance to meet and play with others in their own age group. And because the days aboard are long, youngsters will also be able to spend time with their parents or grandparents, as well as with their peers.

A cruise for children is an educational experience. They will tour the ship's bridge, meet senior officers and learn about the navigation, radar, and communications equipment, as well as being able to see how the ship operates. They will be exposed to different environments, experience many types of food, travel to and explore new places, and participate in any number of exciting activities.

Cruise ships can be full of kids, or they can provide quiet moments. But aboard the busiest ships, adults will rarely get to use the swimming pools alone, they will be overcome with children having a truly good time. One good thing about a ship's swimming pool for kids, however, is the fact that there is no sand to get in their eyes (or anywhere else)!

Many cruise lines, recognizing the needs of families, have added a whole variety of children's programs to their daily activities. Some ships have separate swimming pools and play areas for children, as well as junior discos, video rooms, and teen centers.

75

*Hours of smiles and laughter are found in the Fun Zone aboard Princess Cruises' **Sun Princess**.*

Cruise lines serious about children divide them into five distinct age groups, with various names to match, according to cruise line and program: Toddlers (ages 2-4); Juniors (ages 5-7); Intermediate (ages 8-10); Tweens (ages 11-13); and Teens (ages 14-17). Notably, it often seems to be children under twelve who get the most from a cruise vacation.

DISNEY GOES CRUISING
In late July 1998, Disney Cruise Line entered the family cruise market with a big splash. The giant entertainment company introduced the first of two large ships (each with two funnels) that cater specifically to families with children. The two ships, *Disney Magic* and *Disney Wonder,* are the family cruise ships of the future and cater to 1,750 adults and up to 1,000 children, with the whole of the Disney organization to draw from for the shipboard entertainment program. For more comments, see *Disney Magic* in Part Two.

GENERAL INFORMATION
Parents with babies can rest assured that they will find selected baby foods on board ships that cater to children (along with cribs and high chairs, but do ask your travel agent to check first). If you need something out of the ordinary, or that special brand of baby food, do let your travel agent know well in advance. Most cruise lines are accommodating and will do their best to obtain what is needed, provided enough notice is given. Parents using organic baby foods, such as those obtained from health food stores, should be aware that cruise lines buy their supplies from major general food suppliers and not the smaller specialized food houses.

Although many ships have full programs for children during days at sea, these may be limited when the ship is in port. Ships expect you to take your children with you on organized excursions, and sometimes (though not always) there are special prices for children. If the ship has a playroom, it might be wise to find out if it is open and supervised on all days of the cruise. Do not expect your travel agent to know everything. Either ask the agent to find the answers to your questions, or do some research yourself.

When going ashore, remember that if you want to take your children swimming or to the beach, it is wise to phone ahead to a local hotel with a beach or pool. Whether it is in the Caribbean, the Mediterranean, or the Orient, most hotels will be delighted to show off their property, hoping for future business.

Some cruise ships in the Caribbean area have the use of a "private" island for a day. A lifeguard will be on duty, and there will be water sports and snorkeling equipment you can rent. Remember, however, that the beaches on some "private" islands are fine for 200 passengers, but with 2,000 they become crowded, and standing in line for beach barbecues and changing and toilet facilities becomes a necessary part of the experience.

Although the sun and sea might attract juniors to the warm waters of the Caribbean, children aged seven and over will find a Baltic, Black Sea, or Mediterranean cruise a delight. They will also have a fine introduction to history, languages, and different cultures.

CHILDREN'S RATES

Most cruise lines offer special rates for children sharing their parents' cabin. The cost is often lower than third and fourth person share rates. To get the best possible rates, however, it is wise to book early. And do not overlook booking an inside cabin; you will rarely be in it anyway.

You should note that, although many adult cruise rates include airfare, most children's rates do not! Also, although some lines say children sail "free," they must in fact pay port taxes as well as airfare. The cruise line will get the airfare at the best rate, so there is no need to shop around for the lowest fare.

Unless they have plenty of things to keep them occupied, even the most placid and well-behaved children can become bored and restless. So try to choose a cruise where there are lots of other children, as they will be best equipped to provide the required entertainment.

SINGLE PARENTS

Single parents traveling with child(ren) will have their own special needs, and need not feel left out, either. They will feel more secure than in any hotel. In fact, a cruise provides a safe, convenient way for any single parent and child to be together but also have their own space and, in some cases, a guarantee of peer companionship for the child. Only a handful of cruise lines so far have introduced their versions of the "Single Parent Plan." This offers an economical way for single parents to take their child(ren) on a cruise, with parent and child sharing a two-berth cabin, or parent and children sharing a three-berth cabin. Single parents will pay approximately one-third the normal single-person rate for their children, and there will be plenty of activities for both parent and child(ren) to enjoy.

Courtesy Holland America Line

Kids have fun in the sun while traveling to the next destination on the cruise itinerary.

CHILDREN-FRIENDLY CRUISE LINES

These have been selected by the author for their excellent programs and care: Airtours Sun Cruises, American Hawaii Cruises, Carnival Cruise Lines, Celebrity Cruises, Cunard, Disney Cruise Line, Norwegian Cruise Line, P&O Cruises, Royal Caribbean International, Star Cruises, and Thomson Cruises.

FAMILY REUNIONS

A cruise can provide the ideal place for a family reunion (either with or without children). Here are some tips to take into account when planning one.

→ Let your travel agent do the planning and make all the arrangements (ask for a group discount if the total in your group adds up to more than 15). Make sure that together you choose the right cruise line, for the right reasons.

→ Book 12 months in advance if possible, so that you can arrange cabins close to each other (remember to arrange for everyone to be at the same dinner seating, if the ship operates two seatings).

→ If anyone in the group has a birthday or anniversary, tell your travel agent to arrange a special cake (most cruise lines do not charge extra for this). Special private parties can also be arranged, although there will be an additional cost. If the group is not too large, you may be able to request to dine at the captain's table.

→ Arrange shore excursions as a group (in some ports, private arrangements may prove unbeatable).

→ Finally, get everything in writing (particularly cabin assignments and locations).

BEFORE YOU GO

BAGGAGE

→ There is generally no limit to the amount of personal baggage you can take on your cruise (towels, soap, shampoo, and shower caps are provided aboard most cruise ships). Do allow extra space for purchases on the cruise.

→ Tag your luggage with your name, ship, cabin number, sailing date, and port of embarkation (tags are provided by the cruise line with your tickets). Baggage transfers from airport to ship are generally smooth and problem-free when handled by the cruise line.

→ Liability for loss or damage to baggage is contained in the passenger contract (part of your ticket). Do take out insurance (the policy should extend from the date of departure until two or three days after your return home).

CLOTHING

If you think you might not wear it, don't take it, as closet space aboard many ships is at a premium. So, unless you are on an extended cruise, keep your luggage to a minimum.

For cruises to tropical areas, where the weather is warm to hot with high humidity, casual wear should include plenty of lightweight cottons and other natural fibers. Synthetic materials do not "breathe" as well and often retain heat. Clothes should, however, be as opaque as possible to counteract the ultraviolet rays of the sun. Take a lightweight cotton sweater or windbreaker for the evenings, when the ship's air-conditioning will seem even more powerful after a day in the sun. Pack sunglasses and a hat. Rainstorms in the tropics are infrequent and do not last long, but they can give you a good soaking, so take inexpensive, lightweight rainwear for excursions you go on.

The same is true for cruises to the Mediterranean, Greek Isles, or North Africa, although there will be little or no humidity for most of the year. Certain areas may be dusty as well as dry. In these latitudes, the weather can be changeable and cool in the evenings from October to March, so take extra sweaters and a windbreaker.

For cruises to Alaska, the North Cape, or the Norwegian fjords, take some warm comfortable clothing layers, plus a raincoat or parka for the northernmost port calls. Cruises to Alaska and the Land of the Midnight Sun are operated during the peak summer months, when temperatures are pleasant and the weather less likely to be inclement. Unless you are traveling to northern ports such as St. Petersburg during winter, you will not need thermal underwear. However, you will need it — and a topcoat — if you are taking an adventure cruise to the Antarctic Peninsula or through the Northwest Passage.

In destinations with a strong religious tradition, like Venezuela, Haiti, the Dominican Republic, Colombia, and countries in the Far East, note that shorts or bare shoulders may cause local offense, so cover up.

Aboard ship, dress rules are relaxed during the day, but in the evening what you wear should be tasteful. Men should take a blazer or sports jacket and ties for the dining room and for any "informal" occasions. Transatlantic crossings are normally more elegant and require formal attire.

For formal nights (usually two out of seven), women can wear a long evening gown, elegant cocktail dress, or a smart pants suit. Gentlemen are expected to wear either a tuxedo or dark business suit and tie. These "rules" are less rigid on short and moderately priced cruises. If you are the athletic type, pack sportswear for the gymnasium or aerobics classes.

No matter where in the world you are traveling, comfortable low- or flat-heeled shoes are a *must* for women, except for formal nights. Light, airy walking shoes are best for walking. If you are in the Caribbean or Pan-Pacific region and you are not used to heat and humidity, your ankles may swell, so tight shoes are not recommended. Rubber soles are best for walking on the deck of a ship.

→ **Formal**: Tuxedo or dinner jacket (alternatively a dark suit) for men; evening gown or other appropriate formal attire for women.

→ **Informal**: Jacket and tie for men; cocktail dress, dressy pant suit, or the like for women.

→ **Casual**: Slacks and jacket over sweater or open shirt for men; a blouse with skirt, slacks, or similar comfortable attire for women.

DOCUMENTS

A passport is the most practical proof of your citizenship and identification. Visas are required for some countries (allow time to obtain these). On most cruises, you will hand in your passport to the purser upon embarkation. This helps the ship to clear customs and immigration inspection on arrival in ports of call. Your passport will be returned prior to the ship's arrival in the port of disembarkation.

FLYING...AND JET LAG

Several cruise lines now have "air deviation" desks that enable you to change your air flights and connections, for an additional fee (about $30–$50 per person).

Modern air travel is fast and efficient. Even experienced travelers, however, may occasionally find that the stress of international travel persists long after the flight is over.

Eastbound flights seem to cause more pronounced jet lag than westbound flights. Jet aircraft are generally pressurized to some 8,000 feet (2,400 meters) in altitude, causing discomfort in the ears and the stomach, and swollen feet. A few precautions should reduce the less pleasant effects of flying around the world. Plan as far in advance of your cruise as you possibly can. Take a daytime flight, so that you can arrive at, or close to, your normal bedtime. Try to be as quiet as possible prior to flying, and allow for another five hours of rest after any flight that crosses more than five time zones.

Note: Babies and small children are less affected by changes in time because of their shorter sleeping and waking cycles. But adults generally need more time to adjust. The only way to experience a flight without jet lag is to fly the *Concorde* (London or Paris–New York or New York–London or Paris). At Mach-2 speed, such a flight does not produce the symptoms of jet lag.

MEDICATION

Take any medicine and other medical supplies that you need, plus spare eyeglasses or contact lenses. In many countries it may be difficult to find certain medicines. Others may be sold under different names. If you are taking a long cruise, ask your doctor for names of alternatives, in case the medicine you are taking is not available.

The ship's pharmacy will stock certain standard remedies, but do not expect a supply of the more unusual or obscure medicines. Remember to take along a doctor's prescription for any medication, especially when you are flying into foreign countries to join a ship, as customs may be difficult without documentation, particularly in the Far East.

Also, be advised that if you run out of your medication and you need to get a supply aboard ship, most ships will require that you see the doctor, even if you have a prescription. There is a charge for each visit, plus the cost of any medication.

Let spouses/companions carry a supply of your medicine and medical supplies. Do not pack medication in any luggage to be checked in when flying, but take it in your carry-on.

MONEY MATTERS

Most cruise ships operate primarily in US dollars but some operate in other currencies. Major credit cards and traveler's checks are accepted on board (few lines take personal checks). You sign for drinks and other assorted services, as part of the "cashless cruising" policy. Some large ships now have ATM cash machines.

PETS

Pets are not allowed aboard cruise ships (although a handful of cargo-passenger ships still carry them), with two exceptions. The first is aboard the scheduled transatlantic services of the *QE2*, which has 16 air-conditioned kennels (plus a genuine British lamppost and New York fire hydrant) and cat containers, plus several special cages for birds. The second is aboard the scheduled South Atlantic service from England to Cape Town and the Ascension Islands aboard *St. Helena*.

PHOTOGRAPHY

It is hard to find any situation more ideal for photography than a cruise. Your photographs enable you to share your memories with others at home. Here are some tips:

→ Use low-speed film in tropical areas such as the Caribbean or South Pacific (high-speed film is easily damaged by heat). Take plenty of film with you; standard sizes are available in the ship's shop, but the selection is limited. If you purchase film during a port visit, try to buy from an air-conditioned store, and check the expiration date.

→ Keep film cool, as the latent image on exposed film is fragile and easily affected by heat. There will be professional photographers on board who may develop film for you, for a fee (print film only).

→ When taking photographs in ports of call, respect the wishes of local inhabitants. Ask permission to photograph someone close-up. Most will smile and tell you to go ahead. But some people are superstitious or afraid of having their picture taken and will shy away from you. Do not press the point.

Courtesy of Douglas Ward

Radisson Seven Seas Cruises' **Song of Flower** *travels the River Thames as it goes through Tower Bridge in London.*

LIFE ABOARD

TOP 30 PET PEEVES (MINE AND THOSE OF OTHER PASSENGERS)

→ Passengers who do not possess a credit card (particularly older Asian passengers) are made to feel inferior at the check-in/embarkation desks, particularly in the United States. Some cruise lines have the temerity to ask for a $500 deposit in cash, just for the "privilege" of securing an onboard charge card. No hotel on land does this. Simply refuse, and say that if you cannot trust me, then refund my cruise fare.

→ Aboard the large, high-tech ships, getting Cabin Services, or the "Guest Relations Desk," or the Operator to answer the telephone can be an exercise in frustration, patience, and gross irritation.

→ Aboard many ships, 15 percent is automatically added to wine bills. This means that a wine waiter makes much more money on a more expensive bottle of wine, whether he knows anything about that wine (or how to decant and serve it, for example) or not. For doing just the same job for a wine costing $125 as for a wine costing $15 he makes a lot more. Therefore, *insist* on adding your own gratuity, and politely refuse to be told how much you have to tip.

→ Cruise brochures that use models, and provide the anticipation of an onboard product that a ship cannot deliver; the result is disappointment for passengers. Cruise brochures that state that their ship has a "small ship feel, big ship choice" when it really caters to more than 1,000 passengers (often more than 2,000).

→ Constant, irritating, and repetitive announcements for bingo, horse racing, and the latest gizmo sale in the shops.

→ Any announcement that is repeated. Any announcement that is repeated.

→ Flowers in one's cabin that are never watered or refreshed by the steward.

→ Bathrobes provided but never changed for the duration of the cruise.

→ Skimpy towels.

Courtesy Len Kaufman/Windstar Cruises

Morning aerobics aboard Windstar Cruises' **Wind Surf** *with the skyline of Monte Carlo in the background.*

→ Mini-bar/refrigerators that do not provide limes and lemons for drink mixes.

→ Remote control units that need an instruction manual to understand their operation for turning on the television and getting a video player to work.

→ In-cabin announcements at any time, except for emergencies (they are completely unnecessary for programmed events and shore excursions).

→ Garnishes, when "parsley with everything" seems to be the rule of the seagoing entree experience.

→ Baked Alaska parades.

→ Paper, plastic, or polystyrene plastic cups for drinks of any kind.

→ Paper napkins for meals or informal buffets (they should be linen or cotton).

→ Plastic plates (often too small) for buffets.

→ Buffets where only cold plates are available, even for hot food items.

→ Repetitious breakfast and luncheon buffets and uncreative displays.

→ "Elevator" music playing continuously in passageways and on open decks (even worse: rock music).

→ Artwork placed aboard ships, but with the cruise line not caring or knowing enough about it to place the name of the artist and the year of creation alongside, whether it be a painting or a sculpture.

→ Shopping lecturers, shopping videos, art auctions, and carpet auctions.

→ Shore-side porters who take your bags when you get off the bus, or out of your car, then stand there until you tip them before they move your bags or drop them (worst ports: Ft. Lauderdale and Miami).

→ Cabin stewards/stewardesses who place small folded pieces of paper in cabin door frames to show when their passengers have left their cabins.

→ Audiovisual technicians who think that the volume level of the show should equal that for a rock concert for 250,000 people.

→ Bands scheduled to play in a lounge that do not start playing until passengers walk in and sit down.

→ Private island days, when the tender ride to get to the island is longer than the flight to get to the ship.

→ Ships that ask you to settle your shipboard account before the morning of disembarkation.

→ Long lines and waiting periods for disembarkation.

AIR-CONDITIONING
Cabin temperature can be regulated by an individually controlled thermostat, so you can adjust it to suit yourself. Public room temperatures are controlled automatically. Air temperatures are often kept cooler than you may be used to.

ART AUCTIONS
Aboard many large and mid-size ships, art auctions form part of the entertainment. They are fun participation events, but don't expect to purchase an heirloom, as most of the art pieces are pure drivel. It's funny how so many identical pieces can be found aboard so many other ships!

BABY-SITTING
In some ships, stewards, stewardesses, and other staff may be available as sitters for an hourly charge. Make arrangements at the purser's office.

BEAUTY SALON/BARBER SHOP

Make appointments as soon after boarding as possible (particularly on short cruises). Appointment times fill up rapidly, particularly before social events such as a captain's cocktail party. Charges are comparable to those ashore. Typical services: haircut for men and women, styling, permanent waving, coloring, manicure, pedicure, and leg waxing.

BRIDGE VISITS

Check the *Daily Program* for navigation bridge visits. In some ships, bridge visits are not allowed for insurance and security reasons. In others, although personal visits are forbidden, a *Behind the Scenes* video on how the ship is run may be shown on the cabin television system.

CASHLESS CRUISING

It is now the norm to cruise cash-free, and to settle your account with one payment (by cash or credit card) prior to disembarking on the last day. Often this is arranged by making an imprint of a credit card prior at embarkation, permitting you to sign for everything. Before the end of the cruise, a detailed statement will be delivered to your cabin. Some cruise lines may discontinue its "cashless" system for the last day of the cruise, which can be most irritating. *Note*: Ships visiting a "private island" on a Bahamas/Caribbean itinerary will probably ask you to pay cash for beverages, water sports/scuba diving gear, and other items purchased ashore.

CASINO

Many cruise ships have casinos, where a range of games is played (typically blackjack or 21, roulette, craps, and baccarat). Playing chips and cash change are available. Children under 18 are not allowed in the casino. The casino is closed in port due to international customs regulations, and taking photographs in the casino is usually forbidden. German- and Japanese-registered ships are not permitted to operate casinos that give cash prizes.

Most cruise lines show videos that give information on how to play the various table games, and dealers may also be helpful. Remember that casinos provide entertainment rather than a hard-core gambling environment.

COMMENT CARDS

On the last day of the cruise you are asked to fill out a company "comment card." Some cruise lines offer "incentives" such as a bottle of champagne. Be honest when you fill out this form, it serves as a means of communication between you and the cruise line. Pressure from staff to write "excellent" for everything is rampant aboard cruise ships. But if there *have* been problems with the service or any other aspect of your cruise, do say so.

COMMUNICATIONS

Most ships now have a direct-dial satellite telephone system. In addition, all ships are given an internationally recognized call sign, made up of a combination of several letters and digits. When the ship is at sea, you can call from your cabin (or the ship's radio room) to anywhere in the world:

→ via radiotelephone (a slight/moderate background noise might be noticed).

→ via satellite (which will be as clear as your own home phone).

Direct dial satellite calls (this service started in 1986) are more expensive, but are completed instantly. Some ships also have credit card telephones located in public areas; these also connect instantly, via satellite. Satellite calls can also be made when the ship is in port (radiotelephone calls cannot). Satellite telephone calls cost between $5 and $15 per minute, depending on the type of communications equipment the ship carries (the latest systems are digital). Calls are charged to your onboard account.

Your relatives and friends can reach you by calling the High Seas Operator in most countries (in the United States, dial 1-800-SEA-CALL). The operator will need the name of the ship, together with the ocean code (Atlantic is 871; Pacific is 872; and the Indian Ocean is 873).

CRUISESPEAK

The following terminology is used aboard today's cruise ships. The correct nautical terminology is given, while the words that follow are what many cruise lines now use:

Cabin: Penthouse Suite, Junior Suite, Stateroom, or Room

Cabin Service: Room Service

Passenger: Guest

Purser's Office: Guest Relations Desk or Front Office

CUSTOMS REGULATIONS
All countries vary in the duty-free allowances granted by their own customs service, but you will be informed aboard your cruise ship of the allowable amounts for your nationality and residency.

DAILY PROGRAM
The *Daily Program* contains a list of the day's activities, entertainment, and social events. It is normally delivered to your cabin the evening before the day that it covers. Read it carefully, so that you know what, when, and where things are happening.

DEATH AT SEA
What happens if someone dies at sea? Typically, it happens more on long cruises, where passengers are generally older. Bodies are put in a special refrigeration unit for removal at the port of disembarkation, or the body can be flown home from a wayward port of call (more complicated, owing to the paperwork). Note that flying a body home usually involves a large expense. A burial at sea can also be arranged aboard ship (some people have a body cremated at home, return to their favorite cruise ship, and have the ashes scattered at sea).

DEPARTURE TAX
If you are disembarking in a foreign port and flying home, be advised that there could be a departure tax to pay (in local currency) at the airport.

DISEMBARKATION
During the final part of your cruise, the cruise director will give an informal talk on customs, immigration, and disembarkation (sometimes called "debarkation") procedures. The night before your ship reaches its final destination, you will be given a customs form to fill out. Any duty-free items bought from the shop on board must be included in your allowance (save the receipts in case a customs officer wishes to see them).

The night before arrival, place your main baggage outside your cabin on retiring (or before 4:00am). It will be collected and off-loaded on arrival. Leave out fragile items, liquor, and the clothes you intend to wear for disembarkation and onward travel (it is amazing just how many people pack *everything*, only to find they are in an embarrassing position on disembarkation day). Anything left in your cabin will be considered hand luggage to be hand-carried off when you leave.

On disembarkation day, be aware that breakfast will be early. It might be better to miss breakfast and sleep later, providing announcements on the ship's public address system do not wake you (it may be possible to turn off such announcements). Even worse than early breakfast is the fact that you will be commanded (requested, if you are lucky) to leave your cabin early, only to wait in crowded public rooms (sometimes for hours). To add insult to injury, your cabin steward (after he has received his tip, of course) will knock on the door to take the sheets off the bed so the cabin can be made up for the incoming passengers. Cruise aboard the smaller "upscale" ships and this will not happen.

Before leaving the ship, remember to claim any items you have placed in the ship's safety deposit boxes and leave your cabin key in your cabin. Passengers cannot go ashore until all baggage has been off-loaded, and customs and/or immigration inspections or pre-inspections have been carried out. In most ports, this takes two to three hours after arrival. It is wise to leave at least three hours from the time of arrival to catch a connecting flight or other transportation. Once off the ship, you will identify your baggage on the pier before going through customs inspection (delays are usually minimal). Porters may be there to assist you.

ENGINE ROOM
In almost all passenger ships, the engine room is off-limits to passengers, and visits are not allowed, for insurance and security reasons. In some ships, a technical information leaflet may be available.

On others, a *Behind the Scenes* video may be shown on the cabin television system. For more specific or detailed information, contact a member of the ship's engineering staff via the purser's office.

GIFT SHOPS

The gift shop/boutique/drugstore will offer a selection of souvenirs, gifts, toiletries, and duty-free items, as well as a basic stock of essential items. You will find duty-free items, such as perfumes, watches, and so on, very competitively priced, and buying onboard ship may save you the hassle of shopping ashore. Opening hours are posted at the store and in the *Daily Program*.

HEALTH/FITNESS/SPA FACILITIES

The latest ships have elaborate spas where (for an extra fee) whole days of treatments are on offer. Stress reducing and relaxation treatments are practiced combined with the use of seawater, which contains minerals, micronutrients, and vitamins. Massages might include Swedish remedial massage, shiatsu, and aromatherapy treatments. Indeed, you can even get a massage on your private balcony aboard some ships.

LAUNCH (TENDER) SERVICES

Enclosed or open motor launches (called "tenders") are employed on those occasions when your cruise ship is unable to berth at a port or island. In such cases, a regular launch service is operated between ship and shore for the duration of the port call. Details of the launch service will be provided in the *Daily Program*. When stepping on or off a tender, remember to extend "forearm to forearm" to the person assisting you. Do not grip their hands because this simply has the effect of immobilizing the helper.

LAUNDERETTE

Some ships are fitted with self-service launderettes, equipped with washers, dryers, and ironing facilities (there may be a charge).

LAUNDRY AND DRY CLEANING

Most ships offer a full laundry and pressing service. Some ships may also offer dry-cleaning facilities. A detailed list of services (and prices) can be found in your cabin. Your steward will collect and deliver your laundry or dry cleaning.

LIBRARY

Most cruise ships have a library offering a good selection of books, reference material, and periodicals. A small deposit (refundable on return of the book) is sometimes required when you borrow a book. Note that aboard the small luxury ships, the library is open 24 hours a day, and no deposit is required. Aboard large ships, you will probably find that the library is open only a couple of hours each morning and afternoon. *Oriana* and the *QE2* are examples of ships with full-time, fully qualified librarians. The library is typically where you will find board games like Scrabble, backgammon, and chess.

LIFEBOAT DRILL

There have been few recent incidents requiring the evacuation of passengers, although two cruise ships have been totally lost following collisions (*Jupiter*, 1988, and *Royal Pacific*, 1992). Travel by ship, however, remains one of the safest means of transportation. Even so, it cannot be stressed enough that attendance at lifeboat drill is not only required but makes sense, and participation is mandatory. You must, at the very least, know your boat station and how to get to it in the event of an emergency.

If others are lighthearted about the drill, do not let that affect your seriousness of purpose. Be sure to note your exit and escape pathways and learn how to put on your lifejacket correctly. The drill takes no more than 15 minutes of your time and is a good investment in playing safe (in 1992, the cruise ship *Royal Pacific* sank in 16 minutes following a collision).

A Passenger Lifeboat Drill *must* be conducted on board within 24 hours of leaving port. You will hear an announcement from the bridge, which goes something like this: "Ladies and Gentlemen, may I have your attention, please. This is the captain speaking to you from the bridge. In 15 minutes time, the ship's alarm bells will signal emergency lifeboat drill for all passengers. This is a mandatory drill, conducted in accordance with the requirements of the *Safety of Life at Sea Convention*. There are no exceptions."

Just watching the scenery go by can be a great cruising experience.

Here is an example of a typical announcement from the navigation bridge:

"The emergency signal is a succession of seven or more short blasts followed by one long blast of the ship's whistle, supplemented by the ringing of the electric gongs throughout the ship. On hearing this signal, you should make your way quickly but quietly to your cabin, put on warm clothing and your lifejacket, then follow the signs to your emergency boat station, where you will be kept fully informed over the loudspeakers through which I am speaking to you now."

LOST PROPERTY
Contact the purser's office immediately if you lose or find something on the ship. Notices regarding lost and found property may be posted on the bulletin boards.

MAIL
You can buy stamps and mail letters aboard most ships. Some ships use the postal privileges and stamps of their flag of registration, while others buy local stamps at ports of call. Mail is usually taken ashore by the ship's port agent just before the ship sails for the next port. A list of port agents and mailing addresses will be sent with your tickets and documents before you leave for your cruise, so you can advise friends and family how to send mail to you.

MASSAGE
Make appointments for a massage as soon after embarkation as possible, in order to obtain the time and day of your choice. Larger ships have more staff and offer more flexibility in appointment times. The cost averages just over $1.00 per minute. In some ships, a massage service is available in your cabin (or on your private balcony), if it is large enough to accommodate a portable massage table.

MEDICAL SERVICES
Except for ships registered in England or Norway, there are *no* mandatory international maritime requirements for cruise lines to carry a licensed physician or to have hospital facilities aboard. However, in general, all ships carrying over 50 passengers *do* have hospital facilities and *do* carry at least one licensed doctor aboard ship (ships registered in England and Norway have both, without exception). Usually, there is a reasonably equipped hospital in miniature, although the standard

87

of medical practice and of the physicians themselves may vary from line to line. Most shipboard doctors are generalists; there are no cardiologists or neurosurgeons. Doctors are often employed as outside contractors and therefore will charge for use of their services, including seasickness shots (except for Russian and Ukrainian registered vessels, where medical services are free). UK passengers should note that ships fall outside the UK National Health Service scheme.

Regrettably, many cruise lines place a low priority on providing medical services (there are, however, some exceptions). Most shipboard physicians are not certified in trauma treatment or medical evacuation procedures, for example. Most ships that cater to North American passengers tend to carry doctors licensed in the United States, Canada, or Britain, but aboard many other ships, doctors come from a variety of countries and disciplines. Some medical organizations, such as the American College of Emergency Physicians, have created a special division for cruise medicine.

Cunard's *QE2*, which carries up to 2,825 passengers and crew, has a fully equipped hospital with one surgeon, one doctor, a staff of six nurses, and two medical orderlies; contrast this with Carnival's *Sensation*, which carries up to 3,514 passengers and crew, with just one doctor and two nurses.

There is wide variation between standards and equipment. Obviously, any ship that features long-distance cruises, with several days at sea, should have better medical facilities and a better qualified staff than one that is engaged in a standard seven-day Caribbean cruise, with a port of call to make almost every day.

There is, at present, no agreed industry-wide standard relating to the standard of medical certification that is required by cruise ships. Most ship doctors are necessarily of the general practice type, but often, short-term contracts can mean poor continuity and differing standards.

Ideally, a ship's medical staff should be certified in Advanced Cardiac Life Support. The minimal standard medical equipment should include:

→ Examination room

→ Isolation ward/bed

→ X-ray machine (to verify the existence of broken or fractured bones)

→ Cardiac monitor (EKG) and defibrillator

→ Oxygen-saturation monitor (to determine a patient's blood-oxygen level)

→ External pacemaker

→ Oxygen, suction, and ventilators

→ Hematology analyzer

→ Culture incubator

→ Mobile trolley intensive care unit

Existing health problems that require treatment on board must be reported at the time of booking.

MOVIES

In most cruise ships, a movie theater is an essential part of the ship's public-room facilities. The movies are recent, often selected by the cruise line from a special film- or video-leasing service. Many of the latest ships have replaced or supplemented the ship's movie theater with television sets and video players in each cabin.

NEWS AND SPORTS BULLETINS

The world's news and sports results are reported in the ship's newspaper or placed on the bulletin board that is normally located near the purser's office or in the library. For sports results not listed, ask at the purser's office; it may be possible for the office to obtain the results for you.

PASSENGER LISTS

All ships of yesteryear provided passenger lists with each passenger's name and hometown or region. Today, only a handful of companies carry on the tradition (perhaps some passengers are traveling with someone they should not!).

PHOTOGRAPHS

Professional photographers take pictures of passengers throughout the cruise, including their arrival on board. They cover all main events and social functions, such as the captain's cocktail party. The photographs can be viewed without any obligation to purchase (the price is likely to be in excess of $6.00 for a postcard-sized color photograph).

POSTCARDS AND WRITING PAPER

These are available from the writing room, library, purser's office, or your room steward. Aboard many ships, they are available for a modest sum.

PURSER'S OFFICE

This is also known as the reception office, guest relations, or information desk. Centrally located, this is the nerve center of the ship for general information and problems. Opening hours are posted outside the office and given in the *Daily Program*. In some ships, the purser's office is open 24 hours a day.

RELIGIOUS SERVICES

Interdenominational services are conducted on board, usually by the captain or staff captain. A few older ships (and Costa Cruises' ships) have a small private chapel. Denominational services may be offered by specially invited or fellow-passenger members of the clergy.

ROOM SERVICE

Beverages and snacks are available at most hours. Liquor is normally limited to the hours when the ship's bars are open. Your room steward will advise you of the services that are offered. There is no charge for room service.

SAFETY FIRST

In an increasingly regulated world, the importance of safety cannot be overplayed. The training of crew in relation to safety and security has become extremely important — so much so that new international regulations are due to come into force that will require all crew to undergo basic safety training *before* they are allowed to join and work aboard any cruise ship. No longer will crew members be recruited with the intention of providing on-the-job training.

Safeguards for passengers include lifeboats and life rafts. Since the introduction of the 1983 amendments to Chapter III of the *Safety of Life at Sea* (SOLAS) *Convention 1974* (which came into effect in 1980), much attention has been given to safety. The SOLAS conventions are subscribed to by all member countries of the United Nations, under the auspices of the International Maritime Organization (IMO).

All cruise ships built since July 1, 1986, must have either totally enclosed or partially enclosed lifeboats (only ships built before this date are allowed to have open lifeboats). These have diesel engines that will still operate when the lifeboat is inverted.

The 1990 SOLAS standards on stability and fire protection (mandating the enclosing of all stairways and the installation of sprinkler and smoke detection systems and "low-location" lighting) for all new ship construction took effect on October 1, 1997. Existing ships have another five years to comply (the retrofitting of sprinkler systems in particular is an expensive measure that may not be considered viable by owners of older ships).

October 1, 1997, was the deadline whereby all cruise ships must:

↪ Use smoke detectors and smoke alarms in all passenger cabins, corridors, stairway enclosures, and other public spaces.

↪ Have and use low-level lighting showing routes of escape (such as in corridors and stairways).

↪ Make all fire doors throughout the ship controllable from the ship's navigation bridge, and their status displayed thereon.

↪ Make all fire doors that are held open by hinges capable of release from a remote location (however, fire doors that slide are not required to have that capability until 2000).

↪ Use a general emergency alarm that is audible in all cabins.

In 2010, the use of combustible materials in cruise ship construction (allowed under the previous SOLAS 60 regulations) will be forbidden.

The crew attends frequent emergency drills, the lifeboat equipment is regularly tested, and the fire-detecting devices, and alarm and fire-fighting systems are checked throughout the ship. If you spot fire or smoke, use the nearest fire alarm box, alert a member of staff, or contact the bridge.

SAILING TIME

In each port of call, the ship's sailing and all-aboard times are posted at the gangway. The all-aboard time is usually half an hour before sailing (ships cannot wait for individual passengers who are delayed).

SEASICKNESS

The French term *mal de mer* may sound quaint, but the malady has been nauseating to seafarers since the Phoenicians. Fortunately, seasickness is rare these days, even in rough weather (less than 3 percent of all passengers become seasick). Ships have stabilizers — large underwater "fins" on each side of the hull — to counteract any rolling motion. Nevertheless, it is possible to develop some symptoms — anything from slight nausea to vomiting.

Seasickness occurs when the brain receives confusing messages from the body's sensory organs, causing an imbalance of a mechanism in the inner ear. The mind and brain are accustomed to our walking or riding on a nonmoving surface. If the surface itself moves in another direction, a signal is sent to the brain that something's wrong. Continuous mixed signals result in headaches, clammy skin, dizziness, paleness, and yawning, soon followed by nausea and vomiting. There is still no explanation for the great difference in individual susceptibility to seasickness.

Both old-time sailors and modern physicians have their own remedies, and you can take your choice or try them all (but not at the same time):

↝ When you notice the first movement of a ship, go out on deck and walk back and forth. You will find that your knees, which are our own form of stabilizer, will start getting their feel of balance and counteraction. This is the sign that you are "getting your sea legs."

↝ Get the fresh sea breeze into your face (arguably the best antidote of all), and if nauseated, suck an orange or a lemon.

↝ When on deck, focus on a steady point, such as the horizon.

↝ Eat lightly. Do not make the mistake of thinking a heavy meal will keep your stomach well anchored. It will not.

↝ Dramamine (dimenhydrinate, a sedative, which was introduced just after World War II) will be available in tablet (chewable) form on board the ship.

↝ Transderm Scop, known as "The Patch" (manufactured by Ciba-Geigy), has an ingredient known as scopolamine, which has proven effective. Taken off the market for some while, it was reintroduced in 1997.

↝ If you are really distressed, the ship's doctor can give you an injection that will cure all discomfort. It may also make you drowsy, but the last thing on your mind will be staying awake at the movie.

↝ Try Travel Oil, an aromatherapy oil made by Borealis Healthcare in the UK. It is a natural alternative to drug-based medications. Applied to the temples and across the forehead, there are no side effects.

↝ Another natural preventive is ginger in powder form. Mix half a teaspoon in a glass of warm water or milk, and drink it before sailing. This is said to settle any stomach for a period of up to eight hours.

↝ "Sea Bands" (or "Aquastraps") are a drug-free method of controlling motion sickness. These are slim bands (in varying colors) that are wrapped around the wrist, with a circular "button" that presses against an acupressure point (*nei kuan*) on the lower arm. Attach them a few minutes before you step aboard and wear on both wrists throughout the cruise.

All this being said, bear in mind that in addition to stabilizers in the hull, most cruises are in warm, calm waters and most cruise ships spend much time along the coast or pull into port regularly. The odds are very much against being seasick.

SECURITY

A recognized standard of passenger ship protection exists, following the tragedy of the hijacking of *Achille Lauro* in 1985. Cruise lines reached this recognized standard as a result of several factors: a moral obligation which, like safety, is inherent in the industry; passenger expectation; and the firmer, more formal pressures being applied across the world by governments and coast guards. You may be required to go through metal detection devices at the gangway, and your baggage may be subject to more stringent inspection.

All cabins can be locked, and it is recommended that you keep your cabin locked at all times when you are not there. Old-style keys are made of metal and operate a mechanical lock; most will be plastic key cards that operate electronically coded locks. Cruise lines do not accept responsibility for any money or valuables left in cabins and suggest that you store them in a safety deposit box at the purser's office, or, if one is supplied, in your in-cabin personal safe.

You will be issued a personal boarding pass when you embark (the latest high-tech passes may include your photo, lifeboat station, restaurant seating, and other pertinent information). This serves as identification and must be shown at the gangway each time you board (you may also be asked for a separate photo ID, such as a driver's license). The system of boarding passes is one of many ways in which cruise lines ensure passenger safety.

SHIPBOARD ETIQUETTE

Cruise lines want you to have a good vacation, but there are some rules to be observed.

→ In public rooms, smoking and nonsmoking sections are available. In the dining room, however, cigar and pipe smoking are not permitted at all.

→ If you take a video camera with you, be aware that you are not allowed to tape any of the professional entertainment shows and cabarets due to international copyright infringement regulations.

→ It is all right to be casual when on vacation, but not to enter a ship's dining room in just a bathing suit. Bare feet, likewise, are not permitted. If you are uncomfortable eating with the typical ten-piece dining room cutlery setting, don't fret; some cruise lines now have etiquette classes to help you.

SHIPBOARD INJURY

Slipping, tripping, and falling are the major sources of shipboard injury. This does not mean that ships are unsafe, but there are some things you can do to minimize the chance of injury. If you *do* suffer from injury aboard ship, feel it is the cruise line's fault, and want to take some kind of legal action against the company, you should be aware of the following:

In the United States, Appendix 46, Section 183(b) of the US Civil Code requires that "the injured passenger notify the cruise line in writing within six months from the date of the injury to file a claim and suit must be filed within one year from the date of injury." So, if you file a claim after the one-year period, the cruise line will probably seek a summary judgment for dismissal.

It is imperative that you first *read your ticket*. The passenger ticket is a *legal contract* between passenger and cruise line. It will invariably state that you must file suit in the state (or country) designated in the ticket. Thus, if a resident of California buys a cruise, and the cruise line is based in Florida, then the lawsuit must be filed in Florida. If you reside in the US and you purchase a cruise in the Mediterranean and the cruise line is based in Italy, then you would have to file suit in Italy. This is known as the Forum Clause.

A clause in the ticket typically reads:

"The Carrier's legal responsibility for death, injury, illness, damage, delay, or other loss or detriment of person or property of whatever kind suffered by the Passenger will, in the first instance, be governed by the Athens Convention relating to the Carriage of Passengers and their Luggage by Sea, 1974, with protocols and amendments, together with the further provisions of the International Convention on Limitation of Liability for Maritime Claims, 1976, with revisions and amendments (hereinafter collectively referred to as the "Convention"). The Carrier shall not be liable for any such death, injury, illness, damage, delay, loss, or detriment caused by Act of God, war or warlike operations, civil commotions, labor trouble, interference by Authorities, perils of the sea, or any other cause beyond the control of the Carrier, fire, thefts or any other crime, errors in the navigation or management of the Vessel, or defect in, or unseaworthiness of hull, machinery, appurtenances, equipment, furnishings, or supplies of the Vessel, fault or neglect of pilot, tugs, agents, independent contractors, such as ship's Physician, Passengers or other persons on board not in the Carrier's employ or for any other cause of whatsoever nature except and unless it is proven that such death, injury, illness, damage, delay, loss resulting from Carrier's act or omission was committed with the intent to cause such loss or with knowledge that such loss would probably result therefrom and in that event the Carrier's liability therefore shall not exceed the specified limitations per Passenger in Special Drawing Rights (S.D.R.) as defined in the applicable conventions or in any further revision and/or amendment thereto as shall become applicable."

One area in which passengers may not be able to sue a cruise line is in the event of injury or accident when they are on a shore excursion advertised and sold aboard ship. This is because the tour operators are independent contractors. So, when you buy your shore excursion, ask if the ship's insurance fully covers you under the terms of the passenger ticket contract.

In Your Cabin

Note that aboard many ships, particularly older vessels, there are raised lips separating the bathroom from the sleeping area.

→ Do not hang anything from the fire sprinkler heads located on most cabin ceilings.

→ On older ships, it is wise to note how the door lock works. Some require a key on the inside in order to unlock the door. Leave the key in the lock, so that in the event of a real emergency, you do not have to hunt for the key.

On Deck

→ Aboard older ships, watch for raised lips in doorways leading to open deck areas. Be alert and do not trip over them.

→ Wear sensible shoes with rubber soles (not crepe) when walking on deck or going to pool and lido areas. Do not wear high heels.

→ Walk with caution when the outer decks are wet after being washed, or if they are wet after rain. This warning applies especially to metal decks. There is nothing more painful than falling onto a solid steel deck.

→ Do not throw a lighted cigarette or cigar butt, or knock out your pipe, over the ship's side. The sea might seem like a safe place to throw such items, but they can easily be sucked into an opening in the ship's side or onto an aft open deck area, only to cause a fire.

How to Survive a Shipboard Fire

Shipboard fires generate heat, smoke, and often panic. In the unlikely event that you are in one, try to remain calm and think logically and clearly.

When you board the ship and get to your cabin, check the way from there to the nearest emergency exits fore and aft. Count the number of cabin doorways and other distinguishing features to the exits in case you have to escape without the benefit of lighting, or in case the passageway is filled with smoke and you cannot see clearly. New ships will use the "low location" lighting systems more and more, which are either the electroluminescent or photoluminescent type.

Exit signs are located just above floor level, but aboard older vessels the signs may be above your head, which is virtually useless, as smoke and flames always rise. Note the nearest fire alarm location and know how to use it in case of dense smoke and/or no lighting.

If you are in your cabin and there is fire in the passageway outside, first put on your lifejacket and feel for the cabin door. If the door handle is hot, soak a towel in water and use it to turn the handle of the door. If there is a raging fire in the passageway, cover yourself in wet towels and go through the flames. It may be your only means of escape, unless you have a balcony cabin.

Check the passageway. If there are no flames, or if everything looks clear, walk to the nearest emergency exit or stairway. If there is smoke in the passageway, crawl to the nearest exit. If the exit is blocked, then go to an alternate one.

It may take considerable effort to open a fire door to the exit, as they are heavy. Don't use the elevators, as they may stop at a deck that is on fire or full of smoke.

In the event of fire in your cabin, report it immediately by telephone. Then get out of your cabin if you can and close the door behind you to prevent any smoke or flames from entering the passageway. Finally, sound the alarm and alert your neighbors.

SHORE EXCURSIONS

→ Cruise lines plan and oversee shore excursions assuming that you have not seen a place and aim to show you its highlights in a comfortable manner and at a reasonable price.

→ Buses, rather than taxis or private cars, are often the principal choice of transportation. This cuts costs and allows the tour operator to narrow the selection of guides to only those most competent, knowledgeable, and fluent in whatever language the majority of passengers speak, while providing some degree of security and control.

→ Brochure-Speak: Shore excursion descriptions include artistic license, often written by personnel who have not visited the port of call. All cruise lines should adopt the following definitions in their descriptive literature and for their lectures and presentations: The term "visit" should be taken to mean actually entering the place or building concerned. The term "see" should be taken to mean viewing from the outside (as from a bus, for example).

→ Shore excursions are timed to be most convenient for the greatest number of participants, taking into account the timing of meals on board (these may be altered according to excursion times). Departure times are listed in the descriptive literature and in the *Daily Program*, and may or may not be announced over the ship's public address system. There are no refunds if you miss the excursion.

→ *Note*: If you are hearing impaired, make arrangements with the shore excursion manager to assist you in departing for your excursions at the correct times.

→ The ship's representative supervising the shore excursion program is the eyes and ears of the cruise line, and can recommend to the head office that any excursion be suspended if it is not up to standard. Shore excursion staff will be dockside dispatching the excursions in each port.

→ Most excursions give little in-depth history, and guides are often not acquainted with details beyond a superficial general knowledge.

→ City excursions are basically superficial. To get to know a city intimately, go alone or with a small group. Go by taxi or bus, or walk directly to the places that are of most interest to you.

→ Many ships operate dive-in excursions at a reasonable price that includes all equipment. Instruction is offered on board, and underwater cameras can often be rented, too.

→ When you buy a shore excursion from the cruise line, you are fully covered by the ship's insurance; do it on your own and you are not covered when you step off the ship.

→ Shore excursion booking forms should be forwarded with your cruise tickets and documents. In some ships, they can be booked via the interactive television system in your cabin.

→ Book early, particularly those listed as "limited participation." This means that there are a restricted number of places available, sold on a first come, first served basis. In some ships, where shore excursions can be booked prior to the sailing date, sellouts often occur.

→ For cancellations, most ships require a minimum of 24 hours' notice before the advertised shore excursion departure time. Refunds are at the discretion of the cruise line.

→ Only take along what is necessary; leave any valuables aboard ship, together with any money and credit cards you do not plan to use. Groups of people are often targets for pickpockets in popular sightseeing destinations and major cities. Also, beware of excursion guides who give you a colored disk to wear for "identification." He may be marking you as a "rich" tourist for local shopkeepers.

→ Going solo? If you hire a taxi for sightseeing, negotiate the price in advance, and do not pay until you get back to the ship or to your final destination. If you are with friends, hiring a taxi for a full- or half-day sightseeing trip can often work out far cheaper than renting a car, and you also avoid the hazards of driving. Naturally, prices vary according to destination, but if you can select a driver who speaks your language, and the taxi is comfortable, even air-conditioned, you are ahead.

SHOPPING

→ Many cruise lines that operate in Alaska, the Bahamas, the Caribbean, and the Mexican Riviera openly engage a company that provides the services of a "shopping lecturer." The shopping lecturer promotes selected shops, goods, and services heavily, fully authorized by the cruise line (which receives a commission from the same). This relieves the cruise director of any responsibilities, together with any question about his involvement, credibility, and financial remuneration.

→ Shopping maps, with "selected" stores highlighted, are placed in your cabin. Often, they come with a "guarantee" such as: "Shop with confidence at each of the recommended stores. Each merchant listed on this map has been carefully selected on the basis of quality, fair dealing, and value. These merchants have given Cruise Line X a guarantee of satisfaction valid for thirty (30) days after purchase, excluding passenger negligence and buyers' regret, and have paid a promotional fee for inclusion as a guaranteed store."

→ Know in advance just what you are looking for, especially if your time is limited. But if time is no problem, browsing can be fun.

→ When shopping time is included in shore excursions, be wary of stores recommended by tour guides; the guides are likely to be receiving commissions from the merchants.

Courtesy Windjammer Barefoot Cruises

Warm sun, gentle waves, and a good book — a great way to unwind.

→ Shop around and compare prices before you buy. Good shopping hints and recommendations are often given in the port lecture at the start of your cruise.

→ When shopping for local handicrafts, make sure they have indeed been made locally.

→ Be wary of "bargain-priced" name brands, as they may well be counterfeit and of dubious quality. For watches, check the guarantee. Some shopping information may be available in information literature about the port and this should be available at the ship's shore excursion office.

→ Remember that the ship's shops are also duty free and, for the most part, competitive in price. The shops on board are closed while in port, however, due to international customs regulations.

SPORTS FACILITIES
The variety of sports facilities on board depends on the size of the ship. Facilities typically include: badminton, basketball practice area, golf driving cage, horseshoes, jogging track, miniature putting green, paddle tennis, quoits, ring toss, shuffleboard, skeet shooting, squash (rarely), table tennis, and volleyball.

SUN
Cruising to the sun? Note that the closer you get to the equator the more potent and penetrating are the rays. They are most harmful when the sun is directly overhead. Use a protective sun lotion (15–30 factor), and reapply it every time you go for a swim or soak in the pool or ocean. Start with just 15 minutes' exposure and gradually work your way up to an hour or so. It is better to go home with a suntan than sunburn.

SWIMMING POOLS
Most ships have outdoor or indoor swimming pools, or both. They may be closed in port owing to local health regulations and/or cleaning. Opening hours will be listed in the *Daily Program*. Diving is not allowed, since pools are shallow. Parents should note that most pools are unsupervised. Be aware that some ships use excessive chlorine or bleaching agents for cleaning; these could cause bathing suit colors to run.

TELEVISION
Television programming is obtained from a mixture of satellite feeds and onboard videos. Some ships can lock-on to live international news programs (such as CNN or BBC World News), or to text-only news services, for which cruise lines pay a subscription fee. Satellite television reception is sometimes poor, however, due to the fact that ships constantly move out of the narrow beam being downloaded from the satellite and they therefore cannot "track" the signal as accurately as a land-based facility.

TIPPING (GRATUITIES)
Many travelers feel that the ship should host its passengers, and that the passengers should not host the crew by means of tips, so the question of tipping is awkward and embarrassing. In some ships, there are subtle suggestions made regarding tips; in others, cruise directors get carried away and are too dictatorial regarding tipping. Some ships offer hints on tipping via the in-cabin video system. Some cruise brochures state that "tipping is not required." They may not be required, but they are definitely expected by the ship's staff.

The accepted cruise industry standards for gratuities follows:

→ **Dining room waiter**: $3.00–$4.00 per person per day;

→ **Busboy**: $1.50–$2.00 per day;

→ **Cabin steward/stewardess**: $3.00–$3.50 per person per day;

→ **Butler**: $5.00–$6.00 per person per day.

→ Aboard many ships a gratuity of 10 or 15 percent is automatically added to your bar check.

Tips are given on the last evening of a cruise of up to 14 days' duration. For longer cruises, you would extend half of the tip halfway through and the rest on your last evening. *Note*: In some Greekflagged ships (Royal Olympic Cruises, for example), gratuities are pooled and given to the chief steward, who gives them out at the end of each cruise ($8-$10 per person per day is the norm).

Gratuities are now included in the cruise fare aboard a number of ships (principally those in the luxury end of the market), where no extra tipping is permitted (in theory).

Origin of the Word "Tips"

Before the introduction of postage stamps, coachmen who carried passengers were often asked to carry a letter or other package. A small recompense was given for this service, called a "tip" — which stands for "to insure personal service." Hence, when in the future some special service was provided, particularly in the hospitality industry, tips became an accepted way of saying thank-you for services rendered.

VALUABLES

Many ships now have a small personal safe in each cabin. However, items of special value should be kept in a safety deposit box in the purser's office. You will then have simple and convenient access to your valuables during the cruise.

VISITORS

Passes for visitors to see you on board prior to sailing must be arranged in advance, preferably at the time you make your booking. Announcements will be made when it is time for all visitors to go ashore.

Sadly, bon voyage parties, such as those you may have seen in the movies, are virtually a thing of the past. They are no longer possible (with the exception of ships operating around-the-world cruises) owing to greatly increased security concerns and insurance regulations.

WATER SPORTS

Some small ships have a water sports platform that is lowered from the ship's stern or side. These ships carry windsurfers, water-ski boats, jet skis, water skis, and scuba and snorkel equipment, usually at no extra charge. Some may also feature an enclosed swimming "cage" for areas of the world where unpleasant fish might be lurking.

Although such facilities look good in the cruise brochures, in many cases ships seem reluctant to use them. This is because many itineraries have too few useful anchor ports. Also, the sea must be in an almost flat calm condition, which is seldom the case. Another more prosaic reason is simply because of strict insurance regulations.

WINE AND LIQUOR

The cost of drinks on board is generally lower than on land, since ships have access to duty-free liquor. Drinks may be ordered in the dining room, at any of the ship's bars or from room service. Some lines charge "corkage," a fee to deter passengers from bringing their own wines into the dining room.

In the dining room, you can order wine with your meals from an extensive and reasonably priced wine list. For wine with your dinner, try to place your order at lunchtime, as wine waiters are always at their busiest at the evening meal.

In some ships, a duty-free sales point allows you to purchase wine and liquor for personal consumption in your cabin. You will not normally be permitted to bring these purchases into the dining room or other public rooms, nor indeed any duty-free wine or liquor purchased in port. These regulations are made to protect bar sales, which are a substantial source of onboard revenue for the cruise line.

20 PRACTICAL TIPS FOR A GOOD CRUISE EXPERIENCE

What to Do If...

1. Your luggage does not arrive at the ship.
If you are part of the cruise line's air/sea package, the airline is wholly responsible for locating your luggage and delivering it to the next port. If you arranged your own air transportation it is wholly *your* problem. Always have easy-to-read name and address tags both *inside* as well as *outside* your luggage. Keep track of claim documents and give the airline a detailed itinerary and list of port agents (usually included with your documents).

2. *You* miss the ship.
If you miss the ship's departure (due to late or nonperforming flight connections, etc.), and you are traveling on an air/sea package, the airline will arrange to get you to the ship. If you are traveling "cruise-only," however, and have arranged your own air transportation, then *you* are responsible for onward flights, hotel stays, and transfers. Many cruise lines now have "deviation" desks, where (for a fee) you can adjust airline flights and dates to suit personal preferences. If you arrive at the port just as your ship is pulling away, see the ship's port agent immediately.

3. Your cabin is too small.
Almost all cruise ship cabins are too small! When you book a cruise, you pay for a certain category and type of cabin but have little or no control over which one you actually get. See the hotel manager as soon as possible, explaining what is wrong with the cabin (noisy, too hot, etc.). If the ship is full (and most are nowadays), it will be difficult to change. However, the hotel manager will probably try to move you from known problem cabins, although they are not required to do so.

4. Your cabin has no air-conditioning, is noisy, or there are plumbing problems.
If there is anything wrong in your cabin, or if there is something wrong with the plumbing in your bathroom, bring it to the attention of your cabin steward immediately. If nothing gets better, complain to the hotel manager. Some cabins, for example, are located above the ship's laundry, generator, or galley (hot); others may be above the disco (noisy). If the ship is full, it may be difficult to change.

5. You have noisy cabin neighbors.
First, politely tell your neighbors that you can hear them brushing their hair as the cabin walls are so thin, and would they please not bang the drawers shut at 2:00am! If that does not work, complain to the purser or hotel manager, and ask them to attend to the problem.

6. You have small children and the brochure implied that the ship has special programs for them, but when on board you find out it is not an all-year-round program.
In this instance, either the brochure was misleading, or your travel agent did not know enough about the ship or did not bother to ask the right questions. If you have genuine cause for complaint, then see your travel agent when you get home. Ships generally will try to accommodate your young ones, but may not be covered by their insurance for "looking after" them throughout the day, as the brochure seemed to promise. Again, check thoroughly with your travel agent *before* you book.

7. You do not like your dining room seating.
Most "standard" market ships operate two seatings for dinner (sometimes for all meals). When you book your cruise, you are asked whether you want the first or second seating. The line will make every attempt to please you. But if you want second seating and are given first seating (perhaps a large group has taken over the entire second seating, or the ship is full), there may be little the maître d' can do.

8. You want a table for two and are put at a table for eight.
Again, see the maître d' and explain why you are not satisfied. A little gratuity should prove helpful.

9. You cannot communicate with your dining room waiter.
Dining room waiters are probably of a nationality and tongue completely foreign to yours, and all they can do is smile. This could prove frustrating for a whole cruise, especially if you need something out of the ordinary. See the maître d', and tell him you want a waiter with whom you can communicate. If he does not solve the problem, see the hotel manager.

10. The food is definitely not "gourmet" cuisine as advertised in the brochure.
If the food is not as described (for example, whole lobster in the brochure, but only cold lobster salad once during the cruise, or the "fresh squeezed" orange juice on the breakfast menu is anything but), tell the maître d.'

11. A large group has taken over the ship.
Sometimes, large groups have blocked (pre-booked) several public rooms for meetings (seemingly every hour on the hour in the rooms you want to use). This means the individual passenger (that is you) becomes a second-class citizen. Make your displeasure known to the hotel manager immediately, tell your travel agent, and write a follow-up letter to the line when you return home.

12. A port of call is deleted from the itinerary.
If you only took the cruise because the ship goes to the place you have wanted to go for years, then read the fine print in the brochure *before* you book. A cruise line is under *no* obligation to perform the stated itinerary. For whatever reason (political unrest, weather, mechanical problems, no berth space, safety, etc.), the ship's captain has the ultimate say.

13. You are unwell aboard ship.

Do not worry. There will be a qualified doctor (who generally operates as a concession, and therefore charges) and medical facilities, including a small pharmacy. You will be well taken care of. Although there are charges for medical services rendered, almost all cruise lines offer insurance packages that include medical coverage for most eventualities. It is wise to take out this insurance when you book.

14. You have a problem with a crew member.

Go to the hotel manager or chief purser and explain the problem (for single women this could be a persistent cabin steward with a master door key). No one will do anything unless you complain. Cruise ships try to hire decent staff, but, with so many crew members, there are bound to be a few bad apples. Insist on a full written report of the incident, which must be entered into the ship's daily log by the staff captain (deputy captain).

15. You leave some personal belongings on a tour bus.

If you have left something on a tour bus, and you are back on board your ship, first advise the shore excursion manager or the purser's office. The shore excursion manager will contact the tour operator ashore to ascertain whether any items have been handed in to their office.

16. The cruise line's air arrangements have you flying from Los Angeles via Timbuktu to get to your cruise ship.

Fine if your cruise ship is in Timbuktu (difficult, as it is inland). Most cruise lines that have low rates also use the cheapest air routing to get you to your ship. That could mean flights from a central hub. Be warned: you get what you pay for. Ask questions *before* you book.

17. You fly internationally to take a cruise.

If your cruise is a long distance away from your home, then it makes good sense to fly to your cruise embarkation point and stay for at least a day or two before the cruise. Why? You will be better rested. You will have time to adjust to any time changes. You will step aboard your ship already relaxed and ready for a real vacation.

18. The ship's laundry ruins your clothes.

If any of your clothing is ruined or discolored by the ship's laundry, tell your cabin steward(ess), and then follow up by going to the purser's office and getting it registered as a proper complaint. Get a copy of it, so you can follow up when you get home. Unfortunately, you will probably find a disclaimer on the laundry list saying something to the effect that liability is limited to about $1 per item, which is not a lot. So, although the laundry and dry cleaning facilities generally work well, things can occasionally go wrong just like ashore.

19. You have extra charges on your bill.

Check your itemized bill carefully. Then talk to the purser's office and ask them to show you the charge slips. Make sure you are given a copy of your bill, *after* any modifications have been made.

20. You are unhappy with your cruise experience.

You (or your travel agent) ultimately choose the ship and cruise. But if your ship does not meet your specific lifestyle and interests, or the ship performs less well than the brochure promises, then let your travel agent and the cruise line know as soon as possible. If your grievance is valid, many cruise lines will offer a credit, good towards a future cruise. But do read the fine print on the ticket.

THE PASSENGER'S PRAYER

"Heavenly Father, look down on us, Your humble, obedient passengers who are doomed to travel the seas and waterways of this earth, taking photographs, mailing postcards, buying useless souvenirs, and walking around in ill-fitting swimwear.

"We beseech You, oh Lord, to see that our plane is not hijacked, our luggage is not lost, and that our oversized carry-ons go unnoticed.

"Protect us from surly and unscrupulous taxi drivers, avaricious porters, and unlicensed, English-speaking guides in foreign places.

"Give us this day Divine guidance in the selection of our cruise ships and our travel agents — so that we may find our bookings and dining room reservations honored, our cabins of generous proportions, that our luggage arrives before the first evening meal, and that our beds are made up.

"We humbly ask that our shower curtains do not provoke us into meaningless frustration and destructive thoughts.

"We pray that our cabin telephones work, the operator (human or electrical) speaks our tongue, and that there are no phone calls from our children forcing us to abandon our cruise early.

"Lead us, dear Lord, to good, inexpensive restaurants in the world ashore — where the food is superb, the waiters friendly, and the wine included in the price of a meal.

"Please grant us a cruise director who does not "cream" excessively from the spoils of bingo or horse racing, or does not stress only those jewelry stores from which he accepts an offering.

"Grant us the strength to take shore excursions — to visit the museums, cathedrals, spice stalls, and gift shops listed in the guidebooks.

"And if on our return journey by non-air-conditioned buses we slip into slumber, have mercy on us for our flesh is weak, hot, and tired.

"Give us the wisdom to tip correctly at the end of our voyage. Forgive us for undertipping out of ignorance, and over-tipping out of fear. Please make the chief purser and ship's staff love us for what we are and not for what we can contribute to their worldly goods or company comment forms.

"Dear God, keep our wives from shopping sprees and protect them from bargains they do not need or cannot afford. Lead them not into temptation in St. Thomas or Hong Kong for they know not what they do.

"Almighty Father, keep our husbands from looking at foreign women and comparing them to us. Save them from making fools of themselves in cafés and night clubs. Above all, please do not forgive them their trespasses for they know exactly what they do.

"And when our voyage is over and we return home to our loved ones, grant us the favor of finding someone who will look at our home videos and listen to our stories, so our lives as tourists will not have been in vain. This we ask you in the name of our chosen cruise line, and in the name of American Express, Visa, Mastercard, and our banks. Amen."

QUIPS AND QUOTES

Passengers cruising for the first time are the source of all the following questions to me when I worked aboard ships all those years ago:

"Do the crew sleep on board?"
"How far above sea level are we?"
"Is the island surrounded by water?"
"How does the captain know which port to go to?"
"Can we get off in the Panama Canal?"
"Does the ship generate its own electricity?"
"Does this elevator go up as well as down?"
"Will this elevator take me to my cabin?"
"Why is the sauna so hot?"
"What time's the midnight buffet?"
"Are there two seatings at the midnight buffet?"
"Is dinner in the dining room?"
"Can I please have some hot iced tea?"
"Do we have to stay up until midnight to change our clocks?"
"How many fjords to the dollar?"
"What time's the 2 o'clock tour?"
"Where's the bus for the walking tour?"
"Will we have time to take the shore excursion?"
"If I don't buy a shore excursion, am I allowed off in port?"
"Are the entertainers paid?"

"Why don't we have a Late Night Comedy Spot in the afternoon?"
"Why aren't the dancers fully dressed?"
"How do we know which photos are ours?"
"Will the ship wait for the tour buses to get back?"
"Will I get wet if I go snorkeling?"
"Do the Chinese do the laundry by hand?"
"Is the mail brought in by plane?"
"Does the ship dock in the middle of town?"
"Who's driving the ship if the captain is at the cocktail party?"
"Does the sun always rise on the left side of the ship?"
"Is the doctor qualified?"
"Is trapshooting held outside?"
"I'm married, but can I come to the Singles Party?"
"Should I put my luggage outside the cabin before or after I go to sleep?"

And here are some new ones:
"Can I have an inside cabin with a balcony?"
"Does an *outside* cabin mean it's *outside* the ship?"

In Alaska (Cunard *Princess*):
"Are the glaciers always here?"

In the dining room (*Stella Solaris*):
Me: "Do you have a decanter for this young red wine?"
Wine waiter: "Not unless it's on the wine list."

Overheard in the cigar smoking room (*Century*):
"Where are the no-smoking seats?"

Overheard in the dining room (Cunard *Countess*):
"Waiter, this vichyssoise is cold."
"Was the fish caught this morning by the crew?"

Overheard on an Antarctic cruise (*Hanseatic*):
"Where is the good shopping in Antarctica?"

Overheard on a British islands cruise:
"Windsor Castle is terrific. But why did they build it so close to the airport?"

Overheard on a Greek islands cruise:
"Why did the Greeks build so many ruins?"

Overheard on a round-Japan cruise, in Kagoshima, with Mount Suribaya in the background (*QE2*):
"Can you tell me what time the volcano will erupt? I want to be sure to take a photograph."

Then there is the cruise brochure that describes the cabin layout as: "cabins with double bed, can accommodate a third passenger!" (the now defunct Premier Cruise Lines)

And what about the saying "He let the cat out of the bag?" On board a square-rigger 150 years ago, this would have sent shudders through one's spine — for it meant that a sailor had committed an offense serious enough to have the "cat o' nine tails" extracted from its bag.

The "cat" was a whip made of nine lengths of cord, each being about 18 inches long with three knots at the end, all fixed to a rope handle. It could bring serious injuries, even death upon the victim. It is no longer carried on today's tall ships, having been outlawed by the US Congress in 1850, and then by Britain's Royal Navy in 1879.

ENTERTAINMENT

DID YOU KNOW...?

...that Roy, of the famous Siegfried & Roy (Siegfried Fischbacher and Roy Uwe Ludwig Horn) illusion act, used to be a steward aboard the German liner *Bremen*?

...that the Cunard White Star Line's *Queen Mary* was the first ship to have a system of colored lights that varied according to music (chromosonics)?

...that Verdi wrote an opera to commemorate the opening of the Suez Canal? Its name is *Aida*.

...that the 212-passenger *Seabourn Legend* was the star of the film *Speed 2: Cruise Control*, released in July 1997 in the US? The film was shot on location in Marigot, the capital of the French side of the tiny two-nation Caribbean island of St. Martin/St. Maarten. The filming called for the building of almost a complete "town" at Marigot, into which the ship crashes.

...that *Titanic*, the stage musical, cost $10 million dollars to mount in New York in 1997? That's $2.5 million more than it cost to build the original ship that debuted in 1912. The play debuted at the Lunt-Fontanne Theater in April 1997 (the ship sank on April 14, 1912).

... that the Hollywood film that cost the most, but made the most money was based aboard a passenger liner? The film, *Titanic*, was released in 1997.

...that the cruise ship used in the movie *Juggernaut*, in which seven bombs in oil drums were placed aboard, was *Maxim Gorkiy?* The film starred Richard Harris, David Hemmings, and Anthony Hopkins.

THAT'S ENTERTAINMENT!

After food, the most subjective (and talked-about) part of any mainstream cruise experience is the entertainment program. Menus always present you with a choice of several foods, whereas the same is not often possible with cruise ship entertainment, which has to be diversified and innovative but never controversial. Ask 1,000 people what they would like to see as part of any evening entertainment program, and 1,000 different answers will ensue. It is all a matter of personal taste and choice. Whatever one expects, the days are gone when you would have been entertained by waiters doubling as singers, although a few bar waiters are still known to perform tray-spinning effects to boost their tips!

Many passengers, despite having paid so little for their cruise, expect to see top-notch entertainment, "headline" marquee-name cabaret artists, the world's most "popular" singers, and the most dazzling shows with slick special effects, just as one would find in the best venues in Las Vegas, London, or Paris. There are many reasons why it is not exactly so. International star acts invariably have an entourage that accompanies them to any venue: their personal manager, their musical director (often a pianist or conductor), a rhythm section (with bass player and drummer), even their hairdresser. On land, one-night shows are possible, but on a ship, an artist cannot always disembark after just one night, especially when it involves moving equipment, costumes, and baggage. This makes the whole matter logistically and financially unattractive for all but the very largest ships on fixed itineraries, where a marquee-name act might be considered a marketing draw.

When you are at home you can literally bring the world's top talent into your home via television. Cruise ships are a different matter. Most entertainers do not like to be away from their "home base" for long periods, as they rely on telephone contact. Most do not like the long contracts that the majority of ships must offer in order to amortize the cost.

So many acts working aboard cruise ships are interchangeable with so many other acts also working aboard cruise ships. Ever wonder why? Entertainers aboard ship must also *live* with their audiences for several days (sometimes weeks), something unheard-of on land, as well as work on stages

Courtesy Holland America Line

Costumes add to the scenery of Holland America Line's Copacabana Show.

aboard older ships that were not designed for live performances. However, there is no question that cruise ships are the new location for vaudeville acts, where a guaranteed audience is a bonus for many former club-date acts, as well as fresh acts waiting to break in to the big time on land.

Many older (pre-1970) ships have extremely limited entertainment spaces, and very few ships provide proper dressing rooms and backstage facilities for the storage of costumes, props, or effects, not to mention the extensive sound and lighting equipment most live "name" artists demand or need. Only the latest ships provide the extensive facilities needed for presenting the kind of high-tech shows one would find in Las Vegas, London, or New York, for example. These feature elaborate electronic backdrops, revolving stages, orchestra pits, multislide projection, huge stageside video screens, pyrotechnic capabilities, and the latest light-mover and laser technology. Even the latest ships often lack enough dressing room and hanging space for the 150 costumes required in a single typical ship production show.

However, more emphasis has been placed on entertainment since the mid-1970s. Entertainment on today's large mainstream ships is market-driven. In other words, it is directed toward that segment of the industry that the cruise line's marketing department is specifically targeting (discounting notwithstanding). This is predominantly a family audience, so the entertainment must appeal to as broad an age range as possible — a tall order for any cruise line's director of entertainment.

A cruise line with several ships in its fleet will normally employ an entertainment department that is made up of an entertainment director and several assistants, and most cruise lines have contracts with one or more entertainment agencies that specialize in entertainment for cruise ships.

It is no use, for example, in a company booking a juggler who needs a floor-to-ceiling height of 12 feet but finds that the ship has a show lounge with a height of just 7 feet. ("Couldn't he juggle sideways?" I have heard one cruise company executive ask!); or an acrobatic knife-throwing act (in a moving ship?); or a concert pianist when the ship only has an upright honky-tonk piano; or a singer who sings only in English when the passengers are German-speaking, and so on.

Indeed, the hardest audience to cater to is one of mixed nationalities (each of whom will expect entertainers to cater exclusively to their particular linguistic group). Given that cruise lines are now marketing to more international audiences in order to fill ships, the problem of finding the right entertainment is far more acute.

The more upscale cruise lines offer more classical music, even some light opera, and more fine guest lecturers and world-renowned authors than the seven-day package cruises heading for warm-weather destinations.

One area of entertainment that has become part of the experience, and is expected — particularly aboard large cruise ships — is that of the glamorous "production show." This is the kind of show one would expect to see in any good Las Vegas show palace, with a team of singers and dancers, a production manager, lavish backdrops, extravagant sets, grand lighting, special effects, and stunning custom-designed costumes. Unfortunately, many cruise line executives, who know little or nothing about entertainment, regard plumes and huge peacock feathers paraded by showgirls who step, but cannot dance, as being desirable. Some cruise ships have coarse shows that are not becoming to either dancer or passenger. Such things went out of vogue about 20 years ago. Shows that offer more creative costuming and real dancing win more votes today.

Book back-to-back seven-day cruises (on alternating eastern and western Caribbean itineraries, for example), and you should note that entertainment is generally geared to seven-day cruises. Thus, you will probably find the same two or three production shows and the same acts on the second week of your cruise. The way to avoid seeing everything twice is to pace yourself. Go to some shows during the first week and save the rest for the second week.

Regular passengers will notice that they seem to see the same acts time after time on various ships. For the reasons given above (and more), the criteria narrows the field even though there are many fine land-based acts. In addition, ship entertainers need to enjoy socializing. Successful shipboard acts tend to be good mixers, are presentable when in public, do not do drugs or take excess alcohol, are not late for rehearsals, and must cooperate with the cruise director and his or her staff as well as with the band.

Sadly, with cruise lines forever looking for ways to cut costs, entertainment has of late been a major target for some companies (particularly the smaller ones). Cutting costs translates to bringing on, for example, lower-cost singers (who often turn out to be nonreading, vocally-challenged persons) and bands that cannot read charts (musician-speak for musical arrangements) brought on board by cabaret acts.

SHOW BIZ AT SEA

In today's high-tech world, the putting together of a lavish 45–50-minute production show involves the concerted efforts of a range of experienced people from the world of show business, and a cost of $500,000 to $1 million per show is not unheard-of. Weekly running costs (performers' salaries, costume cleaning and repair, royalties, replacement audio and videotapes, and so on) all add up to an expensive package for what can be a largely unappreciative and critical audience.

WHO'S WHO

Although production companies differ in their approach, the following gives some idea of the various people involved behind the scenes.

Executive Producer

Transfers the show's concept from design to reality. First, the brief from the cruise line's director of entertainment might be for a new production show (the average being two major shows per seven-day cruise). Together they must plan the show. After deciding on an initial concept, they then call in the choreographer, vocal coach, and musical arranger, so everyone agrees on the flow of the show, the story line, and linkage.

Choreographer

Responsible for auditioning the dancers and for creating, selecting, and teaching the routines.

Musical Director

Coordinates all musical scores and arrangements; trains the singers in voice and microphone techniques, projection, accenting, phrasing, memory, and general presentation; and oversees session singers and musicians for the recording sessions, and click-tracks tapes.

Musical Arranger

After the music has been selected, the musical arrangements must be made. Just one song can cost as much as $2000 for a single arrangement for a 12-piece orchestra.

Costume Designer

Provides creative original designs for a minimum of seven costume changes in one show lasting 45 minutes. The costumes must also be practical, as they will be used repeatedly.

Costume Maker

Purchases all materials, and must be able to produce all of the costumes required by the costume designer, in the time frame allotted.

Graphic Designer

Provides all the set designs, whether they are physical one- two- or three-dimensional sets for the stage, or photographic images created on slide film, video, laser disk, or other electronic media. The trend is for digital computer technology to play an increasingly important part in creating the images to be transferred via an electronic medium.

Lighting Designer

Creates the lighting patterns and effects for a production show. Sequences and action on stage must be carefully lit to the best advantage. The completed lighting plot is sent to a software company that will etch the plot into computer-controlled disks to be used every time the show runs.

BANDS/MUSICIANS

Before the big production shows and artists can be booked, bands and musicians must be hired, often for long contracts. Naturally, live musicians are favored for a ship's show band, as they are excellent music readers (necessary for all visiting cabaret artists, not to mention the big production shows). Big bands are often placed in some of the larger ships for special sailings, or for world cruises, on which ballroom dancing plays a large part.

Most musicians work to contracts of about six months. Entertaining lounge duos and solo pianists or singer/pianists are generally hired through an entertainment agency specializing in cruise ships. Steel bands are recruited from the Caribbean, while other specialist bands (such as popular country and western bands) may be invited aboard for special occasions or charters.

OTHER ENTERTAINMENT

Most cruise ships organize acts that, while perhaps not nationally recognized "names," can provide two or three different shows during a seven-day cruise. These will be male/female singers, illusionists, puppeteers, hypnotists, and even circus acts, with wide age-range appeal.

There are comedians, comediennes, and comedy duos who perform "clean" material and who may find employment year-round on what is now known as the "cruise ship circuit." These popular comics enjoy good accommodation, are stars while on board, and often go from ship to ship on a standard rotation every few days. There are raunchy, late-night "adults only" comedy acts in some of the ships with younger, "hip" audiences, but few seem to have enough material for several shows.

The larger a ship, the larger the entertainment program will be. In some ships, the cruise director may "double" as an act, but most companies prefer him/her to be strictly an administrative and social director, allowing more time to be with passengers. Whichever ship and cruise you choose, you will find that being entertained "live" is an experience far superior to that of sitting at home in front of a television set, watching its clinical presentation. That's show business!

NAUTICAL NOTES

DID YOU KNOW...?

...that in 1903 the British liner *Lucania* became the first ship to have wireless equipment, which enabled her to keep in touch with both sides of the Atlantic Ocean at the same time?

...that the first ship-to-shore wireless telegraphy took place on the American passenger ship *St. Paul*, in 1899?

...that the first twin-screw passenger ship was the Compagnie Generale Transatlantique's 3,200-tonne *Washington*, built in 1863 and converted in 1868?

...that the first floating eclipse expedition was led by US astronomer Ted Pedas in 1972, when 800 passengers sailed to a spectacular rendezvous with a total sun eclipse in the North Atlantic?

...that the first passenger ship to exceed 80,000-tonnes was the Compagnie Generale Transatlantique's *Normandie*, which measured at 82,799-tonnes in 1936?

...that the first gravity lifeboats were aboard the Compagnie Generale Transatlantique's *Ile de France* of 1928?

The world of ships is a world of its own, and associated with it is a whole language and culture that can sometimes be confusing — but fascinating — to the newcomer. Here are a few tidbits of nautical information for you, which may contribute to the pleasure of your cruise.

RULES OF THE ROAD

Ships, the largest moving objects made by man, are subject to stringent international regulations. They must keep to the right in shipping lanes, and pass on the right (with certain exceptions). When circumstances raise some doubt, or shipping lanes are crowded, ships use their whistles in the same way an automobile driver uses directional signals to show which way he will turn. When one ship passes another and gives a single blast on its whistle, this means it is turning to starboard (right). Two blasts mean a turn to port (left). The other ship acknowledges by repeating the same signal. Ships switch on navigational running lights at night — green for starboard, red for port, plus two white lights on the masts, the forward one lower than the aft one.

Flags and pennants form another part of a ship's communication facilities and are displayed for identification purposes. Each time a country is visited, its national flag is shown. While entering and leaving a port, the ship flies a blue-and-white vertically striped flag to request a pilot, while a half red, half white flag (divided vertically) indicates that a pilot is on board. Cruise lines also display their own "house" flag from the mast.

A ship's funnel (smokestack) is one other means of identification, each line having its own design and color scheme. The size, height, and number of funnels were points worth advertising at the turn of the century. Most ocean liners of the time had four funnels and were called "four-stackers."

There are numerous customs at sea, many of them older than any maritime law. Superstition has always been an important element, as in the following example quoted from the British Admiralty Manual of Seamanship: "The custom of breaking a bottle of wine over the stem of a ship when it is being launched originates from the old practice of toasting prosperity to a ship with a silver goblet of wine, which was then cast into the sea in order to prevent a toast of ill intent being drunk from the same cup. This was a practice that proved too expensive, and it was replaced in 1690 by the breaking of a bottle of wine over the stem."

WIND SPEEDS

A navigational announcement to passengers is normally made once or twice a day, giving the ship's position, temperature, and weather information.

WHAT IS AN ISLAND?

An island is defined as any land mass smaller than the smallest continent, and completely surrounded by water.

THE COLOR OF SEAWATER

Seawater is colorless. We only see "color" in seawater because quantities of the water play with light. The deep blue of deep seawater is produced in part by the refraction of light particles in the water and by the reflection of the sky. Also, the color blue is absorbed least by seawater. "Green" seas are found closer to land and are the result of greater quantities of suspended matter carried in coastal waters. Thus, the color essentially results from the combination of the blue-looking ocean water and the yellow pigments that result from the decomposition of plant matter. The Red Sea was so named due to the periodic swarming of an alga that stains its surface.

WAVES

Water waves are produced when the air-sea surface interface is distorted by a force such as the wind. Waves provide one of the most important mechanisms for transporting energy from one point to another on the surface of the sea. A restoring force such as gravity, surface tension, or the Coriolis force then acts to return the surface to equilibrium.

Various winds affect the world's weather patterns. Such well-known winds as the Bora, Mistral, Northwind, and Sirocco, among others, play an important part in the makeup of weather at and above sea level. Wind velocity is measured on the Beaufort scale, a method that was devised in 1805 by Commodore Francis Beaufort, later Admiral and Knight Commander of the Bath, for measuring the force of wind at sea. Originally, it measured the effect of the wind on a fully rigged man-of-war (which was usually laden with cannons and heavy ammunition). It became the official way of recording wind velocity in 1874, when the International Meteorological Committee adopted it.

You might be confused by the numbering system for wind velocity. There are 12 velocities, known as "force" on the Beaufort scale. They are as follows:

Force	Speed (mph)	Description/Ocean Surface
0	0–1	Calm; glassy (like a mirror)
1	1–3	Light wind; rippled surface
2	4–7	Light breeze; small wavelets
3	8–12	Gentle breeze; large wavelets, scattered whitecaps
4	13–18	Moderate breeze; small waves, frequent whitecaps
5	19–24	Fresh breeze; moderate waves, numerous whitecaps
6	25–31	Strong breeze; large waves, white foam crests
7	32–38	Moderate gale; streaky white foam
8	39–46	Fresh gale; moderately high waves
9	47–54	Strong gale; high waves
10	55–63	Whole gale; very high waves, curling crests
11	64–73	Violent storm; extremely high waves, froth and foam, poor visibility
12	73+	Hurricane; huge waves, thundering white spray, visibility nil

KNOTS AND LOGS

A knot is a unit of speed measuring one nautical mile. (A nautical mile is equal to one-sixtieth of a degree of the earth's circumference and measures exactly 6,080.2 ft (1,852 km). It is about 800 feet (243 meters) longer than a land mile. Thus, when a ship is traveling at a speed of 20 knots (*note*: this is never referred to as 20 knots per hour), she is traveling at 20 nautical miles per hour.

This unit of measurement has its origin in the days prior to the advent of modern aids, when sailors used a log and a length of rope to measure the distance that their boat had covered, as well as the speed at which it was advancing. In 1574, a tract by William Bourne, entitled *A Regiment for the Sea*, records the method by which this was done. The log was weighted down at one end while the other end was affixed to a rope. The weighted end, when thrown over the stern, had the effect of making the log stand upright, thus being visible. Sailors believed that the log remained stationary at the spot where it had been cast into the water, while the rope unraveled. By measuring the length of rope used, they could ascertain how far the ship had traveled, and were thus able to calculate its speed.

Sailors first tied knots at regular intervals, eventually fixed at 47 feet 3 inches (14.4 meters) along a rope, then counted how many knots had passed through their hands in a specified time (later established as 28 seconds), and measured by the amount of sand that had run out of an hourglass. They then used simple multiplication to calculate the number of knots their ship was traveling at over the period of an hour.

The data gathered in this way were put into a record, called a logbook. Today, a logbook is used to record the day-to-day details of the life of a ship and its crew as well as other pertinent information.

LATITUDE AND LONGITUDE

Latitude signifies the distance north or south of the equator, while longitude signifies distance east or west of the 0 degree at Greenwich Observatory, London. Both are recorded in degrees, minutes, and seconds. At the equator, one minute of longitude is equal to one nautical mile, but as the meridians converge after leaving the equator and meeting at the poles, the size of a degree becomes smaller.

PLIMSOLL MARK

The safety of ships at sea and all those aboard owes much to the 19th-century social reformer Samuel Plimsoll, a member of the British Parliament concerned about the frequent loss of ships due to overloading. In those days, some shipowners would load their vessels down to the gunwales to squeeze every ounce of revenue out of them. They gambled on good weather, good fortune, and good seamanship to bring them safely into port. Consequently, many ships went to the bottom of the sea — the result of their buoyancy being seriously impaired by overloading.

Plimsoll helped to enact legislation that came to be known as the Merchant Shipping Act of 1875. This required shipowners to mark their vessels with a circular disc 12 inches (30.5 centimeters) long bisected by a line 18 inches (45.7 centimeters) long, as a measure of their maximum draft; that is, the depth to which a ship's hull could be safely immersed at sea. The Merchant Shipping Act of 1890 went even further, and required the Plimsoll mark (or line) to be positioned on the sides of vessels in accordance with tables drawn up by competent authorities.

The Plimsoll mark is now found on the ships of every nation. The Plimsoll mark indicates three different depths: the depth to which a vessel can be loaded in fresh water, which is less buoyant than salt water; the depth in summer, when seas are generally calmer; and the depth in winter, when seas are much rougher.

SHIP TALK

Ships and the sea have their own special vocabulary. This list may be of use.

Abeam: off the side of the ship, at a right angle to its length.

Aft: near, toward, or in the rear of the ship.

Ahead: something that is ahead of the ship's bow.

Alleyway: a passageway or corridor.

Alongside: said of a ship when it is beside a pier or another vessel.

Amidships: in or toward the middle of the ship; the longitudinal center portion of the ship.

Anchor Ball: black ball hoisted above the bow to show that the vessel is anchored.

Astern: is the opposite of Ahead (i.e., meaning something behind the ship).

Backwash: motion in the water caused by the propeller(s) moving in a reverse (astern) direction.

Bar: sandbar, usually caused by tidal or current conditions near the shore.

Beam: width of the ship between its two sides at the widest point.

Bearing: compass direction, expressed in degrees, from the ship to a particular objective or destination.

Below: anything beneath the main deck.

Berth: dock, pier, or quay. Also means bed on board ship.

Bilge: lowermost spaces of the infrastructure of a ship.

Boat Stations: allotted space for each person during lifeboat drill or any other emergency when lifeboats are lowered.

Bow: the forward most part of the vessel.

Bridge: navigational and command control center.

Bulkhead: upright partition (wall) dividing the ship into compartments.

Bunkers: the space where fuel is stored; "bunkering" means taking on fuel.

Cable Length: a measured length equaling 100 fathoms or 600 feet.

Chart: a nautical map used for navigating.

Colors: refers to the national flag or emblem flown by the ship.

Companionway: interior stairway.

Course: direction in which the ship is headed, in degrees.

Davit: a device for raising and lowering lifeboats.

Deadlight: a ventilated porthole cover to prevent light from entering.

Disembark (also debark): to leave a ship.

Dock: berth, pier, or quay.

Draft (or draught): measurement in feet from the ship's waterline to the lowest point of its keel.

Embark: to join a ship.

Fantail: the rear or overhang of the ship.

Fathom: distance equal to six feet.

Flagstaff: a pole at the stern of a ship where the flag of the ship's country of registry is flown.

Free Port: port or place that is free of customs duty and regulations.

Funnel: chimney from which the ship's combustion gases are propelled into the atmosphere.

Galley: the ship's kitchen.

Gangway: the stairway or ramp link between ship and shore.

Gross Registered Tonnes (grt): not the weight of a ship but the total navigation of all permanently enclosed spaces above and below decks, with certain exceptions, such as the bridge, radio room, galleys, washing facilities, and other specified areas. It is the basis for harbor dues. International regulations introduced in 1982 required shipowners to remeasure the grt of their vessels (1 grt = 100 cubic feet of enclosed space/2.83 m^3). This unit of measure was invented in England centuries ago for taxation purposes, when wine shipped from France was stored in standard-size casks, called *tonneaux*. Thus a ship carrying twenty casks measured 20 tonnes, and taxes were applied accordingly.

Helm: the apparatus for steering a ship.

House Flag: the flag denoting the company to which a ship belongs.

Hull: the frame and body of the ship exclusive of masts or superstructure.

Leeward: the side that is sheltered from the wind.

Manifest: a list of the ship's passengers, crew, and cargo.

Nautical Mile: one-sixtieth of a degree of the circumference of the Earth.

Pilot: a person licensed to navigate ships into or out of a harbor or through difficult waters, and to advise the captain on handling the ship during these procedures.

Pitch: the rise and fall of a ship's bow that may occur when the ship is under way.

Port: the left side of a ship when facing forward.

Quay: berth, dock, or pier.

Rudder: a finlike device astern and below the waterline, for steering the vessel.

Screw: a ship's propeller.

Stabilizer: a gyroscopically operated retractable "fin" extending from either or both sides of the ship below the waterline to provide a more stable ride.

Starboard: the right side of the ship when facing forward.

Stern: the aftmost part of the ship that is opposite the bow.

Tender: a smaller vessel, often a lifeboat, that is used to transport passengers between the ship and shore when the vessel is at anchor.

Wake: the track of agitated water left behind a ship when in motion.

Waterline: the line along the side of a ship's hull corresponding to the water surface.

Windward: the side toward which the wind blows.

Yaw: the erratic deviation from the ship's set course, usually caused by a heavy sea.

THE BRIDGE

A ship's navigation bridge is manned at all times, both at sea and in port. Besides the captain, who is master of the vessel, other senior officers take "watch" turns for four- or eight-hour periods. In addition, junior officers are continually honing their skills as experienced navigators, waiting for the day when they will be promoted to master.

The captain is always in command at times of high risk, such as when the ship is entering or leaving a port, when the density of traffic is particularly high, or when visibility is severely restricted by poor weather.

Navigation has come a long way since the days of the ancient mariners, who used only the sun and the stars to calculate their course across the oceans. The space-age development of sophisticated navigation devices (using satellites) has enabled us to eliminate the guesswork of early navigation (the first global mobile satellite system came into being in 1979).

A ship's navigator today can establish accurately where the ship is in any weather and at any time. There follows a description of some of the navigation instruments, which will help you understand the complexities of seamanship today.

System Control

The most sophisticated state-of-the-art machinery and navigation systems are such technical marvels that sailors of yesteryear could not even conceive of their invention. The latest navigation system, known as the "Electronic Chart Precise Integrated Navigation System" (ECPINS) combines the electronics of the latest satellite positioning methods (Global Positioning System) with automatic course plotting, video map displays of the oceans, gyrocompass, echo sounders, sonar Doppler log, wind speed, and various sensors to provide a comprehensive, at-a-glance display of the ship in relation to the rest of the world.

The Compass

This is the instrument by which a ship may be steered on a preselected course, and by which bearings of *visible* objects can be taken in order to fix a ship's position on a navigation chart. There are two kinds:

The magnetic compass uses the inherent magnetic forces within and around the Earth;

The gyrocompass, a relatively recent invention, uses the properties of gyroscopic inertia and precession, ideally to align itself to a true north-south position.

*A great viewpoint: aft of the huge funnel aboard Cunard Line's **Queen Elizabeth 2**.*

Steering

Two different methods can be used to steer a ship:

Electrohydraulic steering uses automatic (tele-motor-type) transmission from the wheel itself to the steering gear aft. This is generally used in conditions of heavy traffic, during maneuvers into and out of ports, or when there is poor visibility.

Automatic steering (gyropilot) is used only in the open sea. This system does not require anyone at the wheel because it is controlled by computer. However, aboard all ships, a quartermaster is always at the wheel, for extra safety, and just in case a need should arise to switch from one steering system to another.

Satellite Navigator

Using this latest high-tech piece of equipment, ship's officers can read, on a small television screen, the ship's position in the open ocean anywhere in the world, any time, and in any weather with pinpoint accuracy.

Satellite navigation systems use the information transmitted by a constellation of orbiting satellites. Each is in a normal circular polar orbit at an altitude of 450 to 700 nautical miles, and orbits the Earth in about 108 minutes. Data from each gives the current orbital position every two minutes. Apart from telling the ship where it is, it continuously provides the distance from any given point, calculates the drift caused by currents and so on, and tells the ship when the next satellite will pass.

The basis of the satellite navigation is the US Navy Satellite System (NNSS). This first became operational in January 1964 as the precision guidance system for the Polaris submarine fleet and was made available for commercial use in 1967.

The latest (and more accurate) system is the GPS (Global Positioning System), which is now fitted to an increasing number of ships. This uses 24 satellites (18 of which are on-line at any given time) that provide accuracy in estimating a ship's position to plus or minus six feet. Another variation is the NACOS (Navigational Command System), which collects information from a variety of sources: satellites, radar, gyroscopic compass, speed log, and surface navigational systems as well as engines, thrusters, rudders, and human input. It then displays relevant computations and information on one screen, controlled by a single keyboard.

Radar

Radar is one of the most important discoveries ever made for the development of navigational aids, providing a picture of all solid objects in a range selected by the navigator, which is from a half-mile to a 72-mile radius. Its greatest asset is as an aid to collision avoidance with other ships, although it is of value in finding a position at a distance when navigational marks or charted coastlines are within its range.

Engine Telegraph

These automatic signaling devices are used to communicate orders between the bridge and the engine room. There may be three, one on the bridge and one on each bridgewing.

Bow Thruster

This small two-way handle is used to control the bow thrusters, powerful engines in the bow that push the ship away from the dockside without tugs. Some new ships may also have thrusters positioned at the stern.

Rudder Angle Indicator
This device is normally positioned in front of, and above, the quartermaster. It provides both the commanding officer and the quartermaster with a constant readout of the degrees of rudder angle, either to port (left) or starboard (right).

VHF Radio
This is a radio receiver and transmitter, operating on VHF (Very High Frequency) with a "line-of-sight" range. It is used for communicating with other ships, pilots, port authorities, and so on.

Radio Direction Finder
This operates on radio waves, enabling its operator to take bearings of shore radio stations. By crossing two or more bearings, you find the ship's position.

Depth Indicator
This equipment (which is an echo-sounder) provides a ship with a constant digital monitor readout, together with a printed chart.

Course Recorder
This records and prints all courses followed by the ship at all times.

Clearview Screen
This device makes simple but effective use of centrifugal force, where instead of an automobile-type windshield wiper, a ship has circular screens that rotate at high speed to clear rain or sea spray away, providing those on the bridge with the best possible view in even the worst weather.

Engine Speed Indicators
These provide a reading of the number of revolutions per minute being generated by the engines. Each engine has a separate indicator, giving the speed in forward or reverse.

Facsimile Recorder
This special radio device is designed to receive meteorological and oceanographic maps, satellite pictures, and other pertinent weather information transmitted by maritime broadcast stations throughout the world.

Fire Control
If anyone sounds the fire alarm, an alarm is automatically set off on the bridge. A red panel light will be illuminated on a large plan, indicating the section of the ship that has to be checked so that the crew can take immediate action.

Ships are sectioned into several zones, each of which can be tightly closed off. In addition, almost all ships have a water-fed sprinkler system that can be activated at the touch of a button, or automatically activated when sprinkler vials are broken by fire-generated heat. New electronic fire detection systems are being installed aboard ships in order to increase safety further.

Emergency Ventilation Control
This automatic fire damper system also has a manual switch that is activated to stop or control the flow of air to all areas of the ship, in this way reducing the fanning effect on flame and smoke via air-conditioning and fan systems.

Watertight Doors Control
Watertight doors throughout the ship can be closed off, in order to contain the movement of water flooding the ship. A master switch activates all the doors in a matter of seconds. All watertight doors can be operated electrically and manually, which means that nobody can be trapped in a watertight compartment.

Stabilizers Control
The ship's two stabilizing fins can be extended, housed, or controlled. They normally operate automatically under the command of a gyroscope located in the engine control room.

THE SHIP'S COMPANY

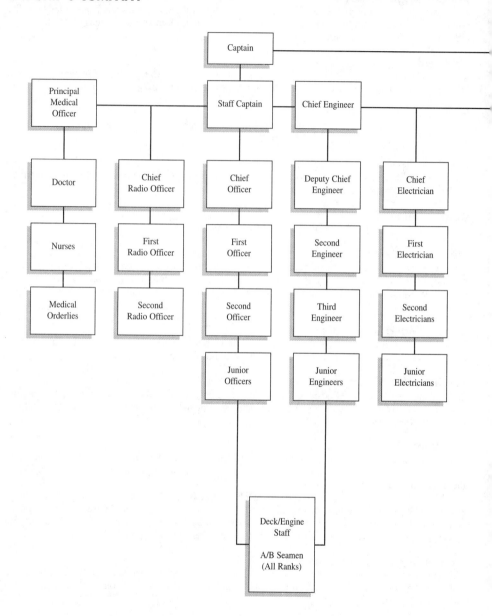

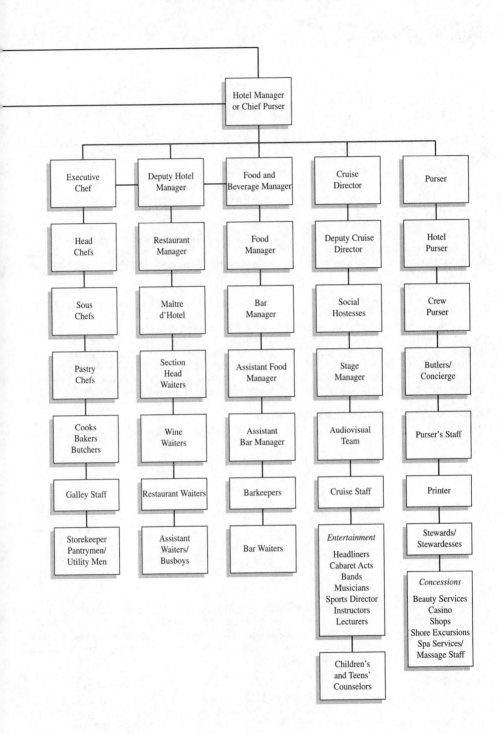

ALTERNATIVE CRUISES

DID YOU KNOW...?

...that the whole disc of the sun is visible for 24 hours a day at some points north of the Arctic Circle? North Cape (May 14–July 29); Hammerfest (May 16–July 27); Tromso (May 20–July 22); Harstad (May 26–July 19); Bodo (June 4–July 8).

COASTAL CRUISES

Europe

There is year-round coastal cruising along the shores of Norway to the Land of the Midnight Sun aboard the ships of the Norwegian Coastal Express Line (known locally as the Hurtig-Ruten, or "Highway 1"). The fleet consists of small, comfortable, working express coastal packet steamers. Their principal job is the delivery of mail, small packaged goods, and foodstuffs, as well as passengers, to the communities spread on the shoreline.

This is a 2,500-mile journey from Bergen in Norway to Kirkenes, close to the Russian border (half of which is north of the Arctic Circle) and takes 12 days. You can join it at any of the 34 ports of call and stay as long as you wish (the ships sail every day of the year). In 1997, the company carried 286,000 passengers.

The service started in 1893 and is run by a combination of three companies. The ships have between 69 and 230 cabins, and they can accommodate between 144 and 490 passengers. The newest ships in the fleet have an elevator that can accommodate a wheelchair passenger.

Archipelago hopping can be done along Sweden's eastern coast, too, by sailing in the daytime and staying overnight in one of the many small hotels. One vessel sails from Norrtalje, north of Stockholm, to Oskarshamn, near the Baltic island of Öland, right through the spectacular Swedish archipelago. You can also cruise from the Finnish city of Lappeenranta to the Estonian city of Viborg without a visa, thanks to perestroika. Point-to-point coastal transportation between neighboring countries, major cities, and commercial centers is big business in Northern Europe.

NORWEGIAN COASTAL EXPRESS SHIPS

SHIP	TONNAGE	BUILT	BERTHS
Harold Jarl	2,568	1960	165
Kong Harald	6,270	1993	490
Lofoten	2,597	1964	228
Midnatsol	4,200	1982	322
Narvik	4,073	1982	314
Nordkapp	11,204	1996	490
Nordlys	6,270	1994	490
Nordnorge	11,204	1997	490
Polarlys	11,204	1996	490
Richard With	6,270	1993	490
Vesteralen	4,073	1983	314

Scotland

The fishing town of Oban, two hours west of Glasgow by road, perhaps seems an unlikely point to start a cruise, but it is the base for one of the world's finest cruise experiences. *Hebridean Princess* is an absolute gem, with Laura Ashley–style interiors. This ship carries passengers around some of Scotland's most magnificent coastline and islands. Take lots of warm clothing, however (layers are ideal), as the weather can be somewhat unkind.

United States

In the US, coastal vessels flying the American flag offer a change of style from big oceangoing cruise ships. On these cruises, informality is the order of the day. Accommodating up to 160 passengers, the ships are more like private parties — there's no pretentiousness. Unlike large cruise ships, these small vessels are rarely out of sight of land. Their operators seek out lesser-known areas, offering in-depth visits to destinations inaccessible to larger ships, both along the eastern coast and in Alaska.

During the last few years, there has been little growth in this segment of the cruise market, although this is now changing. If you are the sort of person who prefers a small country inn to a larger resort, this type of cruise might appeal to you. The ships, each of which measures under 2,500 tonnes and are classified as a "D-class" vessel, are subject neither to the bureaucratic regulations nor the union rules that sounded the death knell for the large US-registered ships.

These vessels are restricted to cruising no more than 20 miles off shore, at a comfortable 12 knots. Public room facilities are limited, and because the vessels are of American registry, there is no casino. For entertainment, passengers are usually left to their own devices. Most vessels are in port during the evening, so you can go ashore for the local nightlife. Getting ashore is extremely easy; passengers can be off in a matter of minutes, with no waiting at the gangway.

Accommodation is in outside-view cabins (some open directly onto the deck, not convenient when it rains), each with a picture window and small bathroom. The cabins are small but cozy, and closet space is very limited, so take only what you absolutely need. There's no room service, and you turn your own bed down at night. Cabins are closer to the engines and generators so noise can be considerable at night. The quietest cabins are at the bow, and most cruising is done during the day so passengers can sleep better at night. Tall passengers should note that the overall length of beds rarely exceeds 6 feet (1.82 meters) maximum.

The principal evening event is dinner in the dining room, which accommodates all passengers at once. This can be a family-style affair, with passengers at long tables, and the food passed around. The cuisine is decidedly American, with fresh local specialties featured.

These vessels usually have three or four decks, and no elevators. Stairs can be on the steep side and are not recommended for people with walking difficulties. This kind of cruise is good for those who do enjoy a family-type cruise experience in pleasant surroundings. The maxim "You just relax, we'll move the scenery" is very appropriate in this case.

A small selection of the coastal and inland cruise vessels are featured in the profiles in Part Two, since they are small and specialized and have limited facilities.

COASTAL CRUISE VESSELS (OVER 10 CABINS)

SHIP	CRUISE LINE	CABINS	REGION
Ambassador I	Marco Polo Cruises	45	Galapagos
Dro Ki Cakau	Captain Cook Cruises	59	Australia
Eclipse	Abercrombie & Kent	24	Galapagos
Executive Explorer	Glacier Bay Tours & Cruises	25	Alaska
Grande Caribe	American Canadian Caribbean Line	48	Alaska
Isabela II	Abercrombie & Kent	20	Galapagos
Nantucket Clipper	Clipper Cruise Line	51	USA
Niagara Prince	American Canadian Caribbean Line	42	USA
Pacific Aurora	Inside Passage Cruises	35	Alaska
Reef Endeavor	Captain Cook Cruises	75	Australia
Santa Cruz	Metropolitan Touring	43	Galapagos
Sea Bird	Lindblad Special Expeditions	35	Alaska
Sea Lion	Lindblad Special Expeditions	35	Alaska
Spirit of Alaska	Alaska Sightseeing/Cruise West	39	Alaska
Spirit of Columbus	Alaska Sightseeing/Cruise West	39	Alaska
Spirit of Discovery	Alaska Sightseeing/Cruise West	25	Alaska
Spirit of Endeavor	Alaska Sightseeing/Cruise West	51	Alaska
Spirit of Glacier Bay	Alaska Sightseeing/Cruise West	43	Alaska
Sydney 2000	Captain Cook Cruises	60	Australia
Temptress Explorer	Temptress Adventure Cruises	48	Central America
Temptress Voyager	Temptress Adventure Cruises	33	Central America
Terra Australis	Cruceros Australis	55	Patagonia
Wilderness Adventurer	Glacier Bay Tours & Cruises	38	Alaska
Wilderness Discoverer	Glacier Bay Tours & Cruises	43	Alaska
Wilderness Explorer	Glacier Bay Tours & Cruises	18	Alaska
Yorktown Clipper	Clipper Cruise Line	69	USA

RIVER AND BARGE CRUISES

Whether you want to cruise down the Nile, along the mighty Amazon or the lesser Orinoco, the stately Volga or the primal Sepik, the magnificent Rhine or the "blue" Danube, along the mystical Irrawaddy (now renamed Ayeyarwady) or the "yellow" Yangtze — to say nothing of the Don and the Dnieper, the Elbe, or Australia's Murray — there's a river vessel and cruise to suit you.

What sort of person enjoys cruising aboard river vessels? Well, anyone who survives well without dressing up, bingo, casinos, discos, or entertainment, and those who want a totally unstructured lifestyle.

European River Cruising

Cruising down one of Europe's great waterways is a soothing experience — it's quite different from sailing on an open sea, where motion has to be taken into consideration (rivers are calm). These cruises provide a constant change of scenery, often passing through several countries, each with its own history and architecture, in a weeklong journey. River vessels are always close to land and provide a chance to visit cities and areas inaccessible to large ships. Indeed, watching stunning scenery slip past your floating hotel is one of the most relaxing and refreshing ways to absorb the beauty that has inspired poets and artists through the centuries. A cruise along the Danube, for example, will take you through four countries and from the Black Forest to the Black Sea.

In 1840–41, the Marquess of Londonderry, a member of the British aristocracy, traveled across Europe along the Rhine and Danube Rivers. He then wrote about these experiences, which were published in 1842, in a book entitled *A Steam Voyage to Constantinople*. And who could forget the romance implied by Johann Strauss's famous waltz "The Blue Danube"? The new Rhine-Main-Danube waterway, at 2,175 miles (3,500 kilometers), is the longest waterway in Europe. It connects 14 countries, from Rotterdam on the North Sea to Sulina and Izmail on the Black Sea, and offers river travelers some of the most fascinating sights anywhere.

River vessels are long and low in the water, and their masts fold down in order to negotiate low bridges. Although small when compared to oceangoing cruise ships, they have a unique and friendly international atmosphere. The most modern of them are air-conditioned and offer the discreet luxury of a small floating hotel, with several public rooms including a dining room, observation lounge, bar, heated swimming pool (some even have a heated indoor pool), sauna, solarium, whirlpool, gymnasium, massage, hairdresser, and shop kiosk.

Although the cabins may be small, with limited closet space (take casual clothing, as informality is the order of the day), they are functional. Most have an outside view (facing the river), with a private bathroom, and will prove very comfortable for a one-week journey. Many cabins in the lat-

Courtesy Douglas Ward

Barge cruising lets you enjoy your cruise experience at a slower pace.

est vessels feature a personal safe, a mini-bar, a television, and an alarm clock/radio. The ceilings are rather low, and the beds are short.

River cruising in Europe has reached a very sophisticated level, and you can be assured of good service and meals of a consistently high European standard. Dining is a pleasant although not always a gourmet experience (the best food is that catered by Austrian and Swiss companies). While lunch is generally a buffet affair, dinners feature a set menu consisting of three or four courses.

Typical rates for river cruises are from $800 to over $3000 per person for a one-week cruise, including meals, cabin with private facilities, side trips, and airport/railway transfers. If you are already in Europe, many cruises can be purchased "cruise-only" for greater flexibility.

Tip: It is best to go for an outside-view cabin on a deck that does not have a promenade deck walkway outside it. Normally, cabins on the lowest deck have a four-berth configuration. It does not matter which side of the vessel you are on, as you will see a riverbank and scenery on both sides.

River Cruising: Russia

Perhaps the best way to get to know Russia is on a river/inland waterway cruise. Often referred to as the "Waterways of the Tsars," the country benefits from a well-developed network of rivers, lakes, and canals. Geographically, river routes for tourists are divided into three main areas: Central European Russia, Northwestern European Russia, and Asian Russia.

Rechtflot is the Russian government's management overlord, with 21 shipping companies and a combined fleet of more than 5,000 vessels. The largest is the United Volga River Shipping Company, which has more than 2,000 river vessels, carrying more than 50 million passengers and about 100 million tonnes of cargo each year. The Moscow River Shipping Company is the next largest, with more than 1,000 vessels; it transports up to 11 million passengers and more than 60 million tonnes of cargo each year.

In the Central Basin, Moscow is the hub of river tourism, and the newly opened waterways between Moscow and St. Petersburg allow a seven-day cruise link between the present and former capitals.

The best known Russian rivers are the Don, Moskva, Neva, and Volga, but the lesser known Belaya, Dvina (and North Dvina) Irtysh, Kama, Ob (longest river in Siberia), Oka, Svir, Tura, and Vyatka connect the great system of rivers and lakes in the vast Russian hinterland.

Many Russian vessels are chartered to foreign (non-Russian) cruise wholesalers and tour packagers. The vessels do vary in quality and facilities. Some are air-conditioned and most are clean.

One unusual Russian river vessel worth mentioning, *Rossiya*, is used for state visits and is extremely elegant and fitted throughout with exceptionally fine materials. Cruises include the services of a cruise manager and lecturers. Some companies also specialize in pre- or post-cruise "home stays" as part of a cultural package.

River Cruising: The Nile

A journey along the Nile — the world's longest (and historically the greatest) river — is a journey back in time, to over 4,000 years before the birth of Christ — when the Pharaohs thought they were immortal. Even though time proved them mistaken, the people who lived along the riverbanks formed one of the greatest civilizations the world has known. The scenery has changed little in over 2,000 years. The best way to see it, of course, is by riverboat.

In all, there are over 7,000 departures every year aboard approximately 200 Nile cruise vessels, many offering standards of comfort, food, and service that vary between very good and extremely poor. Most have a swimming pool, lounge, piano bar, and disco. A specialist lecturer in ancient Egyptian history accompanies almost all sailings, which cruise the 140 miles between Aswân and Luxor in four or five days. Extended cruises, typically of seven or eight days, cover about 295 miles (475 km) and visit Dendera and Abydos. The longest cruises, of 10 to 12 days, cover 590 miles (950 km) and include visits to Sohâg, El Amarna, Tuna El Gabal, and Ashmuneim, ending in Cairo.

Most Nile cruises include sight-seeing excursions, which are accompanied by experienced, trained guides who may reside on board, or who may meet the boat at each call. Multilingual guides also accompany each cruise.

River Cruising: China

There are now several new river vessels featuring cruises along the Yangtze, the world's third-longest river, particularly through the area known as the Three Yangtze River Gorges, a 100-mile stretch between Nanjin Pass in the east and White King City in the west. The Yangtze stretches 3,100 miles (4,989 kilometers) from Shanghai through the very heartland of China. The Three Gorges include the 47-mile-long Xiling Gorge, the 25-mile-long Wu Gorge, and the 28-mile-long Qutang Gorge (known locally as "Wind Box Gorge"). The Lesser Three Gorges (or Three Small Gorges) are also an impressive sight, often part of the main cruise but also reached by small vessels from Wushan. Take a cabin with a balcony. It is worth the extra money, and the view is better. Note that in China, rats and rivers often go together, so beware that rat poison may well be found under your bed. *Note:* Standards of hygiene are generally far lower than you may be used to at home.

Among the best operators are Regal China Cruises (*Elaine, Jeannie,* and *Sheena,* 258 passengers) and Victoria Cruises (*Victoria, Victoria Pearl,* and *Victoria III,* 154 passengers). All have Chinese- and western-style restaurants, a beauty salon, a small health club with sauna, and private mah-jongg and karaoke rooms. Fine Asian hospitality and service prevail, and cabins are always supplied with fresh towels and hot tea. There are several other operators, but do check on the facilities, meet-and-greet service, and the newness of the vessels before booking. The best time of the year to go is May–June, and late August–October (July and early August are extremely hot and humid).

Note that the new $35 billion-plus hydroelectric Sanxia (Three Gorges) Dam, the world's largest (first envisioned by Sun Yat-sen in 1919), is being constructed, essentially blocking off this major tourist attraction and making a 370-mile-long reservoir. It is scheduled for completion in 2003.

Ayeyarwady (Irrawaddy) River (Myanmar)

How about the *Road to Mandalay*? Orient Express Hotels operates a fine river cruise vessel in Myanmar (formerly known as Burma). The river vessel *Road to Mandalay* operates weekly between Mandalay and Pagan, along the Ayeyarwady (formerly Irrawaddy) River. Or there's the small *Pandaw,* a stern-wheeler built in Scotland in 1947.

River Murray (Australia)

The fifth-largest river in the world, the Murray, was the lifeblood of the pioneers who lived on the driest continent on earth. Today, the river flows for more than 1,250 miles (2,765 kilometers) across a third of Australia, her banks forming protected lagoons for an astonishing variety of bird and animal life. Paddlewheel boats such as *Murray Princess* offer all the amenities found aboard America's *Mississippi Queen.* There are even six cabins for the physically disabled.

Barge Cruising: Europe

Smaller and more intimate than river vessels, and more accurately called boats, "hotel barges" ply the inland waterways and canals of Europe from spring to fall, when the weather is best. Barge cruises (usually of 3 to 13 days' duration) offer a completely informal atmosphere, and a slow pace of life, for up to a dozen passengers. They cruise along slowly in the daytime, and moor early each evening, giving you time to pay a visit to a local village and get a restful night's sleep. The inland waterways of Europe all adhere to the CEVNI regulations (Code European des Voies de la Navigation Interieur), a United Nations instrument with international authority and relevance.

Hotel barges tend to be beautifully fitted out with rich wood paneling, full carpeting, custom-built furniture and tastefully chosen fabrics. Each barge has a dining room/lounge-bar and is equipped with passenger comfort in mind. Each barge captain takes pride in his vessel, often acquiring some rare memorabilia to be incorporated into the decor.

Locally grown fresh foods are usually purchased and prepared each day, allowing you to live well and feel like a houseguest. Most barges can also be chartered exclusively so you can just take your family and friends, for example.

The waterways of France especially offer beauty, tranquillity, and a diversity of interests, and barge cruising is an excellent way of exploring an area not previously visited. Most cruises include a visit to a famous vineyard and wine cellar, as well as side trips to places of historic, architectural, or scenic interests. Shopping opportunities are limited, and evening entertainment is always impromptu. You will be accompanied by a crew member familiar with the surrounding countryside. You can even go hot-air ballooning over the local countryside and land to a welcome glass of champagne and your flight certificate. Although ballooning is an expensive extra, the experience of floating within earshot of chateaux and villages, over pastoral landscapes, is something to treasure.

How you dine on board a barge will depend on which barge and area you choose; dining ranges from home-style cooking to outstanding nouvelle cuisine, with all the trimmings.

Barging on the canals often means going through a constant succession of locks. Nowhere is this more enjoyable and entertaining than in the Burgundy region of France where, between Dijon and

Mâcon, for example, a barge can negotiate as many as 54 locks during a six-day cruise. Interestingly, all lockkeepers in France are women!

Rates typically range from $600 to more than $3000 per person for a six-day cruise. I do not recommend taking children. Rates include a cabin with private facilities, all meals, good wine with lunch and dinner, other beverages, use of bicycles, side trips, and airport/railway transfers. Some operators also provide a hotel the night before or after the cruise. Clothing, by the way, is totally casual at all times, but at the beginning and end of the season, the weather can be unreliable, so make sure you take sweaters and rain gear.

Steamboating: United States

The most famous of all river cruises in the United States are those aboard the steamboats of the mighty Mississippi River. Mark Twain, an outspoken fan of Mississippi cruising, at one time said: "When man can go 700 miles an hour, he'll want to go seven again."

The grand traditions of the steamboat era are maintained by the *American Queen*, and by the older, smaller *Delta Queen* and *Mississippi Queen* (Delta Queen Steamboat Company), all of which are powered by steam engines that drive huge wooden paddlewheels at the stern.

The smallest and oldest of the three boats, the 180-passenger *Delta Queen*, was built on Scotland's Clydeside in 1926 and is on the US National Register of Historic Places. She gained attention when President Carter spent a week aboard her in 1979.

Half a century younger, the $27-million, 400-passenger *Mississippi Queen* was built in Jefferson, Indiana, where nearly 5,000 steamboats were built during the 19th century. *Mississippi Queen* was designed by James Gardner of London (creator of Cunard's *QE2*).

The latest, a $60 million, 222-cabin, 436-passenger American-built steamboat, *American Queen* (Delta Queen Steamboat Company), debuted in June 1995. Built by McDermott Shipyard, Morgan City, Louisiana, the riverboat is fitted out with vintage tandem compound horizontal reciprocating steam engines (circa 1930) that originally drove a steam dredge called *Kennedy*. The engines are used to drive the 60-ton stern paddle wheel, with paddles made up of individual bucket boards that are 30 feet long and 2 feet wide. *American Queen* is the 30th steamboat built for the Delta Queen Steamboat Company. Each of the steamboats features one of the rarest of musical instruments — a calliope, or "steam piano," driven by the boat's engine.

Traveling aboard one of the steamboats makes you feel as if you are stepping back into the past, into the world of American folklore. There is a certain charm and old-world graciousness as well as delightful woods, brass, and flowing staircases. And once every year, boats challenge each other in the Great Steamboat Race — a ten-day extravaganza.

Steamboat cruises last from 2 to 12 days, and during the year there are several theme cruises, with big bands and lively entertainment. The steamboats cruise up and down the Mississippi and Ohio rivers. As for food, it is really "Americana" fare, which means steak, and shrimp, Creole sauces, fried foods, and a modicum of fresh vegetables.

Traveling on the river is a great way of taking a vacation and avoiding the crush of congested roads and airports. And of course there are no immigration or customs procedures in the heartland of America.

EXPEDITION/NATURE CRUISES

Passenger Ships Through The Northwest Passage

1984 *Lindblad Explorer*
1985 *World Discoverer*
1986 *World Discoverer*
1988 *Society Explorer*
1991 *Frontier Spirit* (ship returned at Flaxman Island — trip cancelled)
1992 *Frontier Spirit*
1994 *Kapitan Khlebnikov*
1995 *Hanseatic*
1995 *Kapitan Khlebnikov*
1996 *Hanseatic* (ship grounded for ten days — passengers taken aboard *Kapitan Dranitsyn*)
1997 *Hanseatic*
1998 *Kapitan Khlebnikov*
1998 *Hanseatic*

With so many opportunities to cruise in Alaska and in the Baltic, Caribbean, Mediterranean, and Mexican Riviera areas, you may be surprised to discover a small but growing group of enthusiasts heading out for strange and remote waters. But there are countless virtually untouched areas to be visited by the more adventurous, whose motto might be "see it before it is spoiled." Such passengers tend to be more self-reliant and more interested in doing or learning than in being entertained.

Passengers take an active role in almost every aspect of the voyage, which is destination-, exploration-, and nature-intensive. Naturalists, historians, and lecturers (rather than entertainers) are aboard each ship to provide background information and observations about wildlife. Each participant receives a personal logbook, illustrated and written by the wildlife artists and writers who accompany each cruise. The logbook documents the entire voyage and serves as a great source of information as well as a complete mémoire of your cruise. Adventure cruise companies provide expedition parka and waterproof boots, but you will need to take waterproof trousers (for Antarctica and the Arctic).

You can walk on pack ice in the Arctic Circle, explore a gigantic penguin rookery on Antarctica or the Falkland Islands, and search for "lost" peoples in Melanesia. Or you can cruise close to the source of the Amazon, gaze at species of flora and fauna in the Galapagos Islands (Darwin's laboratory), or watch a genuine dragon on the island of Komodo (from a comfortable distance, of course).

Briefings and lectures bring a cultural and intellectual element to expedition cruise vessels. There is no formal entertainment as such; passengers enjoy this type of cruise more for the camaraderie and learning experience. The ships are designed and equipped to sail in ice-laden waters, and yet they have a shallow enough draft to glide over coral reefs.

Expedition cruise vessels can, nevertheless, provide comfortable and even elegant surroundings for up to 200 passengers, and offer first-class food and service. Without traditional cruise ports at which to stop, the ship must be self-sufficient, capable of long-range cruising, as well as environmentally friendly.

DID YOU KNOW...?

...that passengers once asked the operations director of a well-known expedition cruise ship where the best shops were in Antarctica? His reply: "On board, madam!"

...that in 1984, Salen Lindblad Cruising made maritime history by successfully negotiating a westbound voyage through the Northwest Passage, a 41-day epic that started from St. John's, Newfoundland, in Canada, and ended at Yokohama, Japan? The expedition cruise had taken two years of planning and was sold out just days after it was announced. The search for a Northwest Passage to the Orient attracted brave explorers for more than four centuries. Despite numerous attempts and loss of life, including Henry Hudson in 1610, a "white passage" to the East remained an elusive dream. Amundsen's 47-ton ship *Gjoa* eventually navigated the route in 1906, taking three years to do so. It was not until 1943 that a Canadian ship, *St. Roch*, became the first vessel in history to make the passage in a single season. *Lindblad Explorer* became the 34th vessel, and the first cruise vessel, to complete the Northwest Passage.

...that Quark Expeditions had the good fortune of making maritime history in July/August 1991, when its chartered Russian icebreaker, *Sovetskiy Soyuz*, made a spectacular 21-day voyage to negotiate a passage from Murmansk, Russia, to Nome, Alaska, across the North Pole? The ship followed the trail that had been set in 1909 by Admiral Peary, who crossed the North Pole with 56 Eskimos, leaving by sled from Ellesmere Island. Although the polar ice cap had been navigated by the US nuclear submarines *Skate* and *Nautilus,* as well as by dirigible and airplane, this was the first passenger ship to make the hazardous crossing (planning for it took over two years).

...that the most expensive expedition cruise excursion was a cruise/dive to visit the resting place of RMS *Titanic* aboard the two deep ocean submersibles *Mir I* and *Mir II* used in James Cameron's Hollywood blockbuster. Just 60 participants went as observers up-close-and-personal in 1998, and only another 60 will be taken in 1999.

Expedition cruising came about as a result of people wanting to find out more about this remark-able planet of ours, its incredible animal, bird, and marine life. Lars-Eric Lindblad pioneered it in the late 1960s. A Swedish American, he was determined to turn travel into adventure by opening up parts of the world tourists had not visited.

After chartering several vessels for cruises to Antarctica (which he started in 1966), he organized the design and construction of a ship capable of going almost anywhere in comfort and safety.

In 1969, *Lindblad Explorer* was launched. The ship earned an enviable reputation in adventure travel. Lindblad sold the ship to Salen-Lindblad Cruising in 1982. They subsequently resold her to Society Expeditions, who renamed her *Society Explorer* (the ship is presently operated by Abercrombie & Kent as *Explorer*).

Specialist adventure/expedition cruise companies provide in-depth expertise and specially con-structed vessels, usually with ice-hardened hulls that are capable of going into the vast reaches of the Arctic and Antarctica.

Expedition/Nature Cruise Areas

Buddha was once asked to express verbally what life meant to him. He waited a moment — then, without speaking, held up a single rose. Several "destinations" on our planet cannot be adequately described by words. They have instead to be experienced, just as a single rose.

The principal adventure cruise areas of the world are Alaska and the Aleutians, the Amazon and the Orinoco, Antarctica, Australasia and the Great Barrier Reef, the Chilean fjords, the Galapagos Archipelago, Indonesia, Melanesia, the Northwest Passage, Polynesia, and the South Pacific. Baja California and the Sea of Cortez, Greenland, the Red Sea, East Africa, the Réunion Islands and the Seychelles, West Africa and the Ivory Coast, and the South China Seas and China Coast are other adventure cruise destinations growing in popularity.

To put together cruise expeditions, companies turn to knowledgeable sources and advisors. Scientific institutions are consulted; experienced world explorers and naturalists provide up-to-date reports on wildlife sightings, migrations, and other natural phenomena. Although some days are scheduled for relaxation or preparing for the days ahead, participants are kept physically and men-tally active. Speaking of physical activity, it is unwise to consider such an adventure cruise if you are not completely ambulatory.

Antarctica

Perhaps the most intriguing destination on earth is Antarctica, first sighted only in 1820 by the American sealer Nathaniel Palmer, British naval officer Edward Bransfield, and Russian captain Fabian Bellingshausen. For most, it is nothing but a wind-swept frozen wasteland (it has been cal-culated that the ice mass contains almost ninety percent of the snow and ice in the world). For oth-ers, however, it represents the last pristine place on earth, empty of people, commerce, and pollu-tion, yet offering awesome scenery and a truly wonderful abundance of marine and bird life. There are no germs and not a single tree. Over 6,000 people visited the continent in 1997 — the only smoke-free continent on earth — yet the first human to come here did so within a generation of man landing on the moon. There is not a single permanent inhabitant of the continent, whose ice is as much as two miles thick. Its total land mass equals more than all the rivers and lakes on earth and exceeds that of China and India combined. Indeed, icebergs can easily be the size of Belgium! The continent has a raw beauty and an ever-changing landscape.

Once part of the ancient land mass known as Gondwanaland (which also included Africa, South America, India, Australasia, and Madagascar), it is, perhaps, the closest thing on earth to another planet, and it has an incredibly fragile ecosystem that needs international protection.

Although visited by "soft" expedition cruise ships and even "normal"-sized cruise ships with ice-hardened hulls, the more remote "far side" — the Oates and Scott Coasts, McMurdo Sound, and the famous Ross Ice Shelf — can only be visited by real icebreakers such as *Kapitan Dranitsyn, Kapitan Khlebnikov,* and *Yamal* (they carry 100 passengers or fewer), as the winds can easily reach more than 100 mph.

As there are no docks in Antarctica, venturing "ashore" is done by Zodiac rubber inflatable craft, an integral part of the Antarctica experience.

Arctic

The Arctic is defined best as that region north of which no trees grow, and where water is the pri-mary feature of the landscape. The Arctic is an ocean surrounded by continents, whereas Antarctica

*Passengers aboard Hapag-Lloyd's **Hanseatic** take to Zodiacs to explore Antarctica up close.*

is a continent surrounded by ocean. The Arctic Circle is located at 66 degrees, 33 minutes, and 3 seconds north, although this really designates where 24-hour days and nights begin. It is technically a desert (receiving less than 10 inches of rainfall a year) but actually teems with wildlife. It has short, cool summers; long, cold winters; and frequent high winds. Canada's Northwest Territories, which cover 1.3 million square miles, is part of the Arctic region.

Galapagos
A word of advice about the Galapagos Islands: do not even think about taking a cruise with a "non-Ecuadorian flag" ship. The Ecuadorians jealously guard their islands and prohibit the movement of almost all non-Ecuadorian-registered cruise vessels within its boundaries. The best way to see this place that Darwin loved is to fly to Quito and cruise aboard an Ecuadorian-registered vessel. Note that the Galapagos National Park tax is presently about $80 per person.

Greenland
The world's largest island, Greenland, in the Northern Hemisphere's Arctic Circle, is technically a desert that is 82 percent covered with ice (actually compressed snow) that is up to 11,000 feet thick. Greenland's rocks are among the world's oldest (the 3.8 billion-year-old Isukasia formations), and its ecosystem is one of the newest. Forget Alaska, the glacier at Jacobshavn (also known as Ilulissat) is the fastest moving in the world and creates a new iceberg every five minutes. Greenland is said to have more dogs than people, and these provide the principal means of transport for the Greenlanders.

The Environment
Since the increase in environmental awareness, adventurers have banded together to protect the environment from further damage. In the future, only those ships that are capable of meeting new "zero discharge" standards, like those introduced in the Arctic by the Canadian Coast Guard, will be allowed to proceed through environmentally sensitive areas.

Expedition cruise companies are very concerned about the environment (none more than Hapag-Lloyd Seetouristik and Quark Expeditions), and they spend much time and money in educating both crews and passengers about safe environmental procedures.

An "Antarctic Traveler's Code" has been created, the rules of which are enforced by the expedition cruise companies, based on the Antarctic Conservation Act of 1978 to protect and preserve the ecosystem, flora, and fauna of the Antarctic continent. Briefly, the Act makes it unlawful, unless authorized by regulation or permit issued under the Act, to take native animals or birds, to collect any special native plant or introduce species, to enter certain special areas (SPAs), or to discharge or dispose of any pollutants. To "take" means to remove, harass, molest, harm, pursue, hunt, shoot, kill, trap, capture, restrain, or tag any native mammal or bird, or to attempt to do so.

Under the Act, violators are subject to civil penalties, including a fine of up to $10,000 and one year imprisonment for each violation. The Act is found in the library of each adventure/expedition ship that visits the continent.

Will large cruise ships ever cruise in Antarctica? Not in the foreseeable future. Ships are limited to a maximum of 400 passengers, so the likelihood of a mega-ship zooming in on the penguins with 2,000-plus passengers is unlikely.

THE COMPANIES

Abercrombie & Kent
This well-known company operates the older, but still highly suitable *Explorer* (ex-*Society Explorer*).

Hapag-Lloyd Seetouristik
This company operates *Bremen* and *Hanseatic*, small, high-tech expedition cruise vessels. Both ships have fine, rather luxurious appointments (*Bremen* is less luxurious than *Hanseatic*) and are marketed to both English- and German-speaking passengers.

Marine Expeditions
This Canadian company, in essence a Canadian version of Quark Expeditions, charters several Russian vessels for "soft" expedition/nature cruises to several popular areas, including Antarctica. The company applies its own ship names for the duration of the charter; for example *Marine Discovery* (ex-*Maria Yermalova*), *Marine Adventurer* (ex-*Akademic Ioffe*), and *Marine Spirit* (*Akademik Shuleykin*).

Quark Expeditions
Quark Expeditions charters Russian-owned nuclear- or diesel-powered icebreakers fitted with some outstanding amenities and decent creature comforts for up to 100 passengers. The operator specializes in itineraries to the Antarctic, the Arctic, and North Polar regions. Among the vessels chartered are the superb *Kapitan Khlebnikov* and *Yamal*.

Society Expeditions
This company operates *World Discoverer* — a fine expedition cruise vessel, featuring full creature comforts and a range of fascinating itineraries. The ship is often chartered to various societies and specialist tour operators.

Lindblad Special Expeditions
This company operates *Polaris*, a small expedition vessel operating in the Galapagos Islands, which features fine appointments and full creature comforts (see profile section for details). In addition, two small vessels, *Sea Bird* and *Sea Lion* (ex-Exploration Cruise Lines vessels) operate "soft" expedition cruises in protected coastal areas in the United States, including Alaska.

SAIL-CRUISE SHIPS
Thinking of a cruise but really want to sail — to be free as the wind? Been cruising on a conventional large cruise ship that is more like an endurance test? Whatever happened to the *romance* of sailing? Think no more, for the answer, to quote a movie title, is "back to the future."

How about cruising under sail, with towering masts and washing-powder-white sails to power you along? There is simply nothing that beats the thrill of being aboard a multimast tall ship, sailing under thousands of square feet of canvas through waters that mariners have sailed for centuries.

This is cruising in the traditional manner, aboard authentic sailing ships, contemporary copies of clipper ships, or aboard the latest high-tech cruise-sail ships. Even the most jaded passengers enjoy the exhilaration of being under sail.

There are no rigid schedules, and life aboard equates to an unstructured lifestyle, apart from meal times. Weather conditions may often dictate whether a scheduled port visit will be made or not, but passengers sailing on these vessels are usually unconcerned with being ashore anywhere. They would rather savor the thrill of being one with nature, albeit in a comfortable, civilized setting, and without having to do the work themselves.

Real Tall Ships

While we have all been dreaming of adventure, a pocketful of designers and yachtsmen committed pen to paper, hand in pocket and rigging to mast, and came up with a pot-pourri of stunning vessels to delight the eye and refresh the spirit. Look in Part Two for these true, working tall ships: *Royal Clipper*, *Sea Cloud*, *Sir Francis Drake*, *Star Clipper*, and *Star Flyer*.

In the Caribbean, Windjammer Barefoot Cruises also operates a fleet of five tall ships offering very basic fun-and-sun cruises: *Flying Cloud*, *Legacy*, *Mandalay*, *Polynesia*, and *Yankee Clipper*. Only shorts and T-shirts are needed, and you'll need to take your own beach towels (cabin towels are provided). The vessels are not certified by the US Coast Guard (there is one exception) although they do comply with most international safety regulations.

Contemporary Sail-Cruise Ships

To combine sailing with automation (no energy needed), try *Club Med 2* (Club Méditerranée) or *Wind Surf* (Windstar Cruises) — with five tall aluminum masts, they are the world's largest sail-cruise ships — and *Wind Song*, *Wind Spirit*, and *Wind Star* (Windstar Cruises), with four masts. Not a hand touches the sails. They are controlled by computer from the navigation bridge. These ships are contemporary oceangoing robots.

From a yachter's viewpoint, the sail-to-power ratio is laughable. That's why these cruise ships with sails have engine power to get them into and out of port. (The Star Clippers, by contrast, do it by sail alone, except when there is no wind, which is infrequent.). You should be aware that on some itineraries, when there is little wind you could well be under motor power for most of the cruise, with only a few hours spent under sail. The four Windstar Cruises' vessels and one Club Med ship are typically under sail for about 40 percent of the time.

Courtesy Windjammer Barefoot Cruises

*Now this is a totally unique way to travel! Aboard Windjammer Barefoot's **Legacy**.*

It was a Norwegian living in New York, Karl Andren, who first turned the concept of a cruise vessel with sails into reality. "Boyhood dream stuff," he said. The shipyard he chose, the Société Nouvelle des Ateliers et Chantiers du Havre (ACH, as it is known in Le Havre), enjoyed the challenge of building these most unusual vessels.

The shipyard had much experience in the design and construction of cable-laying ships using the hydraulic power of servomechanisms. This was a concept that was adopted for the Windstar's automatic computer-controlled sail rig. Gilbert Fournier, the shipyard president and an expert computer programmer, became fascinated with the project. Three ships (a fourth was planned but never built) were delivered to Windstar Cruises. These ships carry mainly North American passengers, whereas the Club Med vessel caters primarily to French-speaking passengers.

Another slightly smaller but very chic vessel is the ultra-sleek *Le Ponant*. This three-mast ship caters to just 64 French-speaking passengers in elegant, yet casual, high-tech surroundings, developing the original Windstar concept to a very advanced state of 1990s technology.

FREIGHTER TRAVEL

More than 3,000 passengers presently travel by freighter each year, and the number is growing as passengers become further disenchanted with the large resort ships that form a major part of the cruise industry today. Traveling by freighter is also the ultimate way to travel for those seeking a totally unstructured voyage without entertainment or other diversions.

There are approximately 250 cargo ships (freighters and container vessels) offering berths, with German operators now accounting for about more than half of the ships. True freighters — the general breakbulk carrier ships and feeder container vessels, carry up to 12 passengers. Freighter schedules change constantly, depending on the whim of the owner and the cargo to be carried, whereas container ships travel on regular schedules. For the sake of simplicity, they are all termed freighters.

Today's freighters have changed dramatically over the past few years, as cost management and efficiency have become the most relevant factors for successful ship operators. Container ships today are operated as the passenger' liners used to be — running line voyages on set schedules, or name-day voyages, as they are presently termed.

Passengers opting for this type of travel typically include independent types (anyone allergic to traveling in groups), retirees, relocating executives, people with family connections in other countries, graduates returning home from an overseas educational establishment, or professors on sabbatical. Because there are no medical facilities, a maximum age limit is imposed by most freighter companies, and anyone over the age of 65 will be required to produce a medical certificate of good health.

What do you get when you book a freighter voyage? A cabin with double or twin beds, small writing table, and private bathroom. You also get good company, cocktails with conversation, hearty food (you'll eat in one seating with the ship's officers), an interesting voyage, a lot of water, and the allure of days at sea. What don't you get? Entertainment, bingo, horse racing, and other mindless parlor games (unless you take them with you). You will certainly have time to relax and unwind completely, read books (some freighters have a small library), or play card games, or board games with the few other passengers that will be on board.

The accommodation aboard today's freighters will almost always consist of a spacious and well-equipped outside-view cabin high above the water line, with a large window rather than a porthole, comfortable lounge/sitting area, and private facilities.

While freighter travel can be less expensive than regular cruise ship travel on a per day basis (between $75 and $150), remember that freighter voyages are of much longer duration. A typical voyage lasts about 30 days or more, so the cost of a voyage can actually add up to a considerable amount. Most voyages are sold out far in advance (often more than a year ahead), so do plan ahead, and remember to purchase trip cancellation insurance.

What to take with you? Casual clothing, all medication, cosmetics, and personal toiletry items, hair dryer, multivoltage converter plug, washing powder, and other sundry items. There may be a small "shop" on board (for the crew) but only the bare essentials like toothpaste will be available. Remember to take some extra photos of yourself in case the ship makes unannounced port stops and visas are required. The only gratuities you will need to give are for the waiter and cabin steward, at about $1–$2 per day, per person.

The following lines offer *regular* passenger voyages year-round:

American President Lines, Australia New Zealand Direct Lines, Bank Line, Blue Star Line, Canada Maritime, Chilean Lines, Cho Yang Shipping, Columbus Line, Egon Oldendorff, Great

Lakes Shipping, Hamburg-Sud, Hanseatic Shipping Company, Hapag-Lloyd, Ivaran Lines, Lykes Brothers Steamship Company, Mediterranean Shipping Company, Nauru Pacific Line, Safmarine Cruises, and United Baltic Corporation.

Freighter Bookings and Information

Traveltips Cruise & Freighter Association
P.O. Box 580188, Flushing, NY 11358, USA

Freighter World Cruises
180 South Lake Avenue, Suite 335, Pasadena, CA 91101, USA

The Cruise People
88 York Street, London W1H 1DP, England

Strand Voyages
Charing Cross Shopping Concourse, Strand, London WC2N 4HZ, England

CROSSINGS ——————————————

By "crossings," I mean crossings of the North Atlantic, that is, 3,000 miles or so of it, from the Old World to the New World or vice versa, although crossings might also include any other major ocean, such as the Pacific or the Indian Ocean.

Crossing the North Atlantic by ship is an adventure, when time seems to be totally suspended. It really is the most delicious way of enjoying life aboard ship. It actually takes little more than a long weekend. After the embarkation procedures have been completed, you will be shown to the gangway. Cross the gangway from pier to ship and you are in another world. It is a world that provides a complete antidote to the pressures of contemporary life ashore, and it allows you to practice the fine art of doing nothing, if you so wish. After the exhilaration of a North Atlantic crossing, the anticipation of landfall among passengers throughout any ship is nothing short of electric.

The North Atlantic

Hemmed in by the polar ice caps, the Atlantic Ocean divides Europe and Africa from the Americas. It is three times the size of North America and contains the world's longest mountain range, which extends (undersea) over 7,000 miles (11,265 kilometers) and rises over 6,000 feet (1,828 meters) above the ocean floor. The only points of this ridge that rise to the surface are at St. Helena (Ascension), St. Paul's Rocks (the Azores), and Tristan da Cunha. The ocean's average width is 2,500 miles (4,023 kilometers).

Although half the size of the Pacific Ocean, the Atlantic Ocean receives more than half of the water drainage of the world (four times that of the Pacific Ocean). Its average depth is 18,900 feet (5,760 meters) and its greatest depth, which is known as the Milwaukee Depth, goes down beyond 30,240 feet (9,217 meters).

Crossing the North Atlantic by passenger vessel should really be considered an art form. I have done it myself 147 times and still enjoy it immensely. I consider crossings as rests in musical parlance, for both are described as "passages." Indeed, musicians do often "hear" rests in between notes. So if ports of call are the musical notes of a voyage, then the rests are the days at sea — a temporary interlude, when the indulgence of the person and psyche are of paramount importance.

Experienced mariners will tell you that a ship only behaves like a ship when it is doing a crossing, for that's what a real ship is built for. Yet the days when ships were built specifically for crossings are almost gone. The only ship offering a regularly scheduled transatlantic service (a "crossing") is Cunard's *Queen Elizabeth 2*, a 70,327-grt ship designed to hold well against the worst weather the North Atlantic has to offer. Indeed, captains work harder on an Atlantic crossing than on regular cruising schedules.

The most unpredictable weather in the world, together with fog off the Grand Banks of Newfoundland, can mean that the captain will spend torturous hours on the bridge, with little time for socializing. When it is foggy, the crew of *QE2* are often pestered by passengers wanting to know if the ship has yet approached latitude 41°46' north, longitude 50°14' west — where White Star Line's *Titanic* (43,326-tonnes) struck an Arctic iceberg on that fateful April night in 1912.

There is something magical in "doing a crossing." It takes you back to the days when hordes of passengers turned up at the piers of the ports of New York, Southampton, Cherbourg, or

DID YOU KNOW...?

...that the first regular steamship service across the North Atlantic was inaugurated on March 28, 1838, when the 703-ton steamer *Sirius* left London for New York via Cork, Ireland?

...that the winter of 1970–71 was the first time since 1838 that there was no regular passenger service on the North Atlantic?

...that the first scheduled transatlantic advertisement appeared in the *New York Evening Post* on October 27, 1817, for the 424-ton sailing packet *James Monroe* to sail from New York to Liverpool on January 5, 1818, and for *Couvier* to sail from Liverpool to New York on January 1?

...that the following are just some of the personalities that have crossed in the *QE2*? Carl Sagan, Joan Fontaine, Larry Hagman, Ben Lyon, Joan Rivers, Elaine Stritch, and Arthur Schlesinger, Jr.

...that the *QE2* is still the fastest passenger ship in service?

...that since the ship's maiden voyage in 1969, the *QE2* has traveled more than four million nautical miles, and carried almost two million passengers?

...that the amount of paint used to cover the *QE2*'s hull would completely cover one of the towers of New York's World Trade Center?

...that Cunard Line held the record from 1940 to 1996 for the largest passenger ship ever built (RMS *Queen Elizabeth*)?

Hamburg, accompanied by chauffeurs and steamer trunks, jewels and finery, ablaze in a show of what they thought was best in life. Movie stars of the 1920s, 1930s, and 1940s often traveled abroad on the largest liners of the day, to arrive refreshed and ready to dazzle European fans.

Excitement and anticipation precede a crossing. First there is the hubbub and bustle of check-in, then the crossing of the threshold on the gangway before being welcomed into the calmness aboard, and finally escorted to one's accommodation for the next several days. Once the umbilical cord of the gangway is severed, bow and stern mooring lines are cast off, and with three long blasts on the ship's deep whistle, the *QE2* is pried gently from her berth. She sails silently down the waterway, away from the world, as pretty as a picture, as serene as a Rolls-Royce, and as sure as the Bank of England.

Passengers on deck often observe numerous motorboats trying to keep up with the giant liner as she edges down the Hudson River, past Battery Park City, the Statue of Liberty, the restored Ellis Island, then out toward the Verrazano-Narrows Bridge, and out to the open sea.

Coming westbound, arriving in New York by ship is one of the world's thrilling travel experiences. Following a six-day crossing aboard the *QE2*, where five of the days are 25 hours long (they are 23 hours long on an eastbound crossing), *everything else* is an anticlimax.

The *QE2* can also accommodate up to 12 cars per crossing, just in case you really do not want to be parted from your wheels. She also provides kennels, so you can even take your pet, although when crossing eastbound to Southampton, they will have to be quarantined for up to six months. The *QE2* is a distillation of over 150 years of transatlantic traditions and an oasis of creature comforts offered by no other ship.

QE2 is special — part liner, part cruise ship — a legend in her own lifetime, and the only ship offering regularly scheduled crossings throughout the year. Vast amounts of money have been spent on refurbishment over time. During the ship's initial planning stages, naval architect Dan Wallace and director of engineering Tom Kameen were responsible for the ship's design — for a high-speed, twin-screw ship capable of carrying out safely a six-day transatlantic crossing. Cunard's chairman, Sir Basil Smallpiece, invited James Gardner and Dennis Lennon, well-known industrial designers, as general design coordinators.

Gardner concentrated on exterior aesthetics, while Lennon, in addition to designing the restaurant interiors — the basic shape of which had already been determined by structural and operational requirements — was also concerned with the introduction of a design signature that would be immediately apparent throughout the ship; for example, in the staircases and corridors. The aim was that the interior design of the *QE2* would emphasize the "classless" ship concept.

Apart from the *QE2*'s regular crossings, a number of cruise ships feature transatlantic crossings. Although they are little more than repositioning cruises — a way of moving ships that cruise the Mediterranean in summer to the Caribbean in winter, and vice versa — they offer more chances to experience the romance and adventure of a crossing, usually in the spring and in the fall. These are particularly good for those wanting uninterrupted days at sea and plenty of leisure time. Most cruise ships operating repositioning crossings actually cross the Atlantic using the "sunny southern route" — typically departing from southern ports such as Ft. Lauderdale, San Juan, or Barbados, and ending the journey in Lisbon, Genoa, or Copenhagen via the Azores or the Canary Islands off the coast of northern Africa. In this way, they avoid the more difficult weather that is often encountered in the North Atlantic. The crossings take longer, however, and last between eight and twelve days.

WORLD CRUISES AND SEGMENTS

The ultimate classic voyage for any experienced traveler is a round-the-world cruise. This is usually defined as the complete circumnavigation of the earth in a continuous one-way voyage. The ports of call are carefully planned for their interest and diversity, and the entire voyage can last as long as six months.

Ships that sail from cold to warm climates — almost always during January, February, and March, when the weather in the southern hemisphere is at its best — give you the experience of crisp, clear days, sparkling nights, delicious food, tasteful entertainment, superb accommodation, delightful company, and unforgettable memories. It is for some the cultural, social, and travel experience of a lifetime, and for the few who can afford it, an annual event!

The concept of the world sea cruise first became popular in the 1920s, although it has existed since the 1880s (the first around-the-world voyage was actually made by Ferdinand Magellan in 1519). A world cruise aboard a modern ship means experiencing stabilized, air-conditioned comfort in luxury cabins, and extraordinary sight-seeing and excursions on shore and overland. In some ships, every passenger will get to dine with the captain at least once.

A world cruise gives you the opportunity to indulge yourself. Although at first the idea may sound totally extravagant, it need not be, and fares can be as low as $100 per day to more than $3000 per day. Alternately, you can book just a segment of the cruise if that fits your pocket and interest. There is a difference in what you get for your money, however. For example, aboard ships rated at four stars or more, shuttle buses from your ship to the center of town (or attraction) will probably be included; this is not so aboard ships rated three stars or less.

Special Features

Some of the special events planned for a world cruise will typically include:

→ Celebrity entertainers

→ World-renowned lecturers

→ Themed formal balls and parties

→ Equator crossing ceremony

→ International dateline crossing ceremony

→ Overnight and multiday overland shore excursions

→ Personalized stationery

Planning and Preparation

Few enterprises can match the complexity of planning and preparing for a world cruise. For example, more than 675,000 main meals will be prepared in the galleys during a typical *QE2* world cruise. Several hundred professional entertainers, lecturers, bands, and musicians must all be booked about a year in advance of the voyage. Crew changeovers during the cruise must be organized. A ship the size of the *QE2* requires two major crew changes during the three-month-long voyage.

DID YOU KNOW...?

...that the Dollar Steamship Line featured a round-the-world cruise that started October 15, 1910 from New York, aboard the ss *Cleveland*? The cruise was advertised as "one-class, no overcrowding" voyage. The cost was "$650 and up," according to an advertisement placed by the Frank Clark Travel Agency, of the Times Building in New York.

...that a round-the-world cruise was made in 1922–23 by Cunard's *Laconia* (19,680 grt), a three-class ship that sailed from New York? The itinerary included many of the ports of call that are still popular with world cruise travelers today. The vessel accommodated 350 persons in each of its first two classes, and 1,500 in third class, giving a total capacity of 2,200 passengers, more than many ships of today.

...about the lady who went to her travel agent, who asked if she had enjoyed her cruise around the world? The lady replied, "Yes, but next year I want to go somewhere different!"

Because a modern world cruise ship has to be totally self-contained, a warehouse-full of spare parts (electrical, plumbing, and engineering supplies, for example) must be planned for, ordered, loaded, and stored somewhere aboard ship prior to sailing. For just about every shipboard department, the same basic consideration will apply: once at sea, it will be impossible to pick up a replacement projector bulb, air-conditioning belt, table tennis ball, saxophone reed, or anything else that the ship might run out of.

The cruise director will have his/her hands full planning entertainment and social events for a long voyage. It is not like the "old days" when an occasional game of bingo, horse racing, or the daily tote would satisfy passengers.

A cruise line must give advance notice of the date and time that pilots will be needed, together with requirements for tugs, docking services, customs and immigration authorities, or meetings with local dignitaries and the press. Then there is the organization of dockside labor and stevedoring services at each port of call, plus planning and contracting of bus or transportation services for shore excursions. Other preparations include reserving fuel at various ports on the itinerary.

The complexity of the preparations requires the concerted efforts of many departments and people on every continent to bring about, with precise timing, this ultimate cruising experience for travelers.

World Cruise Segments

Cruises to exotic destinations — China, the Orient, the South Pacific, around Africa, the Indian Ocean, and around South America — offer all the delights associated with a world cruise. The cruise can be shorter and hence less expensive, yet offer the same elegance and comfort, splendid food, delightful ambience, and interesting, well-traveled fellow passengers.

An exotic voyage can be a totally self-contained cruise to a specific destination, lasting anywhere from 30 days to more than 100 days. Or you can book a segment of a world cruise to begin at one of its ports of call, getting off at another port. "Segmenting" is ideal for those who wish to be a part of a world cruise but have neither the time nor the money for the prolonged extravagance of a three- to six-month vacation.

Segment cruising necessarily involves flying either to or from your cruise (or both). You can travel to join your exotic cruise at one of the principal ports such as Genoa, Rio de Janeiro, Acapulco, Honolulu, Sydney, Hong Kong, Singapore, Bangkok, Colombo, Mumbai (Bombay), Mombasa, or Athens, depending on the ship and the itinerary.

Ships that roam worldwide during the year offer the most experienced world cruises or segments. Most of these world cruise ships operate at about 75 percent capacity, thus providing considerably more space for passengers than they would normally have.

Going P.O.S.H.

This colloquialism for "grand" or "first-rate" has its origin in the days of ocean steamship travel between England and India. Wealthy passengers would, at some considerable cost, book round-trip

AROUND THE WORLD CRUISES: 2000–2001

This list includes ships presently scheduled to operate an around-the-world cruise in 2000/2001.

SHIP	COMPANY	DAYS	FROM
Aegean I	The World Cruise Company	114	Athens
Albatros	Phoenix Seereisen	100	Genoa
Astor	Transocean Tours	111	Nice
Asuka	NYK Cruises	100	Yokohama
Crystal Symphony	Crystal Cruises	104	Los Angeles
Delphin *	Delphin Seereisen	176	Genoa
Europa	Hapag-Lloyd Seetouristik	160	Lisbon
Maxim Gorkiy	Phoenix Seereisen	120	Genoa
Nippon Maru	Mitsui OSK Passenger Line	100	Yokohama
Ocean Explorer I	The World Cruise Company	127	Athens
Ocean Explorer I	The World Cruise Company	115	Athens
Ocean Explorer I	The World Cruise Company	118	Athens
Olvia	Peace Boat	92	Tokyo
Olvia	Peace Boat	89	Tokyo
Oriana	P&O Cruises	91	Southampton
Queen Elizabeth 2	Cunard	100	New York
Rotterdam	Holland America Line	96	Ft. Lauderdale
Saga Rose	Saga Holidays	100	Southampton
Victoria	P&O Cruises	83	Southampton

* This is an Africa/Caribbean/Latin America Cruise (not a complete around-the-world cruise)

passage as "Port Outward, Starboard Home." They would thus secure a cabin on the cooler side of the ship while crossing the unbearably hot Indian Ocean under the sun. Abbreviated as P.O.S.H., the expression soon came to be applied to first-class passengers who could afford that luxury. (*Brewers Dictionary of Phrase & Fable*, Cassell Ltd.).

However, the reality is that the monsoon winds that blow in and out of the Asian area shift between winter and summer, so that the sheltered side of a ship would change according to the season. Further, in looking at deck plans of ships of the period, most cabins were located *centrally*, with indoor promenades or corridors along each side, so the actual definition of the origin of P.O.S.H. could be said to be taken as artistic license.

DATE (Start)	TO	DATE (Finish)	Millenium Location (31 Dec 1999)
19 Nov 1999	Athens	12 Mar 2000	Buenos Aires
7 Nov 1999	Genoa	15 Feb 2000	Sydney
13 Dec 1999	Venice	1 Apr 2000	Rio de Janeiro
25 Mar 2000	Kobe	3 Jul 2000	
20 Jan 2000	London	4 May 2000	
14 Dec 1999	Palma de Mallorca	6 Jun 2000	Rio de Janeiro
8 Nov 1999	Venice	17 Apr 2000	Sydney
8 Jan 2000	Bremerhaven	7 May 2000	
16 Mar 1999	Yokohama	23 Jun 1999	
19 Nov 1999	Athens	25 Mar 2000	Santiago
25 Mar 2000	Athens	19 Jul 2000	
19 Jul 2000	Athens	14 Nov 2000	
18 Oct 1999	Tokyo	15 Jan 2000	International Date Line
16 Jan 2000	Tokyo	14 Apr 2000	
5 Jan 2000	Southampton	5 Apr 2000	
6 Jan 2000	New York	20 Apr 2000	
6 Jan 2000	Los Angeles	11 Apr 2000	
4 Jan 2000	Southampton	14 Apr 2000	
17 Feb 2000	Southampton	18 May 2000	

Courtesy Holland America Line

The ms **Rotterdam** cruising past St. Mark's Square, Venice, Italy.

FUN FACTS

Cruise ship design is interesting. Aesthetically, the beauty of design lies in curves, and not in straight lines. Today's large cruise ships, designed merely for cruising in warm weather regions and not for voyaging across the North Atlantic (heaven forbid, the delivery voyage was enough), are made of straight lines. They are boxy and cold in appearance, yet of course they provide much more usable space inside the ship. Take a look at *Norway* (the former liner *France*) and you won't find a straight line anywhere. Then take a look at *Imagination* and compare the two.

Norwegian Cruise Line features a "chocoholic" buffet aboard its ships once each cruise. This midnight extravaganza should appease even the most dedicated chocolate lovers.

Cruise lines and charity go hand in hand. Cunard donated some 1,500 pieces of classic furniture from the 1994 refit of *Queen Elizabeth 2* to the Salvation Army for its adult rehabilitation program. Crew members aboard the same ship, when on its annual around-the-world cruise, donate money to buy guide dogs for the blind, or an ambulance for the St. John's Ambulance Brigade in the UK. Princess Cruises made a "sizeable" contribution to UNICEF following the death of Audrey Hepburn in 1993, who christened the company's *Star Princess* (presently operated as *Arcadia* for P&O Cruises). Both Holland America Line and Princess Cruises have contributed heavily to the Raptor Center in Juneau, Alaska.

The sky's the limit! Now you can have a private astrological report including a horoscope analysis provided for you in two special "astroflash" booths set up aboard Norwegian Cruise Lines newest ship, *Norwegian Sky*.

Carnival Cruise Lines will carry over 500,000 seniors (those over 55 years of age) in 1999 aboard its "fun ships" fleet (this number represents about one-third of its passengers).

Naming a ship can be a bubbly sort of bus ness. In fact, so bubbly that when Royal Caribbean International's *Legend of the Seas* was named by Cindy Pritzker on May 16, 1995 in Miami, the company ordered a "sovereign" of champagne (the largest in the world, equal to 34 ordinary bottles of champagne) from Moet & Chandon.

Times were different then. In the mid-1960s there were 12 "bell boys" ("piccolos" in hotelspeak) aboard the Cunard Line's RMS *Queen Elizabeth* and *Queen Mary*. They manned the elevators and opened the doors to the various restaurants. Each day, before they were allowed to work, they all lined up and their fingernails were inspected.

On Valentine's Day (February 14) 1998, some 5,000 couples collectively renewed their wedding vows aboard the ships of Princess Cruises.

Tall ship lovers who are also music lovers may like to know about "The Tall Ship Suite," a work in three movements (The Race Begins – 10 mins:24 secs; The Open Sea – 10 mins:42 secs; Landfall and the Grand Parade of Sail – 6 mins:28 secs). It was jointly composed and orchestrated by Dave Roylance and Bob Gavin. The two composers met in Liverpool in 1980 and composed the suite in 1992 in commemoration of the Grand Regatta Columbus '92. The work is played by the Royal Liverpool Philharmonic Orchestra conducted by Bill Conifer, on an audio compact disc (CD). Also on the disc are two other works by the same composing team: "Ocean Fantasia," a tone poem (18 mins:19 secs), and "Voyager," an orchestral piece (8 mins:11 secs). With strong themes and excellent scoring, this music should be in every tall ship lover's music library.

Part Two:
THE CRUISE SHIPS
AND RATINGS

Mandalay; courtesy Windjammer Barefoot Cruises

HOW SHIPS ARE EVALUATED

I have been evaluating and rating cruise ships and the onboard product professionally since 1980, together with a small team of trained "professional passengers." The ratings are conducted with total objectivity, from a set of predetermined criteria and a modus operandi designed to work globally, not just regionally, across the entire spectrum of oceangoing cruise ships today.

There really is no "best cruise line in the world" or "best cruise ship," only the ship and cruise that is *right for you*. Therefore, different criteria are applied to ships of different sizes, styles, and market segments throughout the world. Since so many new ships are of similar dimensions, but with different decor, more emphasis is placed on the standard of the dining experience, and the service and hospitality aspects of the cruise.

This section includes 241 oceangoing cruise ships in service when this book was completed. Almost all except the newest ships have been carefully evaluated, taking into account more than 400 separate inspection points based on personal cruises, visits and revisits to ships, as well as observations and comments from my reporting team. For the sake of clarity, the resulting scores are first channeled into 20 sections (with 100 points per section possible, the maximum possible score for any ship is, thus, 2,000 points), then into five major at-a-glance sections.

Cruise lines, shipowners, and operators should note that ratings, like stocks and shares, can go down as well as up each year, due to increased competition, the introduction of newer ships with more custom-designed facilities, and other market- or passenger-driven factors.

The ratings more reflect the *standards* of the cruise product delivered to passengers (the software), and less the physical plant (the hardware). Thus, although a ship may be the latest, most stunning vessel in the world in terms of design and decor, if the food, service, staff, and hospitality are not so good, the scores and ratings will reflect these aspects more clearly.

The stars beside the name of the ship at the top of each page relate directly to the Overall Rating. The highest number of stars awarded is five stars (★★★★★), and the lowest is one star. This system is universally recognized throughout the hospitality industry. A plus (+) indicates that a ship deserves just that little bit more than the number of stars attained. However, *it is the number of points achieved rather than the number of stars attained* that perhaps is more meaningful to anyone comparing the ships.

SCORING METHOD: THE RATINGS

Overall Rating	Number of Stars
1851–2000	★★★★★ +
1701–1850	★★★★★
1551–1700	★★★★ +
1401–1550	★★★★
1251–1400	★★★ +
1101–1250	★★★
951–1100	★★ +
801–950	★★
651–800	★ +
601–650	★

WHAT THE RATINGS MEAN

1851–2000 Points ★★★★★ +

You can expect to have an outstanding luxury cruise experience — in fact, it doesn't get any better than this. It should be truly memorable, with the very highest attention to detail, finesse, and personal service. The decor must be tasteful, without glitz, and public room layout may possibly be somewhat in accordance with the principles of *feng shui*. Any ship with this rating should be just about unsurpassable in the cruise industry, and for any ship to reach this level, it has to be very, very special, with the service and hospitality levels to match. There must be the very highest quality surroundings, comfort, and service levels, the finest and freshest quality foods, highly creative menus, and dining alternatives that provide maximum choice and variety. Meals (particularly dinners) are expected to be grand, memorable affairs, correctly served on the finest china. The service staff will take pleasure in providing you with the ultimate personal, yet unobtrusive, attention with the utmost of finesse, and the word "no" should definitely not be in their vocabulary. This really is the very best of the best in terms of refined, unstructured living at sea, and may cause serious damage to your bank statement.

1701–1850   Points   ★★★★★

You can expect to have a really excellent cruise experience that should be extremely memorable, and with the finesse and attention to detail commensurate with the amount of money paid. The service and hospitality levels will be extremely high from all levels of officers and staff, with strong emphasis on hospitality training. Food and service will be commensurate with the high level expected from what is virtually the best that is possible — attentive yet unobtrusive. The food should be quite memorable, with ample taste. Special orders should never present a problem, with a creative cuisine that will be of a very high standard. Entertainment is expected to be of prime quality and variety. Again, the word "no" should not be in the vocabulary of any member of staff aboard a ship with this rating. A cruise aboard a ship with this high rating may well cause damage to your bank statement, particularly if you choose the most spacious grades of accommodation.

1551–1700   Points   ★★★★ +

You should expect to have a high quality cruise experience that will be quite memorable, and just a little short of being excellent in all aspects. Perhaps the attention to detail could be slightly better, but, nonetheless, this should prove to be a fine cruise experience, in a setting that is extremely clean and comfortable, with few lines anywhere, a caring attitude from service personnel, and a good standard of entertainment. The cuisine and service will be well-rounded, with mostly fresh ingredients and varied menus that should appeal to almost anyone, served on high quality china. All in all, this should prove to be a well-rounded cruise experience, probably in a ship that is new or almost new.

1401–1550   Points   ★★★★

You should expect to have a very good quality cruise experience, most probably aboard a modern, highly comfortable ship that will provide a good range of facilities and services. The food and service will be quite decent overall, although decidedly not as "gourmet" and fanciful as the brochures with the always-smiling faces might have you believe. The service on board will be well organized, although it will perhaps be a little robotic and impersonal at times, and only as good as the cruise line's training program allows. However, you should have a good time, and only a moderate amount of damage will be done to your bank statement.

1251–1400   Points   ★★★ +

You should expect to have a decent quality cruise experience, from a ship where the service levels should be good, but perhaps without the finesse that could be expected from a more upscale environment. The crew aboard any ship achieving this score should reflect a positive attitude with regard to hospitality, and a willingness to accommodate your needs, up to a point. Staff training will probably be in need of more attention to detail and flexibility. Food and service levels in the dining room(s) should be reasonably good, although special orders or anything out of the ordinary might prove more difficult.

1101–1250   Points   ★★★

You can expect to have a reasonably decent, middle-of-the-road cruise experience, with a moderate amount of space and quality in furnishings, fixtures, and fittings. Cabins are likely to be a little on the small side. The food and service levels will be quite acceptable, but somewhat inflexible with regard to special orders, as almost everything is standardized. Crew attitude could certainly be improved, the level of hospitality and cleanliness will be moderate but little more, and entertainment will probably be weak. Good, however, for those looking for the reasonable comforts of home without pretentious attitudes, and little damage to one's bank statement.

951–1100   Points   ★★ +

You should expect to have a cruise experience that is below average in terms of accommodation, quality, food, service, and hospitality levels, in surroundings that are completely unpretentious. In particular, the food and its service will probably prove to be most disappointing and rather typical of roadside café standards. There will be little flexibility in the levels of service, hospitality and staff training, which will be no better than poor. Thus, the overall experience will be commensurate with the small amount of money you paid for the cruise.

801–950 Points ★★

You should expect to have a cruise experience of modest quality aboard a ship that is probably in need of more attention to maintenance and service levels, not to mention hospitality. The food is likely to be quite tasteless and homogenized, and of low quality, and service will leave much to be desired in terms of attitude, which will tend to be mediocre at best. Staff training will be minimal, and turnover is likely to be high. The "end-of-pier" entertainment could well leave you wanting to read a good book.

651-800 Points ★ +

You can expect to have only the most basic cruise experience, with little or no attention to detail, from a poorly trained staff that is probably paid low wages and to whom you are just another body. The ship will, in many cases, probably be in need of much maintenance and upgrading, and will probably have few facilities. Cleanliness and hygiene may well be questionable, and there will be absolutely no finesse in personal service levels, with poor attitude from the crew, and dismal entertainment as significant factors in the low score and rating. On the other hand, the price of a cruise is probably extremely inexpensive.

601-650 Points ★

You can expect to have a cruise experience that is the bottom of the barrel, with the least amount of hospitality, and forget about attention to detail. This will be the kind of experience that would equal a stay in the most basic motel, with few facilities, a poorly trained, uncaring staff, most of whom will have undergone a hospitality bypass, and a ship that is in need of better maintenance and upgrading. The low cost of a cruise aboard any cruise ship with this rating should provide a clue to the complete lack of any quality. This will be particularly true in the areas of food, service, and entertainment. In other words, a totally forgettable cruise experience.

The Ratings and Evaluations cover five principal areas, each of which is almost as important as the next:

A) The Ship

B) Accommodation

C) Cuisine

D) Service

E) The Cruise Experience

THE SHIP

This section forms 25 percent of the whole rating system.

Ship: Hardware/Maintenance

This score reflects the general profile and condition of the ship as hardware, its age and maintenance, hull condition, exterior paint, decking and caulking, swimming pool and surrounds, deck furniture, lifeboats, life rafts, and shore tenders. Also reflects interior cleanliness (public restrooms, elevators, floor coverings, wall coverings, stairways, passageways, and doorways), food preparation areas, refrigerators, garbage handling, compacting, and incineration, and waste disposal facilities.

Ship: Outdoor Facilities/Space

This score reflects the overall space per passenger on open decks, crowding, swimming pools/whirlpools and their surrounds, lido deck areas, number and type of deck lounge chairs (with/without cushioned pads) and other deck furniture, outdoor sports facilities, shower stalls and changing facilities, towels, and quiet areas (those without music).

Ship: Interior Facilities/Space/Flow

This score reflects the use of common interior public spaces, including enclosed promenades; passenger flow and points of congestion; ceiling height; lobby areas, stairways, and all passenger hallways; elevators; public restrooms and facilities; signage, lighting, air-conditioning and ventilation; and degree of comfort and density.

Ship: Decor/Furnishings/Artwork

This score reflects the overall interior decor and color scheme; hard and soft furnishings, wood (real, imitation, or veneer) paneling, carpeting (tuft density, color, and practicality), fit and finish (seams and edging), chairs (comfort, height, and support), ceilings and decor treatments, reflective surfaces, artwork (paintings, sculptures, and atrium centerpieces), and lighting.

Ship: Spa/Fitness Facilities

This score reflects any health spa, wellness center, and fitness facilities; location and accessibility; lighting and flooring materials; fitness and muscle-training machines and other equipment; fitness programs; sports and games facilities; indoor swimming pools; whirlpools; grand baths; aqua-spa pools; saunas and steam rooms; rasul, massage, and other treatment rooms; changing facilities; jogging and walking tracks; and promenades.

ACCOMMODATION

This section forms 15 percent of the whole rating system.

Cabins: Suites and Deluxe Grades

This score reflects the design and layout of all grades of suites and deluxe grade cabins, private balconies (whether full floor-to-ceiling partition or part partitions, balcony lighting, balcony furniture). Also beds/berths, furniture (its placement and practicality), and other fittings; closets and other hanging space, drawer space, and bedside tables; vanity unit, bathroom facilities, washbasin, cabinets, and toiletries storage; lighting, air-conditioning, and ventilation; audiovisual facilities; quality and degree of luxury; artwork; bulkhead insulation, noise, and vibration levels. Suites should not be so designated unless the sleeping room is completely separate from the living area. *Note*: Some large cruise ships now have whole decks devoted to superior grade accommodation, with much difference between this accommodation and that of "standard" cabins.

Also the soft furnishings and details such as the information manual (list of services); paper and postcards (including personalized stationery); telephone directory; laundry lists; tea- and coffee-making equipment; flowers (if any); fruit (if any); bathroom personal amenities kits, bathrobes, slippers, and the size, thickness, quality, and material content of towels.

Cabins: Standard Sizes

This score reflects the design and layout (whether outside or inside), beds/berths, furniture (its placement and practicality), and other fittings. Also closets and other hanging space, drawer space, and bedside tables; vanity unit, bathroom facilities, washbasin, cabinets, and toiletries storage; lighting, air-conditioning and ventilation; audiovisual facilities; quality and degree of luxury; artwork; bulkhead insulation, noise, and vibration levels.

Also the soft furnishings and details in cabins, such as the information manual (directory of services); paper and postcards (including personalized stationery); telephone directory; laundry lists; tea- and coffee-making equipment; flowers (if any); fruit (if any); and bathroom amenities kits, bathrobes, slippers, and the size, thickness, quality, and material content of towels.

CUISINE

This section forms 15 percent of the whole rating system and is very important, as food is often the main feature of today's cruises. Cruise lines put maximum emphasis on telling passengers how good their food is, often to the point of being unable to deliver what is promised. Generally, the standard of food is good. The rule of thumb is: if you were to eat out in a good restaurant, what would you expect? Does the ship meet your expectations? Would you come back again for the food?

There are perhaps as many different tastes as there are passengers. The "standard" market cruise lines cater to a wide range of tastes, while the more exclusive cruise lines can offer better quality food, cooked individually to your taste. As in any good restaurant, you get what you pay for.

Food: Dining Room/Cuisine

This score reflects the physical structure of dining rooms; window treatments; seating (alcoves and individual chairs, with or without armrests); lighting and ambience; table set-ups; the quality and condition of linen, china, and cutlery; and table centerpieces (flowers). Also reflects menus, food quality, presentation, food combinations, culinary creativity, variety, design concepts, appeal, taste, texture, palatability, freshness, color, balance, garnishes, and decorations; appetizers, soups, pastas, flambeaus, tableside cooking; fresh fruit and cakes; the wine list (and connoisseur wine list), price range, and wine service.

Food: Informal Dining/Buffets

This score reflects the hardware (including the provision of hot and cold display units, sneeze guards, tongs, ice containers and ladles, and serving utensils); buffet displays (which have become quite disappointing and institutionalized); presentation; trays and set-ups; correct food temperatures; food labeling; breakfast, luncheon, deck buffets, midnight buffets, and late-night snacks; decorative elements such as ice carvings; and staff attitude, service, and communication skills.

Food: Quality of Ingredients

This score reflects the overall quality of ingredients used, including consistency and portion size; grades of meat, fish, and fowl; and the price paid by the cruise line for its food product per passenger per day. It is the quality of ingredients that most dictates the eventual presentation and quality of the finished product as well as its taste. Also included is the quality of tea and coffee (better quality ships are expected to provide better quality tea and coffee).

Food: Afternoon Tea/Bar Snacks

This score reflects the quality and variety of teas, and their presentation; whether mugs or cups and saucers are presented/available; whether milk is served in the correct open containers or in sealed packets; whether tea is self-service or graciously served; whether cakes, scones, and pastries are available, as well as bar/lounge snacks, hot and cold canapes, and hors d'oeuvres.

SERVICE

This section forms 20 percent of the whole rating system.

Service: Dining Room

This score reflects the professionalism of the restaurant staff: maître d' Hotel, dining room managers, head section waiters, waiters and assistant waiters (busboys), and sommeliers and wine waiters. It includes place settings and correct service (serving, taking from the correct side), communication skills, attitude, flair, dress sense (uniform), and finesse. Waiters should note whether passengers are right- or left-handed and, aboard ships with assigned table places, make sure that the cutlery and glasses are placed on the side of preference. Cutlery and wine glasses are also included.

Service: Bars

This score reflects the lighting and ambience; overall service in bars and lounges; noise levels; communication skills (between bartenders and bar staff and passengers); staff attitude, personality, flair and finesse; correct use of glasses (and correct size of glasses); billing and attitude when presenting the bill (aboard those ships where a charge is made).

Service: Cabins

This score reflects the cleaning and housekeeping staff, butlers (for penthouse and suite passengers), cabin stewards/stewardesses and their supervisory staff, attention to detail and cleanliness, in-cabin food service, linen and bathrobe changes, and language and communication skills.

Service: Open Decks

This score reflects steward/stewardess service for beverages and food items around the open decks; service for placement and replacement of towels on deck lounge chairs, self-help towels, and emptying of used towel bins; general tidiness of all associated deck equipment; and the availability of service at nonstandard times (in the evening or early morning, for example).

THE CRUISE EXPERIENCE
This section forms 25 percent of the whole rating system.

Cruise: Entertainment
This score reflects the overall entertainment program and content as designed and targeted to specific passenger demographics. Cruise ship entertainment has to appeal to passengers of widely varying ages and types. Included is the physical plant (stage/bandstand); technical support, lighting, follow spotlight operation and set/backdrop design; sound and light systems (including laser shows); recorded click-tracks and all special effects; variety and quality of large-scale production shows (including story, plot, content, cohesion, creativeness of costumes, relevancy, quality, choreography, and vocal content); cabaret; variety shows; singers; visual acts; bands and solo musicians.

Cruise: Activities Program
This score reflects the variety, quality, and quantity of daytime activities and events. The rating includes the cruise director and cruise staff (including their visibility, availability, ability, and professionalism), sports programs, participation games, special interest programs, port and shopping lecturers, and mind-enrichment lecturers.

This score also reflects any water sports equipment carried (including banana boat, jet skis, scuba tanks, snorkeling equipment, waterski boat and Windsurfers), instruction programs, overall staff supervision, the marina (usually located aft) or side-retractable water sports platforms, and any enclosed swimming area (if applicable).

Cruise: Movies/Television Programming
This score reflects movies screened in onboard theaters, including screen, picture and sound quality; videos screened on the in-cabin television system; other televised programming, including a ship's own television station programming; content; and entertainment value. Cabin television audio channels are also included in this section.

Cruise: Hospitality Standard
This score reflects the level of hospitality of the crew and their attention to detail and personal satisfaction. It includes the professionalism of senior officers, middle management, supervisors, cruise staff, and general crew; social contact, appearance, and dress codes or uniforms; atmosphere and ambience; motivation; communication skills (most important); the general ambience and the attention to detail.

Cruise: Overall Product Delivery
This score reflects the quality of the overall cruise as a vacation experience — what the brochure states and promises (real or implied), which reflects on the level of expectation versus the onboard product delivery.

THE RATING RESULTS — THE AUTHOR'S NOTES
Cruise ship evaluations and ratings have of necessity become tougher and much more complex. Although a ship may be the newest, with all the latest high-tech facilities possible, passengers state that it is the onboard food and service that often disappoints.

Cruise companies defend themselves by stating that their passengers are willing to accept lesser quality with regard to food in return for lower prices. This attitude can only result in a downward spiral that affects food quality, freshness, variety, creativity, and presentation, as well as service, quality of personnel, crew training, safety, maintenance, and other related items.

Cuts are often made by cruise companies in the hopes that passengers will not notice, but in the final analysis, it is all the little things that add up to points lost on the great scorecard.

It is therefore hoped that these ratings will help the cruise companies to take note of their product, listen to their passengers, and return some of the items and the finesse currently missing in the overall cruise vacation experience, while adjusting fares to better reflect long-term growth of this good value-for-money vacation product.

THE SHIP PROFILES AND RATINGS

PREFIXES

Prefixes given before the name of a ship are used to denote the type of propulsion system used:

cs = "club ship" concept

ib = icebreaker (diesel or nuclear)

ms = motor ship (diesel)

msy = motor sailing yacht

mts = motor twin screw (diesel) or motor turbine ship (steam)

mv = motor vessel (diesel)

my = motor yacht

mys = motor (assisted) sailing yacht

RMS = Royal Mail Ship

ss = steamship

ssc = semisubmersible craft (swath)

sts = sail training ship

sy = sailing yacht

tes = turbo-electric ship (steam)

ts = turbine steamer (steam) or twin-screw vessel

tsmv = twin-screw motor vessel

tss = turbine steam ship

tts = turbine twin-screw ship

ys = yacht ship

SHIP SIZE

A large letter, **S**, **M**, **L**, denotes whether the entry is a small ship (up to 500 passengers), a mid-size ship (500–1,000 passengers), or a large ship (over 1,000 passengers).

LIFESTYLE

After the name of each ship, the word LIFESTYLE is followed by STANDARD, PREMIUM, or LUXURY, according to a general classification into which segment of the market the ship falls. It should thus further allow you to choose the right size ship to fit your lifestyle.

→ Those designated STANDARD are the least expensive.

→ Those designated PREMIUM are more expensive, have generally better food, service, and facilities.

→ Those designated LUXURY are the most expensive but will provide the best facilities, food, and service, and the finest cruise experience possible.

CRUISE LINE
The cruise line and the operator may be different if the company that owns the vessel does not market and operate it.

FIRST ENTERED SERVICE
Where two dates are given, the first is the ship's maiden passenger voyage when new, and the second is the date it began service for the present operator.

PROPULSION
The type of propulsion is given (i.e., diesel, diesel-electric, or steam turbine), together with the output (at 100 percent), expressed either as bhp = brake horsepower; kW = kilowatts generated; or shp = shaft horsepower

PROPELLERS
Included is the type of propeller, where known, expressed as:

CP = controllable (or variable) pitch

FP = fixed (or direct) pitch

Pod = azimuthing pod and propeller mounted externally (replacing propellers and shafts)

PASSENGER CAPACITY
The number of passengers is based on:

→ Two beds/berths per cabin, plus all single cabins.

→ All available beds/berths filled (Note: This figure may not always be accurate, as cruise lines often make changes by adding or taking away third/fourth berths according to demand).

PASSENGER SPACE RATIO (TONNES PER PASSENGER)
Achieved by dividing the gross registered tonnage by the number of passengers.

CABIN SIZE RANGE
From the smallest cabin to the largest suite (including private balconies), in square feet and square meters, rounded up to the nearest number.

WHEELCHAIR CABINS
Cabins designed to accommodate passengers with mobility problems.

MOVIE THEATER/SEATS
A "Yes" means that there is a separate, dedicated movie theater, where large-screen movies can be shown throughout the day and evening, and *not* a show lounge that can also screen movies during the day (afternoon) and live shows at night. The number of seats is provided where known.

Note: In the Other Comments section at the bottom of each page, all gratuities are usually at extra cost unless specifically included in the price. Likewise, insurance and port taxes are also at extra cost unless specifically stated as included.

THE CRUISE LINES: MARKET CLASSIFICATION

Luxury

Crystal Cruises
Cunard Line
Hapag-Lloyd Seetouristik (4)
Hebridean Island Cruises
NYK Cruises
Sea Cloud Cruises
Seabourn Cruise Line
Silversea Cruises

Premium

Abercrombie & Kent
Celebrity Cruises
Classical Cruises
Clipper Cruise Line
Club Mediterranee Cruises
Compagnie des Isles du Ponant Cruises
Discoverer Reederei
Fred Olsen Cruise Lines
Holland America Line
Lindblad Special Expeditions
Noble Caledonia
Norwegian Capricorn Line
Orient Lines
P&O Cruises
Princess Cruises
Quark Expeditions
Radisson Seven Seas Cruises
Raymond & Whitcomb
Renaissance Cruises
Saga Shipping
Society Expeditions
Spice Island Cruises
Star Clippers
Swan Hellenic Cruises
Venus Cruise
Windstar Cruises

Standard

Airtours Sun Cruises
Alaska Sightseeing/Cruise West
American Canadian Caribbean Line
American Hawaii Cruises
Arcalia Shipping (3)
Arkona Reisen
Canaveral Cruise Line
Carnival Cruise Lines
Classic International Cruises (3)
Clipper Cruise Line
Commodore Cruise Line
Costa Cruises
Croatia Cruise Lines
Crown Cruise Line
Delphin Seereisen

Direct Cruises
Disney Cruise Line
Festival Cruises (1)
First Choice
First European Cruises (1)
Glacier Bay Cruises & Tours
Golden Sea Cruises
Golden Sun Cruises
Hapag-Lloyd Seetouristik (4)
Hyundai Cruises (Hyundai Merchant Marine)
Imperial Majesty Cruises
Jahn Reisen
Kristina Cruises
Leisure Cruises
Louis Cruise Lines
Mano Cruises
Marine Expeditions (2)
Mediterranean Shipping Cruises
Mitsui OSK Passenger Line
Neckermann Seereisen
New Century Cruise Lines
New Paradise Cruises
Nina Cruise Line
Noble Caledonia
Norwegian Cruise Line
P&O Holidays
Phoenix Seereisen
Premier Cruise Lines
Primexpress Cruises
Regal Cruises
Royal Caribbean International
Royal Olympic Cruises
Star Cruises
Star Line Cruises
Sun Cruises
Tall Ship Adventures
Thomson Cruises
Transocean Tours
Transtours
Windjammer Barefoot Cruises
World Cruise Company (2)
World Explorer Cruises

Notes:
(1) These companies operate under different brand names in Europe and North America.
(2) Marine Expeditions and The World Cruise Company are two brands owned by the same company.
(3) These companies are one and the same.
(4) This company has different ships for different market segments and is thus listed under more than one market classification.

m/v Aegean I
★★ +
(M)

LIFESTYLE:	STANDARD
Cruise Line:	Golden Sun Cruises
Former Names:	*Aegean Dolphin, Narcis, Alkyon*
Gross Tonnage:	11,563
Builder:	Santierul N. Galatz (Romania)
Original Cost:	n/a
Entered Service:	May 1988
Flag:	Greece
Tel. No.:	1130627/7651576788
Fax No.:	1130627
Length (ft/m):	460.9/140.5
Beam (ft/m):	67.2/20.5
Draft (ft/m):	20.3/6.2
Propulsion/Propellers:	diesel (10,296kW)/2 (CP)
Passenger Decks:	8
Total Crew:	200
Pass. Capacity (basis 2):	560
Pass. Capacity (all berths):	682
Pass. Space Ratio (basis 2):	20.6
Pass. Space Ratio (all berths):	16.8
Officers:	Greek
Total Cabins:	280
Size Range (sq ft/m):	134.5–290.6/12.5–27.0
Cabins (outside view):	198
Cabins (inside — no view):	82
Cabins (single occupancy):	0
Cabins (with private balcony):	8

Cabins (wheelchair accessible):	0
Cabin Current:	220 volts
Cabin TV:	Yes (suites only)
Dining Rooms:	1
Elevators:	2
Casino:	Yes
Slot Machines:	Yes
Swimming Pools (outdoors):	1
Swimming Pools (inside):	0
Whirlpools:	0
Fitness Center:	Yes
Sauna/Steam Room:	Yes/No
Massage:	Yes
Self-Service Launderette:	Yes
Movie Theater/Seats:	Yes/176
Library:	Yes
Classification Society:	Lloyd's Register

RATINGS	POSSIBLE SCORE	SCORE ACHIEVED
Ship	500	274
Accommodation	200	108
Food	400	212
Service	400	227
Cruise	500	241
TOTAL	**2,000**	**1,062**

Accommodation: The cabins are mostly outside units, and all feature a refrigerator. They are reasonably spacious for the size of the ship, and are pleasantly decorated, although the storage space is quite limited (not good for a long cruise), and the walls and ceilings are very plain. The cabin soundproofing is poor, and you can hear almost everything that's happening in the adjacent cabin(s). The closet, drawer, and luggage storage space for two is limited. The partly tiled bathrooms are small but adequate, although there is little space for personal toiletry items. Bathrobes may or may not be provided for all passengers (this depends on who charters and operates the vessel).

Dining: The dining room, which is set low down in the ship, features restful colors, has mostly large tables (there are no tables for two), and is a totally nonsmoking room, with two seatings. There is plenty of space around each table, allowing waiters ample room to provide decent service. Features a mixed continental/Greek cuisine, with a rather limited choice, particularly of breads, cheeses, and fruits, which tend to be very standard items.

For informal eating, small self-serve breakfast and lunch buffets are available on the Lido Deck aft, and a popular outdoor gyro and salad bar is set under a large canopy which was added in 1996.

Other Comments: The profile of this ship looks moderately smart, although somewhat square and angular. The ship underwent an extensive $26 million conversion/stretch in 1988. The open deck space can be said to be generally good, but it is definitely not enough when the ship is full, which means it could be difficult to find good sunbathing space.

Inside, the public rooms are fairly tastefully decorated in soft, mostly pastel colors, although there is far too much use of mirrored surfaces. There is a good showroom, laid out in a single-level amphitheater-style, with decent sight lines from most seats. The Belvedere Lounge, which is set high atop the ship and forward, features a smart piano bar and good ocean views. A dialysis station is a bonus. In general, the service could be said to be moderately friendly, although there is certainly no finesse.

This ship really caters primarily to European passengers, and it is often placed under charter to various operators. The ship will provide a cruise in comfortable but very densely populated surroundings, and at a fair price — therefore, you should not expect the spit and polish that other ships might provide in the same price range.

Weak Points: Too many unnecessary and loud announcements (in several languages); narrow gangway in some ports; no cushioned pads for the deck lounge chairs (lying on a towel on plastic ribbing is no fun for more than a few minutes!). Poor attitude and hospitality from most officers and crew members is not acceptable.

WHO'S WHO – THE CAPTAIN

The captain is the master of the ship and has absolute dictatorial rights and control over his vessel, officers, crew, and passengers. He is a seaman first and manager of the ship second. He is also expected to be a generous and worthy host (the social aspect of a captain's job today requires an investment of about a quarter of his time spent with his passengers). When passenger ships are registered for insurance coverage, the captain's credentials and past record are reviewed together with the seaworthiness of the vessel itself.

Although on the bridge there may be several officers with a master's certificate, the captain still maintains unquestioned authority. He wears four gold bars on his sleeves and epaulets.

Every ship has a log, a daily record in which are noted all navigational and pertinent nautical data, details of reports from various department heads, and any relevant information on passengers or crew. Maritime law dictates that only the captain is allowed to sign that the daily entries in the log are correct. If a ship were to be abandoned, the log is the only record of the ship's operation, prevailing conditions, weather information, and geographical locations that could be reviewed. The captain normally attends numerous social functions during the course of a cruise, hosts a table in the dining room, and is often seen during the day on walkabout inspection tours.

c/s Aida

★★★★

(L)

LIFESTYLE:	STANDARD
Cruise Line:	Arkona Touristik
Former Names:	-
Gross Tonnage:	38,600
Builder:	Kvaerner Masa-Yards (Finland)
Original Cost:	DM300 million
Entered Service:	June 1996
Flag:	Bahamas/Liberia
Tel. No.:	663670110
Fax No.:	363669420
Length (ft/m):	634.1/193.3
Beam (ft/m):	90.5/27.6
Draft (ft/m):	20.3/6.2
Propulsion/Propellers:	4 MAN 6cyl L48/60
Passenger Decks:	9
Total Crew:	370
Pass. Capacity (basis 2):	1,186
Pass. Capacity (all berths):	1,230
Pass. Space Ratio (basis 2):	32.5
Pass. Space Ratio (all berths):	31.3
Officers:	German
Total Cabins:	593
Size Range (sq ft/m):	145.3–376.7/13.5–35.0
Cabins (outside view):	391
Cabins (inside — no view):	202
Cabins (single occupancy):	0
Cabins (with private balcony):	4

Cabins (wheelchair accessible):	4
Cabin Current:	110 and 220 volts
Cabin TV:	Yes
Dining Rooms:	3
Elevators:	5
Casino:	No
Slot Machines:	No
Swimming Pools (outdoors):	1
Swimming Pools (inside):	0
Whirlpools:	3
Fitness Center:	Yes
Sauna/Steam Room:	Yes/Yes
Massage:	Yes
Self-Service Launderette:	Yes
Movie Theater/Seats:	Yes/600
Library:	Yes
Classification Society:	Germanischer Lloyd

RATINGS	POSSIBLE SCORE	SCORE ACHIEVED
Ship	500	419
Accommodation	200	148
Food	400	299
Service	400	289
Cruise	500	393
TOTAL	**2,000**	**1,548**

Accommodation: There are five grades: A-outside (182.9 sq ft/17.0 m²); B-outside (145.3 sq ft/13.5 m²); C-inside (156.0 sq ft/14.5 m²); Junior Suite (269.1 sq ft/25.0 m²); Suite (376.7 sq ft/35.0 m²). The accommodation features contemporary decor with a bright, youthful, contemporary look. All cabins are accented with multipatterned fabrics, wood-trimmed cabinetry (with nicely rounded edges), and rattan furniture. The twin beds have duvets and a fabric canopy from headboard to ceiling. Windows feature full pull-down blackout blinds.

Grades A, B, and C have just a small amount of drawer space, but, as you will not need many clothes, this is not really a drawback. Some cabins in grades A, B, and C have one bed and a convertible daytime sofa bed. All cabin bathrooms, which are compact but well designed and practical, feature showers and wall-mounted soap/shampoo dispensers, so there is no wastage of throwaway plastic bottles (environmentally friendly), but you should bring your own conditioner, hand lotion, or any other personal toiletry items. Cotton bathrobes are also provided. Although bathrooms do not feature a hairdryer, one is located in the vanity unit in the cabin. *Note*: There is no toiletries cabinet.

Four Suites have a forward-facing private balcony (all four share the same, ship-wide balcony, as there are no partitions for privacy) and more luxurious furnishings and fittings. Seating in the cabin lounge area is in contemporary rattan chairs. There is a wall unit that houses a television that can be turned for viewing from either lounge or bedroom, and a refrigerator.

Suites and Junior Suites have a generous amount of closet, drawer, and other storage space, a stocked minibar, and a VCR unit. Bathrooms feature a full-size bathtub and a hairdryer.

The cabins are cleaned and beds are made each morning, but not in the evening. For those who may be allergic to natural fibers, down-filled duvets and pillows can be replaced by synthetic ones.

Dining: There are good dining options, with a wide range of food that is available almost 24 hours a day. There are two huge self-service buffet restaurants ("Caribbean" and "Market") and one à la carte restaurant (with waiter and sommelier service).

The standard of food offered at the buffets (which feature numerous food "islands" with the greatest variety in the cruise industry today) is good to excellent, with creative presentation and above average table-clearing service. There is no standing in the long lines so common aboard most other cruise ships today. There is always a fine selection of breads, cheeses, cold cuts, fruits, and make-your-own teas (with a choice of more than 30 types of loose-leaf regular and herbal teas, as well as coffee).

At peak times, the buffet restaurants do remind one of highway cafes (albeit fairly elegant ones), with all their attendant noise, but an excellent selection of foods is provided (there are over 1,200 items of food aboard this ship). You can sit where you want, when you want, and with whom you want, so dining really is a great social occasion. Highly entertaining are the comical, impromptu antics and theatrics performed by some of the entertainment staff (these take place in all restaurants during a typical cruise).

Because of the two large self-serve buffet rooms and dining concept, the actual crew-to-passenger ratio looks poor; this is because there really are no waiters as such (except in the à la carte restaurant), only staff for clearing tables.

The Maritime Restaurant, which has 74 mostly high-back striped seats, set in an intimate dining atmosphere, is open for dinner only and features a set five- or six-course menu that is changed every two or three days. There is no extra charge, except for additional à la carte menu items (featuring such things as sevruga caviar, smoked salmon, châteaubriand, and rib-eye steak), and for wines. Reservations are made each morning of the day you want to eat in the Maritime Restaurant, at the reception desk.

Other Comments: *Aida* has a sleek contemporary profile and is well proportioned, with a swept-back funnel and a large wedge-shaped stern. There is certainly no mistaking the red lips painted on her bows, as well as the blue eyes of Aida (from Verdi's opera of the same name, written to commemorate the opening of the Suez Canal in 1871).

Aida has diesel-mechanical propulsion and is a much larger and more contemporary half-sister to the company's traditional ship, *Arkona*, which is presently under a long-term charter to Seetours (which itself was purchased by Deutsche Seerederei in late 1997). Deutsche Seerederei is part of The Arkona Group, which also operates hotels in five German cities: Eisenbach, Osnabruck, Potsdam, Stralsund, and Wismar.

Aida is a "Club Ship," totally different from any traditional cruise ship and a breath of fresh air to the German cruise industry. The "Club Ship" concept, which stems from the popular Robinson Clubs, is a real fun ship. It includes a whole army of "animateurs" (like the GOs of Club Med, but much, much better) who enjoy doing varied activities by day (as well as acting as tour escorts) and are entertainers at night, acting in the colorful, often funny shows alongside the professional entertainers. The "animateurs" (along with other staff) also interact with passengers throughout the ship and can drink with them at the bars, something not allowed aboard any other ship.

The ship features a wraparound promenade deck outdoors, good for strolling or sitting in a deck lounge chair and just taking in the sea air. Outside on deck, the swimming pool and surrounding area have several cascading levels at the forward end for deck chairs and sun lounging, plus a basketball court, although the pool itself is small.

Inside, there is no wasted space, and the public rooms are open and flow into each other instead of being contained spaces. The "you are here" (deck plan) signs are excellent, and finding your way around is a simple matter. The decor is upbeat and trendy and will appeal to younger passengers, particularly those who may not have cruised before. A large observation lounge is set high atop the ship overlooking the bow. There is a wide array of intimate public rooms and spaces from which to choose.

The fitness, wellness, and sports programming is arguably the most extensive in the cruise industry today. There is an excellent "Wellness Center" located forward, which measures 11,840.6 sq ft (1,100 m^2) and contains two saunas (one seats more than 20 persons and has glass ocean-view walls), massage and other treatment rooms, and a large lounging area. Adjoining the wellness center, forward and outside, is an FKK nudist sunbathing deck. One really popular feature is 30 "Hit Bikes," mountain bikes with tough front and rear suspension units, for conducted biking excursions in each port of call — the concept and concession of Austrian downhill champion skier Erwin Resch.

Central to all social interactions is The Aida Lounge, which features novel "lollipop stick" decorations on the bar counter. The bar itself, at 162.4 ft (49.5 m) long, is certainly the longest bar aboard any cruise ship. The feel is youthful, colorful, unpretentious, casual, relaxed, and sporting.

This really is a family-friendly ship, with plenty of activities for younger family members (children are split into two age groups: Seepferdchen, from 4 to 7 years; Sharks, from 8 to 13 years). There is a diverse selection of children's and youth programs — good for families. Children can make their own menus for the week (together with the chef), and they get to go into the galley to make cookies and other items — a novel idea that more ships could adopt.

The ship caters particularly to first-time cruisegoers and youthful German-speaking couples. The dress code is simple: "casual" (no dinner jackets or ties) at all times.

Alternating seven-night itineraries can be combined for a 14-day cruise holiday. In addition, packages created by tour operators such as Jahn Reisen, Seetours, and TUI can add land stays for an even longer cruise and resort holiday experience. This presents a good amount of flexibility. During the summer, *Aida* sails two alternating itineraries in the Mediterranean from Antalya (Turkey), while in the winter, she sails two alternating itineraries in the Caribbean from Santo Domingo.

About 20 nationalities are represented among the crew, who are really upbeat and cheerful, and want passengers to have a great time. And they do, for this is definitely a young, vibrant fun ship, with plenty of passenger participation in all kinds of events. The brochure accurately describes the lifestyle (only real passengers are used, not models), facilities, and activities aboard this truly refreshing and innovative ship.

All port taxes and gratuities (but not insurance) are included, and with rates of approximately DM250–DM300 per day, it is almost cheaper than staying home and is a better value than almost any land-based vacation. Airlines used in the various fly-cruise programs are Condor and Hapag-Lloyd. Currency aboard: deutschmark.

Weak Points: There is a charge of DM1 for use of the washing machine and DM1 for the dryer in the self-service launderette.

t/s Albatros
★★★ +
(M)

LIFESTYLE:	STANDARD
Cruise Line:	Phoenix Seereisen
Former Names:	*Dawn Princess, FairWind, Sylvania*
Gross Tonnage:	24,803
Builder:	John Brown & Co. (UK)
Original Cost:	n/a
Entered Service:	June 1957/August 1993
Flag:	Bahamas
Tel. No.:	1306132
Fax No.:	1306133
Length (ft/m):	608.2/185.40
Beam (ft/m):	80.3/24.49
Draft (ft/m):	29.3/8.94
Propulsion/Propellers:	steam turbine (18,300kW)/2 (FP)
Passenger Decks:	11
Total Crew:	340
Pass. Capacity (basis 2):	940
Pass. Capacity (all berths):	1,100
Pass. Space Ratio (basis 2):	26.3
Pass. Space Ratio (all berths):	22.5
Officers:	European
Total Cabins:	470
Size Range (sq ft/m):	89.3–240.0/8.3–22.3
Cabins (outside view):	239
Cabins (inside — no view):	231
Cabins (single occupancy):	0
Cabins (with private balcony):	0
Cabins (wheelchair accessible):	0
Cabin Current:	110 volts
Cabin TV:	Yes
Dining Rooms:	2
Elevators:	3
Casino:	Yes
Slot Machines:	Yes
Swimming Pools (outdoors):	3
Swimming Pools (inside):	0
Whirlpools:	0
Fitness Center:	Yes
Sauna/Steam Room:	Yes/No
Massage:	Yes
Self-Service Launderette:	Yes
Movie Theater/Seats:	Yes/n/a
Library:	Yes
Classification Society:	Lloyd's Register

RATINGS	POSSIBLE SCORE	SCORE ACHIEVED
Ship	500	276
Accommodation	200	117
Food	400	278
Service	400	262
Cruise	500	320
TOTAL	**2,000**	**1,253**

Accommodation: There is a wide range of cabin sizes and configurations (28 categories), a throwback to the days when she was a ship operating transatlantic crossings, all of which feature really heavy-duty furniture, fittings, and doors. All of the cabins feature good storage space (many of the larger cabins have wood-paneled walls), although closet and storage space could become limited for long voyages, particularly in the smaller, lower-grade cabins.

The bathrooms are fairly large, with cabinets and shelf space for toiletries in most. Bathrobes are provided for all passengers, as are some personal toiletry amenities.

Anyone booking a suite or one of the top five grades receives Phoenix VIP service, which includes flowers for the cabin, separate check-in desk, and priority disembarkation.

Dining: There are two dining rooms, both of which are charming and comfortable (with high ceilings), but the tables are very close together; this means they are also quite noisy (although some would call this "ambience"). There is one seating.

The menu is moderately creative, the choice is rather limited, and the food is best described as "down-home basic." The service is friendly and attentive, in true European style (the staff do speak German), although there is little finesse in their style of service. Still, it is unpretentious.

Other Comments: This is a lovely, vintage, all-white classic ship with a forthright profile and a single, large, centrally placed funnel. She is sturdily constructed, has a riveted hull that is virtually impossible to find today, and has a deep draft that makes her very stable at sea, having been built as a two-class liner specifically for Cunard Line's transatlantic crossings in the 1950s.

She is an unpretentious ship with an interesting old-world ambience and charm that somehow helps to make up for the lack of finesse associated with more upscale, newer (and thus more expensive) products.

There is plenty of open deck and sunbathing space. There is a second swimming pool (fitted into what was formerly a cargo hold) for the use of children, as Phoenix Seereisen appeals particularly well to families with children. Particularly popular are two decks of sheltered promenade decks, which are ideal for strolling or just sitting on one of the many deck lounge chairs.

Inside the ship, a great deal of the dark wood paneling and trim that was used in her original interiors has been retained. There are also many solid brass accents throughout her interiors and public rooms. There is a fine, serene library, with a good selection of both hardback and paperback books, as well as some reference material.

There are, however, relatively few public rooms from which to choose, they are usually crowded, and it is hard to get away from the smell of stale cigarette smoke. There are also a number of "thresholds" or high sills to step over at doorways, particularly to the outside decks and pool area, and so the ship cannot be recommended to anyone confined to a wheelchair under any circumstances.

Features extensive, interesting destination-intensive itineraries. Young, willing Phoenix Seereisen staff members are aboard every cruise to help with shore excursions. There is a very informal atmosphere and a relaxed, casual dress code.

Although the ship has been generally well maintained, remember that she *is* an old ship, having been designed for transatlantic service, so the layout is somewhat disjointed, and passageways are narrow. Because she is a steamship, you should be aware of the possibility of black soot falling on the aft decks occasionally — in other words, do not wear white!

This ship will prove to be good for a first cruise experience with fellow German-speaking passengers and crew. Phoenix Seereisen always has a good onboard team of social staff to look after you, and the company's cruise directors are very experienced, fun-loving people who really do go out of their way to help you enjoy your cruise experience.

Far from being a new ship, she performs and behaves extremely well, and the resulting product is both entertaining and extremely reasonably priced for the popular market seeking an oceangoing holiday in totally relaxed, unstuffy, and unpretentious surroundings. It represents an excellent value-for-money cruise holiday. The currency aboard is the deutschmark.

m/v Ambasador I
★ +
(S)

LIFESTYLE:	STANDARD
Cruise Line:	Galapagos Cruises
Former Names:	*Jedinstvo/Aquanaut Ambassador/*
	Atlas Ambasador
Gross Tonnage:	2,573
Builder:	Brodogradiliste (Yugoslavia)
Original Cost:	n/a
Entered Service:	1959/1993
Flag:	Ecuador
Tel. No.:	n/a
Fax No.:	n/a
Length (ft/m):	296.2/90.30
Beam (ft/m):	42.7/13.03
Draft (ft/m):	14.0/4.20
Propulsion/Propellers:	diesel (7,060kw)/2 (FP)
Decks:	5
Total Crew:	68
Pass. Capacity (basis 2):	134
Pass. Capacity (all berths):	160
Pass. Space Ratio (basis 2):	19.2
Pass. Space Ratio (all berths):	16.0
Officers:	International
Total Cabins:	62
Size Range (sq ft/m):	n/a
Cabins (outside view):	43
Cabins (inside — no view):	19
Cabins (single occupancy):	0
Cabins (with private balcony):	0

Cabins (wheelchair accessible):	0
Cabin Current:	220 volts (DC)
Cabin TV:	No
Dining Rooms:	1
Elevators:	0
Casino:	No
Slot Machines:	No
Swimming Pools (outdoors):	1
Swimming Pools (inside):	0
Whirlpools:	0
Fitness Center:	No
Sauna/Steam Room:	No/No
Massage:	No
Self-Service Launderette:	No
Movie Theater/Seats:	No
Library:	Yes
Classification Society:	Jugoslavenski Registrar
	Brodova

RATINGS	POSSIBLE SCORE	SCORE ACHIEVED
Ship	500	139
Accommodation	200	71
Food	400	132
Service	400	179
Cruise	500	184
TOTAL	**2,000**	**705**

Accommodation: Although there are more than 10 cabin categories (higher decks command bigger prices), most of the cabins really are very small, with only the most minimal amount of furniture, fittings, and furnishings, and they are barely comfortable. Many cabins have upper/lower berths, and many accommodate three or four persons.

Dining: The dining room is reasonably pleasant, and it accommodates all passengers in a single sitting, but there are no tables for two. The service is quite forgettable, as is the food.

Other Comments: She is a real vintage style of ship (formerly owned and operated by a Yugoslavian shipping company) with a single, squat, blue funnel placed amidships. She is not a handsome vessel, by any stretch of the imagination. There is only a small amount of outdoor deck space for sunning.

Inside the ship there is only one main public room, the main lounge, which is used for just about every public activity. The public passageways are quite dark, and the carpeting is well worn.

This small cruise ship performs cruises of the Galapagos Islands, but not at a very modest price, so do not expect much. Although the ship can carry more passengers, there is a limit of 86 passengers for these cruises, set by the Galapagos National Park regulations.

The Galapagos National Park tax is an additional $80 per person (approximate), payable *in cash* when you land at your incoming airport.

Weak Points: The cruise prices are extremely high for what you get and for such an old vessel with limited facilities. The swimming pool is merely a "dip" pool.

t/s/s Apollon
★★ +
(M)

LIFESTYLE:	STANDARD
Cruise Line:	Royal Olympic Cruises/Direct Cruises
Former Names:	*Star of Texas, Mardi Gras, Empress of Canada*
Gross Tonnage:	28,574
Builder:	Vickers Armstrong (UK)
Original Cost:	UK8,250,000
Entered Service:	April 1962/April 1998
Flag:	Greece
Tel. No.:	761478975/76147896/323919310
Fax No.:	761478977/323919313
Length (ft/m):	650.0/198.13
Beam (ft/m):	86.7/26.45
Draft (ft/m):	29.0/8.83
Propulsion/Propellers:	steam turbine (22,400kW)/2 (FP)
Passenger Decks:	8
Total Crew:	408
Pass. Capacity (basis 2):	914
Pass. Capacity (all berths):	1,256
Pass. Space Ratio (basis 2):	31.2
Pass. Space Ratio (all berths):	23.0
Officers:	Greek
Total Cabins:	457
Size (sq ft/m):	n/a
Cabins (outside view):	193
Cabins (inside — no view):	260
Cabins (single occupancy):	8

Cabins (with private balcony):	0
Cabins (wheelchair accessible):	0
Cabin Current:	110 volts
Cabin TV:	No
Dining Rooms:	2
Elevators:	4
Casino:	Yes
Slot Machines:	Yes
Swimming Pools (outdoors):	2
Swimming Pools (inside):	1
Whirlpools:	0
Fitness Center:	Yes
Sauna/Steam Room:	Yes/No
Massage:	Yes
Self-Service Launderette:	No (has ironing room)
Movie Theater/Seats:	Yes/200
Library:	Yes
Classification Society:	Lloyd's Register

RATINGS	POSSIBLE SCORE	SCORE ACHIEVED
Ship	500	238
Accommodation	200	108
Food	400	200
Service	400	216
Cruise	500	235
TOTAL	**2,000**	**997**

Accommodation: In general, the cabins are reasonably large, with good heavy-duty fittings, and there are many different configurations, a carryover from the days when the ship operated as a former liner; all have private facilities, and all have been refurbished. However, many cabins have upper and lower berths instead of lower beds (Direct Cruises' brochure uses the same terminology for beds or berths, so make sure you get what you want). Some of the upper grades feature several different woods. No cabins have televisions, but they all have telephones and a good amount of closet and drawer space.

Dining: The main dining room has an elegant entrance, portholes, reasonably contemporary decor, and tables for four, six, or eight. Two seatings are featured. The cuisine is decidedly continental in style, and reasonably tasty, but the choice is not extensive. Service, from an international staff, is friendly but frenzied. The wine list is rather limited, but the prices are reasonable. There is also the informal Seaview Buffet Restaurant for casual self-service buffet-style breakfast and lunch, although the fare here is really very basic, with little creativity.

Other Comments: This ship is presently chartered to Direct Cruises after having several varied former lives. Early in 1995, Carnival Cruise Lines sold this ship to Royal Olympic Cruises in a stock swap when both parted company, and companies. Originally, however, she was built for Canadian Pacific for line voyages between England and Canada; this is the reason that she has a covered promenade deck. *Apollo* (the ship's actual name is *Apollon*) is the name used by Direct Cruises. This is a well-constructed former ocean liner that has a large midships funnel; she has been well maintained by her owners.

Sunbathing space on the open deck is limited when the ship is full, as some of the space is taken by seating for the outdoor section of the buffet restaurant. Inside, the numerous public rooms have high ceilings, a carryover from her original operators. You can also see some of the original woods and nicely polished brass fittings from the 1950s, as well as some neat custom-made carpeting. Has an indoor swimming pool and a good movie theater, features not found aboard many new cruise vessels.

This ship provides a reasonable cruise experience in a comfortable mix of contemporary and old-world surroundings, decor and colors. Good for a first, no-frills cruise experience for families seeking a cruise vacation at a very modest price aboard a real vintage ocean liner. For a large part of the year, the ship is under charter to Scotland-based Direct Cruises, in which case the cruise fare includes all gratuities, port charges, and travel insurance. For UK-based passengers, this means no flying, as the ship sails from Greenock, mostly on 14-day cruises.

Weak Points: These include the fact that this high-density ship is old, well worn, and tired in some areas; the gangway is narrow; there are a number of sills or "lips" at various doorways to negotiate.

SATELLITE NAVIGATOR

Using this latest high-tech piece of equipment, ship's officers can read, on a small television screen, the ship's position in the open ocean anywhere in the world, any time, and in any weather with pinpoint accuracy.

Satellite navigation systems use the information transmitted by a constellation of orbiting satellites. Each is in a normal circular polar orbit at an altitude of 450 to 700 nautical miles, and orbits the Earth in about 108 minutes. Data from each gives the current orbital position every two minutes. Apart from telling the ship where it is, it continuously provides the distance from any given point, calculate the drift caused by currents and so on, and tell the ship when the next satellite will pass.

The basis of the satellite navigation is the US Navy Satellite System (NNSS). This first became operational in January 1964 as the precision guidance system for the Polaris submarine fleet, and was made available for commercial use in 1967.

The latest system (and more accurate) is the GPS (Global Positioning System), which is now fitted to an increasing number of ships. This uses twenty-four satellites (eighteen, of which, are on-line at any given, time) that provide accuracy in estimating a ship's position to plus or minus six feet. Another variation is the NACOS (Navigational Command System), which collects information from a variety of sources: satellites, radar, gyroscopic compass, speed log, and surface navigational systems as well as engines, thrusters, rudders, and human input. It then displays relevant computations and information on one screen, controlled by a single keyboard.

m/t/s Arcadia
★ +
(S)

LIFESTYLE:	STANDARD
Cruise Line:	Golden Sun Cruises
Former Names:	*Angelina Lauro, Vicente Puchol, Arcadia*
Gross Tonnage:	5,200
Builder:	Union de Levante (Spain)
Original Cost:	n/a
Entered Service:	1969/May 1990
Flag:	Greece
Tel. No.:	113-2426
Fax No.:	n/a
Length (ft/m):	360.8/110.0
Beam (ft/m):	86.2/16.30
Draft (ft/m):	16.3/4.97
Propulsion/Propellers:	diesel (4,589kW)/2 (FP)
Passenger Decks:	6
Total Crew:	130
Pass. Capacity (basis 2):	270
Pass. Capacity (all berths):	342
Pass. Space Ratio (basis 2):	18.4
Pass. Space Ratio (all berths):	14.5
Officers:	Greek
Total Cabins:	139
Size (sq ft/m):	n/a
Cabins (outside view):	109
Cabins (inside — no view):	30
Cabins (single occupancy):	4
Balcony Cabins:	0

Cabins (wheelchair-accessible):	1
Cabin Current:	220 volts
Refrigerator:	No
Dining Rooms:	1
Sittings:	2
Elevators:	1
Casino:	Yes
Slot Machines:	Yes
Swimming Pools (outdoors):	1
Swimming Pools (inside):	0
Whirlpools:	0
Fitness Center:	Yes
Sauna:	Yes
Massage:	Yes
Self-Service Laundry:	No
Cinema/Theater:	No
Cabin TV:	No
Library:	Yes
Classification Society:	Hellenic Registry

RATINGS	POSSIBLE SCORE	SCORE ACHIEVED
Ship	500	142
Accommodation	200	72
Food	400	150
Service	400	196
Cruise	500	164
TOTAL	**2,000**	**724**

Accommodation: Although this *is* a small ship, the cabins are *extremely* small and come only just equipped with the bare essentials. Closet, drawer, and storage space is very limited, the ceilings are plain, and the bathrooms really are tiny. Four cabins have double beds, while all others have fixed twin beds or lower beds. Some cabins also have third/fourth person upper berths, although if you take one of these, not only do you need to be small, you need to make sure you don't have any luggage.

Dining: The dining room, although small, has large mirrors along both sides, making it appear double the size it actually is (however, there are no windows or portholes). Although noisy, it is somehow mildly charming, with its pastel pink color and warm, very casual ambience. Two seatings are featured. The cuisine is very basic fare (as is the price of a cruise) and so there is little choice in food, and the bread is of poor quality and choice. Adequate basic service, but it is hurried, and there's absolutely no finesse.

Other Comments: She is a small vessel (originally an ex-Spanish ferry) with an all-white hull, which divides superstructure and hull by a red line, and twin funnels; she was, for a short time, operated by the now-defunct Lauro Cruises as *Angelina Lauro*. A recent refurbishment makes the vessel smarter in her new "whites." The tiny aft swimming pool is really only a "cool dip" pool.

The interior decor is "1980s contemporary" and quite tastefully carried out, although there is too much use of reflective surfaces (mirrors), which dates it. Chairs in the public lounges (there are only two) are of the low back tub type, are not comfortable at all, and are prone to tipping over.

This ship has been well worn, and caters principally to European and Asian passengers seeking a small ship on which to cruise the Greek islands with minimum comfort and fuss. There is no finesse and the mixed crew displays only marginal hospitality and poor communication.

<u>Weak Points:</u> Has very low ceilings throughout. Vibration, engine noise, and diesel fumes are very evident in several areas, particularly in the center and aft sections of the vessel. The entertainment is provided at deafening volumes, and there are too many loud announcements.

m/s Arcadia
★★★★
(L)

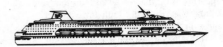

LIFESTYLE:	PREMIUM
Cruise Line:	P&O Cruises
Former Names:	*Star Princess, FairMajesty*
Gross Tonnage:	63,524
Builder:	Chantiers de L'Atlantique (France)
Original Cost:	$200 million
Entered Service:	March 1989/December 1997
Flag:	Great Britain
Tel. No.:	1240247
Fax No.:	1240236
Length (ft/m):	810.3/247.00
Beam (ft/m):	105.6/32.20
Draft (ft/m):	26.9/8.20
Propulsion/Propellers:	diesel-electric (39,000kW)/2 (CP)
Passenger Decks:	11
Total Crew:	650
Pass. Capacity (basis 2):	1,461
Pass. Capacity (all berths):	1,549
Pass. Space Ratio (basis 2):	43.4
Pass. Space Ratio (all berths):	41.0
Officers:	British
Total Cabins:	748
Size Range (sq ft/m):	179.7–529.6/16.7–49.2
Cabins (outside view):	583
Cabins (inside — no view):	165
Cabins (single occupancy):	64

Cabins (with private balcony):	50
Cabins (wheelchair accessible):	8
Cabin Current:	110 and 220 volts
Cabin TV:	Yes
Dining Rooms:	1
Elevators:	9
Casino:	Yes
Slot Machines:	Yes
Swimming Pools (outdoors):	3
Swimming Pools (inside):	0
Whirlpools:	4
Fitness Center:	Yes
Sauna/Steam Room:	Yes/No
Massage:	Yes
Self-Service Launderette:	Yes
Movie Theater/Seats:	Yes/205
Library:	Yes
Classification Society:	Lloyd's Register

RATINGS	POSSIBLE SCORE	SCORE ACHIEVED
Ship	500	379
Accommodation	200	151
Food	400	265
Service	400	279
Cruise	500	362
TOTAL	**2,000**	**1,436**

Accommodation: All inside and outside-view standard-grade cabins are of a decent size and are well equipped with an abundance of drawer and other storage space, some under-bed space for luggage, and walk-in closets. However, you should know that the sound insulation between cabins is extremely poor (televisions late at night can be particularly irritating). A number of cabins also feature third- and fourth-person berths, and some cabins are designated for single occupancy. The large, modular bathrooms have showers (none have bathtubs, as the ship was originally built for American passengers, who prefer showers) and personal toiletry amenity kits.

There are 14 suites and 36 mini-suites (each thoughtfully named after historical P&O ships of the past), and each has a private balcony (the partitions are not of the full floor-to-ceiling type, however, so you will probably hear your neighbors — or smell their smoke). All suites and cabins have large walk-in closets, private safe, refrigerator, television, telephone, and hairdryer. In addition, all suite bathrooms have a bathtub as well as a shower stall, and bathrobes. Room service for breakfast, afternoon tea, and snacks for suite occupants is quite basic, and should be better.

Dining: The multitiered Pacific Restaurant has a two-deck-high center ceiling, but dining in it can be fairly noisy, as the sound seems to reverberate everywhere. There are tables for two, four, six, or eight, mostly in small sections that help give a cozy feel to the room. Two seatings are featured. The food is typical of P&O, unpretentious and not memorable, although the choice is good. The presentation is straightforward, with little use of garnishes. The service is warm and friendly. The Great British Breakfast is always a popular and necessary feature of P&O ships, and *Arcadia* is no exception.

The indoor-outdoor "Conservatory" deck buffet restaurant (open for breakfast and lunch) is small, but there is also a pizzeria, an ice cream bar, a patisserie, an in-pool bar, and a wine bar.

Other Comments: This ship is the third to bear the name *Arcadia* (the name being taken from a mythical region of Greece) for P&O. The first *Arcadia* was launched in 1887, the second, in 1954. This latest (and largest) one has good seagoing characteristics and provides a fine replacement for the company's much-loved *Canberra* (taken out of service in late 1997).

She was originally built for Sitmar Cruises, which was absorbed into Princess Cruises in 1988 (the ship's former operators prior to P&O Cruises). She was extensively refurbished in late 1997, at the Harland & Wolff shipyard in Belfast, and reconfigured specifically for British cruise passengers. The ship is well proportioned and has a decent amount of open deck space for sunbathing around her twin swimming pools (one has a swim-up bar, a first for P&O Cruises) as well as on her open decks aft of the funnel.

When P&O Cruises acquired the ship from its sister company, Princess Cruises, a little "massaging" to her appointments and decor was done for her British passengers. The ship is used for regular cruises of 14 days, as well as an annual three-month-long around-the-world cruise.

Her interiors feature restrained contemporary styling mixed with traditional shipboard decor, including some pleasing art deco touches (chrome balustrades), so nothing jars the senses, is garish, or out of place. Her spacious public rooms, many of which have high ceilings, have tasteful decor. A good selection of artwork provides some warmth to what would otherwise be a rather clinical interior. Has a large, horseshoe-shaped balconied showroom, with adequate sight lines from most seats.

Little vignettes of the former P&O liner *Canberra* and the necessary cricket memorabilia are displayed resplendently in the wood-paneled "The Oval" pub, which also has a dance floor. She provides a traditional large ship cruise ambience for the many British repeat passengers who enjoy such facilities and some degree of anonymity. Families with children will enjoy P&O's excellent children's programs; there are special rooms for children and teenagers (there is also a night nursery).

The focal point of a three-deck-high foyer is highlighted by a stainless steel kinetic sculpture that brings one's attention to the multideck staircases, and afternoon tea dances are a delight here. There is a domed observation lounge atop the ship; because it is a little out of the traffic flow, it is a restful spot for cocktails, although it turns into a nightspot/discotheque for night owls. The Canberra Room houses memorabilia from the famous ship. Aside from the memorabilia, most of *Canberra*'s crew was transferred to *Arcadia*. Features an interesting assortment of worldwide cruise itineraries, and, incidentally, P&O's brochures are always logical in layout and easy to follow.

There is always a good mix of entertainment aboard the ships of P&O Cruises, and this includes the Theater at Sea, production shows, and cabaret acts suited to British taste. The children's playroom, called Peter Pan, is located aft and features an outdoor paddling pool and games area. There is no extra charge for use of the Night Nursery (6:00pm–2:00am).

P&O Cruises has a fine program of special theme cruises (antiques, The Archers, art appreciation, classical music, comedy, cricket, gardening, jazz, motoring, popular fiction, Scottish dance, and sequence dancing are among the themes); check with your travel agent to see what is available at the time you want to cruise.

<u>Weak Points</u>: There is no full wraparound promenade deck outdoors (open port and starboard walking areas stretch only partly along the sides). The stairways and passageways are dull, as are the painted cabin doors; the library is small, has poor lighting and few chairs; obstructed sight lines from many seats in the Palladium Showlounge (on both balcony and main levels).

m/s Arkona
★★★★
(M)

LIFESTYLE:	PREMIUM
Cruise Line:	Arkona Touristik
Former Names:	*Astor (I)*
Gross Tonnage:	18,591
Builder: Howaldtswerke Deutsche Werft (Germany)	
Original Cost:	$55 million
Entered Service:	December 1981/December 1995
Flag:	Liberia
Tel. No.:	1261462
Fax No.:	1261463
Length (ft/m):	539.2/164.35
Beam (ft/m):	74.1/22.60
Draft (ft/m):	20.0/6.11
Propulsion/Propellers:	diesel (13,200kW)/2 (CP)
Passenger Decks:	8
Total Crew:	243
Pass. Capacity (basis 2):	516
Pass. Capacity (all berths):	618
Pass. Space Ratio (basis 2):	36.0
Pass. Space Ratio (all berths):	30.0
Officers:	European
Total Cabins:	258
Size Range (sq ft/m):	150.0–725.0/13.4–65.3
Cabins (outside view):	176
Cabins (inside — no view):	82
Cabins (single occupancy):	0
Cabins (with private balcony):	0
Cabins (wheelchair accessible):	0
Cabin Current:	220 volts
Cabin TV:	Yes
Dining Rooms:	1
Elevators:	3
Casino:	No
Slot Machines:	No
Swimming Pools (outdoors):	1
Swimming Pools (inside):	1
Whirlpools:	0
Fitness Center:	Yes
Sauna/Steam Room:	Yes/No
Massage:	Yes
Self-Service Launderette:	No
Movie Theater/Seats:	No
Library:	Yes
Classification Society:	Germanischer Lloyd

RATINGS	POSSIBLE SCORE	SCORE ACHIEVED
Ship	500	389
Accommodation	200	153
Food	400	310
Service	400	309
Cruise	500	371
TOTAL	**2,000**	**1,532**

Accommodation: There are 14 categories of cabins from which to choose. Boat Deck suite rooms are simply lovely and have just about everything one would need. Most of the other, more standard cabins are also well appointed and decorated, and all feature crisp, clean colors (some might find them plain, as are the ceilings).

The bathrooms are compact but fully tiled, with a good cabinet for toiletries. The ship features good traditional European hotel service from a willing staff. All printed materials, including the brochure, are on recycled paper. Even the toilet paper is made from recycled paper. There is only a limited cabin service menu, however.

Dining: The Arkona Restaurant, located high in the ship, has big, ocean-view picture windows and is reasonably attractive, with dark wood paneling and restful decor; two seatings are featured. The food is adequate to very good, though choice is somewhat limited, but the service, by some charming waitresses, does help. The occasional formal candlelight dinners are romantic, and the daily outdoor deck buffets (for breakfast and luncheon) are varied.

Other Comments: This is a traditional cruise ship, originally constructed for the now defunct Astor Cruises, and has cruised under a charter to Seetours from 1985 until the year 2000 (Seetours was purchased by Deutsche Seetouristik/Arkona Tourisitik in late 1997).

She is a well-constructed modern vessel that has a handsome and well-balanced profile. There is a good amount of open deck and sunbathing space for her size, with some excellent teakwood decking and polished railings. Cushioned pads are provided for all deck lounge chairs. For the sports-minded, there is a large volleyball court.

Has beautifully appointed interior fittings and decor, with much rosewood paneling and trim. Subdued lighting and soothing ambience, highlighted by good artwork throughout. Has good meetings facilities, a fine library, and, perhaps more important, an excellent pub with draught German beer from Rostock.

There is an excellent indoor spa and fitness center, with a good range of facilities that include a swimming pool, fitness center, and three sunbed rooms for tanning sessions. In addition, sophisticated hospital facilities include oxygen multistep therapy.

The atmosphere is a little starchy. There are many cigarette and cigar smokers. Features good traditional European hotel service and mostly German (expensive, under the German flag) staff. The reception desk is open 24 hours daily.

Arkona features good value-for-money cruising in contemporary comfort, and is best recommended for passengers who appreciate quality, fine surroundings, good food, and excellent destination-intensive itineraries, all packaged neatly in a relaxed, informal ambience. Many of the cruises have special themes. Seetours/TUI staff are available aboard every cruise and go out of their way to make sure that you will have an excellent cruise experience in very comfortable surroundings. Has many repeat passengers, who enjoy an extremely friendly, mostly German crew (who provide a fun crew show). Port taxes are included. Gratuities are suggested at DM8–10 per person per day, and are pooled.

<u>Weak Points</u>: There is no wraparound promenade deck outdoors. The show lounge has 10 pillars obstructing the sight lines, and the stage is also the dance floor and cannot be raised for shows; entertainment, therefore, is mostly cabaret-style. Finally, nonsmokers should note that there are many cigarette and cigar smokers, and it is often hard to get away from them.

m/s Astor
★★★★
(M)

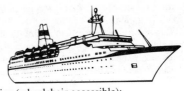

LIFESTYLE: **PREMIUM**

Cruise Line:	Transocean Tours
Former Names:	*Fedor Dostoyevskiy, Astor (II)*
Gross Tonnage:	20,158
Builder: Howaldtswerke Deutsche Werft (Germany)	
Original Cost:	$65 million
Entered Service:	February 1987/April 1997
Flag:	Bahamas
Tel. No.:	1402771/1402772
Fax No.:	1400125
Length (ft/m):	579.0/176.50
Beam (ft/m):	74.1/22.61
Draft (ft/m):	20.0/6.10
Propulsion/Propellers:	diesel (15,400kW)/2 (CP)
Passenger Decks:	7
Total Crew:	300
Pass. Capacity (basis 2):	590
Pass. Capacity (all berths):	650
Pass. Space Ratio (basis 2):	34.1
Pass. Space Ratio (all berths):	31.0
Officers:	Russian/Ukrainian
Total Cabins:	295
Size Range (sq ft/m):	140.0–280.0/13.0–26.0
Cabins (outside view):	199
Cabins (inside — no view):	96
Cabins (single occupancy):	0
Cabins (with private balcony):	0
Cabins (wheelchair accessible):	0
Cabin Current:	220 volts
Cabin TV:	Yes
Dining Rooms:	1
Elevators:	3
Casino:	No
Slot Machines:	No
Swimming Pools (outdoors):	1
Swimming Pools (inside):	1
Whirlpools:	0
Fitness Center:	Yes
Sauna/Steam Room:	Yes/No
Massage:	Yes
Self-Service Launderette:	No (ironing room)
Movie Theater/Seats:	No
Library:	Yes
Classification Society:	Germanischer Lloyd

RATINGS	POSSIBLE SCORE	SCORE ACHIEVED
Ship	500	398
Accommodation	200	157
Food	400	305
Service	400	308
Cruise	500	379
TOTAL	**2,000**	**1,547**

Accommodation: The cabins (there are 18 categories) are all very nicely appointed and tastefully decorated in fresh pastel colors, and have dark wood accents and cabinetry, so they are very restful. There is plenty of closet and drawer space in each cabin, as well as some under-bed storage space for luggage. The bathrooms are very practical, and each has a good-sized toiletries cabinet as well as all the necessary fittings, 100 percent cotton towels, and a bathrobe for each passenger.

In addition, the suites, which have a completely separate bedroom, living room, and bathroom, have a refrigerator as well as a minibar-refrigerator and a large boxed set of bathroom amenities.

However, the cabin service menu is poor and could be better (there is a charge for sandwiches, and little else is available).

Dining: The dining room is reasonably elegant, well laid out, and operates two seatings. It also has two small wings (good for private parties or groups of up to 30). The service throughout is friendly but unpretentious, and the food quality and presentation has received much attention and upgrading, with catering supplied by Zerbone of Italy. Menus are creative, and the quality and presentation are very good. In addition to the regular entrees (three for dinner), there is always a pasta dish and a vegetarian specialty dish.

The buffets are well presented and constantly refreshed, although the choice of foods could still be improved.

Other Comments: *Astor* was the original name for this ship, the larger of two ships bearing this same name in the 1980s, originally built for the now-defunct Astor Cruises. Her previous owners, the now defunct AquaMarin Cruises, again brought back the name *Astor* from her previous name, *Fedor Dostoyevskiy*.

She is a very attractive modern ship with a raked bow, a large squarish funnel, and a nicely balanced contemporary profile. The ship was constructed in the best German tradition (slightly larger than the first *Astor* (now called *Arkona*) and was extensively refurbished in late 1995 before commencing service for

AquaMarin Cruises. She was then was taken over by Transocean Tours in 1996 (she is under charter to Transocean Tours until 2007) following the collapse of AquaMarin Cruises.

This ship represents an excellent mix of traditional and contemporary styling. Built to a high standard (in a German shipyard), fine teakwood decking and polished wooden rails are seen outside almost everywhere.

She has an excellent amount of open deck and sunbathing space, as well as padded cushions for the deck lounge chairs. There is a basketball court for active passengers, and a large deck chess game on an aft deck.

Her interior fittings are of extremely fine quality. There is a supremely comfortable and varied array of public rooms and conference facilities, most of which have high ceilings. A wood-paneled tavern (always with good German lager on draught) is a fine retreat and extremely popular. There is a well-designed interior fitness center and large swimming pool, but the charge of DM10 for use of the sauna is absurd (there should be no charge at any time).

The company features interesting and well-designed destination-intensive worldwide itineraries, and cruises are at a very attractive price. The Russian/Ukrainian hotel staff is friendly without being obtrusive.

This ship, which caters exclusively to German-speaking passengers, provides style, comfort, and elegance, and a fine leisurely cruise experience in a relaxed, spacious setting (there is no crowding anywhere) that is less formal than a ship such as *Europa*. Port taxes, insurance, and gratuities are included in the cruise price. The ship can be booked at any DERPART, Transmarin, or UDR travel agency, and it represents a good choice for those seeking a well-packaged cruise in fine contemporary surroundings. Transocean Tours staff can be found aboard every cruise, some of which are designated as special-theme cruises. The currency aboard is the German deutschmark and the US dollar. Port taxes, insurance and all gratuities to staff are included.

<u>Weak Points</u>: The show lounge has pillars obstructing the sight lines, and the stage is also the dance floor and cannot be raised for shows; entertainment, therefore, is mostly cabaret-style. The bathroom towels are small and should be larger.

m/s Astra II
★★★
(S)

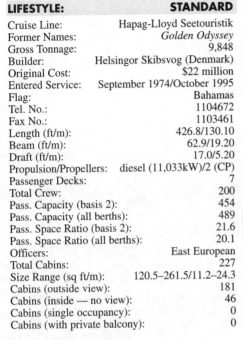

LIFESTYLE:	STANDARD
Cruise Line:	Hapag-Lloyd Seetouristik
Former Names:	*Golden Odyssey*
Gross Tonnage:	9,848
Builder:	Helsingor Skibsvog (Denmark)
Original Cost:	$22 million
Entered Service:	September 1974/October 1995
Flag:	Bahamas
Tel. No.:	1104672
Fax No.:	1103461
Length (ft/m):	426.8/130.10
Beam (ft/m):	62.9/19.20
Draft (ft/m):	17.0/5.20
Propulsion/Propellers:	diesel (11,033kW)/2 (CP)
Passenger Decks:	7
Total Crew:	200
Pass. Capacity (basis 2):	454
Pass. Capacity (all berths):	489
Pass. Space Ratio (basis 2):	21.6
Pass. Space Ratio (all berths):	20.1
Officers:	East European
Total Cabins:	227
Size Range (sq ft/m):	120.5–261.5/11.2–24.3
Cabins (outside view):	181
Cabins (inside — no view):	46
Cabins (single occupancy):	0
Cabins (with private balcony):	0

Cabins (wheelchair accessible):	0
Cabin Current:	110 volts
Cabin TV:	No
Dining Rooms:	1
Elevators:	2
Casino:	No
Slot Machines:	No
Swimming Pools (outdoors):	1
Swimming Pools (inside):	0
Whirlpools:	0
Fitness Center:	Yes
Sauna/Steam Room:	Yes/No
Massage:	Yes
Self-Service Launderette:	No
Movie Theater/Seats:	Yes/154
Library:	Yes
Classification Society:	Lloyd's Register

RATINGS	POSSIBLE SCORE	SCORE ACHIEVED
Ship	500	269
Accommodation	200	108
Food	400	227
Service	400	241
Cruise	500	289
TOTAL	**2,000**	**1,134**

Accommodation: Most of the cabins, although really small, are quite tastefully furnished and decorated, and have a reasonable amount of closet and drawer space, and pleasant artwork (the ceilings are plain, however). The bathrooms really are small, as are the towels. There is little space for one's toiletries, and the plumbing is tired and can be troublesome at times.

Dining: There is a single, comfortable dining room that was enlarged a few years ago. It features one seating for all meals and good quality continental food that is well presented. The menu choice is decent (given the price of a cruise), and the food is geared specifically to German tastes. There is a decent selection of cold cuts and cheeses at the buffets.

While there is not much finesse from the dining room staff, they are quite willing and eager to please. It is just that they have not been sent to the best culinary and hotel schools, so service tends to be basic but with a smile.

Other Comments: This is a fairly handsome-looking, compact ship that was well known in a previous life as Royal Cruise Line's *Golden Odyssey* and has a well-balanced, very compact, almost handsome profile that could be termed "cute." The ship has been fairly well maintained, although she is now more than 20 years old, and that means that plumbing can prove troublesome for such ships.

Originally constructed to accommodate the passenger load of a chartered Boeing 747 jet aircraft, this ship offers comfortable surroundings, at a moderate price, to a well-chosen palette of destinations.

This intimate little ship has already established a loyal following, and for good reason. The ship is clean and tidy throughout, and well maintained; she has a teakwood promenade deck outdoors, which is good for strolling, with several deck lounge chairs available for those who just like to sit, read, and watch the world go by. There is a good selection of public rooms for the size of the ship, with a couple of good bars (naturally, with German lager on draught).

An attentive staff offers fine-tuned personal service that is personable without being condescending, although a sense of tiredness prevails. Ideally suited to passengers who want a small ship atmosphere and who do not like big ships, A*stra II* is presently under a three-year charter to Hapag-Lloyd Seetouristik (this ends in October 2000). The ship is marketed to passengers seeking a decent cruise experience at a low price, with destination-intensive itineraries.

The staff does a good job of keeping their passengers informed, entertained, and very grateful for their presence. Do remember when choosing a cruise that, as in many other areas of life, you get what you pay for. Having said that, this ship will provide a comfortable setting for a first cruise experience in surroundings that are cozy, intimate, and well run.

Weak Points: The gangway is steep and narrow in many ports, and may prove difficult for older passengers. The plumbing is tired and troublesome at times. There are no cushioned pads for the deck lounge chairs. The passenger hallways are narrow. Storage space for luggage in the cabins is very limited.

THE COMPASS

This is the instrument by which a ship may be steered on a pre-selected course, and by which bearings of *visible* objects can be taken in order to fix a ship's position on a navigation chart. There are two kinds:

The magnetic compass uses the inherent magnetic forces within and around the Earth;

The gyrocompass, a relatively recent invention, uses the properties of gyroscopic inertia and precession, ideally to align itself to a true north–south position.

STEERING

Two different methods can be used to steer a ship:

Electrohydraulic steering uses automatic (telemotor-type) transmission from the wheel itself to the steering gear aft. This is generally used in conditions of heavy traffic, during maneuvers into and out of ports, or when there is poor visibility.

Automatic steering (gyropilot) is used only in the open sea. This system does not require anyone at the wheel because it is controlled by computer. However, aboard all ships, a quartermaster is always at the wheel, for extra safety, and just in case a need should arise to switch from one steering system to another.

m/s Asuka
★★★★ +
(M)

LIFESTYLE:	PREMIUM
Cruise Line:	NYK Cruises
Former Names:	-
Gross Tonnage:	28,856
Builder:	Mitsubishi Heavy Industries (Japan)
Original Cost:	$86 million
Entered Service:	December 1991
Flag:	Japan
Tel. No.:	343148652
Fax No.:	343148641
Length (ft/m):	632.5/192.81
Beam (ft/m):	81.0/24.70
Draft (ft/m):	20.3/6.20
Propulsion/Propellers:	diesel (17,300kW)/2 (CP)
Passenger Decks:	8
Total Crew:	262 (includes officers)
Pass. Capacity (basis 2):	600
Pass. Capacity (all berths):	618
Pass. Space Ratio (basis 2):	48.0
Pass. Space Ratio (all berths):	46.6
Officers:	Japanese
Total Cabins:	300
Size Range (sq ft/m):	182.9–649.0/17.0–60.3
Cabins (outside view):	300
Cabins (inside — no view):	0
Cabins (single occupancy):	0
Cabins (with private balcony):	108
Cabins (wheelchair accessible):	2
Cabin Current:	110 volts
Cabin TV:	Yes
Dining Rooms:	1 (+ sushi restaurant)
Elevators:	5
Casino:	Yes
Slot Machines:	Yes
Swimming Pools (outdoors):	1
Swimming Pools (inside):	0
Whirlpools:	3
Fitness Center:	Yes
Sauna/Steam Room:	Yes/Yes
Massage:	Yes
Self-Service Launderette:	Yes
Movie Theater/Seats:	Yes/97
Library:	Yes
Classification Society:	Nippon Kaiji Kyokai

RATINGS	POSSIBLE SCORE	SCORE ACHIEVED
Ship	500	430
Accommodation	200	174
Food	400	341
Service	400	334
Cruise	500	402
TOTAL	**2,000**	**1,681**

Accommodation: There are many categories, but really only five types of suites and cabins, many of them with a small private balcony. All have unobstructed ocean views.

In all grades, all of the blond wood cabinetry has rounded edges, and excellent insulation is provided, as well as a good amount of closet and drawer space, including some lockable drawers. A tea-making unit, refrigerator, bathrobe, slippers, down quilts instead of blankets. All grades feature full, deep bathtubs (while the "club" suite bathrooms are of generous proportions, the standard bathrooms are rather small) and a range of personal toiletry items.

The "club" suites (the most expensive grade) are excellent, have a generous amount of space, and are very well decorated. In addition to all the standard amenities, binoculars are also provided. The bathrooms are of generous proportions. There is no butler service in the "club" suites. Four new suites were added to Panorama Deck 10 in the ship's 1999 dry-dock.

The balcony door handles are awkward.

Dining: The main dining room, which is laid out so that it appears to be in two sections, with ocean-view windows along one side only, has a good amount of space around the tables, although there are very few tables for two. Features two seatings and both Japanese and western cuisine; traditional Japanese breakfast and luncheon, and mainly western-style dinners. The Hotel Okura chain provides the menus and the food. Although there are some good wines, the range of sake is limited.

"Umihiko" is a small à la carte sushi bar that features fresh seafood, beautifully prepared and presented (at extra cost) and a good selection of Japanese sake. It is open also for lunch as well as dinner on some short cruises, and for dinner on longer cruises.

For casual breakfasts and lunches, an informal self-serve Lido Café is provided. This popular eatery was expanded in 1999 and now provides more indoor seating.

A traditional *washitsu* tatami room (the whole floor is covered in tatami mats, no shoes allowed) for special afternoon tea ceremonies.

Other Comments: When introduced, she was the first all-new large ship specially designed for the still slow growing Japanese cruise market, and the largest cruise ship constructed in Japan (for the Japanese market).

The ship has pleasing exterior styling and profile, with a large, squat funnel. There is a good amount of open deck space (Japanese passengers do not use it much, however). There is a wraparound promenade deck outdoors, good for strolling.

The "cake-layer" stacking of the public rooms hampers passenger flow and makes it somewhat disjointed, although the ship's Japanese passengers like the separation of public rooms. There are many intimate public rooms and plenty of space so that there is never a feeling of crowding. There is an excellent, spacious, and true Japanese grand bath. However, the massage room is located away from the grand bath area and would be better if it were integrated.

Features elegant interior decor that is understated, and pleasing color combinations, fine-quality fabrics, soft furnishings, and a relaxing ambience. Fascinating Japanese artwork is featured, including a multideck mural located on the wall of the main foyer staircase. The Mariner's Club, decorated in the style of an English gentlemen's club, is a popular evening spot.

Cellular pay phones are located in one of the deck foyers, good for use when operating short cruises around Japan. Features a good mix of western and traditional Japanese entertainment. Provides good meetings facilities with some of the latest high-tech equipment available.

There are formal and informal nights as far as the dress code goes, while during the day, the dress code is very casual. One nice touch — streamers are still used when the ship is cruising around Japan — a tradition that so many other cruise ships have stopped. Gratuities are neither expected nor allowed. Note that children under 10 are not generally accepted.

<u>Weak Points</u>: The forward staircase is utilitarian and quite plain. The ship is in need of further refurbishment and upgrading in some areas in order to compete effectively in the international marketplace.

m/v Atalante
★ +
(S)

LIFESTYLE:	STANDARD
Cruise Line:	New Paradise Cruises
Former Names:	*Tahitien*
Gross Tonnage:	13,562
Builder:	Direction des Construction et Armes Navales, France
Original Cost:	n/a
Entered Service:	May 1953/December 1992
Flag:	Cyprus
Tel. No.:	3579545600
Fax No.:	3579370298
Length (ft/m):	548.5/167.20
Beam (ft/m):	67.9/20.70
Draft (ft/m):	20.7/6.3
Propulsion/Propellers:	diesel (7,700kW)/2 (FP)
Passenger Decks:	7
Total Crew:	170
Pass. Capacity (basis 2):	484
Pass. Capacity (all berths):	518
Pass. Space Ratio (basis 2):	26.1
Pass. Space Ratio (all berths):	19.2
Officers:	Cypriot/Greek
Total Cabins:	260
Size Range (sq ft/m):	129.1–247.5/12.0–23.0
Cabins (outside view):	171
Cabins (inside — no view):	89
Cabins (single occupancy):	2
Cabins (with private balcony):	0
Cabins (wheelchair accessible):	0
Cabin Current:	220 volts (DC)
Cabin TV:	No
Dining Rooms:	1
Elevators:	0
Casino:	Yes
Slot Machines:	Yes
Swimming Pools (outdoors):	2
Swimming Pools (inside):	0
Whirlpools:	0
Fitness Center:	No
Sauna/Steam Room:	No/No
Massage:	No
Self-Service Launderette:	No
Movie Theater/Seats:	No
Library:	No
Classification Society:	Bureau Veritas

RATINGS	POSSIBLE SCORE	SCORE ACHIEVED
Ship	500	153
Accommodation	200	73
Food	400	146
Service	400	177
Cruise	500	162
TOTAL	**2,000**	**711**

Accommodation: The cabins, in 10 grades, are all rather small and spartan, although most have been redecorated in pastel shades. While many cabins have two lower beds, many also have third- and fourth-person upper Pullman berths. There is limited closet space, but you do not need much clothing for this casual cruise environment. Note that additional cabins that were installed in a 1993 refit are noisy and subject to extreme squeaks, which makes them quite difficult to sleep in. The top-grade cabins also have a refrigerator.

Dining: The Venus Dining Room is located low down in the ship and always seems to have a musty odor. Buffets are featured for most meals, and the food really is quite basic — with few choices and unimaginative presentation. Service is provided mainly by Greek waiters, who are friendly but without finesse. There is also a small cafeteria for casual snacks.

Other Comments: Now well over 40 years of age, the ship, a former passenger-car liner, is showing its age in a number of places, having gone through many changes during her long life. She has a small, squat funnel amidships and a really long foredeck (something that is not generally found aboard new ships). She is a stable ship at sea, with a deep draft, and rides well. There is a generous amount of open deck and sunbathing space, but the outdoor decking is well worn in several places.

The number of public rooms is very limited, and the layout is quite awkward and disjointed. Recent decor changes are for the better, although still much of the interior decor is also dated and worn, yet adequate and comfortable for those who do not want the glitz of newer ships. Much emphasis is placed on duty-free shopping.

This ship is perhaps acceptable for younger, budget-minded passengers wanting to party and travel with just the basics and without the need for much service. The ship operates two- and three-night short, very casual cruises from Cyprus to Egypt and Israel. The currency used on board is the Cyprus Pound.

Weak Points: The nightlife really is disco-loud. There is no finesse anywhere, although the staff is reasonably enthusiastic. There is a steep gangway in some ports.

m/s Aurora
(L)

LIFESTYLE:	STANDARD
Cruise Line:	P&O Cruises
Former Names:	-
Gross Tonnage:	76,000
Builder:	Meyer Werft (Germany)
Original Cost:	$375 million
Entered Service:	May 2000
Flag:	Great Britain
Tel. No.:	n/a
Fax No.:	n/a
Length (ft/m):	885.8/270.0
Beam (ft/m):	105.6/32.2
Draft (ft/m):	25.9/7.9
Propulsion/Propellers:	diesel-electric (40,000kW)/2 (FP)
Decks:	10
Total Crew:	815
Pass. Capacity (basis 2):	1,850
Pass. Capacity (all berths):	1,975
Pass. Space Ratio (basis 2):	41.0
Pass. Space Ratio (all berths):	38.4
Officers:	British
Total Cabins:	934
Size Range (sq ft/m):	150.6–953.0/14.0–88.5
Cabins (outside view):	655
Cabins (inside — no view):	279
Cabins (single occupancy):	0
Cabins (with private balcony):	414

Cabins (wheelchair accessible):	22
	(8 with private balcony)
Cabin Current:	110 and 220 volts
Cabin TV:	Yes
Dining Rooms:	2 main
Elevators:	10
Casino:	Yes
Slot Machines:	Yes
Swimming Pools (outdoors):	3 (1 with magrodome)
Swimming Pools (inside):	0
Whirlpools:	5
Fitness Center:	Yes
Sauna/Steam Room:	Yes/Yes
Massage:	Yes
Self-Service Launderette:	Yes
Movie Theater/Seats:	Yes/200
Library:	Yes
Classification Society:	Lloyd's Register

RATINGS	POSSIBLE SCORE	SCORE ACHIEVED
Ship	500	NYR
Accommodation	200	NYR
Food	400	NYR
Service	400	NYR
Cruise	500	NYR
TOTAL	**2,000**	**NYR**

Note: The score is expected to be similar to that of sister ship *Oriana*.

Accommodation: All cabins, from the largest to the smallest, provide the following common features: polished cherry wood laminates, tea- and coffee-making facilities (a P&O first), as well as a personal safe, refrigerator, television, individually-controlled air-conditioning, sofa, coffee table, and twin beds that convert to a queen-size bed. There are four whole decks of cabins with private balconies (this is about 40 percent of all cabins), and they feature sliding glass floor-to-ceiling doors.

The largest suites are two penthouse suites (named Library Suite and Piano Suite), each spread over two decks in height, connected by a spiral staircase. The living area is on the lower deck (Deck 10), and incorporates a dining suite (a first in a P&O ship) and a private balcony. Upstairs on Deck 11, the bedroom, complete with walk-in closet (and bathroom, in porcelain and polished granite, with twin basins, bathtub, and separate shower enclosure) also incorporates a private balcony. Both suites measure approximately 908.5 sq ft (84.4 m^2) excluding the balconies.

Dining: The two main dining rooms, Alexandria and Medina (each seats 525), feature tables for two, four, six, eight, and ten, and there are two seatings. Medina, the midships restaurant, features Moorish theme decor, while Alexandria, with windows on three sides, features Egyptian decor. Both restaurants feature more tables for two aboard this ship than in the equivalent restaurants aboard sister ship *Oriana*. In addition to the two formal dining rooms, there are several other dining options.

You can have dinner in the 24-hour 120-seat bistro-style restaurant, the Café Bordeaux; or breakfast and lunch in a colorful eatery named The Orangery. Other more casual eating options include the Sidewalk Café (for fast food items), a French patisserie (for pastries and coffee), and, in a first for a P&O cruise ship, a champagne bar. There's also Raffles coffee and chocolate bar (but there are no ceiling fans).

Other Comments: *Aurora* (named after the carnation Dianthus Aurora) is built specifically for the growing British traditional cruise market, is based at Southampton, England, and is a sister ship and running mate to the company's popular *Oriana*. As ships evolve, slight differences in layout occur, as is the case with *Aurora* over sister ship *Oriana*. This ship has a magrodome-covered indoor/outdoor swimming pool (good for all weather conditions).

The focal point of the four-deck-high atrium lobby is a dramatic, calming, 35-feet-high (10.6 meters), Lalique-style sculpture (actually made of fiberglass) of two mythical figures behind a veil of water. At the top of the atrium is the ship's library (larger and in a different location than in *Oriana*), complete with eight computer stations and several audio chairs for CD listening.

Other features include a virtual reality games room, 12 bars (one of them has a fireplace and mahogany paneling, another is a sports bar), golf simulator, business center, and movie theater (so few new ships have these today) that doubles as a concert hall.

Families with children are well catered to, with children's and teenagers' rooms, and a night nursery. In addition, there are 16 cabins with interconnecting doors — good for families with children (or a maid).

For well-being, a gymnasium and aerobics studio is linked to the beauty and health services by a spiral stairway.

The library also houses several writing desks as well as audio chairs (in which you can relax with a good compact disc).

All dance aficionados will be pleased to note that there are four wooden dance floors aboard this ship.

t/s Ausonia
★★★
(M)

LIFESTYLE: **STANDARD**

Cruise Line:	Louis Cruise Lines/First Choice
Former Names:	-
Gross Tonnage:	12,609
Builder:	Cantieri Riuniti dell' Adriatico (Italy)
Original Cost:	n/a
Entered Service:	September 1957/May 1998
Flag:	Cyprus
Tel. No.:	n/a
Fax No.:	n/a
Length (ft/m):	522.5/159.26
Beam (ft/m):	69.8/21.29
Draft (ft/m):	21.4/6.54
Propulsion/Propellers:	steam turbine (12,799kW)/2 (FP)
Passenger Decks:	8
Total Crew:	280
Pass. Capacity (basis 2):	508
Pass. Capacity (all berths):	701
Pass. Space Ratio (basis 2):	24.8
Pass. Space Ratio (all berths):	17.9
Officers:	Greek/Cypriot
Total Cabins:	254
Size Range (sq ft/m):	69.9–269.1/6.5–25.0
Cabins (outside view):	152
Cabins (inside — no view):	102
Cabins (single occupancy):	1
Cabins (with private balcony):	0
Cabins (wheelchair accessible):	0
Cabin Current:	220 volts
Cabin TV:	Upper-grade cabins only
Dining Rooms:	1
Elevators:	1
Casino:	Yes
Slot Machines:	Yes
Swimming Pools (outdoors):	1
Swimming Pools (indoor):	0
Whirlpools:	1
Fitness Center:	Yes
Sauna/Steam Room:	Yes/No
Massage:	Yes
Self-Service Laundry:	No
Movie Theater/Seats:	Yes/125
Library:	Yes
Classification Society:	Registro Navale Italiano

RATINGS	POSSIBLE SCORE	SCORE ACHIEVED
Ship	500	256
Accommodation	200	93
Food	400	260
Service	400	241
Cruise	500	259
TOTAL	**2,000**	**1,109**

Accommodation: From suites to standard inside and outside cabins, all are small and compact, yet reasonably comfortable, in six cabin grades. They have all the basics, including a private bathroom and adequate closet space for frugal packers (drawer space is limited, however).

The uppermost cabin grades feature a full-size bathtub (two suites feature whirlpool baths), while all others have showers. There are several family cabins. Note that some inside and outside standard cabins have upper and lower berths.

Dining: The dining room (totally nonsmoking) is set high up in the vessel, has good ocean views from large picture windows, and features fine china and pleasant table settings. Tables are for four, six, or eight, in two seatings. Features friendly, efficient service with well programmed flair and attention. The cuisine is international in nature and provides a good mix of continental fare, with some regional Mediterranean specialties and British favorites. The selection of fruits and cheeses is perhaps limited. The wine list, while basic, provides an inexpensive range and a decent choice of wines.

Other Comments: This all-white ship has a somewhat classic steamship profile, with a large, single funnel placed amidships. There is a decent amount of open deck and sunning space, although the swimming pool is tiny (it's really only a "dip" pool). She was purchased by Louis Cruise Lines in 1997 and underwent an extensive amount of refurbishing and upgrading in October 1998. Under her previous owners she had not been well maintained during the past few years and is now still in need of a lot of attention to detail. There is a reasonable amount of open deck and sunning space. The ship has also undergone much mechanical and galley upgrading.

Inside the vessel, most of the public rooms are located on one deck (Corfu Deck), so it is easy to find one's way around. Most of the public areas have had upgraded decor and color changes, and they are now lighter and more cheerful, with new soft furnishings.

The number of public lounges and rooms is, however, limited. The Majorca Lounge (main show lounge) is pleasantly decorated, although the sight lines to the stage area are poor due to a large number of pillars obstructing the view; seats on the raised sections on the port and starboard sides are slightly better. There is also a small nightclub, a casino, a duty-free shop, an enclosed "winter garden" lounge/reading area on the starboard side, and a cinema.

This ship is presently under a charter arrangement to the UK's First Choice Holidays and will provide a good, no-frills first cruise experience for those who choose to cruise on a limited budget, with all the basics in place. Hopefully the ship will exceed your expectations.

<u>Weak Points</u>: There are few public rooms. Many passengers are heavy smokers and it is difficult to avoid them. Has a narrow gangway (this can be steep in some ports). You can book the deck you want your cabin to be on, but cabins are assigned by First Choice Cruises.

THE BRIDGE

A ship's navigation bridge is manned at all times, both at sea and in port. Besides the captain, who is master of the vessel, other senior officers take "watch" turns for four- or eight-hour periods. In addition, junior officers are continually honing their skills as experienced navigators, waiting for the day when they will be promoted to master.

The captain is always in command at times of high risk, such as when the ship is entering or leaving a port, when the density of traffic is particularly high, or when visibility is severely restricted by poor weather.

Navigation has come a long way since the days of the ancient mariners, who used only the sun and the stars to calculate their course across the oceans. The space-age development of sophisticated navigation devices (using satellites) has enabled us to eliminate the guesswork of early navigation (the first global mobile satellite system came into being in 1979).

A ship's navigator today can establish accurately where the ship is in any weather and at any time. There follows a description of some of the navigation instruments, which will help you understand the complexities of seamanship today.

m/v Azur
★★★
(M)

LIFESTYLE:	STANDARD
Cruise Line:	Festival Cruises
Former Names:	*Eagle, Azur*
Gross Tonnage:	14,717
Builder:	Dubigeon-Normandie (France)
Original Cost:	n/a
Entered Service:	May 1971/April 1994
Flag:	Panama
Tel. No.:	1332515
Fax No.:	335495215
Length (ft/m):	465.8/142.00
Beam (ft/m):	71.8/21.90
Draft (ft/m):	18.11/5.76
Propulsion/Propellers:	diesel (16,300kW)/2 (CP)
Passenger Decks:	7
Total Crew:	350
Pass. Capacity (basis 2):	720
Pass. Capacity (all berths):	850
Pass. Space Ratio (basis 2):	20.4
Pass. Space Ratio (all berths):	17.3
Officers:	Greek
Total Cabins:	361
Size Range (sq ft/m):	94.7–212.0/8.8–19.7
Cabins (outside view):	148
Cabins (inside — no view):	213
Cabins (single occupancy):	2
Cabins (with private balcony):	0

Cabins (wheelchair accessible):	2
Cabin Current:	220 volts
Cabin TV:	Yes (upper grades only)
Dining Rooms:	1
Elevators:	3
Casino:	Yes
Slot Machines:	Yes
Swimming Pools (outdoors):	2
Swimming Pools (inside):	0
Whirlpools:	0
Fitness Center:	Yes
Sauna/Steam Room:	Yes/No
Massage:	No
Self-Service Launderette:	No
Movie Theater/Seats:	Yes/175
Library:	Yes
Classification Society:	Bureau Veritas

RATINGS	POSSIBLE SCORE	SCORE ACHIEVED
Ship	500	265
Accommodation	200	112
Food	400	259
Service	400	277
Cruise	500	285
TOTAL	**2,000**	**1,198**

Accommodation: Most of the cabins are of a decent size, but many also have upper berths, thus accommodating three or four persons. Note that there are many inside cabins (there are more insides than outsides). These are, naturally, the least expensive, but they have a limited amount of storage space (the under-bed storage space is good, however). Although the cabins are plain, they are furnished and decorated in soft earth tones accented by brightly colored soft furnishings. All have a private bathroom, nicely refurbished with tiled floor, shower, retractable clothes drying line, and good storage space for personal toiletries.

A number of deluxe cabins have a full bathtub/shower combination, hairdryer, illuminated closets, minibar-refrigerator, and plenty of closet, drawer, and under-bed storage space.

There are two outside cabins for the physically challenged, but the ship really cannot be recommended for anyone in a wheelchair, as access to most of it is difficult at best.

The cabin insulation is poor throughout the ship. Housekeeping is provided by a friendly group of Goanese cabin staff.

Dining: The low-ceilinged dining room (totally nonsmoking) is reasonably charming and has large ocean-view windows on three sides, but the chairs are not really comfortable. Two seatings are featured. The food is actually good, and its presentation is attractive, as are the menus. There is a rather limited selection of breads, fruits, and cheeses. The dining room service is provided by waiters, many of whom are multilingual. Meal hours can vary, depending on the itinerary (and shore excursions). The wine list is decent (the wines are young, however), and prices are modest. Informal breakfast and lunch buffets are adequate but never seem to look very attractive, the result of a food concession that is used to the repetition and routine of doing things the same way all the time. There is, however, plenty of food.

Other Comments: This fairly smart, though somewhat stubby-looking ship (the first ship that this relatively new cruise line placed into service) has a very short bow and twin tall funnels and was originally constructed as a cruise-ferry. There is a modest amount of open deck space for sunbathing, and this becomes really tight when the ship is full (which is most of the time). There are no cushioned pads for the plastic deck lounge chairs. The two swimming pools (located on different decks, one atop the ship, the other aft) are very small (more like "dip" pools).

Inside, the layout is a little awkward to get used to at first, with many stairways in the aft section of the ship that have short, steep steps (this is typical of her original cruise-ferry construction). There is a reasonable selection of public rooms and several bars, with light, upbeat decor and the use of many mirrored surfaces (if you wear glasses, reflections could prove to be a problem). The show room has extremely poor sight lines and a low ceiling, although it is good for group meetings and lectures. A cinema (it is unusual for a ship of this size to have one) is used for movies and lectures. There is almost always lively action in the casino (which has its own bar), although the room is somewhat out of the main passenger flow. A two-deck-high indoor volleyball court is a bonus for sports fans, although it is located adjacent to the children's playroom.

The ship looks really neat and tidy in most areas, but in some others she looks unkempt and sloppy, the result of uneven refurbishments.

Festival Cruises has done a good job of creating a totally European product in a short space of time, and garnered a good name for honest, value-for-money cruising. Festival Cruises (known in the US as First European Cruises) provides destination-intensive cruises principally aimed at European passengers. The ship is a popular vessel for those seeking a friendly environment, and should appeal to the young, active set looking for a good first cruise experience to a host of destinations, at an extremely attractive price. Add the ingredients of friendly service, unpretentious but tasty food, and a mix of international passengers speaking many different languages, and what you get is extremely good value for money, despite the fact that the ship is tired and well worn in places.

The ship provides all announcements, daily programs, news, entertainment, and shore excursions in five languages.

Weak Points: It is difficult to find quiet spaces, as music is playing constantly in all public rooms and open spaces (for ambience). Constant announcements in several languages are irritating. The poolside towels are small and thin. The show lounge is really poor. Cinema seats are not staggered, so sight lines can be awkward.

Deck lounge chairs stacked and ready for another day.

m/s Black Prince
★★★
(S)

LIFESTYLE:	STANDARD
Cruise Line:	Fred Olsen Cruise Lines
Former Names:	-
Gross Tonnage:	11,209
Builder:	Fender Werft (Germany)
Original Cost:	$20 million
Entered Service:	1966
Flag:	Norway
Tel. No.:	1313217
Fax No.:	1313217
Length (ft/m):	470.4/143.40
Beam (ft/m):	66.6/20.30
Draft (ft/m):	20.0/6.10
Propulsion/Propellers:	diesel (12,310kW)/2 (CP)
Passenger Decks:	7
Total Crew:	200
Pass. Capacity (basis 2):	446
Pass. Capacity (all berths):	517
Pass. Space Ratio (basis 2):	25.1
Pass. Space Ratio (all berths):	21.6
Officers:	European
Total Cabins:	238
Size Range (sq ft/m):	80.7–226.0/7.5–21.0
Cabins (outside view):	168
Cabins (inside — no view):	70
Cabins (single occupancy):	30
Cabins (with private balcony):	0

Cabins (wheelchair accessible):	2
Cabin Current:	230 volts
Cabin TV:	Yes
Dining Rooms:	2
Elevators:	2
Casino:	Yes
Slot Machines:	No
Swimming Pools (outdoors):	1
Swimming Pools (inside):	1
Whirlpools:	2
Fitness Center:	Yes
Sauna/Steam Room:	Yes/No
Massage:	Yes
Self-Service Launderette:	No
Movie Theater/Seats:	No
Library:	Yes
Classification Society:	Det Norske Veritas

RATINGS	POSSIBLE SCORE	SCORE ACHIEVED
Ship	500	293
Accommodation	200	116
Food	400	215
Service	400	241
Cruise	500	279
TOTAL	**2,000**	**1,144**

Accommodation: There is a wide range of cabin sizes and configurations, and a good percentage of cabins are for single passengers. Many cabins have poor air-conditioning, however, and hard beds. The outside suites are decent (particularly comfortable are the Gran Canaria and Lanzarote suites, with their wood-paneled walls) and nicely appointed. Other cabins are small but nicely equipped and tastefully decorated, for a smaller ship. Note that there is a charge for room service. The upper-grade cabins also have refrigerators.

Dining: The two main dining rooms have big picture windows. There are two seatings (sometimes first- and second-seating diners exchange seatings, a good arrangement). The food is generally of high quality, but there could be more menu choice, particularly at the buffet lunches. Has a very limited, basic wine list. Service is by Filipino stewards.

Other Comments: This is a solidly built ship that has been well maintained but has a rather ungainly profile, and she does tend to pitch heavily in unkind seas.

Features a good indoor fitness/leisure center, complete with an indoor swimming pool (unusual for a small ship, added in 1996) and a spa area.

Very homely, restrained decor, feel, and ambience, with much of the soft furnishings hand-tailored on board. Good wooden stairways throughout, although the steps are a little steep. An ironing room is provided.

This small ship has a friendly feel and ambience, an almost totally Filipino staff, and is well suited to the informal, older, British passenger, but the standards of service are slipping. Still, there are many repeat passengers who would not dream of trying another ship.

Weak Points: It is often difficult to get away from smokers, and the service has become overly casual and sloppy of late. The company lists recommended gratuities of £4.00 per passenger per day.

m/s Black Watch
★★★★
(M)

LIFESTYLE:	STANDARD
Cruise Line:	Fred Olsen Cruise Lines
Former Names:	*Star Odyssey, Westward,*
	Royal Viking Star
Gross Tonnage:	28,492
Builder:	Wartsila (Finland)
Original Cost:	$22.5 million
Entered Service:	June 1972/November 1996
Flag:	Bahamas
Tel. No.:	(47) 51848630
Fax No.:	(47) 51848630
Length (ft/m):	674.1/205.47
Beam (ft/m):	82.6/25.20
Draft (ft/m):	24.7/7.55
Propulsion/Propellers:	diesel (13,400kW)/2 (CP)
Passenger Decks:	8
Total Crew:	330
Pass. Capacity (basis 2):	801
Pass. Capacity (all berths):	892
Pass. Space Ratio (basis 2):	35.5
Pass. Space Ratio (all berths):	31.9
Officers:	European
Total Cabins:	422
Size Range (sq ft/m):	135.6–579.1/12.6–53.8
Cabins (outside view):	375
Cabins (inside — no view):	47
Cabins (single occupancy):	37
Cabins (with private balcony):	9
Cabins (wheelchair accessible):	4
Cabin Current:	110 and 220 volts
Cabin TV:	Yes
Dining Rooms:	1
Elevators:	5
Casino:	Yes
Slot Machines:	Yes
Swimming Pools (outdoors):	2
Swimming Pools (inside):	0
Whirlpools:	3
Fitness Center:	Yes
Sauna/Steam Room:	Yes/Yes
Massage:	Yes
Self-Service Launderette:	Yes
Movie Theater/Seats:	Yes/156
Library:	Yes
Classification Society:	Det Norske Veritas

RATINGS	POSSIBLE SCORE	SCORE ACHIEVED
Ship	500	381
Accommodation	200	157
Food	400	260
Service	400	278
Cruise	500	344
TOTAL	**2,000**	**1,420**

Accommodation: A wide range of cabins provides something for everyone, from spacious suites with real separate bedrooms to small cabins (inside). All are nicely equipped, and there is plenty of good closet, drawer, and storage space. Nonsmoking cabins are also available. Some cabin bathrooms have awkward access. Insulation between cabins is very poor. The towels are of substandard quality.

Dining: The dining room has a high ceiling and provides plenty of space at each table; there are two seatings. Features good cuisine, attractively presented, with an emphasis on seafood. The food is generally of good quality, although the menu variety is somewhat limited, particularly at the buffet lunches (best described as a Scandinavian smorgasbord). The breakfast buffets are repetitious, however. Communication with the Filipino waiters can prove frustrating at times. The self-service beverage station needs improvement. There is a good range of wines. The room service (in-cabin) menu is very limited and unimaginative.

Other Comments: Acquired by Fred Olsen Cruise Lines in late 1996, this handsome ship, originally built for long-distance cruising for the now-defunct Royal Viking Line, has a sharply raked bow and a sleek appearance, and was "stretched" in 1981. There is an excellent amount of open deck and sunbathing space, and a good health-fitness spa high atop ship.

The interior decor is restful, having been made more attractive in a recent refit. Good materials, fabrics (including the use of the Black Watch tartan), and soft furnishings add to a pleasant ambience and warmth. The spacious public rooms have high ceilings, and the staircases are wide and well lit.

There is a good cinema with a steeply tiered floor, and a very pleasant library and lounge for card players. The observation lounge high atop ship has commanding views and is very comfortable as a relaxing lounge.

This comfortable ship has settled in well under the Fred Olsen Cruise Lines brand, and will provide a good cruise experience at a modest price with a friendly staff and good service.

<u>Weak Points</u>: Do remember that she is now an old ship, and that means little problems with plumbing and other idiosyncrasies will occur from time to time.

m/s Bolero
★★★
(M)

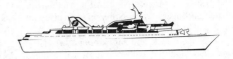

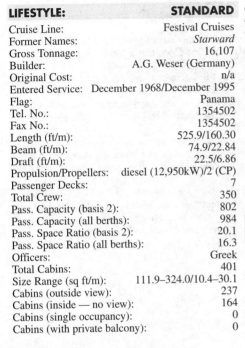

LIFESTYLE:	STANDARD
Cruise Line:	Festival Cruises
Former Names:	*Starward*
Gross Tonnage:	16,107
Builder:	A.G. Weser (Germany)
Original Cost:	n/a
Entered Service:	December 1968/December 1995
Flag:	Panama
Tel. No.:	1354502
Fax No.:	1354502
Length (ft/m):	525.9/160.30
Beam (ft/m):	74.9/22.84
Draft (ft/m):	22.5/6.86
Propulsion/Propellers:	diesel (12,950kW)/2 (CP)
Passenger Decks:	7
Total Crew:	350
Pass. Capacity (basis 2):	802
Pass. Capacity (all berths):	984
Pass. Space Ratio (basis 2):	20.1
Pass. Space Ratio (all berths):	16.3
Officers:	Greek
Total Cabins:	401
Size Range (sq ft/m):	111.9–324.0/10.4–30.1
Cabins (outside view):	237
Cabins (inside — no view):	164
Cabins (single occupancy):	0
Cabins (with private balcony):	0

Cabins (wheelchair accessible):	2
Cabin Current:	110 and 220 volts
Cabin TV:	No
Dining Rooms:	1
Elevators:	4
Casino:	Yes
Slot Machines:	Yes
Swimming Pools (outdoors):	2
Swimming Pools (inside):	0
Whirlpools:	0
Fitness Center:	Yes
Sauna/Steam Room:	Yes/No
Massage:	Yes
Self-Service Launderette:	No
Movie Theater/Seats:	Yes/210
Library:	Yes
Classification Society:	Det Norske Veritas

RATINGS	POSSIBLE SCORE	SCORE ACHIEVED
Ship	500	266
Accommodation	200	111
Food	400	258
Service	400	271
Cruise	500	291
TOTAL	**2,000**	**1,197**

Accommodation: Except for five good-sized suites, the cabins are very compact units that are moderately comfortable, decorated in soft colors accented by colorful soft furnishings. They are, however, adequate, particularly as this company specializes in destination-intensive cruises. While the closet space is limited, there are plenty of drawers, although they are metal and tinny. The bathrooms are small and tight, and the towels are not large, although they are made of 100 percent cotton; the toilets are of the "gentle flush" and not the "barking dog suction" variety as found aboard newer ships. The insulation between cabins could be better (each cabin has a notice asking passengers to keep the audio system to a minimum to avoid "cabin rage" complaints from neighbors).

The five suites (all, strangely, with Jamaican names) are of a good size with a "privacy" curtain between the hallway/closet and the sleeping/lounging area. There is plenty of space to walk in these suites, which feature separate vanity desk, curtained-off closet, plenty of drawer and storage space for luggage, lounge with sofa that converts into an additional bed, drinks table, and two chairs. The bathroom features a small but deep bathtub with shower.

Dining: This ship has a dining room (totally nonsmoking) that is cheerful and charming, with some prime tables overlooking the stern (most are for four, six, or eight). There are two seatings. The company provides good food and a wide menu choice, as in sister ships *Flamenco* and *Azur*. The service is cheerful, friendly, and comes with a smile (remember, this *is* an inexpensive, informal cruise experience, so you should not expect haute cuisine). The wine list is acceptable, but the wines, for the most part, are very young.

In addition, breakfast and lunch buffets are provided indoors at Signals Café, with seating provided outdoors at tables set around the aft swimming pool (space is tight, however, and there simply isn't enough of it). There is a good selection of bread and bread rolls, cold cuts of meat, fresh fruits, and cheeses at the buffets, which are presented reasonably well, given the space limitations.

Other Comments: This ship has a fairly contemporary upper profile with dual swept-back funnels, and is an ideal size for cruising in the Mediterranean region. *Bolero* was formerly a Caribbean-based ship owned and operated by Norwegian Cruise Line. She was acquired in late 1995 by Festival Cruises, the Piraeus-based cruise line "for Europeans."

The open deck and sunbathing space is very limited (some of the decks are of plain steel, painted blue),and cluttered with plenty of white plastic deck lounge chairs and blue/yellow sun umbrellas for shade at the aft outdoor decks. Just forward of her twin blue funnels is an enclosed basketball/volleyball court), while aft of the mast is a large solarium-style shielded housing, with multilevel lounge/bar/disco that is adjacent to one of the ship's two swimming pools.

Inside the ship, there is a good choice of public rooms for this size of vessel, and they feature clean, contemporary furnishings and upbeat, cheerful fabric colors and decor. Has a good, steeply tiered movie theater, with excellent sight lines.

Bolero is a very comfortable vessel that is ideal for Mediterranean cruises, with a warm, friendly upbeat ambience. She is reasonably attractive and should prove to be a good choice for first-time passengers seeking a destination-intensive cruise at very attractive prices. The ship is now positioned for charter to tour operators (for example, in the summer of 2000 she is chartered by First Choice Holidays, specifically for British passengers.

Festival Cruises provides a well-tuned European-style cruise experience in somewhat crowded, though comfortable (and certainly not elegant or glitzy) surroundings, at a very modest price that translates to very good value for money. The staff is very friendly and tries hard to make you feel welcome, like a member of a family.

Weak Points: This is a fairly high-density vessel that really does crowd when full (it is called "ambience"). Has a less than handsome "duck-tailed" sponson stern (this acts rather like a stabilizer). There are no cushioned pads for the deck lounge chairs. The diesel engines are somewhat noisy and tend to "throb" in some parts of the vessel, including those cabins on lower decks. No cabins have a television. There are simply too many repetitive announcements in several languages.

m/s Bremen
★★★★
(S)

LIFESTYLE:	**PREMIUM**
Cruise Line:	Hapag-Lloyd Seetouristik
Former Names:	*Frontier Spirit*
Gross Tonnage:	6,752
Builder:	Mitsubishi Heavy Industries (Japan)
Original Cost:	$42 million
Entered Service:	November 1990/November 1993
Flag:	Bahamas
Tel. No.:	1103404
Fax No.:	1103405
Length (ft/m):	365.8/111.51
Beam (ft/m):	55.7/17.00
Draft (ft/m):	15.7/4.80
Propulsion/Propellers:	diesel (4,855kW)/2 (CP)
Passenger Decks:	6
Total Crew:	94
Pass. Capacity (basis 2):	164
Pass. Capacity (all berths):	184
Pass. Space Ratio (basis 2):	41.1
Pass. Space Ratio (all berths):	36.6
Officers:	European
Total Cabins:	82
Size Range (sq ft/m):	174.3–322.9/16.2–30.0
Cabins (outside view):	82
Cabins (inside — no view):	0
Cabins (single occupancy):	0
Cabins (with private balcony):	18
Cabins (wheelchair accessible):	2

Cabin Current:	110 and 220 volts
Cabin TV:	Yes
Dining Rooms:	1
Elevators:	2
Casino:	No
Slot Machines:	No
Swimming Pools (outdoors):	1
Swimming Pools (inside):	0
Whirlpools:	0
Fitness Center:	Yes
Sauna/Steam Room:	Yes/No
Massage:	No
Self-Service Launderette:	No
Lecture/Film Room:	Yes (seats 164)
Library:	Yes (open 24 hours)
Zodiacs:	12
Helicopter Pad:	Yes
Classification Society:	Lloyd's Register

RATINGS	POSSIBLE SCORE	SCORE ACHIEVED
Ship	500	349
Accommodation	200	150
Food	400	298
Service	400	311
Cruise	500	353
TOTAL	**2,000**	**1,461**

Accommodation: The accommodation comes in only four different configurations. All cabins have an outside view (the lowest deck of cabins have portholes; all others have good-sized picture windows).

All of the cabins are well equipped for the size of the vessel; each features a color television (small), telephone, refrigerator (soft drinks are provided and replenished daily, at no charge), vanity desk, and sitting area with small drinks table. Each has a private bathroom (of the "me first, you next" variety) with tiled floor, shower, toiletries cupboard and good under-sink storage space (there's also an electrical socket for shavers).

Each cabin has moderate (illuminated) closet space, although the drawer space is limited (suitcases can be stored under the beds). The beds feature European cotton duvets. Some cabins (Sun Deck and Bridge Deck) also have a small balcony (but these are tiny), a first for any expedition cruise vessel.

Two Sun Deck suites have a separate lounge area with sofa and coffee table, bedroom (with large wall clock), large walk-in closet, and bathroom with a bathtub and two sinks.

Dining: The dining room features open seating. It is fairly attractive, with pleasing decor and colors; it also has big picture windows. The food is excellent and made with high-quality ingredients. Portions are small, but the presentation is very appealing to the eye. There is a good choice of freshly made breads and pastries, and a good selection of cheeses and fruits. The service is good, with smartly dressed bilingual (German- and English-speaking) waiters and waitresses. As an alternative to the dining room, breakfast and luncheon buffets are available in "The Club" or outside on the Lido Deck (weather permitting), where "The Grill" is also operated for hamburgers and other grilled food items.

Other Comments: This purpose-built expedition cruise vessel (formerly *Frontier Spirit*, for the now-defunct US-based Frontier Cruises) has a handsome, wide, and squat contemporary profile and fairly decent, although not the latest, high-tech equipment. Its wide beam provides decent stability and the vessel's long cruising range and ice-hardened hull provides the ship with access to remote destinations. The ship carries the highest ice classification.

177

Zero-discharge of waste matter is practiced; this means that absolutely nothing is discharged into the oceans that does not meet with the international conventions on ocean pollution (MARPOL). All the equipment for in-depth marine and shore excursions is provided, including a boot-washing station. When the ship goes to cold weather/ice areas such as the Arctic or Antarctic, red parkas (waterproof outdoor jackets) are supplied, as are high waterproof boots (take some waterproof trousers and several pairs of thick socks, plus thermal underwear).

There is almost a wraparound walking deck (you must go up and down the steps at the front of the deck to complete the "wrap"). The ship has an unusual number of public rooms for her size, including a forward-facing observation lounge/lecture room, and a main lounge with high ceiling, bandstand, and bar.

Bremen features fine, well-planned destination-intensive itineraries, with good documentation and port information. The ship provides a high degree of comfort (although not as luxurious as her slightly larger sister *Hanseatic*). There is a 24-hour reception desk, a fine array of expert lecturers, a friendly crew, and no annoying "elevator" music played in the corridors or on the open decks, all of which add to the extremely sound cruise experience you should have aboard this ship.

Bremen is a very comfortable and practical expedition cruise vessel (she is arguably a better expedition vessel than sister *Hanseatic*). Cruises aboard the ship will provide you with a fine learning and expedition experience, and she operates particularly well when featuring Antarctic cruises. The ship underwent an extensive upgrading of her interiors in 1993. The onboard ambience is casual, comfortable, and unstuffy (no tux needed).

For part of the year the ship is under charter to New York-based Raymond and Whitcomb, whose cultural cruises are extremely popular with alumni groups; for the remainder of the year the ship is operated by Hapag-Lloyd Seetouristik. Insurance, port taxes, and all staff gratuities are included.

Weak Points: The swimming pool is very small, as is the open deck space around it, although there are both shaded and open areas. The plastic chairs on deck would be more comfortable with cushions.

m/v Caledonian Star
★★★ +
(S)

LIFESTYLE: **STANDARD**

Cruise Line:	Lindblad Special Expeditions
Former Names:	*North Star, Marburg, Lindmar*
Gross Tonnage:	3,132
Builder:	A.G. Weser Seebeckwerft (Germany)
Original Cost:	n/a
Entered Service:	1966/1984
Flag:	Bahamas
Tel. No.:	330818210
Fax No.:	330818213
Length (ft/m):	292.6/89.20
Beam (ft/m):	45.9/14.00
Draft (ft/m):	20.3/6.20
Propulsion/Propellers:	diesel (3,236kW)/1 (FP)
Passenger Decks:	6
Total Crew:	64
Pass. Capacity (basis 2):	108
Pass. Capacity (all berths):	123
Pass. Space Ratio (basis 2):	29.0
Pass. Space Ratio (all berths):	25.4
Officers:	Scandinavian
Total Cabins:	61
Size Range (sq ft/m):	191.6–269.1/17.8–25.0
Cabins (outside view):	61
Cabins (inside — no view):	0
Cabins (single occupancy):	14
Cabins (with private balcony):	0

Cabins (wheelchair accessible):	0
Cabin Current:	110 and 220 volts
Cabin TV:	No
Dining Rooms:	1
Elevators:	0
Casino:	No
Slot Machines:	No
Swimming Pools (outdoors):	1
Whirlpools:	0
Fitness Center:	Yes
Sauna/Steam Room:	Yes/Yes
Massage:	No
Self-Service Launderette:	No
Lecture/Film Room:	Yes
Library:	Yes
Zodiacs:	10
Helicopter Pad:	No
Classification Society:	Det Norske Veritas

RATINGS	POSSIBLE SCORE	SCORE ACHIEVED
Ship	500	270
Accommodation	200	116
Food	400	267
Service	400	282
Cruise	500	328
TOTAL	**2,000**	**1,263**

Accommodation: The all-outside-view units are very compact, but reasonably comfortable units, decorated in warm, muted tones. All cabins feature a minibar-refrigerator, good closet and drawer space, and a clock. Bathrooms are tight, with little space for the storage of personal toiletry items.

Dining: The dining room is small and fairly charming, but the low-back chairs are small. An open seating is operated (you can sit where you wish, with whomever you wish). The cuisine is European in style with high quality, very fresh ingredients, but not a lot of menu choice. Attentive and friendly service is provided.

Other Comments: She is a reasonably handsome ship that is extremely tidy and has been well cared for. Has an open bridge policy. Carries Zodiac landing craft for in-depth excursions, and there is also an enclosed shore tender. An aft stairway (it is steep) leads down to the landing craft platform.

This ship is very comfortable and unpretentious, with a warm, intimate ambience and a casual dress code that helps make her passengers feel quite at home.

For such a small ship there is a good range of public rooms and facilities (all were nicely refurbished in mid-1998) that includes a good lecture lounge/bar/library, where a selection of videos is stocked for in-cabin use. An excellent set of lecturers that are placed aboard for each cruise make this a real life-enrichment and learning experience for an intellectual (mainly North American and British) clientele wanting to travel and learn, while enveloped in comfortable, unpretentious surroundings (you won't need a tuxedo or any dressy clothes).

This very likable little ship provides a well-tuned destination-intensive, soft expedition-style cruise experience, at a very reasonable price. She attracts a lot of loyal repeat passengers. Her itineraries now include Antarctica, where she started operating in December 1998.

Weak Points: The interior stairways are a little steep. The exterior stairway to the Zodiac embarkation points is also steep. There is noise from the diesel engines (generators) that can prove quite irksome at times, particularly on the lower decks. Communication with staff can also sometimes prove frustrating.

m/s Carnival Destiny
★★★★
(L)

LIFESTYLE:	STANDARD
Cruise Line:	Carnival Cruise Lines
Former Names:	-
Gross Tonnage:	101,353
Builder:	Fincantieri (Italy)
Original Cost:	$400 million
Entered Service:	November 1996
Flag:	Panama
Tel. No.:	335655710
Fax No.:	n/a
Length (ft/m):	892.3/272.0
Beam (ft/m):	116.0/35.3
Draft (ft/m):	27.0/8.2
Propulsion/Propellers:	diesel-electric (63,400kW)/2 (CP)
Passenger Decks:	12
Total Crew:	1,000
Pass. Capacity (basis 2):	2,642
Pass. Capacity (all berths):	3,400
Pass. Space Ratio (basis 2):	38.3
Pass. Space Ratio (all berths):	29.8
Officers:	Italian
Total Cabins:	1,321
Size Range (sq ft/m):	179.7–482.2/16.7–44.8
Cabins (outside view):	806
Cabins (inside — no view):	515
Cabins (single occupancy):	0
Cabins (with private balcony):	480

Cabins (wheelchair accessible):	25
Cabin Current:	110 volts
Cabin TV:	Yes
Dining Rooms:	2
Elevators:	18
Casino:	Yes
Slot Machines:	Yes
Swimming Pools (outdoors):	3 (+1 with magrodome)
Swimming Pools (inside):	0
Whirlpools:	7
Fitness Center:	Yes
Sauna/Steam Room:	Yes/Yes
Massage:	Yes
Self-Service Launderette:	Yes
Movie Theater/Seats:	No
Library:	Yes
Classification Society:	Lloyd's Register

RATINGS	POSSIBLE SCORE	SCORE ACHIEVED
Ship	500	430
Accommodation	200	165
Food	400	219
Service	400	269
Cruise	500	372
TOTAL	**2,000**	**1,455**

Accommodation: Over half of all cabins are outside (and at 225 sq ft/21 m² they are the largest in the standard market). They are spread over four decks and have private balconies (with glass rather than steel balustrades, for better, unobstructed ocean views) extending from the ship's side. The balconies also feature bright fluorescent lighting.

The standard cabins are of good size and come equipped with all the basics, although the furniture is rather square and angular, with no rounded edges. Three decks of cabins (eight on each deck, each with private balcony) overlook the stern (with three days at sea on each of two alternating itineraries, vibration is kept to a minimum).

Eight penthouse suites, each with a large balcony, are lavish in their appointments, although, at only 483 sq ft (44.8 m²) are small when compared to the best suites in many smaller ships. There are also 40 other suites, each of which features a decent-size bathroom and a good amount of lounge space.

In those cabins with balconies (more cabins have balconies aboard this ship than those that do not), the partition between each balcony is open at top and bottom, so you can hear noise from neighbors (or smell their cigarette/cigar smoke). Now that we approach a new century, it is disappointing to see three categories of cabins (both outside and inside) with upper and lower bunk beds (lower beds are far more preferable, but this is how the ship accommodates an extra 600 over and above the lower bed capacity).

The cabins feature soft color schemes and more soft furnishings in more attractive fabrics than any other ship in the fleet. Interactive "Fun Vision" technology lets you choose movies on demand (for a fee). Bathrooms, which have good-size showers, feature good storage space in the toiletries cabinet. Take your own shampoo, conditioner, hand cream, shower cap, or other personal toiletry items as these are not supplied in the cabins (the line believes that passengers like to take their own).

Dining: The ship's two dining rooms (the Galaxy, forward, with windows on two sides, has 706 seats; the Universe, aft, with windows on three sides, has 1,090 seats) are both nonsmoking. Dining in each restaurant is in two seatings. Each spans two decks (a first for any Carnival ship) and incorporates a dozen pyramid-shaped domes and chandeliers and a soft, mellow, peachy color scheme. The Universe dining room features a two-deck-high wall of glass overlooking the stern. There are tables for four, six, and eight (and even a few tables for two that the line tries to keep for honeymooners).

The menus, which have been upgraded somewhat recently, feature a better selection than before, with more choices and improved quality entree items. Although there is a decent wine list, there are no wine waiters. However, the waiters do sing and dance and there are always the expected waiter parades; the dining room is show business — all done in the name of gratuities at the end of your cruise.

The dining room entrances have comfortable drinking areas for predinner cocktails. There are also many options for casual dining, particularly during the daytime. Two decks high is the Sun and Sea Restaurant, the ship's informal international food court–style eatery, which is adjacent to the aft pool and can be covered by a magrodome glass cover in inclement weather. Included in this eating mall are a trattoria (Italian cuisine, with made-to-order pasta dishes), Happy Valley (Chinese cuisine, with wok preparation), a 24-hour pizzeria, and a patisserie (extra charge for pastries), as well as a grill (for fast foods such as hamburgers and hot dogs).

Other Comments: This is Carnival's 11th new ship in the past 15 success-filled years, and the first ship to be built that is unable to transit the Panama Canal due to her size.

She is quite a stunning ship, built to impress at every turn, has the most balanced profile of all the ships in the Carnival Cruise Lines fleet, although the bow itself is extremely short. Amidships on the open deck is the longest water slide at sea (200 feet in length), as well as tiered sunbathing decks positioned between two swimming pools and several hot tubs. As aboard all Carnival ships, there is a "topless" sunbathing area set around the funnel base (can't be seen from the pool deck below).

Inside the ship, Joe Farcus, the interior designer who has designed all of the ship interiors for Carnival Cruise Lines, has outdone himself, but tastefully so. The ship is simply superb, and a fantasy land for the senses (though nowhere near as glitzy as the "*Fantasy*"-class ships). The layout is logical, so finding your way around is a fairly simple matter.

There are three decks full of lounges, 10 bars, and lots of rooms to play in. Like her smaller (though still large) predecessors, this ship features a double-wide indoor promenade, a nine-deck-high, glass-domed rotunda atrium lobby, and a huge (15,000 sq ft/1,393.5 m^2) Nautica Spa. The three-level (non-smoking) Palladium show lounge is stunning and features a revolving stage, hydraulic orchestra pit, superb sound, and seating on three levels (the upper levels being tiered through two decks). There is a proscenium over the stage that acts as a scenery loft (there are two large-scaled Vegas-like razzle-dazzle production shows each cruise). For those that like to gamble, the Millionaire's Club Casino is certainly the largest (and noisiest) at sea; there are also more than 320 slot machines.

An additional feature that this ship has that the *Fantasy*-class ships do not have is the Flagship bar, located in the Rotunda (atrium), which faces forward to the glass-walled elevators. Another new (for Carnival) feature is the sports bar (All Star Bar), with tables that feature (naturally) sports memorabilia.

Children are provided with good facilities, including their own two-level Children's Club (including an outdoor pool), and are well cared for with "Camp Carnival," the line's extensive children's program.

From the viewpoint of safety, passengers will be able to embark directly into the lifeboats from their secured position without having to wait for them to be lowered, thus saving time in the event of a real emergency. Well done.

However, this certainly is a big ship, with lots of people everywhere, and that means some waiting in line, particularly for shore excursions, buffets, embarkation, and disembarkation (although the port of Miami has greatly improved terminal facilities specifically for this ship, with some 90 check-in desks). It also means a very impersonal cruise experience. For such a large ship, there really is not much open deck space per passenger, so on any sea days you can expect some crowds.

Finally, this ship has quickly become one of the ultimate floating Caribbean playgrounds for young, active adults who enjoy constant stimulation and close contact with lots and lots of others — a live board game with every move executed in typically grand, colorful, fun-filled Carnival Cruise Lines style. And what a fine vessel for large incentive groups! Potential passengers of other nationalities should note that this is definitely an all-American experience and product, with all its attendant glitz and jazzy/rock sounds — a real "life on the ocean rave."

<u>Weak Points</u>: The terraced pool deck is really cluttered, and there are no cushioned pads for the deck chairs. Getting away from people and noise is difficult. Disembarking from the ship at the end of the cruise is an unsettling experience, not to mention the crowds and lines at the airport.

m/s Carnival Triumph
(L)

LIFESTYLE:	**STANDARD**
Cruise Line:	Carnival Cruise Lines
Former Names:	-
Gross Tonnage:	102,000
Builder:	Fincantieri (Italy)
Original Cost:	$410 million
Entered Service:	July 1999
Flag:	Panama
Tel. No.:	n/a
Fax No.:	n/a
Length (ft/m):	893.0/272.2
Beam (ft/m):	116.0/35.3
Draft (ft/m):	27.0/8.2
Propulsion/Propellers:	diesel-electric (63,400kW)/2 (CP)
Passenger Decks:	13
Total Crew:	1,150
Pass. Capacity (basis 2):	2,758
Pass. Capacity (all berths):	3,473
Pass. Space Ratio (basis 2):	36.9
Pass. Space Ratio (all berths):	29.2
Officers:	Italian
Total Cabins:	1,379
Size Range (sq ft/m):	179.7–482.2/16.7–44.8
Cabins (outside view):	345
Cabins (inside — no view):	526
Cabins (single occupancy):	0
Cabins (with private balcony):	508

Cabins (wheelchair accessible):	25
Cabin Current:	110 volts
Cabin TV:	Yes
Dining Rooms:	2
Elevators:	18
Casino:	Yes
Slot Machines:	Yes
Swimming Pools (outdoors):	3 (+1 with magrodome)
Swimming Pools (inside):	0
Whirlpools:	7
Fitness Center:	Yes
Sauna/Steam Room:	Yes/Yes
Massage:	Yes
Self-Service Launderette:	Yes
Movie Theater/Seats:	No
Library:	Yes
Classification Society:	Lloyd's Register

RATINGS	POSSIBLE SCORE	SCORE ACHIEVED
Ship	500	NYR
Accommodation	200	NYR
Food	400	NYR
Service	400	NYR
Cruise	500	NYR
TOTAL	**2,000**	**NYR**

For general comments, see *Carnival Destiny*. Although the names of public rooms will be different, most other comments apply.

m/s Carnival Victory
(L)

LIFESTYLE:	STANDARD
Cruise Line:	Carnival Cruise Lines
Former Names:	-
Gross Tonnage:	102,000
Builder:	Fincantieri (Italy)
Original Cost:	$440 million
Entered Service:	Summer 2000
Flag:	Panama
Tel. No.:	n/a
Fax No.:	n/a
Length (ft/m):	893.0/272.2
Beam (ft/m):	116.0/35.3
Draft (ft/m):	27.0/8.2
Propulsion/Propellers:	diesel-electric (63,400kW)/2 (CP)
Decks:	13
Total Crew:	1,150
Pass. Capacity (basis 2):	2,758
Pass. Capacity (all berths):	3,473
Pass. Space Ratio (basis 2):	38
Pass. Space Ratio (all berths):	29.4
Officers:	Italian
Total Cabins:	1,321
Size Range (sq ft/m):	179.7–482.2/16.7–44.8
Cabins (outside view):	345
Cabins (inside — no view):	526
Cabins (single occupancy):	0
Cabins (with private balcony):	508

Cabins (wheelchair accessible):	25
Cabin Current:	110 volts
Cabin TV:	Yes
Dining Rooms:	2
Elevators:	18
Casino:	Yes
Slot Machines:	Yes
Swimming Pools (outdoors):	3 (+1 with magrodome)
Swimming Pools (inside):	0
Whirlpools:	7
Fitness Center:	Yes
Sauna/Steam Room:	Yes/Yes
Massage:	Yes
Self-Service Launderette:	Yes
Movie Theater/Seats:	No
Library:	Yes
Classification Society:	Lloyd's Register

RATINGS	POSSIBLE SCORE	SCORE ACHIEVED
Ship	500	NYR
Accommodation	200	NYR
Food	400	NYR
Service	400	NYR
Cruise	500	NYR
TOTAL	**2,000**	**NYR**

For general comments, see *Carnival Destiny*. Although the names of public rooms will be different, most other comments apply.

m/s Caronia
★★★★ +
(M)

LIFESTYLE: LUXURY

Cruise Line:	Cunard Line
Former Names:	*Vistafjord*
Gross Tonnage:	24,492
Builder:	Swan, Hunter (UK)
Original Cost:	$35 million
Entered Service:	May 1973/May 1984
Flag:	Bahamas
Tel. No.:	1306645
Fax No.:	1305630
Length (ft/m):	626.9/191.09
Beam (ft/m):	82.1/25.05
Draft (ft/m):	27.0/8.23
Propulsion/Propellers:	diesel (17,900kW)/2 (FP)
Passenger Decks:	9
Total Crew:	400
Pass. Capacity (basis 2):	677
Pass. Capacity (all berths):	732
Pass. Space Ratio (basis 2):	36.1
Pass. Space Ratio (all berths):	33.4
Officers:	European/Scandinavian
Total Cabins:	376
Size Range (sq ft/m):	66.7–871.9/6.2–81.0
Cabins (outside view):	324
Cabins (inside — no view):	52
Cabins (single occupancy):	73
Cabins (with private balcony):	25
Cabins (wheelchair accessible):	4
Cabin Current:	110 volts
Cabin TV:	Yes
Dining Rooms:	1
Elevators:	6
Casino:	Yes
Slot Machines:	Yes
Swimming Pools (outdoors):	1
Swimming Pools (inside):	1
Whirlpools:	2
Fitness Center:	Yes
Sauna/Steam Room:	Yes/No
Massage:	Yes
Self-Service Launderette:	Yes
Movie Theater/Seats:	Yes/190
Library:	Yes
Classification Society:	Lloyd's Register

RATINGS	POSSIBLE SCORE	SCORE ACHIEVED
Ship	500	421
Accommodation	200	177
Food	400	345
Service	400	339
Cruise	500	408
TOTAL	**2,000**	**1,690**

Accommodation: The suites with private balconies are superbly equipped and have ample drawer space. All cabins are extremely well appointed and tastefully redecorated (all had new bathrooms installed in a 1994 refit), and all feature a refrigerator, a minibar, a personal safe, European duvets (in two thicknesses), and thick cotton bathrobes. All the wooden furniture has nicely rounded edges.

There are two duplex apartments that are really outstanding. These occupy two levels: the lower level features a large bedroom and bathroom with Jacuzzi bathtub; the upper level features an expansive living room with Bang & Olufsen sound system, treadmill, private bar, large bathroom (with Jacuzzi bathtub), and separate private sauna. Outdoors on deck is a huge private balcony, complete with a two-person hot tub.

All of the cabins also have excellent closet and drawer space (illuminated closets), and VCR units, and each bathroom features a whisper-quiet (nonvacuum) toilet. There is also an excellent range of cabins for single travelers. Some Sun Deck and Promenade Deck suites have obstructed views. Note, however, that the smallest cabins really are small, with little room to move around.

Dining: The dining room is a grand, elegant room and has been expanded for single-seating dining. There are tables for two, four, six, or eight (there are more tables for two in the dining room than in any other cruise ship afloat). This is because the company has recognized that a great number of its passengers are single and enjoy traveling alone.

The senior officers each host a table for dinner each evening. A main feature is single-waiter service in the best European tradition. The tables are a little close together, making it somewhat difficult for waiters to serve in some areas.

The ship features international cuisine offering the highest quality and variety of ingredients (there is an excellent variety of breads at every meal). A cold table is set for such things as breads and cheeses at lunchtime, and passengers can either help themselves or be served by a waiter. Salad items, many salad dressings, juices, and cheeses (a fine selection of more than 40 international cheeses) are always available.

Plate-service is the standard procedure (where vegetables and entrees are set artistically on the main course plate). Extra vegetables can be obtained at any time. This is European-style service in the classic seagoing tradition. Waiters are well trained through a good onboard management structure.

Although tableside flambeaus cannot be done at individual tables, they are done in several central locations, and the waiters collect the finished product to take to their respective tables.

Although the chef has his favorites, the menus are not repeated, even on long voyages. Also, one of the good points about this and other ships in her class (five stars) is that, while the menus are very creative, you can order "off-menu" at any time and create your own delightful cuisine. Little touches in presentation, such as paper doilies under teacups and soup bowls, and towel-wrapped water jugs, make a difference in product delivery.

Apart from the regular menu (several appetizers, three soups, sorbet, five entrees, two salads, several desserts, and a superb selection of international cheeses at every dinner meal), there is always a Cunard Spa menu, a vegetarian menu, as well as diabetic desserts every day.

Different color tablecloths and napkins are featured daily for luncheon and dinner. There is an outstanding, extensive wine list, with prices ranging from $13 to almost $400. Cappuccino and espresso coffees are available at any time in the dining room (or at the Lido Deck Cafe), without charge. There is an excellent selection of breads, tropical fruits, and cheeses.

Tivoli, a completely separate 40-seat Italian à la carte restaurant (an alternative nonsmoking dining spot) is intimate and elegant, and the food is outstanding, from a varied menu that features many special dishes daily. It has the feel of a small, exclusive bistro.

The Lido Deck Cafe is a popular informal dining area that provides a wide range of self-service buffets that have a different theme daily, as well as for breakfast and lunch.

Other Comments: This ship has classic liner styling and profile, and really does *look* like a ship. She is finely proportioned, with beautiful, rounded, flowing lines and a sleek profile, complete with a large midships funnel. Following a refit in late 1999, the ship's name changed from *Vistafjord* to *Caronia* (the third Cunard ship to bear the name, the first two being in 1905 and 1947). The hull is now painted a deep shade of blue, which shows off her lines even more. The ship has been well maintained, and at sea she is stable, smooth, and quiet in operation.

The open decks and sunbathing space are expansive. Built with excellent quality materials throughout. There is a fine teak wraparound promenade deck outdoors, and the deck lounge chairs have cushioned pads. The ship's bell is sounded at noon in fine maritime tradition.

Inside, the spacious and elegant public rooms have high ceilings. Has tasteful decor throughout, improved in her latest refit. Real ballroom/show lounge has a fine, large, wooden dance floor, and a big band for ballroom dancing. Features excellent European and Filipino stewardesses. Conservative, sophisticated, classically oriented entertainment. The wide interior stairwells are subtly illuminated. Few international ships can compete with this ship for the relaxing ambience and service from a well-organized and happy crew. There are refreshingly few announcements and interruptions.

This ship caters especially well to discerning passengers in an elegant, refined, yet friendly style and very comfortable surroundings for adults (children do not fit, nor are there any facilities for them). Although not shiny and new, she has been well cared for, and provides a most pleasant and civilized travel experiences.

Note: Rated as *Vistafjord* prior to name change and refit.

m/s Carousel
★★★
(L)

LIFESTYLE:	STANDARD
Cruise Line:	Airtours Sun Cruises
Former Names:	*Nordic Prince*
Gross Tonnage:	23,149
Builder:	Wartsila (Finland)
Original Cost:	$13.5 million
Entered Service:	July 1971/May 1995
Flag:	Bahamas
Tel. No.:	1310547
Fax No.:	1310547
Length (ft/m):	637.5/194.32
Beam (ft/m):	78.8/24.03
Draft (ft/m):	21.9/6.70
Propulsion/Propellers:	diesel (13,400kW)/2 (CP)
Passenger Decks:	7
Total Crew:	400
Pass. Capacity (basis 2):	1,050
Pass. Capacity (all berths):	1,158
Pass. Space Ratio (basis 2):	22
Pass. Space Ratio (all berths):	19.9
Officers:	International
Total Cabins:	525
Size Range (sq ft/m):	119.4–482.2/11.1–44.8
Cabins (outside view):	340
Cabins (inside — no view):	185
Cabins (single occupancy):	0
Cabins (with private balcony):	0

Cabins (wheelchair accessible):	0
Cabin Current:	110 volts
Cabin TV:	No
Dining Rooms:	1
Elevators:	4
Casino:	Yes
Slot Machines:	Yes
Swimming Pools (outdoors):	1
Swimming Pools (inside):	0
Whirlpools:	0
Fitness Center:	Yes
Sauna/Steam Room:	Yes/No
Massage:	Yes
Self-Service Launderette:	No
Movie Theater/Seats:	No
Library:	Yes
Classification Society:	Det Norske Veritas

RATINGS	POSSIBLE SCORE	SCORE ACHIEVED
Ship	500	310
Accommodation	200	115
Food	400	236
Service	400	253
Cruise	500	312
TOTAL	**2,000**	**1,226**

Accommodation: The cabins are provided in just four grades (Standard, Superior, Promenade, and Deluxe) and six types, making it an easy matter to select your accommodation. Most cabins are of a similar size (dimensionally-challenged comes to mind), and the insulation between them is poor. The cabins also have mediocre closets and very little storage space, yet somehow everyone seems to manage (the ship was built originally for Caribbean cruising). The best advice is therefore to take only casual clothing and only the things you really need. Do note that cabin voltage is 110 volts, so you will need to take adapters for electrical appliances such as a hairdryer. Note that cabins are not assigned until you arrive at the ship. Only the owner's suite features a refrigerator.

Dining: The dining room, which operates in two seatings, is large but noisy, and the tables (for four, six, or eight) are close together. The catering operation is quite good, however, although all the food seems to taste alike. There is a limited selection of breads, cheeses and fruits. Attentive, friendly, but rather frenzied service (particularly for those in the first seating). The wine list is fairly basic, but the prices are very modest, as are the prices for most alcoholic beverages.

Other Comments: This ship, originally built for and operated by Royal Caribbean International, has a fairly handsome, contemporary look with good lines, a nicely raked bow, and large blue funnel (complete with sunburst logo). This ship was acquired by Airtours Sun Cruises (one of the UK's "Big Three" tour companies) in 1995. Airtours is now partly owned by Carnival Corporation, which also owns Carnival Cruise Lines (and others), and provides an activity-filled cruise product in comfortable, but fairly busy surroundings. The ship underwent a $7 million refit in late 1997. While most of the work was below decks, with the fitting of new, better, more powerful generators, some cosmetic work was completed in her interiors.

There is a good, polished wraparound promenade deck outdoors (it can be slippery when wet) and wooden railings. The open deck space for sunbathing is very crowded and noisy when the ship is full (which is most of the time) but makes for a good party ambience.

The interior layout and passenger flow is sound, with clean, bright decor and some good wooden paneling and trim. The dress code is very casual, good for unstuffy, unpretentious cruising. This is a very affordable cruise, particularly for families with children, and Airtours also features a wide selection of pre- and postcruise hotel programs.

Airtours is known for packaging its products really well, and this ship represents an excellent buy for families who want to cruise, but on a limited budget. The company will fly you to and from the ship in one of its own modern jet aircraft, and all transfers to/from the ship are included for good measure. The company really does go out of its way to provide a fine "no-nonsense" good value-for-money vacation, as long as your expectations are not too high. This is *not* the ship if you are looking for a quiet and relaxing vacation. If you have been on a land-based Airtours vacation, you'll know what to expect. The currency is the pound sterling. Tipping is recommended at £5.00 per day. Insurance is included (but you will be charged for it) unless declined.

Weak Points: The cabin hallways are very narrow. There are too many repetitious announcements. Blue-coated social staff provide the lively entertainment but, although they try hard, it *is* rather amateurish.

m/s Celebration
★★★ +
(L)

LIFESTYLE:	STANDARD
Cruise Line:	Carnival Cruise Lines
Former Names:	-
Gross Tonnage:	47,262
Builder:	Kockums (Sweden)
Original Cost:	$130 million
Entered Service:	March 1987
Flag:	Liberia
Tel. No.:	1240526
Fax No.:	n/a
Length (ft/m):	732.6/223.30
Beam (ft/m):	92.5/28.20
Draft (ft/m):	25.5/7.80
Propulsion/Propellers:	diesel (23,520kW)/2 (CP)
Passenger Decks:	10
Total Crew:	670
Pass. Capacity (basis 2):	1,486
Pass. Capacity (all berths):	1,896
Pass. Space Ratio (basis 2):	31.8
Pass. Space Ratio (all berths):	24.9
Officers:	Italian
Total Cabins:	743
Size Range (sq ft/m):	184.0/17.1
Cabins (outside view):	453
Cabins (inside — no view):	290
Cabins (single occupancy):	0
Cabins (with private balcony):	10

Cabins (wheelchair accessible):	14
Cabin Current:	110 volts
Cabin TV:	Yes
Dining Rooms:	2
Elevators:	8
Casino:	Yes
Slot Machines:	Yes
Swimming Pools (outdoors):	3
Swimming Pools (inside):	0
Whirlpools:	2
Fitness Center:	Yes
Sauna/Steam Room:	Yes/No
Massage:	Yes
Self-Service Launderette:	Yes
Movie Theater/Seats:	No
Library:	Yes
Classification Society:	Lloyd's Register

RATINGS	POSSIBLE SCORE	SCORE ACHIEVED
Ship	500	355
Accommodation	200	143
Food	400	221
Service	400	275
Cruise	500	324
TOTAL	**2,000**	**1,318**

Accommodation: The cabins are quite standard and mostly identical in terms of layout and decor (which means they are good for large groups who generally like to have identical cabins for their participants) and are of fairly generous proportions (except for the inside cabins, which are quite small). The cabins are reasonably comfortable and well equipped, although only soap and ice water are supplied in the bathroom (no shampoo, conditioner, or shower cap).

The best accommodation can be found in the 10 suites, each of which has its own private balcony, larger bathroom, and more closet, drawer, and storage space.

Dining: The two dining rooms are cramped when full, and extremely noisy (both are nonsmoking), with low ceilings in the center (raised) sections. There are two seatings. The decor is colorful, to say the least. Do not even think about this ship if you like good food. The meals stress quantity, not quality, and the line does not spend as much on food as some other companies. The buffets are disappointing, although there has been an attempt to improve their variety of late. Although there is a wine list, there are no wine waiters (the waiters are expected to serve both food and wine).

Other Comments: The ship's exterior is rather angular but typical of the space-conscious designs that were introduced in the early 1980s, particularly by Carnival Cruise Lines, in an effort to maximize interior (revenue generating) space. The swimming pools are smaller than one would expect, but the open deck space is good, provided the ship is not full, when, like most ships, the deck always seems crowded.

Inside, this ship has double-width indoor promenades and a very good selection of public rooms in which to play. The flamboyant interior decor in public rooms is stimulating instead of relaxing, as is the colorful artwork. Features New Orleans–themed decor throughout the public rooms, except for some nautical-themed decor in the Wheelhouse Bar/Grill. Huge, very active, noisy casino. The party atmosphere is good for anyone wanting a stimulating cruise experience. Features a wide range of entertainment and activities.

Carnival Cruise Lines excels at providing plenty of entertainment venues and passenger participation activities to keep you occupied.

This ship should prove a good choice for families with children (there are so many places for them to explore). There are good dazzle and sizzle shows on stage, which are good for the whole family. This ship is good if you are taking your first cruise, providing that you like lots of people, noise, and lively action.

<u>Weak Points</u>: There are too many loud announcements. There really is nowhere to go for privacy, peace, and quiet, but then you should choose another ship for that.

SHIP TALK

Cable Length: a measured length equaling 100 fathoms or 600 feet.

Chart: a nautical map used for navigating.

Colors: refers to the national flag or emblem flown by the ship.

Companionway: interior stairway.

Course: direction in which the ship is headed, in degrees.

Davit: a device for raising and lowering lifeboats.

Deadlight: a ventilated porthole cover to prevent light from entering

Disembark (also debark): to leave a ship.

Dock: berth, pier or quay.

Draft (or draught): measurement in feet from the ship's waterline to the lowest point of its keel.

Embark: to join a ship.

Fantail: the rear or overhang of the ship.

Fathom: distance equal to six feet.

Flagstaff: a pole at the stern of a ship where the flag of the ship's country of registry is flown.

Free Port: port or place that is free of customs duty and regulations.

Funnel: chimney from which the ship's combustion gases are propelled into the atmosphere.

Galley: the ship's kitchen.

Gangway: the stairway or ramp link between ship and shore.

m/s Century
★★★★ +
(L)

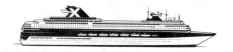

LIFESTYLE:	PREMIUM
Cruise Line:	Celebrity Cruises
Former Names:	-
Gross Tonnage:	70,606
Builder:	Meyer Werft (Germany)
Original Cost:	$320 million
Entered Service:	December 1995
Flag:	Liberia
Tel. No.:	363633911
Fax No.:	363633920
Length (ft/m):	807.1/246.00
Beam (ft/m):	105.6/32.20
Draft (ft/m):	24.6/7.50
Propulsion/Propellers:	diesel (29,250kW)/2 (CP)
Passenger Decks:	10
Total Crew:	858
Pass. Capacity (basis 2):	1,750
Pass. Capacity (all berths):	2,150
Pass. Space Ratio (basis 2):	40.3
Pass. Space Ratio (all berths):	32.8
Officers:	Greek
Total Cabins:	875
Size Range (sq ft/m):	168.9–1,514.5/15.7–140.7
Cabins (outside view):	569
Cabins (inside — no view):	306
Cabins (single occupancy):	0
Cabins (with private balcony):	61
Cabins (wheelchair accessible):	8
Cabin Current:	110 and 220 volts
Cabin TV:	Yes
Dining Rooms:	2
Elevators:	9
Casino:	Yes
Slot Machines:	Yes
Swimming Pools (outdoors):	2
Swimming Pools (inside):	1 hydropool
Whirlpools:	4
Fitness Center:	Yes
Sauna/Steam Room:	Yes/Yes
Massage:	Yes
Self-Service Launderette:	No
Movie Theater/Seats:	Yes/190
Library:	Yes
Classification Society:	Lloyd's Register

RATINGS	POSSIBLE SCORE	SCORE ACHIEVED
Ship	500	450
Accommodation	200	178
Food	400	321
Service	400	324
Cruise	500	423
TOTAL	**2,000**	**1,696**

Accommodation: A wide variety of cabin types includes 18 family cabins, each with two lower beds, two foldaway beds, and one upper berth. All cabins have wood cabinetry and accenting, interactive television and entertainment systems (you can go shopping, book shore excursions, or play casino games, interactively) as well as hairdryers in the bathrooms, and 100 percent cotton towels. However, the standard 24-hour cabin menu is disappointing and very limited. There are no cabins for single occupancy.

All cabins feature a personal safe and minibar-refrigerator (extra cost) and are nicely equipped and decorated, with warm wood-finish furniture and none of the boxy feel of cabins in many ships, due to the angled placement of vanity and audio-video consoles at an angle. In addition, all suites on Deck 10 (and the Sky Deck suites on Deck 12) feature butler service and in-cabin dining facilities. Suites that have private balconies also have floor-to-ceiling windows and sliding doors to balconies (a few have outward opening doors).

For the ultimate in accommodation, choose one of two beautifully decorated Presidential Suites, each of which measures 1,173 sq ft (109.0 m^2). These are located amidships in the most desirable position (each can be combined with the adjacent minisuite via an interconnecting door, to provide a living space of 1,515 sq ft (140.7 m^2). Each has a marble-floored foyer, a living room with mahogany wood floor, and a hand-woven rug. Other features include a separate dining area with six-seat dining table; butler's pantry with wet bar; a wine bar with private label stock, refrigerator, and microwave. There is also a large private balcony with dining table for two, chaise lounge chairs with cushioned pads, hot tub, and dimmer-controlled lighting; master bedroom with king-size bed, dressed with fine fabrics and draperies, Egyptian cotton bed linen, and walk-in closet with abundant storage space. The all-marble bathroom has a jet-spray shower and whirlpool bath.

All grades of accommodation feature interactive Sony audio and video facilities for booking shore excursions, ordering room service, and purchasing goods from the ship's boutiques, so you do not have to leave your quarters if you do not wish to, especially if you do not like the ports of call. The interactive system is available in English, French, German, Italian, and Spanish.

All accommodation designated as suites feature European duvets instead of sheets/blankets, fresh flowers, video player, use of the AquaSpa without charge, and butler service. Electrically operated blinds and other goodies are also standard in some suites.

Dining: A grand staircase connects the upper and lower levels of the splendid two-level dining room. Huge windows overlook the stern (electrically operated blinds feature several different backdrops). Each of the two levels has a separate finishing galley. There are two seatings. The design of the two galleys is excellent, and is such that food that should be hot *does* arrive hot at the table. Three different decorative panels, changed according to theme nights, adorn the huge aft windows.

There is also a large indoor/outdoor Lido cafe called Islands with four separate well-designed self-service buffet lines, as well as two grill serving stations located adjacent to the swimming pools outdoors.

All meals can also be served, course by course for all meals including full dinners, in all suites and cabins, no matter what accommodation grade you choose. For those who cannot live without them, freshly baked pizzas (boxed) can also be delivered, in an insulated pouch, to your cabin.

Celebrity Cruises has established an enviable reputation for fine dining aboard its ships, and this tradition is being continued. Michel Roux designs Celebrity Cruises' menus and exerts tight personal control over their correct cooking and delivery to assure consistency of product. All meals are made from scratch, with nothing precooked or prepackaged ashore. However, the food served as room-service items is decidedly below the standard of food featured in the dining room.

Other Comments: Looks externally like a larger version of the company's popular *Horizon/Zenith*. Well balanced despite its squared-off stern and has the distinctive Celebrity Cruises' "X" funnel ("X" being the Greek letter "C," which stands for Chandris, the former owning company). With a high passenger space ratio for such a large ship, there is no real sense of crowding, and passenger flow is good.

The interior decor is elegant and understated. Technical and engineering excellence prevail, and there is overindulgence in fire and safety equipment. She is a contemporary ship, with fine public rooms, and an array of television and video screens in many of them, provided by Sony. The medical facilities are also excellent.

There is a three-quarter, two-level teakwood promenade deck, and for joggers, a wraparound jogging track atop the ship. A stunning, two-level, 1,000-seat show lounge/theater with side balconies features a huge stage, a split orchestra pit (hydraulic), and the latest in high-tech lighting and sound equipment.

A three-deck-high main foyer (atrium) features one wall with nine large television screens. The atrium is not glitzy, but its decor somehow does not closely match the rest of the ship.

There are 4.5 acres of open deck space, together with a fine array of other public rooms and enhanced passenger facilities. An outstanding AquaSpa has some of the more unusual wellness treatments (including a steamy rasul room), with large panoramic windows and the latest high-tech equipment, all set in a calming environment, complete with shoji screens and Japanese-inspired rock garden.

Wide passageways provide plenty of indoor space for strolling. A small, dedicated movie theater also doubles as a conference and meeting center with all the latest audiovisual technology that includes three-language simultaneous translation and headsets for the hearing-impaired.

Cigar smokers will love Michael's Club, a cigar and cognac room of superb taste. It is a lovely triangular-shaped room that has become a favorite watering place for those who smoke, with large comfortable chairs and decor reminiscent of a real gentlemen's club. Features include a cigar humidor and a choice of almost 20 different cigars. Tastings is the place for those who enjoy the *very best* in coffee, provided by the impeccable Cova of Milan, Italy. It is set around the second level of the atrium, and several display cases show off the extensive range of Cova coffee, chocolates, and alcoholic digestives. This is *the* place to see and be seen. The large casino is packed with slot machines and gaming tables, and even has a satellite-linked ATM machine.

Outstanding are the 500 pieces of art that adorn the ship — a $3.8 million art collection that includes many Andy Warhol favorites and some fascinating contemporary sculptures (look for the colored violins on Deck 7). The "Century Collection" includes a comprehensive survey of the most important artists and the major developments in art since the 1960s.

Century operates Caribbean and Mediterranean cruises (1999 was the first year that Celebrity Cruises featured cruises in Europe). Overall, *Century* is a fine vessel for a big-ship cruise vacation, although some wear and tear and sloppy maintenance show in some areas. The overall product is extremely good. Very good hospitality from a well-dressed staff that is enthusiastic and generally well trained.

Weak Points: Although this is a beautiful ship, the shore excursion operation, embarkation, and disembarkation remain the weak links in the Celebrity Cruises operation, and the cruise staff is young and unpolished. The room service menu is poor, and room service food items are below the standard of food featured in the dining room. The interactive television system is frustrating to use, and the larger suites have three remotes for television/audio equipment (one would be better).

m/s Clelia II
★★★★ +
(S)

LIFESTYLE:	PREMIUM
Cruise Line:	Golden Sea Cruises
Former Names:	*Renaissance Four*
Gross Tonnage:	4,077
Builder:	Cantieri Navale Ferrari (Italy)
Original Cost:	$20 million
Entered Service:	January 1991/March 1998
Flag:	Bahamas
Tel. No.:	1307526
Fax No.:	1307527
Length (ft/m):	289.0/88.1
Beam (ft/m):	50.1/15.3
Draft (ft/m):	13.4/4.1
Propulsion/Propellers:	diesel (3,514kW)/2 (CP)
Passenger Decks:	5
Total Crew:	55
Pass. Capacity (basis 2):	84
Pass. Capacity (all berths):	84
Pass. Space Ratio (basis 2):	48.5
Pass. Space Ratio (all berths):	48.5
Officers:	French
Total Cabins:	42
Size Range (sq ft/m):	210.0–538.2/19.5–50.0
Cabins (outside view):	42
Cabins (inside — no view):	0
Cabins (single occupancy):	0
Cabins (with private balcony):	4

Cabins (wheelchair accessible):	0
Cabin Current:	110 volts
Cabin TV:	Yes
Dining Rooms:	1
Elevators:	1
Casino:	No
Slot Machines:	No
Swimming Pools (outdoors):	1
Swimming Pools (inside):	0
Whirlpools:	1
Fitness Center:	Yes
Sauna/Steam Room:	No/Yes
Massage:	No
Self-Service Launderette:	No
Movie Theater/Seats:	No
Library:	Yes
Classification Society:	Lloyd's Register

RATINGS	POSSIBLE SCORE	SCORE ACHIEVED
Ship	500	399
Accommodation	200	172
Food	400	324
Service	400	334
Cruise	500	384
TOTAL	**2,000**	**1,613**

Accommodation: Excellent all-outside cabins (called suites in the brochure) combine highly polished imitation rosewood paneling with lots of mirrors, and fine, handcrafted Italian furniture. All suites have twin beds that can convert to a queen-size bed, a sitting area with three-person sofa, one individual chair, coffee table, minibar-refrigerator (all drinks are at extra cost), color television and VCR unit, and direct-dial satellite telephone. Note that while closet space is good, space for stowing luggage is tight, and there is little drawer space (each cabin has three drawers, two of which are lockable, plus several open shelves in a separate closet). Also note that there are no music channels in the cabins, and there is no switch to turn announcements off in your cabin.

The number of cabins was reduced from 50 to 42 when the present owners acquired the vessel in 1997, thus providing more space per passenger. Outside each cabin are two brass porthole-shaped lights, which provide a stately, nautical feel to the dark wood-paneled hallways.

The marble bathrooms are compact units that have showers (no bathrooms have a bathtub) with fold-down (plastic) seat, real teakwood floor, marble vanity, large mirror, recessed towel rail (good for storing personal toiletries), and built-in hairdryer. *Note:* there is a high "lip" into the bathroom.

There are also four VIP "apartments," each consisting of two adjoining "suites," thus providing a bedroom, large lounge (with red leather-topped office desk), and two bathrooms (his 'n' hers).

There is one Presidential Apartment (owner's suite) with an en-suite office, two full separate bedrooms and living room (each with three windows), two bathrooms, and private, though narrow, balcony.

Dining: The Golden Star Restaurant, which has an open seating policy (it can seat up to 100), is bright, elegant, and welcoming (nonsmoking). It is on the lowest deck and has portholes rather than windows, due to maritime regulations. There are tables for two, four, six, or eight, and you can sit where you like, with whom you like, when you like in this open seating arrangement. Dinners are normally sit-down affairs, although, depending on the itinerary and length of cruise, there could be an occasional buffet. Breakfast and lunch are usually buffets and can be taken at poolside (weather permitting), in your suite, or in the restaurant.

The cuisine consists of continental dishes complemented by local (regional) delicacies. The food quality, choice, and presentation are all good. While the food is very well presented, the choice of entrees is limited to three for dinner.

Other Comments: This ship, with its royal blue hull and white superstructure, has the look and feel of a contemporary mega-yacht, with handsome styling throughout, although the exterior profile is not particularly handsome. There are two teakwood wraparound promenade decks outdoors. There is a small water sports platform at the stern, and a "Baby Clelia" water jet-propelled shore tender hangs over the stern. The ship also carries jet skis, waterski boat, and sailfish for use when cruising in warm weather areas.

The accommodation is located forward, with public rooms aft. Features pleasing colors and refined and attractive interior decor, with some accent on Greek design. There is a small library, which also houses the video library, a lounge that can accommodate all passengers (good for use as a lecture room), and a piano bar/lounge.

Originally one of a fleet of eight similar-sized ships operated by Renaissance Cruises, this ship was very nicely refurbished for service in early 1998. Greek artists are featured in many pieces of art around the ship, courtesy of the new owners. With her name change (the new name is also the name of the ship's owner), this charming little ship operates Greek island cruises during most of the year. She is very comfortable and inviting, and is close, but not quite the equal of some of the other small premium ships (but neither is the price). This ship provides a destination-intensive, refined, quiet, relaxed cruise for passengers who do not like crowds, dressing up, scheduled activities, or entertainment.

The ship is often placed under charter to companies such as Abercrombie & Kent, Travel Dynamics, and others for much of the year, and operated by Le Ponant (a French ship management company). The officers and crew are almost all French; all provide a certain "savoir faire" and warmth, and are youthful and very creative. No smoking is allowed anywhere inside the ship, only on open decks.

Weak Points: The tiny "dip" pool is not a swimming pool. The open deck and sunbathing space is very limited. The decor consists of plastic woods instead of real woods (it looks almost too perfect in places). There are many slim pillars in the public rooms in odd places. The constant music played throughout the public spaces (including accommodation hallways) is irritating and unnecessary.

m/s Clipper Adventurer
★★★
(S)

LIFESTYLE:	STANDARD
Cruise Line:	Clipper Cruise Line
Former Names:	*Alla Tarasova*
Gross Tonnage:	5,750
Builder:	Brodgradiliste Uljanik (Yugoslavia)
Original Cost:	n/a
Entered Service:	1976/April 1998
Flag:	Bahamas
Tel. No.:	n/a
Fax No.:	n/a
Length (ft/m):	328.1/100.01
Beam (ft/m):	53.2/16.24
Draft (ft/m):	15.2/4.65
Propulsion/Propellers:	diesel (3,884kW)/2 (CP)
Passenger Decks:	3
Total Crew:	84
Pass. Capacity (basis 2):	122
Pass. Capacity (all berths):	122
Pass. Space Ratio (basis 2):	47.1
Pass. Space Ratio (all berths):	47.1
Officers:	European
Total Cabins:	61
Size Range (sq ft/m):	119.0–211.0/11.0–19.6
Cabins (outside view):	61
Cabins (inside — no view):	0
Cabins (single occupancy):	0
Cabins (with private balcony):	0

Cabins (wheelchair accessible):	0
Cabin Current:	220 volts
Cabin TV:	No
Dining Rooms:	1
Elevators:	0
Casino:	No
Slot Machines:	No
Swimming Pools (outdoors):	No
Swimming Pools (inside):	No
Whirlpools:	No
Fitness Center:	No
Sauna/Steam Room:	Yes/No
Massage:	No
Self-Service Launderette:	No
Movie Theater/Seats:	No
Library:	Yes
Classification Society:	RS

RATINGS	POSSIBLE SCORE	SCORE ACHIEVED
Ship	500	292
Accommodation	200	120
Food	400	247
Service	400	242
Cruise	500	274
TOTAL	**2,000**	**1,175**

Accommodation: All of the cabins (there are seven grades, including a dedicated price for single cabin occupancy) have outside views and twin lower beds, with private bathroom with shower, and toilet. The bathrooms are really tiny (of the "me first, you next" variety), however, although they are tiled and come with all the basics. Several of the double-occupancy cabins can be booked by passengers traveling alone (special rates apply).

All cabins feature a private lockable drawer for valuables, a telephone, and individual temperature control. Some cabins have picture windows, while others have portholes, depending on the deck location. Two larger cabins (called suites in the brochure, which they really are not) are quite well equipped for the size of the vessel.

Dining: Pleasant, though with somewhat dark decor, the dining room, which has deep ocean-view windows, seats all passengers at a single seating, the restaurant having been extended aft during her 1998 refit. The food consists of a combination of American and continental cuisine, prepared freshly by chefs trained at some of America's finest culinary institutions. There are limited menu choices, but the food is wholesome and simply but attractively presented. Dining room service is provided by young American waitresses whose bubbly enthusiasm makes up for a lack of training in service finesse.

Other Comments: This small ship (originally one of a series of eight built for the Murmansk Shipping Company) has an ice-strengthened royal blue hull (she has an A-1 ice classification), and a white funnel, bow-thruster, and stabilizers. Although the ship is not new, she went through a $15 million refit/conversion in the winter of 1997/1998, meets the latest international safety codes and requirements, and specializes in operating close-in expedition-style cruising. She carries 10 Zodiac rubber inflatable landing craft for in-depth excursions and wet landings, and has a covered promenade deck of Oregon pine.

She is now a tidy, neat, clean, and quite handsome ship throughout, with attractive, warm decor, lots of polished dark wood paneling and numerous real brass fixtures (like a "real" ship). She is cozy and caters to travelers rather than mere passengers.

The public spaces, however, are limited, with just one main lounge (this was extended forward over a former cargo hold during the refit so that it now accommodates all passengers for lectures) and bar. There is a small library, complete with high wing-back chairs and a decent selection of books. There is no forward observation lounge, although there is an outdoor observation area directly below the bridge. The dress code is casual and on all cruises, Clipper Cruise Line provides its own cruise staff and experienced historians and naturalist lecturers.

She is now a smart-looking vessel, and features cruises to unusual destinations not frequented by the flood of larger vessels. A no-smoking policy throughout all interior areas is in effect, although smoking is permitted on the outside decks. Travel insurance is included in the cruise fare.

<u>Weak Points</u>: The passageways are narrow (it is difficult to pass housekeeping carts), and the stairs are steep on the outer decks.

m/s Clipper Odyssey
★★★★ +
(S)

LIFESTYLE:	PREMIUM
Cruise Line:	Clipper Cruise Line
Former Names:	*Oceanic Odyssey, Oceanic Grace*
Gross Tonnage:	5,218
Builder:	NKK Tsu Shipyard (Japan)
Original Cost:	$40 million
Entered Service:	April 1989/November 1999
Flag:	Bahamas
Tel. No.:	n/a
Fax No.:	n/a
Length (ft/m):	337.5/102.9
Beam (ft/m):	50.5/15.4
Draft (ft/m):	14.1/4.3
Propulsion/Propellers:	diesel (5,192kW)/2 (CP)
Passenger Decks:	5
Total Crew:	52
Pass. Capacity (basis 2):	128
Pass. Capacity (all berths):	128
Pass. Space Ratio (basis 2):	40.7
Pass. Space Ratio (all berths):	40.7
Officers:	European
Total Cabins:	64
Size Range (sq ft/m):	195.9–258.3/18.2–24.0
Cabins (outside view):	64
Cabins (inside — no view):	0
Cabins (single occupancy):	0
Cabins (with private balcony):	8

Cabins (wheelchair accessible):	1
Cabin Current:	115 volts
Cabin TV:	No
Dining Rooms:	1
Elevators:	1
Casino:	No
Slot Machines:	No
Swimming Pools (outdoors):	1
Swimming Pools (inside):	0
Whirlpools:	1
Fitness Center:	Yes
Sauna/Steam Room:	Yes/Yes
Massage:	No
Self-Service Launderette:	No
Movie Theater/Seats:	No
Library:	Yes
Classification Society:	Nippon Kaiji Kyokai

RATINGS	POSSIBLE SCORE	SCORE ACHIEVED
Ship	500	432
Accommodation	200	168
Food	400	345
Service	400	340
Cruise	500	393
TOTAL	**2,000**	**1,678**

Accommodation: The all-outside cabins are tastefully furnished and feature blond wood cabinetry, twin- or queen-size beds, personal safe, minibar-refrigerator, safe, television and VCR player, tea-making unit, three-sided mirror, and cotton bathrobes. Bathrooms feature a deep, full-sized bathtub. The cabins that have private balconies (note that they are *very small* balconies) have awkward door handles. The bathroom toilet seats are high.

Dining: The dining room is very warm and inviting. The cuisine features fresh foods from local ports, in a mix of regional and some western cuisine, with open seating. The service is provided by young, friendly Americans.

Other Comments: This ship features impressive, if somewhat square-ish, contemporary looks and sports twin outboard funnels. She was built originally as a Japanese attempt to copy the Sea Goddess concept specifically outfitted for the Japanese market.

There is a decompression chamber for scuba divers, and water sports equipment is carried, as is a fleet of Zodiacs — inflatable landing craft for "soft" expedition use. Water sports facilities include an aft platform, scuba, snorkel, and water-ski boat. There is plenty of open deck and sunbathing space. The small swimming pool is just a "dip" pool, however. Has a wide teakwood outdoor jogging track.

Inside, nothing jars the senses, as the interior design concept successfully balances East-West color combinations with some Indonesian accents. The ambience is decidedly warm and intimate, and is for those who seek a small ship where entertainment and loud music is not a priority. *Clipper Odyssey* will provide a pleasing antidote to cruising aboard the large ships.

Under new owners Clipper Cruise Line (which takes over the ship as of November 1999), the ship operates three- and four-day cruises from November through April, and ten-day and longer cruises from April to November (islands of the North Pacific region, New Zealand, and Australia's Great Barrier Reef).

m/y/s Club Med 2
★★★★
(S)

LIFESTYLE:	PREMIUM
Cruise Line:	Club Med Cruises
Former Names:	-
Gross Tonnage:	14,983
Builder:	Ateliers et Chantiers du Havre (France)
Original Cost:	$125 million
Entered Service:	December 1992
Flag:	Wallis & Fortuna
Tel. No.:	112175
Fax No.:	112176
Length (ft/m):	613.8/187.1
Beam (ft/m):	65.6/20.00
Draft (ft/m):	16.4/5.00
Type of Vessel:	high-tech sail-cruiser
No. of Masts:	5 (164 ft high)/ 7 computer-controlled sails
Sail Area (sq ft/sq m):	26,910/2,500
Main Propulsion:	engines/sails
Propulsion/Propellers:	diesel (9,120kW)/2 (CP)
Passenger Decks:	8
Total Crew:	200
Pass. Capacity (basis 2):	394
Pass. Capacity (all berths):	409
Pass. Space Ratio (basis 2):	38.0
Pass. Space Ratio (all berths):	36.6
Officers:	French
Total Cabins:	197
Size Range (sq ft/m):	193.8–322.0/18.0–30.0

Cabins (outside view):	196
Cabins (inside — no view):	0
Cabins (single occupancy):	0
Cabins (with private balcony):	0
Cabins (wheelchair accessible):	0
Cabin Current:	110 and 220 volts
Cabin TV:	Yes
Dining Rooms:	2
Elevators:	2
Casino:	No
Slot Machines:	No
Swimming Pools (outdoors):	2
Whirlpools:	0
Fitness Center:	Yes
Sauna/Steam Room:	Yes/No
Massage:	Yes
Self-Service Launderette:	No
Library:	Yes
Classification Society:	Bureau Veritas

RATINGS	POSSIBLE SCORE	SCORE ACHIEVED
Ship	500	410
Accommodation	200	164
Food	400	293
Service	400	292
Cruise	500	387
TOTAL	**2,000**	**1,546**

Accommodation: The cabins are very nicely equipped, have an inviting decor that includes blonde wood cabinetry. They feature a minibar-refrigerator, 24-hour room service (but you pay for food), personal safe, television, plenty of storage space, bathrobes, and hairdryers. There are 6 four-person cabins, and some 35 doubles are fitted with an extra Pullman berth — good for young families, although this makes them a little more cramped when occupied.

Dining: There are two lovely dining rooms, each of which has tables for one, two, or more. A single open seating is featured for all meals. The Odyssey Restaurant has a delightful open terrace for informal meals. Complimentary wines and beers are available with lunch and dinner. Afternoon tea is a delight. The cuisine itself provides French, continental, and Japanese specialties, and the presentation is good.

Other Comments: She is one of a pair of the world's largest high-tech sail-cruisers. This vessel is part cruise ship, part yacht, and is rather like a larger version of the earlier Windstar vessels. Five huge masts provide seven computer-controlled sails.

There are extensive water sports facilities and an aft marina platform. Water sports equipment includes 12 Windsurfers, 3 sailboats, 2 water-ski boats, several kayaks, 20 single scuba tanks, snorkels, and 4 motorized water sport boats.

Inside the ship, other facilities include a computer workshop, and a golf simulator (for which there is an extra charge) instead of a fitness center. Your cruise can also be combined with a Club Med Village Vacation.

The onboard activities come under the direction of a large team of young, energetic GOs (Gentile Ordinaires), who, like their compatriots on land, have the full run of the ship. Although enthusiastic, the entertainment is rather clownlike and very amateurish, although everyone seems to have fun.

This vessel is excellent for the more upscale active singles and couples who might like casual elegance rather than the wilder vacation experience one might find at some Club Med resorts, and for those who enjoy water sports. No gratuities are expected or accepted, as at all Club Med resorts.

m/s Columbus
★★★ +
(S)

LIFESTYLE:	STANDARD
Cruise Line:	Hapag-Lloyd Seetouristik
Former Names:	-
Gross Tonnage:	14,903
Builder:	MTW Schiffswerft (Germany)
Original Cost:	$69 million
Entered Service:	July 1997
Flag:	Bahamas
Tel. No.:	330990810/630990811
Fax No.:	330990812/330990815
Length (ft/m):	472.8/144.13
Beam (ft/m):	70.5/21.50
Draft (ft/m):	16.8/5.15
Propulsion/Propellers:	diesel (10,560kW)/2 (CP)
Passenger Decks:	8
Total Crew:	170
Pass. Capacity (basis 2):	410
Pass. Capacity (all berths):	423
Pass. Space Ratio (basis 2):	36.3
Pass. Space Ratio (all berths):	35.2
Officers:	German
Total Cabins:	205
Size Range (sq ft/m):	129.1–322.9/12.0–30.0
Cabins (outside view):	158
Cabins (inside — no view):	47
Cabins (single occupancy):	0
Cabins (with private balcony):	2

Cabins (wheelchair accessible):	0
Cabin Current:	110 volts
Cabin TV:	Yes
Dining Rooms:	1
Elevators:	3
Casino:	No
Slot Machines:	No
Swimming Pools (outdoors):	1
Swimming Pools (inside):	0
Whirlpools:	0
Fitness Center:	Yes
Sauna/Steam Room:	Yes/No
Massage:	Yes
Self-Service Launderette:	No
Movie Theater/Seats:	No
Library:	Yes
Classification Society:	Germanischer Lloyd

RATINGS	POSSIBLE SCORE	SCORE ACHIEVED
Ship	500	347
Accommodation	200	146
Food	400	269
Service	400	292
Cruise	500	329
TOTAL	**2,000**	**1,383**

Accommodation: The standard cabins are really small, and many of them are inside. All but ten cabins feature lower berths, but the 16 categories established really are a lot for this size of ship. Except for two forward-facing suites, there are no balcony cabins. The cabin decor is bright and upbeat, and a good amount of closet and shelf space is provided. The bathrooms are fully tiled and have large shower stalls (none have bathtubs). All cabins feature a minibar-refrigerator (all items are at extra cost, as in hotels ashore), personal safe, and hairdryer (bathrobes are available on request, for a small surcharge).

There are eight suites (each is at least double the size of a standard cabin), and each has a curtained partition between the lounge and sleeping areas, with a wall unit that houses a television that can be turned 360 degrees for viewing from either the lounge or the bedroom. Two of the suites located at the bow each have a narrow private veranda (with two teak lounge chairs and a coffee table), bedroom (with a large wall clock) and lounge area separated by a curtain, two televisions, and an excellent amount of closet, drawer, and shelf space. The cabinetry, with its walnut finish and birds-eye pattern, makes these suites feel warm and luxurious. All the suites have a small room service menu. The bathrooms have a large shower (it is big enough for two), hairdryer, and under-sink storage space. There is 24-hour room service. Limited room service menu available for all cabins. Turn-down service.

Dining: There is one large main dining room located at the stern, with large ocean-view windows on three sides, and it seats all passengers in one seating, with assigned tables. There are tables for two (there are just two tables for two) up to 16 — good for family reunions. The cuisine features unstuffy presentation and is fairly good, although the menu selection is quite limited (choice of two or three entrees for dinner). There is an excellent selection of fresh-baked breads and rolls every day.

Breakfast and lunch can be taken in the bright but casual setting of the Palm Garden, which is also the ship's very comfortable observation lounge. Light dinners also can be taken in the Palm Garden, where a small dance floor adds another dimension.

Other Comments: This ship has a smart contemporary profile, with a single large funnel (painted in Hapag-Lloyd's orange/blue colors). Hapag-Lloyd Seetouristik has chartered the ship from the German owner, Conti Reederei, until 2002.

The ship also features an ice-hardened hull, which is useful for cold-weather cruise areas. In addition, the bridge "wings" can fold inward (as do the overhang lights) flush with the ship's side so that the vessel can enter the locks in the US/Canada Great Lakes region, including the St. Lawrence Seaway and Welland Canal, for which the ship was specifically built.

The ship has a good passenger space ratio. Each deck has a distinctly different color scheme and carpeting, making it easy to find one's way around. There is a reasonable range of public rooms to choose from, most of which are located in a "cake-layer" vertical stacking aft of the accommodation. Although the ceilings in the public rooms are plain and unimaginative (except for the Palm Garden), the decor is really bright and upbeat, and very different from all other ships in the Hapag-Lloyd fleet. The most popular room is arguably the delightful multifunction Palm Garden, which is also the ship's forward-facing observation lounge.

The fit and finish of the ship is a little utilitarian (the mottled grey walls are a little cold, but a contrast to the splashes of color found in carpeting and other decorative touches). The artwork chosen is, for the most part, minimal and uncoordinated, yet it all works together to provide cheerful surroundings. Ship buffs will be pleased to find some superb original photographs from the Hapag-Lloyd archives adorning the stairways.

She is a good ship for the standard market German-speaking traveler, and, as such, she offers excellent value for the money in very comfortable, unpretentious surroundings. However, you should know that the level of "luxury" is well below that of Hapag-Lloyd's *Europa*, and the experience is completely different (so is the cruise price).

First-time cruise passengers in particular will find this a fresh, comfortable, casual, and unpretentious ship for a cruise vacation. You don't need to buy a new wardrobe, and you can leave your tuxedo at home; for this ship you need only informal and casual clothes.

Well-planned itineraries and destination-intensive cruises are featured. Of particular note are the Great Lakes cruises, which are only possible because of the pencil-slim design of *Columbus* (the last oceangoing cruise vessel to operate Great Lakes cruises was *World Discoverer* in 1974).

<u>Weak Points</u>: The swimming pool is small (more like a "dip" pool), as is the open deck space. The standard cabins are also very small. There is no wraparound promenade deck outdoors. The layout and sight lines (including several pillars) in the show lounge are poor.

m/v CostaAllegra
★★★
(M)

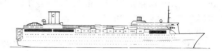

LIFESTYLE:	STANDARD
Cruise Line:	Costa Cruises
Former Names:	*Annie Johnson*
Gross Tonnage:	28,430
Builder:	Mariotti Shipyards (Italy)
Original Cost:	$175 million
Entered Service:	December 1992
Flag:	Liberia
Tel. No.:	1252216
Fax No.:	1252217
Length (ft/m):	616.1/187.8
Beam (ft/m):	83.9/25.6
Draft (ft/m):	23.9/7.3
Propulsion/Propellers:	diesel (19,200kW)/2 (CP)
Passenger Decks:	8
Total Crew:	400
Pass. Capacity (basis 2):	820
Pass. Capacity (all berths):	1,072
Pass. Space Ratio (basis 2):	34.7
Pass. Space Ratio (all berths):	26.5
Officers:	Italian
Total Cabins:	410
Size Range (sq ft/m):	105.4–265.8/9.8–24.7
Cabins (outside view):	218
Cabins (inside — no view):	192
Cabins (single occupancy):	0
Cabins (with private balcony):	10

Cabins (wheelchair accessible):	8 (inside)
Cabin Current:	110/220 volts
Cabin TV:	Yes
Dining Rooms:	1
Elevators:	4
Casino:	Yes
Slot Machines:	Yes
Swimming Pools (outdoors):	1
Swimming Pools (inside):	0
Whirlpools:	2
Fitness Center:	Yes
Sauna/Steam Room:	Yes/Yes
Massage:	Yes
Self-Service Launderette:	No
Movie Theater/Seats:	No
Library:	Yes
Classification Society:	Registro Navale Italiano

RATINGS	POSSIBLE SCORE	SCORE ACHIEVED
Ship	500	311
Accommodation	200	130
Food	400	218
Service	400	249
Cruise	500	302
TOTAL	**2,000**	**1,210**

Accommodation: The standard cabins are quite light and airy, with splashes of fabric colors and wood accenting, and they are laid out in a practical manner. However, they are small, and there is little closet and drawer space, so take only casual clothing. There are many small inside cabins, and all cabins suffer from poor soundproofing. Many cabins also have Pullman berths for a third or fourth occupant. The bathrooms are compact, although they do feature good shower enclosures, with sliding circular door instead of the usual limp curtain. The cabin service menu is extremely limited.

On Rousseau Deck there are three forward-facing suites (the largest accommodation on board), each of which features a living room, dinette, and wet bar. Another 10 slightly smaller mini-suites feature a small balcony, but it is really not very private, as it can be seen from the walking track on the deck above.

Dining: The Montmartre Restaurant, which seats about 475, is fairly spacious and has large glass window views to the stern, while the port side and starboard side feature large portholes. It is a very noisy room, with tables for four, six, eight, or ten (there are no tables for two). Dinner is later when the ship operates in Europe. The cuisine is mostly continental, with many Italian dishes featured, and the service from a bubbly staff is generally excellent. Good pasta dishes are served daily (the pasta is made fresh on board daily). The wine list is modest, but there are no wine waiters; instead, the waiters serve the wine (when they have time).

The Yacht Club is the informal dining spot, with two small centrally located buffet lines. As for breakfast and lunch buffets, Costa Cruises comes way down the list; they are rather plain, repetitive, and unimaginative, and fresh (ripe) fruit and cheese selections are poor. For ice cream lovers, a gelati cart provides welcome relief at least once each day.

Other Comments: Originally a container ship that has undergone a skillful transformation into contemporary cruise vessel, she is a jazzy, rather angular-looking ship with a low-slung appearance. There are three bolt upright yellow funnels that take a little getting used to, but have become somewhat of a signature for almost all ships in the fleet (exception: *CostaRiviera*). Slightly longer and larger than her sister ship *CostaMarina*, this ship enjoys a much better standard of interior fit and finish. Has an interesting glass-enclosed stern.

There is a high glass-to-steel ratio, with numerous glass domes and walls admitting light, as well as Murano glass light fixtures in some places. There is a good amount of outdoor deck and sunbathing space, although there is no forward observation lounge. Cushioned pads are provided for the deck lounge chairs outdoors.

The decks are named after famous painters. This ship features surprisingly nice interior decor, with cool, restful colors and soft furnishings, as well as domed ceilings and a big use of glass. In the Folies Bergeres show lounge, some 14 pillars obstruct the sight lines to the semicircular stage from many seats.

CostaAllegra will provide a decent first cruise experience for young adults who enjoy European-style service and a real upbeat, almost elegant atmosphere with an Italian accent and lots of noise. However, few of the officers and crew are actually Italian, as one might expect.

<u>Weak Points</u>: There are few public restrooms. The children's room is too small, and the ship is simply not equipped to handle large numbers of children, which are aboard in the summer and at peak holiday periods. The many loud and extended announcements (in several languages) quickly become tiresome — there are no quiet spots to be found anywhere. The open hours for the small library are really minimal. Tipping envelopes state the amount you are expected to give.

m/s CostaAtlantica
(L)

LIFESTYLE:	STANDARD
Cruise Line:	Costa Cruises
Former Names:	-
Gross Tonnage:	84,000
Builder:	Kverner Masa-Yards (Finland)
Original Cost:	$400 million
Entered Service:	July 2000
Flag:	Liberia
Tel. No:	n/a
Fax No:	n/a
Length (ft/m):	957/291.7
Beam (ft/m):	106/32.3
Draft (ft/m):	25.5/7.8
Propulsion/Propellers:	diesel-electric (34,000kW)/2 azimuthing pods
Passenger Decks:	14
Total Crew:	906
Pass. Capacity (basis 2):	2,112
Pass. Capacity (all berths):	2,680
Pass. Space Ratio (basis 2):	39.7
Pass. Space Ratio (all berths):	31.3
Officers:	Italian
Total Cabins:	1,056
Size Range (sq ft/m):	n/a
Cabins (outside view):	843 (including suites)
Cabins (inside — no view):	213
Cabins (single occupancy):	0
Cabins (with private balcony):	736
Cabins (wheelchair accessible):	8
Cabin Current:	110/220 volts
Cabin TV:	Yes
Dining Rooms:	1 (+ 1 specialty restaurant)
Elevators:	n/a
Casino:	Yes
Slot Machines:	Yes
Swimming Pools (outdoors):	2 (+1 indoor/outdoor)
Swimming Pools (inside):	0
Whirlpools:	Yes
Fitness Center:	Yes
Sauna/Steam Room:	Yes/Yes
Massage:	Yes
Self-Service Launderette:	No
Movie Theater/Seats:	No
Library:	Yes
Classification Society:	Registro Navale Italiano

RATINGS	POSSIBLE SCORE	SCORE ACHIEVED
Ship	500	NYR
Accommodation	200	NYR
Food	400	NYR
Service	400	NYR
Cruise	500	NYR
TOTAL	**2,000**	**NYR**
Expected Score Range:		**1400-1600**

Accommodation: This latest new ship for Costa Cruises provides a healthy proportion of outside-view to inside (no view) cabins. All accommodation features twin beds that can be easily converted into a queen-size bed, individually controlled air-conditioning, television, and telephone.

Some of the most desirable cabins will be the suites with private balconies in a quiet and protected (from the wind) location on four aft-facing decks, with some fine views overlooking the stern of the ship.

Dining: The main dining room is large, with ocean-view windows on three sides. There are two seatings, with both smoking and nonsmoking sections. Themed evenings are a part of the Costa Cruises tradition, one of which includes a "Roman Bacchanal" as part of the fun.

There will also be one specialty restaurant for alternative dining, a first for a Costa Cruises ship.

Perhaps the place that most people will want to see and be seen is in Caffe Florian, a replica of the famous indoor/outdoor cafe of the same name in St. Mark's Square, Venice (ideal for drinks, aperitifs, and music).

Other Comments: She is Costa Cruises' largest ship (with the same exterior design and internal layout as that of *Carnival Spirit*). She sports the familiar, instantly recognizable yellow upright funnels, with one large funnel and two small exhaust funnels set farther back, in a slightly different arrangement from the tri-funnel clusters of previous newbuilds.

There are two centrally located swimming pools outdoors, with one centrally located pool that can be used in inclement weather due to its magrodome cover. Families with children will note that one swimming pool incorporates a long water slide.

Inside, although few details were available at press time, the design is an extension of that found in previous newbuilds for Costa Cruises, particularly that of *CostaVictoria*.

This new ship will operate seven-night Mediterranean cruises during the summer.

m/v CostaClassica
★★★ +
(L)

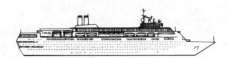

LIFESTYLE:	STANDARD
Cruise Line:	Costa Cruises
Former Names:	-
Gross Tonnage:	52,950
Builder:	Fincantieri (Italy)
Original Cost:	$325 million
Entered Service:	January 1992
Flag:	Liberia
Tel. No.:	1252243
Fax No.:	1252244
Length (ft/m):	718.5/220.61
Beam (ft/m):	98.4/30.8
Draft (ft/m):	25.0/7.60
Propulsion/Propellers:	diesel (22,800kW)/2 (CP)
Passenger Decks:	10
Total Crew:	600
Pass. Capacity (basis 2):	1,308
Pass. Capacity (all berths):	1,764
Pass. Space Ratio (basis 2):	40.4
Pass. Space Ratio (all berths):	30.0
Officers:	Italian
Total Cabins:	654
Size Range (sq ft/m):	185.1–430.5/17.2–40.0
Cabins (outside view):	438
Cabins (inside — no view):	216
Cabins (single occupancy):	0
Cabins (with private balcony):	10

Cabins (wheelchair accessible):	6 (inside)
Cabin Current:	110/220 volts
Cabin TV:	Yes
Dining Rooms:	1
Elevators:	8
Casino:	Yes
Slot Machines:	Yes
Swimming Pools (outdoors):	2
Swimming Pools (inside):	0
Whirlpools:	4
Fitness Center:	Yes
Sauna/Steam Room:	Yes/Yes
Massage:	Yes
Self-Service Launderette:	No
Movie Theater/Seats:	No
Library:	Yes
Classification Society:	Registro Navale Italiano

RATINGS	POSSIBLE SCORE	SCORE ACHIEVED
Ship	500	388
Accommodation	200	154
Food	400	218
Service	400	282
Cruise	500	326
TOTAL	**2,000**	**1,368**

Accommodation: The cabins are of a fairly generous size. They have cherry wood veneered cabinetry and include a vanity desk unit with a large mirror. There are useful sliding doors to bathroom and closets, and good soundproofing. The soft furnishings are of good quality, but the room service menu is disappointing. The suites feature more space (although they are not large), and handwoven bedspreads.

Dining: The dining room has a lovely indented clean white ceiling, but is extremely noisy (there are two seatings), and there are a good number of tables for two, as well as tables for four, six, or eight. Changeable wall panels help create a European Renaissance atmosphere, albeit at the expense of blocking off windows. Dinner on European cruises is late. Reasonable continental cuisine, with many Italian (salty) dishes, but presentation, quality, and service are poor and really basic. There is a wine list, but there are no wine waiters.

The outdoors Alfresco Café is moderately good. Unfortunately, breakfast and luncheon buffets are really poor and unimaginative, with little variety, and long lines are typical. The selection of bread, rolls, fruits, and cheeses is disappointing.

Other Comments: This all-white ship has a slab-sided profile, which is topped by Costa Cruises' unmistakable trio of tall yellow funnels. This ship has brought Costa into the mainstream, Italian-style.

Inside, she features contemporary, innovative Italian design and styling that is best described as befitting European tastes. There is an excellent range of public rooms, lounges, and bars from which to choose. A number of specially designed good business and meeting facilities can be found; the rooms provide multi-flexible configurations.

Has some fascinating artwork, including six hermaphrodite statues in one lounge. There is a fine, if unconventional multitiered amphitheater-style showroom, but the seats are bolt upright and are downright uncomfortable for more than a few minutes. The multilevel atrium is stark and angular, and cold.

The marble-covered staircases look pleasant, but are uncarpeted, really do not work well aboard a cruise ship, and are institutional (not to mention just a little dangerous if water or drinks are spilled on them when the ship is moving).

Perhaps the interior is best described as an innovative design project that almost works. A forward observation lounge/night club sits atop ship like a lump of cheese, and, unfortunately, fails to work well as a night club.

The staff is reasonably friendly, and, although the "spit and polish" of fine service is definitely missing, they will help you to have an enjoyable cruise (especially when pushing for gratuities). Sadly, the dress code has become very casual throughout, even on formal nights. Most passengers will be Italian, with a generous sprinkling of other European nationalities. One night (typically towards the end of each cruise) is reserved for a "Roman Bacchanal," which means that passengers dress up toga-style for dinner and beyond.

<u>Weak Points</u>: There is no wraparound promenade deck outdoors. There are too many loud, repetitious, and irritating announcements. Shore excursions are very expensive. Tipping envelopes provided in your cabin state the amount you are expected to give.

m/s CostaMarina
★★★
(M)

LIFESTYLE:	STANDARD
Cruise Line:	Costa Cruises
Former Names:	-
Gross Tonnage:	25,558
Builder:	Marriotti Shipyards (Italy)
Original Cost:	$130 million
Entered Service:	July 1990
Flag:	Liberia
Tel. No.:	1252245
Fax No.:	1252246
Length (ft/m):	571.8/174.25
Beam (ft/m):	84.6/25.75
Draft (ft/m):	26.1/8.20
Propulsion/Propellers:	diesel (19,152kW)/2 (CP)
Passenger Decks:	8
Total Crew:	400
Pass. Capacity (basis 2):	776
Pass. Capacity (all berths):	1,005
Pass. Space Ratio (basis 2):	32.9
Pass. Space Ratio (all berths):	25.4
Officers:	Italian
Total Cabins:	388
Size Range (sq ft/m):	104.4–264.8/9.7–24.6
Cabins (outside view):	183
Cabins (inside — no view):	205
Cabins (single occupancy):	0
Cabins (with private balcony):	0
Cabins (wheelchair accessible):	0
Cabin Current:	110/220 volts
Cabin TV:	Yes
Dining Rooms:	1
Elevators:	8
Casino:	Yes
Slot Machines:	Yes
Swimming Pools (outdoors):	1
Swimming Pools (inside):	0
Whirlpools:	3
Fitness Center:	Yes
Sauna/Steam Room:	Yes/Yes
Massage:	Yes
Self-Service Launderette:	No
Movie Theater/Seats:	No
Library:	Yes
Classification Society:	Registro Navale Italiano

RATINGS	POSSIBLE SCORE	SCORE ACHIEVED
Ship	500	310
Accommodation	200	130
Food	400	218
Service	400	249
Cruise	500	302
TOTAL	**2,000**	**1,209**

Accommodation: Both the outside and inside (no-view) cabins are quite comfortable, yet they have very plain, almost clinical, decor and no warmth. In other words, they really are quite basic units. Bathrooms are functional, but there is little space for personal toiletry items. The illuminated cabin numbers outside each cabin are quite novel. The room service menu is very poor.

Dining: The dining room, which is located at the stern, has excellent ocean views on three sides, is reasonably spacious, and reached by escalator. There are two seatings. The lime green color, however, is less than attractive; in fact it is rather institutional. There are only two tables for two, other tables being for four, six, or eight. The table candlelights are of poor quality. The ship serves good commercial pasta, and features mainly continental cuisine. The service is adequate, but there are few Italians in the dining room, as one might expect.

Other Comments: She is an interesting, though very angular-looking, mid-sized ship, the first of two such ships (her almost identically designed, though slightly longer sister ship is *CostaAllegra*). There is a high glass-to-steel ratio, with numerous glass domes and walls. Has a cutaway stern which is virtually replaced by a glass wall (which are in fact the dining room windows), and a stark upright cluster of three yellow funnels.

There is generally good passenger flow throughout her public room spaces. Most public rooms are located above the accommodation decks and feature several bars and lounges useful for social meetings. This very Italian ship will provide a good first cruise experience for young adults, although it is much better suited to European passengers.

<u>Weak Points</u>: The fit and finish of this vessel is below the standard of competing ships in the same price category. There is a very limited amount of open deck and sunbathing space. There is no forward observation lounge. Has a tiny swimming pool. There are simply too many cabins (inside). There are poor sight lines in the showroom, with too many pillars (14 of them). The library is really poor. Tipping envelopes provided in your cabin state the amount you are expected to give.

s/s CostaRiviera
★★★
(M)

LIFESTYLE:	STANDARD
Cruise Line:	Costa Cruises
Former Names:	*American Adventure/*
	CostaRiviera/Guglielmo Marconi
Gross Tonnage:	30,000
Builder:	Cantieri Riuniti dell' Adriatico (Italy)
Original Cost:	$33.7 million (reconstruction)
Entered Service:	October 1963/May 1995
Flag:	Liberia
Tel. No.:	1252214
Fax No.:	1252215
Length (ft/m):	700.1/213.4
Beam (ft/m):	94.1/28.71
Draft (ft/m):	23.9/7.3
Propulsion/Propellers:	steam turbine
	(32,800kW)/2 (FP)
Passenger Decks:	8
Total Crew:	500
Pass. Capacity (basis 2):	974
Pass. Capacity (all berths):	1,819
Pass. Space Ratio (basis 2):	32.3
Pass. Space Ratio (all berths):	17.3
Officers:	Italian
Total Cabins:	487
Size Range (sq ft/m):	150.6–209.9/14.0–19.5
Cabins (outside view):	285
Cabins (inside — no view):	202
Cabins (single occupancy):	0
Cabins (with private balcony):	0
Cabins (wheelchair accessible):	0
Cabin Current:	110/220 volts
Cabin TV:	No
Dining Rooms:	1
Elevators:	7
Casino:	Yes
Slot Machines:	Yes
Swimming Pools (outdoors):	1
Swimming Pools (inside):	0
Whirlpools:	3
Fitness Center:	Yes
Sauna/Steam Room:	Yes/Yes
Massage:	Yes
Self-Service Launderette:	No
Movie Theater/Seats:	Yes/180
Library:	Yes
Classification Society:	Registro Navale Italiano

RATINGS	POSSIBLE SCORE	SCORE ACHIEVED
Ship	500	299
Accommodation	200	115
Food	400	230
Service	400	245
Cruise	500	263
TOTAL	**2,000**	**1,152**

Accommodation: There is a wide variety of cabin sizes, styles and configurations from which to choose. Many cabins are large enough for families of five or six, while many others will accommodate three or four persons. The cabin insulation is not good, however, and the bathrooms are small, compact units, with little space to place or store personal toiletry items. All cabins have a telephone.

Dining: The dining room, which has portholes and not windows, is large and bubbly (noisy), although it is plain and unattractive (especially the ceiling). There are two seatings. Reasonable continental food is provided; this includes plenty of pasta, pizza, and buffets, but desserts are poor. Decent enough service comes with a smile from an international staff. It is *not* for those who like a quiet dining experience.

Other Comments: This ship is a reconstructed former two-class ocean liner which was completely refurbished in 1993 in theme-park style for families, refurbished again in 1994 for Italian family cruising, and updated again in 1998. Solidly built ship that is stable and quiet at sea, with no vibration. Rides well, due to her deep draft. Built-up fore and aft decks provide a good amount of open deck and sunbathing space. The interior decor and styling, and everything else are geared to families. Good array of public rooms, including a cinema with a balcony level. A new lobby provides more light and room, and is now two decks high.

Has a very casual, bubbly ambience, and a very relaxed dress code. This ship will provide a cruise in relatively comfortable, family-filled surroundings for a modest price, with activities designed for participation, which means lots of noise. Particularly caters to an Italian family clientele.

Weak Points: The internal layout is a little disjointed; this is because the ship was originally built as a two-class ocean liner. There is no forward observation lounge. Do expect lines for embarkation and disembarkation (depending on itinerary), buffets, and shore excursions. The many announcements quickly become tedious. Everywhere there is noise, and a lot of cigarette smoke. Cleanliness could be better in some areas. The air-conditioning is quite noisy in many cabins, and there is very little adjustment. Tipping envelopes provided in your cabin and tell you the amount you are expected to give.

m/v CostaRomantica
★★★ +
(L)

LIFESTYLE:	STANDARD
Cruise Line:	Costa Cruises
Former Names:	-
Gross Tonnage:	53,049
Builder:	Fincantieri (Italy)
Original Cost:	$325 million
Entered Service:	November 1993
Flag:	Liberia
Tel. No.:	1252227
Fax No.:	1252231
Length (ft/m):	718.5/220.61
Beam (ft/m):	98.4/30.89
Draft (ft/m):	25.0/7.60
Propulsion/Propellers:	diesel (22,800kW)/2 (CP)
Passenger Decks:	10
Total Crew:	600
Pass. Capacity (basis 2):	1,356
Pass. Capacity (all berths):	1,779
Pass. Space Ratio (basis 2):	39.1
Pass. Space Ratio (all berths):	29.8
Officers:	Italian
Total Cabins:	678
Size Range (sq ft/m):	185.1–430.5/17.2–40.0
Cabins (outside view):	462
Cabins (inside — no view):	216
Cabins (single occupancy):	0
Cabins (with private balcony):	10

Cabins (wheelchair accessible):	6 (inside)
Cabin Current:	110/220 volts
Cabin TV:	Yes
Dining Rooms:	1
Elevators:	8
Casino:	Yes
Slot Machines:	Yes
Swimming Pools (outdoors):	2
Swimming Pools (inside):	0
Whirlpools:	4
Fitness Center:	Yes
Sauna/Steam Room:	Yes/Yes
Massage:	Yes
Self-Service Launderette:	No
Movie Theater/Seats:	No
Library:	Yes
Classification Society:	Registro Navale Italiano

RATINGS	POSSIBLE SCORE	SCORE ACHIEVED
Ship	500	389
Accommodation	200	154
Food	400	218
Service	400	282
Cruise	500	326
TOTAL	**2,000**	**1,369**

Accommodation: The 16 suites (with floor-to-ceiling windows) and 18 mini-suites are really lovely (except for the balconies of the ten suites on Madrid Deck, where a solid steel half-wall blocks the view; a glass half-wall and polished wood rail wood be better). A sliding door separates the bedroom from the living room, and bathrooms are of a decent size. Cherry wood walls and cabinetry help make these suites warm and very attractive. The six suites at the forward section of Monte Carlo Deck are the largest, and have huge glass windows with superb forward views, but no balconies.

All other cabins are of a standard, though generous size, and all have nicely finished cherry wood cabinetry and walls (the ceilings are plain). However, the cabin bathrooms and showers are small. There are a good number of triple and quad cabins that are ideal for families with children. The company's in-cabin food service menu is very basic.

Dining: The dining room is better designed and a little less noisy than in her sister ship of the same size — *CostaClassica*, and there are several tables for two, as well as tables for four, six, or eight. There are two seatings. Features reasonable continental cuisine, but the presentation, quality, and service need improving. There is a poor selection of bread rolls, fruits, and cheeses. The pasta dishes and cream sauces, however, are very good. Although there is a wine list, there are no wine waiters.

For informal dining there is a much improved and more practical buffet layout than in her sister ship, but it is far too small, and buffets are very much standard fare, really unimaginative and noncreative, with the exception of some good commercial pasta dishes. One would expect Italian waiters, but, sadly, this is not the case now, with most of the waiters coming from countries other than Italy (many are from the Philippines).

Other Comments: This bold, contemporary ship has an upright yellow funnel cluster of three, typical of Italian styling today. Costa is well established in Europe, and its Italian-style cruising is something it does well. Sadly, there is no wraparound promenade deck outdoors, and so contact with the sea is minimal, although there is some good open space on several of the upper levels.

She has a much nicer interior design than her sister ship, *CostaClassica*, and the decor is decidedly warmer. The layout and flow are somewhat disjointed, however. Has a good number of business and conference facilities, with several flexible meeting rooms for groups of different sizes. The decor is decidedly Italian, chic, and very tasteful, and should appeal to both Europeans and sophisticated North Americans.

The multilevel atrium is open and spacious, and features a revolving mobile sculpture. The amphitheater-style, two-deck-high, multitiered showroom is good, and has interesting artwork, but the stark upright seating is really uncomfortable. The sight lines to the stage from many seats are obstructed by ten large pillars. There is also a small chapel (in a different location to that in her sister ship), and several intimate public rooms, lounges, and bars.

Costa Cruises does a good job of providing first-time cruise passengers with a well-packaged vacation that is a mix of sophistication and basic fare, albeit accompanied by rather loud music and an international staff that seems to have lost direction. During the summer, this ship cruises in the Mediterranean region, while during the winter she cruises in the Caribbean (when there are more American passengers than Europeans).

<u>Weak Points</u>: Announcements are many and loud. The reception desk staff is very poor and impersonal, like in a bad hotel, and cigarette smoke is everywhere. Tipping envelopes provided in your cabin state the amount you are expected to give.

m/v CostaVictoria
★★★★
(L)

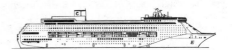

LIFESTYLE:	STANDARD
Cruise Line:	Costa Cruises
Former Names:	-
Gross Tonnage:	75,200
Builder:	Bremer Vulkan (Germany)
Original Cost:	$388 million
Entered Service:	July 1996
Flag:	Liberia
Tel. No.:	363653510
Fax No.:	363653520
Length (ft/m):	823.0/251.00
Beam (ft/m):	105.5/32.25
Draft (ft/m):	25.6/7.80
Propulsion/Propellers:	diesel (30,000kW)/2 (CP)
Passenger Decks:	10
Total Crew:	800
Pass. Capacity (basis 2):	1,928
Pass. Capacity (all berths):	2,464
Pass. Space Ratio (basis 2):	38.9
Pass. Space Ratio (all berths):	31.0
Officers:	Italian
Total Cabins:	964
Size Range (sq ft/m):	120.0–430.5/11.1–40.0
Cabins (outside view):	573
Cabins (inside — no view):	391
Cabins (single occupancy):	0
Cabins (with private balcony):	0
Cabins (wheelchair accessible):	6
Cabin Current:	110 and 220 volts
Cabin TV:	Yes
Dining Rooms:	2
Elevators:	12
Casino:	Yes
Slot Machines:	Yes
Swimming Pools (outdoors):	2
Swimming Pools (inside):	1
Whirlpools:	4
Fitness Center:	Yes
Sauna/Steam Room:	Yes/Yes
Massage:	Yes
Self-Service Launderette:	Yes
Movie Theater/Seats:	No
Library:	Yes
Classification Society:	Registro Navale Italiano

RATINGS	POSSIBLE SCORE	SCORE ACHIEVED
Ship	500	418
Accommodation	200	158
Food	400	220
Service	400	273
Cruise	500	337
TOTAL	**2,000**	**1,406**

Accommodation: There are six large Panorama suites (each has third/fourth pullman berths in a separate, tiny, train-like compartment) and 14 mini-suites (the six suites feature Laura Ashley-style fabrics), all with butler service. Sixty-five percent of all other cabins are outside, but they are small (for two). While the suites are not large, all other cabins are of rather mean dimensions. Some (only 16) of the cabins (inside) accommodate four, while all other cabins are for two or three persons.

All cabins feature wood cabinetry, with a fair amount of closet and drawer space for two for a one-week cruise, excellent air-conditioning, minibar-refrigerator, and electric blackout window blind (there are no curtains). The ocean-view cabins have large picture windows. The cabin bathrooms are small but well appointed, and (sensibly) have a sliding door. There are six cabins for the physically handicapped (each has two bathrooms); all are well located, and adjacent to elevators in the center of the ship.

Note that the personal safe is difficult to reach, and cabin stewards simply have too many cabins to clean, and no help, which means that service is less than desirable.

Dining: The two main dining rooms (there are two seatings) are the Fantasia and Sinfonia, which are separated by the main galley. They are expansive (there are a few tables for two, most being for four, six, or eight) and feature marble and pine walls. The cuisine is good basic fare, and so the presentation is adequate. Perhaps somewhat lacking is the use of garnishes to dress the plates. As you would expect, there is always plenty of pasta. Aboard an Italian ship, one would expect a dining room full of Italian waiters, but, sadly, this is not so, for there are none. Romantic candlelight dining featured on formal nights.

The ship also features casual breakfast and lunch buffets with indoor/outdoor seating (under a canvas sailcloth canopy for the outdoor section), although the buffet displays are very disappointing. There is also a pizzeria (it is open afternoons and evenings), good for casual fast-food devotees who may be used to frozen/reheated commercial pizzas.

Other Comments: The ship's exterior profile is similar to that of an enlarged version of the popular and very successful *CostaClassica* and *CostaRomantica*, with huge upright yellow funnels. A sister ship, *CostaOlympia* was scheduled for delivery in 1998, but was not completed due to shipyard bankruptcy. Having replaced all its older tonnage in the past few years, Costa Cruises now has a good contemporary fleet, operating in the Caribbean, Mediterranean, and South America.

Has a fully enclosed bridge. There is an outdoor wraparound promenade deck (but it is full of deck lounge chairs) as well as a wraparound jogging track.

Inside the ship is a lovely four-deck-high forward-facing observation lounge (Concorde Plaza) with a "beam-me-up" glass elevator; in the center is a cone-shaped waterfall (huge video screens flank the walls), while "pod" balconies overlook the room's center; it is a stunning space, and has its own bar. Sadly, thick floor-to-ceiling pillars obstruct sight lines from most seats.

The seven-deck-high "planetarium" atrium (a novel, but somewhat impractical design) has four glass elevators that travel up to a clear crystal dome (you can see the weather outside through it). The upper-most level of the atrium is the deck where two outside swimming pools are located, together with four blocks of showers, and an ice cream bar and grill. There is a large forward shopping area, adjacent to the atrium. Ship lovers should look in the Tavernetta Lounge (aft) for ten paintings of past and present Costa Cruises ships. There is also a small chapel.

Unusual for a new ship (and welcomed by European passengers) is a pleasant but small indoor swimming pool, and sauna (it is tiny, and there are no adjacent changing or locker facilities, which makes it very user-unfriendly). Also adjacent is a steam room, and gymnasium (limited assortment of equipment), as well as a covered walking/jogging track. There is also a tennis court. Sunbathers on the forwardmost section of the outdoor deck close to the mast have their own showers (excellent) and no music (good).

Where this ship differs from most large ships is in her distinct European interior decor, with decided-ly Italian styling. The ship is modern without being glitzy, and bold without being brash.

Weak Points: When inside, there is absolutely no feeling that this is a ship. There are not enough seats in the show lounge. There are no fresh flowers in evidence anywhere. The service is decidedly loud and casu-al (make that sloppy and inconsistent) and there is little real hospitality. The telephone numbering system is incredibly complicated (try remembering 05313 for the information desk or 06718 to book a massage).

The live music everywhere is loud, very loud, and there are too many repetitive announcements. Tipping envelopes provided in your cabin state the amount you are expected to give. The indigo blue interior walls look pleasant enough, but in the event of a power failure they would make the vessel appear pitch black.

m/s Crown Dynasty
★★★ +
(M)

LIFESTYLE:	STANDARD
Cruise Line:	Crown Cruise Lines
Former Names:	*Norwegian Dynasty, Crown Majesty,*
	Cunard Dynasty, Crown Dynasty
Gross Tonnage:	19,089
Builder:	Union Navale de Levante (Spain)
Original Cost:	$100 million
Entered Service:	July 1993/October 1999
Flag:	Panama
Tel. No.:	1337757
Fax No.:	1337761
Length (ft/m):	537.4/163.81
Beam (ft/m):	73.8/22.5
Draft (ft/m):	17.7/5.40
Propulsion/Propellers:	diesel (13,200kW)/2 (CP)
Passenger Decks:	7
Total Crew:	320
Pass. Capacity (basis 2):	802
Pass. Capacity (all berths):	916
Pass. Space Ratio (basis 2):	23.8
Pass. Space Ratio (all berths):	20.8
Officers:	European
Total Cabins:	401
Size Range (sq ft/m):	139.9–349.8/13.0–32.5
Cabins (outside view):	277
Cabins (inside — no view):	124
Cabins (single occupancy):	0

Cabins (with private balcony):	10
Cabins (wheelchair accessible):	4
Cabin Current:	110 and 220 volts
Cabin TV:	Yes
Dining Rooms:	1
Elevators:	4
Casino:	Yes
Slot Machines:	Yes
Swimming Pools (outdoors):	1
Swimming Pools (inside):	0
Whirlpools:	3
Fitness Center:	Yes
Sauna/Steam Room:	Yes/No
Massage:	Yes
Self-Service Launderette:	No
Movie Theater/Seats:	No
Library:	No
Classification Society:	Det Norske Veritas

RATINGS	POSSIBLE SCORE	SCORE ACHIEVED
Ship	500	367
Accommodation	200	148
Food	400	242
Service	400	289
Cruise	500	335
TOTAL	**2,000**	**1,381**

Accommodation: The cabins, although small, are nicely furnished, trimmed with wood and feature large picture windows. They come quite well equipped, complete with vanity desk unit, a good amount of drawer space, curtained windows, and personal safe. Bathrooms are somewhat compact, but are nicely fitted out and have an excellent shower stall. However, the cabins unfortunately have very poor soundproofing; passengers in cabins on Deck 4 in particular are disturbed by anyone running or jogging on the deck above.

Dining: The dining room (nonsmoking) is pleasing and attractive, with large ocean-view windows on three sides. However, it is rather cramped, and there are no tables for two. The ambience, however, is quite warm. There are two seatings for dinner, and one for breakfast and lunch. A varied menu is provided.

Other Comments: This really is a very handsome mid-sized ship. There is a reasonably good amount of open deck and sunbathing space. The ship is under a long-term charter to Crown Cruise Line from the ship's owner, Neptun Maritime Group of Helsinki, Finland.

There is a well-designed five-deck-high, glass-walled atrium, offset to the starboard side. The off-center stairways seem to add a sense of spaciousness to a clever interior design. The interior decor in public spaces is warm and inviting. The artwork is colorful and pleasant, but it certainly is not outstanding.

The show lounge sits longitudinally with amphitheater-style seating in several tiers.

Crown Cruise Line (run by the same owners as Commodore Cruise Line) is positioning itself as a premium cruise line that aims to provide a reasonably priced cruise product in clean, decent surroundings. The ship will operate seven-night Bermuda cruises during the summer (from Philadelphia), featuring weekends in Bermuda, and seven-night Caribbean cruises during the winter.

<u>Weak Points</u>: Do expect lines for the buffets, tenders, and the few elevators. The health spa is extremely tight, and the show lounge has congestion problems, is poorly designed for passenger movement, and several pillars obstruct the sight lines to the stage.

m/v Crown Princess
★★★★
(L)

LIFESTYLE:	PREMIUM
Cruise Line:	Princess Cruises
Former Names:	-
Gross Tonnage:	69,845
Builder:	Fincantieri Navali (Italy)
Original Cost:	$276.8 million
Entered Service:	July 1990
Flag:	Liberia
Tel. No.:	1150543
Fax No.:	1150544
Length (ft/m):	811.0/247.2
Beam (ft/m):	105.8/32.26
Draft (ft/m):	26.5/8.10
Propulsion/Propellers:	diesel-electric (24,000kW)/2 (CP)
Passenger Decks:	11
Total Crew:	696
Pass. Capacity (basis 2):	1,590
Pass. Capacity (all berths):	1,910
Pass. Space Ratio (basis 2):	43.9
Pass. Space Ratio (all berths):	36.5
Officers:	Italian
Total Cabins:	795
Size Range (sq ft/m):	1989.4–574.8/17.6–53.4
Cabins (outside view):	624
Cabins (inside — no view):	171
Cabins (single occupancy):	0

Cabins (with private balcony):	184
Cabins (wheelchair accessible):	10
Cabin Current:	110 and 220 volts
Cabin TV:	Yes
Dining Rooms:	1 (main)
Elevators:	9
Casino:	Yes
Slot Machines:	Yes
Swimming Pools (outdoors):	2
Swimming Pools (inside):	0
Whirlpools:	4
Fitness Center:	Yes
Sauna/Steam Room:	Yes/Yes
Massage:	Yes
Self-Service Launderette:	Yes
Movie Theater/Seats:	Yes/169
Library:	Yes
Classification Society:	Registro Navale Italiano

RATINGS	POSSIBLE SCORE	SCORE ACHIEVED
Ship	500	382
Accommodation	200	156
Food	400	271
Service	400	299
Cruise	500	401
TOTAL	**2,000**	**1,509**

Accommodation: In general, the cabins are well designed and have large bathrooms as well as good soundproofing. Walk-in closets, refrigerator, personal safe, and an interactive video system are provided in all cabins. Twin beds convert to queen-size beds in standard cabins. Bathrobes and personal toiletry amenities are standard, too. Note that the handicapped cabins have obstructed views.

The 14 most expensive suites (each of which has a large private balcony) are very well laid out, with a practical design that positions most things in just the right place. The bedroom is separated from the living room by a heavy wooden door, and there are televisions in both rooms. The closet and drawer space is very generous, and there is enough of it even for long cruises.

Dining: The dining room (all dining rooms aboard Princess Cruises ships are nonsmoking) is large, but lacks tables for two, although the line's marketing tag line states that this is "The Love Boat" line. Some of the most desirable tables overlook the stern. There are two seatings. The cuisine is, for the most part, disappointing (it is stodgy, with poor creativity and presentation) although there has been more creativity of late. The pasta dishes are good, however, usually served by section headwaiters. The general service level is quite reasonable, but it always seems hurried, particularly for those who are at the first seating. The wine list is average, with a heavy emphasis on Californian wines.

There is an excellent pizzeria, however, for informal meals; this is particularly popular at lunchtime and in the afternoons. Themed late-night buffets are provided, but afternoon teas are poor. For sweet snacks during the day, a Patisserie (items are at extra charge) is located in the spacious lobby.

Other Comments: This was the first ship in the 70,000-tonne range for Princess Cruises, and provided a foretaste of even larger ships for this successful company. The ship has an interesting, jumbo-airplane look to it when viewed from the front, with a dolphin-like upper structure, and a large upright funnel placed aft.

Inside, however, innovative and elegant styling is mixed with traditional features and a spacious interior layout. The interior spaces are well designed, although the layout itself is somewhat disjointed. An understated decor of soft pastel shades is highlighted by some very colorful artwork.

An observation dome, set high atop the ship like the head of a dolphin, features a large casino, numerous rubber trees, a dance floor, and live music. The ship has decent health and fitness facilities. A striking, elegant three-deck-high atrium features a grand staircase with fountain sculpture (real, stand-up cocktail parties are held here). Characters Bar, located adjacent to the pizzeria on the open deck forward, has wonderful drink concoctions and some unusual glasses.

This ship provides a very pleasant cruise in elegant and very comfortable surroundings, and fine-tuned staff will make you feel welcome. Princess Cruises provides white-gloved stewards to take you to your cabin when you embark, another nice touch. *Crown Princess* has undergone an extensive refit (remodeled atrium and dining room, new 24-hour Lido restaurant and evening bistro, and new children's center). She operates a series of cruises in Europe in 2000, combining these with a winter season in the Caribbean.

Weak Points: The open deck space is very limited for the size of the ship and the number of passengers carried, and, sadly, there is no forward observation viewpoint outdoors. There is no wraparound promenade deck outdoors (the only walking space being along the sides of the ship). In fact, there is little contact with the outdoors at all. The sunbathing space is really limited when the ship is full, although with passenger age range often of 50 years old and above, perhaps this is not quite so crucial. There are too many support pillars in the public rooms that obstruct the sight lines and flow. Inside, the layout is disjointed, and takes getting used to. Galley fumes seem to waft constantly over the aft open decks.

m/v Crystal Harmony
★★★★★
(M)

LIFESTYLE:	LUXURY
Cruise Line:	Crystal Cruises
Former Names:	-
Gross Tonnage:	49,400
Builder:	Mitsubishi Heavy Industries (Japan)
Original Cost:	$240 million
Entered Service:	July 1990
Flag:	Bahamas
Tel. No.:	1103237
Fax No.:	1103234
Length (ft/m):	790.5/240.96
Beam (ft/m):	97.1/29.60
Draft (ft/m):	24.6/7.50
Propulsion/Propellers:	diesel-electric (32,800kW)/2 (CP)
Passenger Decks:	8
Total Crew:	545
Pass. Capacity (basis 2):	940
Pass. Capacity (all berths):	1,010
Pass. Space Ratio (basis 2):	51.4
Pass. Space Ratio (all berths):	48.9
Officers:	Scandinavian/Japanese
Total Cabins:	480
Size Range (sq ft/m):	182.9–947.2/17.0–88.0
Cabins (outside view):	461
Cabins (inside — no view):	19
Cabins (single occupancy):	0
Cabins (with private balcony):	260

Cabins (wheelchair accessible):	4
Cabin Current:	115 and 220 volts
Cabin TV:	Yes
Dining Rooms:	3 (2 alternative restaurants)
Elevators:	8
Casino:	Yes
Slot Machines:	Yes
Swimming Pools (outdoors):	2 (1 with magrodome)
Swimming Pools (inside):	0
Whirlpools:	2
Fitness Center:	Yes
Sauna/Steam Room:	Yes/Yes
Massage:	Yes
Self-Service Launderette:	Yes
Movie Theater/Seats:	Yes/270
Library:	Yes
Classification Society:	Lloyd's Register/Nippon Kaiji Kyokai

RATINGS	POSSIBLE SCORE	SCORE ACHIEVED
Ship	500	452
Accommodation	200	175
Food	400	345
Service	400	346
Cruise	500	443
TOTAL	**2,000**	**1,761**

Accommodation: Deck 10 Penthouses: Four spectacular Crystal penthouses measure 948-982 sq ft (88.0-91.2 m²) and feature a huge private balcony and lounge, separate master bedroom with king-sized bed and electric curtains, large walk-in closets, and stunning ocean-view bathrooms. These really are the epitome of fine, private, pampered living at sea, and all the priority perks.

Other Deck 10 Suites: All of the other suites on this deck are worth the asking price, have plenty of space (all of them feature a private balcony), including a separate lounge with large sofa, coffee table and chairs, and a separate sleeping area. The bathrooms are quite large, and extremely luxurious. In fact, any of the suites on this deck are equipped with everything necessary for refined, private living at sea.

Five butlers feature the best in personal service in all the top category suites on this deck (with a total of 132 beds), where all room service food arrives on sterling silver trays, and all laundry is included, as are afternoon tea trolley service and evening hors d'oeuvres.

Deck 9/8/7/5 Cabins: Many of the cabins feature a private balcony (in fact, 50 percent of all cabins have private balconies), and are extremely comfortable, although a little tight for space. They are very compact units, and it's one-way traffic past the bed, but there is a reasonable amount of drawer and storage space (the drawers *are* small, however) although the closet hanging space is somewhat limited for long voyages. Some cabins in grades G and I have lifeboat-obstructed views. All cabins have color televisions, video player units, mini-refrigerator, personal safe, small sofa, coffee table, and excellent soundproofing. The bathrooms, although well appointed, are of the "you first, me next" variety (and size), but they do come with generously sized personal toiletry items and amenities.

Regardless of the accommodation category you select, duvets and down pillows are provided, as are lots of other niceties.

Dining: There are several dining choices aboard this lovely ship. The dining room is moderately elegant, with plenty of space around each table, well-placed waiter service stations and a good number of tables for two, as well as tables for four, six, or eight. It is noisy at times (particularly in the raised, center section), making it difficult to carry on a conversation at the larger tables in the center (raised) section. The food is attractively presented and well served in a friendly but correct manner. It is of a high standard, with good quality ingredients used throughout (meat quality could be improved, however). Features a mixture of European specialties and North American favorites. The menus are extremely varied, and special orders are available (including caviar and other niceties). All in all, the food is most acceptable and, with the choice of the two alternative dining spots, provides consistently high marks from passengers.

Sadly, dinner in the main dining room is in two seatings (the early seating is simply too rushed), although with two alternative restaurants, off-menu choices, a fine hand-picked European staff, and excellent service, dining is often memorable. Note that smoking and nonsmoking sections are provided. However, there is no physical barrier between the two, so nonsmokers could find themselves seated next to smokers.

Pasta specialties are made each day on request to the headwaiters. For those who enjoy caviar, it is available, although it is sevruga (malossol) and not beluga. The wine list is superb.

Afternoon tea (and coffee) in the Palm Court is good. The choice of sandwiches, cakes, and pastries is good (although I am concerned about cutbacks). Needless to say, service is generally excellent.

The two alternative dining spots — Prego (features fine pasta dishes), and Kyoto, with pseudo-Japanese specialties (there is no extra charge, other than a recommended $5 waiter gratuity per meal that should be included in the cruise fare) are intimate, have great views, and feature fine food. There should be separate entrances for these two alternative restaurants (at present a single entrance serves both). Both are totally nonsmoking.

Other Comments: She is a handsome, contemporary ship with raked clipper bow and well-balanced, sleek flowing lines. Excellent open deck, sunbathing space, and sports facilities that include a paddle tennis court. One of two outdoor swimming pools has a swim-up bar and can be covered by a magrodome. There is almost no sense of crowding anywhere, a superb example of comfort by design, quality construction, and engineering. There is a wraparound teakwood deck for walking, and an abundance of open deck and sunbathing space.

Inside, the design shows that form follows function superbly well. There is a fine assortment of public entertainment lounges and small intimate rooms (except for a night club/lounge that is simply too large for the number of late-night passengers frequenting it), and passenger flow is excellent. Outstanding are the Vista (observation) Lounge and the supremely tranquil, elegant Palm Court, one of the nicest rooms afloat. A Business Center features laptop computers, printers, satellite faxes, and phones.

There is an excellent book and video library. The theater features high-definition video projection and special headsets for the hearing-impaired. There is a self-service launderette on each deck, particularly useful for long voyages. Fine-quality fabrics and soft furnishings, china, flatware, and silver are used throughout. Features an excellent array of in-cabin television programming, as well as close-captioned videos for the hearing-impaired. Smokers will enjoy a fine range of cigars available in the Vista Lounge. The decorations on the Christmas cruise are simply stunning.

This very friendly, well-trained, highly professional staff, and excellent teamwork (with one of the lowest turnover of staff in the industry) is under the direction of a solid, all-European middle management. It is the extra attention to detail that makes a cruise aboard this ship so special, such as few announcements, and no background music anywhere. The company pays attention to its fine base of repeat passengers, and makes subtle changes in operations in order to constantly fine-tune its product.

This ship has just about everything for the discerning, seasoned traveler who wants and is prepared to pay for good style, space, and the comfort and the facilities of a large vessel capable of longer voyages. She is, without doubt, an outstanding example of the latest style in contemporary grand hotels afloat and provides abundant choices and flexibility. Following a refit in 1997, some of the public rooms have been expanded (most notably the casino) and refurbished. In 1999, both ships took on board a "Connoisseurs Club" which operates in the Avenue Saloon and incorporates the very best in premium brands of liquor and cigars for those who can appreciate (and pay for) such things.

You will be surrounded by a cocoon of fine comfort and pampering to the highest degree, although it is let down to some degree by the two seatings for dinner. Insurance and gratuities are extra, although they should be included at this price level.

m/s Crystal Symphony
★★★★★
(M)

LIFESTYLE:	LUXURY
Cruise Line:	Crystal Cruises
Former Names:	-
Gross Tonnage:	51,044
Builder:	Masa-Yards (Finland)
Original Cost:	$300 million
Entered Service:	March 1995
Flag:	Bahamas
Tel. No.:	630916820/30/40/50/60
Fax No.:	1306716
Length (ft/m):	777.8/237.10
Beam (ft/m):	98.0/30.20
Draft (ft/m):	24.9/7.60
Propulsion/Propellers:	diesel-electric (33,880kW)/2 (CP)
Passenger Decks:	8
Total Crew:	545
Pass. Capacity (basis 2):	940
Pass. Capacity (all berths):	1,010
Pass. Space Ratio (basis 2):	53.1
Pass. Space Ratio (all berths):	50.5
Officers:	Scandinavian
Total Cabins:	480
Size Range (sq ft/m):	201.2–981.7/18.7–91.2
Cabins (outside view):	480
Cabins (inside — no view):	0
Cabins (single occupancy):	0

Cabins (with private balcony):	276
Cabins (wheelchair accessible):	7
Cabin Current:	110 and 220 volts
Cabin TV:	Yes
Dining Rooms:	3
Elevators:	8
Casino:	Yes
Slot Machines:	Yes
Swimming Pools (outdoors):	2 (1 with magrodome)
Swimming Pools (inside):	0
Whirlpools:	2
Fitness Center:	Yes
Sauna/Steam Room:	Yes/Yes
Self-Service Launderette:	Yes
Massage:	Yes
Movie Theater/Seats:	Yes/143
Library:	Yes
Classification Society:	Lloyd's Register

RATINGS	POSSIBLE SCORE	SCORE ACHIEVED
Ship	500	457
Accommodation	200	178
Food	400	345
Service	400	345
Cruise	500	444
TOTAL	**2,000**	**1,769**

Accommodation: The spacious, well-designed accommodation includes two spectacular 982 sq ft (91.2 m²) Crystal penthouses with a huge balcony and lounge, bedroom with queen-sized bed, and stunning ocean-view bathroom with large whirlpool bath. Butlers feature the best in personal service in the top category suites on Penthouse Deck 10, where all room service food arrives on sterling silver trays, and lots of extra goodies are provided for occupants. All other cabins (called "penthouses" by Crystal Cruises) on Deck 10 are worth the asking price, being extremely spacious, supremely comfortable, and quiet units equipped with everything necessary for refined, private living at sea, including VCR units.

More than 50 percent of all cabins have private balconies; they are well equipped, and extremely comfortable, with excellent sound insulation. The balcony partitions, however, do not go from floor to ceiling, so you *can* hear your neighbors. Even in the lowest category of standard cabins, there is plenty of drawer space, but the closet hanging space may prove somewhat limited for long voyages. Has generously sized personal bathroom amenities, duvets, and down pillows. European stewardesses provide excellent service and attention.

Some cabins (grades G and I), although no public rooms, have obstructed views. Except for the penthouse suites, cabin bathrooms are somewhat compact. A privacy curtain should be placed between entrance and sleeping area in all non-Penthouse Deck cabins.

Dining: The main dining room is elegant, with crisp design and plenty of space around each table, well placed waiter service stations and ample tables for two. The main dining room is well laid out, and features a raised, circular central section, although it is somewhat noisy at times, and not conducive to a fine dining experience. There are tables for two (many of them positioned adjacent to large windows), four, six, or eight.

The food is attractively presented and well served (mix of plate and silver service). It is of a high standard, with fine-quality ingredients used. European dishes are predominant. Menus are extremely varied, and feature a good selection of meat, fish, and vegetarian dishes. Special (off-menu) orders *are* available, as are caviar and other culinary niceties.

Overall, the food is most acceptable for a large ship and, with the choice of the two alternative dining spots, receives high passenger praise. Dinner in the main dining room is in two seatings, although with two alternative restaurants, off-menu choices, a fine European staff and excellent service, dining can be memorable. Fresh pasta and dessert flambeau specialties are made tableside each day by the headwaiters.

Afternoon tea in the Palm Court is a delightful daily event. The Lido provides breakfast and luncheon buffets that are fairly standard fare.

Two alternative dining rooms, the 75-seat Prego (serving Italian cuisine), and the 84-seat Jade Garden (serving contemporary Chinese dishes), are appreciably larger and set on a lower deck (Deck 6) than those aboard her sister ship, and each restaurant has a separate entrance and theme decor. They both provide an excellent standard of culinary fare, with food cooked to order at no extra charge (but the recommended $5 waiter gratuity per meal should be included in the cruise fare).

In addition, The Bistro provides a fine array of snacks, cakes, coffees, and teas throughout the day, with unusual, Crystal Cruises-logo china that can also be purchased in one of the ship's boutiques.

Other Comments: This is a contemporary ship that has a nicely raked clipper bow and well-balanced lines. While some might not like the "apartment block" look of the ship's exterior, it is the look of the future, as balconies become the norm. This ship has an excellent amount of open deck, sunbathing space, and sports facilities. The aft of two outdoor swimming pools can be covered by a magrodome in inclement weather. There is no sense of crowding anywhere, a superb example of comfort by design, high quality construction, and engineering. Has a wide wraparound teakwood deck for walking, uncluttered by lounge chairs.

The interior decor is restful, with color combinations that do not jar the senses. Has a good mixture of public entertainment lounges and small intimate rooms. Outstanding is the Palm Court, a forward observation lounge that is tranquil, and one of the nicest rooms afloat (it is larger than aboard the sister ship). There is an excellent book, video, and CD-ROM library (combined with a Business Center). The theater (smaller than aboard the sister ship) features high-definition video projection and headsets for the hearing-impaired. Useful self-service launderette on each deck. Fine-quality fabrics and soft furnishings, china, flatware, and silver are used. Excellent in-cabin television programming (including CNN and ESPN), and close-captioned videos for the hearing-impaired.

In 1999, both ships took on board a "Connoisseurs Club" which operates in the Avenue Saloon and incorporates the very best in premium brands of liquor and cigars for those who can appreciate (and pay for) such things.

This ship has just about everything for the discerning, seasoned traveler who wants and is prepared to pay good money for fine style, abundant space, and the comfort and the facilities of a large vessel capable of extended voyages. The one thing that lets the product down is the dining room operation in two seatings.

Crystal Cruises takes care of its ships, and its staff, and it is the staff that makes the cruise experience really special. They are a fine-tuned, well-trained group who stress hospitality at all times. The ship achieves a high rating because of her fine facilities, service, and crew. It is the extra attention to detail that makes a cruise with this ship so special, such as very few announcements. Gratuities should be included on a ship so highly rated (they can, however, be pre-paid).

m/s Dalmacija
★★
(S)

LIFESTYLE:	STANDARD
Cruise Line:	Croatia Cruise Lines
Former Names:	-
Gross Tonnage:	5,650
Builder:	Brodogradiliste Uljanik (Yugoslavia)
Original Cost:	n/a
Entered Service:	1965
Flag:	Croatia
Tel. No.:	n/a
Fax No.:	n/a
Length (ft/m):	383.4/116.87
Beam (ft/m):	54.1/16.51
Draft (ft/m):	17.3/5.28
Propulsion/Propellers:	diesels (11,030kW)/2 (FP)
Passenger Decks:	5
Total Crew:	112
Pass. Capacity (basis 2):	284
Pass. Capacity (all berths):	300
Pass. Space Ratio (basis 2):	19.8
Pass. Space Ratio (all berths):	18.8
Officers:	Croatian
Cabins:	142
Size (sq ft/m):	n/a
Cabins (outside view):	93
Cabins (inside — no view):	55
Cabins (single occupancy):	0
Cabins (with private balcony):	0

Cabins (wheelchair accessible):	0
Cabin Current:	220 volts
Dining Rooms:	1
Elevators:	0
Casino:	No
Slot Machines:	No
Swimming Pools (outdoors):	1
Swimming Pools (inside):	0
Whirlpools:	0
Fitness Center:	No
Sauna/Steam Room:	No
Massage	No
Cinema/Theater:	No
Cabin TV:	No
Library:	Yes
Classification Society:	n/a

RATINGS	POSSIBLE SCORE	SCORE ACHIEVED
Ship	500	212
Accommodation	200	94
Food	400	189
Service	400	207
Cruise	500	193
TOTAL	**2,000**	**895**

Accommodation: The cabins really are very small, and most have only a limited amount of drawer space, although the closet space is reasonably adequate (for short cruises). Each cabin has its own private bathroom, which is very small and utilitarian, with a tiny shower stall in which you will be invited to dance with the shower curtain.

Dining: This ship has a dining room that is pleasant, with cheerful decor and service, dining is in one seating with assigned tables. The service staff is friendly and attentive, although the service really is just basic. The choice of meals is very limited, and the food is generally overcooked. There is little choice of fresh fruits, cheeses, and breads. The wine list is poor.

Other Comments: This ship has an all-white exterior, and presents a reasonably clean-looking small ship profile. She is a cozy, very high-density ship that does not pretend to be glamorous. She is clean and tidy throughout, however, having undergone a refurbishment in 1997. Her limited number of public rooms feature wood accenting, which helps warm the otherwise plain decor.

There is a small outdoor swimming pool (which is really a "dip" pool), an entertainment lounge, photo shop, small fitness center, and two bars.

She caters primarily to European passengers looking for a destination-intensive cruise in comfortable, but not elegant, surroundings, at a modest price, without the finesse and fuss of a lot of other ships. The ship is often under charter to various tour packagers, and so the standard of product delivery, food, and service can differ.

Weak Points: There is a limited amount of open deck and sunbathing space. Passenger hallways are really dark and dreary, and lighting throughout is inconsistent.

m/s Dawn Princess
★★★★ +
(L)

LIFESTYLE:	**PREMIUM**
Cruise Line:	Princess Cruises
Former Names:	-
Gross Tonnage:	77,000
Builder:	Fincantieri (Italy)
Original Cost:	$300 million
Entered Service:	May 1997
Flag:	Liberia
Tel. No.:	363657010
Fax No.:	363657020
Length (ft/m):	856.2/261.0
Beam (ft/m):	105.8/32.25
Draft (ft/m):	26.0/7.95
Propulsion/Propellers:	diesel-electric (46,080kW)/2 (FP)
Passenger Decks:	10
Total Crew:	900
Pass. Capacity (basis 2):	1,950
Pass. Capacity (all berths):	2,250
Pass. Space Ratio (basis 2):	39.4
Pass. Space Ratio (all berths):	34.2
Officers:	British/Italian
Total Cabins:	975
Size Range (sq ft/m):	158.2–610.3/14.7–56.7
Cabins (outside view):	609
Cabins (inside — no view):	372
Cabins (single occupancy):	0
Cabins (with private balcony):	410
Cabins (wheelchair accessible):	19
Cabin Current:	110 and 220 volts
Cabin TV:	Yes
Dining Rooms:	2 main/3 others
Elevators:	11
Casino:	Yes
Slot Machines:	Yes
Swimming Pools (outdoors):	4
Swimming Pools (inside):	0
Whirlpools:	5
Fitness Center:	Yes
Sauna/Steam Room:	Yes
Massage:	Yes
Self-Service Launderette:	Yes
Movie Theater/Seats:	No
Library:	Yes
Classification Society:	Registro Navale Italiano

RATINGS	POSSIBLE SCORE	SCORE ACHIEVED
Ship	500	442
Accommodation	200	168
Food	400	271
Service	400	299
Cruise	500	406
TOTAL	**2,000**	**1,586**

Accommodation: Although the cabins are a little small, they are well designed and functional in layout, and have earth tone colors accentuated by splashes of color from the bedspreads. Proportionately, there are quite a lot of inside cabins. Many of the outside cabins have private balconies (more than any other Princess Cruises ship to date except *Grand Princess*), and all seem to be well soundproofed, although the balcony partition is not floor to ceiling type, so you can hear your next door neighbors clearly. Note: The balconies are very small, and only large enough for two small chairs. Good closet and abundant drawer and other storage space is provided in all cabins — plenty for a seven-night cruise. The cabin bathrooms are practical, and come complete with all the little details one needs, although they really are tight, one person at-a-time units. A decent shower stall, some shelving for toiletries, and real glasses are provided.

The suites and mini-suites are very well laid out, with larger bathrooms, Jacuzzi bathtubs and a large, separate shower, as well as a separate bedroom, and television sets in both bedroom and lounge areas. The suites also have a dining room table and four chairs.

Dining: There are two main dining rooms (both are nonsmoking); each of which has its own galley and each is split into multitier sections, which help create a feeling of intimacy, although there is a lot of noise from the waiter stations, which are adjacent to many tables. Breakfast and lunch are provided in an open seating arrangement, while dinner is in two seatings. The food, its presentation and delivery are somewhat disappointing, but adequate (this is banquet catering, after all), and let this otherwise beautifully decorated ship down.

There is also a patisserie (for cappuccino/espresso coffees and pastries), a wine/caviar bar, and a pizzeria (complete with cobblestone floors and wrought iron decorative features), and excellent pizzas (there are six to choose from).

The Horizon Buffet is open almost 24 hours a day, and, at night, features an informal dinner setting with sit-down waiter service and a small bistro menu (available from 6:00pm to 2:00am). The buffet displays are, for the most part, unappetizing and repetitious. The cabin service menu is very limited, and presentation of the food items featured is quite poor.

Other Comments: Although large, this all-white ship has a good profile, and is well balanced by its large funnel, which contains a deck tennis/basketball/volleyball court in its sheltered aft base. There is a wide, teak wraparound promenade deck outdoors, some real teak steamer-style deck chairs (complete with royal blue cushioned pads), and 93,000 sq ft (8,640 m²) of outdoor space. A great amount of glass area on the upper decks provides plenty of light and connection with the outside world.

The ship, while large, almost has an intimate feel to her, which is what the interior designers intended. Her interiors are very pretty and warm, with attractive colors and welcoming decor that includes some very attractive wall murals and other artwork. The signs around the ship could be improved, however.

There is a wide range of public rooms to choose from, with several intimate rooms and spaces so that you do get the feel of being overwhelmed by large spaces. Features tasteful decor, with attractive color combinations that are warm and do not clash (nothing is brash). The interior focal point is a huge four-deck-high atrium lobby with winding, double stairways, complete with two panoramic glass-walled elevators.

The main public entertainment rooms are located under three cabin decks. There is plenty of space, the traffic flow is good, and the ship absorbs people well. There are two showrooms, one at each end of the ship; one is a superb 550-seat, theater-style show lounge (movies are also shown here) and the other is a 480-seat cabaret-style lounge, complete with bar.

A glass-walled health spa complex is located high atop ship and includes a gymnasium with high-tech machines. One swimming pool is "suspended" aft between two decks (there are two other pools, although they are not large for the size of the ship).

The library is a very warm room and has six large buttery leather chairs for listening to compact audio discs, with ocean-view windows. There is a conference center for up to 300, as well as a business center, with computers, copy, and fax machines. The collection of artwork is good, particularly on the stairways, and helps make the ship feel smaller than it is, although in places it doesn't always seem coordinated. The casino, while large, is not in the main flow and so does not generate the "walk-through" factor found aboard many ships.

The most traditional room aboard is the Wheelhouse Lounge/Bar, which is decorated in the style of a turn-of-the-century gentleman's club, whose focal point is a large ship model from the P&O collection archives.

At the end of the day, as is the case in most large ships today, if you live in the top suites, you will be well attended; if you do not, you will merely be one of a very large number of passengers. One nice feature is the captain's cocktail party, held in the four-deck-high main atrium so you can come and go as you please — no standing in line if you don't want to.

Weak Points: There is no escape from unnecessary and repetitious announcements that intrude. The swimming pools are small for so many passengers, and the pool deck is cluttered with deck lounge chairs (plastic). Waiting for tenders in anchor ports can prove irritating, but typical of large ship operations. Charging for the machines in the self-service launderette is trifling.

m/s Delphin
★★★ +
(S)

LIFESTYLE:	STANDARD
Cruise Line:	Delphin Seereisen
Former Names:	*Kazakhstan II/Belorussiya*
Gross Tonnage:	16,214
Builder:	Wartsila (Finland)
Original Cost:	$25 million
Entered Service:	January 1975/December 1993
Flag:	Malta
Tel. No.:	1257506/624945111
Fax No.:	1257507/624945115
Length (ft/m):	512.5/156.24
Beam (ft/m):	71.8/21.90
Draft (ft/m):	20.3/6.20
Propulsion/Propellers:	diesel (13,250kW)/2 (CP)
Passenger Decks:	8
Total Crew:	234
Pass. Capacity (basis 2):	466
Pass. Capacity (all berths):	556
Pass. Space Ratio (basis 2):	35.6
Pass. Space Ratio (all berths):	29.8
Officers:	Ukrainian
Total Cabins:	233
Size Range (sq ft/m):	150.0–492.0/14.0–45.7
Cabins (outside view):	128
Cabins (inside — no view):	105
Cabins (single occupancy):	0
Cabins (with private balcony):	0
Cabins (wheelchair accessible):	0
Cabin Current:	220 volts
Cabin TV:	Yes
Dining Rooms:	1
Elevators:	2
Casino:	No
Slot Machines:	No
Swimming Pools (outdoors):	1
Swimming Pools (inside):	0
Whirlpools:	0
Fitness Center:	Yes
Sauna/Steam Room:	Yes/Yes
Massage:	Yes
Self-Service Launderette:	Yes
Movie Theater/Seats:	No
Library:	Yes
Classification Society:	Germanischer Lloyd

RATINGS	POSSIBLE SCORE	SCORE ACHIEVED
Ship	500	314
Accommodation	200	126
Food	400	247
Service	400	278
Cruise	500	314
TOTAL	**2,000**	**1,279**

Accommodation: The Boat Deck suites (located forward) are extremely large and well equipped, with an absolute abundance of drawers and good closet space, and all feature blond wood furniture, and a refrigerator. The bathrooms are very spacious, and come with full-sized bathtubs and large toiletries cabinet; bathrobes are also provided.

All other cabins are compact, yet adequate, although there is little drawer space, making storage space tight on long cruises, which this ship often features. All of the beds have duvets, and all cabins receive fresh flowers each cruise. The bathrooms are small, but there is good space for toiletry items.

Dining: Has a single, large dining room, with a high ceiling, big picture windows, and pleasing, elegant decor; seats all passengers in one seating. The catering remains a weak point, but has improved during the past two years.

The food is, for the most part, attractively presented (although inconsistent), and very reasonable. The choice is good and includes selections for vegetarians. While standard white and red table wines are included for lunch and dinner, there is also an additional wine list with a reasonably good selection at moderate prices. The breakfast and lunch buffets, which are provided in The Lido, are decent enough, and the gala buffet is excellent. Service comes with a smile from attractive Ukrainian waitresses, although communicating with them can prove awkward at times.

Other Comments: This smart-looking modern ship has a rather square funnel, and was very well refitted and refurbished throughout following a shipyard rollover incident (when she was named *Belorussiya*).

New facilities were added which improved almost all the public areas and added new health/fitness and spa facilities and an improved outdoor pool/lido deck (the circular pool is small, however). The promenade decks outdoors are quite good (although there are "lips" to step over in the forward section). The interior decor is very tasteful, and enhanced by several flower bouquets and colorful artwork throughout.

This ship will provide a comfortable cruise experience for German-speaking passengers at an extremely attractive price. It is not a luxury product, nor does it pretend to be, but she is a very comfortable and friendly ship in which to cruise. She attracts many repeat passengers because of the excellent itineraries and good service levels. The company continues to spend money on little refinements throughout the ship, which are appreciated by the many loyal repeat passengers. Delphin Seereisen's own onboard cruise director and staff are excellent. Port taxes and insurance are included.

Finally, the company also has an outstanding new (in 1998) river vessel, *Delphin Queen*, which operates along the River Danube.

THE POPULARITY OF CRUISING

In 1998, over eight million people worldwide took a cruise, packaged and sold by cruise lines through tour operators and travel agents. The most recent (1998) breakdown of passengers by nationality choosing to take an oceangoing cruise vacation is provided below (taken from figures supplied by the Maritime Evaluations Group):

United States	5,500,000
UK*	635,000
Asia (not including Japan)	800,000
Germany	283,000
Canada	250,000
Italy	250,000
Australasia	200,000
Japan	200,000
France	165,000
Rest of Europe	120,000
Cyprus**	75,000
Freighter Passengers	3,000
TOTAL	**8,481,000**

*This figure includes 130,000 British passengers who took a two- to seven-day cruise from Cyprus in conjunction with a resort/hotel stay.

**Local Cyprus market.

Additional - River Cruise Passengers: Britain: 145,000; Germany: 117,500; France: 60,000; Japan: 30,000

ms Disney Magic
★★★★ +
(L)

LIFESTYLE:	PREMIUM
Cruise Line:	Disney Cruise Line
Former Names:	-
Gross Tonnage:	83,338
Builder:	Fincantieri (Italy)
Original Cost:	$350 million
Entered Service:	July 1998
Flag:	Bahamas
Tel. No.:	330851612/13/17/18
Fax No.:	330851611/16
Length (ft/m):	964.5/294.00
Beam (ft/m):	105.7/32.22
Draft (ft/m):	26.2/8.0
Propulsion/Propellers:	diesel-electric (38,000kW)/ 2 (FP)
Passenger Decks:	12
Total Crew:	945
Pass. Capacity (basis 2):	1,750
Pass. Capacity (all berths):	3,325
Pass. Space Ratio (basis 2):	47.6
Pass. Space Ratio (all berths):	25.5
Officers:	European/Norwegian
Total Cabins:	875
Size Range (sq ft/m):	180.8–968.7/16.8–90.0
Cabins (outside view):	720
Cabins (inside — no view):	155
Family Cabins:	80

Cabins (with private balcony):	388
Cabins (wheelchair accessible):	12
Cabin Current:	110 volts
Cabin TV:	Yes
Dining Rooms:	3 main (+1 Alternative +1 Cafe)
Elevators:	12
Casino:	No
Slot Machines:	0
Swimming Pools (outdoors):	3
Swimming Pools (inside):	0
Whirlpools:	6
Fitness Center:	Yes
Sauna/Steam Room:	Yes/Yes
Massage:	Yes
Self-Service Launderette:	Yes (3)
Movie Theater/Seats:	Yes/270
Library:	No
Classification Society:	Lloyd's Register

RATINGS	POSSIBLE SCORE	SCORE ACHIEVED
Ship	500	447
Accommodation	200	172
Food	400	211
Service	400	303
Cruise	500	420
TOTAL	**2,000**	**1,553**

Accommodation: Spread over six decks, there are several types of suites and cabins from which to choose; all have been designed for practicality and have space-efficient layouts that are well laid out. Most cabins have common features such as a neat vertical steamer trunk used for clothes storage, a hairdryer located at a vanity desk (or in the bathroom), and bathrobes for all passengers. Many cabins have third- and fourth pull-down berths that can be raised totally into the ceiling when not in use, but the standard inside and outside cabins, while acceptable for two, are extremely tight with three or four. The decor is practical, creative, and very colorful, with lots of neat styling touches. Cabins with refrigerators can have them stocked with one of three packages (at extra cost, of course).

The bathrooms, although compact (due to the fact that the toilet is separate from the rest of the bathroom), are really functional units, designed with split-use facilities so that more than one person can use them at the same time (good for families); many have bathtubs (really shower tubs).

The suites, quite naturally, offer much more space and goodies such as VCR units, CD players, large screen televisions, and extra beds that are useful for larger families. Some of the suites are, however, beneath the pool deck, teen lounge, or informal cafe, so there could be lots of noise as the ceiling insulation is poor (but cabin to cabin insulation is good).

Wheelchair-bound passengers have a variety of cabin sizes and configurations to choose from, including suites with a private balcony and extra-large bathrooms with excellent roll-in showers, and good closet and drawer space (most of the vessel is quite accessible).

A 24-hour room service is available (suite occupants also get concierge service); the room service menu is limited, however, as is the cabin breakfast menu. There is a 15 percent service charge for beverage deliveries.

Dining: There are three main dining rooms (all are nonsmoking), each with over 400 seats, two seatings, and unique themes. Lumiere's has *Beauty and the Beast*; Parrot Cay has a pseudo-Caribbean theme; and Animator's Palate (the most visual of the three) features food and electronic art that makes the evening

223

decor change from black and white to full-color. You will get to eat in all three dining rooms in what is termed "rotation" dining — you move together with your assigned waiter and assistant waiter to each dining room in turn, thus providing a different dining experience (each has a different decor, different menus). *Note*: As you will have the same waiter in each of the three restaurants, any gratuities go only to "your" waiter. Parrot Cay and Lumiere's have open seating for breakfast and lunch (the lunch menu is pitiful). The noise level in all three dining rooms is extremely high.

In addition, Palo is an elegant 140-seat reservations-only alternative restaurant (with a $5 cover/gratuity charge) featuring Italian cuisine. It has a 270-degree view, and is for adults only (no "Munchkins" allowed); the à la carte cuisine is cooked to order, and the wine list is good (prices are high). Make your reservations as soon as you board or miss out on the only decent food aboard this ship.

For casual eating there's Topsider's — an indoor/outdoor cafe featuring low-quality, self-serve breakfast and lunch buffets with very poor choice and presentation, and a buffet dinner for children (mostly fried foods). There is an ice cream and frozen yogurt bar (Scoops) that opens too infrequently. There are other fast food outlets for hamburgers, veggie burgers, hot dogs (Pluto's), inedible pizza, and sandwiches (Pinocchio's — open at varying times throughout the day but not in the evening).

Overall, the food has improved since the ship was first introduced, and is now more attractively presented, although there are still few green vegetables. Vegetarians and those seeking healthy spa alternatives will be totally underwhelmed, as will those who want spa (light) cuisine. Guest chefs from Walt Disney World Resort prepare signature dishes each cruise.

Other Comments: This ship's profile has tried to combine streamlining with tradition and nostalgia, and has two large red and black funnels designed to remind you of the ocean liners of the past (she is the first cruise ship built with two funnels since the 1950s. However, one of the funnels is a dummy, but contains a variety of public spaces, including a neat ESPN sports bar and a broadcast center). The ship's whistle even plays "When You Wish Upon A Star" (sort of). The bow features handsome gold scrollwork that is more often seen adorning the tall ships of yesteryear. There is a wraparound promenade deck outdoors for strolling.

Disney Cruise Line has not added ostentatious decoration to the ship's exterior. However, Mickey's ears are painted on the funnels; there is also a special 85-foot-long (25.9 m) paint stripe that cleverly incorporates Disney characters into the whimsical yellow paintwork along each side of the hull at the bow. Cute: The ship's exterior colors are also those of Mickey Mouse himself (call it a well-planned coincidence). Also of note is a 15-foot-tall (4.5 m) Goofy hanging upside down in a bosun's chair, painting the stern of the vessel.

Inside, the ship is quite stunning, although poorly finished in several places. The Art Deco theme of the old ocean liners has been tastefully carried out (check out the stainless steel/pewter Disney detailing on the handrails and balustrades in the three-deck-high lobby). Most public rooms have high ceilings. The decor is actually more reminiscent of New York's Radio City Music Hall. The interior detailing is stunning, much of it whimsical — pure Disney. The lobby provides a real photo opportunity that should not be missed — a 6-feet (1.8 m) high bronze statue of Mickey in the role of a ship's helmsman (there is probably some pixie dust around somewhere, too!). Mickey is also visible in many other areas, albeit somewhat subtly (for Disney). If you can't sleep, try counting the number of times Mickey's logo appears — it's an impossible task!

There are two large shops and an abundance of Disney-theme clothing, soft toys, collectibles, and specialty items. Features a superb, 1040-seat Walt Disney Theatre (spread over four decks but without a balcony), piano bar, adults-only night club/disco, family lounge, dedicated cinema (where classic Disney films are shown, as well as first-run movies).

On deck, a sports deck features a paddle tennis court, table tennis, basketball court, and shuffleboard, as well as a golf driving range. An ESPN Skybox Bar features 12 televisions of differing sizes for live sports events and noisy conversation (cigar smokers welcome). There are three outdoor pools; one pool for adults only (in theory), one for children, and one for families (guess which one has Mickey's ears painted into the bottom of the pool?). However, there's music everywhere, and it's virtually impossible to find a quiet spot. The children's pool features a long yellow water slide (available at specified times), held up by a Mickey's hand.

For fitness devotees, a fitness spa, measuring 8,500 sq ft (789.6 m^2) has ocean-view windows that overlook the navigation bridge below. There are several treatment rooms, and a "rain forest" with scented steam rooms, although the pounding from the basketball court located directly above makes relaxing spa treatments impossible, and thus a waste of money.

The children's entertainment areas measure 13,000 sq ft (1,207.7 m^2), and more than 30 counselors are aboard for any given cruise. There is also a separate teen club and video game arcade. A child drop-off service works in the evenings, private babysitting services are available ($11 per hour), as are character "tuck-ins" for children, and character breakfasts and lunches. Strollers are available, at no charge, and parents can be provided with beepers, so that they can also enjoy their time alone, away from the kids for much of the day.

Entertainment and the activities programming for families and children are outstanding. Stage shows feature Disney themes; "Hercules — A Muse-ical Comedy," "Voyage of the Ghost Ship" (a lighthearted look at cruising), "Disney Dreams" (a bedtime story with Peter Pan, Aladdin, the Little Mermaid, and others); sadly, all are performed without a hint of a live orchestra, although lighting and staging are excellent. A show called "Island Magic," which features only Disney characters, is performed the day before reaching Castaway Cay, and is the only show featuring a "live" orchestra. On the four-day cruise, an additional local Bahamian show takes place outdoors at the middle swimming pool.

For adults, there is "Beat Street," an entertainment area for the adults that includes a wacky Hollywood-style street, and three entertainment rooms. "Sessions" is a jazz piano lounge, complete with private headphones for listening to music of all types when no live music is scheduled; "Rockin' Bar D" (for ear-splitting rock 'n roll and country music); and "Off-Beat" (for improvisational comedy involving the audience). During the day, creative enrichment programs have been added.

Although Nassau is decidedly unappealing and not very tourist-friendly, the highlight of the itinerary is undoubtedly Disney's private island, Castaway Cay. It is an outstanding private island (perhaps the benchmark for *all* private islands), with its own pier so that the ship can dock alongside — a cruise industry first. There is a post office with its own special Bahamas/Disney stamp, and a whole host of dedicated, well thought-out attractions and amenities for all ages (including a large adults-only beach, complete with massage cabanas).

Disney characters are aboard for all cruises and lots of photo opportunities; they come out to play mainly when children's activities are scheduled. All the artwork throughout the ship's public areas comes from Disney films or animation features, with many original drawings dating from the early thirties. One neat onboard service is that any photographs taken by the ship's photographers are automatically delivered to your cabin — no more searching on endless boards.

This ship should appeal to couples, single parents, and families alike (there are few activities for couples during the daytime, but plenty of entertainment at night). Whether cruising with 1,000 (or more) kids aboard will make for a relaxing vacation for those without kids depends on how much noise one can absorb (there will probably be even more juniors aboard at peak vacation periods). Disney always points out that 25 percent of Walt Disney World's visitors are adults (these are the *real* kids). What is definite is that if you bring children, they will have so much fun that they will not want to leave at the end of the cruise. Members of Disney's Vacation Club can exchange points for cruises.

At Port Canaveral, a special terminal has been constructed (a copy of the original Ocean terminal used by the transatlantic liners *Queen Elizabeth* and *Queen Mary* in Southampton, England). Embarkation and disembarkation is an entertainment event rather than the hassle-laden affair that it has become for many cruise lines with large ships (if all the buses do not arrive together).

Features year-round three- and four-day cruises to the Bahamas — part of a seven-night vacation package that includes a three- or four-day stay at a Walt Disney World resort hotel in Orlando (the cruise then forms the second half of the vacation). It's all tied up in one encapsulated, well-controlled and seamless environment that promises escape and adventure. You can also book just the cruise without the resort stay. Transfers between Walt Disney World resorts in Orlando and the ship are included. Special buses feature vintage 1930s/1940s style interior decor (30 sets of Mickey's face and ears can be found in the blue fabric of each seat); five of the 45 custom-made buses are outfitted to carry wheelchair passengers.

Disney Magic is the cruise industry's floating theme park — a sea-going never-never land that has been rated on its own, in common with all other ships in this book. This rating does not include any additional three- or four-day stay at a Disney World resort, which forms part of the total Disney Cruise Line vacation (although it is now possible to book just the cruise).

You should be aware that this is a highly programmed, strictly timed and regimented onboard experience, with tickets, lines, and reservations necessary for almost everything. Since its introduction, the product has improved, almost to the point that Disney understands that cruise ships are different to operate than theme parks. Take only *casual* clothing (that's casual with a capital "C," folks) and wish upon a star — that's really all you'll need to do to enjoy yourself aboard this stunning ship.

Weak Points: There's absolutely no dance floor with live orchestra for adults (other than the disco-style country-style "Rockin Bar D" in Beat Street). The elevators are very small, and so is the gymnasium (for a large ship). It is very expensive for a short cruise, gratuities are extra, and 15 percent is added to all bar/beverage/wine accounts. Don't even think about it if you don't like Disney, kids, lining up and registering for things, or moderate food and service with low-grade hospitality attitude. Lines at various outlets can prove irritating, as can trying to get through to Guest Services by telephone. The food product and delivery has improved — but falls short of less expensive cruise products. There is no library — something that many regular cruise passengers miss.

m/s Disney Wonder
★★★★ +
(L)

LIFESTYLE:	PREMIUM
Cruise Line:	Disney Cruise Line
Former Names:	-
Gross Tonnage:	85,000
Builder:	Fincantieri (Italy)
Original Cost:	$350 million
Entered Service:	August 1999
Flag:	Bahamas
Tel. No.:	n/a
Fax No.:	n/a
Length (ft/m):	964.5/294.00
Beam (ft/m):	105.7/32.22
Draft (ft/m):	26.2/8.0
Propulsion/Propellers:	diesel-electric (38,000kW)/ 2 (FP)
Passenger Decks:	12
Total Crew:	945
Pass. Capacity (basis 2):	1,750
Pass. Capacity (all berths):	3,325
Pass. Space Ratio (basis 2):	48.5
Pass. Space Ratio (all berths):	25.5
Officers:	European/Norwegian
Total Cabins:	875
Size Range (sq ft/m):	180.8–968.7/16.8–90.0
Cabins (outside view):	720
Cabins (inside — no view):	155
Family Cabins:	80

Cabins (with private balcony):	388
Cabins (wheelchair accessible):	12
Cabin Current:	110 volts
Cabin TV:	Yes
Dining Rooms:	3 main (+1 Alternative +1 Cafe)
Elevators:	12
Casino:	No
Slot Machines:	0
Swimming Pools (outdoors):	3
Swimming Pools (inside):	0
Whirlpools:	6
Fitness Center:	Yes
Sauna/Steam Room:	Yes/Yes
Massage:	Yes
Self-Service Launderette:	Yes (3)
Movie Theater/Seats:	Yes/270
Library:	Yes
Classification Society:	Lloyd's Register

RATINGS	POSSIBLE SCORE	SCORE ACHIEVED
Ship	500	447
Accommodation	200	172
Food	400	211
Service	400	303
Cruise	500	420
TOTAL	**2,000**	**1,553**

This ship, sister to *Disney Magic*, has a more sophisticated ambience due to the fact that her interiors were designed by Adam Tihani, one of New York's top interior designers. For other comments, see *Disney Magic*.

s/s Dolphin IV
★★
(M)

LIFESTYLE:	STANDARD
Cruise Line:	Cape Canaveral Cruise Lines
Former Names:	*Ithaca/Amelia De Melo/Zion*
Gross Tonnage:	13,000
Builder: Howaldtswerke Deutsche Werft (Germany)	
Original Cost:	n/a
Entered Service:	March 1956/February 1996
Flag:	Bahamas
Tel. No.:	n/a
Fax No.:	n/a
Length (ft/m):	502.9/153.30
Beam (ft/m):	65.1/19.87
Draft (ft/m):	25.9/7.90
Propulsion/Propellers:	steam turbine (7,723kW)/1 (FP)
Passenger Decks:	6
Total Crew:	290
Pass. Capacity (basis 2):	588
Pass. Capacity (all berths):	718
Pass. Space Ratio (basis 2):	22.1
Pass. Space Ratio (all berths):	18.1
Officers:	Greek
Total Cabins:	285
Size Range (sq ft/m):	72.1–258.3/6.7–24.0
Cabins (outside view):	206
Cabins (inside — no view):	79
Cabins (single occupancy):	0
Cabins (with private balcony):	0
Cabins (wheelchair accessible):	0
Cabin Current:	110 and 220 volts
Cabin TV:	No
Dining Rooms:	1
Elevators:	1
Casino:	Yes
Slot Machines:	Yes
Swimming Pools (outdoors):	1
Swimming Pools (inside):	0
Whirlpools:	0
Fitness Center:	No
Sauna/Steam Room:	No/No
Massage:	Yes
Self-Service Launderette:	No
Movie Theater/Seats:	No
Library:	No
Classification Society:	Lloyd's Register

RATINGS	POSSIBLE SCORE	SCORE ACHIEVED
Ship	500	222
Accommodation	200	97
Food	400	174
Service	400	207
Cruise	500	242
TOTAL	**2,000**	**942**

Accommodation: The cabins are very small and have very plain, basic decor. However, they may be judged almost comfortable and adequate for the short cruises made by this ship. Cabins on the lower decks suffer from noise (and the smell of diesel fuel) from the engine-room.

Dining: The dining room is an attractive room and has a warm ambience, but it is narrow and has a low ceiling. There are two seatings. The food is indifferent, and the ingredients are not the best, but it is a good value for the budget-minded. The service is hurried and lacks any finesse, although the staff is friendly and tries to please. Fairly attractive buffet displays, but there could be more creativity.

Other Comments: She is a fairly attractive older ship (well over 40 years old), with pleasing lines, even with its now very noticeable center-sag. The open deck and sunbathing areas are very cramped due to high passenger density, and the plastic chairs and tables are in need of help.

The ship's public rooms are nicely decorated in clean, crisp, contemporary colors, albeit with much use of reflective surfaces (mirrors). There is a good shopping area, although it really is full of tacky items, more for souvenirs and gifts than anything else.

The showroom is really poor, and the stage would be better at the opposite end (the seating is also uncomfortable for long periods). Also, the discotheque is small and claustrophobic. Has a moderately friendly staff and ambience, but the entertainment is weak and decidedly low budget — typical of what you would find in a poor night club ashore in southern Florida.

This ship has a lively atmosphere for short, fun cruises for the young and active set seeking fun in a very casual, party-like setting, but she's a tired old lady. I wonder how much longer she can compete with the bright new ships that offer more space and better facilities, and indeed more of everything. Operates two- and four-night Bahamas cruises.

Weak Points: This is a very high-density ship, and it is difficult to find a quiet corner anywhere. Some of the staff (particularly those at the Purser's Office/Reception Desk) need to be sent to charm school.

m/v Don Juan
★★
(S)

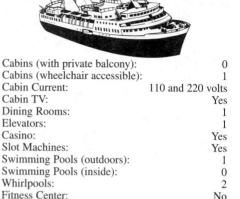

LIFESTYLE:	STANDARD
Cruise Line:	Royal Hispania Cruises
Former Names:	*Melia Don Juan, Crown del Mar,*
	Las Palmas de Gran Canarias
Gross Tonnage:	10,000
Builder:	Union Navale de Levante (Spain)
Original Cost:	n/a
Entered Service:	1967/July 1994
Flag:	Panama
Tel. No.:	1351264
Fax No.:	1351264
Length (ft/m):	428.8/130.70
Beam (ft/m):	62.9/19.20
Draft (ft/m):	18.0/5.50
Propulsion/Propellers:	diesel-electric
	(11,769kW)/2 (CP)
Passenger Decks:	6
Total Crew:	195
Pass. Capacity (basis 2):	448
Pass. Capacity (all berths):	469
Pass. Space Ratio (basis 2):	22.3
Pass. Space Ratio (all berths):	21.3
Officers:	Spanish
Total Cabins:	209
Size Range (sq ft/m):	n/a
Cabins (outside view):	130
Cabins (inside — no view):	79
Cabins (single occupancy):	0

Cabins (with private balcony):	0
Cabins (wheelchair accessible):	1
Cabin Current:	110 and 220 volts
Cabin TV:	Yes
Dining Rooms:	1
Elevators:	1
Casino:	Yes
Slot Machines:	Yes
Swimming Pools (outdoors):	1
Swimming Pools (inside):	0
Whirlpools:	2
Fitness Center:	No
Sauna/Steam Room:	Yes/No
Massage:	Yes
Self-Service Launderette:	No
Movie Theater/Seats:	No
Library:	No
Classification Society:	Lloyd's Register

RATINGS	POSSIBLE SCORE	SCORE ACHIEVED
Ship	500	234
Accommodation	200	94
Food	400	175
Service	400	230
Cruise	500	214
TOTAL	**2,000**	**947**

Accommodation: Five suites, located just below the navigation bridge, command forward views; they are well furnished, and have full bathtubs (most others have showers). No private balconies. The standard cabins are adequate at best, and have almost no drawer space, little closet space, and very small bathrooms.

Dining: The dining room is set low down and has ocean views, but it is a little dark and somber. There are two seatings, and tables are for four, six, or eight persons. The cuisine is barely adequate, and menu choice is very limited. The service is below international standards, there is no finesse, and it is hard to communicate. The dining times are late (typically at 8:00pm and 10:00pm for dinner).

The casual breakfast and lunch buffets are very poor, with little creativity, almost nonexistent presentation, and not much variety — with many of the same items repeated each day.

Other Comments: This former Spanish ferry, which was refurbished in 1994, now sports a more modern, though somewhat angular look, aided by a royal blue hull and topped off with gold stripes. There is a decent amount of open deck space, but there are no cushioned pads for deck lounge chairs.

Inside, soft earth tone colors are used in the decor. There is a three-deck high atrium, with a circular staircase, although it is narrow. Most of the public rooms are set below the accommodation decks, except for one forward observation lounge. The showroom is set between accommodation decks, which means it is particularly noisy at night for some passenger cabins located close by. Some flower bouquets would add warmth to the ambience.

This is a high-density ship that will provide a moderately comfortable cruise experience, but forget the word "luxury," for this really is a basic vessel with limited public rooms and facilities. Perhaps it represents good value for Spanish-speaking passengers who are not yet used to better ships, but when compared to other ships in the international marketplace, this company has a lot to learn about the hospitality industry.

<u>Weak Points</u>: The ceilings are rather low in many places (due to the fact that the ship was originally constructed as a ferry). The price of drinks is very high, and the poor quality of food is deplorable.

m/s Ecstasy
★★★ +
(L)

LIFESTYLE:	STANDARD
Cruise Line:	Carnival Cruise Lines
Former Names:	-
Gross Tonnage:	70,367
Builder:	Kvaerner Masa-Yards (Finland)
Original Cost:	$275 million
Entered Service:	June 1991
Flag:	Liberia
Tel. No.:	1244233
Fax No.:	n/a
Length (ft/m):	855.8/260.60
Beam (ft/m):	104.0/31.40
Draft (ft/m):	25.9/7.89
Propulsion/Propellers:	diesel-electric (42,240kW)/2 (CP)
Passenger Decks:	10
Total Crew:	920
Pass. Capacity (basis 2):	2,040
Pass. Capacity (all berths):	2,594
Pass. Space Ratio (basis 2):	34.4
Pass. Space Ratio (all berths):	27.1
Officers:	Italian
Total Cabins:	1,020
Size Range (sq ft/m):	173.2–409.7/16.0–38.0
Cabins (outside view):	618
Cabins (inside — no view):	402
Cabins (single occupancy):	0
Cabins (with private balcony):	54
Cabins (wheelchair accessible):	22
Cabin Current:	110 volts
Cabin TV:	Yes
Dining Rooms:	2
Elevators:	14
Casino:	Yes
Slot Machines:	Yes
Swimming Pools (outdoors):	3
Swimming Pools (inside):	0
Whirlpools:	6
Fitness Center:	Yes
Sauna/Steam Room:	Yes/Yes
Massage:	Yes
Self-Service Launderette:	Yes
Movie Theater/Seats:	No
Library:	Yes
Classification Society:	Lloyd's Register

RATINGS	POSSIBLE SCORE	SCORE ACHIEVED
Ship	500	395
Accommodation	200	151
Food	400	221
Service	400	270
Cruise	500	348
TOTAL	**2,000**	**1,385**

Accommodation: As in sister ships *Elation, Fantasy, Fascination, Imagination, Inspiration, Paradise*, and *Sensation*, the standard cabins are plain and marginally comfortable, spacious enough and practical, with good storage space and well-designed bathrooms. Those booking one of the 28 outside suites will find whirlpool bathtubs, and eclectic decor and furniture. These are mildly attractive, but nothing special, being much smaller than those aboard the ships of a similar size of several competing companies.

Dining: The two dining rooms have attractive decor and colors, but are large, crowded and noisy. There are two seatings. The food is adequate, although Carnival Cruise Lines has made several improvements. The service is quite robotic, closely timed, and inflexible, although waiters are willing and reasonably friendly (the first seating is frenzied). The wine list is quite decent, although there are no wine waiters.

Other Comments: This is one of the successful *Fantasy*-class of eight almost identical ships.

The general passenger flow is good, and the interior design is clever, functional, and extremely colorful. The neon lighting in the interior decor takes a little getting used to at first. There is a vintage Rolls Royce motor car located on the principal, double-width indoor promenade. The health spa and fitness facilities are decent. A stunning, 10-ton sculpture graces marble and glass atrium that spans seven decks. The library has delightful decor, but there are few books. The Chinatown Lounge features hanging lanterns and smoking dragon. The balconied show lounge is large, but 20 pillars do obstruct the views from several seats.

This ship will provide a great introduction to cruising for the novice passenger seeking an action-packed short cruise experience, with a real swinging party atmosphere, and minimum fuss and finesse. This is cruising in theme-park fantasyland, and the dress code is extremely casual. The staff will help you have organized fun, and that is what Carnival does best. Want to party? Then this should prove to be a great ship for you. Features three- and four-day cruises to the Bahamas year-round.

Weak Points: This ship is not for those who want a quiet, relaxing cruise experience. There are simply too many annoying announcements, and a great deal of hustling for drinks.

m/s Elation
★★★ +
(L)

LIFESTYLE:	STANDARD
Cruise Line:	Carnival Cruise Lines
Former Names:	-
Gross Tonnage:	70,367
Builder:	Kvaerner Masa-Yards (Finland)
Original Cost:	$300 million
Entered Service:	March 1998
Flag:	Panama
Tel. No.:	33558311
Fax No.:	33558311
Length (ft/m):	855.0/260.60
Beam (ft/m):	104.0/31.40
Draft (ft/m):	25.9/7.90
Propulsion/Propellers:	diesel-electric (42,842kW)/2 pods (CP)
Passenger Decks:	10
Total Crew:	920
Pass. Capacity (basis 2):	2,040
Pass. Capacity (all berths):	2,594
Pass. Space Ratio (basis 2):	34.4
Pass. Space Ratio (all berths):	26.7
Officers:	Italian
Total Cabins:	1,020
Size Range (sq ft/m):	173.2–409.7/16.0–38.0
Cabins (outside view):	618
Cabins (inside — no view):	402
Cabins (single occupancy):	0
Cabins (with private balcony):	54
Cabins (wheelchair accessible):	22
Cabin Current:	110 volts
Cabin TV:	Yes
Dining Rooms:	2
Elevators:	14
Casino:	Yes
Slot Machines:	Yes
Swimming Pools (outdoors):	3
Swimming Pools (inside):	0
Whirlpools:	6
Fitness Center:	Yes
Sauna/Steam Room:	Yes/Yes
Massage:	Yes
Self-Service Launderette:	Yes
Movie Theater/Seats:	No
Library:	Yes
Classification Society:	Lloyd's Register

RATINGS	POSSIBLE SCORE	SCORE ACHIEVED
Ship	500	395
Accommodation	200	151
Food	400	223
Service	400	270
Cruise	500	348
TOTAL	**2,000**	**1,387**

Accommodation: As in her sister ships in the same (*Fantasy*-class) series, the cabins are almost all identical in size, shape, fittings, and decoration. There are 28 outside suites with whirlpool bathtubs, and some fascinating, eclectic decor, and furniture. The standard cabin ceilings are very plain, and amenities consist only of ice water and soap, so bring shampoo and conditioner (shower cap for ladies) and other personal toiletry items.

Dining: There are two large, lively dining rooms (both are nonsmoking) with Carnival's usual efficient (fast), programmed, well-practiced service and delivery. There are two seatings. The improved cuisine is acceptable, but it still is not the company's strong point (you get what you pay for, remember). There is a wine list, but there are no wine waiters.

For casual meals, there's The Lido, which, aboard this ship, has some improvements and additions worthy of note, such as an orange juice machine, where you put in oranges and out comes fresh juice (better than the concentrate stuff supplied in the dining room). There's also a sushi bar. Things are looking up, which means more choices.

Other Comments: This is the seventh in a series of eight mega-ships of the same series and identical internal configuration. It is a very successful design for this successful company that targets the mass market, and particularly the first-time cruisegoer. *Elation* has a bold, forthright, angular appearance that is typical of today's space-creative designs. What is new, however, is the Azipod propulsion system, which gives the ship more maneuverability, while reducing required machinery space and vibration at the stern. There is a banked outdoor jogging track.

Splashy, showy, public rooms and interior colors — pure Las Vegas and ideal for those who love it. The theme of the interior decor is composers and their compositions (most of the public rooms have musical names), and the colors, while bright, are less so than aboard previous ships in this series. As in her sister ships, there is a dramatic six-deck-high atrium, appropriately dressed to impress, topped by a large glass dome, and featuring a fascinating, entertaining artistic centerpiece. Has expansive open deck areas and a good, expansive health spa. There are public entertainment lounges, bars and clubs galore, with something for everyone, including a children's playroom, larger than aboard the previous ships in this series. Some busy colors and design themes abound in the handsome public rooms; these are connected by wide indoor boulevards and beg your attention and indulgence. There is also a good art collection, much of it bright and vocal. The library is a fine room, as aboard most Carnival ships (but there are few books). One neat feature (not found aboard previous ships in this series) is an atrium bar, complete with live classical music — something new for this company.

Features a lavish, yet almost elegant multitiered 1,010-seat showroom and the line's fine, loud, high-energy razzle-dazzle shows. A large, three-deck-high glass-enclosed health spa is always a busy place, including a gymnasium full of the latest high-tech muscle-pumping machinery. A large casino invites almost nonstop action. Good for those who like big city life ashore and want it on their vacation. Operates seven-night Mexican Riviera cruises year-round from the port of Los Angeles, but the ship is arguably better than the ports of call!

<u>Weak Points</u>: This is another ship that provides a rather impersonal cruise experience, as the ship is large and there are so many other passengers. There are many repetitive announcements.

s/s Emerald
★★★
(M)

LIFESTYLE: **STANDARD**

Cruise Line: Louis Cruise Lines/Thomson Cruises
Former Names: *Regent Rainbow, Diamond Island,*
Santa Rosa, Samos Sky
Gross Tonnage: 26,431
Builder: Newport News Shipbuilding (USA)
Original Cost: $25 million
Entered Service: June 1958/April 1997
Flag: Cyprus
Tel. No.: 1125514
Fax No.: 1125515
Length (ft/m): 599.0/182.57
Beam (ft/m): 84.0/25.60
Draft (ft/m): 27.5/8.38
Propulsion/Propellers: steam turbine
(16,400kW)/2 (FP)
Passenger Decks: 10
Total Crew: 420
Pass. Capacity (basis 2): 990
Pass. Capacity (all berths): 1,172
Pass. Space Ratio (basis 2): 26.6
Pass. Space Ratio (all berths): 22.5
Officers: Greek/European
Total Cabins: 500
Size Range (sq ft/m): 124.8–304.6/11.6–28.3
Cabins (outside view): 338
Cabins (inside — no view): 162
Cabins (single occupancy): 10

Cabins (with private balcony): 0
Cabins (wheelchair accessible): 2
Cabin Current: 110 and 220 volts
Cabin TV: Yes
Dining Rooms: 1
Elevators: 3
Casino: Yes
Slot Machines: Yes
Swimming Pools (outdoors): 1
Swimming Pools (inside): 0
Whirlpools: 2
Fitness Center: Yes
Sauna/Steam Room: Yes/No
Massage: Yes
Self-Service Launderette: No
Movie Theater/Seats: No
Library: Yes
Classification Society: American Bureau of
Shipping

RATINGS	POSSIBLE SCORE	SCORE ACHIEVED
Ship	500	292
Accommodation	200	120
Food	400	220
Service	400	255
Cruise	500	290
TOTAL	**2,000**	**1,177**

Accommodation: This ship has a varied mix of cabins both old and new that offer a wide range of configurations from which to choose, presented in just three main categories: premier, superior, and standard (although there are, in effect, seven price levels). You should note that cabins are not assigned until you are at the embarkation port for check-in. This ad-hoc method of assigning cabins means that those who arrive first probably will get the best cabins, in the best locations.

Many of the original cabins are quite spacious, with good closet and drawer space, while newer ones are a little more compact, and have poor insulation. Continental breakfast in your cabin will cost about $7.50 (£4.50) per person extra (each time). There is also a 24-hour cabin service menu for snacks, all at extra cost.

Dining: The dining room has large ocean-view windows and an interesting, neat orchestra balcony. There are two seatings. The food quality and presentation are good for the cost of a cruise. The service is friendly and quite attentive, although you should not expect grand hotel-style service. There is also a self-service buffet for breakfast and lunch.

Other Comments: After being laid up for over 10 years, this American-built (and solidly built, at that), former ocean liner underwent a great amount of reconstruction (costing $72 million) in 1992 in Greece, with more again in 1997, when she was purchased by Louis Cruise Lines. With new upper decks added, her profile is not exactly handsome, and the open deck and sunbathing space is limited when the ship is full, although there are a good number of deck lounge chairs. There is, however, a good wraparound promenade deck outdoors, and there are plenty of deck chairs.

The ship's interiors are very pleasant and surprisingly comfortable, featuring warm decor that is contemporary without being at all brash. Many of the public rooms have high ceilings, which provides a spacious ocean liner feel to the ship, and there are some lovely wrought iron railings on the stairways. The artwork, unfortunately, does look like the low budget stuff it is and could do with being upgraded further.

The entertainment will generally be of typical low-budget quality, and the sight lines in the show lounge are really poor particularly from the port and starboard side seating areas, where there is obstruction from 12 thick pillars. For short cruises, the ship provides a range of public spaces that, in turn, promotes a good party ambience and a number of bars for drinking in. There is a large casino with a high ceiling.

During the summer, the ship is based on Palma Majorca, under charter to Thomson Cruises. *Emerald* operates Mediterranean cruises, and is quite well suited for this task. Note that the gratuities are included. Thomson's wholly-owned airline is Britannia Airways, which will probably fly you to your port of embarkation. Despite the minor criticisms, this ship manages to provide a decent cruise experience, and therefore achieves a very respectable rating.

Weak Points: The high density of this vessel means that there is little room to move about when full, although cruise lines often translate this to "ambience."

QUESTIONS TO ASK YOUR TRAVEL AGENT

→ Is air transportation included in the cabin rate quoted? If not, what will be the extra cost?

→ What other extra costs will be involved? These can include port charges, insurance, gratuities, shore excursions, laundry, and drinks.

→ What is the cruise line's cancellation policy?

→ If I want to make changes to my air arrangements, routing, dates, and so on, will the insurance policy cover everything in case of missed or cancelled flights?

→ Does your agency deal with only one, or several different insurance companies?

→ Does the cruise line offer advance booking discounts or other incentives?

→ Do you have preferred suppliers, or do you book any cruise on any cruise ship?

→ Have you sailed aboard the ship I want to book, or that you are recommending?

→ Is your agency bonded and insured? If so, by whom?

→ If you book the shore excursions offered and recommended by the cruise line, is insurance coverage provided?

m/s Enchanted Capri
★★ +
(S)

LIFESTYLE: **STANDARD**

Cruise Line:	Black Sea Shipping Company
Former Names:	*Island Holiday, Arkadiya,*
	Azerbaydzhan
Gross Tonnage:	15,410
Builder:	Wartsila (Finland)
Original Cost:	$25 million
Entered Service:	January 1976/June 1998
Flag:	Bahamas
Tel. No.:	1400740
Fax No.:	1400740
Length (ft/m):	512.5/156.24
Beam (ft/m):	72.3/22.05
Draft (ft/m):	20.5/6.20
Propulsion/Propellers:	diesel (13,430kW)/2 (CP)
Passenger Decks:	8
Total Crew:	300
Pass. Capacity (basis 2):	488
Pass. Capacity (all berths):	637
Pass. Space Ratio (basis 2):	31.5
Pass. Space Ratio (all berths):	24.2
Officers:	American/European
Total Cabins:	244
Size Range (sq ft/m):	150.6–427.3/14.0–39.7
Cabins (outside view):	126
Cabins (inside — no view):	118
Cabins (single occupancy):	0

Cabins (with private balcony):	0
Cabins (wheelchair accessible):	0
Cabin Current:	220 volts
Cabin TV:	suites only
Dining Rooms:	1
Elevators:	1
Casino:	Yes
Slot Machines:	Yes
Swimming Pools (outdoors):	1
Swimming Pools (inside):	0
Whirlpools:	0
Fitness Center:	Yes
Sauna/Steam Room:	No/No
Massage:	Yes
Self-Service Launderette:	No
Movie Theater/Seats:	Yes/145
Library:	No
Classification Society:	Det Norske Veritas

RATINGS	POSSIBLE SCORE	SCORE ACHIEVED
Ship	500	255
Accommodation	200	113
Food	400	208
Service	400	232
Cruise	500	266
TOTAL	**2,000**	**1,074**

Accommodation: The suites and deluxe cabins are quite large and very nicely furnished (particularly those in the front of the vessel), and have wood paneled walls and cabinetry, and an abundance of closet and drawer space. Boat Deck cabins also feature a refrigerator. Other cabins are small, have clean lines and are quite simply furnished, without much closet and drawer space, but they are quite adequate and comfortable. There are really too many inside cabins. The cabin insulation in general is quite poor.

Dining: There is one rather plain, but brightly decorated dining room, and two seatings. The service is provided by waiters of mixed nationality, who are reasonably friendly. The cuisine is very so-so, with limited choice, and it is presented in a very basic meat and potatoes fashion that is not as good as the menu desecription would have you believe. The wine list is also basic, with mostly California wines represented.

Other Comments: She is a fairly smart looking ship, originally one of a series of five almost identical vessels built for the Black Sea Shipping Company. This ship is quite basic, with an informal, unpretentious ambience. She is now under a five-year charter to the south Florida-based Commodore Cruise Line, until 2003.

There is a reasonable amount of open deck and sunbathing space for the size of the ship, although it does tend to be quite tight and cluttered. Much used, however, are the sports facilities, which include a basketball court. The outdoor swimming pool is located aft, and is circular and quite deep, but very small.

Inside, there is just a handful of public rooms, lounges, and bars from which to spend time in, but the casino is a good size, and was created in a 1998 makeover from what used to be the ship's second dining room.

She now operates two- and five-night cruises from New Orleans, and provides a good way for novice cruise passengers to test the waters before trying a longer cruise. The company also operates the older *Enchanted Isle*. The crew is quite friendly and attentive.

<u>Weak Points</u>: Service levels are spotty and inconsistent, and more training is needed. The ship has a steep, narrow gangway in ports of call. There is no wraparound promenade deck outdoors, no observation lounge, and a poor library.

s/s Enchanted Isle
★★★
(M)

LIFESTYLE:	STANDARD
Cruise Line:	Commodore Cruise Line
Former Names:	*Commodore Hotel, Enchanted Isle,*
	Bermuda Star, Brasil, Edam, Veendam,
	Monarch Star, Argentina
Gross Tonnage:	23,395
Builder:	Ingalls Shipbuilding (USA)
Original Cost:	$26 million
Entered Service:	December 1958/February 1995
Flag:	Panama
Tel. No.:	1333171
Fax No.:	1333201
Length (ft/m):	617.5/188.22
Beam (ft/m):	88.1/26.88
Draft (ft/m):	27.2/8.30
Propulsion/Propellers:	steam turbine
	(19,000kW)/2 (FP)
Passenger Decks:	9
Total Crew:	350
Pass. Capacity (basis 2):	729
Pass. Capacity (all berths):	840
Pass. Space Ratio (basis 2):	32.0
Pass. Space Ratio (all berths):	27.8
Officers:	European
Total Cabins:	366
Size Range (sq ft/m):	103.3–292.7/9.6–27.2
Cabins (outside view):	290
Cabins (inside — no view):	76

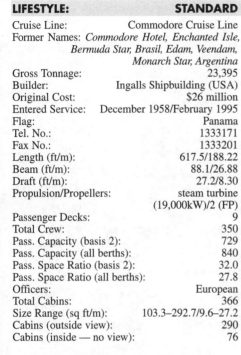

Cabins (single occupancy):	3
Cabins (with private balcony):	0
Cabins (wheelchair accessible):	0
Cabin Current:	110 volts
Cabin TV:	Yes
Dining Rooms:	1
Elevators:	3
Casino:	Yes
Slot Machines:	Yes
Swimming Pools (outdoors):	1
Swimming Pools (inside):	0
Whirlpools:	0
Fitness Center:	Yes
Sauna/Steam Room:	Yes/No
Massage:	Yes
Self-Service Launderette:	No
Movie Theater/Seats:	Yes/200
Library:	Yes
Classification Society:	Lloyd's Register

RATINGS	POSSIBLE SCORE	SCORE ACHIEVED
Ship	500	276
Accommodation	200	110
Food	400	220
Service	400	255
Cruise	500	273
TOTAL	**2,000**	**1,134**

Accommodation: The cabins are quite spacious, and feature solid, but old-style, heavy-duty furniture and fittings, and a decent amount of closet and drawer space, depending on the cabin grade chosen. The bathrooms are, for the most part, of a decent size, but many of the old plumbing fittings are exposed and often prove frustrating.

Dining: The dining room is located on a lower deck and really needs more light. There are two seatings. The food is very basic fare, the menu choice is rather limited, and the wine list is downright poor. The buffets are minimal, and presentation needs some more creativity. The service is attentive and friendly, but there is certainly no finesse.

Other Comments: This ship, originally built for Moore-McCormack Lines, has a pleasing profile, typical of a compact ocean liner. Has a large, but false funnel (the exhaust gasses are dispersed via two slim funnels located further aft). Thanks to her deep draft, she is a stable ship at sea. *Enchanted Isle* has been quite well looked after over the years (she has had a great number of name changes), and now has a rather homey, matronly look and ambience. Has good exterior teakwood decking and plenty of open deck space.

There is a good choice of public rooms, and passenger flow is quite good, as the ship seems to absorb people well. The interior is by no means glamorous, but provides unpretentious surroundings and decor reminiscent of quiet ocean liners, although it is somewhat dated and worn. The show lounge, while comfortable, has poor sight lines. The casino is not particularly inviting, but is well used. Gentleman dance hosts are aboard every sailing.

This ship will provide a basic, but fairly decent first-time cruise experience, in a fun atmosphere, at a down to earth price, providing you do not expect too much. Don't go for the food, but go to get a taste of the cruising life.

m/s Enchantment of the Seas
★★★★
(L)

LIFESTYLE:	STANDARD
Cruise Line:	Royal Caribbean International
Former Names:	-
Gross Tonnage:	74,137
Builder:	Kvaerner Masa-Yards (Finland)
Original Cost:	$300 million
Entered Service:	July 1997
Flag:	Norway
Tel. No.:	625890011
Fax No.:	325790012
Length (ft/m):	915.6/279.1
Beam (ft/m):	105.6/32.2
Draft (ft/m):	24.9/7.6
Propulsion/Propellers:	diesel-electric (50,400kW)/2 (FP)
Passenger Decks:	11
Total Crew:	760
Pass. Capacity (basis 2):	1,950
Pass. Capacity (all berths):	2,446
Pass. Space Ratio (basis 2):	38.0
Pass. Space Ratio (all berths):	30.3
Officers:	Norwegian/International
Total Cabins:	975
Size Range (sq ft/m):	158.2–1,033.3/14.7–96.0
Cabins (outside view):	576
Cabins (inside — no view):	399
Cabins (single occupancy):	0
Cabins (with private balcony):	212

Cabins (wheelchair accessible):	14
Cabin Current:	110 and 220 volts
Cabin TV:	Yes
Dining Rooms:	1
Elevators:	9
Casino:	Yes
Slot Machines:	Yes
Swimming Pools (outdoors):	1
Swimming Pools (inside):	1 (indoor/outdoor w/glass roof)
Whirlpools:	6
Fitness Center:	Yes
Sauna/Steam Room:	Yes/Yes
Massage:	Yes
Self-Service Launderette:	No
Movie Theater/Seats:	No
Library:	Yes
Classification Society:	Det Norske Veritas

RATINGS	POSSIBLE SCORE	SCORE ACHIEVED
Ship	500	434
Accommodation	200	247
Food	400	169
Service	400	302
Cruise	500	383
TOTAL	**2,000**	**1,535**

Accommodation: All of the standard cabins have twin beds that convert to a queen-size bed. There is a reasonably good amount of closet space for a one-week cruise, and an adequate amount of drawer space, although under-bed storage for luggage is limited. The bathrooms are practical, but the decor is plain. The category A and B cabins also have a VCR unit.

Dining: The 1,195-seat dining room is spread over two decks, with both levels connected by a grand, sweeping staircase. There are two seatings. General comments regarding the food operation aboard the company's *Legend of the Seas* and *Splendour of the Seas* apply, but some further options have been introduced to provide a little more flexibility.

A large, informal Windjammer Café, which features a great expanse of ocean-view glass windows, is where breakfast and lunch buffets are available as an alternative to the dining room.

There is an intimate terrace Champagne Bar located forward of the lower level of the two-deck-high dining room and just off the atrium for those who might like to taste something a little out of the ordinary, in a setting that is bright and contemporary. There is a good use of tropical plants throughout the public rooms, which helps to counteract the clinical pastel wall colors.

Other Comments: This is one of two of a recent breed of ships for this popular cruise line (her sister ship is *Grandeur of the Seas*), introduced in December 1996. She looks long, with her single funnel located well aft, has a nicely rounded stern (rather like the *Sovereign of the Seas*-class ships), and a Viking Crown Lounge set amidships. This, together with the forward mast, provides three distinct focal points in her exterior profile. There is a wraparound promenade deck outdoors (there are no cushioned pads for the deck lounge chairs, however).

A large Viking Crown Lounge (a trademark of all Royal Caribbean International ships) sits between funnel and mast, and overlooks the forward section of the swimming pool deck, as aboard *Legend of the Seas/Splendour of the Seas*, with access provided from stairway off the central atrium.

Inside is a seven-deck-high Centrum (atrium), which provides a central focal and meeting point (the Purser's Desk and Shore Excursion Desk are located on one level). Many public entertainment rooms and facilities can be located off the atrium.

There are two showrooms; one (the principal show lounge, 875 seats), for big production shows; the other (the secondary show lounge, 575 seats), for smaller shows and adult cabarets. The children's and teens' facilities are good, much expanded from previous ships in the fleet.

This ship is quite pretty, and will provide a good cruise vacation, particularly for first-time passengers seeking comfortable surroundings typical of what would be found in a Hyatt Hotel style setting, with fabrics and soft furnishings that blend together to provide a contemporary resort environment. The food is typical of what one would find in a big-city brasserie — adequate in quantity and nicely presented, but made from premixed ingredients. This company provides a well organized, but rather homogeneous cruise experience, with the same old passenger participation activities and events that have been provided for the past 25 years.

Weak Points: There are too many announcements, and constant contemporary pop music played around the swimming pool throughout the day and night (difficult to get away from).

m/s Europa
(S)

LIFESTYLE:		LUXURY
Cruise Line:		Hapag-Lloyd Seetouristik
Former Names:		-
Gross Tonnage:		28,600
Builder:		Kvaerner Masa-Yards (Finland)
Original Cost:		DM260 million
Entered Service:		September 1999
Flag:		Bahamas
Tel. No.:		n/a
Fax No.:		n/a
Length (ft/m):		651.5/198.6
Beam (ft/m):		78.7/24.0
Draft (ft/m):		19.6/6.0
Propulsion/Propellers:		diesel-electric
		(21,600 kW)/2 pods (CP)
Passenger Decks:		7
Total Crew:		267
Pass. Capacity (basis 2):		408
Pass. Capacity (all berths):		450
Pass. Space Ratio (basis 2):		70.0
Pass. Space Ratio (all berths):		63.5
Officers:		German
Total Cabins:		204
Size Range (sq ft/m):		355.2–710.4/33.0–66.0
Cabins (outside view):		204
Cabins (inside — no view):		0
Cabins (single occupancy):		0
Cabins (with private balcony):		168

Cabins (wheelchair accessible):	2
Cabin Current:	110 and 220 volts
Cabin TV:	Yes
Dining Rooms:	3
Elevators:	4
Casino:	Yes
Slot Machines:	Yes
Swimming Pools (outdoors):	1
Swimming Pools (inside):	1 (indoor/outdoor with magrodome)
Whirlpools:	1
Fitness Center:	Yes
Sauna/Steam Room:	Yes/Yes
Massage:	Yes
Self-Service Launderette:	Yes (2)
Movie Theater/Seats:	Yes/60
Library:	Yes
Classification Society:	Germanischer Lloyd

RATINGS	POSSIBLE SCORE	SCORE ACHIEVED
Ship	400	NYR
Accommodation	200	NYR
Food	400	NYR
Service	400	NYR
Cruise	500	NYR
TOTAL	**2,000**	**NYR**

Accommodation: The accommodation (in four configurations and 12 price categories) consists of all-outside view suites: two penthouse grand suites, ten penthouse deluxe suites, 156 suites with balcony, and 36 standard suites. There are two suites (with private balcony) for the handicapped, and eight suites with interconnecting doors (good for families). Almost all suites have a private balcony, but perhaps the most sought after accommodation will be the 12 suites (six on each of two decks) that overlook the stern. All suites have unobstructed views.

Each suite features blond wood cabinetry and accenting (with rounded edges). There is a refrigerator/mini-bar, with soft drinks supplied at no extra charge; writing/vanity desk and sofa with large table in a separate lounge area; personal safe (which can be opened with your suite keycard), illuminated closets, umbrella, shoe horn, clothes brush, and European duvets instead of blankets.

In a cruise industry first, an integrated color television and superb "infotainment" system — 24 hours per day video-on-demand (no charge) is featured, so *you* choose when *you* want to watch a movie. Internet access is provided via the superb Loewe *digital* television (with per second billing). A modem socket is also provided should you decide to bring your own laptop computer.

All suites have a teak-floor entrance hall, and 24-hour room service. The walk-in closets provide a generous amount of storage space for even the longest voyages. All suites feature 100 percent air-circulation system, another cruise industry first. Western European butlers and cabin stewardesses are featured.

The marble-tiled bathrooms are extremely well designed, in light decor, and include a large cabinet for personal toiletry items. All suites feature a full-sized bathtub as well as a separate shower enclosure, with retractable clothesline. Thick, 100 percent luxurious cotton bathrobes are provided, as are slippers and a large array of famous name brand personal toiletry amenities.

For those desiring even more exclusivity, Penthouse Deck accommodation (two Penthouse Grand suites and ten Penthouse Deluxe suites) offer more space, butler service, complimentary bar set-up, laundry and ironing service, a voucher for one massage, caviar on request, canapes, petit-fours, and other niceties at no extra charge. The two Penthouse Grand suites also feature a private sauna, as well as larger balconies and extensive forward views from their prime location one deck above the navigation bridge.

Dining: There is one main, formal dining room, with seats for all passengers in one seating (there are 446 seats), with assigned tables, and both smoking and nonsmoking sections provided. Both full silver service and plated service is featured (silver service for entrees and plated presentation for all other dishes), as are tableside flambees. Table settings include Rosenthal china, 150-gram weight Robbe & Berking silverware, and Riedel glasses. The cuisine is extremely international, with many German favorites featured. The quality of food items is extremely high. Beluga, sevruga, and ossetra caviar are all available on request (at extra cost). An extensive wine list is featured, including a fine selection of connoisseur wines.

Dining options include two small alternative restaurants, one Euro-Asian (Oriental), one Italian (Venezia), both of which are adjacent to and forward of the main restaurant, for more casual dining but in beautifully-appointed surroundings. These are available by reservation, at no extra charge. The Oriental Restaurant features Bauscher china; the chinaware in Venezia is specially made by Rosenthal.

For more casual dining, there is a Lido café for breakfast, lunch, and dinner. Rosenthal china and themed evening dining are featured.

Other Comments: This ship's fine, sleek appearance should please even the most critical among passengers, with her sweeping lines, graceful profile, and the Hapag-Lloyd orange/blue funnel. She is the first Hapag-Lloyd ship to feature "pod" propulsion, designed to reduce vibration and improve efficiency and handling. The ship also carries seven Zodiac landing craft for use during close-up shore excursions. For those times when the Zodiac shore boats are used, port and starboard boot-washing/changing rooms are provided. There is a jogging track for the sporting, as well as an FKK (FreiKoerperKultur) deck for those who enjoy nude sunbathing, and a full teakwood wraparound outside promenade deck. The deck lounge chairs are aluminum with teak armrests and hydraulic reclining section.

Europa is *the* most spacious cruise ship in the world, and the company's (smaller) replacement for the previous *Europa*, which, during her 17-year history, amassed a fine clutch of loyal devotees and consistently high ratings for her fine service standards. However, during the former *Europa*'s last year in service, the standards were decidedly lower.

Reducing the size of the vessel and the number of passengers aboard this brand new ship has enabled Hapag-Lloyd to once again reach and maintain the high standards for which the company has become known, and which passengers expect and demand. A concierge is now available for all passengers.

Besides being the most spacious, she is also the most luxuriously appointed cruise ship in the world, with the finest of soft furnishings chosen for her interiors, which blend traditional with modern designs and materials in a subtle manner. As in her former larger sister, public rooms include a Club Belvedere (where delightful, intimate classical recitals are a regular feature), a Grand Lounge (this is the main showroom, which has a U-shaped seating configuration). In addition, there is a Clipper Lounge, Atrium Piano Bar (set opposite the reception and shore excursion desks), and a sidewalk Havana Bar set off to one side of a winding indoor promenade, for those Cuban cigars and fine almagnacs, calvados, and cognacs, poured tableside. A library, meeting room, hobby room (for arts and crafts), children's playroom, and electronic golf simulator room.

In a radical departure for Hapag-Lloyd Seetouristik, there is a casino, called Casino Royal (the previous *Europa* did not have one). In another first, a multi-deck central atrium is featured, together with two glass-walled elevators, operated by "piccolos" on embarkation day. Other features include a business center, an electronic golf simulator room (plus golf driving ranges and a deck tennis court on the open deck), and special rooms for children (complete with video games). A concierge is available to all passengers, for those special arrangements both aboard and ashore.

There is also an extensive health spa and beauty salon, operated by the well-known spa/cosmetics firm Lancaster, who provide the staff for the several types of massage featured, as well as full-day spa packages and many other rejuvenative treatments.

This ship will appeal to all those who desire to be aboard what is arguably the most luxurious and finest of new ships today. For the German-speaking market, nothing else comes close. Combined with a well-trained staff whose aim is to serve and please passengers in the most sumptuous surroundings, the tradition of luxury cruising is carried to the highest expression. Port taxes and all gratuities are included, although further tipping is permitted.

m/v Explorer
★★ +
(S)

LIFESTYLE:	STANDARD
Cruise Line:	Abercrombie & Kent
Former Names:	*Society Explorer*
	Lindblad Explorer, World Explorer
Gross Tonnage:	2,398
Builder:	Nystad Varv Shipyard (Finland)
Original Cost:	$2.5 million
Entered Service:	1969/March 1993
Flag:	Liberia
Tel. No.:	1241223
Fax No.:	1241223
Length (ft/m):	239.1/72.88
Beam (ft/m):	46.0/14.03
Draft (ft/m):	13.7/4.20
Propulsion/Propellers:	diesel (2,795kW)/1 (FP)
Passenger Decks:	6
Total Crew:	71
Pass. Capacity (basis 2):	100
Pass. Capacity (all berths):	114
Pass. Space Ratio (basis 2):	23.9
Pass. Space Ratio (all berths):	21.0
Officers:	European
Total Cabins:	50
Size Range (sq ft/m):	81.8–161.4/7.6–15.0
Cabins (outside view):	50
Cabins (inside — no view):	0
Cabins (single occupancy):	8
Cabins (with private balcony):	0

Cabins (wheelchair accessible):	0
Cabin Current:	220 volts
Cabin TV:	No
Dining Rooms:	1
Elevators:	0
Casino:	No
Slot Machines:	No
Swimming Pools (outdoors):	1
Whirlpools:	0
Exercise Room:	Yes
Sauna/Steam Room:	Yes/No
Massage:	Yes
Self-Service Launderette:	No
Lecture/Film Room:	Yes
Library:	Yes
Zodiacs:	Yes
Helicopter Pad:	No
Classification Society:	Det Norske Veritas

RATINGS	POSSIBLE SCORE	SCORE ACHIEVED
Ship	500	229
Accommodation	200	94
Food	400	239
Service	400	247
Cruise	500	286
TOTAL	**2,000**	**1,095**

Accommodation: The cabins are extremely small and utilitarian, and there is very little closet, drawer, and storage space. Even so, they are just about adequate for this type of cruising (call them cozy), where you need only very casual clothing. The bathrooms (and the towels) are really tiny, however, and there is little room for your personal toiletry items. National Geographic maps are provided in all cabins.

Dining: The dining room is cheerful and intimate, although somewhat noisy, but it does seat all passengers in one seating with assigned tables. Features creatively presented food, although the choice is quite limited, as is the wine list. Smiling, attentive, and genuinely friendly service, but it is quite casual.

Other Comments: Although she is a small vessel, she is well fitted out with all the necessary equipment for successful in-depth exploration cruising, including a fleet of ten Zodiac rubber landing craft. She is now aging and showing many signs of wear and tear, and cannot compete effectively with the newer expedition-style ships, despite recent refurbishment. She does, however, have an ice-hardened hull and a well-balanced profile, and she is extremely maneuverable.

There are few public rooms, but the interior decor is quite tasteful and cheerful, and the ambience is decidedly intimate. There is a large reference library of books associated with nature and wildlife. There are good lecturers and nature specialists on board for each cruise, provided by specialist operators Abercrombie & Kent.

When cruising in the Antarctic region, she often carries fresh fruits and other produce, and medication to the research stations, and also to some of the isolated islands in the South Atlantic. The ship also files an annual Environmental Impact Assessment with the United States Environmental Protection Agency, and follows tough guidelines for waste disposal.

This is cruising for the serious "in-your-face" adventurer who wants to explore specialized areas of the world yet have some of the most basic creature comforts of home within reach. All shore excursions and gratuities are included.

<u>Weak Points</u>: The original modern-day expedition cruise vessel is now old and a little quirky.

t/s/s Fair Princess
★★ +
(M)

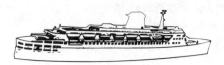

LIFESTYLE:	STANDARD
Cruise Line:	P&O Holidays
Former Names:	*Fair Princess, Fairsea, Fairland, Carinthia*
Gross Tonnage:	24,724
Builder:	John Brown & Co. (UK)
Original Cost:	£21 million
Entered Service:	June 1956/1997
Flag:	Bahamas
Tel. No.:	n/a
Fax No.:	n/a
Length (ft/m):	608.2/185.40
Beam (ft/m):	80.3/24.49
Draft (ft/m):	28.5/8.71
Propulsion/Propellers:	steam turbine (18,300kW)/2 (FP)
Passenger Decks:	11
Total Crew:	450
Pass. Capacity (basis 2):	890
Pass. Capacity (all berths):	1,100
Pass. Space Ratio (basis 2):	27.7
Pass. Space Ratio (all berths):	22.4
Officers:	International
Total Cabins:	464
Size Range (sq ft/m):	89.3–240.0/8.3–22.3
Cabins (outside view):	230
Cabins (inside — no view):	234
Cabins (single occupancy):	0

Cabins (with private balcony):	0
Cabins (wheelchair accessible):	0
Cabin Current:	110 volts
Cabin TV:	Yes
Dining Rooms:	2
Elevators:	3
Casino:	Yes
Slot Machines:	Yes
Swimming Pools (outdoors):	3
Swimming Pools (inside):	0
Whirlpools:	0
Fitness Center:	Yes
Sauna/Steam Room:	Yes/No
Massage:	Yes
Self-Service Launderette:	No
Movie Theater/Seats:	Yes (with balcony)/330
Library:	Yes
Classification Society:	Lloyd's Register

RATINGS	POSSIBLE SCORE	SCORE ACHIEVED
Ship	500	269
Accommodation	200	107
Food	400	196
Service	400	226
Cruise	500	236
TOTAL	**2,000**	**1,034**

Accommodation: The cabins are generally quite spacious for an older ship, and have heavy-duty furnishings and fittings. The cabin bathrooms are now quite antiquated. There are many cabins with third and fourth berths, and there are many more inside cabins than ocean-view cabins.

Dining: The two dining rooms have been reconfigured to provide more space and better flow. They do get crowded and noisy. They have tables for two, six, or eight and two seatings. The cuisine is low-budget and quantity, not quality, prevails. Fairly attentive service, but there is little finesse. There is also a pizzeria.

Other Comments: This solidly constructed former ocean liner has classic, but dated, lines and profile, which translates to good seaworthiness. However, down in the engine room, some parts are definitely well worn and can create occasional breakdowns, although the ship has now settled down well to her new life "down under." The open deck and sunbathing spaces are quite good, unless the ship is full. There is also a jogging track. The ship's Promenade Deck aft area was expanded in a recent refit. Inside, the art-deco interiors on the Promenade Deck are quite elegant, but otherwise the interior decor and the color schemes are mundane. Has an adequate old-style library, and there are facilities for families with children which are just so-so.

This high-density ship represents reasonable value for those who do not expect much, but the experience is quite basic, rough, and rowdy. Having said that, the ship now has quite a loyal following, particularly of those who simply do not like the newer, shoebox-shaped ships. This princess really is quite old and tired (and has been breaking down regularly over the recent past), and is very crowded when full.

Weak Points: There is absolutely no sophistication anywhere. Do expect lines for embarkation, disembarkation and shore tenders. The public rooms are reasonably comfortable, but barely adequate for the number of passengers carried, and it is difficult to get away from smokers. There are too many announcements.

m/s Fantasy
★★★ +
(L)

LIFESTYLE: **STANDARD**

Cruise Line:	Carnival Cruise Lines
Former Names:	-
Gross Tonnage:	70,367
Builder:	Kvaerner Masa-Yards (Finland)
Original Cost:	$225 million
Entered Service:	March 1990
Flag:	Liberia
Tel. No.:	1242660
Fax No.:	n/a
Length (ft/m):	855.8/263.6
Beam (ft/m):	103.0/31.4
Draft (ft/m):	25.9/7.9
Propulsion/Propellers:	diesel-electric (42,240kW)/2 (CP)
Passenger Decks:	10
Total Crew:	920
Pass. Capacity (basis 2):	2,044
Pass. Capacity (all berths):	2,634
Pass. Space Ratio (basis 2):	34.4
Pass. Space Ratio (all berths):	26.7
Officers:	Italian
Total Cabins:	1,022
Size Range (sq ft/m):	173.2–409.7/16.0–38.0
Cabins (outside view):	620
Cabins (inside — no view):	402
Cabins (single occupancy):	0

Cabins (with private balcony):	54
Cabins (wheelchair accessible):	22
Cabin Current:	110 volts
Cabin TV:	Yes
Dining Rooms:	2
Elevators:	14
Casino:	Yes
Slot Machines:	Yes
Swimming Pools (outdoors):	3
Swimming Pools (inside):	0
Whirlpools:	6
Fitness Center:	Yes
Sauna/Steam Room:	Yes/Yes
Massage:	Yes
Self-Service Launderette:	Yes
Movie Theater/Seats:	No
Library:	Yes
Classification Society:	Lloyd's Register

RATINGS	POSSIBLE SCORE	SCORE ACHIEVED
Ship	500	395
Accommodation	200	151
Food	400	221
Service	400	270
Cruise	500	348
TOTAL	**2,000**	**1,385**

Accommodation: All of the standard cabins are alike, fairly spacious, and have enough storage space for a one-week cruise, and, although the decor is bright it is also rather spartan. Only the 28 outside suites have whirlpool bathtubs, and a decor that is more pleasant for being less plain.

Dining: The two large dining rooms, both with ocean-view windows (both nonsmoking), are noisy, but the decor is attractive, though rather vivid. There are two seatings. The food is very disappointing even though it has been upgraded steadily over the past couple of years. The service is basic, and pushy, with absolutely no finesse. Although there is a wine list, there are no wine waiters.

Other Comments: Although externally angular and not handsome, this is one of a series of eight identical (and very successful) mega-ships built for Carnival Cruise Lines. Features vibrant colors and extensive use of neon lighting for sensory stimulation. Almost vibration-free service. Has a six-deck-high atrium, topped by a large glass dome, features spectacular artistic centerpiece. Has expansive open deck areas, but they quickly become inadequate when the ship is full.

Inside, this ship has public entertainment lounges, bars, and clubs galore, with something for everyone (except quiet space). Has a fine library and reading room, but few books. Her handsome public rooms connected by wide indoor boulevards, beat a futuristic theme, and are painted in dazzling colors. The multitiered showroom is quite lavish, but 20 pillars do obstruct the views from several seats. Dramatic three-deck-high glass enclosed health spa. Banked jogging track. The large casino has almost nonstop action.

The real fun begins at sundown, when Carnival really excels in sound, lights, and razzle-dazzle shows. From the futuristic Electricity Disco to the ancient Cleopatra's Bar, this ship will entertain you well. Based in Port Canaveral, the ship offers three- and four-day Bahamas cruises year-round. What should be of great interest to families is a special partnership with Universal Studios' travel company, which packages a cruise together with a land stay and choice of three theme parks: Universal Studios, Wet 'n Wild, and Sea World.

Weak Points: There are simply too many annoying, and loud, intrusive announcements.

m/s Fascination
★★★ +
(L)

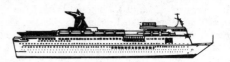

LIFESTYLE:	STANDARD
Cruise Line:	Carnival Cruise Lines
Former Names:	-
Gross Tonnage:	70,367
Builder:	Kvaerner Masa-Yards (Finland)
Original Cost:	$315 million
Entered Service:	July 1994
Flag:	Panama
Tel. No.:	1346374
Fax No.:	n/a
Length (ft/m):	855.0/260.60
Beam (ft/m):	103.0/31.4
Draft (ft/m):	25.9/7.9
Propulsion/Propellers:	diesel-electric (42,240kW)/2 (CP)
Passenger Decks:	10
Total Crew:	920
Pass. Capacity (basis 2):	2,040
Pass. Capacity (all berths):	2,594
Pass. Space Ratio (basis 2):	34.4
Pass. Space Ratio (all berths):	26.7
Officers:	Italian
Total Cabins:	1,020
Size Range (sq ft/m):	173.2–409.7/16.0–38.0
Cabins (outside view):	618
Cabins (inside — no view):	402
Cabins (single occupancy):	0

Cabins (with private balcony):	54
Cabins (wheelchair accessible):	22
Cabin Current:	110 volts
Cabin TV:	Yes
Dining Rooms:	2
Elevators:	14
Casino:	Yes
Slot Machines:	Yes
Swimming Pools (outdoors):	3
Swimming Pools (inside):	0
Whirlpools:	6
Fitness Center:	Yes
Sauna/Steam Room:	Yes/Yes
Massage:	Yes
Self-Service Launderette:	Yes
Movie Theater/Seats:	No
Library:	Yes
Classification Society:	Lloyd's Register

RATINGS	POSSIBLE SCORE	SCORE ACHIEVED
Ship	500	395
Accommodation	200	151
Food	400	221
Service	400	270
Cruise	500	348
TOTAL	**2,000**	**1,385**

Accommodation: The standard cabins are quite functional and of a good size. The decor is bright but somewhat plain and uninspiring; each features a small vanity desk, twin beds that convert to a queen-size bed (some of the lower grade cabins have upper/lower berths), a fairly decent amount of closet and drawer space.

There are 28 outside suites, each with a king-size bed, whirlpool tub and more elegant decor, fittings, and soft furnishings. Take your own shampoo and conditioner (none are provided, although soap is).

Dining: The two seatings in the two large, noisy dining rooms (both are nonsmoking) come with Carnival's typically usual efficient, assertive, fast service. Improved cuisine is so-so, but first-time cruise passengers seem to accept it. The buffets are rather run-of-the-mill, with little creativity. Although there is a wine list (with some good California whites and reds), there are no wine waiters.

Other Comments: This is one of a series of eight identical mega-ships built for Carnival that reflects the fine creative interior design work of Joe Farcus. Features a somewhat ungainly exterior profile, but the space created has been well used. Has expansive open deck areas, but never enough when the ship is full (the aft decks tend to be less noisy, whereas all the activities are focused around the main pool). A well-defined "topless" sunbathing area can be found around the funnel base on Verandah Deck.

Inside, a dramatic atrium lobby spans six decks, and features cool marble and hot neon topped by a large glass dome and a spectacular artistic centerpiece called "Nucleus" which illustrates the kleig lights of a Hollywood premiere, according to the ship's designer, Joe Farcus. The ship offers public entertainment lounges, bars, and clubs galore, with something for everyone.

The interior decor aboard all Carnival ships is themed; this one sports a sophisticated Hollywood theme that begs your indulgence. The principal public rooms are all connected by a double indoor boulevard. Excellent photo opportunities exist with some superb life-like figures from the movies. Look for Marilyn Monroe and James Dean outside the casino at Stars Bar, Humphrey Bogart and Ingrid Bergman at the piano at Bogart's Cafe, Sophia Loren and Paul Newman are close by, and Vivien Leigh and Clark

243

Gable can be found in Tara's Library. Meanwhile, John Wayne is at the entrance to the Passage to India Lounge, while Edward J. Robinson is inside; outside the Diamonds Are Forever discotheque are none other than Elizabeth Taylor and Elvis Presley. There's also Lena Horne and Sydney Poitier outside the Beverly Hills Bar, while inside are Katharine Hepburn and Spencer Tracy. Oh, and just in case you want to gamble, you'll find Lucille Ball outside the casino. Incidentally, all the slot machines aboard all Carnival ships are linked into a big prize, called naturally, Megacash.

The multitiered showroom is quite lavish, and features good, but raucous, razzle-dazzle shows (sight lines are obscured from seats behind or adjacent to 20 pillars). Has a dramatic, well-segmented three-deck-high glass-enclosed health spa and gymnasium with the latest muscle-pump equipment. There is a large shop, but it is stuffed to the gills with low quality merchandise.

However, the real fun begins at sundown, when Carnival excels in decibels. This ship will entertain you in timely fashion. With such an enormous ship to play on, you will never be bored and even may forget to get off in port! There's no doubt that Carnival does "fun" better than anyone else, and if you want to party and live it up, then this ship should do it.

Weak Points: There are less announcements in a military training camp.

m/v Flamenco
★★★ +
(M)

LIFESTYLE:	STANDARD
Cruise Line:	Festival Cruises
Former Names:	*Southern Cross, Star/Ship Majestic,*
	Sun Princess, Spirit of London
Gross Tonnage:	17,042
Builder: Cantieri Navale Del Tirreno & Riuniti (Italy)	
Original Cost:	n/a
Entered Service:	November 1972/December 1997
Flag:	Bahamas
Tel. No.:	1104553
Fax No.:	1104553
Length (ft/m):	535.7/163.30
Beam (ft/m):	73.4/22.4
Draft (ft/m):	22.4/6.85
Propulsion/Propellers:	diesel (13,450kW)/2 (CP)
Passenger Decks:	7
Total Crew:	350
Pass. Capacity (basis 2):	798
Pass. Capacity (all berths):	987
Pass. Space Ratio (basis 2):	21.3
Pass. Space Ratio (all berths):	17.2
Officers:	Greek
Total Cabins:	401
Size Range (sq ft/m):	996.8- 236.8/9.0–22.0
Cabins (outside view):	272
Cabins (inside — no view):	129
Cabins (single occupancy):	4
Cabins (with private balcony):	0

Cabins (wheelchair accessible):	2
Cabin Current:	110 and 220 volts
Cabin TV:	Yes
Dining Rooms:	1
Elevators:	4
Casino:	Yes
Slot Machines:	Yes
Swimming Pools (outdoors):	1 (+children's wading pool)
Swimming Pools (inside):	0
Whirlpools:	0
Fitness Center:	Yes
Sauna/Steam Room:	No/No
Massage:	Yes
Self-Service Launderette:	No
Movie Theater/Seats:	Yes/186
Library:	Yes
Classification Society:	Lloyd's Register

RATINGS	POSSIBLE SCORE	SCORE ACHIEVED
Ship	500	311
Accommodation	200	122
Food	400	267
Service	400	283
Cruise	500	309
TOTAL	**2,000**	**1,292**

Accommodation: There are twelve cabin grades. Those described as deluxe suites are reasonably spacious, with separate sleeping and living areas. All other inside and outside-view cabins are on the small side, but quite well equipped, with colorful soft furnishings. However, the cabin walls are really thin, which means you will be able to hear your next-door neighbors brushing their teeth. There is little drawer space. The cabin telephone system is rather antiquated and should be updated. The bathrooms are compact units, but adequate, and feature 100 percent cotton towels; the toilets are of the "gentle flush" and not the "barking dog suction" variety as found aboard newer ships.

Dining: The Galaxy Restaurant (totally nonsmoking) is quite attractive, and with its high ceiling and ocean-view porthole-shaped windows, provides a light and airy space. However, it can be extremely noisy as the tables are very close together (as aboard Festival Cruises' other ships), as well as close to the waiter stations. There are two seatings. The service standards are good, and being fine-tuned constantly. The quality of food and its presentation are reasonably good. There is a limited choice of breads, rolls, cheeses, and fruits, which all tend to be quite standard. Informal self-service buffets for breakfast and lunch are quite decent, however, and well presented in the Satellite Cafe.

Other Comments: This ship has a fairly handsome 1970s profile, with a rakish superstructure, an all-white hull, and a single large blue funnel. She underwent a $9 million refurbishment in late 1997, after being acquired from her from her former owners, the now-defunct CTC Cruise Lines.

There is a reasonable open deck and sunbathing space for a ship of this size, although it is tight when full, and there are no cushioned pads for the deck lounge chairs.

Inside the ship, the layout is practical, making it easy to find your way around. The public rooms received a facelift during the 1997 refurbishment by her new owners. All of the public rooms are quite comfortable, with attractive decor and soft furnishings, while tasteful colors mixed with the extensive use of reflective surfaces provide an upbeat, contemporary feel, yet comfortable feel. Particularly nice is the

Piano Bar/Casino lounge area, with its warm wood room dividers and long bar. Do remember, however, this is not a new ship, and cannot compare with the latest vessels. Where this company does score highly, is in the friendliness of the crew, which is very international.

This ship provides very good value for money, and a comfortable cruise experience in relaxed surroundings. Festival Cruises (called First European Cruises in the US) specializes in "cruising for Europeans." The languages (and therefore announcements) used throughout the ship are typically English, French, German, Italian, and Spanish. The itineraries are well designed and include several sea days on longer voyages.

Weak Points: She is a high-density vessel, so there will be some crowding during embarkation and disembarkation, as well as for tenders and buffets. There is no wraparound promenade deck outdoors, although you *can* walk around the front sections of one of the open decks. There are too many loud announcements, in several languages. Nonsmokers should be aware that many passengers, officers, and staff are heavy smokers.

WHOS' WHO – THE CHIEF PURSER

The chief purser's office is the financial, business, accommodation, and information center of any ship. The purser's department handles all matters relating to money (including currency exchange), mail, and communications; accepts valuables for safekeeping; and provides a complete information service, sometimes around the clock. The purser is alos responsible for all passenger and crew accounts, purchasing and requisitioning of supplies, shipboard concessions, the onboard printing of items such as the Daily Program and menus, and manning the telephone switchboard, if the ship does not have an automatic system. The purser's domain also includes relations with customs and immigration officials in all ports of call.

The purser has two main assistants: the hotel purser and the crew purser. The hotel purser is in charge of all passenger business, including accommodation (often under the direction of a berthing officer), while the crew purser handles all matters relating to the ship's personnel and contracts.

s/y Flying Cloud
(S)

LIFESTYLE:	STANDARD
Cruise Line:	Windjammer Barefoot Cruises
Former Names:	*Oisseau des Isles*
Gross Tonnage:	400
Builder:	Ancione Chantiers Dibignon (France)
Entered Service:	1935/1968
Flag:	Equatorial Guinea
Tel. No.:	n/a
Fax No.:	n/a
Length (ft/m):	208.0/63.3
Beam (ft/m):	32.0/9.7
Draft (ft/m):	16.0/4.8
Type of Vessel:	barquentine
No. of Masts:	3
Sail Area (sq ft/sq m):	10,500.5/975.5
Main Propulsion:	sail power
Propulsion/Propellers:	diesel/1 (FP)
Decks:	3
Total Crew:	28
Pass. Capacity (basis 2):	66
Pass. Capacity (all berths):	66
Pass. Space Ratio (basis 2):	5.8
Pass. Space Ratio (all berths):	5.8
Officers:	International
Total Cabins:	33
Size Range (sq ft/m):	60.2–148.0/5.6–13.7
Cabins (outside view):	18
Cabins (inside - no view):	15

Cabins (single occupancy):	0
Cabins (with private balcony):	0
Cabins (wheelchair accessible):	0
Cabin Current:	110 volts
Cabin TV:	Yes (3 cabins only)
Dining Rooms:	1
Elevators:	0
Casino:	0
Slot Machines:	0
Swimming Pools (outdoors):	0
Whirlpools:	0
Fitness Center:	No
Sauna/Steam Room:	No/No
Massage:	No
Self-Service Launderette:	No
Library:	Yes
Classification Society:	None

RATINGS	POSSIBLE SCORE	SCORE ACHIEVED
Ship	500	NYR
Accommodation	200	NYR
Food	400	NYR
Service	400	NYR
Cruise	500	NYR
TOTAL	**2,000**	**NYR**
Expected Score Range:		**900-1100**

Accommodation: There are four grades of accommodation. All are dimensionally challenged, particularly when compared to standard cruise ships, but this is a casual cruise experience and you will need few clothes anyway. All are equipped with upper and lower berths, and most of them are quite narrow.

Dining: There is one dining room, and meals are all casual in style and service. Breakfast is served on board, as is dinner, while lunch could be either on board or at a beach, picnic-style.

Other Comments: This ship was built in 1935 for the French Navy and served as a cadet training vessel. Her interior decor includes such things as stained glass windows, a spiral staircase, and lots of lovely wood, having been refurbished when Windjammer Barefoot Cruises purchased her in 1968.

Aboard one of the Windjammer Barefoot Cruises' fleet you can let the crew do all the work, or you can lend a hand at the helm yourself, if you feel so inclined. One neat thing to do is just to sit or lie in the nets at the bows of the vessel, without a care in the world – it's a great feeling.

The mood is free and easy, the ships are equipped very simply, and only the most casual clothes are required (T-shirts and shorts). Shoes are optional, although you may need them if you go off in one of the ports. Quite possibly the most used item will be your bathing suit — better take more than one! Smoking is allowed only on the open decks.

Entertainment in the evenings consists of — you and the crew. You can put on a toga, take or create a pirate outfit, and join in the fun. This is cruising free 'n' easy style — none of that programmed big-ship production show stuff here.

Jammin' aboard a Windjammer (first-time passengers are called "crewmates" while repeat passengers are called "jammers") is no-frills cruising (it could be called an "anti-cruise") in a no-nonsense, friendly environment, for the young at heart and those who don't need programmed activities. It's all about going to sea and the romance of being at sea under sail. Those who enjoy beaches, scuba diving, and snorkeling around the Caribbean will be best suited to a Windjammer Barefoot Cruises cruise.

Part Two: The Cruise Ships and Ratings

Although itineraries (well, islands) are provided in the brochure, the captain actually decides which islands to go to in any given area, depending on sea and weather conditions. *Flying Cloud* features year-round cruises in the British and US Virgin Islands. Brochure rates might seem inexpensive, but you'll need to add on the airfare in order to get the true cost. Tips to the crew are suggested — at $50 per week!

Complies with all international safety regulations, with the exception of the 1966 fire safety standards. Sails from Tortola (British Virgin Islands). Other ships of the fleet in this book: *Legacy, Mandalay, Polynesia,* and *Yankee Clipper*.

Windjammer Barefoot Cruises' **Flying Cloud,** *seen here at anchor.*

m/v Fuji Maru
★★★ +
(S)

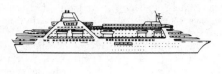

LIFESTYLE:	STANDARD
Cruise Line:	Mitsui OSK Passenger Line
Former Names:	-
Gross Tonnage:	23,340
Builder:	Mitsubishi (Japan)
Original Cost:	$55 million
Entered Service:	April 1989
Flag:	Japan
Tel. No.:	1200467
Fax No.:	1200470
Length (ft/m):	547.9/167.00
Beam (ft/m):	78.7/24.00
Draft (ft/m):	21.4/6.55
Propulsion/Propellers:	diesel (15,740kW)/2 (CP)
Passenger Decks:	8
Total Crew:	190
Pass. Capacity (basis 2):	328
Pass. Capacity (all berths):	603
Pass. Space Ratio (basis 2):	71.1
Pass. Space Ratio (all berths):	38.7
Officers:	Japanese
Total Cabins:	164
Size Range (sq ft/m):	182.9–376.7/17.0–35.0
Cabins (outside view):	164
Cabins (inside — no view):	0
Cabins (single occupancy):	0
Cabins (with private balcony):	0

Cabins (wheelchair accessible):	2
Cabin Current:	100 volts
Cabin TV:	Yes
Dining Rooms:	1
Elevators:	5
Casino:	Yes
Slot Machines:	No
Swimming Pools (outdoors):	1
Swimming Pools (inside):	0
Whirlpools:	0 (4 Japanese Baths)
Fitness Center:	Yes
Sauna/Steam Room:	Yes/No
Massage:	Yes
Self-Service Launderette:	Yes
Movie Theater/Seats:	Yes/142
Library:	Yes
Classification Society:	Nippon Kaiji Kyokai

RATINGS	POSSIBLE SCORE	SCORE ACHIEVED
Ship	500	358
Accommodation	200	137
Food	400	287
Service	400	284
Cruise	500	331
TOTAL	**2,000**	**1,397**

Accommodation: There are two suites that are quite lovely, with separate bedroom and living room. The deluxe cabins are also of a good standard, and come with a vanity/writing desk, minibar-refrigerator, and full-sized, deep bathtub. Almost all of the other (standard) cabins are furnished very simply, but they are good for seminar and school cruises (they are much too small for any long voyages). The cabin insulation is reasonable, but could be better. The bathrooms are small and utilitarian, with old-style fixtures and some exposed plumbing. The folded blankets, a MOPAS (Mitsui OSK Passenger Line) tradition, are lovely.

Dining: The single, large dining room is quite attractive and has a high ceiling, but rather bright lighting, which makes it look more like a school cafeteria dining hall. Both Japanese and Western cuisine are featured for all meals, in one seating. The food itself is of a good standard, with simple, but colorful, presentation, and a good variety. There are several beverage machines around the ship for those who are used to them ashore (again, these are much appreciated by those attending seminars and training session cruises).

Other Comments: This ship has a well thought out, and a flexible design for multifunctional uses, but its principal use is for incentives, conventions, as a seminar and training ship, and only occasionally for individual passengers. The outdoor decks are quite spartan and little used.

Her interiors are plain and a little clinical, although there is some good artwork throughout to brighten things up. There are extensive lecture and conference facilities. The largest and most flexible lecture hall is two decks high, seats 600, and converts into a sports stadium or exhibition hall for industrial product introductions. The lobby is quite elegant and open and is part of a two-level atrium.

The ship features a classic, wood-paneled library. Other features include two Japanese-style grand baths and a traditional washitsu tatami mat room. A Hanaguruma owner's room is elegant for small formal functions. The Sakura Salon is soothing, with a blend of western and traditional Japanese design. The media and television systems throughout the ship include much high-tech equipment (bilingual multiplex televisions are located in all crew cabins).

This is a fascinating exhibition, training, and educational charter cruise ship that has reasonably up-to-date facilities, although it is not ideally designed for individual passengers. As in any ship for Japanese passengers, tipping is not allowed. There are many more modern ships in the international marketplace (also serving Japanese passengers), with better facilities, more dining choices, and a less utilitarian feel and ambience, and so the score for this ship has been adjusted slightly downwards accordingly.

<u>Weak Points</u>: The waste of open deck space and poor maintenance of it. Plastic, utilitarian deck furniture. The lighting is too bright, which also increases the noise level, and so there is little ambience.

RULES OF THE ROAD

Ships, the largest moving objects made by man, are subject to stringent international regulations. They must keep to the right in shipping lanes, and pass on the right (with certain exceptions). When circumstances raise some doubt, or shipping lanes are crowded, ships use their whistles in the same way an automobile driver uses directional signals to show which way he will turn. When one ship passes another and gives a single blast on its whistle, this means it is turning to starboard (right). Two blasts mean a turn to port (left). The other ship acknowledges by repeating the same signal. Ships switch on navigational running lights at night — green for starboard, red for port, plus two white lights on the masts, the forward one lower than the aft one.

Flags and pennants form another part of a ship's communication facilities and are displayed for identification purposes. Each time a country is visited, its national flag is shown. While entering and leaving a port, the ship flies a blue and vertical striped flag to request a pilot, while a half red, half white flag (divided vertically) indicates that a pilot is on board. Cruise lines also display their own "house" flag from the mast.

A ship's funnel (smokestack) is one other means of identification, each line having its own design and color scheme. The size, height, and number of funnels were points worth advertising at the turn of the century. Most ocean liners of the time had four funnels and were called "four-stackers."

There are numerous customs at sea, many of them older than any maritime law. Superstition has always been an important element, as in the following example quoted in the British Admiralty Manual of Seamanship: "The custom of breaking a bottle of wine over the stem of a ship when it is being launched originates from the old practice of toasting prosperity to a ship with a silver goblet of wine, which was then cast into the sea in order to prevent a toast of ill intent being drunk from the same cup. This was a practice that proved too expensive, and it was replaced in 1690 by the breaking of a bottle of wine over the stem."

m/s Funchal
★★ +
(S)

LIFESTYLE:	STANDARD
Cruise Line:	Classic International Cruises
Former Names:	-
Gross Tonnage:	9,563
Builder:	Helsingor Skibsvog (Denmark)
Original Cost:	n/a
Entered Service:	October 1961/May 1986
Flag:	Panama
Tel. No.:	1330320
Fax No.:	1336716
Length (ft/m):	503.6/153.51
Beam (ft/m):	62.5/19.08
Draft (ft/m):	20.3/6.20
Propulsion/Propellers:	diesel (7,356kW)/2 (FP)
Passenger Decks:	6
Total Crew:	155
Pass. Capacity (basis 2):	430
Pass. Capacity (all berths):	524
Pass. Space Ratio (basis 2):	22.2
Pass. Space Ratio (all berths):	18.2
Officers:	Greek/Portuguese
Total Cabins:	222
Size Range (sq ft/m):	102.2–252.9/9.5–23.5
Cabins (outside view):	151
Cabins (inside — no view):	71
Cabins (single occupancy):	14
Cabins (with private balcony):	0

Cabins (wheelchair accessible):	0
Cabin Current:	220 volts
Cabin TV:	No
Dining Rooms:	2
Elevators:	3
Casino:	Yes
Slot Machines:	Yes
Swimming Pools (outdoors):	1
Swimming Pools (inside):	0
Whirlpools:	0
Fitness Center:	Yes
Sauna/Steam Room:	Yes/No
Massage:	No
Self-Service Launderette:	No
Movie Theater/Seats:	No
Library:	Yes
Classification Society:	Rinave Portuguesa

RATINGS	POSSIBLE SCORE	SCORE ACHIEVED
Ship	500	233
Accommodation	200	101
Food	400	242
Service	400	250
Cruise	500	271
TOTAL	**2,000**	**1,097**

Accommodation: The cabins are compact, yet tastefully appointed units, and come in both twin and double-bedded configurations. Each now has a private bathroom (all were refurbished in1997/98), and there is just enough closet and drawer space providing you don't pack too many clothes. The cabins are decorated in very plain colors, accented with colorful soft furnishings. All cabin bathrooms have soap, shampoo, shower cap, shoeshine and sewing kits, and bathrobe.

Dining: There are two dining rooms, Coimbra (which also doubles as a video screening room after dinner) and Lisboa; both have large ocean-view picture windows, are tastefully decorated, and have a very homely and cozy old-world atmosphere. There is one seating. The food is European in style (and includes plenty of fresh fish) and is surprisingly good, as is the service from friendly Portuguese waiters. There is a decent selection of breads, cheeses, and fruits, and the wine list, while not extensive, includes a good selection of Portuguese wines at very modest prices.

Other Comments: This ship has a real classic sixties profile with well balanced, rounded lines, and pleasing real wooden decks (not a hint of artificial grass anywhere), including one outdoor deck with two sheltered promenades, although they do not completely encircle the ship.

Inside, one deck houses all the main public rooms, the most appealing of which is the Porto Bar, which is reminiscent of a late nineteenth century drinking club with its wood paneled walls, furniture, and lovely bar. A highly polished wooden spiral stairway is a beautiful, classic piece of decoration not found in today's ships, and is reminiscent of the days of the transatlantic steamers of the early twentieth century.

The mostly Portuguese staff is friendly, caring, and quite attentive, although a little reserved at first. This ship is popular with Europeans and Scandinavians during the summer and Brazilians during the winter (anyone used to new cruise ships would probably find the ship too eclectic). She features destination-intensive cruises in a comfortable, old-world atmosphere, ideally suited to couples and solo passengers seeking good value for money and a good balance of sea days and port days.

She attracts a great number of loyal repeat passengers, who sail again and again because of the charming, mostly Portuguese crew and Greek captains. *Funchal* is like an old, well-worn shoe — comfortable, but in need of help, and so she hovers just a tad under the three-star level (a two-and-a-half star vessel with a three-star heart). The ship is good if you enjoy small, vintage vessels with all their accompanying eccentricities. The feeling of camaraderie and friendliness from her loyal crew (many of whom have been aboard the ship for many years) offsets some of the hardware negatives. Often operates under charter to various tour packagers and operators.

Weak Points: Much of the ship's exterior paintwork is sloppy. The show lounge is extremely poor. A lack of proper maintenance in her early life has resulted in some of the exterior plating being well worn and thin.

WIND SPEEDS

A navigational announcement to passengers is normally made once or twice a day, giving the ship's position, temperature, and weather information.

Various winds affect the world's weather patterns. Such well-known winds as the Bora, Mistral, Northwind, Sirocco, among others, play an important part in the makeup of weather at and above sea level. Wind velocity is measured on the Beaufort Scale, a method that was first devised in 1805 by Commodore Francis Beaufort, later Admiral and Knight Commander of the Bath, for measuring the force of wind at sea. Originally, it measured the effect of the wind on a fully rigged man-of-war (which was usually laden with cannons and heavy ammunition). It became the official way of recording wind velocity in 1874, when the International Meteorological Committee adopted it.

You might be confused by the numbering system for wind velocity. There are twelve velocities, known as "force" on the Beaufort Scale. They are as follows:

Force	Speed (mph)	Description/Ocean Surface
0	0-1	Calm; glassy (like a mirror)
1	1-3	Light wind; rippled surface
2	4-7	Light breeze; small wavelets
3	8-12	Gentle breeze; large wavelets, scattered whitecaps
4	13-18	Moderate breeze; small waves, frequent whitecaps
5	19-24	Fresh breeze; moderate waves, numerous whitecaps
6	25-31	Strong breeze; large waves, white foam crests
7	32-38	Moderate gale; streaky white foam
8	39-46	Fresh gale; moderately high waves
9	47-54	Strong gale; high waves
10	55-63	Whole gale; very high waves, curling crests
11	64-73	Violent storm; extremely high waves, froth and foam, poor visibility
12	73+	Hurricane; huge waves, thundering white spray, visibility nil

m/v Galapagos Discovery
★★ +
(S)

LIFESTYLE:	STANDARD
Cruise Line:	Klein Tours
Former Names:	*Bali Sea Dancer, Illiria*
Gross Tonnage:	3,852
Builder:	Cantieri Navale Pellegrino (Italy)
Original Cost:	n/a
Entered Service:	1962/October 1998
Flag:	Ecuador
Tel. No.:	673505710
Fax No.:	673505731
Length (ft/m):	332.6/101.40
Beam (ft/m):	48.0/14.66
Draft (ft/m):	16.4/5.02
Propulsion/Propellers:	diesel (4,281kW)/2 (FP)
Passenger Decks:	4
Total Crew:	55
Pass. Capacity (basis 2):	110
Pass. Capacity (all berths):	148
Pass. Space Ratio (basis 2):	35.0
Pass. Space Ratio (all berths):	26.0
Officers:	International
Total Cabins:	55
Size Range (sq ft/m):	77.0–336.0/7.1–31.2
Cabins (outside view):	48
Cabins (inside — no view):	7
Cabins (single occupancy):	0
Cabins (with private balcony):	0

Cabins (wheelchair accessible):	0
Cabin Current:	110 volts
Cabin TV:	No
Dining Rooms:	1
Elevators:	0
Casino:	No
Slot Machines:	No
Swimming Pools (outdoors):	1
Swimming Pools (inside):	0
Whirlpools:	0
Fitness Center:	Yes
Sauna/Steam Room:	No/No
Massage:	Yes
Self-Service Launderette:	No
Conference Room/Seats:	Yes/100
Library:	Yes
Classification Society:	American Bureau of Shipping

RATINGS	POSSIBLE SCORE	SCORE ACHIEVED
Ship	500	256
Accommodation	200	111
Food	400	211
Service	400	225
Cruise	500	239
TOTAL	**2,000**	**1,042**

Accommodation: There are five suites and 49 double occupancy cabins. Some have queen-sized beds, some have twin beds that convert to a queen-sized bed, and some are fixed twins. All of the cabins are a little on the small side, but they do have some wood accents and trim, and come with a telephone, and personal safe. All cabins feature a private bathroom with shower (two suites have a full-sized bathtub as well as a separate shower stall), hairdryer and magnifying mirror, although space for personal toiletry items is very limited. There really is little closet and drawer space.

The suites have separate lounge and sleeping areas, with queen-sized beds; lounge features include a desk (with computer outlet), two chairs, and minibar-refrigerator.

Dining: The teak-paneled dining room is quite charming, but it is a little tight when the ship is full, although there is a good amount of space around each table. There is one, open seating. The cuisine is centered on international fare, with some local specialties, and should be quite adequate considering the cuising region. Features open seating dining (you may sit where and with whom you like). Breakfast and lunch are presented buffet-style, and an additional lunch buffet is available on a sun terrace. Has a decent wine list, but the wines are expensive.

Other Comments: This small, very pleasant, relaxed ship was originally constructed for charter cruises in the Mediterranean, but presently operates year-round in the Galapagos Islands. She is quite a clean ship throughout and has been well maintained, despite her age. The ship also carries two Zodiac inflatable rubber craft, as well as a glass bottom boat that can accommodate 20 persons.

Inside appointments and the limited number of public rooms have pleasing decor, color-rich fabrics, and soft furnishings. The use of much wood paneling and brass helps to keep an elegant feel to the vessel. The main lounge has interesting box-fluted columns and oversized armchairs. There is a well-stocked reference library (and a nonworking fireplace). There are some interesting works of art in her public rooms. One unusual facility is a Conference Room that can seat up to 100, and can be split into three separate meeting rooms. The library is equipped with computers (with Internet access) and a video player.

The ship's owners and operators, Klein Tours, of Ecuador, provide a comfortable destination-oriented cruise experience for those seeking to get close to the natural, ecologically interesting world off the coast of Ecuador. Six guides are carried as part of the crew, and the ship operates three-, four- and seven-night cruises.

Weak Points: The swimming pool is tiny (it is really just a "dip" pool). The ceilings are very plain and uninteresting.

KNOTS AND LOGS

A knot is a unit of speed measuring one nautical mile. (A nautical mile is equal to one-sixtieth of a degree of the earth's circumference and measures exactly 6,080.2 ft (1,852 km). It is about 800 ft (243 m) longer than a land mile. Thus, when a ship is traveling at a speed of 20 knots (*note*: this is never referred to as 20 knots per hour), she is traveling at 20 nautical miles per hour.

This unit of measurement has its origin in the days prior to the advent of modern aids, when sailors used a log and a length of rope to measure the distance that their boat had covered, as well as the speed at which it was advancing. In 1574, a tract by William Bourne, entitled *A Regiment for the Sea*, records the method by which this was done. The log was weighted down at one end while the other end was affixed to a rope. The weighted end, when thrown over the stern, had the effect of making the log stand upright, thus being visible. Sailors believed that the log remained stationary at the spot where it had been cast into the water, while the rope unraveled. By measuring the length of rope used, they could ascertain how far the ship had traveled, and were thus able to calculate its speed.

Sailors first tied knots at regular intervals, eventually fixed at 47 feet 3 inches (14.4 meters) along a rope, then counted how many knots had passed through their hands in a specified time (later established as 28 seconds), and measured by the amount of sand that had run out of an hourglass. They then used simple multiplication to calculate the number of knots their ship was traveling at over the period of an hour.

The data gathered in this way were put into a record, called a logbook. Today, a logbook is used to record the day-to-day details of the life of a ship and its crew, as well as other pertinent information.

m/s Galapagos Explorer II
★★★ +
(S)

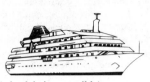

LIFESTYLE:	**PREMIUM**
Cruise Line:	Canodros
Former Names:	*Renaissance Three*
Gross Tonnage:	3,990
Builder:	Cantieri Navale Ferrari (Italy)
Original Cost:	$20 million
Entered Service:	August 1990/January 1998
Flag:	Liberia
Tel. No.:	1250166
Fax No.:	1250167
Length (ft/m):	289.6/88.30
Beam (ft/m):	50.1/15.30
Draft (ft/m):	11.9/3.65
Propulsion/Propellers:	diesel (3,514kW)/2 (CP)
Passenger Decks:	5
Total Crew:	72
Pass. Capacity (basis 2):	100
Pass. Capacity (all berths):	111
Pass. Space Ratio (basis 2):	39.9
Pass. Space Ratio (all berths):	35.9
Officers:	International
Total Cabins:	50
Size Range (sq ft/m):	231.4–282.0/21.5–26.2
Cabins (outside view):	50
Cabins (inside — no view):	0
Cabins (single occupancy):	0
Cabins (with private balcony):	4

Cabins (wheelchair accessible):	0
Cabin Current:	110 volts
Cabin TV:	Yes
Dining Rooms:	1
Elevators:	1
Casino:	Yes
Slot Machines:	Yes
Swimming Pools (outdoors):	1
Swimming Pools (inside):	0
Whirlpools:	1
Fitness Center:	No
Sauna/Steam Room:	Yes/No
Massage:	No
Self-Service Launderette:	No
Movie Theater/Seats:	No
Library:	No
Classification Society:	Registro Navale Italiano

RATINGS	POSSIBLE SCORE	SCORE ACHIEVED
Ship	500	361
Accommodation	200	156
Food	400	244
Service	400	287
Cruise	500	317
TOTAL	**2,000**	**1,365**

Accommodation: The accommodation is located forward, with public rooms aft. Pleasant, all-outside cabins feature a large picture window and combine gorgeous, highly polished imitation rosewood paneling with lots of mirrors, hand-crafted Italian furniture and wet bar (pre-stocked when you book, and all items are at extra cost). All cabins feature a queen-sized bed, a sitting area, and most things you need, including a minibar-refrigerator, television, VCR unit, and hairdryer. The cabins have small closets, however; space for luggage is tight, and there is little drawer space (there are, however, two lockable drawers).

The bathrooms, which are small, have showers (none have bathtubs) with a fold-down seat, real teakwood floors and marble vanities.

Dining: The dining room, which features a single (open) seating, is small and elegant, and is in three sections. It is on the lowest deck and has portholes (construction regulations requirement), although it is quite cozy and welcoming, and there are tables for two, four, six, and even eight. Sit where you like, with whom you like, and at what time you like on the first night, after which you sit at the same table for the duration of the cruise.

The meals are self-service buffet-style cold foods for breakfast and lunch (sometimes lunch will be on deck), with local delicacies featured. Food quality, choice, and presentation are all fairly decent, but not that memorable. There is limited choice, particularly with regard to the entrees.

Other Comments: Originally constructed as one of a fleet of four small, identical, and intimate cruise vessels for Renaissance Cruises, out of a total fleet of eight ships (the second four were slightly larger). This vessel is comfortable and inviting, although it has not been particularly well maintained. Water sports facilities include an aft platform, sailfish, snorkel equipment, and several Zodiacs.

Has contemporary mega-yacht looks and handsome styling, and there is a wooden promenade deck outdoors. Inside, the limited number of public rooms feature decor that is quite smart and restful. The main lounge also doubles as a lecture room, but the piano bar is perhaps the best place to relax in the evening.

This ship will provide a destination-intensive, refined, quiet, and relaxed cruise for passengers who do not like crowds, dressing up, scheduled activities, or entertainment. Naturalist guides that have been trained at the Darwin Station lead the guided shore excursions, which are included in the fare.

This ship operates three-, four-, and seven- night Galapagos cruises year-round from San Cristobal, sold through various tour operators. Liquor, beer, cocktails, and soft drinks are included in the fare, but wine and champagne are not. Also included are guided visits to the islands. The brochure rates *do not* include Galapagos Islands visitor tax (to be *paid in cash* at Guayaquil or Quito airports or in the islands), or other island taxes. Shore visits take place in "pangas" (local lingo for "dinghies").

<u>Weak Points</u>: The tiny "dip" pool is not a swimming pool. The open deck and sunbathing space is quite cramped. Plastic wood instead of real wood everywhere (looks too perfect). While the service is without finesse, the crew is quite willing. The small library is attractive, but book selection is poor. The ship does not sail well in inclement weather.

SHIP TALK

Abeam: off the side of the ship, at a right angle to its length.

Aft: near, toward, or in the rear of the ship.

Ahead: something that is ahead of the ship's bow.

Alleyway: a passageway or corridor.

Alongside: said of a ship when it is beside a pier or another vessel.

Amidships: in or toward the middle of the ship; the longitudinal center portion of the ship.

Anchor Ball: black ball hoisted above the bow to show that the vessel is anchored.

Astern: is the opposite of Ahead (i.e., meaning something behind the ship).

Backwash: motion in the water caused by the propeller(s) moving in a reverse (astern) direction.

Bar: sandbar, usually caused by tidal or current conditions near the shore.

Beam: width of the ship between its two sides at the widest point.

Bearing: compass direction, expressed in degrees, from the ship to a particular objective or destination.

Below: anything beneath the main deck.

Berth: dock, pier, or quay. Also means bed on board ship.

Bilge: lowermost spaces of the infrastructure of a ship.

Boat Stations: allotted space for each person during lifeboat drill or any other emergency when lifeboats are lowered.

Bow: the forward most part of the vessel.

Bridge: navigational and command control center.

Bulkhead: upright partition (wall) dividing the ship into compartments.

Bunkers: the space where fuel is stored; "bunkering" means taking on fuel.

m/s Galaxy
★★★★ +
(L)

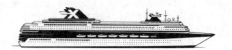

LIFESTYLE: **PREMIUM**

Cruise Line:	Celebrity Cruises
Former Names:	-
Gross Tonnage:	77,713
Builder:	Meyer Werft (Germany)
Original Cost:	$320 million
Entered Service:	December 1996
Flag:	Liberia
Tel. No.:	363653411/663653410
Fax No.:	363753420
Length (ft/m):	865.8/263.9
Beam (ft/m):	105.6/32.20
Draft (ft/m):	25.2/7.70
Propulsion/Propellers:	diesel (31,500kW)/2 (CP)
Passenger Decks:	10
Total Crew:	909
Pass. Capacity (basis 2):	1,870
Pass. Capacity (all berths):	2,681
Pass. Space Ratio (basis 2):	41.5
Pass. Space Ratio (all berths):	28.9
Officers:	Greek
Total Cabins:	935
Size Range (sq ft/m):	171.0–1,514.5/15.88–140.7
Cabins (outside view):	639
Cabins (inside — no view):	296
Cabins (single occupancy):	0
Cabins (with private balcony):	220

Cabins (wheelchair accessible):	8
Cabin Current:	110 and 220 volts
Cabin TV:	Yes
Dining Rooms:	2
Elevators:	10
Casino:	Yes
Slot Machines:	Yes
Swimming Pools (outdoors):	2
Swimming Pools (inside):	1 indoor/outdoor (magrodome)
Whirlpools:	4
Fitness Center:	Yes
Sauna/Steam Room:	Yes/Yes
Massage:	Yes
Self-Service Launderette:	No
Movie Theater/Seats:	Yes/200
Library:	Yes
Classification Society:	Lloyd's Register

RATINGS	POSSIBLE SCORE	SCORE ACHIEVED
Ship	500	455
Accommodation	200	182
Food	400	321
Service	400	324
Cruise	500	415
TOTAL	**2,000**	**1,697**

Accommodation: The largest suites are the two Presidential Suites, located amidships. Each is a 1,173 sq ft (108.9 m^2) penthouse with its own butler's pantry and has an interconnecting door (when joined with the next-door suite it becomes an impressive 1,515 sq ft (140.7 m^2) apartment.

Most of the Deck 10 suites and cabins are of generous proportions, are beautifully equipped, and have balconies with full floor-to-ceiling partitions, as well as VCR units. The Sky Deck suites are also excellent, with huge balconies (the partitions are not quite of the floor-to-ceiling type), wall clock, large floor-to-ceiling mirrors, marble-topped vanity/writing desk, excellent closet and drawer space, and even dimmer-controlled ceiling lights.

All of the standard inside and outside cabins are of a good size and come nicely furnished with twin beds that can convert to a queen-sized unit. The bathrooms, in particular, are spacious and come well equipped (with generous-size showers, hairdryers, and space for personal toiletry items). Sadly, there are no cabins for singles. Baby-monitoring telephones are also in all cabins.

All cabins feature interactive television for booking shore excursions, ordering room service, playing electronic casino games, and purchasing goods from the ship's boutiques. So, you do not have to leave your quarters if you do not wish to, especially if you do not like the ports of call (available in English, French, German, Italian, and Spanish).

Most of the suites with private balconies have floor-to-ceiling windows and sliding doors to balconies (a few have outward opening doors). All accommodation designated as suites feature duvets on the beds instead of sheets/blankets. In-suite massage service is available (with the right balcony, such as those in the Sky Suites, this is an excellent service). Some suites at the stern have balconies, although they can be overlooked, and are not so private.

Dining: There is a huge two-level dining room (and two seatings) reminiscent of the dining halls aboard the ocean liners of the 1930s, with a grand staircase between both levels and perimeter alcoves that provide more intimate dining spaces. Each level of the dining room has its own separate galley, and the

257

noise level in the two sections is quite acceptable (more noise is noticeable on the larger, lower level, however). The cuisine is based on menus created by Michel Roux, and executed by the chefs and cooks on board. The food has lots of taste (in particular the sauces that accompany many of the main dishes) and has fine color balance.

Just outside the lower-level entrance, a champagne and caviar bar serves ossetra and sevruga caviar nicely presented with all the trimmings.

For informal breakfasts and lunches, there is the two-level lido cafe with several serving lines (features warm wood-accented decor), and eight bay windows provide some really prime seating spots. There are also two poolside grills; one located adjacent to the midships pools, the other wedged into the aft pool.

In addition, Tasting's is a coffee lounge and bar for specialty coffees and pastries. For passengers in the two Presidential and 48 other suites, in-cabin dining is an option. However, the food served as room-service items is decidedly below the standard of food featured in the dining room. For those that cannot live without them, freshly baked pizzas (in a box) can be delivered, in an insulated pouch, to your cabin.

Celebrity Cruises is known for its excellent cuisine and presentation, and, although it is more difficult to deliver aboard the new, larger ships, Celebrity Cruises seems to have got it just right.

Other Comments: Slightly longer than sister ship *Century* (by 14 m), the extra length provides room for a third swimming pool, which is covered by a large glass magrodome. Although there are over 4.5 acres of space on the open deck, it seems small when the ship is full.

Inside, there are two foyers (atriums); one is a four-deck-high main foyer, and the second is a three-deck-high atrium. There is a 1,000-seat show lounge with large side balconies and good sight lines from just about every seat. There is also a small, dedicated movie theater, which doubles as a conference and meeting center with all the latest audiovisual technology that includes three-language simultaneous translation and headsets for the hearing-impaired.

The AquaSpa, which has proved extremely popular aboard *Century*, contains 9,040 sq ft (839.8 m²) of space dedicated to well-being and body treatments, and includes a large fitness/exercise area, complete with all the latest high-tech muscle machines and video cycles.

The ship has a superb, somewhat whimsical collection of artwork, which casts an eclectic look at life in some of its many forms. The collection is the result of the personal work of Christina Chandris, wife of the company's chairman. The "zero announcement" policy is much appreciated by passengers.

Apart from the "front of house" aspects of this ship, it is the "back of house" facilities, the design and flow of the main galley (2,200 m²), where the ship really shines. The consideration for safety is second to none. Also has excellent tender loading platforms.

"Stratosphere," the ship's large combination observation lounge and discotheque, provides what is probably the best viewing room when the ship operates Alaska cruises.

For a big-ship cruise experience, this one has it all. *Galaxy* delivers an outstanding product that is worth much more than the cruise fare charged.

<u>Weak Points</u>: The one area of congestion is the Photo Gallery, when passenger flow at peak evening times is poor. Although improved, shore excursions are still a weak point of this operation.

258

m/v Grande Caribe
★★ +
(S)

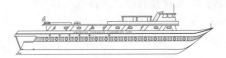

LIFESTYLE: **STANDARD**

Cruise Line:	American Canadian Caribbean Line
Former Names:	-
Gross Tonnage:	99
Builder:	Blount Industries (USA)
Original Cost:	$8 million
Entered Service:	June 1997
Flag:	USA
Tel. No.:	n/a
Fax No.:	n/a
Length (ft/m):	183.0/55.7
Beam (ft/m):	40.0/12.1
Draft (ft/m):	6.5/1.9
Propulsion/Propellers:	diesel (1,044kW)/2 (CP)
Passenger Decks:	3
Total Crew:	17
Pass. Capacity (basis 2):	100
Pass. Capacity (all berths):	100
Pass. Space Ratio (basis 2):	0.99
Pass. Space Ratio (all berths):	0.99
Officers:	American
Total Cabins:	50
Size Range (sq ft/m):	72.0–96.0/6.6–8.9
Cabins (outside view):	41
Cabins (inside — no view):	9
Cabins (single occupancy):	0
Cabins (with private balcony):	0

Cabins (wheelchair accessible):	0
Cabin Current:	110 volts
Cabin TV:	No
Dining Rooms:	1
Elevators:	0
Casino:	0
Slot Machines:	0
Swimming Pools (outdoors):	0
Swimming Pools (inside):	0
Whirlpools:	0
Fitness Center:	0
Sauna/Steam Room:	0/0
Massage:	0
Self-Service Launderette:	No
Movie Theater/Seats:	0
Library:	Yes
Classification Society:	American Bureau of Shipping

RATINGS	POSSIBLE SCORE	SCORE ACHIEVED
Ship	500	253
Accommodation	200	108
Food	400	237
Service	400	233
Cruise	500	264
TOTAL	**2,000**	**1,095**

Accommodation: The cabins are all extremely small, relatively spartan units, with very little closet space (but just enough drawers), and small bathrooms. There are 48 cabins, each with twin beds convertible to queen-sized beds (there is good storage space under the beds). There is no room service menu, and only soap is supplied. Each cabin has its own air conditioner, so passengers do not have to share air with the rest of the ship (and other passengers). Refreshingly, there are no cabin keys.

Dining: The dining room seats all passengers in a single, open seating, so you dine with whomever you wish. Dining tables convert to card tables for use between meals. Passengers are welcome to bring their own alcohol, as the company does not sell it aboard ship. The service is provided by effervescent, young American waitresses, although there is no finesse.

Other Comments: This is the largest and the most contemporary of the Blount-built vessels. During passenger emergency drill, passengers are taught how to use fire extinguishers — a very useful piece of training.

This vessel has a shallow draft, which enables it to cruise into off-the-beaten-path destinations and also features a retractable navigation bridge. *Grande Caribe*, together with sister vessel *Grande Mariner* (but not *Niagara Prince*) have stabilizers. An underwater video camera allows passengers to see what a scuba diver might see underneath the ship, while seated in (dry) comfort in the lounge, on large-screen television monitors. Underwater lights, which should attract fish and other marine life, are also fitted.

The style is unpretentious and very casual (no jackets or ties) both day and night. There are two 24-passenger launches (one of which is a glass bottom boat), and some snorkeling equipment.

There is one lounge/bar, located on a different deck to the dining room — a departure for ACCL from the company's former vessels. Water sports facilities include a glass-bottom boat, and sunfish sailboat.

This vessel will be good for anyone who does not want crowds, or entertainment of any kind, or a high standard of service. All of the gratuities given by passengers are pooled and shared by all the staff (although you should note that the suggested daily rate is very high for the product delivered).

m/v Grande Mariner
★★ +
(S)

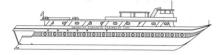

LIFESTYLE:	STANDARD
Cruise Line:	American Canadian Caribbean Line
Former Names:	-
Gross Tonnage:	99
Builder:	Blount industries (USA)
Original Cost:	$8 million
Entered Service:	June 1998
Flag:	USA
Tel. No.:	n/a
Fax No.:	n/a
Length (ft/m):	183.0/55.7
Beam (ft/m):	40.0/12.1
Draft (ft/m):	6.5/1.9
Propulsion/Propellers:	diesel (1,044kW)/2 (CP)
Passenger Decks:	3
Total Crew:	17
Pass. Capacity (basis 2):	100
Pass. Capacity (all berths):	100
Pass. Space Ratio (basis 2):	0.99
Pass. Space Ratio (all berths):	0.99
Officers:	American
Total Cabins:	50
Size Range (sq ft/m):	72.0–96.0/6.6–8.9
Cabins (outside view):	41
Cabins (inside — no view):	9
Cabins (single occupancy):	0
Cabins (with private balcony):	0
Cabins (wheelchair accessible):	0
Cabin Current:	110 volts
Cabin TV:	No
Dining Rooms:	1
Elevators:	0
Casino:	0
Slot Machines:	0
Swimming Pools (outdoors):	0
Swimming Pools (inside):	0
Whirlpools:	0
Fitness Center:	0
Sauna/Steam Room:	0/0
Massage:	0
Self-Service Launderette:	No
Movie Theater/Seats:	0
Library:	Yes
Classification Society:	American Bureau of Shipping

RATINGS	POSSIBLE SCORE	SCORE ACHIEVED
Ship	500	253
Accommodation	200	108
Food	400	237
Service	400	233
Cruise	500	264
TOTAL	**2,000**	**1,095**

For comments, see *Grande Caribe*.

m/s Grandeur of the Seas
★★★★
(L)

LIFESTYLE:	STANDARD
Cruise Line:	Royal Caribbean International
Former Names:	-
Gross Tonnage:	74,137
Builder:	Kvaerner Masa-Yards (Finland)
Original Cost:	$300 million
Entered Service:	December 1996
Flag:	Liberia
Tel. No.:	363654710
Fax No.:	363654720
Length (ft/m):	915.6/279.1
Beam (ft/m):	105.6/32.2
Draft (ft/m):	24.9/7.6
Propulsion/Propellers:	diesel-electric (50,400kW)/2 (FP)
Passenger Decks:	11
Total Crew:	760
Pass. Capacity (basis 2):	1,950
Pass. Capacity (all berths):	2,446
Pass. Space Ratio (basis 2):	38.0
Pass. Space Ratio (all berths):	30.3
Officers:	International
Total Cabins:	975
Size Range (sq ft/m):	158.2–1,033.3/14.7–96.0
Cabins (outside view):	576
Cabins (inside — no view):	399
Cabins (single occupancy):	0
Cabins (with private balcony):	212

Cabins (wheelchair accessible):	14
Cabin Current:	110 and 220 volts
Cabin TV:	Yes
Dining Rooms:	1
Elevators:	9
Casino:	Yes
Slot Machines:	Yes
Swimming Pools (outdoors):	1
Swimming Pools (inside):	1 (indoor/outdoor w/glass roof)
Whirlpools:	6
Fitness Center:	Yes
Sauna/Steam Room:	Yes/Yes
Massage:	Yes
Self-Service Launderette:	No
Movie Theater/Seats:	No
Library:	Yes
Classification Society:	Det Norske Veritas

RATINGS	POSSIBLE SCORE	SCORE ACHIEVED
Ship	500	432
Accommodation	200	169
Food	400	247
Service	400	302
Cruise	500	383
TOTAL	**2,000**	**1,533**

Accommodation: The suites are very well appointed and have very pleasing decor, with good wood and color accenting (the largest suite even has a baby grand piano). Category A and B cabins also have VCR units. All standard cabins have twin beds that convert to a queen-size bed, ample closet space for a one-week cruise, and a good amount of drawer space, although under-bed storage space is not good for large suitcases. Bathrooms have nine mirrors. The plastic buckets for champagne/wine are really shoddy.

Dining: The dining room, which seats 1,195, is a huge, two-deck-high banquet room with huge windows that span its two decks. There are two seatings. General comments regarding the food operation aboard *Legend of the Seas* and *Splendour of the Seas* apply, but some innovative options are also included (even fish knives are available in this ship), although presentation is inconsistent. There is an intimate Champagne Bar, and the popular, informal Windjammer Cafe (with 790 seats) is better, with more food islands.

Other Comments: Always evolving, the ships in the Royal Caribbean International fleet, this ship is no exception, and presents a nice long profile, with a funnel placed well aft (almost a throwback to some ship designs used in the 1950s). She has a well-rounded stern (as have the three *Sovereign of the Seas*-class ships) and a Viking Crown Lounge in the center, just forward of the funnel. This lounge, together with the forward mast and aft funnel, provides three distinct focal points in her exterior profile. The Viking Crown Lounge sits between funnel and mast and overlooks the forward section of the swimming pool deck, as aboard *Legend of the Seas/Splendour of the Seas*, with access provided by a multi-deck atrium. No cushioned pads are provided for the plastic-webbed deck lounge chairs.

There is a wraparound promenade deck outdoors, with a seven-deck-high atrium inside. A delightful champagne terrace bar sits forward of the lower level of the two-deck-high dining room.

There are two showrooms. One is the principal show lounge, for the big production shows, and has excellent sight lines from 98 percent of the 875 seats; the other is the secondary show lounge, for smaller shows and adult cabaret, with 575 seats. Good children's and teens' facilities, much expanded from previous ships in the fleet.

This is another new ship design for Royal Caribbean International (her sister ship is *Enchantment of the Seas*), with what, inside, has proven to be a good passenger flow. The vessel has a good, varied collection of artworks (including several sculptures), principally by British artists, with classical music, ballet, and theater themes. The casino has a fascinating, somewhat theatrical, glass-covered but under-floor exhibit.

This ship will be good for first-time cruise passengers who want fine, very comfortable surroundings, and all the very latest in facilities, entertainment lounges, and high-tech sophistication in one neat, well-packaged, fine-tuned cruise vacation, with plenty of music and entertainment.

CABIN AMENITIES

Cabins provide some, or all, of the following:

→ Private bathroom (generally small and compact) fitted with shower, wash basin, and toilet. Higher grade cabins and suites may have full-size bathtubs. Some even have a whirlpool bath and/or bidet, a hairdryer, and more space.

→ Electrical outlets for personal appliances, usually 110 and/or 220 volts.

→ Multichannel radio, television (regular satellite channels or closed circuit), and VCR.

→ Two beds or a lower and upper berth (possibly, another one or two upper berths) or a double-, queen-, or king-size bed. In some ships, twin beds can be pushed together to form a double.

→ Telephone, for inter-cabin or ship-to-shore communication.

→ Depending on cabin size, a chair, or chair and table, or sofa and table.

→ Vanity/desk unit with chair or stool.

→ Personal safe.

→ Closet space, some drawer space, plus storage room under beds for suitcases.

→ Bedside night stand/table unit.

→ Towels, soap, shampoo, and conditioner.

m/s Grand Princess
★★★★ +
(L)

LIFESTYLE:	PREMIUM
Cruise Line:	Princess Cruises
Former Names:	-
Gross Tonnage:	108,806
Builder:	Fincantieri (Italy)
Original Cost:	$450 million
Entered Service:	May 1998
Flag:	Liberia
Tel. No.:	363677211
Fax No.:	363677220/363677320
Length (ft/m):	951.4/290.0
Beam (ft/m):	118.1/36.0
Draft (ft/m):	26.2/8.0
Propulsion/Propellers:	diesel-electric (42,000kW)/2 (FP)
Passenger Decks:	13
Total Crew:	1,100
Pass. Capacity (basis 2):	2,600
Pass. Capacity (all berths):	3,100
Pass. Space Ratio (basis 2):	41.8
Pass. Space Ratio (all berths):	35.0
Officers:	British/Italian
Total Cabins:	1,300
Size Range (sq ft/m):	161.4–764.2/15.0–71.0
Cabins (outside view):	928
Cabins (inside — no view):	372
Cabins (single occupancy):	0
Cabins (with private balcony):	710

Cabins (wheelchair accessible):	28
	(18 outside/10 inside)
Cabin Current:	110 and 220 volts
Cabin TV:	Yes
Dining Rooms:	3 main, 2 others
Elevators:	14
Casino:	Yes
Slot Machines:	Yes
Swimming Pools (outdoors):	4
Swimming Pools (inside):	0
Whirlpools:	9
Fitness Center:	Yes
Sauna/Steam Room:	Yes/Yes
Massage:	Yes
Self-Service Launderette:	Yes
Movie Theater/Seats:	No
Library:	Yes
Classification Society:	Registro Navale Italiano

RATINGS	POSSIBLE SCORE	SCORE ACHIEVED
Ship	500	447
Accommodation	200	176
Food	400	283
Service	400	304
Cruise	500	427
TOTAL	**2,000**	**1,637**

Accommodation: There are six types of cabins and configurations: (a) grand suite, (b) suite, (c) mini-suite, (d) outside double with balcony, (e) outside double, and (f) inside (no-view) double. There are, however, 35 different brochure price categories; the choice is bewildering for both travel agents and passengers. Pricing depends on two things, size and location.

(a) The plushest suite is the Grand Suite, which has a hot tub accessible from both the private balcony and the bedroom, two bedrooms, a lounge, two bathrooms, and a huge walk-in closet.

(b/c) Suites (with private balcony) have a separate living room (with sofa bed) and bedroom (with a television in each). The bathroom is quite large and features both a bathtub and shower stall. The mini-suites also have a private balcony and feature a separate living and sleeping area (with a television in each). The bathroom is also quite spacious and features both a bathtub and shower stall. The differences between the suites and mini-suites are basically in the size and appointments, the suite being more of a square shape while mini-suites are more rectangular and have few drawers. Both suites and mini-suites feature butler service (known in Princess Cruises' language as Grand Class Gold), really plush bathrobes, and fully tiled bathrooms with ample open shelf storage space. Passengers in suites and mini-suites receive "Grand Class Gold" service and have priority attention, including speedy embarkation and disembarkation privileges.

(d/e/f) Both inside and outside-view (the outsides come either with or without private balcony) cabins are of a functional, practical, design, although almost no drawers are provided. They are very attractive, with warm, pleasing decor and fine soft furnishing fabrics; 80 percent of the outside cabins have a private balcony. The tiled bathrooms have a good amount of open shelf storage space for personal toiletries.

Additionally, two family suites consist of two suites with an interconnecting door, plus a large balcony and can sleep up to ten (if at least four are children, or up to eight people if all are adults).

All accommodation occupants receive turndown service and chocolates on pillows, as well as bathrobes and toiletry amenity kits (larger, naturally, for suite/mini-suite occupants). You should note that the majority of the outside cabins on Emerald Deck have views obstructed by the lifeboats. Sadly, there are no cabins for singles.

In-cabin television programming includes BBC World Service, CNNfn, ESPN, and TNT.

Dining: As befits the size of the ship, there is a wide variety of informal dining options, more than aboard any other Princess Cruises ship to date. For formal meals there are three principal dining rooms, Botticelli (504 seats), Da Vinci (486 seats), and Michelangelo (486 seats), assigned according to the location of your cabin. There are two seatings. All three are nonsmoking and split into multi-tier sections in a non-symmetrical design similar to those seen in *Dawn Princess* and *Sun Princess*, breaking what are quite large spaces into many smaller sections, for better ambience. Each dining room has its own galley.

Several other dining areas are provided: a Trattoria (for pizzas and other Italian fare; reservation only, cover charge $3.50 per person), as well as the Painted Desert (southwestern American food; by reservation only, cover charge $3.50 per person). A coffee bar/patisserie (extra charge), wine/caviar bar (extra charge), a poolside hamburger grill and pizza bar are additional dining spots for casual bites.

Specially designed dinnerware and high-quality linens and silverware are featured by Dudson of England (dinnerware), Frette Egyptian cotton table linens, and silverware by Hepp of Germany.

Other Comments: The design for this large vessel, presently the world's largest (though not longest) cruise ship, is indicative of what is to come in the future for the big players in this industry. She presents a surprisingly bold, forthright profile, with a racy "spoiler" effect at her galleon-like transom stern (this acts as a stern observation lounge by day, and a stunning disco by night). She really is quite a ship although she is too wide to transit the Panama Canal, with many balcony cabins overhanging the hull.

There is a good sheltered teakwood promenade deck, which almost wraps around (three times round is equal to one mile) and a walkway that goes right to the (enclosed, protected) bow of the ship. The outdoor pools have various beach-like surroundings. One lap pool has a pumped "current" to swim against.

Unlike the outside decks, there is plenty of space inside the ship (but there are also plenty of passengers), and a wide array of public rooms to choose from, with many "intimate" (this is a relative word) spaces and places to play. The passenger flow has been well thought out and works with little congestion. The decor is very attractive, with lots of beiges and earth tones (well suited to both American and European tastes). In fact, she is the culmination of the best of all that Princess Cruises has to offer from its many years of operating a fine-quality product.

Four areas center on swimming pools, one of which is two decks high and is covered by a magrodome, itself an extension of the funnel housing. A large health spa complex surrounds one of the swimming pools (you can have a massage or other spa treatment in an ocean-view treatment room). High atop the stern of the ship is a ship-wide glass-walled disco pod (I have nicknamed it the ETR — energy transfer room). It looks like an aerodynamic "spoiler" and is positioned some 150.1 ft (45.75 m) above the waterline, with spectacular views from the extreme port and starboard side windows (you can look along the ship's side and onto lots of "private" balconies).

An extensive collection of artwork has been chosen, and this complements the interior design and colors well. If you see something you like, you will be able to purchase it on board — it's almost all for sale.

This ship features the first oceangoing Wedding Chapel. The ship's captain can legally marry (American) couples, due to the ship's Liberian registry and a special dispensation (which should be verified in the planning stage, according to where you reside). So, what better way to be married *and* have your honeymoon in one location that moves with you. Princess Cruises offers three wedding packages — Pearl, Emerald, and Diamond; the fee includes registration and official marriage certificate. However, to get married *and* take your close family members and entourage with you on your honeymoon is going to cost a lot of money (do you really want your family with you on your honeymoon!). The "Hearts & Minds" chapel is also useful for "renewal of vows" ceremonies.

Another neat feature is the motion-based "virtual reality" room with its enclosed motion-based rides and a "blue screen" studio, where passengers can star in their own videos. Features an excellent library/CD-ROM computer room, and a separate card room. For children, there is a two-deck-high playroom, teen's room, and a host of specially trained counselors.

For entertainment, Princess Cruises prides itself on its glamorous all-American production shows, and the shows aboard this ship ("Gotta Sing, Gotta Dance," "Glamour," and "Swing Time") will not disappoint. Neither will the comfortable show lounges (the largest of which features $3 million in sound and light equipment, as well as a nine-piece orchestra, and a scenery loading bay that connects directly from stage to a hull door for direct transfer to the dockside). Two other entertainment lounges help spread things around. Casino lovers should enjoy what is presently the largest casino at sea, with more than 260 slot machines (all with dolphin-shaped handles); there are blackjack, craps, and roulette tables, plus newer games such as Let It Ride Bonus, Spanish 21, and Caribbean Draw Progressive. But the highlight could well be Neptune's Lair, a multimedia gaming extravaganza.

Ship lovers should enjoy the wood-paneled Wheelhouse Bar, finely decorated with memorabilia and ship models tracing part of parent company P&O's history (British India Line's *Kenya* is a focal point model).

Princess Cays, Princess Cruises' own "private island" in the Caribbean, is "yours" (along with a couple of thousand other passengers) for a day (but you need to take a shore tender to get to and from it, and this can take some time). A high-tech hospital is provided, with live SeaMed tele-medicine link-ups with specialists at the Cedars-Sinai Medical Center in Los Angeles available for emergency help; it's the first such seagoing system in the world.

The ship operates seven-night Caribbean cruises during the winter and 12-day Mediterranean cruises during the summer and provides you with a stunning, grand playground in which to roam when you are not ashore. Princess Cruises delivers a fine, well-packaged vacation product, with a good sense of style, at an attractive, highly competitive price, and this ship will appeal to those that really enjoy a big city to play in, with all the trimmings and lots of fellow passengers. The ship is full of revenue centers, however, which are designed to help you part with even more money than what is paid for in the price of your cruise ticket.

Whether this really can be considered a relaxing vacation is a moot point, but with *so many choices* and "small" rooms to enjoy, the ship has been extremely well designed, and the odds are that you'll have a fine cruise vacation. If you choose a Mediterranean cruise, it is wise to add a post-cruise stay option, as disembarkation is rudely early.

Weak Points: If you are not used to large ships, it will take you some time to find your way around (take good walking shoes), despite the company's claim that this vessel offers passengers a "small ship feel, big ship choice." The cabin bath towels are small, and drawer space is very limited, particularly for the 12-day Mediterranean cruises. The automated telephone system is really frustrating, and luggage delivery needs to be more efficient. Lines form for many things, but particularly for the purser's office and for open seating breakfast and lunch in the three main dining rooms. Long lines for shore excursions and shore tenders are also a fact of life aboard large ships such as this, as is waiting for elevators at peak times.

m/s Hanseatic
★★★★★
(S)

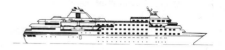

LIFESTYLE: **LUXURY**

Cruise Line:	Hapag-Lloyd Seetouristik
Former Names:	-
Gross Tonnage:	8,378
Builder:	Rauma Yards (Finland)
Original Cost:	$68 million
Entered Service:	March 1993
Flag:	Bahamas
Tel. No.:	1103730
Fax No.:	1103726
Length (ft/m):	402.9/122.80
Beam (ft/m):	59.1/18.00
Draft (ft/m):	15.5/4.71
Propulsion/Propellers:	diesel (5,880kW)/2 (CP)
Passenger Decks:	7
Total Crew:	122
Pass. Capacity (basis 2):	184
Pass. Capacity (all berths):	194
Pass. Space Ratio (basis 2):	45.5
Pass. Space Ratio (all berths):	43.1
Officers:	German
Total Cabins:	92
Size Range (sq ft/m):	231.4–470.3/21.5–43.7
Cabins (outside view):	92
Cabins (inside — no view):	0
Cabins (single occupancy):	0
Cabins (with private balcony):	0

Cabins (wheelchair accessible):	2
Cabin Current:	220 volts
Cabin TV:	Yes
Dining Rooms:	1
Elevators:	2
Swimming Pools (outdoors):	1
Whirlpools:	1
Exercise Room:	Yes
Sauna/Steam Room:	Yes/No
Massage:	Yes
Self-Service Launderette:	No
Lecture/Film Room:	Yes (seats 160)
Library:	Yes
Zodiacs:	14
Helicopter Pad:	Yes
Classification Society:	Det Norske Veritas

RATINGS	POSSIBLE SCORE	SCORE ACHIEVED
Ship	500	434
Accommodation	200	172
Food	400	345
Service	400	343
Cruise	500	446
TOTAL	**2,000**	**1,740**

Accommodation: The all-outside cabins, located in the forward section of the ship, are large and very well equipped and include a separate lounge area next to a large picture window (which has a pull-down blackout blind as well as curtains) and refrigerator. All furniture is in warm woods such as beech, and everything has rounded edges. Wood trim accents the ceiling perimeter and acts as a divider between bed and lounge areas. Each cabin has a mini-bar, a television, a VCR unit, two locking drawers, and plenty of closet and drawer space, as well as two separate cupboards and hooks for all-weather outerwear.

All cabin bathrooms have a large bathtub, two toiletries cabinets, wall-mounted hairdryer, and bathrobe. There are only two types of cabins; 34 have double beds, others have twin beds. Towels, bed linens, and pillowcases are of 100 percent cotton, and individual cotton-filled duvet covers are provided.

The suites and cabins on Bridge Deck have impeccable butler service and full in-cabin dining privileges, as well as personalized stationery. Soft drinks are supplied in the cabin refrigerator and replenished daily at no charge (all liquor is at extra cost, however). A very relaxed ambience prevails on board.

Dining: The dining room is elegant, warm, and welcoming, and features large picture windows on two sides as well as aft, and table settings are graced with fine Rosenthal china and silverware. There is one seating. The cuisine and service are absolutely first rate, but are more informal than, for example, aboard the larger *Europa* (which is at or close to the same price level). Top quality ingredients are always used, and most items are purchased fresh when available.

The meals are very creative and nicely presented, and each is appealing to the eye as well as to the palate. There is always an excellent selection of breads, cheeses, desserts, and pastry items. Note that when operating in the Arctic or Antarctic, table set-ups are often minimal, due to the possible movement of the ship (stabilizers cannot be used in much of the Antarctic region), so cutlery is provided and changed for each course.

In March 1996, the ship added an alternative dining room. The Columbus Lounge, which is an informal, open seating, self-serve (or waiter service) buffet-style eatery by day, changes into an Oriental dining room at night. Reservations are required (you make them in the morning of the day you want to dine there), but there is no extra charge, and there is no tipping at any time. Also, on each cruise a full Viennese tea-time is featured, as well as a regular daily tea-time. Table wines are included for dinner.

Other Comments: *Hanseatic* was designed and constructed specifically to provide worldwide exploration-style cruises in luxurious contemporary surroundings. As such, she looks like the practical vessel she was designed to be. The ship is extremely environmentally-friendly and features the latest, "zero-discharge," non-polluting waste disposal system, including pollution-filtered incinerator, full biological sewage treatment plant, and large storage capacity. This is one of the few ships that will allow you to sign up for an engine room tour.

She is an outstanding ship for the best in destination-intensive exploration voyages and is under long-term charter to specialist operator Hanseatic Tours (part of the Hapag-Lloyd group). Features a fully enclosed bridge (with an open bridge policy, so that passengers can visit the bridge at almost any time) and an ice-hardened hull with the highest passenger vessel classification of 1A1 Super. The ship also features the very latest in high-tech navigation equipment.

A fleet of 14 Zodiac inflatable craft (all named after famous explorers) is used for in-depth shore landings. These craft provide the ship with tremendous flexibility in itineraries and provide excellent possibilities for up-close wildlife viewing in natural habitats, with small numbers of passengers. Rubber boots, parkas, and a boot-washing and storage room are provided for passengers, particularly useful for Arctic and Antarctic cruises.

Inside, the ship is equipped with fine-quality luxury fittings and soft furnishings. There is a choice of several public rooms, all of them well furnished and decorated, and all of them have high ceilings, which helps to provide an impression of space; the result is that the ship feels much larger than her actual size. The library/observation lounge provides a good selection of hardback books and videos in both the English and German languages.

Hanseatic provides destination-intensive, nature, and life-enrichment cruises and expeditions in elegant, but unstuffy surroundings, to some of the world's most fascinating destinations, at a suitably handsome price. The passenger maximum is generally kept to about 150, which means plenty of comfort and lots of space for everyone.

The ship really is at her best when operating in Arctic and Antarctic regions (inform passengers are advised not to consider these areas). Safety is paramount, particularly when operating in the Antarctic and in this the ship excels with professionalism, pride, and skilled seamanship. The ship always operates in two languages, English and German (many staff speak several languages) and caters well to both sets of passengers. All port taxes, insurance, gratuities, Zodiac trips, and most shore excursions (except when the ship operates in Europe) are included.

Hapag-Lloyd Seetouristik specializes in providing outstanding, well-planned itineraries. Where this ship really scores, however, is in her Antarctic sailings, where the experience of her captain and cruise director and the crew really shine. The lectures, briefings, and amount of information provided about the itinerary and ports of call are outstanding. Outstanding lecturers and naturalists accompany each cruise.

Weak Points: There are few negative things about this ship. She is principally marketed to German-speaking and English-speaking passengers, so other nationalities may find it hard to integrate. There are no marine quality telescopes mounted outdoors (there should be). There is, at present, no privacy curtain between cabin door and the sleeping area (there should be).

m/v Hebridean Princess
★★★★ +
(S)

LIFESTYLE:	LUXURY
Cruise Line:	Hebridean Island Cruises
Former Names:	*Columba*
Gross Tonnage:	2,112
Builder:	Hall Russell (Scotland)
Original Cost:	n/a
Entered Service:	1964/April 1989
Flag:	Great Britain
Tel. No.:	1440772
Fax No.:	1440772
Length (ft/m):	235.0/71.6
Beam (ft/m):	46.0/14.0
Draft (ft/m):	10.0/3.0
Propulsion/Propellers:	diesel (1,790kW)/2 (FP)
Passenger Decks:	5
Total Crew:	37
Pass. Capacity (basis 2):	49
Pass. Capacity (all berths):	49
Pass. Space Ratio (basis 2):	43.1
Pass. Space Ratio (all berths):	43.1
Officers:	British
Total Cabins:	30
Size Range (sq ft/m):	144–340/13.4–31.6
Cabins (outside view):	23
Cabins (inside — no view):	6
Cabins (single occupancy):	11
Cabins (with private balcony):	4

Cabins (wheelchair accessible):	0
Cabin Current:	240 volts
Cabin TV:	Yes
Dining Rooms:	1
Elevators:	0
Casino:	No
Slot Machines:	No
Swimming Pools (outdoors):	0
Swimming Pools (inside):	0
Whirlpools:	0
Fitness Center:	Yes
Sauna/Steam Room:	No/No
Massage:	No
Self-Service Launderette:	No
Movie Theater/Seats:	No
Library:	Yes
Classification Society:	Lloyd's Register

RATINGS	POSSIBLE SCORE	SCORE ACHIEVED
Ship	500	425
Accommodation	200	177
Food	400	350
Service	400	341
Cruise	500	406
TOTAL	**2,000**	**1,699**

Accommodation: All cabins have different color schemes and names (there are no numbers, and, refreshingly, no door locks, so don't ask for the door key). All are individually designed (no two cabins are identical) and created, with sweeping chintz curtains and drapes over the beds. They really are quite delightful and come in a range of configurations (some with single, some with double, and some with twin beds), including four that have a private balcony (lovely), but all feature a refrigerator. All but two cabins have a private bathroom with bath or shower; all have real Victorian bathroom fittings (some are even gold-plated), and brass cabin portholes that actually open. Three of the newest cabins added are outfitted in Scottish Baronial style. Some cabins also have a VCR unit.

Dining: Features a totally nonsmoking dining room with ocean-view windows, and tables that are laid with lace overlays. There is one seating. Some chairs have armrests while some do not. The outstanding cuisine is about the same quality and presentation as the Sea Goddess ships. Fresh produce is purchased locally, a welcome change from the mass catering of most ships. Although there are no flambé items (the galley has electric, not gas, cookers), what is created is beautifully presented and of the very highest standard. And the desserts are simply out of this world!

Breakfast menus alternate every two days and feature special dishes in addition to the traditional Scottish fare (try the "porridge and a wee dram" — it sets you up for the whole day). Although there is waiter service for most things, there is also a delightful buffet table display for breakfast and luncheon. This little ship features a very decent wine list, with extremely moderate prices. There are also many wonderful whiskeys (more than 45 of them) and vintage cognacs available (try the 50-year-old Remy Martin Louis XIII). Highly personal and attentive service from British/Scottish staff.

Other Comments: Small is beautiful! This utterly charming little ship has stately home service and a warm, totally cosseted, traditional country house ambience. The Tiree Lounge has a real brick-walled fireplace, and a very cozy bar with a wide variety of whiskeys (the selection of single malts is excellent) and cognacs for connoisseurs. Use of the ship's small boats, speedboat, bicycles, and fishing gear are included in the price, as are entrance fees to gardens, castles, and other attractions. The destination-intensive cruises have very creative itineraries. Specialist guides accompany all cruises.

Inspector Hercules Poirot would be very much at home here. Who needs mega-ships when you can take a retro-cruise aboard this absolute gem of a ship. Sheer pleasure is a week (or more) aboard *Hebridean Princess* — a superb Scottish Island Fling. Direct bookings are accepted. Presently the only cruise vessel in the world with an all-UK crew, she is one of the world's most well-kept travel secrets. A polished gem, she is especially popular with single passengers, and more than 50 percent of her passengers are repeaters. If you cruise from Oban, you will be met at Glasgow station (or airport) and taken to/from the ship by private coach (motor — not horse-drawn).

Weak Points: Although this vessel is strong, she does have structural limitations and noisy engines that cause some vibration (however, the engines do not run at night, and the ship anchors before bedtime, providing soul-renewing peace and tranquility). Drinks are not, but should, at this price, be included. It is often cold (and very wet) in the Scottish islands, so take plenty of warm clothing for layering.

m/s Holiday
★★★ +
(L)

LIFESTYLE:	STANDARD
Cruise Line:	Carnival Cruise Lines
Former Names:	-
Gross Tonnage:	46,052
Builder:	Aalborg Vaerft (Denmark)
Original Cost:	$170 million
Entered Service:	July 1985
Flag:	Bahamas
Tel. No.:	1103216
Fax No.:	n/a
Length (ft/m):	726.9/221.57
Beam (ft/m):	92.4/28.17
Draft (ft/m):	25.5/7.77
Propulsion/Propellers:	diesel (22,360kW)/2 (CP)
Passenger Decks:	9
Total Crew:	660
Pass. Capacity (basis 2):	1,452
Pass. Capacity (all berths):	1,800
Pass. Space Ratio (basis 2):	31.7
Pass. Space Ratio (all berths):	25.5
Officers:	Italian
Total Cabins:	726
Size Range (sq ft/m):	182.9–189.4/17.0–17.6
Cabins (outside view):	447
Cabins (inside — no view):	279
Cabins (single occupancy):	0
Cabins (with private balcony):	10

Cabins (wheelchair accessible):	15
Cabin Current:	110 volts
Cabin TV:	Yes
Dining Rooms:	2
Elevators:	8
Casino:	Yes
Slot Machines:	Yes
Swimming Pools (outdoors):	3
Swimming Pools (inside):	0
Whirlpools:	2
Fitness Center:	Yes
Sauna/Steam Room:	Yes/No
Massage:	Yes
Self-Service Launderette:	Yes
Movie Theater/Seats:	No
Library:	Yes
Classification Society:	Lloyd's Register

RATINGS	POSSIBLE SCORE	SCORE ACHIEVED
Ship	500	355
Accommodation	200	143
Food	400	221
Service	400	275
Cruise	500	324
TOTAL	**2,000**	**1,318**

Accommodation: Carnival Cruise Lines has always tried to provide an adequate amount of space in passenger cabins, and the cabins aboard *Holiday* are no exception. They are quite functional and provide all the basics; bathrooms are practical units, with decent-sized shower stalls. The only toiletry amenities provided, however, are soap and ice water, so you should take your own shampoo (ladies may also need to take a shower cap).

Dining: There are two dining rooms (and two seatings in each); both are large and have low ceilings, making the raised center sections seem crowded (intimate?), and noisy because they are always full. The food is characterized by quantity, not quality, with little taste. The service is quite average, robotic, and hurried.

The buffets are very basic, as is the selection of breads, rolls, fruit, and cheeses. There are no wine waiters, although there is a surprisingly decent wine list.

Other Comments: This is a bold, high-sided, all-white contemporary ship with short, rakish bow and stubby stern typical of so many recently built ships. Has a distinctive, large, swept-back wing-tipped funnel in Carnival Cruise Lines colors of red, white, and blue.

Inside, the passenger flow is quite good. There are numerous public rooms on two entertainment decks to choose from and play in, and these flow from a double-width indoor promenade. A real red and cream bus is located right in the middle of one of the two promenades, and this is used as a snack cafe.

There is a stunning, multitiered showroom, although the sight lines are restricted from some seats that are located behind the several pillars.

The bright (very bright) interior decor has a distinct Broadway theme. The Carnegie Library (which has very few books) is the only public room that is not bright. The casino is good, and there is around-the-clock action. There is plenty of dazzle and sizzle entertainment, while "Camp Carnival" takes care of the junior cruisers (facilities include virtual-reality machines).

This ship, now over 10 years old, is ideal for a first cruise experience in glitzy, very lively surroundings, and for the active set who enjoy constant stimulation, loud music, and a fun-filled atmosphere, at an attractive price. The line does not provide finesse, nor does it claim to. There is no doubt that Carnival does a great job of providing a fun venue, but many passengers say that once is enough, and after you will want to move to a more upscale experience.

Weak Points: There is almost constant hustling for drinks, but at least it is done with a knowing smile. A cruise aboard this ship is a noisy affair, and not relaxing at all (good if you want big-city nightlife).

THE GALLEY

The galley ("kitchen" for landlubbers) is the heart of all food preparation on board. At any time of the day or night, there is plenty of activity, whether it is baking fresh bread at 2:00am, making meals and snacks for passengers and crew around the clock, or decorating a special birthday cake. The staff, from executive chef to pot-washer, all work together as a team, each designated a specific role, with little room for error.

The galley and preparation areas consist of the following sections (the names in parentheses are the French names given to the person who is the specialist in the area of expertise):

Fish Preparation Area (Poisonnier): This area contains freezers and a fully equipped preparation room, where fish is cleaned and cut to size before it is sent to the galley.

Meat Preparation Area (Butcher/Rotisseur): This area contains separate freezers for meat and poultry. These temperatures are kept at approximately 10°F. There are also defrosting areas (35°F to 40°F). Meat and poultry are sliced and portioned before being sent to the galley.

Vegetable Preparation Area (Entremetier): Vegetables are cleaned and prepared in this area.

Sauce Preparation Area (Saucier): This is where the sauces are prepared.

Soup Preparation Area (Potagier): Soups are made in huge tureens.

Cold Kitchen (Garde Manger): This is the area where all cold dishes and salads are prepared, from the simplest sandwich (for room service, for example) to the works of art that grace the buffets. The area is well equipped with mixing machines, slicing machines and refrigeration cabinets where prepared dishes are stored until required.

Bakery and Pastry Shop (Baker): This area provides the raw ingredients for preparing food, and contain dough mixers, refrigerators, proving ovens, ovens, and containers in all manner of shapes and sizes. Dessert items, pastries, sweets, and other confectionery are prepared and made here.

Pantry: This is where cheese and fruits are prepared, and where sandwiches are made.

Dishwashing Area: This area contains huge conveyor-belt dishwashing machines. Wash and rinse temperatures are carefully controlled to comply with public health regulations. This is where all cooking utensils are scrubbed and cleaned, and where the silverware is scrupulously polished.

m/v Horizon
★★★★ +
(L)

LIFESTYLE:	PREMIUM
Cruise Line:	Celebrity Cruises
Former Names:	-
Gross Tonnage:	46,811
Builder:	Meyer Werft (Germany)
Original Cost:	$185 million
Entered Service:	May 1990
Flag:	Liberia
Tel. No.:	1243527/1243554/1243555
Fax No.:	1243532
Length (ft/m):	681.1/207.60
Beam (ft/m):	95.1/29.0
Draft (ft/m):	23.6/7.2
Propulsion/Propellers:	diesel (19,960kW)/2 (CP)
Passenger Decks:	9
Total Crew:	642
Pass. Capacity (basis 2):	1,354
Pass. Capacity (all berths):	1,660
Pass. Space Ratio (basis 2):	34.5
Pass. Space Ratio (all berths):	28.1
Officers:	Greek
Total Cabins:	677
Size Range (sq ft/m):	172–340/15.48–30.6
Cabins (outside view):	533
Cabins (inside — no view):	144
Cabins (single occupancy):	0
Cabins (with private balcony):	0

Cabins (wheelchair accessible):	4
Cabin Current:	110 volts
Cabin TV:	Yes
Dining Rooms:	1
Elevators:	7
Casino:	Yes
Slot Machines:	Yes
Swimming Pools (outdoors):	2
Swimming Pools (inside):	0
Whirlpools:	0
Fitness Center:	Yes
Sauna/Steam Room:	Yes/No
Massage:	Yes
Self-Service Launderette:	No
Movie Theater/Seats:	No
Library:	Yes
Classification Society:	Lloyd's Register

RATINGS	POSSIBLE SCORE	SCORE ACHIEVED
Ship	500	416
Accommodation	200	161
Food	400	317
Service	400	322
Cruise	500	402
TOTAL	**2,000**	**1,618**

Accommodation: All of the standard inside and outside cabins have good quality fittings with lots of wood accenting, are tastefully decorated, and are of an above-average size, with an excellent amount of closet and drawer space, and reasonable insulation between cabins. The bathrooms have a very generous shower area, and a small range of toiletries is provided (the bathroom towels are a little small, however), as is storage space for personal toiletry items.

The largest cabins are the suites on Deck 10, which feature butler service and have a separate bedroom and lounge and larger bathroom complete with whirlpool bathtub. All accommodation designated as suites feature European duvets on the beds instead of sheets/blankets. However, no cabins have private balconies (they were not yet in vogue when this ship was constructed).

Dining: Celebrity Cruises has achieved an enviable reputation for providing outstanding quality food, fine presentation, and service. The dining room, which also has two "wings" (good for small groups), is set on a single level with raised central section, is large, yet it feels almost intimate. It is quite elegant, and there are several tables for two. There are two seatings. The chairs do not have armrests, however, due to space limitations. There are separate menus for vegetarians and children. The wine list is quite extensive, and the prices are quite reasonable.

An informal Coral Seas cafe features decent buffets for breakfast (including an omelet station) and lunch (including a pasta station and vegetarian salad bar); waiters take your trays of food and escort you to tables. At night, the informal café changes into an alternative dining venue for those who want good food, but in a more casual setting than the main restaurant, with items such as grilled salmon, steaks, and rotisserie chicken, as well as specialties that change frequently (ideal for families with children).

An outdoor grill serves fast-food items such as hamburgers and hot dogs. Caviar, at extra cost, is available in the America's Cup Club. For those that cannot live without them, freshly baked pizzas (in a box) can be delivered, in an insulated pouch, to your cabin.

Other Comments: This is quite a handsome, contemporary ship (the first in a series of newbuilds for Celebrity Cruises), with any sharp angles softened by clever exterior styling (blue striping along the ship's hull break up the monotonous all-white exterior of so many of today's ships). There is a good amount of open deck space and cushioned pads for poolside deck lounge chairs.

Inside, the public rooms are quite spacious, feature high ceilings, and provide very good passenger flow throughout. Elegant furnishings and appointments are the norm, with fine-quality fabrics used throughout. Soothing pastel colors are relaxing, but not boring. The wood-paneled casino has a stately look (outside is a satellite-linked BankAtlantic ATM machine, with a $5 access charge).

The two-level show lounge has excellent sight lines from most seats, including the balcony level. There is nothing brash or glitzy about this ship anywhere, although the decor is a little plain in places. The two-deck-high lobby is has a peachy Miami Beach art-deco hotel look. A self-service launderette would have proven useful for longer cruises. Much appreciated by many passengers is the "zero announcement" policy.

An extensive refurbishment in October 1998 saw the addition, on December 8, of a grand "Michael's Club" cigar smoking lounge in what was formerly the underused disco (it includes a bar, fireplace, extremely comfortable chairs, and leather sofas). A new library was added, complete with audio CD listening seats, a card room and a small business area with two computers/printers for passenger use. Also added, on Deck 7, was a small, delightful art deco-style martini bar (with 26 martinis to choose from). A room dedicated to the display of artwork (for art auctions) was added. The health spa has also been expanded. This now includes a seraglio (rasul) treatment room, a relocated beauty salon, enlarged fitness/exercise areas, and five massage and other treatment rooms. A new Cova Café has replaced what was formerly the Plaza Bar. (Cova is the name of the Milan-based coffeehouse that also makes exclusive chocolates and liqueurs. Celebrity Cruises has an exclusive agreement with Pasticceria Confetteria Cova.) This ship delivers a well-defined North American cruise experience at a very modest price. Note that the rating score was given in 1998 before the new additions were put in place.

<u>Weak Points</u>: The room-service food items are far below the standard of food featured in the dining room. Unlike the company's larger *Century, Galaxy,* and *Mercury,* there is no AquaSpa thalassotherapy pool. Participation activities are verging on the mindless and should be upgraded.

m/s Hyundai Bongnae
★★★
(M)

LIFESTYLE:	STANDARD
Cruise Line:	Hyundai Merchant Marine
Former Names:	*SuperStar Sagittarius, Sun Viking*
Gross Tonnage:	18,556
Builder:	Wartsila (Finland)
Original Cost:	$17.5 million
Entered Service:	December 1972/January 1998
Flag:	Norway
Tel. No.:	1312151
Fax No.:	1312151
Length (ft/m):	563.2/171.69
Beam (ft/m):	78.8/24.03
Draft (ft/m):	20.6/6.30
Propulsion/Propellers:	diesel (13,400kW)/2 (CP)
Decks:	8
Total Crew:	341
Pass. Capacity (basis 2):	714
Pass. Capacity (all berths):	818
Pass. Space Ratio (basis 2):	25.9
Pass. Space Ratio (all berths):	22.6
Officers:	International
Total Cabins:	357
Size Range (sq ft/m):	118.4–236.8/11.0–22.0
Cabins (outside view):	240
Cabins (inside — no view):	117
Cabins (single occupancy):	0
Cabins (with private balcony):	0

Cabins (wheelchair accessible):	0
Cabin Current:	110 volts
Cabin TV:	No
Dining Rooms:	1
Elevators:	4
Casino:	Yes
Slot Machines:	Yes
Swimming Pools (outdoors):	1
Swimming Pools (inside):	0
Whirlpools:	0
Fitness Center:	Yes
Sauna/Steam Room:	Yes/No
Massage:	Yes
Self-Service Launderette:	No
Movie Theater/Seats:	No
Library:	Yes
Classification Society:	Det Norske Veritas

RATINGS	POSSIBLE SCORE	SCORE ACHIEVED
Ship	500	279
Accommodation	200	112
Food	400	270
Service	400	260
Cruise	500	324
TOTAL	**2,000**	**1,245**

Accommodation: Almost all the cabins aboard this ship are extremely small (in fact they are among the smallest in the cruise industry), and can best be described as only moderately comfortable. They have very little closet, drawer, and storage space, so do take only the absolutely minimal in casual clothing (no ties or formal wear are needed anyway). While they are small, they have pleasant colors for the soft furnishings. The bathrooms, too, are very small and utilitarian, with little space for personal toiletries.

Dining: The single dining room has pleasing decor and is reasonably attractive, with its large picture ocean-view windows. There are two seatings. There are tables for four, six, or eight (there are no tables for two). The food presented is now very simple fare, with rice and pickled vegetables the mainstay of the cuisine.

Other Comments: She is a well-proportioned mid-size ship with fairly contemporary styling that is typical of the 1970s. She was originally built for Royal Caribbean Cruise Line, who operated her for more than 20 years.

There is a moderate amount of open deck and sunbathing space, but this becomes very tight when the ship is full, and a polished wood wraparound deck outdoors. The ship retains a neat bar/lounge, which is located part way up the funnel.

The public rooms are decorated in the style and colors that were popular in the 1970s, some of which now look dated. Star Cruises acquired this ship from Royal Caribbean International and placed her in service in January 1998. But it was not long before she was sold again, to Hyundai Merchant Marine for cruises in Southeast Asia and specifically so that local market passengers could visit Mount Kumgang in North Korea, which Hyundai is helping to develop into a tourist destination.

Weak Points: This really is a high-density ship, which means that public rooms are always busy. Long wait for elevators, in buffet lines, and for disembarkation in ports. At the time of going to press, it was learned that the ship might cater to international passengers. However, anyone sailing aboard this ship should note that the food is extremely basic and simple fare and will not in any way compare with international cuisine.

m/s Hyundai Kumgang
★★★★
(M)

LIFESTYLE:		**STANDARD**
Cruise Line:		Hyundai Merchant Marine
Former Names:		*SuperStar Capricorn, Golden Princess, Sunward, Birka Queen, Royal Viking Sky*
Gross Tonnage:		28,078
Builder:		Wartsila (Finland)
Original Cost:		$22.5 million
Entered Service:		June 1973/February 1997
Flag:		Panama
Tel. No.:		657336988
Fax No.:		657333622
Length (ft/m):		674.1/205.47
Beam (ft/m):		82.6/25.20
Draft (ft/m):		24.7/7.55
Propulsion/Propellers:		diesel (13,400kW)/2 (CP)
Decks:		8
Total Crew:		600
Pass. Capacity (basis 2):		804
Pass. Capacity (all berths):		1,366
Pass. Space Ratio (basis 2):		34.9
Pass. Space Ratio (all berths):		20.5
Officers:		International
Total Cabins:		429
Size Range (sq ft/m):		135.6–579.1/12.6–53.8
Cabins (outside view):		358
Cabins (inside — no view):		71
Cabins (single occupancy):		2
Cabins (with private balcony):		10
Cabins (wheelchair accessible):		0
Cabin Current:		110 and 220 volts
Cabin TV:		Yes
Dining Rooms:		1
Elevators:		5
Casino:		Yes
Slot Machines:		Yes
Swimming Pools (outdoors):		2
Swimming Pools (inside):		1
Whirlpools:		1
Fitness Center:		Yes
Sauna/Steam Room:		Yes/Yes
Massage:		Yes
Self-Service Launderette:		Yes
Movie Theater/Seats:		No
Library:		Yes
Classification Society:		Det Norske Veritas

RATINGS	POSSIBLE SCORE	SCORE ACHIEVED
Ship	500	382
Accommodation	200	155
Food	400	288
Service	400	302
Cruise	500	371
TOTAL	**2,000**	**1,498**

Accommodation: There are nine suites that are spacious and nicely equipped, and each has a separate bedroom and a large living area, including sofa, coffee table, and chairs; there is also a private outdoor balcony.

All other cabins are reasonably well appointed and have good closet, drawer, and reasonable storage space. Most bathrooms are sound, although some, on the lower decks, have awkward access.

Dining: The spacious dining room has a high ceiling, is quiet, and provides a reasonably elegant setting for cuisine that is now very simple fare, with rice and pickled vegetables the mainstay of the cuisine. There are two seatings.

Other Comments: Has handsome outer styling. Has a nicely balanced profile and lines, with a sharply raked bow. Good amount of open deck and sunbathing space; in fact, there is plenty of space everywhere. Good wraparound promenade deck outdoors, as well as decent fitness and sports facilities.

Inside, the ship features decor that is quite attractive and tasteful. There are lots of public rooms to choose from, including a karaoke lounge and private karaoke rooms. The casino action is lively.

This ship, which was stretched in 1982, should provide a decent cruise experience in spacious, nicely furnished surroundings. She was purchased by Star Cruises in 1996 and went through an extensive $5-million refit that added an indoor swimming pool and a video arcade. At present, she is under charter to Hyundai Merchant Marine, for cruises in Southeast Asia, for Korean passengers, specifically to North Korea, to visit the famous mountain, Mount Kumgang near the demilitarized zone in Kangwon Province, which Hyundai is helping to develop into an international tourist destination.

The ship's operational staff is provided by Star Cruises. There are a great number of Chinese among the hotel service crew.

<u>Weak Points</u>: At press time, it was learned that the ship might cater to international passengers. However, anyone sailing aboard this ship should note that the food is extremely basic and simple fare.

m/s Hyundai Pungak
★★★ +
(M)

LIFESTYLE:	PREMIUM
Cruise Line:	Hyundai Merchant Marine
Former Names:	*Island Princess, Island Venture*
Gross Tonnage:	19,907
Builder:	Rheinstahl Nordseewerke (Germany)
Original Cost:	$25 million
Entered Service:	February 1972/August 1974
Flag:	Great Britain
Tel. No.:	1440214
Fax No.:	1440214
Length (ft/m):	553.6/168.74
Beam (ft/m):	80.8/24.64
Draft (ft/m):	24.5/7.49
Propulsion/Propellers:	diesel (13,400kW)/2 (CP)
Passenger Decks:	7
Total Crew:	350
Pass. Capacity (basis 2):	610
Pass. Capacity (all berths):	717
Pass. Space Ratio (basis 2):	32.6
Pass. Space Ratio (all berths):	27.7
Officers:	International
Total Cabins:	305
Size Range (sq ft/m):	125.9–441.3/11.7–41.0
Cabins (outside view):	238
Cabins (inside — no view):	67
Cabins (single occupancy):	2
Cabins (with private balcony):	0
Cabins (wheelchair accessible):	2
Cabin Current:	110 and 220 volts
Cabin TV:	Yes
Dining Rooms:	1
Elevators:	4
Casino:	Yes
Slot Machines:	Yes
Swimming Pools (outdoors):	2
Swimming Pools (inside):	0
Whirlpools:	0
Fitness Center:	Yes
Sauna/Steam Room:	Yes/No
Massage:	Yes
Self-Service Launderette:	No
Movie Theater/Seats:	Yes/250
Library:	Yes
Classification Society:	Lloyd's Register

RATINGS	POSSIBLE SCORE	SCORE ACHIEVED
Ship	500	320
Accommodation	200	127
Food	400	271
Service	400	293
Cruise	500	355
TOTAL	**2,000**	**1,366**

Accommodation: The suites are quite large and well designed, with plenty of space to move around in. Most other cabins have ample room, are well appointed, and have plenty of closet and drawer space. The top category cabins have a full bathtub, while all others have a shower enclosure. None of the cabins has a private balcony.

Dining: Features a pleasant dining room, with two seatings. The food presented now is very simple fare, with rice and pickled vegetables the mainstay of the cuisine.

Other Comments: This ship, which has been operated by Princess Cruises since 1972, has a very attractive profile and exterior styling. As the former *Island Princess*, she was, together with her sister ship *Pacific Princess*, one of the pair of original "Love Boats" in the American television series *The Love Boat*. Hyundai Cruises acquired the ship in 1999. The ship has lines that are quite pleasing and well rounded.

The public areas are quite spacious, and there are numerous public rooms, with wide passageways and some high ceilings. There is a two-deck-high lobby, with several shops and offices located on the upper level. Tasteful decor is featured throughout, with pastel colors and fine artwork that is pleasing to the eye, if a little bland. The forward observation lounge also acts as an indoor buffet dining area. The "theater-in-the-round" show lounge has banquette-style seating in several tiers.

The ship, which has been well maintained, is quite elegant, with comfortable surroundings for the older passenger who wants plenty of space and does not want to be part of the larger, more impersonal ships.

The ship is now operating year-round in Southeast Asian waters, almost exclusively for South Korean passengers.

<u>Weak Points</u>: There is no wraparound promenade deck outdoors. At the time of going to press, it was learned that the ship might cater to international passengers. However, anyone sailing aboard this ship should note that the food is extremely basic and simple fare, and will not in any way compare with international cuisine.

m/s Imagination
★★★ +
(L)

LIFESTYLE:	STANDARD
Cruise Line:	Carnival Cruise Lines
Former Names:	-
Gross Tonnage:	70,367
Builder:	Kvaerner Masa-Yards (Finland)
Original Cost:	$330 million
Entered Service:	July 1995
Flag:	Panama
Tel. No.:	1347673
Fax No.:	n/a
Length (ft/m):	855.0/260.6
Beam (ft/m):	103.0/31.4
Draft (ft/m):	25.9/7.9
Propulsion/Propellers:	diesel-electric (42,240kW)/2 (CP)
Passenger Decks:	10
Total Crew:	920
Pass. Capacity (basis 2):	2,040
Pass. Capacity (all berths):	2,594
Pass. Space Ratio (basis 2):	34.4
Pass. Space Ratio (all berths):	26.7
Officers:	Italian
Total Cabins:	1,020
Size Range (sq ft/m):	173.2–409.7/16.0–38.0
Cabins (outside view):	618
Cabins (inside — no view):	402
Cabins (single occupancy):	0
Cabins (with private balcony):	54
Cabins (wheelchair accessible):	22
Cabin Current:	110 volts
Cabin TV:	Yes
Dining Rooms:	2
Elevators:	14
Casino:	Yes
Slot Machines:	Yes
Swimming Pools (outdoors):	3
Swimming Pools (inside):	0
Whirlpools:	6
Fitness Center:	Yes
Sauna/Steam Room:	Yes/Yes
Massage:	Yes
Self-Service Launderette:	Yes
Movie Theater/Seats:	No
Library:	Yes
Classification Society:	Lloyd's Register

RATINGS	POSSIBLE SCORE	SCORE ACHIEVED
Ship	500	395
Accommodation	200	151
Food	400	221
Service	400	270
Cruise	500	348
TOTAL	**2,000**	**1,385**

Accommodation: The Verandah Suites have rather eclectic colors and designs, but they are very comfortable (although the balconies are very narrow). Standard cabins are just that — standard cabins. They are functional, of cookie-cutter likeness, but have a reasonably good amount of closet and drawer space. The bathrooms are practical, as are the large shower units. Soap and ice water are provided.

Dining: There are two large, colorful, noisy dining rooms (both are nonsmoking), each with two seatings. Each has the usual efficient, programmed, assertive service. The improved cuisine is fair, but certainly not memorable. One plus is a 24-hour pizzeria. Shorts are permitted for one dinner each cruise.

Other Comments: Has a forthright, angular appearance typical of today's space-creative designs. This is the fifth in a series of eight identically-sized Carnival ships that reflects the talents of interior designer Joe Farcus, whose philosophy is that the cruise ship environment should provide fantasy and an escape from routine.

Like all Carnival ships, this one has themed decor for her interiors; for this ship classical mythology and ethereal decor can be found throughout the public rooms, which are connected by a double-width indoor boulevard. The ship has expansive open deck areas and a good, well-segmented health spa, and there is also a $1-million art collection, with many items in public areas featuring some timeless mosaics.

Ship buffs will enjoy six Stephen Card paintings of clipper ships, positioned in the Grand Bar. The Victorian-era-style library is a curious room, with intentionally mismatched furnishings, fine oriental rugs, and even a few books. Lavish, yet elegant multitiered showroom (but with 20 pillars obstructing sight lines), and fine, colorful, razzle-dazzle shows. Has an ATM machine located outside the large casino (all the slot machines aboard all Carnival ships are linked into a Megacash give-away).

Weak Points: Some may well complain of sensory overload. There are many loud, rather repetitive announcements. There are virtually no quiet spaces aboard to get away from crowds. Aggressive hustling for drinks means there is plenty of service everywhere. However, this ship will entertain those who are young at heart in fine fashion, and make them forget about solid ground for a while.

s/s Independence
★★ +
(M)

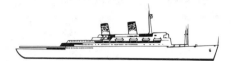

LIFESTYLE:	STANDARD
Cruise Line:	American Hawaii Cruises
Former Names:	*Oceanic Independence, Sea Luck I*
Gross Tonnage:	20,221
Builder:	Bethlehem Shipbuilders (USA)
Original Cost:	$25 million
Entered Service:	February 1951/June 1980
Flag:	USA
Tel. No.:	808-847-3172
Fax No.:	808-848-0406
Length (ft/m):	682.4/208.01
Beam (ft/m):	89.1/27.18
Draft (ft/m):	30.1/9.19
Propulsion/Propellers:	steam turbine (40,456kW)/2 (FP)
Passenger Decks:	9
Total Crew:	317
Pass. Capacity (basis 2):	866
Pass. Capacity (all berths):	1,021
Pass. Space Ratio (basis 2):	23.3
Pass. Space Ratio (all berths):	19.8
Officers:	American
Total Cabins:	446
Size Range (sq ft/m):	75.0–575.0/7.0–53.5
Cabins (outside view):	206
Cabins (inside — no view):	240
Cabins (single occupancy):	26

Cabins (with private balcony):	0
Cabins (wheelchair accessible):	2
Cabin Current:	110 volts
Cabin TV:	No
Dining Rooms:	2
Elevators:	4
Casino:	No
Slot Machines:	No
Swimming Pools (outdoors):	2
Swimming Pools (inside):	0
Whirlpools:	0
Fitness Center:	Yes
Sauna/Steam Room:	Yes/No
Massage:	Yes
Self-Service Launderette:	Yes
Movie Theater/Seats:	Yes/144
Library:	Yes
Classification Society:	American Bureau of Shipping

RATINGS	POSSIBLE SCORE	SCORE ACHIEVED
Ship	500	256
Accommodation	200	101
Food	400	213
Service	400	240
Cruise	500	282
TOTAL	**2,000**	**1,092**

Accommodation: There is a wide range of cabin types, with more than 50 different configurations to choose from (a carry-over from her nights as a three-class liner), all of which offer ample room to move in. There is adequate closet and drawer space and fairly bright decor, with Hawaii-themed soft furnishings. However, all the cabinetry is made of steel and is absolutely lacking in warmth (the metal drawers are particularly tinny). Also, the cabin bathrooms are small. Overall, the cabins are adequate, but they do reflect the age of the vessel.

Six large "solarium suites," with skylights, are located without access from inside the ship, which means you must go up the forward stairs and out on deck to get to them (fine if it's not raining or windy).

Dining: The dining rooms are set low down, without the benefit of an ocean view (the bi-level forward section is more elegant), but it is fairly cheerful, and has tables for two to ten persons. There are two seatings. The cuisine is American, with the norm being quantity, not quality. The first evening's dinner is buffet-style. The informal buffet area is good, but buffets are predictable, not creative. Fresh local fruits are plentiful, as are snacks and hors d'oeuvres.

Other Comments: American built, crewed, and registered (originally constructed for the 1950s transatlantic trade between New York and the Mediterranean), she, together with her former sister ship *Constitution* (which sank while under tow in November 1997 after being laid-up for some time), were among the first ships to have air-conditioning. This all-white ship has expansive open deck space for sun-worshippers, particularly on her aft, tiered sections, and features a wraparound teakwood promenade deck outdoor.

Originally designed as a three-class ship (but now operated as a one-class vessel) her layout is somewhat awkward and disjointed, and staggered elevators, hidden stairwells and dead-end corridors all add to the confusing interior layout.

This ship features spacious public rooms with high ceilings (although they never were as attractive as aboard her former sister ship *Constitution*). There are reasonably good facilities for meetings. The Hawaii-themed decor is a natural for the ship's operating area. Has heavy-duty, "neo-art deco" furniture and fittings, designed for unkind oceans. Hardwood floors, ceiling fans, and large plants add up to a tropical 1950s ambience. Local Hawaiian artists have their artwork featured on board.

The ambience and dress code are decidedly casual, and the entertainment is understandably regional. Fortunately, such things as bingo and horse racing are low-key, and not daily. Those intending to marry should look into the company's *Nani Kai* (Bountiful Seas) wedding package.

Because a laid-back atmosphere prevails, Aloha smiles come pouring from the friendly staff. This is a destination-intensive operation aboard a ship that is quite tired, despite a $30-million renovation in 1994. On top of the cruise fare, there is a Hawaii State Tax of 4.166 percent in addition to port charges and, for singles, a single supplement (plus gratuities). Airfare is also an additional cost, and 15 percent is added to all drinks and wine purchases. Having said all the above, there is something utterly magical about seeing the Hawaiian islands by ship, and this ships provides the means in a modicum of comfort. Complimentary shuttles to nearby shopping areas are provided at each port of call — a welcome touch.

Weak Points: The ship is now over 40 years old, and although she has been through some refurbishment, she is looking decidedly sad and tired in many places. The show lounge is not large enough and is always crowded. Drink prices are high. There are no stabilizers, so the ship *can* certainly roll in inclement weather.

m/s Inspiration
★★★ +
(L)

LIFESTYLE:	STANDARD
Cruise Line:	Carnival Cruise Lines
Former Names:	-
Gross Tonnage:	70,367
Builder:	Kvaerner Masa-Yards (Finland)
Original Cost:	$270 million
Entered Service:	April 1996
Flag:	Panama
Tel. No.:	1354562
Fax No.:	n/a
Length (ft/m):	855.0/260.6
Beam (ft/m):	103.0/31.4
Draft (ft/m):	25.9/7.9
Propulsion/Propellers:	diesel-electric (42,240kW)/2 (CP)
Passenger Decks:	10
Total Crew:	920
Pass. Capacity (basis 2):	2,040
Pass. Capacity (all berths):	2,594
Pass. Space Ratio (basis 2):	34.4
Pass. Space Ratio (all berths):	26.7
Officers:	Italian
Total Cabins:	1,020
Size Range (sq ft/m):	173.2–409.7/16.0–38.0
Cabins (outside view):	618
Cabins (inside — no view):	402
Cabins (single occupancy):	0

Cabins (with private balcony):	54
Cabins (wheelchair accessible):	22
Cabin Current:	110 volts
Cabin TV:	Yes
Dining Rooms:	2
Elevators:	14
Casino:	Yes
Slot Machines:	Yes
Swimming Pools (outdoors):	3
Swimming Pools (inside):	0
Whirlpools:	6
Fitness Center:	Yes
Sauna/Steam Room:	Yes/Yes
Massage:	Yes
Self-Service Launderette:	Yes
Movie Theater/Seats:	No
Library:	Yes
Classification Society:	Lloyd's Register

RATINGS	POSSIBLE SCORE	SCORE ACHIEVED
Ship	500	395
Accommodation	200	151
Food	400	221
Service	400	270
Cruise	500	348
TOTAL	**2,000**	**1,385**

Accommodation: The outside suites are decorated in a jazzy style and have whirlpool tubs, although they are not large. The standard cabins provide a comfortable home away from home, are of good size, but are also quite plainly decorated. Take your own shampoo and shower cap, however, as the company provides only ice water and soap in the cabins.

Dining: There are two large (rather noisy, or perhaps that should be better translated as "lively") dining rooms; each has two seatings. The cuisine *has* been improved somewhat by this cruise line during the past few years, but it is definitely not Carnival's strong point (it is, for example, difficult to ask for anything remotely unusual or off-menu). Service is attentive, but too fast and assertive, and does not have any finesse. The wine list is definitely not for lovers of fine wines, and there are no wine waiters.

What has noticeably improved is the quality of food available at the informal food outlets such as the Brasserie Bar and Grill, which also includes a pizzeria (open 24 hours).

Other Comments: Bold and forthright all-white ship has a large wing-tipped funnel in red, white, and blue; at its base is a "topless" area for sunbathing.

Like her seven sister ships of the same size, this ship also features a seven-deck-high atrium topped by a glass dome. The atrium features scrolled shapes resembling the necks and heads of violins and a marble staircase. There are expansive open-deck areas and an excellent, three-deck-high glass-enclosed health spa. There are public entertainment lounges, bars, and clubs galore, with something for just about everyone. The public rooms connect to wide indoor boulevards.

Various colors and design themes have been used throughout, although the ship does feature somewhat softer decor than on some of Carnival's ships. Includes a $1-million art collection. Particularly fascinating is the avant-garde rendition of the famed Mona Lisa in Pablo's Lounge. The decor itself is themed after the arts (in an art nouveau style) and literature.

The Shakespeare Library is a stunning, stately room (25 of his quotations adorn the oak veneer. Another dazzling room is the Rock and Roll Discotheque, with its guitar-shaped dance floor and video dance club and dozens of video monitors around the room. The ship also features a lavish, multitiered showroom (although some 20 pillars cause some seats to have obstructed sight lines) and high-energy razzle-dazzle shows. The casino is large, but always humming with hopeful action.

Weak Points: There are no cushioned pads for the deck lounge chairs, which are plastic and hard to sit on with just a towel for any length of time. There is constant, aggressive hustling for drinks. There are many announcements. There is too much use of plastic on board, particularly in the informal food service areas.

Finally, the company's brochure tells it exactly like it is, by providing a good look at the unpretentious lifestyle of its passengers. This ship provides a fine adult playground for those that like to party. It will entertain you well, but do not go for the food, go for the fun, the almost non-stop, all-too-predictable action and participation activities, and for a way to visit the Caribbean in a well-packaged manner that would best be described as a compact Las Vegas afloat.

s/s IslandBreeze
★★ +
(L)

LIFESTYLE:	STANDARD
Cruise Line:	Premier Cruise Lines/Thomson Cruises
Former Names:	*Festivale, Transvaal Castle, S.A. Vaal*
Gross Tonnage:	31,793
Builder:	John Brown & Co. (UK)
Original Cost:	n/a
Entered Service:	January 1962/May 1996
Flag:	Bahamas
Tel. No.:	1103150
Fax No.:	1103150
Length (ft/m):	760.1/231.70
Beam (ft/m):	90.1/27.49
Draft (ft/m):	31.9/9.75
Propulsion/Propellers:	steam turbine (32,800kW)/2 (FP)
Passenger Decks:	9
Total Crew:	612
Pass. Capacity (basis 2):	1,158
Pass. Capacity (all berths):	1,487
Pass. Space Ratio (basis 2):	27.4
Pass. Space Ratio (all berths):	21.3
Officers:	International
Total Cabins:	579
Size Range (sq ft/m):	49.5–166.8/4.6–15.5
Cabins (outside view):	269
Cabins (inside — no view):	310
Cabins (single occupancy):	0
Cabins (with private balcony):	10
Cabins (wheelchair accessible):	0
Cabin Current:	110 volts
Cabin TV:	No
Dining Rooms:	1
Elevators:	4
Casino:	Yes
Slot Machines:	Yes
Swimming Pools (outdoors):	2 (+ children's paddling pool)
Swimming Pools (inside):	0
Whirlpools:	0
Fitness Center:	Yes
Sauna/Steam Room:	Yes/No
Massage:	Yes
Self-Service Launderette:	No (has ironing room)
Movie Theater/Seats:	Yes/202
Library:	Yes
Classification Society:	Lloyd's Register

RATINGS	POSSIBLE SCORE	SCORE ACHIEVED
Ship	500	267
Accommodation	200	109
Food	400	216
Service	400	235
Cruise	500	260
TOTAL	**2,000**	**1,087**

Accommodation: In general, the cabins are small when compared to those of ships of a similar size. There are a large number of bunk beds (third and fourth berths), but there is only just enough closet and drawer space for this style of informal cruising. Heavy-duty fittings were standard aboard older ships such as this. In general, the bathrooms are of a good size, although the lighting is poor. Some of the large cabins are especially good for families. Note that the outside cabins on Veranda Deck have obstructed views.

When under charter to Thomson Cruises, there are four principal cabin categories; suites, premier, superior, and standard (although there are eight price levels), and specific cabins are not assigned until you arrive at the embarkation port for check-in. When operated under the Thomson Cruises banner, continental Breakfast in your cabin will cost about $7.50 (£4.50) per person extra (each time). There is also a 24-hour cabin service menu for snacks, all at extra cost.

Dining: The dining room, located low down, is bright, cheerful, and noisy (and it is nonsmoking, although smokers gather outside, so smoke can be smelled in the dining room anyway). There are two seatings. There are no tables for two. The food quality is quite adequate, with a good variety. The service is quite reasonable, but is hurried and lacks polish.

An informal cafe is suited to self-service buffets for those that do not want to bother with the dining room, but the selection of food presented here is very standardized and not very creative.

Other Comments: This is one of the real classic former ocean liners (originally *Transvaal Castle*), with a well-balanced profile and long, tiered foredeck. She looks like a real ship, and has a fine amount of open deck space. She is also being well maintained.

Her interiors retain much of the original wood and brass fittings intact from her former days as a Union Castle liner on the Southampton to Cape Town run (Union Castle disbanded in the 1970s). Most of the changes have taken place on the Promenade Deck. There is a good array of public rooms, including a

5,000 sq ft (464.5 m²) casino. Ship enthusiasts will like the fascinating steel art deco staircase. The show lounge features two shows in the evenings, to accommodate the two dinner seatings.

This ship now does dual-duty, being operated by Premier Cruise Lines during the winter and by Thomson Cruises (based in Naples) during the summer months (gratuities are included for Thomson's British passengers, and air travel will probably be provided by Britannia Airways, owned by Thomson). *IslandBreeze* provides an adequate older-ship experience, with lively casino action, for the young at heart who seek a low-budget cruise in comfortable, unstuffy surroundings, with no finesse, but lots of atmosphere — in a vintage ocean liner. And in keeping with her ocean liner image, the officers are well dressed and visible in public areas.

Weak Points: It is almost impossible to find any "quiet" space anywhere. The layout is not easy to master. The strange color schemes are eclectic, a leftover from her days as a Carnival Cruise Lines ship. The signs are confusing (it is difficult to find the "you are here" spots, or what deck you are on when exiting elevators, for example). The staff is not overly friendly and hustles for drinks, and communication is a problem for some. You should expect low-budget entertainment; in addition, the Piccadilly show lounge is poor and has very limited sight lines. The public address system is as poor as the cruise staff.

m/v Italia Prima
★★★
(M)

LIFESTYLE:	STANDARD
Cruise Line:	Nina Cruise Line
Former Names:	*Fridtjof Nansen,*
	Volkerfreundschaft,
	Stockholm
Gross Tonnage:	15,000
Builder:	Varco Chiapella (Italy)
Original Cost:	$150 million (reconstruction)
Entered Service:	February 1948/May 1994
Flag:	Italy
Tel. No.:	115-2210/115-2214
Fax No.:	115-2211/115-2215
Length (ft/m):	525.2/160.10
Beam (ft/m):	68.8/21.04
Draft (ft/m):	24.6/7.5
Propulsion/Propellers:	diesel (11,200kW)/2 (CP)
Passenger Decks:	7
Total Crew:	280
Pass. Capacity (basis 2):	540
Pass. Capacity (all berths):	600
Pass. Space Ratio (basis 2):	27.7
Pass. Space Ratio (all berths):	25.0
Officers:	Italian
Total Cabins:	260
Size Range (sq ft/m):	129.2–376.7/12.0–35.0
Cabins (outside view):	221
Cabins (inside — no view):	39
Cabins (single occupancy):	0

Balcony Cabins:	8
Wheelchair Cabins:	0
Cabin Current:	110 and 220 volts
Cabin TV:	Yes
Dining Rooms:	1
Elevators:	2
Casino:	Yes
Slot Machines:	Yes
Swimming Pools (outdoors):	1
Swimming Pools (inside):	0
Whirlpools:	1
Gymnasium:	Yes
Sauna/Steam Room:	Yes/Yes (Turkish Bath)
Massage:	Yes
Self-Service Launderette:	No
Movie Theater/Seats:	Yes/400
Library:	Yes
Classification Society:	Registro Navale Italiano

RATINGS	POSSIBLE SCORE	SCORE ACHIEVED
Ship	500	303
Accommodation	200	127
Food	400	207
Service	400	228
Cruise	500	238
TOTAL	**2,000**	**1,103**

Accommodation: All of the cabins have a mini-bar, television, and personal safe. Each cabin has a large Italian fresco above the bed, although the ceilings are very plain. All cabin bathrooms feature a bathtub, as well as a good amount of indented space for one's personal toiletries.

Eight suites feature a small private balcony, although the sight lines are not good, as well as a separate lounge, with table and chairs. The bathrooms in the suites and junior suites feature Jacuzzi bathtubs.

Note that the cabins on Sole Deck forward have lifeboat-obstructed views and those on Portofino Deck may, late at night, be subject to noise from the public rooms located on the deck above.

Dining: The single, large dining room is set low down in the center of the vessel. It is quite attractive and has tables for two, four, six, and eight. There is one seating. As you might expect, Italian cuisine is featured, with decent pasta dishes. There is a good selection of Italian wines. Standard house wines are included for lunch and dinner (this depends on the charterer/operator). There is a limited selection of breads, fruits, and cheeses; too much use of canned fruits, and a poor cabin service menu.

For casual meals, there is also a self-serve buffet for breakfast and lunch (Il Giardino), although the selection is very basic.

Other Comments: This ex-ocean liner made history when, as *Stockholm*, she rammed and sank the *Andrea Doria* in July 1956. She was reconstructed as a cruise ship in 1994 using her old, riveted hull, but with a completely new superstructure and a somewhat ungainly profile, she took on a new lease of life. However, the ship's maneuverability at slow speeds is quite poor, and stability is questionable, despite the addition of a sponson stern. There is a wraparound teak promenade deck outdoors, and heavy, real wood "steamer" deck chairs are provided, although there are no cushioned pads for them. The sunbathing space outdoors is, however, very limited, and definitely not sufficient when the ship is full.

Her interiors are decorated in contemporary Italian style. There is a good selection of public rooms to choose from, including a 400-seat auditorium for meetings, and a number of smart boutiques. The contemporary decor is quite upbeat and fresh and is complemented by a good selection of colorful art-work. There is also a Turkish bath, which is quite an unusual feature aboard cruise vessels today, as is the small chapel.

Italia Prima, however, really is a high-density ship. The ship is often under charter to various tour oper-ators, and cruises are sold through a number of outlets in several countries in Europe. Thus, the standard of product delivery can thus be inconsistent at best, and the actual scores should be used only as a guideline.

Although the ship has attractive interiors, your cruise experience will depend on what is spent on the food and the service staff, whose attitude and communication skills lack any kind of finesse. The ship sails from Havana (Cuba) on seven-night cruises within the Caribbean (a Cuban visa is necessary). The cur-rencies used aboard ship are the Italian lire and US dollar.

<u>Weak Points</u>: The "you are here" deck plans are not easy to read. The small swimming pool is really only a "dip" pool. There is no forward observation lounge. The hallways on the accommodation decks are quite narrow. Sight lines in the single-level show lounge are poor. In the cinema, the seats are not stag-gered and so the sight lines are poor. The steep gangway is designed for European, not Caribbean, ports.

m/t/s Jason
★★
(S)

LIFESTYLE:	STANDARD
Cruise Line:	Royal Olympic Cruises
Former Names:	*Eros*
Gross Tonnage:	5,250
Builder:	Cantieri Riuniti dell' Adriatico (Italy)
Original Cost:	n/a
Entered Service:	April 1967
Flag:	Greece
Tel. No.:	1130175
Fax No.:	1130175
Length (ft/m):	333.0/101.50
Beam (ft/m):	52.6/16.06
Draft (ft/m):	17.5/5.34
Propulsion/Propellers:	diesel (8,090kW)/2 (FP)
Passenger Decks:	6
Total Crew:	139
Pass. Capacity (basis 2):	272
Pass. Capacity (all berths):	302
Pass. Space Ratio (basis 2):	19.3
Pass. Space Ratio (all berths):	17.3
Officers:	Greek
Total Cabins:	136
Size Range (sq ft/m):	72.1–182.9/6.7–17.0
Cabins (outside view):	100
Cabins (inside — no view):	36
Cabins (single occupancy):	0
Cabins (with private balcony):	0
Cabins (wheelchair accessible):	0
Cabin Current:	220 volts
Cabin TV:	No
Dining Rooms:	1
Elevators:	1
Casino:	Yes
Slot Machines:	Yes
Swimming Pools (outdoors):	1
Swimming Pools (inside):	0
Whirlpools:	0
Fitness Center:	No
Sauna/Steam Room:	No/No
Massage:	No
Self-Service Launderette:	No
Movie Theater/Seats:	No
Library:	Yes
Classification Society:	Lloyd's Register

RATINGS	POSSIBLE SCORE	SCORE ACHIEVED
Ship	500	206
Accommodation	200	86
Food	400	201
Service	400	218
Cruise	500	198
TOTAL	**2,000**	**909**

Accommodation: The cabins are very small, yet they are quite cozy and inviting, and most come with a sofa bed that converts to a daytime sitting area. The bathrooms are extremely small, with little room for storage of toiletries. Note, however, that many of the shower stalls are in poor condition.

Dining: The dining room is reasonably charming and features large picture windows, comfortable seating, and some interesting tapestries. There are two seatings. The cuisine is decidedly continental, with some regional Greek dishes, although there is really too much use of canned foods. The service, provided by Greek waiters, is reasonably warm, friendly, and quite attentive, but lacks any degree of polish. The dining room seating and table assignments are normally handled by the maître d' upon embarkation.

Other Comments: This little ship has a traditional, rather low, profile. Her simple layout means that it is easy to find one's way around in a few minutes. There is a decent amount of outdoor deck and sunbathing space. Maintenance around the ship leaves much to be desired, however.

Inside, the decor is best described as well worn, drab, and not very inviting. There is some interesting artwork, as well as a reasonable library, although most of the books are old and well used. The main lounge is on one level, so the sight lines are poor, and the chairs are not very comfortable.

This ship will provide a reasonable, fairly comfortable cruise experience in some degree of classical style, without the crowds, at a fair price, but she is a high-density ship sixties-vintage vessel whose maintenance and operation leave much to be desired. Good for those who simply do not like larger ships. *Jason* operates mostly under charter to various tour operators, and so the onboard product, food presented, and service levels often change to accommodate the requests of the charterers. Do remember that when you pay cheap, you get cheap. Gratuities (suggested at $9 per person per day) are pooled among the crew.

<u>Weak Points</u>: The ship's maintenance needs serious attention. Poor standard of housekeeping, include badly stained items, such as towels and blankets not taken out of service. The cabin and bathroom maintenance are poor and includes a lot of shoddy patchwork.

m/s Jubilee
★★★ +
(L)

LIFESTYLE:	STANDARD
Cruise Line:	Carnival Cruise Lines
Former Names:	-
Gross Tonnage:	47,262
Builder:	Kockums (Sweden)
Original Cost:	$134 million
Entered Service:	July 1986
Flag:	Panama
Tel. No.:	1240503
Fax No.:	n/a
Length (ft/m):	733.0/223.40
Beam (ft/m):	92.5/28.20
Draft (ft/m):	24.7/7.5
Propulsion/Propellers:	diesel (23,520kW)/2 (CP)
Passenger Decks:	10
Total Crew:	670
Pass. Capacity (basis 2):	1,486
Pass. Capacity (all berths):	1,896
Pass. Space Ratio (basis 2):	31.8
Pass. Space Ratio (all berths):	24.9
Officers:	Italian
Total Cabins:	743
Size Range (sq ft/m):	182.9–419.8/17.0–39.0
Cabins (outside view):	453
Cabins (inside — no view):	290
Cabins (single occupancy):	0
Cabins (with private balcony):	10

Cabins (wheelchair accessible):	14
Cabin Current:	110 volts
Cabin TV:	Yes
Dining Rooms:	2
Elevators:	8
Casino:	Yes
Slot Machines:	Yes
Swimming Pools (outdoors):	3
Swimming Pools (inside):	0
Whirlpools:	2
Fitness Center:	Yes
Sauna/Steam Room:	Yes/No
Massage:	Yes
Self-Service Launderette:	Yes
Movie Theater/Seats:	No
Library:	Yes
Classification Society:	Lloyd's Register

RATINGS	POSSIBLE SCORE	SCORE ACHIEVED
Ship	500	355
Accommodation	200	143
Food	400	221
Service	400	275
Cruise	500	324
TOTAL	**2,000**	**1,318**

Accommodation: The cabins are quite spacious, are neatly appointed, and have attractive, though spartan, decor. Especially nice are the ten large suites on Veranda Deck. The outside cabins feature large picture windows. Soap and ice water are provided.

Dining: There are two dining rooms (both are nonsmoking). They are quite attractive, but have low ceilings and a raised center section that is somewhat cramped. There are two seatings. The food, although upgraded, is still very much a low-budget affair. Poor selection of breads, rolls, and fruit (too much canned fruit). The service is hurried — there being little time for attention to detail or anything out of the ordinary. There are no wine waiters, although there is a reasonably good wine list.

Other Comments: She has a bold, forthright all-white profile, but a very short, rakish bow. Sports Carnival's distinctive swept-back wing-tipped, red, white, and blue funnel.

Inside, there are flamboyant, vivid colors in all the public rooms except for the somewhat elegant Churchill's Library, which, sadly, is almost devoid of books. A large casino has almost round-the-clock action. Numerous public rooms are spread throughout two entertainment decks. Excellent double-width promenade deck features a white gazebo. Stimulating multitiered Atlantis Lounge showroom has huge theater stage.

This ship, now 10 years old, provides novice cruisers with an excellent first cruise experience in comfortable surroundings. Fun-filled, noisy, almost non-stop action provides a stimulating vacation, targeted particularly to those who like to party and have fun. Excellent for families with children, and especially good for singles who want constant action (sleep *before* you cruise). Provides very good value, with plenty of dazzle and sizzle entertainment and constant activities, which Carnival does it so well particularly for first-time cruise passengers.

Weak Points: There are many annoying and unnecessarily loud announcements. Constant hustling for drinks is the norm.

m/v Kapitan Khlebnikov
★★★ +
(S)

LIFESTYLE:	STANDARD
Cruise Line:	Murmansk Shipping/Quark Expeditions
Former Names:	-
Gross Tonnage:	12,288
Builder:	Wartsila (Finland)
Original Cost:	n/a
Entered Service:	1981
Flag:	Russia
Tel. No.:	1400676
Fax No.:	1400676
Length (ft/m):	434.6/132.49
Beam (ft/m):	87.7/26.75
Draft (ft/m):	27.8/8.50
Propulsion/Propellers:	diesel-electric (16,412kW)/3 (CP)
Passenger Decks:	6
Total Crew:	60
Pass. Capacity (basis 2):	108
Pass. Capacity (all berths):	116
Pass. Space Ratio (basis 2):	115.9
Pass. Space Ratio (all berths):	105.9
Officers:	Russian
Total Cabins:	54
Size Range (sq ft/m):	150.6–269/14.0–25.0
Cabins (outside view):	54
Cabins (inside — no view):	0
Cabins (single occupancy):	0
Cabins (with private balcony):	0

Cabins (wheelchair accessible):	0
Cabin Current:	220 volts
Cabin TV:	No
Dining Rooms:	1
Elevators:	1
Casino:	No
Slot Machines:	No
Swimming Pools (outdoors):	0
Swimming Pools (inside):	1
Whirlpools:	0
Fitness Center:	Yes
Sauna/Steam Room:	Yes-2/No
Massage:	No
Lecture/Film Room:	No
Library:	Yes
Zodiacs:	4
Helicopter Pad:	Yes (1 helicopter)
Classification Society:	RS

RATINGS	POSSIBLE SCORE	SCORE ACHIEVED
Ship	500	315
Accommodation	200	135
Food	400	244
Service	400	250
Cruise	500	343
TOTAL	**2,000**	**1,287**

Accommodation: The cabins are spread over four decks, and all have private facilities and plenty of storage space. Although nothing special, they are quite comfortable, with two lower berths, large closets, and portholes that actually open. The bathrooms are practical units.

Dining: The dining room is plain and unpretentious and is totally nonsmoking; there is one seating, with assigned tables. Features real hearty food, in generous portions (with an emphasis on fish), served by waitresses in a dining room that is comfortable and practical. The cuisine and its production and presentation are overseen by Scandinavian advisors, and western foods are brought in specifically for these chartered voyages.

Other Comments: This is a real, working icebreaker, one of a fleet of ten that are available for various charters. The ship has an incredibly thick hull, a forthright profile, and a bow like an inverted whale head. The funnel is placed amidships, and the accommodation block is placed forward. An open bridge policy allows passengers to visit the bridge at almost any time. Strong diesel-electric engines allow her to plow through ice several feet thick. There is plenty of open deck and observation space and a heated indoor swimming pool. There is always a team of excellent naturalists and lecturers aboard. Heavy parka and boots are provided for passengers, who really become participants in this kind of hands-on expedition cruising. A helicopter is usually carried and can be used by all passengers for sightseeing forays.

This vessel is particularly good for tough expedition cruising and will provide practical surroundings; a friendly, experienced, and dedicated crew; and excellent value for the money in true expeditionary style.

Weak Points: The ship offers only basic cruise amenities and a very spartan, no-frills decor. Also, you should be prepared for the tremendous roaring noise when the ship breaks through pack ice.

m/s Kristina Regina
★★ +
(S)

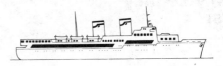

LIFESTYLE:	STANDARD
Cruise Line:	Kristina Cruises
Former Names:	*Borea, Bore*
Gross Tonnage:	4,295
Builder:	Oskarshamn Shipyard (Sweden)
Original Cost:	n/a
Entered Service:	1960/1987
Flag:	Finland
Tel. No.:	1623154
Fax No.:	1623154
Length (ft/m):	327.4/99.80
Beam (ft/m):	50.1/15.30
Draft (ft/m):	17.3/5.30
Propulsion/Propellers:	diesel (3,233kW)/2 (FP)
Passenger Decks:	6
Total Crew:	55
Pass. Capacity (basis 2):	290
Pass. Capacity (all berths):	370
Pass. Space Ratio (basis 2):	14.8
Pass. Space Ratio (all berths):	11.6
Officers:	Finnish
Total Cabins:	145
Size Range (sq ft/m):	64.5–124.8/6.0–11.6
Cabins (outside view):	112
Cabins (inside — no view):	33
Cabins (single occupancy):	0
Cabins (with private balcony):	0

Cabins (wheelchair accessible):	0
Cabin Current:	220 volts
Cabin TV:	Deluxe cabins only
Dining Rooms:	2 (1 for buffets/1 à la carte)
Elevators:	0
Casino:	No
Slot Machines:	No
Swimming Pools (outdoors):	0
Swimming Pools (inside):	0
Whirlpools:	0
Fitness Center:	No
Sauna/Steam Room:	Yes/No
Massage:	No
Self-Service Launderette:	No
Movie Theater/Seats:	No
Library:	Yes
Classification Society:	Lloyd's Register

RATINGS	POSSIBLE SCORE	SCORE ACHIEVED
Ship	500	233
Accommodation	200	110
Food	400	238
Service	400	233
Cruise	500	238
TOTAL	**2,000**	**1,052**

Accommodation: There is a wide assortment of cabin sizes and configurations. Some cabins have queen-sized bed; others have two beds, while others have upper and lower berths. All cabins have a shower and toilet, radio, telephone, but not much else, and they are really tiny, as are the bathrooms. As the cabins have very little closet and drawer space, do take only what's really necessary. There are also five allergy-free cabins, as well as several interconnecting cabins.

Dining: The dining room is charming and features continental (European) cuisine, with a distinct accent on fish, seafood, and fresh berries. The breads and cheeses are also good. There is one seating at assigned tables, and fine, hearty, and friendly service comes with a smile.

Other Comments: This lovely old-world ship was built specifically for close-in northern European coastal and archipelago cruises, and was extensively refurbished in 1990. She is one of few ships left today that has two funnels and is owned by a single family.

Features include a wraparound wooden promenade deck outdoors. There are few public rooms (there is, however, a small conference room), but she does have some beautiful hardwoods and lots of brass feature throughout her interior decor. The Scandinavian artwork is also quite fascinating. The ship exudes old-world charm. Has a well-designed auditorium that doubles as a movie theater. The onboard currency is both in US dollars and Finnish marks. Non-alcoholic drinks are complementary.

Her itineraries take her to the Baltic States and Russia, into White Sea ports, and occasionally to Scotland. Weak Points: This is a high-density ship, so there is little room to move about inside when full.

s/y Legacy
(S)

LIFESTYLE: **STANDARD**

Cruise Line:	Windjammer Barefoot Cruises
Former Names:	*France II*
Gross Tonnage:	1,740
Builder:	Forges et al Mediterraneee du Havre (France)
Entered Service:	1959/1997
Flag:	Equatorial Guinea
Tel. No.:	n/a
Fax No.:	n/a
Length (ft/m):	294.0/89.6
Beam (ft/m):	40.0/12.1
Draft (ft/m):	23.0/7.0
Type of Vessel:	barquentine
No. of Masts:	4
Sail Area (sq ft/sq m):	19,900/1848.7
Main Propulsion:	sail power
Propulsion/Propellers:	diesel/1 (FP)
Decks:	4
Total Crew:	43
Pass. Capacity (basis 2):	122
Pass. Capacity (all berths):	122
Pass. Space Ratio (basis 2):	14.2
Pass. Space Ratio (all berths):	14.2
Officers:	International
Total Cabins:	61
Size Range (sq ft/m):	75.0–159.0/6.9–14.7
Cabins (outside view):	46
Cabins (inside — no view):	15
Cabins (single occupancy):	0
Cabins (with private balcony):	0
Cabins (wheelchair accessible):	0
Cabin Current:	110 volts
Cabin TV:	1 (Burke's Berth)
Dining Rooms:	1
Elevators:	0
Casino:	0
Slot Machines:	0
Swimming Pools (outdoors):	0
Whirlpools:	0
Fitness Center:	0
Sauna/Steam Room:	No/No
Massage:	No
Self-Service Launderette:	No
Library:	Yes
Classification Society:	American Bureau of Shipping

RATINGS	POSSIBLE SCORE	SCORE ACHIEVED
Ship	500	NYR
Accommodation	200	NYR
Food	400	NYR
Service	400	NYR
Cruise	500	NYR
TOTAL	**2,000**	**NYR**
Expected Score Range:		**900-1100**

When built, she served as a meteorological research and exploration vessel for the French Government before being converted into a traditional tall ship by Windjammer Barefoot Cruises in 1989. Sails from Fajardo (Puerto Rico). For other comments about the lifestyle, see *Flying Cloud*.

m/s Legend of the Seas
★★★★
(L)

LIFESTYLE:	STANDARD
Cruise Line:	Royal Caribbean International
Former Names:	-
Gross Tonnage:	69,130
Builder:	Chantiers de l'Atlantique (France)
Original Cost:	$325 million
Entered Service:	May 1995
Flag:	Liberia
Tel. No.:	363600716
Fax No.:	363600712
Length (ft/m):	867.0/264.20
Beam (ft/m):	105.0/32.00
Draft (ft/m):	23.9/7.3
Propulsion/Propellers:	diesel (40,200kW)/2 (CP)
Passenger Decks:	11
Total Crew:	720
Pass. Capacity (basis 2):	1,800
Pass. Capacity (all berths):	2,076
Pass. Space Ratio (basis 2):	38.3
Pass. Space Ratio (all berths):	33.2
Officers:	Norwegian
Total Cabins:	900
Size Range (sq ft/m):	137.7–1,147.4/12.8–106.6
Cabins (outside view):	575
Cabins (inside — no view):	327
Cabins (single occupancy):	0
Cabins (with private balcony):	231

Cabins (wheelchair accessible):	17
Cabin Current:	110 and 220 volts
Cabin TV:	Yes
Dining Rooms:	1
Elevators:	11
Casino:	Yes
Slot Machines:	Yes
Swimming Pools (outdoors):	2 (1 with sliding roof)
Swimming Pools (inside):	0
Whirlpools:	4
Fitness Center:	Yes
Sauna/Steam Room:	Yes/Yes
Massage:	Yes
Self-Service Launderette:	No
Movie Theater/Seats:	No
Library:	Yes
Classification Society:	Det Norske Veritas

RATINGS	POSSIBLE SCORE	SCORE ACHIEVED
Ship	500	432
Accommodation	200	169
Food	400	245
Service	400	295
Cruise	500	387
TOTAL	**2,000**	**1,528**

Accommodation: Royal Caribbean International has realized that small cabins do not happy passengers make. The company therefore set about designing a ship with much larger standard cabins than in any of the company's previous vessels (except sister ship *Splendour of the Seas*). Some cabins on Deck 8 also have a larger door for wheelchair access in addition to the 17 cabins for the physically handicapped, and the ship is very accessible, with ample ramped areas and sloping decks. All cabins have a sitting area and beds that convert to double configuration, and there is ample closet and drawer space, although there is not much space around the bed (and the showers could have been better).

Cabins with balconies have glass railings rather than steel/wood to provide less intrusive sight lines. The largest accommodation, named the Royal Suite, is a superb living space for those that can afford the best. It is beautifully designed, finely decorated, and features a baby grand piano, a whirlpool bathtub, and other fine amenities. Several quite sitting areas are located adjacent to the best cabins amidships. Seventeen cabin categories is really too many. Sadly, there are no cabins for singles.

Dining: The two-deck-high dining room has dramatic two-deck-high glass side walls, so many passengers both upstairs and downstairs can see both the ocean and each other in reflection (it would, perhaps, have been even better located at the stern), but it is quite noisy when full (call it atmosphere). There are two seatings. There is also a cavernous indoor-outdoor cafe, located toward the bow and above the bridge, as well as a good-sized snack area, which provide more informal dining choices.

Meals, choices, and presentation were much improved of late. In addition, full vegetarian menus were also introduced. Royal Caribbean International delivers generally good food and service, with waiters who are smartly dressed and very attentive. Special orders are seldom possible, however, and there is neither good caviar, nor tableside carving or flambeau items.

Other Comments: This ship's contemporary profile looks somewhat unbalanced (but it soon grows on you), and she does have a nicely tiered stern. The pool deck amidships overhangs the hull to provide an extremely wide deck, while still allowing the ship to navigate the Panama Canal. With engines placed midships, there is little noise and no noticeable vibration, and the ship has an operating speed of up to 24 knots.

The interior decor is quite colorful, but too glitzy for European tastes. The outside light is brought inside in many places, with an extensive amount of glass area that provides contact with sea and air (there is, in fact, over two acres of glass). Features an innovative single-level sliding glass roof (not a magrodome) over the more formal setting of one of two swimming pools, thus providing a multi-activity, all-weather indoor-outdoor area, called Solarium. The glass roof provides shelter for the Roman-style pool and adjacent health and fitness facilities (which are superb) and slides aft to cover the miniature golf course when required (both cannot be covered at the same time, however).

Golfers might enjoy the 18-hole, 6,000 sq ft (557.5 m^2) miniature golf course, aptly named Legend of the Links (it is the first of its kind in any cruise ship). It has the topography of a real championship course, complete with trees, foliage, grass, bridges, water hazards, and lighting for play at night. The holes themselves are 155–230 sq ft (14.3–21.3 m^2).

Inside, there are two full entertainment decks sandwiched between five decks full of cabins. The tiered and balconied show lounge, which covers two decks, is expansive and has excellent sight lines and very comfortable seats. Several large-scale production shows are provided here, and there is an orchestra pit, which can be raised or lowered as required. A multitiered seven-deck-high atrium lobby, complete with a huge stainless steel sculpture, connects with the impressive Viking Crown Lounge via glass-walled elevators. The casino is really expansive, overly glitzy, and absolutely packed. The library, outside of which is a bust of Shakespeare, is a fine facility, with over 2,000 books.

There is, sadly, no separate cinema. The casino could be somewhat disorienting, with its mirrored walls and lights flashing everywhere, although it is no different to those found in Las Vegas fantasy gaming halls. As with any large ship, you can expect to find yourself standing in lines for embarkation, disembarkation, buffets, and shore excursions, although the company does its best to minimize such lines.

Representing natural evolution, this ship is an outstanding new cruise vessel for the many repeat passengers who enjoy Royal Caribbean International's consistent delivery of a well-integrated, fine-tuned, very comfortable and well-liked product. With larger cabins, excellent decor, and contemporary style, *Legend of the Seas* has taken Royal Caribbean International passengers, most of whom are typically from middle-America, into a much upgraded cruise experience from that of the company's other ships. The ship provides a very cost-effective cruise for all ages. Similar comments apply to sister ship *Splendour of the Seas.*

m/v Le Levant
★★★★ +
(S)

LIFESTYLE: **PREMIUM**

Cruise Line:	Compagnie des Isles du Ponant/ Classical Cruises
Former Names:	-
Gross Tonnage:	3,504
Builder:	Leroux & Lotz (France)
Original Cost:	$35 million
Entered Service:	January 1999
Flag:	Wallis and Fortuna
Tel. No.:	81322804320
Fax No.:	81322804330
Length (ft/m):	328.0/100.00
Beam (ft/m):	45.9/14.00
Draft (ft/m):	11.4/3.50
Propulsion/Propellers:	diesel (3,000 kW)/2 (CP)
Passenger Decks:	5
Total Crew:	50
Pass. Capacity (basis 2):	90
Pass. Capacity (all berths):	90
Pass. Space Ratio (basis 2):	38.9
Pass. Space Ratio (all berths):	38.9
Officers:	French
Total Cabins:	45
Size Range (sq ft/m):	199.1/18.5
Cabins (outside view):	45
Cabins (inside — no view):	0
Cabins (single occupancy):	0
Cabins (with private balcony):	0

Cabins (wheelchair accessible):	0
Cabin Current:	110 and 220 volts
Cabin TV:	Yes
Dining Rooms:	2
Elevators:	1
Casino:	No
Slot Machines:	No
Swimming Pools (outdoors):	1
Swimming Pools (inside):	0
Whirlpools:	0
Fitness Center:	Yes
Sauna/Steam Room:	No/Yes
Massage:	No
Self-Service Launderette:	No
Movie Theater/Seats:	No
Library:	Yes
Classification Society:	Bureau Veritas

RATINGS	POSSIBLE SCORE	SCORE ACHIEVED
Ship	500	424
Accommodation	200	173
Food	400	312
Service	400	319
Cruise	500	381
TOTAL	**2,000**	**1,609**

Accommodation: There are 45 ocean-view cabins (the brochure says "suites") and all are located mid-ships and forward, in five different price categories. Each cabin features a large ocean-view window, inlaid wood furniture and accenting, designer fabrics, two beds that convert to a queen-size bed, a television, a VCR, a refrigerator, a personal safe, and personal amenity kits in the marble-appointed bathrooms, all of which feature a shower (no bathtubs).

Dining: There are two dining rooms; the first is a wood-paneled main Dining Room (one seating only), which has round and oval tables; the second is the more informal Veranda Restaurant, with a panoramic view overlooking the stern. Dining is in open seating, with unassigned seats, so you can dine with whomever you wish. Complimentary wines are included for lunch and dinner, and the cuisine is, naturally, classic French.

Other Comments: This new high-class vessel looks like a streamlined private mega-yacht, and has quite a stunning low profile appearance with its royal blue (ice-hardened) hull and blue/white superstructure. She sports two slim funnels that extend over port and starboard sides to carry any soot away from the vessel (somewhat like the design of the first four former Renaissance Cruises vessels). Built in a yacht shipyard in St. Malo, France. An open-bridge policy is featured, so that passengers may visit the bridge whenever they wish (except when maneuvering in difficult conditions). She sports a stern "marina" platform for scuba diving, snorkeling, or swimming. Two special landing craft are carried for shore visits, hidden in the stern, as well as six inflatable Zodiacs runabouts for landings in "soft" expedition areas such as the Amazon.

Inside, the vessel features contemporary, clean, and uncluttered decor. The public rooms are elegant and refined, with much use of wood trim and accenting throughout. Particularly pleasing is the wood-paneled library, a feature so often lacking aboard many ships today. There is also one grand salon, which accommodates all passengers, and is used by day as a lecture room, and by night as the main lounge/bar. A resident scuba divemaster is aboard for all Caribbean sailings. In addition, Classical Cruises features life-enrichment lecturers aboard each cruise, as well as tour leaders.

This ship, under charter to New York-based Classical Cruises, operates cruises to some off-beat destinations and cruise regions. During the summer of 2000 she will be in the Great Lakes, sailing between Toronto and Chicago (her pencil-slim beam allows her to navigate the locks). During the fall of 2000 she heads to Canada/New England, and even as far north as Hudson Bay and the Northern Territories of Canada. During the winter months she heads to the Caribbean and South America.

The company also owns and operates *Le Ponant*, a chic ultra-sleek sailing vessel. This is all-inclusive cruising, with all port charges, gratuities, shore excursions, and port charges included in the cruise fare. The crew is almost entirely French.

<u>Weak Points</u>: Although you can walk around the uppermost accommodation deck, there really is no wraparound promenade deck. No cabins have balconies.

WHAT IS AN ISLAND?

An island is defined as any land mass smaller than the smallest continent, and completely surrounded by water.

THE COLOR OF SEAWATER

Seawater is colorless. We only see "color" in seawater because quantities of the water play with light. The deep blue of deep seawater is produced in part by the refraction of light particles in the water and by the reflection of the sky. Also, the color blue is absorbed least by seawater. "Green" seas are found closer to land and are the result of greater quantities of suspended matter carried in coastal waters. Thus, the color essentially results from the combination of the blue-looking ocean water and the yellow pigments that result from the decomposition of plant matter. The Red Sea was so named due to the periodic swarming of an alga that stains its surface.

WAVES

Water waves are produced when the air-sea surface interface is distorted by a force such as the wind. Waves provide one of the most important mechanisms for transporting energy from one point to another on the surface of the sea. A restoring force such as gravity, surface tension, or the Coriolis force then acts to return the surface to equilibrium.

m/y/s Le Ponant
★★★★
(S)

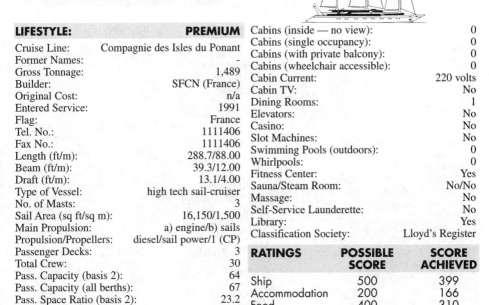

LIFESTYLE:	PREMIUM
Cruise Line:	Compagnie des Isles du Ponant
Former Names:	-
Gross Tonnage:	1,489
Builder:	SFCN (France)
Original Cost:	n/a
Entered Service:	1991
Flag:	France
Tel. No.:	1111406
Fax No.:	1111406
Length (ft/m):	288.7/88.00
Beam (ft/m):	39.3/12.00
Draft (ft/m):	13.1/4.00
Type of Vessel:	high tech sail-cruiser
No. of Masts:	3
Sail Area (sq ft/sq m):	16,150/1,500
Main Propulsion:	a) engine/b) sails
Propulsion/Propellers:	diesel/sail power/1 (CP)
Passenger Decks:	3
Total Crew:	30
Pass. Capacity (basis 2):	64
Pass. Capacity (all berths):	67
Pass. Space Ratio (basis 2):	23.2
Pass. Space Ratio (all berths):	22.2
Officers:	French
Total Cabins:	32
Size Range (sq ft/m):	139.9/13.0
Cabins (outside view):	32

Cabins (inside — no view):	0
Cabins (single occupancy):	0
Cabins (with private balcony):	0
Cabins (wheelchair accessible):	0
Cabin Current:	220 volts
Cabin TV:	No
Dining Rooms:	1
Elevators:	No
Casino:	No
Slot Machines:	No
Swimming Pools (outdoors):	0
Whirlpools:	0
Fitness Center:	Yes
Sauna/Steam Room:	No/No
Massage:	No
Self-Service Launderette:	No
Library:	Yes
Classification Society:	Lloyd's Register

RATINGS	POSSIBLE SCORE	SCORE ACHIEVED
Ship	500	399
Accommodation	200	166
Food	400	310
Service	400	319
Cruise	500	346
TOTAL	**2,000**	**1,540**

Accommodation: Crisp, clean blond woods and pristine white cabins feature double or twin beds, mini-bar, personal safe, and private bathroom. All cabins feature portholes, crisp artwork, and a refrigerator. There is a limited amount of storage space, however, and few drawers. The cabin bathrooms are quite small, but efficiently designed.

Dining: The lovely Karukera dining room (open seating) features complimentary wines and good food. There is fresh fish every day, and meals are true "affaires gastonomiques." There is also a charming outdoor cafe under canvas sailcloth awning.

Other Comments: Ultrasleek, very efficient, this latest generation of sail-cruise ship has three masts that rise 16.7 meters above the water line. This captivating ship has plenty of room on her open decks for sunbathing. Water sports facilities include an aft marina platform, windsurfers, water ski boat, and scuba and snorkel equipment.

Very elegant, no glitz interior design is clean, stylish, functional, and ultra-high-tech throughout. Three public lounges have pastel decor, soft colors, and great European flair.

One price fits all. Marketed mainly to young, sophisticated French-speaking passengers who love yachting and the sea. Tres French, and tres chic. The company also has a stunning mega-yacht cruise vessel, *Le Levant*. Gratuities are not "required," but they are expected.

m/s Maasdam
★★★★
(L)

LIFESTYLE: **PREMIUM**

Cruise Line:	Holland America Line
Former Names:	-
Gross Tonnage:	55,451
Builder:	Fincantieri (Italy)
Original Cost:	$215 million
Entered Service:	December 1993
Flag:	The Netherlands
Tel. No.:	624295813
Fax No.:	1302514
Length (ft/m):	719.3/219.30
Beam (ft/m):	101.0/30.80
Draft (ft/m):	24.6/7.50
Propulsion/Propellers:	diesel-electric (34,560kW)/2 (CP)
Passenger Decks:	10
Total Crew:	557
Pass. Capacity (basis 2):	1,266
Pass. Capacity (all berths):	1,627
Pass. Space Ratio (basis 2):	43.8
Pass. Space Ratio (all berths):	34.0
Officers:	Dutch
Total Cabins:	632
Size Range (sq ft/m): 186.2–1,124.8/17.3–104.5	
Cabins (outside view):	502
Cabins (inside — no view):	131
Cabins (single occupancy):	0

Cabins (with private balcony):	150
Cabins (wheelchair accessible):	6
Cabin Current:	110 and 220 volts
Cabin TV:	Yes
Dining Rooms:	1
Elevators:	12
Casino:	Yes
Slot Machines:	Yes
Swimming Pools (outdoors):	1
Swimming Pools (inside):	1 (magrodome)
Whirlpools:	2
Fitness Center:	Yes
Sauna/Steam Room:	Yes/No
Massage:	Yes
Self-Service Launderette:	Yes
Movie Theater/Seats:	Yes/249
Library:	Yes
Classification Society:	Lloyd's Register

RATINGS	POSSIBLE SCORE	SCORE ACHIEVED
Ship	500	418
Accommodation	200	162
Food	400	282
Service	400	299
Cruise	500	387
TOTAL	**2,000**	**1,548**

Accommodation: The accommodation ranges from small inside (no-view) cabins to a large penthouse suite, in 17 categories.

The 148 inside (no-view) and 336 outside (with a view) standard cabins feature twin beds that convert to a queen-size bed, and there is a separate living space with sofa and coffee table. However, although the drawer space is generally good, the closet space is actually very tight, particularly for long cruises (although more than adequate for a seven-night cruise). The bathrooms are tiled and compact but practical — they come with a good range of personal toiletry amenities. Bathrobes are also provided, as are hairdryers. The bathrooms are quite well laid out, but the bathtubs are small units better described as shower tubs. Some cabins have interconnecting doors, good for families with children or older couples with their own butler/maid or nurse (*Maasdam, Ryndam,* and *Veendam* only, not *Statendam*).

On Navigation Deck 28 suites have accommodation for up to four. These suites also feature in-suite dining as an alternative to the dining room, for private, reclusive meals. These are very spacious, tastefully decorated and well laid out, and feature a separate living room, bedroom with two lower beds (convertible to a king-size bed), a good size living area, a dressing room, plenty of closet and drawer space, and a marble bathroom with Jacuzzi tub.

The largest accommodation of all is a penthouse suite; there is only one, located on the starboard side of navigation Deck). It features a king-size bed, walk-in closet with superb drawer space, an oversize whirlpool bath and separate shower enclosure, a living room, a dressing room, a large private balcony, a pantry, mini-bar/refrigerator, a guest toilet, and floor to ceiling windows.

Dining: The two-level dining room, located at the stern is quite dramatic, and has a grand staircase (although few seem to use it), panoramic views on three sides, and a music balcony. Fine Rosenthal china is featured. Features open seating for breakfast and lunch and two seatings for dinner. While the food and service seem to have improved somewhat, dinner is still not the memorable experience it should be (however, you should remember that this is mass catering). The waiter stations in the dining room are very noisy for anyone seated adjacent to them.

Instead of the more formal dining room, the Lido Buffet is open for casual dinners on several nights each cruise (typically three nights on a seven-night cruise), in an open-seating arrangement. Tables are set with crisp linens, flatware, and stemware. A set menu is featured, and this includes a choice of four entrees.

There is also an extensive, dual-line (self-serve) Lido Buffet (one side is for smokers, the other side for nonsmokers) for casual breakfasts and lunches. For the buffets, there is much use of canned fruits (good for older passengers with no teeth) and packeted items, although there are several commercial low-calorie salad dressings. The choice of cheeses (and accompanying crackers) is very poor. The beverage station also lets it down, for it is no better than those found in family outlets ashore in the US. In addition, a poolside grill provides basic American hamburgers and hot dogs.

Other Comments: This is one of a series of four almost identical ships in the same series, the others being *Statendam*, *Ryndam*, and *Veendam*. The exterior styling is rather angular (some would say boxy — the funnel certainly is), although it is softened and balanced somewhat by the fact that the hull is painted black. There is a full wraparound teakwood promenade deck outdoors, excellent for strolling and, thankfully, no sign of artificial grass anywhere. The deck lounge chairs are wood, and come with comfortable cushioned pads.

Inside, an asymmetrical layout breaks up the interiors and helps to reduce bottlenecks and congestion. The decor is softer, more sophisticated, and far less eclectic than in sister ship *Statendam* (the first in this series of what the company terms *Statendam*-class ships), while the interiors of the latest in the series, *Ryndam* and *Veendam* seem to improve further on the theme. In general, however, a restrained approach to interior styling is taken using a mixture of contemporary materials combined with traditional woods and ceramics. There is, fortunately, little "glitz" anywhere.

What is outstanding is the array of artwork throughout the ship (costing about $2 million), assembled and nicely displayed to represent the fine Dutch heritage of Holland America Line and to present a balance between standard itineraries and onboard creature comforts. Also noticeable are the fine flower arrangements throughout the public areas and foyers, used to good effect to brighten up what to some is dull decor.

Atop the ship, with forward facing views that wrap around the sides is the Crow's Nest Lounge. By day it makes a fine observation lounge (particularly in Alaska), while by night it turns into a night club with extremely variable lighting.

A three-deck-high atrium foyer is quite stunning, although its sculptured centerpiece makes it look a little crowded, and leaves little room in front of the purser's office. A hydraulic magrodome (glass) roof covers the reasonably sized swimming pool/whirlpools and central Lido area (whose focal point is a large dolphin sculpture) so that this can be used in either fine or inclement weather.

The two-deck-high show lounge is basically well designed, but the ceiling is low and the sight lines from the balcony level are poor. Has a large and quite lovely and relaxing reference library. The company keeps its ships very clean and tidy throughout, and there is good passenger flow throughout.

Maasdam, *Ryndam*, *Statendam*, and *Veendam* are well built, and have fairly decent interior fit and finish. Holland America Line is constantly fine-tuning its performance as a cruise operator and its regular passengers (almost all of whom are North American; there are few international passengers) find the company's ships very comfortable and well run. The company continues its strong maritime traditions, although the present food and service components still let the rest of the cruise experience down. The line does not add an automatic 15 percent gratuity for beverage purchases, unlike many other cruise lines.

What is always enjoyed by Holland America Line's many repeat passengers is the fact that social dancing is always on the menu. The company also offers cappuccino and espresso coffees, and free ice cream during certain hours of the day aboard its ships, as well as hot hors d'oeuvres in all bars — something other major lines seem to have dropped or charge extra for. In the final analysis, however, the score for this ship (and her sisters *Ryndam*, *Statendam*, and *Veendam*) ends up just a disappointing tad under what it could be if the food and food service staff was better (more professional training might help).

Weak Points: The service staff is Indonesian, and, although quite charming (for the most part), communication with them often proves frustrating for many passengers, and service is spotty and inconsistent. Note that passengers are forced to eat at the Lido Café on days when the dining room is closed for lunch (this is typically once or twice per cruise, depending on ship and itinerary). The single escalator is virtually useless. There is no bell push outside the suites. There is an extra charge for the self-service laundry machines ($1.50).

m/s Majesty of the Seas

★★★ +

(L)

LIFESTYLE:	STANDARD
Cruise Line:	Royal Caribbean International
Former Names:	-
Gross Tonnage:	73,941
Builder:	Chantiers de l'Atlantique
Original Cost:	$300 million
Entered Service:	April 1992
Flag:	Norway
Tel. No.:	1313370
Fax No.:	1313370
Length (ft/m):	879.9/268.2
Beam (ft/m):	105.9/32.3
Draft (ft/m):	24.9/7.6
Propulsion/Propellers:	diesel (21,844kW)/2 (CP)
Passenger Decks:	14
Total Crew:	822
Pass. Capacity (basis 2):	2,350
Pass. Capacity (all berths):	2,744
Pass. Space Ratio (basis 2):	31.4
Pass. Space Ratio (all berths):	26.9
Officers:	Norwegian
Total Cabins:	1,175
Size Range (sq ft/m):	118.4–446.7/11.0–41.5
Cabins (outside view):	732
Cabins (inside — no view):	443
Cabins (single occupancy):	0
Cabins (with private balcony):	62
Cabins (wheelchair accessible):	4
Cabin Current:	110 volts
Cabin TV:	Yes
Dining Rooms:	2
Elevators:	11
Casino:	Yes
Slot Machines:	Yes
Swimming Pools (outdoors):	2
Swimming Pools (inside):	0
Whirlpools:	2
Fitness Center:	Yes
Sauna/Steam Room:	Yes/No
Massage:	Yes
Self-Service Launderette:	No
Movie Theater/Seats:	Yes/200
Library:	Yes
Classification Society:	Det Norske Veritas

RATINGS	POSSIBLE SCORE	SCORE ACHIEVED
Ship	500	381
Accommodation	200	141
Food	400	245
Service	400	286
Cruise	500	341
TOTAL	**2,000**	**1,394**

Accommodation: Except for a few suites, all other cabins are small (particularly by today's standards) – simply because the company's policy has always been one of getting passengers out into the public areas. They are quite attractively decorated in a basic way, but the bathrooms are small and utilitarian. The cabin space is the weak point of a cruise aboard this ship. Special "family suites," located amidships, sleep four.

Dining: The two musical-themed dining rooms are large, attractive, and colorful (sadly, there are no tables for two). There are two seatings. The dining operation is well orchestrated, with emphasis on highly pro-grammed (insensitive), extremely hurried service.

The food is consistently average and certainly not memorable. Features French, Oriental, Italian, Caribbean, and American theme nights, with waiters/busboys in appropriate costumes. There is a reason-ably extensive wine list. The staff is overly friendly, even intrusive.

Other Comments: Royal Caribbean International's trademark Viking Crown lounge and bar surrounds the funnel and provides a stunning view. The open deck space is very cramped when full, as aboard any large ship, although there seems to be plenty of it. There is a basketball court for sports lovers.

This ship has a spacious, well-designed interior, with excellent deck plans and signs. A beautiful, well-stocked library adds a touch of class. The five-deck-high Centrum is the focal point of a large atrium lobby, and there are two glass-walled elevators. The entertainment program is very good, and includes good children's/teens' programs and cheerful youth counselors.

This is basically a well run, fine-tuned, highly programmed cruise product geared particularly to those seeking an action-packed cruise vacation in seven days, at a moderately good price, with around 2,500 fellow passengers.

Weak Points: There are too many loud, intrusive announcements. The officers, junior officers, and staff often forget that hospitality is the key to happy passengers.

s/y Mandalay
(S)

LIFESTYLE	STANDARD
Cruise Line:	Windjammer Barefoot Cruises
Former Names:	*Vema, Hussar*
Gross Tonnage:	420
Builder:	Cox & Stevens (UK)
Entered Service:	1923/1982
Flag:	Equitorial Guinea
Tel No:	n/a
Fax No:	n/a
Length (ft/m):	236.0/71.9
Beam (ft/m):	33.0/10.0
Draft (ft/m):	15.0/4.5
Type of Vessel:	barquentine
No. of Masts:	3
Sail Area (sq.ft/sq.m):	12,002.1/1,114.8
Main Propulsion:	sail power
Propulsion/Propellers:	diesel/1 (FP)
Decks:	3
Total Crew:	36
Pass. Capacity (basis 2):	72
Pass. Capacity (all berths):	72
Pass. Space Ratio (basis 2):	10.0
Pass. Space Ratio (all berths):	5.8
Officers:	International
Total Cabins:	36
Size Range (sq ft/m):	65.0 – 100.1/6.0 – 9.3
Cabins (outside view):	36
Cabins (inside - no view):	6
Cabins (single occupancy):	0
Cabins (with private balcony):	2
Cabins (wheelchair accessible):	0
Cabin Current:	110 volts
Cabin TV:	No
Full-Service Dining Rooms:	1
Elevators:	0
Casino:	No
Slot Machines:	No
Swimming Pools (outdoors):	0
Whirlpools:	0
Fitness Center:	No
Sauna/Steam Room:	No/No
Massage:	No
Self-Service Launderette:	No
Library:	Yes
Classification Society:	none

RATINGS	POSSIBLE SCORE	SCORE ACHIEVED
Ship	500	NYR
Accommodation	200	NYR
Food	400	NYR
Service	400	NYR
Cruise	500	NYR
TOTAL	**2,000**	**NYR**
Expected Score Range:		**900-1100**

Originally built for the American financier E. F. Hutton, she was then sold to shipping magnate George Vettelman. She was acquired by Windjammer Barefoot Cruise in 1982. Sails from Antigua and Grenada. For other comments regarding Windjammer Barefoot Cruises, see *Flying Cloud*.

m/v Marco Polo
★★★★
(M)

LIFESTYLE:	PREMIUM
Cruise Line:	Orient Lines
Former Names:	*Aleksandr Pushkin*
Gross Tonnage:	20,502
Builder:	VEB Mathias-Thesen Werft (Germany)
Original Cost:	n/a
Entered Service:	April 1966/November 1993
Flag:	Bahamas
Tel. No.:	630869310
Fax No.:	1306216
Length (ft/m):	578.4/176.28
Beam (ft/m):	77.4/23.60
Draft (ft/m):	26.8/8.17
Propulsion/Propellers:	diesel (14,444kW)/2 (CP)
Passenger Decks:	8
Total Crew:	356
Pass. Capacity (basis 2):	848
Pass. Capacity (all berths):	915
Pass. Space Ratio (basis 2):	24.1
Pass. Space Ratio (all berths):	22.4
Officers:	European
Total Cabins:	425
Size Range (sq ft/m):	93.0–484.0/8.6–44.9
Cabins (outside view):	294
Cabins (inside — no view):	133
Cabins (single occupancy):	2 (many doubles sold for single occupancy)

Cabins (with private balcony):	0
Cabins (wheelchair accessible):	2
Cabin Current:	110 and 220 volts
Cabin TV:	Yes
Dining Rooms:	2
Elevators:	4
Casino:	Yes
Slot Machines:	Yes
Swimming Pools (outdoors):	1
Swimming Pools (inside):	0
Whirlpools:	3
Fitness Center:	Yes
Sauna/Steam Room:	Yes/No
Massage:	Yes
Self-Service Launderette:	No
Movie Theater/Seats:	No
Library:	Yes
Classification Society:	Bureau Veritas

RATINGS	POSSIBLE SCORE	SCORE ACHIEVED
Ship	500	390
Accommodation	200	144
Food	400	321
Service	400	315
Cruise	500	353
TOTAL	**2,000**	**1,523**

Accommodation: The cabins, which come in a profusion of different sizes and configurations, are pleasantly decorated and adequate in size, but nothing special, except for some rich wood accenting. Occupants of upper-grade cabins also get slippers and bathrobe. The weak point of each cabin is its bathroom, which is very small, with little space for anything, although they do have hairdryers. Although cabin furnishings and details are not the high point of this ship, the overall effect is quite cheerful. Note that some Upper Deck and Sky Deck cabins have lifeboat-obstructed views. There should be (but there isn't) 24-hour room service, particularly in light of the fact that many passengers are of senior years.

Dining: The main dining room is nicely decorated, is practical in design, and functions well, but it is noisy, and the tables are very close together. There are two seatings. There are tables for two to ten, and fine place settings and china. The food itself is of a very high standard, with good presentation. The wine list is very limited.

Raffles is the place for informal breakfasts and lunches. On assorted evenings each cruise it also becomes an alternative dining spot, for about 75 persons; reservations are required, but there is no extra charge.

Other Comments: Originally constructed as one of five almost identical sister ships for the Russian/Ukrainian fleet, this vessel has a fine "real-ship" profile, a strong ice-strengthened hull, and huge storage spaces for long voyages. After being completely refitted and refurbished, she now features well-designed, destination-intensive cruises, at very realistic prices. She is fitted with the latest navigational aids and biological waste treatment center, and carries ten Zodiac landing craft for in-depth shore trips in eco-sensitive areas. This is a very comfortable vessel throughout and she rides well. There is a helicopter landing pad atop the ship.

There is a wide range of public rooms, and a sense of spaciousness pervades, as most have high ceilings. Features very tasteful interior decor, with careful use of mirrored surfaces, and colors that do not clash but are relaxing without being boring.

This ship features well-planned destination-intensive cruises, and offers extremely fine value for money in very comfortable, elegant but unpretentious surroundings and a friendly and accommodating Filipino crew help make a cruise aboard her a very pleasant experience. A 10 percent gratuity is added to all bar and wine accounts. *Marco Polo* was purchased by Norwegian Cruise Line in May 1998, but continues to operate under the Orient Lines brand name.

Weak Points: There are not enough elevators. Expect lines for the small shore tenders, when operated at anchor ports.

COMMUNICATIONS

Most ships now have a direct-dial satellite telephone system. In addition, all ships are given an internationally recognized call sign, made up of a combination of several letters and digits. When the ship is at sea, you can call from your cabin (or the ship's radio room) to anywhere in the world:

➜ via radiotelephone (a slight/moderate background noise might be noticed);

➜ via satellite (which will be as clear as your own home phone).

Direct dial satellite calls (this service started in 1986) are more expensive, but are completed instantly. Some ships also have credit card telephones located in public areas; these also connect instantly, via satellite. Satellite calls can also be made when the ship is in port (radiotelephone calls cannot). Satellite telephone calls cost between $5 and $15 per minute, depending on the type of communications equipment the ship carries (the latest systems are digital). Calls are charged to your onboard account.

Your relatives and friends can reach you by calling the *High Seas Operator* in most countries (in the United States, dial 1-800-SEA-CALL). The operator will need the name of the ship, together with the ocean code (Atlantic is 871; Pacific is 872; and the Indian Ocean is 873).

t/s Maxim Gorkiy
★★★ +
(M)

LIFESTYLE:	STANDARD
Cruise Line:	Phoenix Seereisen
Former Names:	*Hanseatic, Hamburg*
Gross Tonnage:	24,981
Builder:	Howaldtswerke Deutsche Werft (Germany)
Original Cost:	£5.6 million
Entered Service:	March 1969/January 1974
Flag:	Bahamas
Tel. No.:	1305670/1402204
Fax No.:	1305671/1402205
Length (ft/m):	638.8/194.72
Beam (ft/m):	87.3/26.62
Draft (ft/m):	27.0/8.25
Propulsion/Propellers:	steam turbine (16,900kW)/2 (FP)
Passenger Decks:	10
Total Crew:	340
Pass. Capacity (basis 2):	650
Pass. Capacity (all berths):	788
Pass. Space Ratio (basis 2):	38.4
Pass. Space Ratio (all berths):	31.7
Officers:	Russian/Ukrainian
Total Cabins:	326
Size Range (sq ft/m):	145.3–296.0/13.5–27.0
Cabins (outside view):	210
Cabins (inside — no view):	116
Cabins (single occupancy):	2

Cabins (with private balcony):	0
Cabins (wheelchair accessible):	0
Cabin Current:	220 volts
Cabin TV:	Yes
Dining Rooms:	3
Elevators:	4
Casino:	No
Slot Machines:	No
Swimming Pools (outdoors):	1
Swimming Pools (inside):	1
Whirlpools:	0
Fitness Center:	Yes
Sauna/Steam Room:	Yes/No
Massage:	Yes
Self-Service Launderette:	Yes
Movie Theater/Seats:	Yes/290
Library:	Yes
Classification Society:	Det Norske Veritas

RATINGS	POSSIBLE SCORE	SCORE ACHIEVED
Ship	500	334
Accommodation	200	137
Food	400	288
Service	400	299
Cruise	500	327
TOTAL	**2,000**	**1,385**

Accommodation: There are 18 cabin categories. Most cabins are generally quite spacious. Many cabins have wood paneling and trim and comfortable decor. The bathrooms are large and have full-sized bath-tubs in all except 20 cabins; there is plenty of room for toiletries. The deluxe cabins are very good, come fully equipped, and have huge picture windows, while most others have portholes. In-cabin Russian and German satellite TV programs.

Anyone booking a suite or one of the top five grades receives Phoenix VIP service, which includes flowers for the cabin, a separate check-in desk, and priority disembarkation.

Dining: There are three restaurants (all are one seating, with assigned tables), and all three are located low down in the ship, but they are cheerfully decorated, and were modernised during a 1993 refurbishment. There is always excellent lager on draught. Moderately decent food is served, and wine at lunch and din-ner is included in the cruise fare, but more choice, and better presentation would be welcome.

The service is quite attentive and courteous from the well-meaning staff, although it is somewhat hur-ried even though there is only one seating for all meals. Cushions would be a welcome addition to some of the banquette seating.

Other Comments: This all-white ship was originally built for the transatlantic service of the now defunct Deutsche Atlantik Linie, and has long, pleasing lines and outer styling. The ship is easily identified by its platform-topped funnel, which is designed to disperse smoke away from the aft, tiered, open decks. Generally well maintained, with more facilities added during the last refurbishment. There is a generous amount of open deck and sunbathing space, and deck lounge chairs have cushioned pads. Open deck sports include a large basketball court aft of the funnel.

Inside, there are some handsome, well-designed public rooms, and passenger flow is good. A gener-ous amount of wood paneling was used in her construction — most of it still looks good, although some refinishing is needed in some areas. The decor is dark and somewhat dull, although it is quite relaxing and soporific. The show lounge, an important room, is decent enough, although it does not have enough seating; the stage and lighting facilities could also be improved. The gymnasium is small, and much of the equipment needs updating. There are two relaxing winter gardens with large ocean-view windows. One nice facility is the indoor swimming pool — always good for those times when the outdoor pool can't be used because of inclement weather.

Maxim Gorkiy will provide a very good cruise experience in comfortable, quite elegant, but very traditional surroundings, at a modest price, although you should remember that this is an older ship that does not have the latest in facilities. Particularly targeted to German-speaking passengers who appreciate good value and well-planned, destination-intensive itineraries. The friendly, attentive service staff is Russian and Ukrainain. Port taxes, insurance, and gratuities are included.

Phoenix Seereisen has, over the years, attained almost a cult status among her passengers, in that the company provides a consistently fine, very popular product for those seeking a casual cruise experience and lifestyle among friendly passengers who enjoy life. Where passengers are required to fly to join their cruises, the airline most used by Phoenix Seereisen is LTU. The currency on board is the deutschmark.

m/v Melody
★★★ +
(L)

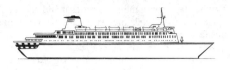

LIFESTYLE:	STANDARD
Cruise Line:	Mediterranean Shipping Cruises
Former Names:	*Star/Ship Atlantic, Atlantic*
Gross Tonnage:	36,500
Builder:	C.N.I.M. (France)
Original Cost:	$100 million
Entered Service:	April 1982/June 1997
Flag:	Panama
Tel. No.:	335315710/635315710
Fax No.:	335315712/635315713
Length (ft/m):	671.9/204.81
Beam (ft/m):	89.7/27.36
Draft (ft/m):	25.5/7.80
Propulsion/Propellers:	diesel (22,070kW)/2 (CP)
Passenger Decks:	9
Total Crew:	535
Pass. Capacity (basis 2):	1,076
Pass. Capacity (all berths):	1,600
Pass. Space Ratio (basis 2):	33.9
Pass. Space Ratio (all berths):	22.8
Officers:	Italian
Total Cabins:	549
Size Range (sq ft/m):	137.0–427.0/12.7–39.5
Cabins (outside view):	392
Cabins (inside — no view):	157
Cabins (single occupancy):	0
Cabins (with private balcony):	0

Cabins (wheelchair accessible):	Yes
Cabin Current:	110 volts
Cabin TV:	Yes
Dining Rooms:	1
Elevators:	4
Casino:	Yes
Slot Machines:	Yes
Swimming Pools (outdoors):	1
Swimming Pools (inside):	1
Whirlpools:	3
Fitness Center:	Yes
Sauna/Steam Room:	Yes/No
Massage:	Yes
Self-Service Launderette:	No
Movie Theater/Seats:	Yes/227
Library:	Yes (2 book racks)
Classification Society:	American Bureau of Shipping

RATINGS	POSSIBLE SCORE	SCORE ACHIEVED
Ship	500	354
Accommodation	200	150
Food	400	215
Service	400	241
Cruise	500	299
TOTAL	**2,000**	**1,259**

Accommodation: Six suites have plenty of space for families of four and feature a decent walk-in closet. The bathroom is large and has a full-size bathtub, oversize sink (large enough to bathe twins in), and an uncomfortable square toilet.

Other cabins (both outside and inside) are of a good size, and have ample closet and drawer space. Many cabins have upper berths — good for families, although with four persons there would be little space for anything else, such as luggage. The cabin insulation is extremely poor, however (you can hear your neighbors brushing their hair), and the room service menu is quite basic.

Dining: The dining room, located on a lower deck, is large and quite attractive, but the tables are much too close together, and it is difficult for waiters to serve properly. Also, the chairs do not have armrests, and the noise level is extremely high. There are two seatings, and the cuisine is Italian-continental. The food quality generally is adequate for the price paid, but dishes, when presented, are not as good as the menu description would have you believe. There is a limited wine list. Service is provided by an attentive multi-national staff, although there it needs polishing. The buffets are quite poor when compared to many other ships in this standard category.

Other Comments: This ship (originally built for the now defunct Home Lines, then operated by Premier Cruise Lines) has a short, stubby bow and squat funnel. Her hull is all in white.

There is a good amount of outdoor deck space, but noise levels can be high when the ship is full, and there are many families with children.

The interior is quite spacious, with plenty of public rooms, most of which have high ceilings. The decor is somewhat somber in places, and lighting is very subdued. There is a generous amount of stainless steel and teak wood trim. A large observation lounge is wasted as an informal eating area. There is a good indoor-outdoor pool area (covered by a magrodome in inclement weather).

For families, there is a fairly good children's program during the peak periods, and several children's (and teen's) counselors. In any event, this ship (the largest in the MSC fleet so far) will provide a good basic cruise experience for families, at a fair price, in comfortable, modern surroundings, in typical MSC style, and that means lots of extra charges. Typically about 60 percent of passengers will be Italian, while the rest may be a mix of other Europeans.

Weak Points: The almost constant, loud, and repetitive announcements are annoying and intrusive, particularly when the ship is in port. There is no wraparound promenade deck outdoors, nor are cushioned pads provided for the deck lounge chairs. Just four elevators for this number of passengers is simply not enough.

Useful Expressions in Italian

Good morning/ Good afternoon.	**Buon giorno.**	bwon **joar**noa
Please ...	**Per favore ...**	pair fah**voa**ray
Thank you.	**Grazie.**	**graa**tseeay
Yes/No.	**Sì/No.**	see/no
Excuse me.	**Mi scusi.**	mee **skoo**zee
Do you speak English?	**Parla inglese?**	**pahr**lah eeng**glay**say
Where is ...?	**Dov'è ...?**	doa**vai**
How far?	**Quanto dista?**	**kwahn**toa **dee**stah
How long?	**Quanto tempo?**	**kwahn**toa **tehm**poa
How much is it?	**Quant'è?**	kwahn**tai**
Waiter/ Waitress!	**Cameriere/ Cameriera!**	kahmayree**air**ay/ kahmayree**air**ah
I don't understand.	**Non capisco.**	noan kah**pee**skoa
When does ... open/close?	**Quando apre/ chiude ...?**	**kwahn**doa **ah**pray/ kee**oo**day
What time is it?	**Che ore sono?**	kay **oa**ray **soa**noa
Where are the toilets?	**Dove sono i gabinetti?**	**doa**vay **soa**noa ee gahbee**neht**tee
Help me, please.	**Mi aiuti, per favore.**	mee ahee**oo**tee pair fah**voa**ray
I'd like ...	**Vorrei ...**	vor**rai**ee

m/s Mercury
★★★★ +
(L)

LIFESTYLE:	PREMIUM
Cruise Line:	Celebrity Cruises
Former Names:	-
Gross Tonnage:	77,713
Builder:	Meyer Werft (Germany)
Original Cost:	$320 million
Entered Service:	November 1997
Flag:	Liberia
Tel. No.:	335151711/335151721
Fax No.:	335151712/335151722
Length (ft/m):	865.8/263.90
Beam (ft/m):	105.6/32.20
Draft (ft/m):	25.2/7.70 (24.2/7.40)
Propulsion/Propellers:	diesel (31,500kW)/2 (CP)
Passenger Decks:	10
Total Crew:	909
Pass. Capacity (basis 2):	1,870
Pass. Capacity (all berths):	2,681
Pass. Space Ratio (basis 2):	41.5
Pass. Space Ratio (all berths):	28.9
Officers:	Greek
Total Cabins:	948 (954)
Size Range (sq ft/m):	171.0–1,514.5/15.8–140.7
Cabins (outside view):	639 (650)
Cabins (inside — no view):	296
Cabins (single occupancy):	0
Cabins (with private balcony):	220

Cabins (wheelchair accessible):	8
Cabin Current:	110 and 220 volts
Cabin TV:	Yes
Dining Rooms:	2
Elevators:	10
Casino:	Yes
Slot Machines:	Yes
Swimming Pools (outdoors):	2
Swimming Pools (inside):	1 indoor/outdoor (magrodome)
Whirlpools:	4
Fitness Center:	Yes
Sauna/Steam Room:	Yes
Massage:	Yes
Self-Service Launderette:	No
Movie Theater/Seats:	Yes/183
Library:	Yes
Classification Society:	Lloyd's Register

RATINGS	POSSIBLE SCORE	SCORE ACHIEVED
Ship	500	454
Accommodation	200	182
Food	400	321
Service	400	325
Cruise	500	415
TOTAL	**2,000**	**1,697**

Accommodation: The accommodation is extremely comfortable throughout this ship, regardless of which cabin grade you choose. Naturally, if you choose a suite you will find more space, butler service (whether you want it or not), more and better amenities, and more personal service than if you choose any of the standard cabin grades.

Occupants of all accommodation designated as suites (Decks 10 and 12) get gold cards to open their doors (and priority service throughout the ship, free cappuccino/espresso coffees served by a butler, welcome champagne, flowers, a VCR unit, and use of the AquaSpa thalassotherapy pool). All occupants of standard (inside and outside) cabins have white cards. Suites that have private balconies also have floor-to-ceiling windows and sliding doors to balconies (a few suites have outward opening doors).

There are two Presidential Suites, located amidships. These provide spectacular living spaces, perhaps even better than those in *Century* and *Galaxy*, depending on your personal taste. There is a separate bedroom (with high-tech Sony multimedia entertainment center), large lounge (complete with dining table), huge walk-in closet with mountains of drawers, and king-sized marble-tiled bathroom.

There is in-suite dining for the two Presidential and 12 Century Suites, as well as for the 24 Sky Suites (1202/1203/1236/1237 have enormous fully private balconies, while the others are only semi-private). All suites feature full butler service, personalized stationery, and business cards. If you choose one of the forwardmost Sky Deck suites, however, be warned that you may well be subject to constant music and noise from the pool deck (one deck below) between 8am and 6:00 pm (not good if you want to relax). The closet and drawer space provided in these suites is superb. In the bathrooms of the Sky Suites, the shaving mirror is positioned too high, and the television cannot be viewed from the bed. Push-button bell and privacy curtains should be, but are not, provided. In-suite massage is available (this really is pleasant when provided on the balcony of the Sky Suites).

The standard (inside and outside) cabins are quite spacious and nicely decorated with cheerful fabrics and marble-topped vanity unit. The bathrooms are generous with space and tiled from floor to ceiling, and the power showers are extremely practical units.

All cabins feature interactive television for booking shore excursions, ordering cabin service items and purchasing goods from the ship's boutiques, so you do not have to leave your quarters if you do not wish to, especially if you do not like the ports of call. The system works in English, French, German, Italian, and Spanish. There are five channels of music, all available from the television; therefore, you cannot have music without having a picture). All cabins are also equipped with a "baby monitoring telephone system" which allows you to telephone your cabin while you are elsewhere aboard ship, and to have a two-way intercom to "listen in." Automatic "wake-up" calls can also be dialed in. All accommodation designated as suites have duvets on the beds instead of sheets/blankets.

Dining: The two-level formal dining room, located at the ship's stern, is really grand and elegant (each level has its own full galley); a grand staircase connects the two levels. Large picture windows look out to sea on three sides; at night, large blinds (with scenes of Manhattan, the name of the dining room) roll down electronically to cover the stern-facing windows. There are two seatings. The same excellent cuisine that has made Celebrity Cruises the shining star of the contemporary cruise industry is directed by three-star Michelin chef, Michel Roux. The menus are creative, and the food is very attractively presented. There is also an excellent wine list, and real wine waiters (unlike so many other large ship companies), although prices are high (particularly for good champagne), and the wine vintages are young — very young.

There are also several informal dining spots as an alternative to the main dining room: a Lido Café, with four main serving lines; a poolside grill, and another indoor/outdoor grill located b the aft swimming pool. The Lido Cafe has fine wood paneling and is much more elegant than the informal dining areas found aboard most ships today and has some seating in bay window areas with great ocean views.

In the center of the ship is Tastings, a delightful coffee/tea lounge; in one corner is a presentation of goodies made by COVA, the chocolatier from Milan — an exclusive to Celebrity Cruises.

Finally, for those that cannot live without them, freshly baked pizzas (in a box) can be ordered and delivered, in an insulated pouch, to your cabin.

Other Comments: She is quite a stunning ship, both inside and outside. As aboard her identical sister *Galaxy*, there is a 1,000-seat show lounge, with side balconies, and no pillars to obstruct views (there are three high-tech "dazzle and sizzle" production shows per seven-night cruise, although they consist mainly of running, jumping, smoke, colored laser lighting, and little story line intelligence). Other facilities include a three-deck-high main foyer with marble floored lobby and waterfall; over 4.5 acres of open deck space (poolside lounge chairs have cushioned pads, those on other decks do not); a magrodome-covered indoor-outdoor pool; AquaSpa thalassotherapy pool (with several "active" water jet stations), and assorted treatment rooms, including a "rasul" mud treatment room. There is also "Michael's Club," a cigar/cognac room that overlooks the atrium; a small but luxurious cinema; and a large casino (extremely glitzy, with confusing and congested layout). The children's facilities are good (open until 10:00pm, it is called the "Fun Factory") as well as an outdoor play area and paddling pool.

The decor includes plenty of wood (or wood-look) paneling and accenting throughout, and many refinements have been made during the three-ship "Century Series" that Celebrity Cruises has introduced in the past few years. The ship also houses a $3.5-million living art collection with true, museum-quality pieces. The health/fitness facilities are among the nicest aboard any ship and have been well thought out and designed for quiet, efficient operation, with everything in just the right place.

This ship will provide you with a finely packaged cruise vacation in elegant surroundings. The ship is efficiently run. There are many more staff per passengers than would be found aboard other ships of the same size in the premium category, and hence service in general is very good indeed.

Weak Points: Getting Cabin Service or the Guest Relations Desk to answer the phone (to order breakfast, for example, if you don't want to do so via the interactive television) is a matter of luck, timing, and patience (a sad reminder of the automated age and lack of personal contact). The library is disappointingly small and poorly located away from the main flow of passengers. There is a charge for using the Aquaspa/sauna/steam room complex. The room-service menu is poor, and food items are decidedly below the standard of food featured in the dining room.

While under the direction of its former owner John Chandris, Celebrity Cruises managed to create a superb quality cruise vacation product virtually unbeatable at the prices charged in the Alaska and Caribbean markets, representing outstanding value for money. However, given the subtle changes that have occurred since Celebrity Cruises was integrated into the Royal Caribbean International family in late 1997, it has become evident that slippage of product delivery standards and staff have occurred, and the latest score reflects these changes.

m/s Mermoz
★★
(M)

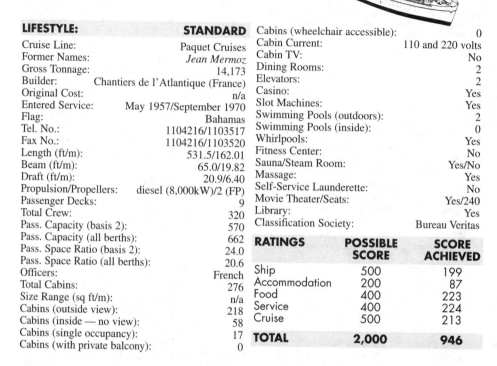

LIFESTYLE:	STANDARD
Cruise Line:	Paquet Cruises
Former Names:	*Jean Mermoz*
Gross Tonnage:	14,173
Builder:	Chantiers de l'Atlantique (France)
Original Cost:	n/a
Entered Service:	May 1957/September 1970
Flag:	Bahamas
Tel. No.:	1104216/1103517
Fax No.:	1104216/1103520
Length (ft/m):	531.5/162.01
Beam (ft/m):	65.0/19.82
Draft (ft/m):	20.9/6.40
Propulsion/Propellers:	diesel (8,000kW)/2 (FP)
Passenger Decks:	9
Total Crew:	320
Pass. Capacity (basis 2):	570
Pass. Capacity (all berths):	662
Pass. Space Ratio (basis 2):	24.0
Pass. Space Ratio (all berths):	20.6
Officers:	French
Total Cabins:	276
Size Range (sq ft/m):	n/a
Cabins (outside view):	218
Cabins (inside — no view):	58
Cabins (single occupancy):	17
Cabins (with private balcony):	0

Cabins (wheelchair accessible):	0
Cabin Current:	110 and 220 volts
Cabin TV:	No
Dining Rooms:	2
Elevators:	2
Casino:	Yes
Slot Machines:	Yes
Swimming Pools (outdoors):	2
Swimming Pools (inside):	0
Whirlpools:	Yes
Fitness Center:	No
Sauna/Steam Room:	Yes/No
Massage:	Yes
Self-Service Launderette:	No
Movie Theater/Seats:	Yes/240
Library:	Yes
Classification Society:	Bureau Veritas

RATINGS	POSSIBLE SCORE	SCORE ACHIEVED
Ship	500	199
Accommodation	200	87
Food	400	223
Service	400	224
Cruise	500	213
TOTAL	**2,000**	**946**

Accommodation: The cabins are quite small and only equipped with basic facilities, but they are tastefully furnished, cozy, and quite comfortable, with solid fixtures and lots of wood everywhere. All cabins have only lower beds. There is a fair amount of closet and drawer space, but the cabin bathrooms are very small (and there is little room for storage of toiletry items). Bathrobes are provided for all passengers.

Dining: The cuisine has changed a little since its Paquet Cruises days (pre-1994). One seating is featured, with assigned tables. There is a fine Grill (Renaissance Grill), with wicker furniture, as well as the regular dining room (Massalia — named after one of Paquet Cruises' former ships). The food is creatively presented. Wine is complimentary with dinner. The wine cellar is extensive and contains many thousands of bottles.

Other Comments: The ship has traditional 1950s lines and a now very dated profile. There is a reasonable amount of open deck and sunbathing space, however, for sun-loving French passengers.

Has somewhat chic art deco-style interior decor that is rather eclectic, with a pastel color scheme and a "colonial" ambience. Typically French in atmosphere and service. The spa and solarium are good spaces, with a main emphasis on hydrotherapy treatments.

The annual Classical Music Festival At Sea is a popular cultural delight for classical music and opera buffs. Much of the artwork and ship models are of interest to ship lovers.

This ship has a fine, perhaps somewhat eclectic French character, and is for those who enjoy being aboard an older ship, with all its quirks and idiosyncracies, albeit for a moderate price. The dress code is casual during the day, but dressy at night. *Mermoz* is getting a bit long in the tooth and should be replaced. However, she is still one of the only French-flag ships still in operation, so French passengers continue to sail aboard her. The currency on board is French francs.

<u>Weak Points</u>: There is no forward observation lounge. She is tired and worn out, and should be replaced.

ms Millennium
(L)

LIFESTYLE:	PREMIUM
Cruise Line:	Celebrity Cruises
Former Names:	-
Gross Tonnage:	91,000
Builder:	Chantiers de l'Atlantique (France)
Original Cost:	$350 million
Entered Service:	June 2000
Flag:	Liberia
Tel No:	n/a
Fax No:	n/a
Length (ft/m):	964.5/294.0
Beam (ft/m):	105.6/32.2
Draft (ft/m):	26.2/8.0
Propulsion/Propellers:	gas turbine/
	2 azimuthing pods (39,000kW)
Passenger Decks:	11
Total Crew:	999
Pass. Capacity (basis 2):	1,950
Pass. Capacity (all berths):	2,450
Pass. Space Ratio (basis 2):	46.6
Pass. Space Ratio (all berths):	37.1
Officers:	Greek
Total Cabins:	975
Size Range (sq ft/m):	165.1–1,637.2/15.34–152.1
Cabins (outside view):	780
Cabins (inside - no view):	195
Cabins (single occupancy):	0
Cabins (with private balcony):	590

Cabins (wheelchair accessible):	26 (17 with private balcony)
Cabin Current:	110 and 220 volts
Cabin TV:	Yes
Dining Rooms:	1 main, 1 specialty
Elevators:	10
Casino:	Yes
Slot Machines:	Yes
Swimming Pools (outdoors):	2
Swimming Pools (inside):	1 (with magrodome)
Whirlpools:	4
Fitness Center:	Yes
Sauna/Steam Room:	Yes/Yes
Massage:	Yes
Self-Service Launderette:	No
Movie Theater/Seats:	Yes/368
Library:	Yes
Classification Society:	Lloyd's Register

RATINGS	POSSIBLE SCORE	SCORE ACHIEVED
Ship	500	NYR
Accommodation	200	NYR
Food	400	NYR
Service	400	NYR
Cruise	500	NYR
TOTAL	**2,000**	**NYR**
Expected Score Range:		**1600-1800**

Accommodation: Almost half of the ship's cabins have a "private" balcony. There are several types of suites, but those at the stern of the ship have huge private balconies that are not overlooked from above. Suites on different decks overhang the starboard side of the ship (opposite a group of glass-walled elevators), providing stunning ocean views.

Dining: The main dining room is two decks high and has a grand staircase to connect the two levels, each of which has its own galley. There are two seatings. A specialty restaurant is also available, adjacent to the conference center. However, with only 180 seats, not all passengers will be able to experience it even once during a cruise. As with Celebrity Cruises' other ships, there are several dining options, particularly for those seeking more casual eateries. Full-service in-cabin dining is also available.

Other Comments: This ship is a slightly enlarged and elongated version of the company's successful trio *Century, Galaxy,* and *Mercury.* Jon Bannenberg designed the exterior, which displays racy lines that include her royal blue and white hull. This is the first Celebrity Cruises ship to be fitted with a "pod" propulsion system, coupled with a gas turbine powerplant.

Inside the ship, you can expect the same high-class decor and public rooms that have made other ships in the fleet so popular and user-friendly.

A group of four glass elevators travel through the port side of the atrium.

m/v Minerva
★★★★ +
(S)

LIFESTYLE:	PREMIUM
Cruise Line:	Swan Hellenic Cruises
Former Names:	-
Gross Tonnage:	12,500
Builder:	Marriotti (Italy)
Original Cost:	n/a
Entered Service:	April 1996
Flag:	Bahamas
Tel. No.:	630947710
Fax No.:	330947711
Length (ft/m):	436.3/133.0
Beam (ft/m):	65.6/20.0
Draft (ft/m):	19.6/6.0
Propulsion/Propellers:	2 x diesels (3,480kW)/2 (CP)
Passenger Decks:	6
Total Crew:	157
Pass. Capacity (basis 2):	356
Pass. Capacity (all berths):	474
Pass. Space Ratio (basis 2):	35.1
Pass. Space Ratio (all berths):	26.3
Officers:	European
Total Cabins:	178
Size Range (sq ft/m):	140.1–277.0/13.02–25.74
Cabins (outside view):	126
Cabins (inside — no view):	52
Cabins (single occupancy):	4
Cabins (with private balcony):	12

Cabins (wheelchair accessible):	4
Cabin Current:	220 volts
Cabin TV:	Yes
Dining Rooms:	1
Elevators:	2
Casino:	No
Slot Machines:	No
Swimming Pools (outdoors):	1
Swimming Pools (inside):	0
Whirlpools:	0
Fitness Center:	Yes
Sauna/Steam Room:	Yes/No
Massage:	Yes
Self-Service Launderette:	Yes
Movie Theater/Seats:	Yes/96
Library:	Yes
Classification Society:	Registro Navale Italiano

RATINGS	POSSIBLE SCORE	SCORE ACHIEVED
Ship	500	429
Accommodation	200	165
Food	400	306
Service	400	303
Cruise	500	391
TOTAL	**2,000**	**1,594**

Accommodation: The range of accommodation is well thought out and all have excellent closet and storage space, a television and a VCR; the suites and deluxe cabins also feature a refrigerator. The cabin bathrooms are totally white and have showers (except for the suites, which have bathtubs and green/black marble floors), but the plumbing fixtures were poorly installed. Cabin electrical sockets are of the standard English, square, three-pin type. Hairdryers are provided in all suites and are available on request in all other cabins. All suite occupants are provided with high-powered binoculars. However, there is no "privacy curtain" between entryway and sleeping area in the suites.

Dining: Features open seating dining (dine with whomever you wish) in both the main restaurant and the informal indoor/outdoor cafe. The menus are quite simple, but the food is attractively presented and has good taste. Dining room service is provided by East European and Filipino crew members. Some "quiet tables" are provided for breakfast for those who like to eat without talking — a welcome touch. Coffee and tea are available 24 hours a day in the self-service Bridge Cafe.

Other Comments: Originally intended to be a spy ship for the Soviet navy, the keel was purchased by V-Ships (the ship's resent owners), who then took the hull to Italy, where she was converted into a ship specifically tailored to the requirements of Swan Hellenic Cruises as charterer. She replaced *Orpheus*, which Swan Hellenic had chartered for the previous 21 years. She has a well-balanced profile, with a single, central funnel. There is ample open and shaded deck space for this size ship, and a teakwood wraparound promenade deck.

Inside, there is an excellent selection of public rooms that includes a vast, well-stocked library, with its classical themed decor. The decor generally is contemporary, yet restrained (for European passengers with good taste). Cigar smokers will appreciate the special smoking room and humidor service; the high-back leather chairs provide an air of exclusivity.

The ship has fine wool carpets throughout, with an Oriental motif running through the passageways and public rooms. Perhaps the most used public room in the ship is the library, with its fine range of reference books (many of university standard). Passengers take delight in playing the multitude of puzzles and games. The reception desk is manned 24 hours a day.

Perhaps the most striking detail of interior decoration is the outstanding array of artwork aboard this ship. It is everywhere, in all passageways, on stairwells, in all public rooms, and cabins (most of it provided by Swan Hellenic passengers, and more is being added all the time). The one disappointment is in the plain white ceilings in the public rooms.

This really is cruising for the intelligent passenger (most of whom are professional people ashore) who yearns to learn more about life and times in civilizations past and present, albeit in a refined, comfortable setting. Features well planned, in-depth itineraries and shore excursions (the majority of which are included in the cruise fare) accompanied by some fine lecturers, and all gratuities and shore excursions are included (these are carried out with almost military precision). Note that this ship is not for children.

m/s Mistral
(L)

LIFESTYLE:	STANDARD
Cruise Line:	Festival Cruises
Former Names:	-
Gross Tonnage:	47,900
Builder:	Chantiers de l'Atlantique (France)
Original Cost:	$245 million
Entered Service:	July 1999
Flag:	Wallis & Fortuna (France)
Tel No:	n/a
Fax No:	n/a
Length (ft/m):	708.6/216.0
Beam (ft/m):	94.6/28.84
Draft (ft/m):	22.4/6.85
Propulsion/Propellers:	diesel-electric (31,680kW)/ 2 (FP)
Passenger Decks:	12
Total Crew:	480
Pass. Capacity (basis 2):	1,196
Pass. Capacity (all berths):	1,715
Pass. Space Ratio (basis 2):	40.0
Pass. Space Ratio (all berths):	27.9
Officers:	European
Total Cabins:	598
Size Range (sq ft/m):	139.9 – 236.8/13.0 – 22.0
Cabins (outside view):	275
Cabins (inside — no view):	223
Cabins (single occupancy):	0
Cabins (with private balcony):	80

Cabins (wheelchair accessible):	2
Cabin Current:	110 and 220 volts
Cabin TV:	Yes
Dining Rooms:	2
Elevators:	6
Casino:	Yes
Slot Machines:	Yes
Swimming Pools (outdoors):	1
Swimming Pools (inside):	0
Whirlpools:	1 (thalassotherapy)
Fitness Center:	Yes
Sauna/Steam Room:	Yes/Yes
Massage:	Yes
Self-Service Launderette:	No
Movie Theater/Seats:	No
Library:	Yes
Classification Society:	Bureau Veritas

RATINGS	POSSIBLE SCORE	SCORE ACHIEVED
Ship	500	NYR
Accommodation	200	NYR
Food	400	NYR
Service	400	NYR
Cruise	500	NYR
TOTAL	**2,000**	**NYR**
Expected Score Range:		**1400-1600**

Accommodation: There are three basic types of cabins in 11 different grades: suites (each of which has a private balcony), ocean-view standard cabins, and inside standard cabins. In addition, there are two inside wheelchair accessible cabins for the handicapped. Good planning means that no outside-view cabins have obstructed views of lifeboats, as aboard many ships today.

All of the cabins feature twin beds that convert to a queen-size unit, bold and colorful bedspreads, a personal safe, a color television/video player combination, a telephone, and a good amount of closet and drawer space for a one-week cruise. The bathrooms, although not large, do have a good-size shower enclosure and decent stowage space for personal toiletry items.

The suites, quite naturally, feature more space, larger closets, more drawers, and better storage space, plus a two-person sofa, a coffee table and an additional armchair, vanity desk, and floor-to-ceiling mirrors.

Dining: There are two dining rooms (and two seatings for meals), which can be configured in any of several different ways. Both have ocean-view windows. The principal dining room (L'Etoile, which seats 600) has round tables for two, four, six, or eight and a small podium complete with baby grand piano. The second dining room (Rialto, which seats 380) is used for both informal meals and as an alternative restaurant (perhaps with one or several "themes") and also has tables for two, four, or six.

The food featured by Festival Cruises is quite sound (it is provided by a separate maritime catering company), and, with varied menus and good presentation, should prove a highlight for most passengers. The wine list features a wide variety of wines at fairly reasonable prices.

In addition, there is a casual cafeteria for informal buffet-style breakfasts and lunches, with ocean-view windows, as well as a pleasant little coffee bar, also with ocean-view windows.

Other Comments: *Mistral* is an all-white ship, with a single blue funnel, and blue and yellow bands to separate hull from superstructure. She is the first brand new for this growing European cruise line, which caters almost exclusively to European passengers, and two more ships of the same type will soon follow.

The company's older *Azur, Bolero,* and *Flamenco* will, more than likely, be positioned for full charters in the future, in order to differentiate the old from the new tonnage.

Mistral is owned by a consortium of French investors and is being operated under long-term charter to Festival Cruises, a vibrant young company that is growing rapidly. She is the largest ship sailing under the French flag (it is actually Wallis & Fortuna, a French possession). The ship's profile is similar to that of most new cruise ships.

The ship is comparable in size to Celebrity Cruises' *Horizon* and *Zenith* and has slightly fewer cabins and, therefore, a better space ratio, which means the ship absorbs passengers well.

The lido deck surrounding the outdoor swimming pool also features whirlpool tubs and a large bandstand is set in raised canvas-covered pods. All the deck lounge chairs have cushioned pads.

Inside, the layout and passenger flow is very good, as are the "you are here" deck signs. The deck names are those of European capitals, the two decks of public rooms being Paris Deck and Rome Deck. The interior decor is light and cheerful without being glitzy in any way (with not even a hint of colored neon) and there is much use of blond wood panelling and rich, textured soft furnishings. The names of public rooms, bars, and lounges are named after European places or establishments.

There is a smoking room, which has all the hallmarks of a gentleman's club of former times, as well as a piano bar. The library has real writing desks (something many ships seem to omit today).

The main show lounge is tiered and has good sight lines from most seats (banquette-style seating is featured), and there is a small balcony level at the rear. There's also a bar/lounge on the lower (main) level at the entrance to the show lounge. High atop the ship is an observation lounge with a twist — it faces aft, instead of forward, a nice change. The room also doubles as a disco for the late-night set. A conference center adds facilities that are good for meetings.

There is also a good-sized spa/beauty complex, set forward of the mast. This includes a fitness center with lots of muscle-toning equipment and lifecycles/life-rowing machines and a view over the bow of the ship through large floor-to-ceiling windows. There are six rooms for massage and other body treatments, as well as a sauna each for men and women, plus an aerobics exercise room. Adjacent is a video game room for teens, as well as a children's center.

The ship operates seven-night Mediterranean cruises from Italy during the summer and fall, and seven-night Caribbean cruises during the winter. As the ship operates in several languages (remember that this means all announcements will be in several languages also), a good number of multilingual cruise staff and reception desk staff are featured at all key points. All prices aboard ship are quoted only in euros, the new common European currency. *Mistral* was built for a European company and constructed by Europeans. The interior design is by Europeans, with European decor and colors, for European passengers, with European food, service, and entertainment. In other words, as the company so strongly states, this is a ship *for Europeans.*

Weak Points: There is no full wrap-around promenade deck outdoors, although there is a partial walking deck on both port and starboard sides under the lifeboats, as well as an oval jogging track atop ship.

m/s Monarch of the Seas
★★★ +
(L)

LIFESTYLE: STANDARD

Cruise Line:	Royal Caribbean International
Former Names:	-
Gross Tonnage:	73,941
Builder:	Chantiers de l'Atlantique
Original Cost:	$300 million
Entered Service:	November 1991
Flag:	Norway
Tel. No.:	1312764
Fax No.:	1312764
Length (ft/m):	879.9/268.2
Beam (ft/m):	105.9/32.30
Draft (ft/m):	24.9/7.60
Propulsion/Propellers:	diesel (21,844kW)/2 (CP)
Passenger Decks:	14
Total Crew:	822
Pass. Capacity (basis 2):	2,354
Pass. Capacity (all berths):	2,744
Pass. Space Ratio (basis 2):	31.0
Pass. Space Ratio (all berths):	26.9
Officers:	Norwegian
Total Cabins:	1,177
Size Range (sq ft/m):	119.4–446.7/11.1–41.5
Cabins (outside view):	732
Cabins (inside — no view):	445
Cabins (single occupancy):	0
Cabins (with private balcony):	62
Cabins (wheelchair accessible):	4
Cabin Current:	110 volts
Cabin TV:	Yes
Dining Rooms:	2
Elevators:	11
Casino:	Yes
Slot Machines:	Yes
Swimming Pools (outdoors):	2
Swimming Pools (inside):	0
Whirlpools:	2
Fitness Center:	Yes
Sauna/Steam Room:	Yes/No
Massage:	Yes
Self-Service Launderette:	No
Movie Theater/Seats:	Yes/200
Library:	Yes
Classification Society:	Det Norske Veritas

RATINGS	POSSIBLE SCORE	SCORE ACHIEVED
Ship	500	381
Accommodation	200	141
Food	400	245
Service	400	286
Cruise	500	341
TOTAL	**2,000**	**1,394**

Accommodation: This ship has small cabins, but the company's philosophy is that you will not spend much time in your cabin. The suites are quite spacious, but most cabins are small, comfortable, and attractively decorated, except for the very plain ceilings. Special "family suites," located amidships, sleep four. The in-cabin food service menu is quite poor (too much standardization).

Dining: The two musical-themed dining rooms are large (sadly, there are no tables for two), but have consistently good, but fast, service and reasonable banquet food (nothing is memorable). There are two seatings. Most nights are themed (French, Oriental, Italian, Caribbean, American), as they have been for years, with waiters and busboys in appropriate costumes. Features dessert parades. The wine list is average.

Other Comments: Almost identical in size and appearance to her sister ship *Sovereign of the Seas* (the first of a trio, the third being *Monarch of the Seas*), but with improved internal layout, public room features, passenger flow, and signs. A basketball court is provided for sports fans.

RCI's trademark Viking Crown lounge and bar surrounds funnel and provides a stunning view. Following grounding (just prior to Christmas 1998), the ship underwent the replacement of 460 tonnes of bottom shell plating. At the same time, a new facility for toddlers was created. The children's and teens' programs are good, overseen by enthusiastic youth counselors, and a busy but sound entertainment program.

There are many public rooms and spaces to play in, including a five-deck-high atrium, which really is the interior focal point of the ship, and glass elevators. There is a fine library.

Monarch of the Seas provides a wide range of facilities, with consistently sound, but highly programmed service from a reasonably attentive, though rather insensitive young staff.

<u>Weak Points</u>: There are too many announcements. Because the public rooms are mostly located aft, there is often a long wait for elevators, particularly at peak times (after dinner, shows).

m/y Monet
★★★ +
(S)

LIFESTYLE:	PREMIUM
Cruise Line:	Leisure Cruises
Former Names:	-
Gross Tonnage:	1,395
Builder:	Brodoremont Shipyard (Croatia)
Original Cost:	n/a
Entered Service:	May 1998
Flag:	Malta
Tel. No.:	n/a
Fax No.:	n/a
Length (ft/m):	223.4/68.1
Beam (ft/m):	33.1/10.1
Draft (ft/m):	11.5/3.5
Propulsion/Propellers:	diesel (1,000kW)/1 (CP)
Passenger Decks:	4
Total Crew:	29
Pass. Capacity (basis 2):	56
Pass. Capacity (all berths):	58
Pass. Space Ratio (basis 2):	24.9
Pass. Space Ratio (all berths):	24.0
Officers:	Croatian
Total Cabins:	30
Size Range (sq ft/m):	92.0–151.0/8.5–14.0
Cabins (outside view):	26
Cabins (inside — no view):	0
Cabins (single occupancy):	4
Cabins (with private balcony):	0

Cabins (wheelchair accessible):	0
Cabin Current:	220 volts
Cabin TV:	Yes
Dining Rooms:	1
Elevators:	0
Casino:	No
Slot Machines:	No
Swimming Pools (outdoors):	1 (splash pool)
Swimming Pools (inside):	0
Whirlpools:	2
Fitness Center:	Yes
Sauna/Steam Room:	No/No
Massage:	No
Self-Service Launderette:	No
Movie Theater/Seats:	No
Library:	Yes
Classification Society:	Bureau Veritas

RATINGS	POSSIBLE SCORE	SCORE ACHIEVED
Ship	500	297
Accommodation	200	108
Food	400	297
Service	400	256
Cruise	500	305
TOTAL	**2,000**	**1,263**

Accommodation: The all-outside cabins come in four size categories. All of them feature hardwood cabinetry and fine soft furnishings, a television and VCR unit, multiple music channels, a telephone, a hairdryer, and a vanity desk with lighted mirror. All have lower beds, in either a twin-bed or double-bed arrangement (two cabins can accommodate three persons) and a tiny bathroom with shower. There is also one owner's suite.

Dining: The Nymphea Restaurant, which has large square ocean-view picture windows, is intimate and quite charming; the decor and colors are light and contemporary (the dining rooms chairs do not, however, have armrests). Meals are cooked individually to order — no mass catering here — and there is one seating for all.

Other Comments: *Monet*: how refreshingly different to have a ship named after an immortal French artist. She is a small, all-white vessel, and is good for for up-close, in-depth coastal cruising, and also carries one Zodiac inflatable landing craft.

Her interior decor is quite charming, with warm colors used throughout her limited public spaces and brass and chrome on her stairways. The housekeeping staff is from the Philippines.

She is presently being operated on behalf of Leisure Cruises, a Switzerland-based company that also operates the larger ms *Switzerland*. She operates Mediterranean cruises during the summer months and itineraries in the Persian Gulf. The dress code is totally relaxed, and informality rules. Nice little ship for those who do not like lines, hubbub, or crowds.

s/s **Monterey**
★★ +
(M)

LIFESTYLE:	STANDARD
Cruise Line:	Mediterranean Shipping Cruises
Former Names:	*Free State Mariner*
Gross Tonnage:	20,040
Builder:	Bethlehem Steel Corp. (USA)
Original Cost:	n/a
Entered Service:	December 1952/August 1988
Flag:	Panama
Tel. No.:	1333517
Fax No.:	1333522
Length (ft/m):	563.6/171.81
Beam (ft/m):	80.3/24.50
Draft (ft/m):	29.3/8.95
Propulsion/Propellers:	steam turbine (14,400kW)/1 (FP)
Passenger Decks:	4
Total Crew:	280
Pass. Capacity (basis 2):	576
Pass. Capacity (all berths):	638
Pass. Space Ratio (basis 2):	34.7
Pass. Space Ratio (all berths):	31.6
Officers:	Italian
Total Cabins:	294
Size Range (sq ft/m):	64.5–344.4/6.5–32.0
Cabins (outside view):	167
Cabins (inside — no view):	127
Cabins (single occupancy):	0
Cabins (with private balcony):	0
Cabins (wheelchair accessible):	0
Cabin Current:	110 volts
Cabin TV:	Suites only
Dining Rooms:	1
Elevators:	2
Casino:	Yes
Slot Machines:	Yes
Swimming Pools (outdoors):	1
Swimming Pools (inside):	0
Whirlpools:	2
Fitness Center:	Yes
Sauna/Steam Room:	Yes/No
Massage:	Yes
Self-Service Launderette:	No
Movie Theater/Seats:	Yes/107
Library:	Yes
Classification Society:	American Bureau of Shipping

RATINGS	POSSIBLE SCORE	SCORE ACHIEVED
Ship	500	262
Accommodation	200	114
Food	400	214
Service	400	234
Cruise	500	263
TOTAL	**2,000**	**1,087**

Accommodation: There is a wide choice of cabin sizes and configurations — but only the top three categories have full bathtubs. Has extremely spacious suites; other cabins are very quite roomy, well-appointed units, but most have tinny metal drawers (a carry-over from her former years as a Matson Line ship).

The cabins located forward on Boat Deck have lifeboat-obstructed views, but other cabins on this deck are quite large; all have a window, plenty of closet and drawer space, together with a vanity desk, coffee table, sofa, and chair. Bathrobes are provided for all passengers.

Dining: The charming two-level dining room is set low down, and decorated in soft earth tones, so the ambience is quite cozy, although it is noisy when full. There are two seatings. Features continental cuisine, with some excellent pasta dishes. There is only the most basic selection of breads, cheeses, and fruits. The service is friendly and attentive, in typical Italian style, but it is somewhat frenzied. There is also a casual café, with fine views over the aft pool deck and stern, for basic breakfast and lunch buffets, and an Italian gelato cart.

Other Comments: This ship has a traditional 1950s (now somewhat dated) liner profile. She was built originally for the United States Maritime Commission as a C-4 cargo vessel before becoming a Matson Lines ship in 1956, with a name change to *Monterey*. She is very stable at sea, with an almost vertical bow and an overhanging aircraft-carrier-like stern that is not at all handsome when viewed from ashore, but provides a good amount of open deck space around the white-tiled swimming pool and Jacuzzis. There are also partly enclosed port and starboard walking promenades, although, sadly, they do not wrap around the vessel. On the navigation bridge is a neat, original spirit level.

The ship was refurbished in a moderate art deco style, and a new sports deck was added several years ago. There is a reasonable amount of sheltered and open deck space, and some forward open observation deck space atop some suites, which were added in the late 1980s.

Inside, there are a reasonable number of public rooms to choose from. All of them have high ceilings, but little elegance. There is too much cold steel and not enough warmth in the interior decoration, although this is being addressed as decor changes are made. Rising through three decks is a large, slim totem pole, a carry-over from her limited days as a ship operating under the banner of Aloha Pacific Cruises.

The crew features a number of Italians, and they provide a friendly atmosphere, but there is really little finesse in service.

This ship will cruise you in reasonable style and surroundings, with mainly European, and particularly Italian speaking passengers (about 60 percent). Currency aboard: lire. Port taxes are included.

Weak Points: There is no forward observation lounge. There are far too many loud, repetitive, and unnecessary annoucements, often in five languages. There is a charge for the sauna, which is located inside the beauty salon and operated by the concession.

SHIP TALK

Cable Length: a measured length equaling 100 fathoms or 600 feet.

Chart: a nautical map used for navigating.

Colors: refers to the national flag or emblem flown by the ship.

Companionway: interior stairway.

Course: direction in which the ship is headed, in degrees.

Davit: a device for raising and lowering lifeboats.

Deadlight: a ventilated porthole cover to prevent light from entering

Disembark (also debark): to leave a ship.

Dock: berth, pier or quay.

Draft (or draught): measurement in feet from the ship's waterline to the lowest point of its keel.

Embark: to join a ship.

Fantail: the rear or overhang of the ship.

Fathom: distance equal to six feet.

Flagstaff: a pole at the stern of a ship where the flag of the ship's country of registry is flown.

Free Port: port or place that is free of customs duty and regulations.

Funnel: chimney from which the ship's combustion gases are propelled into the atmosphere.

Galley: the ship's kitchen.

Gangway: the stairway or ramp link between ship and shore.

m/v Nantucket Clipper
★★★ +
(S)

LIFESTYLE:	STANDARD
Cruise Line:	Clipper Cruise Line
Former Names:	-
Gross Tonnage:	1,471
Builder:	Jeffboat (USA)
Original Cost:	$9 million
Entered Service:	December 1984
Flag:	USA
Tel. No.:	n/a
Fax No.:	n/a
Length (ft/m):	207.0/63.00
Beam (ft/m):	37.0/11.20
Draft (ft/m):	8.0/2.40
Propulsion/Propellers:	diesel (700kW)/2 (FP)
Passenger Decks:	4
Total Crew:	32
Pass. Capacity (basis 2):	102
Pass. Capacity (all berths):	102
Pass. Space Ratio (basis 2):	14.4
Pass. Space Ratio (all berths):	14.4
Officers:	American
Total Cabins:	51
Size Range (sq ft/m):	120.5–137.7/11.2–12.8
Cabins (outside view):	51
Cabins (inside — no view):	0
Cabins (single occupancy):	0
Cabins (with private balcony):	0
Cabins (wheelchair accessible):	0
Cabin Current:	110 volts
Cabin TV:	No
Dining Rooms:	1
Elevators:	0
Casino:	No
Slot Machines:	No
Swimming Pools (outdoors):	0
Swimming Pools (inside):	0
Whirlpools:	0
Fitness Center:	No
Sauna/Steam Room:	No/No
Massage:	No
Self-Service Launderette:	No
Movie Theater/Seats:	No
Library:	Yes
Classification Society:	American Bureau of Shipping

RATINGS	POSSIBLE SCORE	SCORE ACHIEVED
Ship	500	293
Accommodation	200	121
Food	400	277
Service	400	265
Cruise	500	309
TOTAL	**2,000**	**1,265**

Accommodation: The all-outside cabins (in four categories) are very small but somehow comfortable if you do not expect much. They are relatively tastefully furnished, with wood-accented trim and good sound insulation. The beds are twins and are bolted to the deck and wall. The bathrooms are tight, but, thoughtfully, a night-light is provided, although there's little space for your toiletries.

Dining: The dining room is warm and inviting and has large picture windows. There is a single seating, and you can sit with whomever you wish, although meals are at fixed times. There are no tables for two. Features simple and plain American cuisine that is quite tasty, although the menu choice is limited, and the portions are small. The chefs are from the Culinary Institute of America, and all ingredients are fresh. The chocolate chip cookies are popular and are served at various times, usually provided in the lounge.

Other Comments: This small, shallow draft vessel is specially built for coastal and inland cruises and is very maneuverable. Well maintained, although now showing signs of aging.

Note that this extremely high-density ship has only two public rooms — the dining room and an observation lounge, where most passengers congregate in the evening. Passengers can visit the bridge at any time. Not recommended for night owls, and passengers should be over 50 years of age.

The service is by young, friendly all-American college-age types. This is most definitely an "Americana" experience for those seeking particularly to learn more about the coastal ports around the US. Casual and unstructured lifestyle, rather like a small (but certainly not luxurious) country club afloat, with some attention to detail. This should not be compared with big ship ocean cruising.

There are always one or two lecturers aboard each sailing, which highlights the learning experience that is an essential part of cruising with Clipper Cruise Lines. Now, if only the ship would carry a few bicycles! A nonsmoking policy throughout all interior areas was put into effect December 1996.

Weak Points: There is high engine noise level when underway. The per diem price is high for what you get, and airfare is extra. The wraparound teakwood walking deck outdoors is narrow.

m/v Niagara Prince
★★ +
(S)

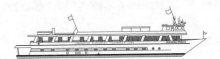

LIFESTYLE: **STANDARD**

Cruise Line:	American Canadian Caribbean Line
Former Names:	-
Gross Tonnage:	99
Builder:	Blount Industries (USA)
Original Cost:	$7.5 million
Entered Service:	November 1994
Flag:	USA
Tel. No.:	n/a
Fax No.:	n/a
Length (ft/m):	177.0/53.9
Beam (ft/m):	40.0/12.1
Draft (ft/m):	6.7/2.0
Propulsion/Propellers:	diesel (1044kW)/2 (CP)
Passenger Decks:	3
Total Crew:	17
Pass. Capacity (basis 2):	84
Pass. Capacity (all berths):	94
Pass. Space Ratio (basis 2):	1.1
Pass. Space Ratio (all berths):	1.0
Officers:	American
Total Cabins:	48
Size Range (sq ft/m):	72.0–96.0/6.6–8.9
Cabins (outside view):	40
Cabins (inside — no view):	2
Cabins (single occupancy):	6
Cabins (with private balcony):	0

Cabins (wheelchair accessible):	0
Cabin Current:	110 volts
Cabin TV:	No
Dining Rooms:	1
Elevators:	0
Casino:	0
Slot Machines:	0
Swimming Pools (outdoors):	0
Swimming Pools (inside):	0
Whirlpools:	0
Fitness Center:	0
Sauna/Steam Room:	No/No
Massage:	0
Self-Service Launderette:	No
Movie Theater/Seats:	0
Library:	Yes
Classification Society:	American Bureau of Shipping

RATINGS	POSSIBLE SCORE	SCORE ACHIEVED
Ship	500	232
Accommodation	200	95
Food	400	235
Service	400	241
Cruise	500	284
TOTAL	**2,000**	**1,087**

Accommodation: No smoking is allowed in any cabin aboard this vessel. The air-conditioning consists of recirculated air. Beds in 75 percent of the cabins can be made up as two singles or a queen-size bed (ten cabins have a third berth).

Dining: The dining room is operated in a single, open seating, with tables for four, six, eight, or ten. Meals are served family style. The cuisine features good, wholesome Americana fare, with fresh-baked breads and regional dishes. There are, perhaps, too many high-cholesterol, fatty foods for the older passengers carried. A bring-your-own-bottle policy exists for those who want wine with dinner, or any alcoholic beverages (mixers however, are available).

Other Comments: The vessel is equipped with a unique, retractable wheelhouse for passage under low bridges on island waterway itineraries, and there is also a small platform for those who want to swim off the stern. There is also a glass-bottom boat and a Sunfish sailboat. See other comments for the company's *Grande Prince*.

An underwater video camera allows passengers to see what a scuba diver might see underneath the ship, while seated in (dry) comfort in the lounge, on large-screen television monitors. Underwater lights, which should attract fish and other marine life, are also fitted.

Cruising aboard the vessels of American Canadian Caribbean Line is for those who do not want or need pampering, much service, or entertainment. This ship is enjoyed by a high rate of repeat passengers, however, who want a simple, unpretentious lifestyle. Take only casual clothing. All gratuities are pooled by the entire complement of staff.

m/s Nieuw Amsterdam
★★★★
(L)

LIFESTYLE:	PREMIUM
Cruise Line:	Holland America Line
Former Names:	-
Gross Tonnage:	33,930
Builder:	Chantiers de l'Atlantique (France)
Original Cost:	$150 million
Entered Service:	July 1983
Flag:	The Netherlands
Tel. No.:	1302552
Fax No.:	1302553
Length (ft/m):	704.2/214.66
Beam (ft/m):	89.4/27.26
Draft (ft/m):	24.6/7.52
Propulsion/Propellers:	diesel (21,600kW)/2 (CP)
Passenger Decks:	10
Total Crew:	510
Pass. Capacity (basis 2):	1,214
Pass. Capacity (all berths):	1,350
Pass. Space Ratio (basis 2):	28.0
Pass. Space Ratio (all berths):	25.1
Officers:	Dutch
Total Cabins:	607
Size Range (sq ft/m):	150.6–296.0/14.0–27.5
Cabins (outside view):	413
Cabins (inside — no view):	194
Cabins (single occupancy):	0
Cabins (with private balcony):	0

Cabins (wheelchair accessible):	4
Cabin Current:	110 and 220 volts
Cabin TV:	Yes
Dining Rooms:	1
Elevators:	7
Casino:	Yes
Slot Machines:	Yes
Swimming Pools (outdoors):	2
Swimming Pools (inside):	0
Whirlpools:	1
Fitness Center:	Yes
Sauna/Steam Room:	Yes/No
Massage:	Yes
Self-Service Launderette:	Yes
Movie Theater/Seats:	Yes/230
Library:	Yes
Classification Society:	Lloyd's Register

RATINGS	POSSIBLE SCORE	SCORE ACHIEVED
Ship	500	383
Accommodation	200	153
Food	400	282
Service	400	300
Cruise	500	380
TOTAL	**2,000**	**1,498**

Accommodation: The cabins are quite spacious, well-appointed, and practical, with decent furniture and fittings, pleasing wood paneling, good counter and storage space, and bathrooms that are of a reasonable size. The top three categories of cabins have full bathtubs while all others have showers. Several cabins have king- or queen-size beds. The cabin insulation, however, is very poor. Some cabins on Boat and Navigation Decks have obstructed views.

Dining: The dining room is quite large and attractive, with warm decor and ample space. Breakfast and lunch are served in an open seating (so you may get a different table and different waiters for each meal), and in two seatings for dinner (where you do have the same table each evening). The food is presentable, but it certainly is not memorable, although the quality has improved somewhat. The Indonesian waiters do try hard, but communication with them is often frustrating.

Instead of the more formal dining room, the Lido Buffet is open for casual dinners on several nights each cruise (typically three nights on a seven-night cruise), in an open-seating arrangement. Tables are set with crisp linens, flatware, and stemware. A set menu is featured, and this includes a choice of four entrees.

Other Comments: There is a nicely raked bow, although the angular exterior design makes the ship look squat and somewhat boxy. There is a good amount of open deck space, and the traditional teak decks outdoors include a wraparound promenade deck.

The ship has quite a spacious interior design and layout, and the soothing color combinations do not jar the senses, although they are rather dark. There is much polished teak and rosewood paneling throughout. Features a fine, well-displayed collection of seventeenth- and eighteenth-century artwork and Dutch artifacts. The Crow's Nest observation lounge, located atop the ship, is a good retreat for many. The Explorers' Lounge is relaxing for after-meal coffee and live chamber music. The main lounge, which has a small balcony level, is reminiscent of the former ocean liners era. The flower bouquets throughout the ship add warmth to the ambience.

This ship is good for older passengers wanting pleasant surroundings and fairly bland food. *Note*: The line does not add an automatic 15 percent for beverage purchases, unlike many others. The company provides cappuccino and espresso coffees, and free ice cream during certain hours of the day aboard its ships, as well as hot hors d'oeuvres in all bars — something other major lines seem to have dropped or charge extra for.

However, the latest batch of ships has more space, better facilities, and more options, which leaves this ship losing a few points in relation to the increased competition in the international marketplace.

Weak Points: There is a considerable amount of vibration at the stern, particularly during slow maneuvering. The charge of $1.50 for self-service washing machines in the launderette is pitiful.

Holland America Line's *Nieuw Amsterdam.*

m/s Nippon Maru
★★★★
(S)

LIFESTYLE:	STANDARD
Cruise Line:	Mitsui OSK Passenger Line
Former Names:	-
Gross Tonnage:	21,903
Builder:	Mitsubishi Heavy Industries (Japan)
Original Cost:	$59.4 million
Entered Service:	September 1990
Flag:	Japan
Tel. No.:	1200462
Fax No.:	1200462
Length (ft/m):	546.7/166.65
Beam (ft/m):	78.7/24.00
Draft (ft/m):	21.4/6.55
Propulsion/Propellers:	diesel (15,740kW)/2 (CP)
Passenger Decks:	7
Total Crew:	160
Pass. Capacity (basis 2):	408
Pass. Capacity (all berths):	607
Pass. Space Ratio (basis 2):	53.6
Pass. Space Ratio (all berths):	36.0
Officers:	Japanese
Total Cabins:	204
Size Range (sq ft/m):	150.6–430.5/14.0–40.0
Cabins (outside view):	189
Cabins (inside — no view):	15
Cabins (single occupancy):	0
Cabins (with private balcony):	0

Cabins (wheelchair accessible):	2
Cabin Current:	100 volts
Cabin TV:	Yes
Dining Rooms:	1
Elevators:	5
Casino:	Yes
Slot Machines:	No
Swimming Pools (outdoors):	1
Swimming Pools (inside):	0
Whirlpools:	4 (Japanese baths)
Fitness Center:	Yes
Sauna/Steam Room:	Yes/No
Massage:	Yes
Self-Service Launderette:	Yes
Movie Theater/Seats:	Yes/135
Library:	Yes
Classification Society:	Nippon Kaiji Kyokai

RATINGS	POSSIBLE SCORE	SCORE ACHIEVED
Ship	500	383
Accommodation	200	138
Food	400	287
Service	400	295
Cruise	500	338
TOTAL	**2,000**	**1,441**

Accommodation: Most of the cabins are located forward. The suites are quite large and feature a separate bedroom and living room with a solid wall divider except for the doorway (where there is a curtain but no door). A large sofa, four chairs, and a coffee table occupy one section of the lounge; there is also a vanity/writing desk. Good amount of closet and drawer space and two beds. The bathroom is quite small, however, although there is a small vanity desk with make-up mirror. Slippers and bathrobe are provided.

The deluxe cabins are quite nicely decorated, and the living area has a table and two chairs, and two beds (they cannot be pushed together).

The standard cabins are spartan and clinical (adequate for convention and seminar cruise passengers, however, and those that don't mind just the basics). Many of these have a third (or third and fourth) pull-down Pullman bed. The lighting is minimal and utilitarian.

Dining: The dining room is quite basic and features both traditional Japanese cuisine and some western dishes. Features one seating for leisure cruises and two seatings for ship charter cruises. The food presentation is quite decent but rather plain, and menu choice is limited, although quite welcome by most passengers.

Other Comments: Has a single, large, orange, swept-back funnel aft of midships, with an exterior styling that is very traditional and not very modern. The teakwood decking outdoors is good. The ship was specifically built and outfitted for Japanese passengers and the Japanese seminar/lecture marketplace.

Inside, the public rooms have very high ceilings, high-quality furnishings, and soothing color combinations. The interior decor, however, including the ceilings in public areas, is plain and unexciting. Elegant, dramatic six-deck-high atrium. Features true Japanese baths, and a washitsu tatami room. Children's activities personnel are placed onboard only for leisure cruises.

This ship is principally for older Japanese passengers (those of "silver" years) who want to cruise at moderate rates in pleasant, but not luxurious, surroundings. Tipping is not allowed.

<u>Weak Points</u>: Cheap plastic deck furniture is difficult to keep clean and looks unkempt. The seats in the theater should be staggered; they are not very comfortable.

m/s Noordam
★★★★
(L)

LIFESTYLE:	**PREMIUM**
Cruise Line:	Holland America Line
Former Names:	-
Gross Tonnage:	33,930
Builder:	Chantiers de l'Atlantique (France)
Original Cost:	$160 million
Entered Service:	April 1984
Flag:	The Netherlands
Tel. No.:	1302541
Fax No.:	1302537
Length (ft/m):	704.2/214.66
Beam (ft/m):	89.4/27.26
Draft (ft/m):	24.2/7.40
Propulsion/Propellers:	diesel (21,600kW)/2 (CP)
Passenger Decks:	10
Total Crew:	530
Pass. Capacity (basis 2):	1,214
Pass. Capacity (all berths):	1,350
Pass. Space Ratio (basis 2):	28.0
Pass. Space Ratio (all berths):	25.1
Officers:	Dutch
Total Cabins:	607
Size Range (sq ft/m):	150.6–296.0/14.0–27.5
Cabins (outside view):	413
Cabins (inside — no view):	194
Cabins (single occupancy):	0
Cabins (with private balcony):	0

Cabins (wheelchair accessible):	4
Cabin Current:	110 and 220 volts
Cabin TV:	Yes
Dining Rooms:	1
Elevators:	7
Casino:	Yes
Slot Machines:	Yes
Swimming Pools (outdoors):	2
Swimming Pools (inside):	0
Whirlpools:	1
Fitness Center:	Yes
Sauna/Steam Room:	Yes/No
Massage:	Yes
Self-Service Laundry:	Yes
Movie Theater/Seats:	Yes/230
Library:	Yes
Classification Society:	Lloyd's Register

RATINGS	POSSIBLE SCORE	SCORE ACHIEVED
Ship	500	383
Accommodation	200	153
Food	400	282
Service	400	300
Cruise	500	380
TOTAL	**2,000**	**1,498**

For comments, see sister ship *Nieuw Amsterdam.*

m/s Nordic Empress
★★★ +
(L)

LIFESTYLE:	STANDARD
Cruise Line:	Royal Caribbean International
Former Names:	-
Gross Tonnage:	48,563
Builder:	Chantiers de l'Atlantique (France)
Original Cost:	$170 million
Entered Service:	June 1990
Flag:	Liberia
Tel. No.:	1243540
Fax No.:	1243547
Length (ft/m):	692.2/211.00
Beam (ft/m):	100.7/30.70
Draft (ft/m):	24.9/7.60
Propulsion/Propellers:	diesel (16,200kW)/2 (CP)
Passenger Decks:	12
Total Crew:	671
Pass. Capacity (basis 2):	1,600
Pass. Capacity (all berths):	2,020
Pass. Space Ratio (basis 2):	30.2
Pass. Space Ratio (all berths):	24.0
Officers:	Scandinavian
Total Cabins:	800
Size Range (sq ft/m):	1176.2–269.1/10.8–25.0
Cabins (outside view):	471
Cabins (inside — no view):	329
Cabins (single occupancy):	0
Cabins (with private balcony):	69

Cabins (wheelchair accessible):	4
Cabin Current:	110 volts
Cabin TV:	Yes
Dining Rooms:	1
Elevators:	7
Casino:	Yes
Slot Machines:	Yes-220
Swimming Pools (outdoors):	1 (+ 1 wading pool)
Swimming Pools (inside):	0
Whirlpools:	4
Fitness Center:	Yes
Sauna/Steam Room:	Yes/No
Massage:	Yes
Self-Service Launderette:	No
Movie Theater/Seats:	No
Library:	No
Classification Society:	Det Norske Veritas

RATINGS	POSSIBLE SCORE	SCORE ACHIEVED
Ship	500	360
Accommodation	200	126
Food	400	246
Service	400	279
Cruise	500	344
TOTAL	**2,000**	**1,355**

Accommodation: Nine cabins have private balconies overlooking the stern (these consist of two owner's suites and seven "superior" ocean-view cabins). The other cabins with private balconies also have a decent amount of living space, and a small sofa, coffee table and chair, and vanity desk. Almost all of the other cabins are dimensionally challenged, though reasonably comfortable, particularly for the short cruises this ship operates during the winter season. All cabins have twin beds that convert to a queen-size configuration. The bathrooms are nicely laid out, and have a decent amount of space for toiletry items.

Dining: Two-level, musical-themed dining room is delightful, though noisy, and has huge windows overlooking the stern. There are two seatings. The entire dining room operation is well orchestrated, the emphasis being on highly programmed service, with a small modicum of finesse. The food is consistently fair, but certainly not memorable (it is hotel banquet food, after all).

Other Comments: She is a fine contemporary ship with short bow and squared-off stern that looks quite stunning. Designed specifically for the short-cruise market, for which the ship is well suited. There is a polished wraparound wooden promenade deck outdoors, and a dramatic use of glass-enclosed viewing spaces, which provide good contact from the upper, open decks to the sea. Inside, a stunning nine-deck-high atrium is the focal point. Passenger flow is generally good. Lots of crystal and brass are used to good effect to reflect light. An ingenious use of lighting effects provides illuminating interiors that make you feel warm. Three-level casino. There is a superb outdoor pool deck designed for evenings under the stars. The Viking Crown Lounge, aft of the funnel, is a two-level nightclub/disco for the late-night set.

Nordic Empress is a glamorous ship with high passenger density, but the ship features an adequate array of activities for all ages. The ship will operate New York–Bermuda cruises in the summer of 2000, then reposition to San Juan for three- and four-night cruises during the winter season.

Weak Points: The two-level show room has poor sight lines in the upper lateral balconies. The constant, loud announcements are irritating.

s/s Norway
★★★ +
(L)

LIFESTYLE:	STANDARD
Cruise Line:	Norwegian Cruise Line
Former Names:	*France*
Gross Tonnage:	76,049
Builder:	Chantiers de l'Atlantique (France)
Original Cost:	$80 million
Entered Service:	February 1962/June 1980
Flag:	Bahamas
Tel. No.:	1104603
Fax No.:	1104604
Length (ft/m):	1035.1/315.50
Beam (ft/m):	109.9/33.50
Draft (ft/m):	35.4/10.80
Propulsion/Propellers:	steam turbine (29,850kW)/4 (FP)
Passenger Decks:	12
Total Crew:	920
Pass. Capacity (basis 2):	2,026
Pass. Capacity (all berths):	2,370
Pass. Space Ratio (basis 2):	37.5
Pass. Space Ratio (all berths):	32.8
Officers:	Norwegian
Total Cabins:	1,013
Size Range (sq ft/m):	99.0–958.0/9.2–89.0
Cabins (outside view):	642
Cabins (inside — no view):	371
Cabins (single occupancy):	20

Cabins (with private balcony):	56
Cabins (wheelchair accessible):	11
Cabin Current:	110 volts
Cabin TV:	Yes
Dining Rooms:	2 (+ 1 bistro)
Elevators:	13
Casino:	Yes
Slot Machines:	Yes
Swimming Pools (outdoors):	2
Swimming Pools (inside):	1 (plus Aquacize Pool)
Whirlpools:	2
Fitness Center:	Yes
Sauna/Steam Room:	Yes/No
Massage:	Yes
Self-Service Launderette:	No
Movie Theater/Seats:	Yes/813
Library:	No
Classification Society:	Bureau Veritas

RATINGS	POSSIBLE SCORE	SCORE ACHIEVED
Ship	500	366
Accommodation	200	146
Food	400	239
Service	400	282
Cruise	500	360
TOTAL	**2,000**	**1,393**

Accommodation: There is a really wide range of suites and cabins in about 20 different grades — from really luxurious and spacious outside suites that can accommodate four — to tiny inside cabins. All have high ceilings, long beds, good closet and drawer space, and a decent range of amenities. Many of the bathrooms feature full-size bathtubs, while others have shower enclosures.

Outstanding owner's suites are extremely lavish, and new suites on two decks atop the ship are very comfortable (however, all suite occupants should have had a private dining room). There are many cabins suitable for families of four, five, or even six.

Dining: There are two large dining rooms (both are nonsmoking) and two seatings in each. The nicest is the Windward, with its fine domed ceiling, and wall murals retained from her former days as the first-class dining room, while the Leeward (the former tourist-class restaurant) has a fine balcony level. There are few tables for two, however, and the tables are close together. The food is not memorable and the menus are often uninspiring and quite disappointing, although there are different themes each night for dinner. There is quite a poor selection of breads, rolls, cheeses, and fruits. The service ranges from poor to good. The cuisine in general can be said to be similar to American hotel banquet food, no more. There is a good wine list with moderate prices, but there are few vintage wines for those who enjoy good wines.

Le Bistro is an informal alternative dining spot that provides for a change from the two restaurants (and the attendant noise). It offers a taste of Italy in a contemporary "South Miami Beach" style, at no extra charge (it always seems difficult to get a table, however).

The casual, outdoor buffet area is useful for those out on deck, but it is always crowded, with long lines to get to what can best be described as "food as it shouldn't be presented." It never looks good, despite staff efforts to restock the displays.

Other Comments: Originally built as the ocean liner ss *France*, she was once known for her food and service when operating transatlantic crossings. She is still quite a majestic-looking ship, with two large funnels and a long foredeck, but the ship's interiors, food, and service have almost no resemblence to her former days as an ocean liner. She was converted to become a Caribbean cruise vessel in 1979, at a cost of $130 million. Some major structural alterations a few years ago added two new glass-enclosed decks atop the ship; the new decks provide an additional 135 outside suites and junior suites, and lower the profile of the two wing-tip funnels considerably, but the balconies are not very private. Two large landing craft provide fast, efficient transportation ashore.

Recent refurbishments have also kept her interiors refreshed. Some rooms feature art deco touches reminiscent of the former ocean liner she once was. There are two different color schemes in the forward and aft sections, which help first-time passengers to find their way around.

The public rooms are, for the most part, quite pleasing, and many have high ceilings. Soft furnishings and much marble have kept the interiors fresh. The outdoor decks are well varnished, but the artificial grass on the ship's top deck is just not right. Features a good indoor Roman Spa, set low down in the ship, with a good range of spa programs (all at extra cost). There is an extensive jogging track, although it cannot be used before 8:00am (it is located above some of the most expensive cabins). The Club Internationale is an elegant carryover from her former days (when it was the first-class lounge) and is still the perfect meeting place for cocktails and sophisticated evenings. There is an excellent proscenium Saga Theatre, complete with large balcony level, for dazzle and sizzle production shows. Large active casino invites you to spend your money, and it is noisy. Sadly, the former library has been changed into a perfume shop. A new Sports Illustrated Bar replaced Checkers Lounge in her winter 1998 refit.

Take the family, as children and teens will have a fine time aboard this ship, with lots of activities and children's staff. She is so large there are plenty of places to play.

This ship, formerly the grand classic transatlantic liner *France*, was for many years the world's largest cruise ship (she is still the longest). *Norway* is now a floating contemporary resort and should prove fascinating for active passengers and families with children of all ages. *Norway* provides an action-packed, sun-filled Caribbean cruise in comfortable but rather overpopulated surroundings, for a reasonable price. Plenty of entertainment and social activities add up to a large part in the onboard offerings, which means there is music and noise almost everywhere, and the same silly audience participation events that have been featured for the past 20 years or more.

Passengers from the UK should note that all onboard gratuities are included, as are port taxes (the pricing structure is quite different from that provided in North America and other countries). In the summer of 1998 she sailed in the Mediterranean area, going back to the future by taking her former name, *France*, as the lure and romance of ocean liners continues.

<u>Weak Points</u>: The open deck and sunbathing space is quite poor, particularly when the ship is full, which is almost always. *Norway* does not dock anywhere because of its size and deep draft (a problem for the nonambulatory) and passengers must go ashore by tender boats (this can take a considerable amount of time). The Roman Spa fitness facilities incur a hefty extra charge, plus an extra 12 percent tip. There are just too many loud announcements, making for too much of a holiday camp atmosphere.

m/s Norwegian Crown
★★★★
(L)

LIFESTYLE:	STANDARD
Cruise Line:	Norwegian Cruise Line
Former Names:	*Crown Odyssey*
Gross Tonnage:	34,242
Builder:	Meyer Werft (Germany)
Original Cost:	$178 million
Entered Service:	June 1988/March 1996
Flag:	Bahamas
Tel. No.:	1104673
Fax No.:	1104674
Length (ft/m):	615.9/187.75
Beam (ft/m):	92.5/28.20
Draft (ft/m):	23.8/7.26
Propulsion/Propellers:	diesel (21,330kW)/2 (CP)
Passenger Decks:	10
Total Crew:	470
Pass. Capacity (basis 2):	1,004
Pass. Capacity (all berths):	1,221
Pass. Space Ratio (basis 2):	34.1
Pass. Space Ratio (all berths):	28.0
Officers:	Norwegian
Total Cabins:	502
Size Range (sq ft/m):	1543.9–613.5/14.3–57.0
Cabins (outside view):	404
Cabins (inside — no view):	98
Cabins (single occupancy):	0
Cabins (with private balcony):	16

Cabins (wheelchair accessible):	4
Cabin Current:	110 volts
Cabin TV:	No
Dining Rooms:	1
Elevators:	4
Casino:	Yes
Slot Machines:	Yes
Swimming Pools (outdoors):	1
Swimming Pools (inside):	1
Whirlpools:	4
Fitness Center:	Yes
Sauna/Steam Room:	Yes/No
Massage:	Yes
Self-Service Launderette:	Yes
Movie Theater/Seats:	Yes/215
Library:	Yes
Classification Society:	Lloyd's Register

RATINGS	POSSIBLE SCORE	SCORE ACHIEVED
Ship	500	404
Accommodation	200	157
Food	400	237
Service	400	286
Cruise	500	350
TOTAL	**2,000**	**1,434**

Accommodation: The suites are quite spacious; each is decorated in a different style and comes with nicely finished wood cabinetry. Most other cabins have good closet and drawer space and are well equipped, although almost all cabins are showing signs of wear and tear. The cabin soundproofing is good, and non-smoking cabins are available.

Dining: The large dining room is noisy, and there are two seatings. It features a stained-glass ceiling, comfortable seating, and is totally nonsmoking. The cuisine is not gourmet either in quality or presentation, yet it is more than adequate for the expectations of Norwegian Cruise Line's passengers. The waiters are generally good, and provide bubbly, attentive service, although the lack of finesse shows. There is a decent, well-priced wine list, although the wines are almost all quite young.

Other Comments: This is a well designed and built ship. She has quite a handsome exterior profile, while inside there is generally good passenger flow, ample space, and fine-quality interiors. However, these interiors are now showing signs of hard wear in many places and more maintenance is needed.

Features a full teakwood wraparound promenade deck outdoors. There are, however, no padded mattresses for the deck lounge chairs.

Inside, the ship has a spacious layout and a good array of public rooms. Generous amounts of warm woods and marble used in the decor, but there are lots of mirrored surfaces. Excellent Roman-style indoor spa, pool, and facilities, unusual for a Caribbean ship, but excellent for cruises to Alaska. There is a good theater-style show room, but the sight lines could be better.

This ship, for many years a favorite of passengers of the now defunct Royal Cruise Line, is excellent particularly for the young-at-heart passenger, and it exudes quality, style, and charm, for a really moderate cruise price.

Passengers from the UK should note that all onboard gratuities are included, as are port taxes.

m/s **Norwegian Dream**
★★★★
(L)

LIFESTYLE:	**STANDARD**
Cruise Line:	Norwegian Cruise Line
Former Names:	*Dreamward*
Gross Tonnage:	50,760
Builder:	Chantiers de l'Atlantique (France)
Original Cost:	$240 million
Entered Service:	December 1992
Flag:	Bahamas
Tel. No.:	1305510
Fax No.:	1305507
Length (ft/m):	754.0/229.80
Beam (ft/m):	93.5/28.50
Draft (ft/m):	22.3/6.80
Propulsion/Propellers:	diesel (18,480kW)/2 (CP)
Passenger Decks:	10
Total Crew:	614
Pass. Capacity (basis 2):	1,730
Pass. Capacity (all berths):	2,159
Pass. Space Ratio (basis 2):	29.3
Pass. Space Ratio (all berths):	23.5
Officers:	Norwegian
Total Cabins:	865
Size Range (sq ft/m):	139.9–349.8/13.0–32.5
Cabins (outside view):	695
Cabins (inside — no view):	170
Cabins (single occupancy):	0
Cabins (with private balcony):	48

Cabins (wheelchair accessible):	6 (+ 30 for hearing-impaired)
Cabin Current:	110 volts
Cabin TV:	Yes
Dining Rooms:	4
Elevators:	11
Casino:	Yes
Slot Machines:	Yes
Swimming Pools (outdoors):	2
Swimming Pools (inside):	0
Whirlpools:	4
Fitness Center:	Yes
Sauna/Steam Room:	Yes/No
Massage:	Yes
Self-Service Launderette:	No
Movie Theater/Seats:	No
Library:	Yes
Classification Society:	Det Norske Veritas

RATINGS	POSSIBLE SCORE	SCORE ACHIEVED
Ship	500	398
Accommodation	200	155
Food	400	241
Service	400	288
Cruise	500	350
TOTAL	**2,000**	**1,432**

Accommodation: There are 15 grades of cabins. The majority of cabins are outside and feature wood-trimmed cabinetry and warm decor, with multicolored soft furnishings, but there is almost no drawer space (the closets have open shelves, however), so take minimal clothing. All cabins have a sitting area, but this takes away any free space, making movement pretty tight. The bathrooms are small but practical, although there is little space for storage of personal toiletry items.

There are 18 suites (12 of which have a private entrance and private balcony), each with separate living room and bedroom, fine-quality cabinetry, and lots of closet and drawer space. Occupants of suites receive "concierge" service, which provides extra personal attention. In addition, 16 suites and 70 cabins have inter-connecting doors, good for families or perhaps those that want separate "his and hers" living spaces. There are several cabins specially equipped for the hearing-impaired. Note that all cabins on the port side of the ship are designated nonsmoking.

Dining: There are three main dining rooms: The Sun Terrace, The Terraces (arguably the nicest, with windows that look out over the ship's tiered aft decks), and the enlarged, midships-located Four Seasons (now with 452 seats). All are nonsmoking and feature the same menu and food, in two seatings. The Four Seasons is now the largest and has some prime tables at ocean-view window seats in a section that extends from the ship's port and starboard sides in half-moon shapes (nice for lunch, but it's either dark or the curtains are drawn for dinner). The dining room you are assigned to depends on the accommodation you book (you cannot choose).

In addition, The Bistro features informal evening dining at no extra charge in more intimate surroundings. A Sports Bar features breakfast, luncheon, and teatime snacks (it is a small space for this number of passengers, and the offerings are quite poor). There's also a poolside pizzeria and a small coffee lounge.

The food is adequate, but not memorable, like the service. The wine list is quite decent, and well put together, with moderate prices, although you won't find any good vintage wines. There are many types of beer (including some on draught in the popular Sports Bar & Grill) to choose from. The cutlery is very ordinary (there are no fish knives). There is no afternoon tea.

You can eat breakfast or lunch in any of the dining rooms when it's "open seating." A lavish "choco-holics" buffet is featured once each cruise, a firm favorite among NCL repeaters.

Other Comments: Built first, this sister ship to *Norwegian Wind* had a fairly handsome profile (despite a large, square funnel) that was well balanced before she underwent a "chop and stretch" operation in the spring of 1998. Following the stretch her exterior shape is now not as handsome. The lifeboats are inboard. There is a rubber-covered promenade deck outdoors. The tiered pool deck is neat, as are the multideck aft sun terraces.

A completely new midsection was added as part of the stretch. Included in the 131.2 ft (40 m) section were 251 new passenger cabins and 50 crew cabins, together with several new or enlarged public rooms (although there simply are not enough) including a 60-seat conference center. Some innovative features were incorporated in the original design, and these have been kept and enhanced. The passenger flow is generally good; indeed, the ship seems to absorb passengers quite well for much of the time, except at peak traffic times between dinner seatings.

The design provides smaller public rooms rather than the large hangers found aboard so many other ships. The pastel interior colors used are quite soothing, and she is considered by many to be a pretty ship inside. The entrance lobby could be warmer (flowers please).

This ship has proven highly successful for Norwegian Cruise Line's younger, active, sports-minded passengers, and provides a good alternative to the larger ships and their larger passenger numbers, although there are plenty of other passengers to keep you company. UK-origin passengers should note that all onboard gratuities are included, as are port taxes.

<u>Weak Points</u>: The room service menu is still poor and could be improved. The outdoor stairways are numerous and confusing. The carpeted steel interior stairwell steps are quite tinny. When the ship was "stretched" it reduced the amount of outdoor space per passenger, and this is reflected in increased density around the pools. There simply are not enough public rooms to absorb the increase in passengers.

m/s Norwegian Majesty
★★★ +
(L)

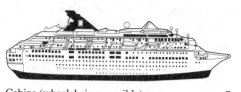

LIFESTYLE:	STANDARD
Cruise Line:	Norwegian Cruise Line
Former Names:	*Royal Majesty*
Gross Tonnage:	40,876
Builder:	Kvaerner Masa-Yards (Finland)
Original Cost:	$229 million
Entered Service:	September 1992/November 1997
Flag:	Panama
Tel. No.:	1336557
Fax No.:	1336563
Length (ft/m):	680.0/207.20
Beam (ft/m):	90.5/27.60
Draft (ft/m):	20.3/6.20
Propulsion/Propellers:	diesel (21,120kW)/2 (CP)
Passenger Decks:	9
Total Crew:	702
Pass. Capacity (basis 2):	1,460
Pass. Capacity (all berths):	1,790
Pass. Space Ratio (basis 2):	27.9
Pass. Space Ratio (all berths):	22.8
Officers:	Norwegian
Total Cabins:	730
Size Range (sq ft/m):	118.4–374.5/11.0–34.8
Cabins (outside view):	481
Cabins (inside — no view):	249
Cabins (single occupancy):	0
Cabins (with private balcony):	0

Cabins (wheelchair accessible):	7
Cabin Current:	110 and 220 volts
Cabin TV:	Yes
Dining Rooms:	2 (+ Bistro)
Elevators:	6
Casino:	Yes
Slot Machines:	Yes
Swimming Pools (outdoors):	2
Swimming Pools (inside):	0
Whirlpools:	3
Fitness Center:	Yes
Sauna/Steam Room:	Yes/No
Massage:	Yes
Self-Service Launderette:	No
Movie Theater/Seats:	Yes/100
Library:	Yes
Classification Society:	Lloyd's Register

RATINGS	POSSIBLE SCORE	SCORE ACHIEVED
Ship	500	393
Accommodation	200	158
Food	400	241
Service	400	255
Cruise	500	331
TOTAL	**2,000**	**1,378**

Note: This rating was done before the "stretch" operation that increased the ship's size and capacity.

Accommodation: The suites feature butler service and are well equipped (they also have VCR units as well as televisions), though they are not really large. Most other cabins are on the small side, but very comfortable, and with excellent bathroom showers. There are 132 cabins designated for nonsmokers. All cabins are provided with ironing boards (but no irons). Some cabins have obstructed views (check the deck plans carefully).

Dining: There are two main dining rooms (Seven Seas, with 636 seats, and the more intimate Four Seasons, which was added when the ship was "stretched" in 1999) with 266 seats. Both are totally non-smoking. However, they are quite noisy and the tables are rather close together, which means that correct service is difficult. There are two seatings. The food, menu, creativity and service are basically sound, but the choice of bread rolls, cheese, and fruits is limited. Dinners are "themed" each evening, something that has been popular with NCL passengers for years.

There is also a 56-seat Le Bistro Restaurant, which serves Italian and continental cuisine for alternative dinners in a more intimate environment (no reservations are needed).

For casual, self-serve meals, Café Royale is an intimate buffet restaurant with 112 seats; it is open for breakfast, lunch, and snacks. A 40-seat coffee bar/lounge serves a variety of coffees, coffee-flavored drinks, "flaming" specialty drinks, and teas.

Other Comments: This smart, stylish, contemporary cruise ship, originally constructed for the now-defunct Royal Cruise Line, has a good profile and is generally a well-designed vessel. However, the open deck and sunbathing space is limited, and there are no cushioned pads for the plastic deck chairs. The ship underwent a $53.3 million "stretch" and refurbishment operation in the spring of 1999, which added new cabins, new and larger public rooms, more open deck space and two new elevators, and refreshed all other existing public spaces. Also added a children's pool in addition to one for adults. The profile is now even sleeker and more aerodynamic.

Inside, she is quite a pretty ship, tastefully appointed, with lots of teak and brass accents, discreet lighting, soothing colors, and no glitz. Wide passageways provide a feeling of inner spaciousness. The ship has a nice touch of elegance and open walking areas provide a fine feel to it. The circular lobby is bright and classical in appearance. Has three good conference/group meeting rooms.

The observation lounge (Royal Observatory) has become a sports bar and lounge, complete with sports memorabilia (it used to contain models and plans of nineteenth-century sailing ships). The showroom, however, is poorly designed, with 14 pillars obstructing the sight lines.

This ship will provide you with a comfortable cruise experience in warm, fairly elegant surroundings, with generally good food, and a modicum of hospitality. The ship is based in Boston during the summer season for seven-night cruises to Bermuda (the crew even wear Bermuda shorts), while during the winter she is based in Miami for seven-night Caribbean cruises. UK-based passengers should note that all onboard gratuities are included, as are port taxes.

<u>Weak Points</u>: There are many repetitive, loud announcements, and the increased amount of squeezing for onboard revenue makes a cruise aboard her less enjoyable than many would like it to be.

m/s Norwegian Sea
★★★ +
(L)

LIFESTYLE:	STANDARD
Cruise Line:	Norwegian Cruise Line
Former Names:	*Seaward*
Gross Tonnage:	42,276
Builder:	Wartsila (Finland)
Original Cost:	$120 million
Entered Service:	June 1988
Flag:	Bahamas
Tel No:	1104601
Fax No:	1104602
Length (ft/m):	708.6/216.00
Beam (ft/m):	95.1/29.00
Draft (ft/m):	22.9/7.00
Propulsion/Propellers:	diesel (21,120kW)/2 (CP)
Passenger Decks:	9
Total Crew:	630
Pass. Capacity (basis 2):	1,508
Pass. Capacity (all berths):	1,798
Pass. Space Ratio (basis 2):	28.0
Pass. Space Ratio (all berths):	23.5
Officers:	Norwegian
Total Cabins:	755
Size Range (sq ft/m):	109.7–269.1/10.2–25.0
Cabins (outside view):	512
Cabins (inside):	243
Cabins (for one person):	0
Cabins (with private balcony):	0
Cabins (wheelchair accessible):	4
Cabin Current:	110 volts
Cabin TV:	Yes
Dining Rooms:	2
Elevators:	6
Casino:	Yes
Slot Machines:	Yes
Swimming Pools (outdoors):	2
Swimming Pools (inside):	0
Whirlpools:	2
Fitness Center:	Yes
Sauna/Steam Room:	Yes/No
Massage:	Yes
Self-Service Launderette:	No
Movie Theater/Seats:	No
Library:	No
Classification Society:	Det Norske Veritas

RATINGS	POSSIBLE SCORE	SCORE ACHIEVED
Ship	500	375
Accommodation	200	148
Food	400	237
Service	400	284
Cruise	500	348
TOTAL	**2,000**	**1,392**

Accommodation: There are 16 cabin categories. This ship was built before balcony cabins came into vogue, so there are none. The cabins are of average size for a standard cruise ship (which translates to "somewhat cramped for two") although they are quite tastefully appointed and comfortable, with warm, pastel colors, bright soft furnishings, and a touch of art deco styling; however, the walls and ceilings are quite plain and simple. Audio channels are available via the television, although the picture cannot be turned off. The bathrooms are efficient units that are quite well designed, although they are quite basic; hairdryers (they are weak) are included in all bathrooms.

If you book a suite or one of two upper-grade cabins, you'll get a little more space, a lounge area with table and sofa that converts into another bed (good for families), European duvets, and a refrigerator (top three catgories only). The bathrooms also feature a bathtub, shower, and retractable clothesline.

Dining: There are two principal dining rooms (Four Seasons, with 372 seats, and Seven Seas, with 476 seats). They are both comfortable, and feature pastel decor. The dining room you are assigned depends on the accommodation you book, but both are nonsmoking and have two seatings. The cuisine, for a mass-market ship, ranges from adequate to reasonably good. Vegetables (few green ones are used) tend to be overcooked. Fish and poultry items are good. Meat is disappointing. The emphasis is on Tex-Mex cuisine, with a wide choice of hot and spicy courses. The service is, on the whole, adequate, nothing more, and proves that good staff that can communicate well are quite difficult to find.

In addition to the two dining rooms, there are other alternative dining spots. For casual breakfast and lunch there's the Big Apple Café (436 seats), which has indoor and outdoor seating. There is also the intimate 82-seat Le Bistro, open for informal dinners, and Gatsby's is a popular wine bar that features a good wine and champagne list. Le Bistro and Gatsby's are both located high in the ship and have large ocean-view picture windows. The selection of wines is good, but the glasses are small. The breakfast and luncheon buffets are quite poor and should have more variety and better ingredients.

Other Comments: This angular, yet reasonably attractive vessel has a contemporary European cruise-ferry profile with a sharply raked bow and sleek mast and funnel. There is a full wraparound promenade deck outdoors (although it is a plain steel deck, painted nautical blue).

This ship is quite well designed, with generally sound passenger flow and no major areas of congestion, and an abundance of public rooms and open interior spaces, many with high ceilings. The interior decor is designed to remind you of sea and sky by stressing the colors of coral, blue, and mauve. Although the hallways and stairways are quite plain, two glass-walled stairways provide good connection with sea and sky. There is a good gymnasium/fitness center for those who want to work their muscles; it is located around the mast and is accessible only from the outside deck (clearly not good when it rains).

The Crystal Court lobby is two decks high and is pleasing without being overwhelming, although at times it appears quite cluttered. It has a tubed crystal and water sculpture and seatback-less seating around its perimeter.

The 770-seat theater-showroom (called "Cabaret") provides large-scale dazzle and sizzle shows with lots of energy and volume (including a shortened version of the musical "Grease"), although 12 thick pillars obstruct the sight lines from many seats. There is also a large nightclub (again there are several pillars obstructing sight lines), and a disco (correctly called "Boomers"). For those seeking a more intimate lounge, the mahogany-paneled Oscar's Lounge is the place to go.

This ship will provide a cruise in good taste for first-time cruise passengers who want to have fun in comfortable surroundings, at a sensible, competitive price. If you like sports bars, country 'n western music, hoedowns, and amateurish participation games, this ship will prove a lot of fun.

Weak Spots: Cluttered and unclean open decks. Food buffets (very poor presentation and quality of ingredients). Food service and supervision need work. Badly dented and scuffed panels in the accommodation hallways are unattractive. The steps on the stairways are tinny. There is no library. The constant background music in the hallways is irritating. There is too much use of artificial grass on the upper outdoor decks (this gets very soggy when wet). There are no cushioned pads for the deck lounge chairs. The cruise staff is very young and rather amateurish.

m/s Norwegian Sky
(L)

LIFESTYLE:	STANDARD
Cruise Line:	Norwegian Cruise Line
Former Names:	-
Gross Tonnage:	80,000
Builder:	Lloyd Werft (Germany)
Original Cost:	$332 million
Entered Service:	August 1999
Flag:	Bahamas
Tel. No.:	n/a
Fax No.:	n/a
Length (ft/m):	853.0/260.0
Beam (ft/m):	105.8/32.25
Draft (ft/m):	26.2/8.00
Propulsion/Propellers:	diesel (50,000kW)/2 (CP)
Passenger Decks:	12
Total Crew:	750
Pass. Capacity (basis 2):	2,002
Pass. Capacity (all berths):	2,450
Pass. Space Ratio (basis 2):	39.9
Pass. Space Ratio (all berths):	32.6
Officers:	Norwegian
Total Cabins:	1,001
Size Range (sq ft/m):	120.5–488.6/11.2–45.4
Cabins (outside view):	574
Cabins (inside — no view):	427
Cabins (single occupancy):	0
Cabins (with private balcony):	252

Cabins (wheelchair accessible):	6
Cabin Current:	110 volts
Cabin TV:	Yes
Dining Rooms:	2 main, 3 alternative
Elevators:	12
Casino:	Yes
Slot Machines:	Yes
Swimming Pools (outdoors):	2
Swimming Pools (inside):	0
Whirlpools:	5
Fitness Center:	Yes
Sauna/Steam Room:	Yes/Yes
Massage:	Yes
Self-Service Launderette:	No
Movie Theater/Seats:	No
Library:	Yes
Classification Society:	Registro Navale Italiano

RATINGS	POSSIBLE SCORE	SCORE ACHIEVED
Ship	500	NYR
Accommodation	200	NYR
Food	400	NYR
Service	400	NYR
Cruise	500	NYR
TOTAL	**2,000**	**NYR**
Expected Score Range:		**1400-1600**

Accommodation: All of the standard outside-view and inside (no view) cabins feature two lower beds that can convert to a queen-size bed, a small lounge area with sofa and table, and a decent amount of closet and drawer space. Over 200 outside-view cabins each have their own private balcony. Each cabin has a small vanity/writing desk, color television, personal safe, climate control, and — in a cruise industry first — a laptop computer connection socket.

Junior suites — 21 of them — feature a private teakwood balcony; these suites face aft in a secluded position and overlook the ship's wash.

The largest accommodation can be found in the eight suites that each feature a Jacuzzi tub outside on their huge, private, forward-facing teakwood floor balconies, slightly better bathrooms, lounge area, separate bedroom, more space, and large, circular windows.

Dining: There are two main dining rooms (Four Seasons, with 564 seats, and Seven Seas, with 604 seats). Both are nonsmoking, and each has two seatings. Adjacent is a third, smaller dining room, Horizons Restaurant, with 84 seats, which is available as an à la carte dining option. Other dining options include the 84-seat Le Bistro, an alternative dining spot for more casual eating; and a sports bar and grill (complete with a wall of television screens and live satellite-televised sports action), a pizzeria, a wine bar, a champagne bar, and an ice-cream bar.

Other Comments: This ship was created from the hull of what was to be *CostaOlympia*, which was purchased for $40 million and not completed when the shipyard went into bankruptcy. Norwegian Cruise Line thus was able to build this ship in about 20 months, almost half of the time it would normally have taken. The amount of outdoor space is very good, and the pool deck, with its two swimming pools and four Jacuzzi tubs, features an electric "skymobile" beverage cart.

There is a two-level, 1,000-seat show lounge, with large proscenium stage for the high-energy dazzle and sizzle shows that NCL passengers enjoy, and Cameron Mackintosh features the first seagoing production of one of his musicals. However, the sight lines are obstructed in a number of seats by several slim pillars.

A separate cabaret lounge is equipped with what NCL states is the longest bar at sea, at 98.4 ft (30 m) long. At present, however, this honor goes to *Aida* — owned by NCL but under charter to Arkona Reisen of Germany. Other features include a large casino, shopping arcade, children's playroom (there is also a splash pool in a prime open deck area forward atop ship), a video arcade, a large health/fitness spa (including an aerobics room and separate gymnasium), and several treatment rooms.

Other facilities include a conference room, library, and beauty salon, Churchill's cigar smoking lounge (adjoining the Windjammer Bar) for cigars and cognac, and an Internet Café, while those with a black belt in shopping might appreciate the fact that all the shops on board are run by Columbian Emeralds (this is a cruise industry first).

Sports fans will appreciate the basketball/volleyball court, baseball batting cage, golf-driving range, platform tennis, shuffleboard, and table tennis facilities, and a sports bar with 24-hour live satellite television coverage of sports events and major games. Joggers will find a wraparound jogging track outdoors.

Norwegian Sky tries to be all things to all people, and is NCL's latest, and best (with staff hand-picked from the company's other ships), resort at sea. The ship is based in Seattle (Seattle is a new cruise turnaround port, whereas almost all other Alaska-bound cruise vessels depart from Vancouver). During the winter season, she features seven-night Caribbean cruises.

<u>Weak Points</u>: Anyone in the Four Seasons dining room wanting to use the restroom must exit the dining room and go across the atrium to locate the nearest one. The ceilings in the cabins are very plain and uninteresting.

m/s Norwegian Star
★★★★
(M)

LIFESTYLE:	STANDARD
Cruise Line:	Norwegian Capricorn Line
Former Names:	*Royal Odyssey, Royal Viking Sea*
Gross Tonnage:	28,078
Builder:	Wartsila (Finland)
Original Cost:	$22.5 million
Entered Service:	November 1973/December 1998
Flag:	Bahamas
Tel. No.:	1104504
Fax No.:	1104511
Length (ft/m):	674.2/205.50
Beam (ft/m):	83.6/25.50
Draft (ft/m):	23.9/7.30
Propulsion/Propellers:	diesel (13,400kW)/2 (CP)
Passenger Decks:	8
Total Crew:	380
Pass. Capacity (basis 2):	848
Pass. Capacity (all berths):	1,150
Pass. Space Ratio (basis 2):	33.1
Pass. Space Ratio (all berths):	24.4
Officers:	Norwegian
Total Cabins:	400
Size Range (sq ft/m):	119.4–612.4/11.1–56.9
Cabins (outside view):	354
Cabins (inside — no view):	46
Cabins (single occupancy):	0
Cabins (with private balcony):	9
Cabins (wheelchair accessible):	0
Cabin Current:	110 and 220 volts
Cabin TV:	Yes
Dining Rooms:	1 (+ 1 bistro)
Elevators:	5
Casino:	Yes
Slot Machines:	Yes
Swimming Pools (outdoors):	1
Swimming Pools (inside):	0
Whirlpools:	3
Fitness Center:	Yes
Sauna/Steam Room:	Yes/No
Massage:	Yes
Self-Service Launderette:	No
Movie Theater/Seats:	Yes/156
Library:	No
Classification Society:	Det Norske Veritas

RATINGS	POSSIBLE SCORE	SCORE ACHIEVED
Ship	500	379
Accommodation	200	156
Food	400	249
Service	400	287
Cruise	500	356
TOTAL	**2,000**	**1,427**

Accommodation: There are 12 grades of accommodation, from expansive owner's suites to small inside (no-view) cabins.

There are four owner's suites (one with a view of the bow being just under the navigation bridge) with twin or queen-size bed. The other three (located on the port side of Promenade Deck) have a queen-size bed, separate lounge with refrigerator, private balcony, large windows, and bathroom with full-size bathtub and shower.

All other cabins (most of which are outside) are well appointed, with good closet, drawer, and storage space, although some bathrooms in the lower categories have awkard access. Some of the newer cabins have whirlpool bathtubs. Nonsmoking cabins are available. Note that tinny drawers in the cabins remain from her former days as a Royal Viking Line ship. Bathrobes are provided for suite passengers only.

Dining: The dining room has a high ceiling and is quite spacious. Dining is in two seatings, with assigned tables for two, four, six, or eight. Breakfast and luncheon can also be taken outdoors by the swimming pool. Regional foods are featured, including a good choice of breads and tropical fruits. The hot food choice is quite good, and the presentation of entrees has been beefed up to cater to the tastes of Australasian passengers.

There is also an informal dining spot called Le Bistro, where casual dining makes for an alternative to the dining room for those who do not wish to dress for dinner. In addition, there is a sports bar and grill.

Other Comments: This ship has a smart, almost contemporary profile, with well-balanced lines and a delightful, sharply raked bow, something not found on the newest cruise ships today. She also has a decent draft, which makes her eminently suitable for the (sometimes) unkind waters around Australia and New Zealand, the ship's principal cruising regions. The ship has been quite well maintained (she started life as one of three original Royal Viking Line sister ships in the 1970s operating world-wide cruises) and has a wide expanse of open deck, sunbathing space, and several sports areas, including a large paddle tennis court.

Inside, the public rooms are quite elegant and have high ceilings. The spa and fitness facilities are generally good. The casino has tasteful decor.

This ship was "stretched" in 1983, and a major multimillion dollar reconstruction took place in 1997, when more cabins were added (sadly, the library was taken away). Also added was a "Kids Korner" playroom, and a video arcade (although there really are few other facilities for children, the ship being better suited to older adults). Families with children are catered to with an extensive program. According to age, children are called Nippers (3 to 6 years old); Navigators (7 to 12 years old); Legends (13 to 17 years old).

This ship is presently sailing under a joint venture between Norwegian Capricorn Line and Norwegian Cruise Line. The ship provides a well programmed cruise experience for those passengers who do not want to cruise aboard the megaships. The ship is based in Sydney, Australia, and started operating seven- to 20-day cruises (plus a couple of occasional short "taster" cruises) in December 1998. Summer cruises feature New Zealand and Tasmania, while winter cruises feature the Coral Sea and Australia's Queensland coast. Most passengers are from Australasia, but the ship is also marketed to North American and British passengers.

<u>Weak Points</u>: Although she is a very smart-looking vessel, the ship *is* getting old and the design has been superceded by more trendy ships in other markets.

m/s Norwegian Wind
★★★★
(L)

LIFESTYLE:	STANDARD
Cruise Line:	Norwegian Cruise Line
Former Names:	*Windward*
Gross Tonnage:	50,760
Builder:	Chantiers de l'Atlantique (France)
Original Cost:	$240 million
Entered Service:	June 1993
Flag:	Bahamas
Tel. No.:	1305713/1305715
Fax No.:	1305714/1305716
Length (ft/m):	754.0/229.8
Beam (ft/m):	93.5/28.5
Draft (ft/m):	22.3/6.8
Propulsion/Propellers:	diesel (18,480kW)/2 (CP)
Passenger Decks:	10
Total Crew:	614
Pass. Capacity (basis 2):	1,732
Pass. Capacity (all berths):	2,156
Pass. Space Ratio (basis 2):	29.3
Pass. Space Ratio (all berths):	23.5
Officers:	Norwegian
Total Cabins:	866
Size Range (sq ft/m):	139.9–349.8/13.0–32.5
Cabins (outside view):	696
Cabins (inside — no view):	170
Cabins (single occupancy):	0
Cabins (with private balcony):	48

Cabins (wheelchair accessible):	6 (+ 30 for hearing impaired)
Cabin Current:	110 volts
Cabin TV:	Yes
Dining Rooms:	2
Elevators:	10
Casino:	Yes
Slot Machines:	Yes
Swimming Pools (outdoors):	2
Swimming Pools (inside):	0
Whirlpools:	2
Fitness Center:	Yes
Sauna/Steam Room:	Yes/No
Massage:	Yes
Self-Service Launderette:	No
Movie Theater/Seats:	No
Library:	Yes
Classification Society:	Det Norske Veritas

RATINGS	POSSIBLE SCORE	SCORE ACHIEVED
Ship	500	398
Accommodation	200	155
Food	400	241
Service	400	288
Cruise	500	350
TOTAL	**2,000**	**1,432**

For comments, see *Norwegian Dream.*

s/s OceanBreeze
★★ +
(M)

LIFESTYLE:	STANDARD
Cruise Line:	Imperial Majesty Cruise Line
Former Names:	*Azure Seas, Calypso, Monarch Star, Southern Cross*
Gross Tonnage:	21,486
Builder:	Harland & Wolff (UK)
Original Cost:	n/a
Entered Service:	March 1955/May 1992
Flag:	Liberia
Tel. No.:	1246254
Fax No.:	1246255
Length (ft/m):	603.8/184.06
Beam (ft/m):	80.0/24.41
Draft (ft/m):	26.1/7.97
Propulsion/Propellers:	steam turbine (14,900kW)/2 (FP)
Decks:	9
Total Crew:	380
Pass. Capacity (basis 2):	776
Pass. Capacity (all berths):	1,012
Pass. Space Ratio (basis 2):	27.6
Pass. Space Ratio (all berths):	21.2
Officers:	Greek
Total Cabins:	388
Size Range (sq ft/m):	96.8–398.2/9.0–37.0
Cabins (outside view):	298
Cabins (inside — no view):	90
Cabins (single occupancy):	0

Cabins (with private balcony):	0
Cabins (wheelchair accessible):	0
Cabin Current:	110 and 220 volts
Cabin TV:	Suites only
Dining Rooms:	1
Elevators:	2
Casino:	Yes
Slot Machines:	Yes
Swimming Pools (outdoors):	1
Swimming Pools (inside):	0
Whirlpools:	1
Fitness Center:	Yes
Sauna/Steam Room:	Yes/No
Massage:	No
Self-Service Launderette:	No
Movie Theater/Seats:	Yes/55
Library:	Yes
Classification Society:	Bureau Veritas

RATINGS	POSSIBLE SCORE	SCORE ACHIEVED
Ship	500	263
Accommodation	200	110
Food	400	215
Service	400	244
Cruise	500	263
TOTAL	**2,000**	**1,095**

Accommodation: There is a wide variety of cabin shapes and sizes, and most of them are, for the most part, reasonably comfortable and nicely decorated in earth tones and pastel colors. Although they are not large, they are reasonably well appointed and have heavy-duty fittings (she is an old ship). There are 12 larger suites, some of which have a forward view; these come with a separate bedroom and living area.

Dining: The Caravelle Restaurant is located low down in the ship, but has a warm, cheerful ambience. There are two seatings. The cuisine is generally quite sound, and there is plenty of it, but it certainly is not gourmet food, despite what the brochure claims, and the variety is quite basic. The service is reasonable and attentive, but somewhat rushed. There is a limited choice of cheeses and fresh fruits.

Other Comments: *OceanBreeze* is a vintage ship, which was originally built to operate line voyages from England to Australia in the 1950s for the now-defunct Shaw Savill Line. The ship has a long, low profile and is easily identified by its single funnel set almost at the stern.

Over the years, the ship has been maintained quite well, although she is now showing her age in several areas — she is, after all, over 40 years old! Her large amounts of wooden open decks are in good condition, while a refurbishment in 1997 revitalized some of the public rooms. One nice feature is her steam turbine propulsion, which translates to no vibration, unlike most of the newer diesel or diesel-electric powered ships.

The ship has some interesting art deco features in her interior decoration, a carryover from her former days as a transocean liner. There is a generous amount of open deck and sunbathing space. There is a two-level casino. The children's program is good for those families with youngsters. This is a good ship for those wanting a pleasant cruise vacation for a very modest price, in casual surroundings.

This ship operates two-day cruises from Port Canaveral to the Bahamas. *OceanBreeze* should prove to be good for an inexpensive, no-frills cruise aboard one of the few former ocean liners still operating.

<u>Weak Points</u>: Do expect lines for embarkation, disembarkation, shore excursions, and buffets. There are many smokers among the passengers. Many crew members do not speak English well.

s/s Ocean Explorer I
(M)

LIFESTYLE:	STANDARD
Cruise Line:	The World Cruise Company
Former Names:	*Sapphire Seas, Emerald Seas,*
	Atlantis, President Roosevelt, Leilani,
	LaGuardia, General Richardson
Gross Registered Tonnage:	20,071
Builder:	Federal Shipbuilding (USA)
Original Cost:	n/a
Entered Service:	December 1944/November 1999
Flag:	Panama
Tel. No.:	1361726
Fax No.:	1362727
Length (ft/m):	622.6/189.77
Beam (ft/m):	75.5/23.04
Draft (ft/m):	26.5/8.10
Propulsion/Propellers:	steam turbine
	(14,000kW)/2 (FP)
Decks:	9
Total Crew:	425
Pass. Capacity (basis 2):	875
Pass. Capacity (all berths):	1,050
Pass. Space Ratio (basis 2):	22.9
Pass. Space Ratio (all berths):	19.1
Officers:	Greek
Total Cabins:	402
Size Range (sq ft/m):	120.0–300.0/11.1–27.8
Cabins (outside):	248
Cabins (inside — no view):	154
Cabins (single occupancy):	0

Cabins (with private balcony):	0
Cabins (wheelchair-accessible):	2
Cabin Current:	110 and 220 volts
Refrigerator:	No
Cabin TV:	some
Dining Rooms:	1
Elevators:	4
Casino:	No
Slot Machines:	No
Swimming Pools (outdoors):	1
Swimming Pools (inside):	0
Whirlpools:	0
Fitness Center:	Yes
Sauna/Steam Room:	Yes/Yes
Massage:	Yes
Self-Service Launderette:	No
Movie Theater/Seats:	Yes/158
Library:	Yes
Classification Society:	American Bureau

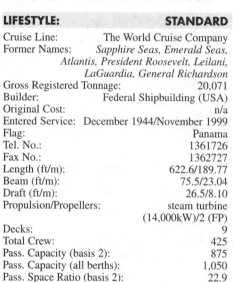

RATINGS	POSSIBLE SCORE	SCORE ACHIEVED
Ship	500	NYR
Accommodation	200	NYR
Food	400	NYR
Service	400	NYR
Cruise	500	NYR
TOTAL	**2,000**	**NYR**
Expected Score Range:		**1000-1200**

Accommodation: There are 11 cabin grades; these include suites, mini-suites, and outside-view and inside cabins. While there certainly are some tiny cabins, most are of reasonably generous proportions, and some have large bathrooms. Single passengers can book in a limited number of selected cabins at no additional surcharge. There is a room service menu, although there is an extra charge for room service.

Dining: The Palm dining room, which is located low down in the ship, has nostalgic old-world decor that is moderately cheerful. Open seating is operated, which means that you can dine when you want, and with whom you wish. The cuisine is definitely not a strong point, with food best described as marginally acceptable, although lacking in quality, variety, and presentation. Remember, however, that the cuisine is provided to a budget, and the prices being charged for a cruise are very modest.

Other Comments: This really classic, vintage ship is only one of a handful of ships with two funnels. She has an extremely strong hull built to quality specifications, with a "ducktail" sponson stern added for stability. For many years, the ship operated short cruises (between Miami and Nassau for Admiral Cruises) but was laid-up following her arrest in 1996 in the Mediterranean, and sold at auction. She is now under charter to the Canada-based World Cruise Company for continuous around-the-world cruises.

There is a good amount of open deck and sunning space. Passengers can visit the ship's navigation bridge at almost any time. The ship carries four Zodiac inflatable rubber landing craft for shore landings in eco-sensitive areas.

There are several good-size public rooms, most of which have high ceilings; they are located along one principal deck that houses most of the public rooms. The interior decor is quite conservative, perhaps even a little somber in places. Has a pleasant library and reading area.

This ship should provide a moderately comfortable cruise experience, with a very casual dress code and a decidedly unstuffy, unpretentious atmosphere. The onboard currency is the US dollar. You should not expect much from this ship however — it does not compare with the more upscale ships normally associated with around-the-world cruises. However, there is a good program of life-enrichment lecturers, whose subjects include the humanities, social sciences, and science and nature.

Weak Points: She is an old ship and cannot compete with the facilities provided aboard more contemporary vessels. There is no wraparound promenade deck outdoors. There are no public restrooms close to the restaurant.

CABIN AMENITIES

Cabins provide some, or all, of the following:

→ Private bathroom (generally small and compact) fitted with shower, wash basin, and toilet. Higher grade cabins and suites may have full-size bathtubs. Some even have a whirlpool bath and/or bidet, a hairdryer, and more space.

→ Electrical outlets for personal appliances, usually 110 and/or 220 volts.

→ Multichannel radio, television (regular satellite channels or closed circuit), and VCR.

→ Two beds or a lower and upper berth (possibly, another one or two upper berths) or a double-, queen-, or king-size bed. In some ships, twin beds can be pushed together to form a double.

→ Telephone, for inter-cabin or ship-to-shore communication.

→ Depending on cabin size, a chair, or chair and table, or sofa and table.

→ Vanity/desk unit with chair or stool.

→ Personal safe.

→ Closet space, some drawer space, plus storage room under beds for suitcases.

→ Bedside night stand/table unit.

→ Towels, soap, shampoo, and conditioner.

s/s **Oceanic**
★★ +
(L)

LIFESTYLE:	STANDARD
Cruise Line:	Premier Cruise Lines
Former Names:	*Oceanic*
Gross Tonnage:	38,772
Builder:	Cantieri Riuniti dell' Adriatico (Italy)
Original Cost:	$40 million
Entered Service:	April 1965/April 1986
Flag:	Bahamas
Tel. No.:	1120520
Fax No.:	1120520
Length (ft/m):	782.1/238.40
Beam (ft/m):	96.5/29.44
Draft (ft/m):	28.2/8.60
Propulsion/Propellers:	steam turbine (45,100kW)/2 (FP)
Decks:	10
Total Crew:	565
Pass. Capacity (basis 2):	1,124
Pass. Capacity (all berths):	1,800
Pass. Space Ratio (basis 2):	34.4
Pass. Space Ratio (all berths):	21.5
Officers:	International
Total Cabins:	562
Size Range (sq ft/m):	139.9–454.2/13.0–42.2
Cabins (outside view):	252
Cabins (inside — no view):	310
Cabins (single occupancy):	0
Cabins (with private balcony):	21
Cabins (wheelchair accessible):	1
Cabin Current:	110 volts
Cabin TV:	Yes
Dining Rooms:	1
Elevators:	5
Casino:	Yes
Slot Machines:	Yes
Swimming Pools (outdoors):	2
Swimming Pools (inside):	0
Whirlpools:	3
Fitness Center:	Yes
Sauna/Steam Room:	No/No
Massage:	Yes
Self-Service Launderette:	No
Movie Theater/Seats:	No
Library:	Yes
Classification Society:	Bureau Veritas

RATINGS	POSSIBLE SCORE	SCORE ACHIEVED
Ship	500	263
Accommodation	200	124
Food	400	222
Service	400	220
Cruise	500	264
TOTAL	**2,000**	**1,093**

Accommodation: There are eight deluxe suites (each of which has a private balcony), 65 suites (13 of which have a private balcony), while the rest are a mixture of inside (no-view) and outside (sea-view) cabins. There is a wide choice of cabin grades, sizes, and shapes. All cabins have heavy-duty furniture and are quite well equipped, although many are now in need of refurbishment. Many of the cabins feature double beds.

Dining: The dining room, which is totally nonsmoking for both of the two seatings, is large and cheerful, but extremely noisy when full. Features reasonably decent food and service (it was upgraded somewhat in 1998) considering the cruise fare, but there is a limited selection of breads, cheeses, and fruits.

Other Comments: Built originally as an ocean liner (now owned by Cruise Holdings of Miami, and operated by Premier Cruise Lines), several years ago the ship underwent a successful conversion to provide cheap and cheerful family cruises. Also known as the Big Red Boat. There is a reasonable amount of open deck space for sunbathing, but it becomes cramped (and noisy) when the ship is full, and there are no cushioned pads for the deck lounge chairs. The swimming pool atop the ship has a magrodome roof for bad weather.

Her interiors feature reasonably contemporary decor and cheerful, bright soft furnishing colors and fabrics. Has good enclosed promenades for strolling or sitting. This ship provides a good cruise experience for families with children by featuring many youth counselors. The many different cruise-and-stay packages are well designed and provide a variety of possibilities for extending your vacation to include land-based theme parks and resorts.

This ship will provide a family with a fun-filled cruise aboard a classic ship setting, but it does tend to remind one of a summer camp at sea, particularly when school vacations mean that lots (and I mean *lots*) of children will have the run of the ship. It is much less expensive than the Disney Cruise Line product, but then the Disney ships are brand new, whereas *Oceanic* is not.

Weak Points: The constant repetitive announcements are really irritating. The interiors could do with some more attention to detail and cleanliness.

m/s Ocean Majesty
★★★ +
(M)

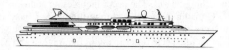

LIFESTYLE:	STANDARD
Cruise Line:	Majestic International Cruises
Former Names:	*Homeric, Olympic, Ocean Majesty, Kypros Star, Juan March*
Gross Tonnage:	10,417
Builder:	Union Navale de Levante (Spain)
Original Cost:	$65 million
Entered Service:	1966/April 1994
Flag:	Greece
Tel. No.:	1132141
Fax No.:	1132142
Length (ft/m):	443.8/135.30
Beam (ft/m):	62.9/19.20
Draft (ft/m):	19.5/5.95
Propulsion/Propellers:	diesel (12,200kW)/2 (CP)
Decks:	8
Total Crew:	235
Pass. Capacity (basis 2):	535
Pass. Capacity (all berths):	621
Pass. Space Ratio (basis 2):	19.4
Pass. Space Ratio (all berths):	16.7
Officers:	Greek
Total Cabins:	273
Size Range (sq ft/m):	96.8–182.9/9.0–17.0
Cabins (outside view):	186
Cabins (inside — no view):	87
Cabins (single occupancy):	11
Cabins (with private balcony):	8

Cabins (wheelchair accessible):	2
Cabin Current:	110 and 220 volts
Cabin TV:	Suites only
Dining Rooms:	1
Elevators:	3
Casino:	Yes
Slot Machines:	Yes
Swimming Pools (outdoors):	1
Swimming Pools (inside):	0
Whirlpools:	1
Fitness Center:	Yes
Sauna/Steam Room:	Yes/No
Massage:	Yes
Self-Service Launderette:	No
Movie Theater/Seats:	No
Library:	Yes
Classification Society:	American Bureau of Shipping

RATINGS	POSSIBLE SCORE	SCORE ACHIEVED
Ship	500	324
Accommodation	200	141
Food	400	248
Service	400	259
Cruise	500	302
TOTAL	**2,000**	**1,274**

Accommodation: Most of the cabins (there are too many cabin categories for a ship of this size) are small but quite functional, with a decent amount of closet and drawer space. The ceilings are very plain, and the soundproofing could be better, but the overall impression is that they are neat and tidy. All cabins have twin lower beds or double beds, and no upper/lower berths.

The bathrooms are bright and functional, with good lighting, but do lack space for storage of personal toiletry items.

Although there are two wheelchair accessible cabins, you should be aware that wheelchair access throughout much of the ship will prove difficult, and is not recommended.

Dining: The dining room (there are two seatings) is set low down and, although it is reasonably attractive, it is also extremely noisy, particularly at tables that are adjacent to the waiter stations, which seem to be everywhere. There are few tables for two, and most passengers dine at large tables that seat eight. The cuisine is continental in style, with a decent enough selection of menu items, highlighted by Greek specialties and signature dishes. There is a small selection of breads, fruits, and cheeses, and the buffets are generally simple, unimaginative, and repetitive affairs that have been improved somewhat since being catered by an Italian maritime catering company.

Other Comments: This ship has a pleasing, balanced, somewhat handsome profile, with an aft funnel. Her name, *Ocean Majesty*, however, seems a little ill-suited to a small ship such as this. A former Spanish ro-ro vessel (sister vessel to the present *Don Juan*, but with a much better designed layout and use of space), she underwent an extensive transformation into a smart cruise vessel (this was completed in 1994), with the exception of hull, shaft, and propellers. The conversion was done well, although her built-up stern is not particularly handsome. There is a good amount of open deck space for the size of the vessel, although the plastic deck furniture is tacky.

There are several good public rooms, bars, and lounges, furnished with good quality materials and soft furnishing fabrics. The decor includes an abundance of highly polished mirrored surfaces.

Cruising aboard this ship will provide a busy, destination-oriented experience in surroundings that are very casual, yet comfortable; in other words, you will not need to take any dressy clothes. The ship is of an ideal size for cruising in the Aegean and Mediterranean areas, and can get into many ports that larger ships cannot.

You should note that this ship is often chartered to various tour operators and packagers, which means that the standards of product delivery can vary on board (in fact almost every year the ship seems to be under a different operator). During each summer, the ship is under charter to the UK's Page & Moy for cruises to Northern Europe and the Baltics (during these charters the food and its presentation is improved).

Weak Points: This is a high-density vessel, so expect lines for shore excursions and buffets. Has a somewhat awkward interior layout and steep interior stairways with short steps.

BAGGAGE

→ There is generally no limit to the amount of personal baggage you can take on your cruise (towels, soap, shampoo, and shower caps are provided aboard most cruise ships). Do allow extra space for purchases on the cruise.

→ Tag your luggage with your name, ship, cabin number, sailing date, and port of embarkation (tags are provided by the cruise line with your tickets). Baggage transfers from airport to ship are generally smooth and problem-free when handled by the cruise line.

→ Liability for loss or damage to baggage is contained in the passenger contract (part of your ticket). Do take out insurance (the policy should extend from the date of departure until two or three days after your return home).

m/s Ocean Princess
★★★★ +
(L)

LIFESTYLE:	PREMIUM
Cruise Line:	Princess Cruises
Former Names:	-
Gross Tonnage:	77,000
Builder:	Fincantieri (Italy)
Original Cost:	$300 million
Entered Service:	February 2000
Flag:	Liberia
Tel. No.:	n/a
Fax No.:	n/a
Length (ft/m):	856.2/261.00
Beam (ft/m):	105.8/32.25
Draft (ft/m):	26.0/7.95
Propulsion/Propellers:	diesel-electric (28,000kW)/2 (FP)
Decks:	10
Total Crew:	900
Pass. Capacity (basis 2):	1,950
Pass. Capacity (all berths):	2,250
Pass. Space Ratio (basis 2):	39.4
Pass. Space Ratio (all berths):	34.2
Officers:	British/Italian
Total Cabins:	975
Size Range (sq ft/m):	158.2–610.3/14.7–56.7
Cabins (outside view):	609
Cabins (inside — no view):	372
Cabins (single occupancy):	0

Cabins (with private balcony):	410
Cabins (wheelchair accessible):	19
Cabin Current:	110 and 220 volts
Cabin TV:	Yes
Dining Rooms:	2 main/3 others
Elevators:	11
Casino:	Yes
Slot Machines:	Yes
Swimming Pools (outdoors):	4
Swimming Pools (inside):	0
Whirlpools:	5
Fitness Center:	Yes
Sauna/Steam Room:	Yes/Yes
Massage:	Yes
Self-Service Launderette:	Yes
Movie Theater/Seats:	No
Library:	Yes
Classification Society:	Registro Navale Italiano

RATINGS	POSSIBLE SCORE	SCORE ACHIEVED
Ship	500	442
Accommodation	200	168
Food	400	271
Service	400	299
Cruise	500	406
TOTAL	**2,000**	**1,586**

This is the fourth in a series of identical sister ships (the others being *Dawn Princess*, *Sea Princess*, and *Sun Princess*), and has been common-rated with them. For comments, see *Dawn Princess*.

m/t/s Odysseus
★★ +
(S)

LIFESTYLE:	STANDARD
Cruise Line:	Royal Olympic Cruises
Former Names:	*Aquamarine, Marco Polo,*
	Princesa Isabel
Gross Tonnage:	12,000
Builder:	Society Espanola Shipyard (Spain)
Original Cost:	n/a
Entered Service:	1962/Spring 1987
Flag:	Greece
Tel. No.:	1130652
Fax No.:	1130252
Length (ft/m):	483.1/147.30
Beam (ft/m):	61.2/18.67
Draft (ft/m):	24.1/7.35
Propulsion/Propellers:	diesel (6,766kW)/2 (CP)
Decks:	7
Total Crew:	194
Pass. Capacity (basis 2):	454
Pass. Capacity (all berths):	484
Pass. Space Ratio (basis 2):	26.4
Pass. Space Ratio (all berths):	24.7
Officers:	Greek
Total Cabins:	226
Size Range (sq ft/m):	102.2–279.8/9.5–26.0
Cabins (outside view):	183
Cabins (inside — no view):	43
Cabins (single occupancy):	0

Cabins (with private balcony):	0
Cabins (wheelchair accessible):	0
Cabin Current:	110 volts
Cabin TV:	No
Dining Rooms:	2
Elevators:	1
Casino:	Yes
Slot Machines:	Yes
Swimming Pools (outdoors):	1
Swimming Pools (inside):	0
Whirlpools:	4
Fitness Center:	Yes
Sauna/Steam Room:	Yes/No
Massage:	Yes
Self-Service Launderette:	No
Movie Theater/Seats:	Yes/145
Library:	Yes
Classification Society:	Lloyd's Register

RATINGS	POSSIBLE SCORE	SCORE ACHIEVED
Ship	500	288
Accommodation	200	116
Food	400	213
Service	400	223
Cruise	500	251
TOTAL	**2,000**	**1,091**

Accommodation: The attractive, fairly spacious, mostly outside-view cabins have convertible sofabeds that convert from a sofa during the day into a bed by night (sadly, very few cabins have genuine double beds). There is a decent amount of closet and drawer space (for short cruies), and tasteful wood trim accents the cabinetry. The cabin bathrooms, however, are really quite small, (particularly the shower stalls) and basic. Any in-cabin food/beverage service tends to be very basic, without the finesse found aboard more expensive vessels.

Dining: The dining room is reasonably charming, though it does tend to be noisy, due to the ceiling height and the location of waiter stations. There are two seatings (both smoking and nonsmoking sections are available). The food is typically continental and features several Greek dishes. Warm, attentive service is provided in typical Greek fashion, but the menu choice is rather limited. The quality and selection of breads, cheeses, and fruits could be better. Note that dining room seating and table assignments are done by the maître d' upon embarkation. An informal dining spot (Marine Club) is available for casual breakfast and lunches, although the selection is very limited.

Other Comments: This attractive-looking vessel has a balanced profile, and was acquired and completely reconstructed by Epirotiki Cruise Line (now part of Royal Olympic Cruises) in 1987. There is ample open deck and sunbathing space. Has twin teak-decked sheltered promenade walking areas.

There is a decent range of public rooms, almost all of which feature pleasing Mediterranean decor, with warm colors, and some interesting artwork. Almost all of the public rooms are located on one principal deck, so finding them is easy. The Taverna is especially popular with the younger set.

This ship is really for those who want to cruise at a modest cost, in warm surroundings, aboard a comfortable smaller vessel that features interesting and popular destination-intensive itineraries in the Aegean and Mediterranean areas. The ship is often placed under charter to tour operators specializing in "learning enrichment" vacations, and the cruises are sold by a number of cruise-tour companies in various countries. This means that passengers are likely to consist of a wide mix of nationalities, and daily programs and announcements, therefore, will probably be in several languages.

Gratuities (suggested at $9 per person per day) are pooled among the crew (you give them to the Chief Steward).

Weak Points: The company provides little port information for passengers wishing to go ashore individually, but heavily sells its own shore excursion programs. The staff hospitality factor is poor, and more training is needed.

MEDICATION

Take any medicine and other medical supplies that you need, plus spare eyeglasses or contact lenses. In many countries it may be difficult to find certain medicines. Others may be sold under different names. If you are taking a long cruise, ask your doctor for names of alternatives, in case the medicine you are taking is not available.

The ship's pharmacy will stock certain standard remedies, but do not expect a supply of the more unusual or obscure medicines. Remember to take along a doctor's prescription for any medication, especially when you are flying into foreign countries to join a ship, as customs may be difficult without documentation, particularly in the Far East.

Also, be advised that if you run out of your medication and you need to get a supply aboard ship, most ships will require that you see the doctor, even if you have a prescription. There is a charge for each visit, plus the cost of any medication.

Let spouses/companions carry a supply of your medicine and medical supplies. Do not pack medication in any luggage to be checked in when flying, but take it in your carry-on.

m/s Olvia
★★
(S)

LIFESTYLE:	STANDARD
Cruise Line:	K&O Cruises
Former Names:	*Kareliya, Leonid Brezhnev*
Gross Tonnage:	15,791
Builder:	Wartsila (Finland)
Original Cost:	$25 million
Entered Service:	December 1976/October 1998
Flag:	Liberia
Tel. No.:	1261557/1261565
Fax No.:	1261564
Length (ft/m):	512.6/156.27
Beam (ft/m):	71.8/21.90
Draft (ft/m):	19.4/5.92
Propulsion/Propellers:	diesel (13,430kW)/2 (CP)
Decks:	8
Total Crew:	250
Pass. Capacity (basis 2):	468
Pass. Capacity (all berths):	660
Pass. Space Ratio (basis 2):	33.7
Pass. Space Ratio (all berths):	23.9
Officers:	Ukrainian
Total Cabins:	234
Size Range (sq ft/m):	90.4–409.0/8.4–38.0
Cabins (outside view):	110
Cabins (inside — no view):	124
Cabins (single occupancy):	0
Cabins (with private balcony):	0

Cabins (wheelchair accessible):	0
Cabin Current:	220 volts
Refrigerator:	Boat Deck cabins only
Cabin TV:	Boat Deck cabins only
Dining Rooms:	2
Elevators:	2
Casino:	Yes
Slot Machines:	Yes
Swimming Pools (outdoors):	1 (+ child pool)
Swimming Pools (inside):	0
Whirlpools:	0
Fitness Center:	Yes
Sauna/Steam Room:	Yes/No
Massage:	Yes
Self-Service Laundry:	No
Movie Theater/Seats:	Yes/140
Library:	Yes
Classification Society:	Ukraine Register of Shipping

RATINGS	POSSIBLE SCORE	SCORE ACHIEVED
Ship	500	208
Accommodation	200	97
Food	400	175
Service	400	172
Cruise	500	190
TOTAL	**2,000**	**842**

Accommodation: Two forward Boat Deck suites are large, well appointed. They have large beds with good under-bed storage drawers, plenty of closet and drawer space, sofa, chairs and glass-topped coffee table, as well as a large bathroom with full-size bathtub and bidet. Another ten Boat Deck suites also have plenty of space and a bathroom that includes a full-size bathtub and bidet. All Boat Deck suites and cabins have windows that actually open, a nice change from the forced air-conditioning system. Bathrobes should be, but are not provided for the suite occupants (neither are personal toiletries such as shampoo or body lotion).

All of the other cabins are on the small side, but adequate for short cruises, though very cramped for any form of long voyage. All have a telephone and three-channel radio, although there really is very little closet and drawer space (definitely not enough for cruises longer than seven days). The cabin bathrooms are small and utilitarian, with little space for toiletries. Note that there is no cabin service menu, although (in general) towels are changed twice daily and bed linen twice weekly.

Dining: There are two dining rooms (in general, both are nonsmoking, although this really depends on the charterer and cruise itinerary of the vessel) and two seatings. They are basic rooms, and not very attractive, but they are noisy. Service is by Ukrainian waitresses who try hard, although without any finesse, and so much more training is needed. The menus are very limited, and presentation, garnishes, and food quality all could be improved greatly. There is a very limited selection of breads, fruits, cheeses, and salad dressings.

Other Comments: This small (by today's standards) but sharp-looking vessel sports a large, square funnel. The ship is one of several of the same size and type originally built to carry both vehicles and passengers, but converted more for cruise ship use several years ago.

Has a moderately comfortable interior, although the decor is rather plain, uncoordinated, and decidedly dated. Her newer facilities (added during various refits) provide more public rooms and choices for passengers. The library is small and the choice of books is poor.

There are several small public rooms, most of which are cozy bars. The Music Salon is the equivalent of a show lounge, and has raised seating along the port and starboard sides; however, views to the stage area are obstructed by ten slim pillars. The Dneipr Bar and Sadko Lounge are the two main bars, while Kiji Bar also acts as the ship's discotheque. Direct-dial satellite credit-card telephones are positioned in several of the foyer areas, although there is no privacy.

There is a separate cinema, located low down in the ship (it occupies space on what was a former car deck), and, although it is tiered, the seating is not staggered, so the sight lines are not as good as they could be. A good-size basketball court is positioned between mast and funnel — essential for the Ukrainian staff, but seldom used by passengers. There is a large sauna and relaxation facility.

This ship has fairly comfortable, reasonably cozy surroundings, although you should not expect any degree of finesse in service levels. The training of the Ukrainian service staff needs much attention, particularly in the dining rooms, where western standards simply have not been reached. Even though some of the staff seems to be willing, the management and supervision really is by outdated methods and needs to be brought more up-to-date. Perhaps more noticeable than anything else is the completely outdated old style of operations.

Much of this ship's cruising life is spent under charter to various operators or organizations, which really means that the standard of product delivery can and does vary according to the type of cruises featured by the charterer (and thus the price paid by passengers).

Weak Points: The condition and cleanliness of exterior open decks, stairways, and railings are poor and need attention. There are too many crew announcements, all of which are put through into the cabins at all hours. There are more inside than outside-view cabins. There is a long, steep gangway in many ports. Noticeably lacking in the ship's interiors are fresh flowers.

m/v Olympic Countess
★★★
(M)

LIFESTYLE: **STANDARD**

Cruise Line:	Royal Olympic Cruises
Former Names:	*Awani Dream I, Cunard Countess*
Gross Tonnage:	17,593
Builder:	Burmeister & Wein (Denmark)
Original Cost:	£12 million
Entered Service:	August 1976/1998
Flag:	Panama
Tel. No.:	1132632
Fax No.:	1132656
Length (ft/m):	536.6/163.56
Beam (ft/m):	74.9/22.84
Draft (ft/m):	19.0/5.82
Propulsion/Propellers:	diesel (15,670kW)/2 (CP)
Decks:	8
Total Crew:	350
Pass. Capacity (basis 2):	846
Pass. Capacity (all berths):	959
Pass. Space Ratio (basis 2):	20.7
Pass. Space Ratio (all berths):	18.3
Officers:	Greek
Total Cabins:	423
Size Range (sq ft/m):	87.1–264.8/8.1–24.6
Cabins (outside view):	281
Cabins (inside — no view):	142
Cabins (single occupancy):	0
Cabins (with private balcony):	0

Cabins (wheelchair accessible):	0
Cabin Current:	110 and 220 volts
Cabin TV:	No
Dining Rooms:	1
Elevators:	2
Casino:	Yes
Slot Machines:	Yes
Swimming Pools (outdoors):	1
Swimming Pools (inside):	0
Whirlpools:	2
Fitness Center:	Yes
Sauna/Steam Room:	Yes/No
Massage:	No
Self-Service Launderette:	No
Movie Theater/Seats:	Yes/126
Library:	Yes
Classification Society:	Lloyd's Register

RATINGS	POSSIBLE SCORE	SCORE ACHIEVED
Ship	500	326
Accommodation	200	121
Food	400	247
Service	400	251
Cruise	500	295
TOTAL	**2,000**	**1,240**

Accommodation: The cabins are mostly of a standard (compact) size, and come in light colors and plain but pleasant decor. They are best described as space-efficient units with metal fixtures and poor insulation — you can talk to your neighbors without having to use the telephone! The cabins on the lowest deck (Poseidon Deck) suffer from vibration and the odor of diesel fuel. The cabin bathrooms are small modular units, good for one, just about impossible for two.

Dining: The single dining room has large ocean-view picture windows on two sides, and seating is mostly at tables for four, six, or eight. There are two seatings. Reasonable banquet food is standard, tailored for American and European passengers. Out-of-the-ordinary requests are difficult. Limited fresh fruit and cheese selection. Good, cheerful service from an attentive Greek staff.

Other Comments: Originally built for Cunard as an informal Caribbean cruise vessel, she was purchased in late 1997 by Royal Olympic Cruises from her former operators, the now defunct Awani Dream Cruises, of Indonesia, who purchased the vessel from Cunard. The ship still displays a contemporary profile, with crisp, clean lines and a distinctive swept-back funnel.

Inside the ship, there is a good selection of public rooms to choose from, and most of them have attractive, light colors and cheerful decor.

Aft of the show lounge, which is a single-level room with raised seating on its port and starboard sides (several pillars obstruct sight lines), there is a good indoor-outdoor entertainment lounge/night club that incorporates a large aft open deck area — an excellent facility, particularly for warm-weather cruises.

Passengers seeking a casual, destination-intensive cruise will probably like this comfortable vessel, which is a change from the newer, larger ships of today, and is well suited to cruising in the Aegean/Mediterranean region.

Weak Points: This is a very high-density ship. The outside decks still need attention. Too many loud and unnecessary announcements do not a relaxing cruise make.

m/s Olympic Voyager
(M)

LIFESTYLE: **STANDARD**

Cruise Line:	Royal Olympic Cruises
Former Names:	-
Gross Tonnage:	25,000
Builder:	Blohm & Voss (Germany)
Original Cost:	$165 million
Entered Service:	July 2000
Flag:	Greece
Tel. No.:	n/a
Fax No.:	n/a
Length (ft/m):	590.5/180.0
Beam (ft/m):	83.6/25.5
Draft (ft/m):	23.2/7.1
Propulsion/Propellers:	diesel (37,800kW)/2 (CP)
Decks:	8
Total Crew:	360
Pass. Capacity (basis 2):	840
Pass. Capacity (all berths):	920
Pass. Space Ratio (basis 2):	29.7
Pass. Space Ratio (all berths):	27.1
Officers:	Greek
Total Cabins:	420
Size Range (sq ft/m):	134.5–516.6/12.5–48.0
Cabins (outside view):	274
Cabins (inside — no view):	126
Cabins (single occupancy):	0
Cabins (with private balcony):	12
Cabins (wheelchair accessible):	4
Cabin Current:	110 and 220 volts
Cabin TV:	Yes
Dining Rooms:	1
Elevators:	4
Casino:	Yes
Slot Machines:	Yes
Swimming Pools (outdoors):	1
Swimming Pools (inside):	0
Whirlpools:	0
Fitness Center:	Yes
Sauna/Steam Room:	Yes/No
Massage:	Yes
Self-Service Launderette:	Yes
Movie Theater/Seats:	No
Library:	Yes
Classification Society:	Germanischer Lloyd

RATINGS	POSSIBLE SCORE	SCORE ACHIEVED
Ship	500	NYR
Accommodation	200	NYR
Food	400	NYR
Service	400	NYR
Cruise	500	NYR
TOTAL	**2,000**	**NYR**
Expected Score Range:		**1400-1600**

Accommodation: The standard inside and outside-view cabins are quite compact, but with a practical layout, and the decor includes warm blond wood cabinetry, accents, and facings, and pleasing soft furnishings. The bathrooms are small, but have a good shower enclosure and storage facilities for toiletry items. There are 16 cabins in the forward section that have bay windows. These extend over the side of the ship, while 12 suites located high atop the ship and in the fowardmost section have large private balconies.

Dining: The dining room is located aft and has picture windows on three sides. There are two seatings, and there are tables for two, four, six, or eight.

Other Comments: This is the first new ship ever ordered by this company and is intended to take the company into the contemporary cruise market with new ships. She displays a compact outer design, complete with royal blue hull. There is a streamlined funnel.

The exterior hull design is similar to that found in naval frigates, with a slender fore-body, and two engine rooms (forward and midships) capable of providing a 27-knot speed (and even some additional power in reserve). The ship is thus designed for destination-intensive (port-hopping) itineraries that can be covered in a shorter time, which allows passengers more time in each port. There is no full wraparound promenade deck outdoors, although you can walk around three-quarters of the vessel. The swimming pool is located aft and is quite small.

The interior design combines contemporary conveniences with quiet, restrained decor intended to remind one of the Mediterranean region the ship is designed for. Most of the public rooms are located on one principal deck in a horizontal-flow layout that makes it easy to find your way around quickly, with a slightly winding open passageway that links several leisure lounges in one neat "street scene." A smoking room is also featured, located just forward of the casino, for cigar and cognac devotees.

Expert guest lecturers will accompany each cruise. In common with other ships in the fleet, it is expected that all gratuities are pooled among the crew (you give them to the chief steward).

351

m/s Oriana
★★★★ +
(L)

LIFESTYLE:	PREMIUM
Cruise Line:	P&O Cruises
Former Names:	-
Gross Tonnage:	69,153
Builder:	Meyer Werft (Germany)
Original Cost:	£200 million
Entered Service:	April 1995
Flag:	Great Britain
Tel. No.:	1453403
Fax No.:	1453404
Length (ft/m):	853.0/260.0
Beam (ft/m):	105.6/32.2
Draft (ft/m):	25.9/7.9
Propulsion/Propellers:	diesel (47,750kW)/2 (CP)
Decks:	10
Total Crew:	760
Pass. Capacity (basis 2):	1,810
Pass. Capacity (all berths):	1,849
Pass. Space Ratio (basis 2):	38.4
Pass. Space Ratio (all berths):	35.0
Officers:	British
Total Cabins:	914
Size Range (sq ft/m):	150.6–500.5/14.0–46.5
Cabins (outside view):	594
Cabins (inside — no view):	320
Cabins (single occupancy):	112
Cabins (with private balcony):	118

Cabins (wheelchair accessible):	8
Cabin Current:	110 and 220 volts
Cabin TV:	Yes
Dining Rooms:	2
Elevators:	10
Casino:	Yes
Slot Machines:	Yes
Swimming Pools (outdoors):	3
Swimming Pools (inside):	0
Whirlpools:	5
Fitness Center:	Yes
Sauna/Steam Room:	Yes/Yes
Massage:	Yes
Self-Service Launderette:	Yes
Movie Theater/Seats:	Yes/189
Library:	Yes
Classification Society:	Lloyd's Register

RATINGS	POSSIBLE SCORE	SCORE ACHIEVED
Ship	500	442
Accommodation	200	173
Food	400	297
Service	400	323
Cruise	500	402
TOTAL	**2,000**	**1,637**

Accommodation: There is a wide range of well-equipped cabin configurations and categories, including family cabins with extra beds (110 cabins can accommodate up to four persons). Some suites and cabins with balconies have an interconnecting door, and include a trouser press, ironing board, and iron — neatly tucked into a cupboard — binoculars, umbrella, a large atlas, and a second television as well as a sliding glazed panel between bedroom and sitting room. The bathrooms are somewhat disappointing, with an ordinary sink (I expected a marble unit). The whirlpool bathtubs are good, however, although they have high sides to step over. All in all, the suites, and particularly the bathrooms, are disappointing when compared with similar-size suites on other ships (they do, however, have a VCR player).

There is much use of rich, warm limed oak or cherry wood in the cabins, which makes even the least expensive four-berth cabin seem inviting. There is also a good number of cabins for single passengers. Standard cabin bathrooms are compact, but they do have art deco–style cabinets and lighting.

Dining: The two restaurants, Peninsular and Oriental, allocated according to the cabin grade and cabin chosen, are midships and aft. Both are moderately handsome (each has tables for two, four, six, or eight). Both have interesting ceilings, chandeliers, and decor; the chinaware is Wedgwood, the silverware Elkington. The Oriental Restaurant has windows on three sides, including the stern. Two seatings are featured in each restaurant.

"Eat and run" instead of "dining" tends to be the norm. Besides the Anton Mosimann–designed signature dishes, the meals are fairly nonmemorable, "Middle-England" standard (unpretentious) fare, and presentation lacks creativity. Afternoon tea, particularly, is disappointing, with a poor selection of teas.

The Conservatory Cafe offers breakfast and lunch buffets, and 24-hour self-service beverage stands. On selected evenings, it becomes an alternative restaurant featuring Indian cuisine, popular with the ship's mainly British clientele.

The former aerobics room (which was not used very much) has been turned into a pizzeria — popular particularly with children and teenage passengers.

Other Comments: The ship is quite conventional: evolutionary rather than revolutionary, but the first new ship for P&O Cruises for over 25 years. Capable of speedy long-distance cruising, it has the largest stabilizers of any ship, covering an area of 231 sq ft (21.5 m^2). She is a ship that takes *Canberra*'s traditional appointments and public rooms and adds more up-to-date touches, together with better facilities and passenger flow, and a feeling of timeless elegance.

For a little diversion, early references to the name *Oriana* are contained in sixteenth-century English romances. Various musical anthologies were composed to celebrate Elizabeth I as *Oriana*, culminating in a collection of 26 madrigals published by Thomas Morley in 1601 under the title "The Triumphs of Oriana." Although attributed to 23 different composers, each madrigal ends with the words "Long Live Fair Oriana."

Back to the ship. Her interiors are gentle, welcoming, and restrained. Splendid amount of open deck and sunbathing space, an important plus for her outdoors-loving British passengers. Has an extra-wide wraparound promenade deck outdoors. The stern superstructure is nicely rounded and has several tiers that overlook the aft decks, pool, and children's outdoor facilities.

Inside, the layout is well-designed and provides good horizontal passenger flow and wide passageways. Very noticeable are the fine, detailed ceiling treatments. Being a ship for all types of people, specific areas have been designed to attract different age groups and lifestyles.

There is a four-deck-high atrium and waterfall; it is elegant but not glitzy, topped by a dome of Tiffany glass. The large number of public entertainment rooms provides plenty of choice. The Theatre Royal, designed by John Wyckham, is decorated in rich reds and created specifically for drama and light theatrical presentations. It has individually air-conditioned seats, an orchestra pit, revolving stage, and excellent acoustics. The theater seats would provide better stage sight lines if they were staggered, however. A night club, the Pacific Lounge, has too many pillars that obstruct the view. Anderson's Lounge (named after the founder of the Peninsular Steam Navigation Company in the 1830s) features a series of nineteenth-century marine paintings and is decorated in the manner of a British gentlemen's club. Although there is no fireplace, it is the most popular lounge.

The fine, restful library has a good range of hardback books (and a real librarian), skillfully crafted tables, and some extremely comfortable chairs. Lord's Tavern is, without doubt, the most sporting place to pitch a beverage or two, decorated as it is in cricket memorabilia (indeed, the house of the ship's interior designer, John McNeece, stands on the site of the original Lord's cricket ground in London). Thackeray's (writing room) is named after William Makepeace Thackeray, a P&O passenger in 1844. Carpeting throughout the ship is of excellent quality, much of it custom designed and made (100 percent wool). There are some outstanding pieces of sculpture that add a touch of a floating museum, and original artworks by all-British artists that include several tapestries and sculptures.

The health spa is located forward and atop ship, is fairly large, and provides all the latest alternative treatment therapies. The coed sauna is a large facility (most ships have separate saunas for men and women).

Children and teens have "Club Oriana" programs with their own rooms ("Peter Pan" and "Decibels") and their own outdoor pool. There is also a special night nursery for small children (ages 2 to 5). The cabins also have a baby-listening device.

There is a wide variety of entertainment aboard the ships of P&O Cruises, as well as a good program of theme cruises (antiques, The Archers, art appreciation, classical music, comedy, cricket, gardening, jazz, motoring, popular fiction, Scottish dance, and sequence dancing are examples). Check with your travel agent to see what is available at the time you want to take your cruise.

Oriana provides a good cruise experience for British passengers (of all dialects) who do not want to fly to join a cruise ship, and the product has been undergoing fine-tuning since the ship first debuted. A fine British brass band send-off accompanies all sailings. Port taxes included for UK passengers. For gratuities (optional), allow £3.00 per person, per day.

<u>Weak Points</u>: During school holidays, you should be aware that there will be many children aboard; this can be a cause of irritation and frustration to many older passengers. Smokers seem to be everywhere. Passenger contact from the cruise "entertainment staff" is quite poor.

m/v Orient Venus
★★★★
(S)

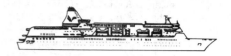

LIFESTYLE:	STANDARD
Cruise Line:	Venus Cruise
Former Names:	-
Gross Tonnage:	21,884
Builder:	Ishikawajima Heavy Industries (Japan)
Original Cost:	$150 million
Entered Service:	July 1990
Flag:	Japan
Tel. No.:	1201731
Fax No.:	1201731
Length (ft/m):	570.8/174.00
Beam (ft/m):	78.7/24.00
Draft (ft/m):	21.3/6.52
Propulsion/Propellers:	diesel (13,830kW)/2 (CP)
Decks:	6
Total Crew:	120
Pass. Capacity (basis 2):	390
Pass. Capacity (all berths):	606
Pass. Space Ratio (basis 2):	56.1
Pass. Space Ratio (all berths):	36.1
Officers:	Japanese
Total Cabins:	195
Size Range (sq ft/m):	182.9–592.0/17.0–55.0
Cabins (outside view):	195
Cabins (inside — no view):	0
Cabins (single occupancy):	0
Cabins (with private balcony):	2

Cabins (wheelchair accessible):	0
Cabin Current:	110 volts
Cabin TV:	Yes
Dining Rooms:	2
Elevators:	3
Casino:	No
Slot Machines:	No
Swimming Pools (outdoors):	1
Swimming Pools (inside):	0
Whirlpools:	0
Fitness Center:	Yes
Sauna/Steam Room:	No/No
Massage:	No
Self-Service Launderette:	Yes
Movie Theater/Seats:	Yes/606
Library:	Yes
Classification Society:	Nippon Kaiji Kyokai

RATINGS	POSSIBLE SCORE	SCORE ACHIEVED
Ship	500	353
Accommodation	200	124
Food	400	291
Service	400	287
Cruise	500	350
TOTAL	**2,000**	**1,405**

Accommodation: There are just four cabin grades. The all-outside standard cabins, many of which have upper berths for third/fourth passengers, have decor that is best described as plain, with a reasonable amount of closet space and little drawer space. The largest suites (of which there are two) have an expansive lounge area with large, plush armchairs, coffee table, window-side chairs and drinks table, floor-to-ceiling windows, and a large private balcony. There is a separate sleeping room (curtained off from the living room) with twin- or queen-size bed, vanity/office desk, and large bathroom. All grades of accommodation feature a tea drinking set (with electric hot water kettle), color television, telephone, and stocked refrigerator.

Dining: The main dining room, which operates one seating with assigned tables, is quite attractive, and there is plenty of space around the dining tables. In addition, an alternative Romanesque Grill is unusual, with its classic period Roman decor and a high, elegant ceiling. Features reasonably good, but rather commercial, Japanese cuisine (washoku) exclusively.

Other Comments: *Orient Venus* is the first cruise ship built for her owners, who are operators of several Japanese ferries. This is a conventional-shaped ship with a reasonably graceful profile. There is a decent amount of open deck and sunbathing space, which is not often used. There is also an expansive amount of open deck space for sunbathing, aft of funnel. Inside the ship, the Night and Day Lounge set at funnel base looks forward over the swimming pool. Windows of the Orient is a small, attractive, peaceful forward observation lounge. The conference facilities are excellent and consist of both main and small conference rooms with 620 movable seats. There is a fine array of public rooms with tasteful and very inviting decor. The horseshoe-shaped main lounge has very good sight lines to the platform stage.

This cruise ship, with its Western-style decor, will provide its mostly Japanese corporate passengers with extremely comfortable surroundings, and a superb cruise and seminar/learning environment.

Weak Points: The ship does not really cater to individual passengers well. The decor is rather plain in many public rooms. The crew-to-passenger ratio is quite poor, but typical of seminar-intensive ships.

m/t/s Orpheus
★★
(S)

LIFESTYLE:	STANDARD
Cruise Line:	Royal Olympic Cruises
Former Names:	*Thesus, Munster I, Munster*
Gross Tonnage:	5,092
Builder:	Harland & Wolff (UK)
Original Cost:	n/a
Entered Service:	1952/1969
Flag:	Greece
Tel. No.:	1133165
Fax No.:	1131336
Length (ft/m):	374.8/114.26
Beam (ft/m):	50.1/15.30
Draft (ft/m):	16.0/4.88
Propulsion/Propellers:	diesel (4,119kW)/2 (FP)
Decks:	6
Total Crew:	140
Pass. Capacity (basis 2):	304
Pass. Capacity (all berths):	310
Pass. Space Ratio (basis 2):	16.7
Pass. Space Ratio (all berths):	16.4
Officers:	Greek
Total Cabins:	152
Size Range (sq ft/m):	99.8–226.0/9.28–21.00
Cabins (outside view):	117
Cabins (inside — no view):	35
Cabins (single occupancy):	7
Cabins (with private balcony):	0

Cabins (wheelchair accessible):	0
Cabin Current:	220 volts
Cabin TV:	No
Dining Rooms:	1
Elevators:	0
Casino:	No
Slot Machines:	No
Swimming Pools (outdoors):	1
Swimming Pools (inside):	0
Whirlpools:	0
Fitness Center:	No
Sauna/Steam Room:	No/No
Massage:	No
Self-Service Launderette:	No
Movie Theater/Seats:	No
Library:	Yes
Classification Society:	Lloyd's Register

RATINGS	POSSIBLE SCORE	SCORE ACHIEVED
Ship	500	209
Accommodation	200	81
Food	400	202
Service	400	208
Cruise	500	214
TOTAL	**2,000**	**914**

Accommodation: The cabins (in six grades) are very compact but very nicely appointed for an older ship, and, thus, adequate for short cruises. There is a limited amount of closet, drawer, and under-bed storage space, so take only minimal clothing. The bathrooms, however, are really short on space.

Dining: The dining room is reasonably attractive and features an open seating policy. Features attentive, friendly service from the Greek waiters, but they are very casual. The food itself is reasonable, but certainly not memorable, and the selection of breads, cheeses, and fruits is limited. Dining room seating and table assignments are done by the maitre d' upon embarkation.

Other Comments: Has a traditional small ship profile, with a small, squat funnel. She is a charming older ship that has been reasonably well maintained. There is ample open deck and sunbathing space for a ship of this size, including a wraparound promenade deck outdoors, and there is also a small outdoor pool and bar, as well as a forward observation area outside on Apollo Deck.

There are few public rooms, but they are comfortable and have Mediterranean decor, good fabrics, and interesting regional artwork. Informality is the order of the day throughout, and dress codes are very casual (no formal nights).

The company features a number of guest lecturers who provide informed, yet informal presentations aboard all cruises. During the summer, the ship typically operates three- and four-night cruises from Piraeus. Gratuities (suggested at $9 per person per day) are pooled among the crew (you give them to the chief steward).

Weak Points: The high density of this vessel means that public rooms are always crowded when the ship is full. She is now an old lady and it is, perhaps, time for her to see retirement.

m/v Pacific Princess
★★★ +
(M)

LIFESTYLE:	PREMIUM
Cruise Line:	Princess Cruises
Former Names:	*Sea Venture*
Gross Tonnage:	20,636
Builder:	Rheinstahl Nordseewerke (Germany)
Original Cost:	$25 million
Entered Service:	May 1971/April 1975
Flag:	Great Britain
Tel. No.:	1440212
Fax No.:	1440212
Length (ft/m):	553.6/168.74
Beam (ft/m):	80.8/24.64
Draft (ft/m):	25.2/7.70
Propulsion/Propellers:	diesel (13,240kW)/2 (CP)
Decks:	7
Total Crew:	350
Pass. Capacity (basis 2):	640
Pass. Capacity (all berths):	717
Pass. Space Ratio (basis 2):	32.2
Pass. Space Ratio (all berths):	28.7
Officers:	British
Total Cabins:	320
Size Range (sq ft/m):	125.9–441.3/11.7–41.0
Cabins (outside view):	250
Cabins (inside — no view):	70
Cabins (single occupancy):	2
Cabins (with private balcony):	0

Cabins (wheelchair accessible):	2
Cabin Current:	110 and 220 volts
Cabin TV:	Yes
Dining Rooms:	1
Elevators:	4
Casino:	Yes
Slot Machines:	Yes
Swimming Pools (outdoors):	2
Swimming Pools (inside):	0
Whirlpools:	0
Fitness Center:	Yes
Sauna/Steam Room:	Yes/No
Massage:	Yes
Self-Service Launderette:	No
Movie Theater/Seats:	Yes/250
Library:	Yes
Classification Society:	Lloyd's Register

RATINGS	POSSIBLE SCORE	SCORE ACHIEVED
Ship	500	327
Accommodation	200	127
Food	400	269
Service	400	293
Cruise	500	354
TOTAL	**2,000**	**1,370**

Accommodation: The suites and all other (nonsuite) cabins are fairly spacious and well appointed, functional and comfortable without being overdone. The decor, however, now seems a little dated and rather plain, and could do with brightening. The bathrooms are practical, and bathrobes are provided for all passengers.

Dining: The dining room (nonsmoking) is located on a lower deck, but has nice, light decor and feels comfortable and spacious. There are assigned tables and two seatings. Good service and fairly good food although standards have been slipping as a result of discounted fares.

Other Comments: This ship was first operated by the now-defunct Flagship Cruises, and was sold to Princess Cruises in 1975. She is a well-proportioned, handsome medium-size ship with a relatively high superstructure and graceful lines. Princess Cruises has spent a considerable sum of money in her upkeep, and she has been quite well maintained. There is plenty of good open deck space and several sunbathing areas, although, sadly, there is no wraparound promenade deck outdoors. One swimming pool has a magrodome roof for use in inclement weather.

Inside, the spacious public areas have wide passageways and high ceilings. Has tasteful earth-toned decor throughout, with complementary artwork. There is a decent movie theater. As for entertainment, the production shows and general entertainment are adequate. Smartly dressed officers and crew help to add a feeling of passenger care.

This ship is definitely for the older passenger. Fairly elegant and moderately expensive, it offers a stylish cruise in very comfortable and elegant surroundings.

m/s Pacific Venus
★★★★ +
(M)

LIFESTYLE:	STANDARD
Cruise Line:	Venus Cruise
Former Names:	-
Gross Tonnage:	26,518
Builder:	Ishikawajima Heavy Industries (Japan)
Original Cost:	$114 million (Yen13 billion)
Entered Service:	April 1998
Flag:	Japan
Tel. No.:	343128110
Fax No.:	343128140
Length (ft/m):	601.7/183.4
Beam (ft/m):	82.0/25.0
Draft (ft/m):	21.3/6.5
Propulsion/Propellers:	diesel (13,636 kW)/2 (CP)
Decks:	7
Total Crew:	180
Pass. Capacity (basis 2):	532
Pass. Capacity (all berths):	720
Pass. Space Ratio (basis 2):	49.8
Pass. Space Ratio (all berths):	36.8
Officers:	Japanese
Total Cabins:	266
Size Range (sq ft/m):	164.6–699.6/15.3–65.0
Cabins (outside view):	250
Cabins (inside — no view):	16
Cabins (single occupancy):	0
Cabins (with private balcony):	20
Cabins (wheelchair accessible):	1
Cabin Current:	110 volts
Cabin TV:	Yes
Dining Rooms:	2
Elevators:	4
Casino:	Yes
Slot Machines:	No
Swimming Pools (outdoors):	1 (+ 1 for children)
Swimming Pools (inside):	0
Whirlpools:	1
Fitness Center:	Yes
Sauna/Steam Room:	No/Yes
Massage:	Yes
Self-Service Launderette:	Yes (2)
Movie Theater/Seats:	Yes/94
Library:	Yes
Classification Society:	Nippon Kaiji Kyokai

RATINGS	POSSIBLE SCORE	SCORE ACHIEVED
Ship	500	433
Accommodation	200	159
Food	400	332
Service	400	329
Cruise	500	416
TOTAL	**2,000**	**1,669**

Accommodation: There are six different types of accommodation: royal suites, suites, deluxe cabins, state cabins (in four different price grades), and standard cabins, all located from the uppermost to lowermost decks, respectively.

The four Royal Suites are decorated in two different styles — one contemporary, one more traditional Japanese style. Each of them features a private balcony, with sliding door (teak table and two chairs), an expansive lounge area with large sofa and plush armchairs, coffee table, windowside chairs and drinks table, floor-to-ceiling windows, and a video player. There is a separate bedroom, with twin- or queen-size bed, vanity/writing desk, large walkin closet with personal safe, and a large bathroom with a tiny Jacuzzi bathtub. The bathroom has ocean-view windows, separate shower, and his/hers sinks.

Sixteen suites also feature a private balcony (with teak table and two chairs), a good-size living area with vanity/writing desk, dining table, chair and curved sofa, separate sleeping area, bathroom with deep bathtub that is slightly larger than the Royal suites, and single large sink. There is ample lighted closet and drawer space (two locking drawers instead of a personal safe), and a video player.

The 20 Deluxe cabins have large picture windows fronted by a large, curtained arch, sleeping area with twin (or queen) beds, plus a daytime sofa that converts into a third bed.

The 210 state cabins (172 of which have upper berths for third passengers) have decor that is best described as basic, with a reasonable closet but little drawer space.

The 16 standard cabins are really plain, but accommodate three persons, although drawer and storage space is tight.

All cabin grades feature: a tea drinking set (with electric hot water kettle), color television, telephone, stocked minibar-refrigerator (all items are included in the cruise price). Bathrooms feature a hairdryer and an extensive array of Shisedo personal toiletry items (particularly in the suites, which include aftershave, hair liquid, hair tonic, skin lotion, body lotion, milky lotion, shampoo, rinse, razor, toothbrush, toothpaste, sewing kit, showercap, hairbrush, clothes brush and shoehorn). All room service menu items are available at extra charge. All passengers receive a *yukata*; in addition, suite occupants get a plush bathrobe.

Dining: The main dining room (Primavera) is located aft and has ocean views on three sides. There is one seating, and tables are for six, ten or twelve. The food consists of both Japanese and western items; the menu is varied and the food is attractively presented.

A second, intimate, yet moderately stately 42-seat alternative restaurant, called Grand Siecle features an à la carte menu, which incurs an extra charge for everything; it is decorated in Regency style; it has lovely wood paneling and a detailed, indented ceiling.

Other Comments: Venus Cruise is part of Japan Cruise Line, which is itself a joint venture between Shin Nohonakai, Hankyu, and Kanpu ferry companies (operating more than 20 ferries). The company also owns and operates the slightly smaller and more basic *Orient Venus,* which is used principally for the charter and incentive group market. *Pacific Venus,* which is being operated for individual cruises (no charters) is one deck higher than her sister ship, is slightly longer and beamier, and is, in fact, the second-largest cruise vessel built by a Japanese shipyard.

There is a good amount of open deck space aft of the funnel, good for deck sports, while protected sunbathing space is provided around the small swimming pool (all deck lounge chairs have cushioned pads). The base of the funnel itself is the site of a day/night lounge, which overlooks the swimming pool (it is slightly reminiscent of the lounges that Royal Caribbean International features aboard its vessels). There is a wraparound (rubber coated) promenade deck outdoors.

Inside the ship, the high passenger space ratio means that there is plenty of space per passenger. The decor is clean and fresh, with much use of pastel colors and blond woods. One deck (Deck 7) features a double-width indoor promenade off which the dining rooms are located. The three-deck-high atrium has a crystal chandelier as its focal point.

Facilities include male and female Grand Baths, which include bathing pool and health/cleansing facilities. There are special rooms for meetings and conference organizers, for times when the ship is chartered. There is a piano salon with colorful low-back chairs, a large main hall (with a finely sculptured high ceiling and 720 moveable seats — production shows are performed here), a 350-seat main lounge for cabaret shows, small theater, library and card room, casino, two private karaoke rooms, Japanese chashitsu (tatami) room for tea ceremonies, and a beauty salon. There is also a 24-hour vending machine corner (juice, beer, camera film, and other items), self-service launderette (no charge), and several (credit card/coin) public telephone booths.

Overall, this company provides a well-packaged cruise in a ship which presents a very comfortable, serene environment. The dress code is relaxed and no tipping is allowed.

<u>Weak Points</u>: There are few cabins with private balcony. The open walking promenade decks are bare steel (there is no wraparound promenade deck).

m/s Paradise
★★★ +
(L)

LIFESTYLE:	STANDARD
Cruise Line:	Carnival Cruise Lines
Former Names:	-
Gross Tonnage:	70,367
Builder:	Kvaerner Masa-Yards (Finland)
Original Cost:	$300 million
Entered Service:	November 1998
Flag:	Panama
Tel. No.:	335583312
Fax No.:	n/a
Length (ft/m):	855.0/260.60
Beam (ft/m):	103.0/31.40
Draft (ft/m):	25.9/7.90
Propulsion/Propellers:	diesel-electric (42,842kW)/2 pods (CP)
Decks:	10
Total Crew:	920
Pass. Capacity (basis 2):	2,040
Pass. Capacity (all berths):	2,594
Pass. Space Ratio (basis 2):	34.4
Pass. Space Ratio (all berths):	26.7
Officers:	Italian
Total Cabins:	1,020
Size Range (sq ft/m):	173.2–409.7/16.0–38.0
Cabins (outside view):	618
Cabins (inside — no view):	402
Cabins (single occupancy):	0
Cabins (with private balcony):	26
Cabins (wheelchair accessible):	22
Cabin Current:	110 volts
Cabin TV:	Yes
Dining Rooms:	2
Elevators:	14
Casino:	Yes
Slot Machines:	Yes
Swimming Pools (outdoors):	3
Swimming Pools (inside):	0
Whirlpools:	6
Fitness Center:	Yes
Sauna/Steam Room:	Yes/Yes
Massage:	Yes
Self-Service Launderette:	Yes
Movie Theater/Seats:	No
Library:	Yes
Classification Society:	Lloyd's Register

RATINGS	POSSIBLE SCORE	SCORE ACHIEVED
Ship	500	395
Accommodation	200	151
Food	400	221
Service	400	270
Cruise	500	353
TOTAL	**2,000**	**1,390**

Like a breath of fresh air, this is a totally *nonsmoking* ship (and that includes the crew), including all open decks. There is a fine of $250 for *anyone* caught smoking, and you will be put off at the next port. Passengers must sign a document agreeing to this policy prior to embarkation. For general comments, see *Elation*.

359

m/s Paul Gauguin
★★★★ +
(S)

LIFESTYLE:	LUXURY
Cruise Line:	Radisson Seven Seas Cruises
Former Names:	-
Gross Tonnage:	18,800
Builder:	Chantiers de l'Atlantique (France)
Original Cost:	$150 million
Entered Service:	January 1998
Flag:	Wallis & Fortuna
Tel. No.:	n/a
Fax No.:	n/a
Length (ft/m):	513.4/156.50
Beam (ft/m):	72.1/22.00
Draft (ft/m):	16.8/5.15
Propulsion/Propellers:	diesel-electric (9,000kW/2 (FP)
Decks:	7
Total Crew:	206
Pass. Capacity (basis 2):	320
Pass. Capacity (all berths):	320
Pass. Space Ratio (basis 2):	58.7
Pass. Space Ratio (all berths):	58.7
Officers:	European
Total Cabins:	160
Size Range (sq ft/m):	200.0–534.0/18.5–49.6
Cabins (outside view):	160
Cabins (inside — no view):	0
Cabins (single occupancy):	0
Cabins (with private balcony):	80
Cabins (wheelchair accessible):	1
Cabin Current:	110 volts
Cabin TV:	Yes
Dining Rooms:	2
Elevators:	4
Casino:	Yes
Slot Machines:	Yes
Swimming Pools (outdoors):	1
Swimming Pools (inside):	0
Whirlpools:	0
Fitness Center:	Yes
Sauna/Steam Room:	No/Yes
Massage:	Yes
Self-Service Launderette:	No
Movie Theater/Seats:	No
Library:	Yes
Classification Society:	Bureau Veritas

RATINGS	POSSIBLE SCORE	SCORE ACHIEVED
Ship	500	425
Accommodation	200	169
Food	400	326
Service	400	320
Cruise	500	405
TOTAL	**2,000**	**1,645**

Accommodation: The outside-view cabins, half of which boast private balconies, are very nicely equipped, although they are strictly rectangular (none have more interesting shapes). Most have large windows, except those on the lowest accommodation deck, which have portholes. Each has queen- or twin-size beds (convertible to queen), and wood-accented cabinetry with rounded edges. A mini-bar/refrigerator (stocked with complimentary soft drinks), VCR unit, personal safe, hair dryer and umbrella are standard. The marble-look appointed bathrooms have a bathtub and a shower. Bathrobes are provided for all passengers, and soft drinks and mineral water are complimentary.

The two largest suites have a private balcony at the front and side of the vessel. Although there is a decent amount of in-cabin space, with a beautiful long vanity unit (and plenty of drawer space), the bathrooms are disappointingly small and plain, and too similar to all other standard cabin bathrooms.

Dining: The main dining room, L'Etoile, features lunch and dinner, while La Veranda, an alternative dining spot, is open for breakfast, lunch, and dinner. Both dining rooms provide open seating, which means that passengers can choose when they want to dine and with whom. This provides a good opportunity to meet new people for dinner each evening. La Veranda provides dinner by reservation, with alternating French and Italian menus; the French menus are provided by Chef Jean-Pierre Vigato, a two-star Michelin chef with his own restaurant in Paris (Apicius).

The dining operation is well orchestrated, with cuisine and service of a high standard. Complimentary standard table wines are served with dinner (although a connoisseur selection is available, at extra cost, for real wine lovers), and mineral water, fruit juices, and soft drinks are complimentary throughout the ship — a nice touch.

In addition, an outdoor bistro provides informal cafe fare on deck aft of the pool, while the Connoisseur Club offers a luxurious retreat for cigars, cognacs, and wine tasting.

Other Comments: This smart-looking vessel also has a retractable aft marina platform, and carries two waterskiing boats and two inflatable craft for water sports, as well as scuba and snorkeling gear. Built by a French company, managed and operated by the US-based Radisson Seven Seas Cruises, this ship is extremely spacious. While she could carry more passengers, under French law operating in the Polynesian islands, she is unable to do so.

Inside, both the artwork and the decor have a real French Polynesia look and feel. The interior colors are quite restful, but a trifle bland.

Expert lecturers on Tahiti and Gauguin accompany each cruise, and a Fare (pronounced "foray") Tahiti Gallery offers books, videos, and other materials on the unique art, history, and culture of the islands; three original Gauguin sketches are displayed under glass. There is a good health spa program with treatment services provided by Carita of Paris, although the changing facilities are very limited, there is no sauna, and use of the steam room incurs an extra charge (it should be free). Water sports facilities include a retractable aft marina platform and waterskiing, Windsurfers, kayaks, and scuba and snorkeling equipment are all available.

The library is pleasant enough, although it really could be larger. This ship (a more deluxe version of the company's popular *Song of Flower*) presents Radisson Seven Seas Cruises with the opportunity to score very high marks with her passengers, as the company is known for its attention to detail and passenger care.

A no-tie policy means the dress code is very relaxed — every day. The standard itinerary means that the ship only docks in Papeete, and shore tenders are used in all other ports. There is little entertainment, as the ship stays overnight in several ports. The ship's high crew-to-passenger ratio translates to highly personalized service. All gratuities to staff are included.

Weak Points: Although it sounds exotic, the itinerary is only marginally interesting to the well traveled, the best island experience being in Bora Bora. The ship's shallow draft means there could be some movement, as she is high-sided for her size. Minimum purchase rule in ship's boutique is irritating (due to local government rules); the same is true of the casino (you must pay $10 to play; again, local government rules). The spa is very small, and the fitness room is windowless.

m/s Polaris
★★★
(S)

LIFESTYLE:	STANDARD
Cruise Line:	Lindblad Special Expeditions
Former Names:	*Lindblad Polaris, Oresund*
Gross Tonnage:	2,214
Builder:	Aalborg Vaerft (Denmark)
Original Cost:	n/a
Entered Service:	1960/May 1987
Flag:	Ecuador
Tel. No.:	330817811
Fax No.:	330817815
Length (ft/m):	236.6/72.12
Beam (ft/m):	42.7/13.03
Draft (ft/m):	13.7/4.30
Propulsion/Propellers:	diesel (2,354kW)/2 (CP)
Decks:	4
Total Crew:	44
Pass. Capacity (basis 2):	82
Pass. Capacity (all berths):	84
Pass. Space Ratio (basis 2):	27.0
Pass. Space Ratio (all berths):	26.3
Officers:	Ecuadorian
Total Cabins:	41
Size Range (sq ft/m):	99.0–229.2/9.2–21.3
Cabins (outside view):	41
Cabins (inside — no view):	0
Cabins (single occupancy):	0
Cabins (with private balcony):	0

Cabins (wheelchair accessible):	0
Cabin Current:	220 volts
Cabin TV:	No
Dining Rooms:	1
Elevators:	0
Casino:	No
Slot Machines:	No
Swimming Pools (outdoors):	0
Whirlpools:	0
Exercise Room:	No
Sauna/Steam Room:	Yes/No
Massage:	No
Self-Service Launderette:	No
Lecture/Film Room:	No
Library:	Yes
Zodiacs:	8
Helicopter Pad:	No
Classification Society:	Bureau Veritas

RATINGS	POSSIBLE SCORE	SCORE ACHIEVED
Ship	500	271
Accommodation	200	113
Food	400	258
Service	400	258
Cruise	500	310
TOTAL	**2,000**	**1,210**

Accommodation: The cabins, all of which are above the waterline, are fairly roomy and nicely appointed, but there is little drawer space. Some have been refurbished and feature large (lower) beds. Each has a hair dryer; refreshingly, cabin keys are not used. The cabin bathrooms are really tiny, however, so take only what you need. Note that there is no cabin service menu.

Dining: The dining room has big picture windows and a wraparound view. Seating is now at individual tables (formerly family style) in a leisurely single seating. Has good food, with a major emphasis on local fish and seafood dishes. There is also a fine wine list. Breakfast and lunch are buffet-style. Has friendly service from an attentive staff.

Other Comments: This "soft" expedition cruise vessel, of modest proportions, sports a dark blue hull and white superstructure. She has been well maintained and operated. Sports a fantail and improved aft outdoor lounge area. Carries several Zodiac inflatable rubber landing craft, as well as a glass bottom boat.

Inside, although there are few public rooms, the Scandinavian-style interior furnishings and decor are very tidy and welcoming, accented by lots of wood trim. Has a friendly, very intimate atmosphere on board, with Filipino service staff. Features a good team of lecturers and nature observers, whose daily recaps are a vital part of the experience. A restful, well-stocked library helps passengers learn more about the region and the natural world.

This is a good small vessel, which now operates year-round nature-intensive "soft" expedition cruises around the Galapagos Islands. This is an area to which the ship is well suited (only 90 passengers from any one ship are allowed at any one time in the Galapagos Islands, where tourism is managed well by the Equadoreans). In fact, this ship is among the best suited to this region. All port charges are included in this product, which is marketed by Lindblad Special Expeditions and Noble Caledonia, together with other specialist packagers.

s/y Polynesia
(S)

LIFESTYLE:	STANDARD
Cruise Line:	Windjammer Barefoot Cruises
Former Names:	*Argus*
Gross Tonnage:	430
Builder:	Haan & Oerlemans (Holland)
Original Cost:	n/a
Entered Service:	1938/1975
Flag:	Equatorial Guinea
Tel. No.:	n/a
Fax No.:	n/a
Length (ft/m):	248.0/75.5
Beam (ft/m):	36.0/10.9
Draft (ft/m):	18.0/5.4
Type of Vessel:	topsail schooner
No. of Masts:	4
Sail Area (sq ft/sq m):	18,000/1,672.2
Main Propulsion:	sail power
Propulsion/Propellers:	diesel/1 (FP)
Decks:	4
Total Crew:	45
Pass. Capacity (basis 2):	110
Pass. Capacity (all berths):	122
Pass. Space Ratio (basis 2):	3.9
Pass. Space Ratio (all berths):	3.5
Officers:	International
Total Cabins:	57
Size Range (sq ft/m):	68.0–104.0/6.3–9.6
Cabins (outside view):	14
Cabins (inside — no view):	41

Cabins (single occupancy):	0
Cabins (with private balcony):	0
Cabins (wheelchair accessible):	0
Cabin Current:	110 volts
Cabin TV:	No
Dining Rooms:	1
Elevators:	0
Casino:	No
Slot Machines:	No
Swimming Pools (outdoors):	0
Whirlpools:	0
Fitness Center:	No
Sauna/Steam Room:	No/No
Massage:	No
Self-Service Launderette:	No
Library:	Yes
Classification Society:	None

RATINGS	POSSIBLE SCORE	SCORE ACHIEVED
Ship	500	NYR
Accommodation	200	NYR
Food	400	NYR
Service	400	NYR
Cruise	500	NYR
TOTAL	**2,000**	**NYR**
Expected Score Range:		**900-1100**

She was originally built as part of the great Portuguese Grand Banks fleet. She was featured in the May 1952 edition of *National Geographic* magazine and in the late maritime writer Allen Villers's book *The Quest of the Schooner Argus*. She was acquired by Windjammer Barefoot Cruises in 1975. Sails from St. Maarten. For other comments regarding Windjammer Barefoot Cruises, see *Flying Cloud*.

m/t/s Princesa Amorosa
★★ +
(S)

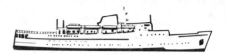

LIFESTYLE: **STANDARD**

Cruise Line:	Louis Cruise Lines
Former Names:	*Galaxias, Galaxy, Scottish Coast*
Gross Tonnage:	5,026
Builder:	Harland & Wolff (UK)
Original Cost:	n/a
Entered Service:	1957/July 1990
Flag:	Cyprus
Tel. No.:	n/a
Fax No.:	n/a
Length (ft/m):	342.2/104.32
Beam (ft/m):	52.6/16.06
Draft (ft/m):	15.7/4.81
Propulsion/Propellers:	diesel 4,781kW)/2 (FP)
Decks:	6
Total Crew:	130
Pass. Capacity (basis 2):	284
Pass. Capacity (all berths):	327
Pass. Space Ratio (basis 2):	17.6
Pass. Space Ratio (all berths):	15.3
Officers:	Cypriot/Greek
Total Cabins:	142
Size Range (sq ft/m):	107.6–172.2/10.0–16.0
Cabins (outside view):	115
Cabins (inside — no view):	27
Cabins (single occupancy):	0
Cabins (with private balcony):	0
Cabins (wheelchair accessible):	0
Cabin Current:	220 volts
Cabin TV:	No
Dining Rooms:	1
Elevators:	0
Casino:	Yes
Slot Machines:	Yes
Swimming Pools (outdoors):	1
Swimming Pools (inside):	0
Whirlpools:	0
Fitness Center:	No
Sauna/Steam Room:	No/No
Massage:	No
Self-Service Launderette:	No
Movie Theater/Seats:	No
Library:	Yes
Classification Society:	Lloyd's Register

RATINGS	POSSIBLE SCORE	SCORE ACHIEVED
Ship	500	218
Accommodation	200	90
Food	400	227
Service	400	230
Cruise	500	226
TOTAL	**2,000**	**991**

Accommodation: Most cabins are outside and comfortable, with crisp Mediterranean colors and some wood trim, but they are small, and bathrooms do show their age. The cabins and bathrooms are very small. Note that cabins located above the disco are very noisy late at night.

Dining: The dining room has portholes and is reasonably attractive. There are two seatings. The food is decidedly Mediterranean, with some reasonable choice and surprisingly good presentation. In addition, a full vegetarian menu is available. The service is cheerful, and the staff does try hard to make this aspect of a cruise perhaps the best part. Both à la carte and buffet meals are featured.

Other Comments: This is an older vessel that has fairly spacious open decks for her size. Seeing the bridge is like stepping back in time, with many shiny brass instruments. The swimming pool is really only a "dip" pool, nothing more.

    Inside the ship, the limited number of public rooms have been nicely refurbished. There is an interesting maroon wrought iron staircase whose balustrades show the ship's former British heritage.

    Earth-tone colors have been used to good effect in the interior decor, creating a mild sense of spaciousness. There is a pleasant lounge and bar for socializing, with comfortable seating and warm decor. The ambience aboard is delightfully warm and friendly.

    Purchased by Louis Cruise Lines in 1989, she offers good "no frills" seven-night Greek Isles/Mediterranean cruises for those without high expectations, particularly well suited to the local Cypriot market, where the ship has a loyal following.

    <u>Weak Points</u>: There is a steep, narrow gangway in some ports. There are too many announcements.

m/v Princesa Victoria
★★
(M)

LIFESTYLE:	STANDARD
Cruise Line:	Louis Cruise Lines
Former Names:	*The Victoria, Victoria,*
	Dunottar Castle
Gross Tonnage:	15,007
Builder:	Harland & Wolff (UK)
Original Cost:	n/a
Entered Service:	July 1936/January 1993
Flag:	Cyprus
Tel. No.:	1101627
Fax No.:	1101630
Length (ft/m):	572.8/174.60
Beam (ft/m):	71.9/21.92
Draft (ft/m):	27.8/8.50
Propulsion/Propellers:	diesel (10,450kW)/2 (FP)
Decks:	7
Total Crew:	230
Pass. Capacity (basis 2):	566
Pass. Capacity (all berths):	750
Pass. Space Ratio (basis 2):	26.5
Pass. Space Ratio (all berths):	20.0
Officers:	Cypriot/Greek
Total Cabins:	287
Size Range (sq ft/m):	156.0–258.3/14.5–24.0
Cabins (outside view):	216
Cabins (inside — no view):	71
Cabins (single occupancy):	8

Cabins (with private balcony):	0
Cabins (wheelchair accessible):	0
Cabin Current:	115 volts
Cabin TV:	Yes
Dining Rooms:	1
Elevators:	3
Casino:	Yes
Slot Machines:	Yes
Swimming Pools (outdoors):	2
Swimming Pools (inside):	0
Whirlpools:	0
Fitness Center:	Yes
Sauna/Steam Room:	Yes/No
Massage:	No
Self-Service Launderette:	No
Movie Theater/Seats:	Yes/250
Library:	Yes
Classification Society:	Lloyd's Register

RATINGS	POSSIBLE SCORE	SCORE ACHIEVED
Ship	500	218
Accommodation	200	91
Food	400	204
Service	400	211
Cruise	500	213
TOTAL	**2,000**	**937**

Accommodation: The standard cabins are fairly spacious, and feature heavy-duty furniture and fittings. The suite rooms are cavernous, and the large bathrooms come with deep, full bathtubs, something not seen on today's cruise vessels.

Dining: The dining room is set low down but is comfortable and has a fine two-deck-high center section with barrel-shaped ceiling, music balcony, and lots of wood paneling. There are two seatings. The standard of cuisine is good, particularly bearing in mind the price you pay. There are three entrees, as well as a complete vegetarian menu. Salads, bakery items, and fruits are reasonable.

Other Comments: This ship was originally built for the Union Castle Line, before being operated for many years by Chandris Cruises prior to her purchase by Louis Cruise Lines. She has been extremely well maintained, despite her age. There is a generous amount of open deck space and twin outdoor swimming pools (although there are no showers on deck).

Inside, the center stairway is built in true art deco style. There is a friendly, old-world ambience on board. The Riviera Club is a contemporary room that is totally out of keeping with the rest of ship.

Provides a good cruise experience for first-time cruisers and for those seeking to optimize their hotel vacation in Cyprus. She really is an old ship, however, and so she does not have the kind of ultra-contemporary facilities that most modern ships feature.

Weak Points: The repetitive announcements are annoying. There is little separation of smokers and nonsmokers, and the ship is old and worn in many places.

m/t/s Princess Danae
★★★
(M)

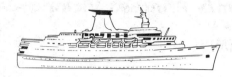

LIFESTYLE:	STANDARD
Cruise Line:	Arcalia Shipping/ Classic International Cruises
Former Names:	*Baltica, Danae, Therisos Express, Port Melbourne*
Gross Tonnage:	17,074
Builder:	Swan, Hunter (UK)
Original Cost:	n/a
Entered Service:	July 1955/1997
Flag:	Panama
Tel. No.:	1346425
Fax No.:	1346425
Length (ft/m):	532.7/162.39
Beam (ft/m):	70.0/21.34
Draft (ft/m):	41.9/12.80
Propulsion/Propellers:	diesel (9,850kW)/2 (FP)
Decks:	7
Total Crew:	240
Pass. Capacity (basis 2):	560
Pass. Capacity (all berths):	670
Pass. Space Ratio (basis 2):	30.4
Pass. Space Ratio (all berths):	25.4
Officers:	European
Total Cabins:	280
Size Range (sq ft/m):	200.0–270.0/18.5–25.0
Cabins (outside view):	215
Cabins (inside — no view):	65
Cabins (single occupancy):	0

Cabins (with private balcony):	6
Cabins (wheelchair accessible):	0
Cabin Current:	220 volts
Cabin TV:	No
Dining Rooms:	1
Elevators:	2
Casino:	Yes
Slot Machines:	Yes
Swimming Pools (outdoors):	1
Swimming Pools (inside):	0
Whirlpools:	2
Fitness Center:	Yes
Sauna/Steam Room:	Yes/No
Massage:	Yes
Self-Service Launderette:	No
Movie Theater/Seats:	Yes/275
Library:	Yes
Classification Society:	American Bureau of Shipping

RATINGS	POSSIBLE SCORE	SCORE ACHIEVED
Ship	500	288
Accommodation	200	116
Food	400	234
Service	400	223
Cruise	500	240
TOTAL	**2,000**	**1,101**

Accommodation: Most cabins are of good size (in eight categories) and feature heavy-duty furniture and fittings with ample closet and drawer space. The insulation between cabins is not very good. Note that the cabins located under the disco can suffer from thumping noise late at night. The lower-grade cabins are really plain. While 210 cabin bathrooms have a bathtub and shower, 70 have a shower only.

Dining: The dining room is decorated quite nicely and has a high ceiling. Features open seating dining (dine with whomever you wish). Features continental/European cuisine and service that is fairly attentive, although the noise level is high from the open waiter stations.

Other Comments: She is a solidly built ship, with good lines and a reasonably balanced profile. She was operated for many years by Costa Cruises before being purchased by Arcalia Shipping, her present owners. There is a decent amount of open deck space for sunbathing.

There is a pleasing traditional shipboard ambience aboard, combined with a mixture of both traditional and contemporary features including many original interior appointments of decent quality. There are a number of spacious public rooms, although the decor is somewhat conservative. A new bar amidships was recently added. There is a roomy, traditional movie theater.

This ship underwent a refurbishment early in 1996, but the fit and finish of the areas that were changed is extremely poor. She provides a moderately comfortable, though by no means glamorous, cruise experience for her passengers, many of whom are from South America. Provides Caribbean cruises from Santo Domingo in winter, from Brazil during the summer, and Mediterranean cruises during some summer months. The ship is often placed under charter with various tour operators (of various nationalities), and so the character of the ship changes, as does the level of food and service provided (the principal constituent parts of the cruise experience). In other words, use the rating only as a guide, as the actual product can be inconsistent.

<u>Weak Points</u>: Sadly, there is no forward observation lounge. There is little finesse in the hospitality department, and service is perfunctory, at best.

366

m/v Professor Khromov
★★
(S)

LIFESTYLE:	**STANDARD**
Cruise Line:	Quark Expeditions/Murmansk Shipping
Former Names:	-
Gross Tonnage:	2,142
Builder:	Wartsila (Finland)
Original Cost:	n/a
Entered Service:	1983
Flag:	Russia
Tel. No.:	n/a
Fax No.:	n/a
Length (ft/m):	234.9/71.6
Beam (ft/m):	42/12.8
Draft (ft/m):	15.0/4.6
Propulsion/Propellers:	diesel (2,327kW)/2 (CP)
Decks:	3
Total Crew:	25
Pass. Capacity (basis 2):	36
Pass. Capacity (all berths):	36
Pass. Space Ratio (basis 2):	59.5
Pass. Space Ratio (all berths):	59.5
Officers:	Russian
Total Cabins:	18
Size Range (sq ft/m):	n/a
Cabins (outside view):	18
Cabins (inside — no view):	0
Cabins (single occupancy):	0
Cabins (with private balcony):	0
Cabins (wheelchair accessible):	0
Cabin Current:	220 volts
Cabin TV:	No
Dining Rooms:	1
Elevators:	0
Casino:	0
Slot Machines:	0
Swimming Pools (outdoors):	0
Swimming Pools (inside):	0
Whirlpools:	0
Fitness Center:	No
Sauna/Steam Room:	Yes/No
Massage:	No
Self-Service Launderette:	No
Movie Theater/Seats:	0
Library:	Yes
Classification Society:	Russian KMLI

RATINGS	POSSIBLE SCORE	SCORE ACHIEVED
Ship	500	227
Accommodation	200	87
Food	400	203
Service	400	188
Cruise	500	242
TOTAL	**2,000**	**947**

Accommodation: With the exception of a single "suite," almost all other cabins are very small, spartan, and rather clinical. Those on the lowest deck share a bathroom.

Dining: There are two dining rooms, and all passengers are accommodated in a single seating. The meals are hearty international fare, with no frills. When under charter to Quark Expedition/Noble Caledonia, a western chef oversees the food operation. The cuisine itself is best describes as hearty fare.

Other Comments: This vessel was originally specially constructed for polar and oceanographic research and should not be taken as a cruise ship, although it was converted and refurbished in 1992 to carry passengers. Has an ice-hardened steel hull, which is good for Arctic and Antarctic cruising. All passengers have access to the navigation bridge. There are several Zodiac landing craft for close-in shore excursions and nature observation trips.

Inside, the limited public rooms consist of a library and a lounge/bar. The dining room also serves as a lecture room. This ship does have good medical facilities.

This is expedition-style cruising, in a very small ship with limited facilities. However, it provides a somewhat primitive, but genuine adventure experience to places others only dream about. The bigger ships cannot get this close to Antarctica, but this little vessel will sail you close to the face of the ice continent. The same comments apply to sister ship *Professor Molchanov*.

t/s/m/v Queen Elizabeth 2

★★★★★ to ★★★ +

(L)

LIFESTYLE:	LUXURY/PREMIUM
Cruise Line:	Cunard Line
Former Names:	-
Gross Tonnage:	70,327
Builder:	Upper Clyde Shipbuilders (UK)
Original Cost:	£29 million
Entered Service:	May 1969
Flag:	Great Britain
Tel. No.:	1440412
Fax No.:	1441331
Length (ft/m):	962.93/293.50
Beam (ft/m):	105.1/32.03
Draft (ft/m):	32.4/9.87
Propulsion/Propellers:	diesel-electric (99,900kW)/2 (CP)
Decks:	13
Total Crew:	1,004
Pass. Capacity (basis 2):	1,715
Pass. Capacity (all berths):	1,890
Pass. Space Ratio (basis 2):	41.0
Pass. Space Ratio (all berths):	37.2
Officers:	British
Total Cabins:	910
Size Range (sq ft/m):	107.0–785.0/10.0–73.0
Cabins (outside view):	659
Cabins (inside — no view):	251
Cabins (single occupancy):	105
Cabins (with private balcony):	32
Cabins (wheelchair accessible):	4
Cabin Current:	110 and 220 volts
Cabin TV:	Yes
Dining Rooms:	5
Elevators:	13
Casino:	Yes
Slot Machines:	Yes
Swimming Pools (outdoors):	1
Swimming Pools (inside):	1 (+ AquaSpa pool)
Whirlpools:	4
Fitness Center:	Yes

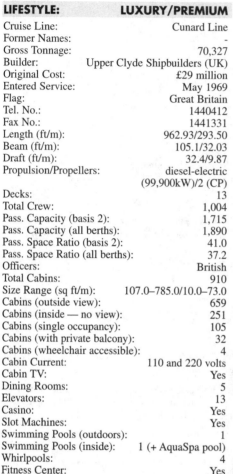

Sauna/Steam Room:	Yes/Yes
Massage:	Yes
Self-Service Launderette:	Yes
Movie Theater/Seats:	Yes/530
Library:	Yes
Classification Society:	Lloyd's Register

GRILL CLASS

RATINGS	POSSIBLE SCORE	SCORE ACHIEVED
Ship	500	446
Accommodation	200	177
Food	400	367
Service	400	360
Cruise	500	435
TOTAL	**2,000**	**1,785**

CARONIA CLASS

RATINGS	POSSIBLE SCORE	SCORE ACHIEVED
Ship	500	416
Accommodation	200	152
Food	400	335
Service	400	328
Cruise	500	416
TOTAL	**2,000**	**1,647**

MAURETANIA CLASS

RATINGS	POSSIBLE SCORE	SCORE ACHIEVED
Ship	500	350
Accommodation	200	99
Food	400	286
Service	400	281
Cruise	500	382
TOTAL	**2,000**	**1,398**

Accommodation: There is a wide range of accommodation from which to choose, much of which features fine wood-paneled walls, generous closet and drawer space, thick, real wood furniture, and large, marble bathrooms. From sumptuous, understated two-level suites with private balconies, walk-in closets, refrigerators, mini-bars, and bathrooms large enough for four, to modest inside cabins that are compact but quite well equipped, you pay for the amount of space and grade you want. The accommodation you choose will determine in which of the ship's five restaurants you will dine.

Dining: There are five principal restaurants (all of which include many tables for two, unlike so many ships today) and two informal dining spots: The Lido and The Grill. In order of excellence they are Queens Grill, Britannia Grill and Princess Grill, Caronia Restaurant, and Mauretania Restaurant. One-seating dining is featured in all except the Mauretania Restaurant, which has two seatings (depending on the ship's passenger capacity). There are both smoking and nonsmoking sections in all restaurants. The menus are extremely varied, creative, and well balanced, and include a good choice of spa/light cuisine and healthy eating items. Alternative dining is available in The Lido (with a casual dress code for dinner), complete with its own galley and bar and separate poolside grill. The luncheon and midnight buffets provide a good range of foods, although at peak times there are lines.

Fine à la carte dining (with everything cooked to order à la minute) was introduced in the Queens Grill in early 1997 to great acclaim, but taken away in 1999 in what *regular* passengers see as a cost-cutting measure by Cunard Line's new owners. Also missing are the smoked salmon carving station and the lunchtime cheese trolley. However, the Queens Grill is still arguably the finest dining experience at sea, comparable to some of the best shoreside gourmet restaurants anywhere, with tableside carvings, flambeaus, and outstanding presentation by dedicated British traditional restaurant managers and head waiters. Some frequent travelers, however, prefer the more intimate Britannia Grill or Princess Grill. All three grills feature a limited selection of à la carte items, sadly the same items every day.

In 1997, the Caronia Restaurant and Mauretania Restaurant switched locations (and back again in 1998). The Queens Grill was completely redecorated and refurbished, and is now better than ever, with individual seating rather than the previous banquettes eating along the inner walls.

The cuisine features many traditional British favorites, together with extensive French dishes as well as regional specialties from around the world.

Other Comments: *Queen Elizabeth 2* is a true *ocean liner*, with a dark blue hull and single large funnel, that performs a regular schedule of transatlantic crossings as well as several cruises each year, plus an annual round-the-world cruise (typically from January to April). She is still the fastest as well as the most integrated ocean liner in the world (it is important to think of this ship as an *ocean liner* rather than as a cruise ship in the more contemporary sense of the word). An excellent range of joint travel programs and tour configurations is integrated into the marketing of this ship. It is also pleasing to note that the dress code is *mostly formal*, in contrast to so many ships where formal dress has all but disappeared.

Originally constructed as a steam turbine ship, she underwent a $160 million refit in Bremen, Germany, in 1986. Her original steam turbines were extracted and exchanged for a diesel-electric propulsion system, resulting in greater speed, better economy, and more reliability. A new, fatter funnel was constructed, designed to better keep any soot off her expansive open decks. She sports a long foredeck (rather like the long snout of a 4.5 liter vintage Bentley) unsurpassed by any other cruise ship today. That foredeck makes her look powerful, yet at the same time sleek and so graceful.

The ship has undergone a number of extensive multimillion dollar interior refurbishments that have included numerous structural changes designed to facilitate passenger flow and provide greater dining space. Fine wood paneling and more traditional furnishings have replaced her original laminates and tacky 1960s decor. The decor is now more reminiscent of the ocean liners of yesteryear — just what her passengers expect.

At the end of 1999, the ship underwent a further $33.1 million refurbishment (including $19 million on technical items). Following the 1999 refit, bathrooms in all accommodation grades will have been entirely replaced; they now all feature marble fixtures and jazzy art deco–style toiletry cabinets. Several new suites were added. Other facilities include a large library with over 6,000 books, combined with multimedia CD-ROM center and Cunard memorabilia shop; there is also a dedicated florist. The Club Lido magrodome-covered pool was replaced with an informal buffet bistro-like dining area (The Lido) The latest enhancements have provided grace, pace, and space in what is a ship for all reasons.

Transatlantic Crossings: She is still the fastest passenger ship presently in service, and even at a speed of close to 30 knots there is little vibration at the stern. Features a wide range of facilities and public rooms with high ceilings, including garage space for 12 cars.

She is a city at sea, and, like any city, there are several parts of town. There are *three* distinct classes: Grill Class, Caronia Class, and Mauretania Class. Grill Class accommodation consists of outstanding penthouse suites (with butler service only in the Sun Deck and Sports Deck suites) and large outside-view cabins (with standard cabin service in One Deck and Two Deck cabins). Dining is in one of three grill rooms: Queens Grill (named after former Cunard transatlantic liners *Queen Elizabeth* and *Queen Mary*), Britannia Grill, or Princess Grill, according to cabin grade chosen. Caronia Class accommodation consists of outside-view double cabins, and inside and outside single cabins, with dining in the Caronia Restaurant (high noise level). Mauretania Class accommodation features lower-priced cabin grades, but dining is in two seatings in the Mauretania Restaurant (a fine restaurant with many dining alcoves) when the ship is full, and one seating when the ship is not full.

All passengers enjoy the use of all public rooms, except for the Queens Grill Lounge (reserved exclusively for Grill Class passengers). The Queens Grill has its own separate galley, the best waiters and service, a fine, formal atmosphere for dinner, and food that can be best described as memorable (you can also order from the à la carte menu, as well as "off-menu"). The Britannia Grill, Princess Grill, and Mauretania Restaurant share the same galley, but the service and setting in the intimate Britannia Grill and Princess

Grill is far superior. The Caronia and Mauretania Restaurants have good, creative, and varied menus, but service is provided by the least experienced waiters.

Grill Class and Caronia Class passengers have separate open deck space and assigned chairs (these incur an extra charge) but join all other passengers for major shows, other entertainment events, and social functions. Grill Class is the most sophisticated way to cross the Atlantic; Caronia Class (formerly known as first class) is good but not quite what it used to be, while Mauretania Class (formerly known as transatlantic class) provides comfortable travel in a price-sensitive setting.

In the final analysis, *Queen Elizabeth 2* is the last of the transatlantic liners and a very civilized experience (good for those who do not like to fly, and for those who enjoy the grace and pace of this ship). The enormous amount of personal luggage allowed is also useful — especially for relocating between continents (or for extended vacations). Arriving in either New York or Southampton after six days of not having to lift a finger is actually a bittersweet anticlimax for most passengers — a disquieting reminder that life ashore has to be faced after the calming, quieting effect of *QE2* on one's innermost being. Indeed, there is probably nothing more pleasing to the soul than a transatlantic crossing, being cosseted in the finery of dining in either of the three grill restaurants with their superb cuisine and dining experiences. All gratuities are included, but 15 percent is added to all bar and wine bills.

Cruises: After refits in 1994 and 1996, public rooms and passenger facilities were refreshed and color-coordinated for the better. The Penthouse Suites are truly superb and quiet — and are among the most refined living spaces at sea (all bathrooms were replaced in 1996). The Heritage Trail, a shipwide display consisting of 26 exhibits of Cunard ocean liner history and ship models that ship buffs will find fascinating, if haphazardly located. It includes a stunning 16-foot-long illuminated model of the company's 1907 *Mauretania* (strangely located outside the Caronia Restaurant, while a model of the former *Caronia* is located in the Mauretania Restaurant). There is a great abundance of memorabilia items (some are for sale in the memorabilia bookshop/library).

Facilities: Grand Lounge (a dedicated show lounge with thrust stage, three seating tiers, and high-tech sound system); Tour and Travel Center (for shore excursions, theater tickets, and other concierge services); Shopping Concourse, which features good brand-name merchandise at high European prices; Cunard Collection shop that features high-quality clothing and special Cunard logo items. The Yacht Club is a delightfully nautical, practical, and popular aft-facing room that becomes a nightclub (afternoon recorded classical concerts here are a bonus). An extensive indoor spa includes a ten-station AquaSpa and several comfortable treatment rooms (treatments are at extra cost); fitness center and beauty salons for men and women; a safety deposit center and passenger accounts office; a large Computer Learning Center; an automated telephone system.

More facilities: The Queens Room is a real ballroom, with a large dance floor, for society dancing to a big band, whereas during the day it is a stately "quiet" room with comfortable chairs. The Midships Lobby, the ship's embarkation point, has a distinctive, ocean liner image and feel, with fine birds-eye maple woodwork and wraparound murals of the former and present Cunard Queens. A large computer center (with daily lectures) is a real bonus. There is also a dedicated florist and flower shop, and a large self-service launderette (no charge). The Lido, a large, informal bistro dining spot with 24-hour hot beverage stations, is also a bonus on cruises (espresso and cappuccino coffees are free). The elegant Chart Room Bar (formerly the Midships Bar) is a charming, quiet drinking spot (it contains a piano from the liner *Queen Mary*).

And more facilities: There is a large movie theater/concert hall (with 530 seats) complete with balcony level and nine-foot-long Bosendorfer piano; the Golden Lion Pub comes complete with Victorian decor and selection of over 20 beers (both bottled and draught). There is also a superb library, much loved by passengers (without doubt the best at sea, with over 6,000 books in several languages), which, combined with a memorabilia bookshop, features real professional librarians. The Player's Club Casino features fitting art deco and blonde wood decor.

QE2 has British officers, although the hotel staff is a very international mix, fairly attentive and service-oriented, though many do not speak English well, as is the case aboard so many ships today. Features good quality entertainment and fine lecture programs. Has an excellent laundry and dry-cleaning facilities. Fine English nannies and children's facilities. This ship offers refined living at sea for those in upper-grade accommodation, otherwise she is just a large ship, albeit with some superb facilities. Tender ports should be avoided whenever possible, however, although the double-deck shore tenders used are fine, practical units.

More about *QE2*: Physically challenged passengers will appreciate four cabins specially equipped for wheelchair-bound passengers, created using the guidelines of the American Disabled Association (ADA). The cabin door is wide enough for a wheelchair (no "lip"); the bathroom door slides open electronically at the touch of a button (located at wheelchair height), and the floor is flat. The full-length bathtub has special assist handles, and the toilet has grab bars. Closets have hanging rails with hydraulically balanced lever that lowers them towards the outside of the closet, to the right height. There is an intercom, alarm, and remote controls for lighting, curtains, and doors. These cabins are also good for the hearing-impaired, with three brightly colored, lighted signs on the cabin bulkhead, as well as a telephone system for the deaf. While these cabins are specially designed for the physically challenged, their ingenious design would not upset a regular passenger.

The famous Ocean Liner Express, which runs between London's Waterloo Station and Southampton Docks, pulls right up alongside the Ocean Terminal to connect with all transatlantic sailings of the ship. This special train consists of refurbished and carpeted first-class carriages from the 1950s, richly paneled and fitted with individual deep-upholstery seats, and complimentary hot canapés and champagne are served. Passengers traveling from London to Southampton can complete all formalities and ship check-in procedures on the train, and simply walk directly on board *QE2* on arrival. Baggage loaded onto the train's baggage carriage in Waterloo is delivered directly to your cabin.

The Cunard/British Airways *Concorde* program is worth experiencing. Combining a *QE2* transatlantic crossing with a one-way British Airways *Concorde* flight is, without doubt, the ultimate way to go. Six days one way, and three hours, fifteen minutes the other is one of the great travel experiences available today. And, with special, Cunard-subsidized fares, there is no excuse for not indulging, at least once in your life. All gratuities are now included.

In 1997 *QE2* became the first cruise ship to have an e-mail address (QE2@cruisemail.com.). She has traveled more than 4 million miles, and features the best of high-tech facilities blended with traditional ocean liner facilities. She is much like a well-worn shoe — comfortable, but a little worn, tired and frayed around the edges in places, which makes her a difficult ship to evaluate. Sadly, there are fewer British crew members serving in her than passengers expect, and less crew speak English when in passenger areas. However, she has a wonderful, loyal following, and provides the *only* civilized way to cross the North Atlantic Ocean with the space, pace, and grace of a real Cunard liner.

If you occupy one of the top-level suites (Grill Class), with butler service and all the trimmings of finery, your experience should be quite wonderful. However, for the many that occupy lower-grade accommodation (Caronia Class and Mauretania Class), you may find that the ship does not quite come up to the high expectations that most passengers have. Will she survive the onslaught of the mega-ships? Yes, simply because she isn't one of them, and she does have a lifestyle that somehow will still be in vogue when all around her have become floating nightclubs.

<u>Weak Points</u>: The exterior paintwork always seems to show the ship as less than the immaculate ship she should be. Sadly, there is no forward observation lounge (there was when the ship was first constructed). What's missing are the grand, flowing staircases, the air of romance, the high standard of maintenance and hotel service personnel of the ocean liners of former years. The show lounge is poor when compared with those aboard newer ships, and the sight lines are also quite poor. The cabins on Five Deck are a disgrace and should be taken out of service (Four Deck cabins are only marginally better). Following recent refurbishments, small, intimate hideaway bars are fewer in number. You cannot have just a sauna, or use of the steam room, without paying a charge for a "Spa Experience" package. As a "classless" cruise ship, the layout is disjointed, but as a transatlantic liner, the layout is designed to keep you in your place.

m/v R One
★★★★ +
(M)

LIFESTYLE:	PREMIUM
Cruise Line:	Renaissance Cruises
Former Names:	-
Gross Tonnage:	30,277
Builder:	Chantiers de l'Atlantique (France)
Original Cost:	$150 million
Entered Service:	July 1998
Flag:	Liberia
Tel. No.:	363677910
Fax No.:	363677921
Length (ft/m):	593.7/181.0
Beam (ft/m):	83.5/25.5
Draft (ft/m):	19.5/6.0
Propulsion/Propellers:	diesel (18,600kW)/2 (CP)
Decks:	9
Total Crew:	373
Pass. Capacity (basis 2):	684
Pass. Capacity (all berths):	824
Pass. Space Ratio (basis 2):	44.2
Pass. Space Ratio (all berths):	36.7
Officers:	European
Total Cabins:	342
Size Range (sq ft/m):	145.3–962.0/13.5–293.2
Cabins (outside view):	317
Cabins (inside — no view):	25
Cabins (single occupancy):	0
Cabins (with private balcony):	232
Cabins (wheelchair accessible):	3
Cabin Current:	110 and 220 volts
Cabin TV:	Yes
Dining Rooms:	4
Elevators:	4
Casino:	Yes
Slot Machines:	Yes
Swimming Pools (outdoors):	1
Swimming Pools (inside):	0
Whirlpools:	2 (+ 1 thalassotherapy)
Fitness Center:	Yes
Sauna/Steam Room:	No/Yes
Massage:	Yes
Self-Service Launderette:	Yes
Movie Theater/Seats:	No
Library:	Yes
Classification Society:	Bureau Veritas

RATINGS	POSSIBLE SCORE	SCORE ACHIEVED
Ship	500	423
Accommodation	200	164
Food	400	309
Service	400	303
Cruise	500	394
TOTAL	**2,000**	**1,593**

Accommodation: There are eight cabin categories. All of the standard inside and outside-view cabins (the lowest four grades) are extremely compact units, and extremely tight for two persons. They feature twin beds (or queen-size bed), with good under-bed storage areas, a personal safe, vanity desk with large mirror, good closet and drawer space (all in rich, dark woods), and bathrobe. Color televisions carry a major news channel (CNN, where obtainable), plus a sports channel and several movie channels.

The cabins with private balconies (66 percent of all cabins) have partial balcony partitions, not full ones, sliding glass doors, and, due to good design and layout, only 14 cabins on Deck 6 have lifeboat-obstructed views. The bathrooms, which have tiled floors and plain walls, are compact, standard units, and include a shower stall with a strong, removable hand-held shower unit, hair dryer, toiletries storage shelves and retractable clothesline. Personal toiletries include soap, shampoo, body lotion, shower cap, and shoe shine kit.

There are 52 mini-suites, which are really large cabins, as the sleeping and lounge areas are not divided. While not overly large, the bathrooms feature a good-size bathtub and good space for storing personal toiletry items. The living area features a refrigerated mini-bar, a lounge area with breakfast table, and a balcony with two plastic chairs and a table.

The ten Owner's Suites are the most spacious of accommodation units, and are beautiful, large living spaces located in the forward and aft sections of the accommodation decks (particularly nice are those that overlook the stern, on Decks 6, 7, and 8). They have more extensive private balconies that really are private and cannot be overlooked by anyone on the decks above. There is an entrance foyer, living room, bedroom (the bed faces the sea, which can be seen through the floor-to-ceiling windows and sliding glass door), CD player (with selection of audio discs), bathroom with Jacuzzi bathtub, and a small guest bathroom.

Dining: Flexibility and choice are what the R-class ships' dining facilities are all about. There are four different restaurants: The Club Restaurant, which is the equivalent of a main dining room, has 338 seats and a raised central section. There are large ocean-view windows on three sides, several prime tables over-looking the stern, and a small bandstand for occasional live dinner music. The menu changes daily for lunch and dinner. The Italian Restaurant has 96 seats, windows along two sides, and a set menu (togeth-er with added daily chef's specials). The Grill Room is an "American steak house," has 98 seats and win-dows along two sides, and has a set menu (together with added daily chef's specials). The Panorama has seats for 154 indoors (not enough during the winter months) and 186 outdoors (it's too cold to sit outside in the winter months). It is open for breakfast, lunch, and casual dinners. It is the ship's self-serve buffet restaurant, and it incorporates a small pizzeria. Excellent salads, meat carving station, and a decent selec-tion of cheeses are featured daily.

All restaurants feature open seating dining, so you dine when you want, with whom you wish, although reservations are necessary in the Italian Restaurant and The Grill, where there are mostly tables for four or six (there are few tables for two). Service in all the restaurants is excellent, and very attentive. In addition, there is a Poolside Grill Bar, and a patisserie called Sweets, located in the upper level of the two-deck-high lobby. Note that all cappuccino and espresso coffees are at extra cost, even when ordered in the restaurants.

Other Comments: Renaissance Cruises is the cruise industry's first totally nonsmoking cruise line. The R-class ships are a series of six such ships, and a real departure for Renaissance Cruises, who have tradi-tionally operated smaller vessels. The exterior design manages to balance the ship's high sides by com-bining a deep blue hull with the white superstructure and large, square blue funnel.

A lido deck features a swimming pool and good sunbathing space, while one of the aft decks has a thalassaotherapy pool (part of a spa package and incurs an extra charge). A jogging track circles the swimming pool deck (but one deck above). The uppermost outdoors deck includes a golf driving net and shuffleboard court.

The interior decor is quite stunning and elegant, a throwback to ship decor of the ocean liners of the 1920s and 1930s. This includes detailed ceiling cornices, both real and faux wrought iron staircase railings, leather-paneled walls, tromp l'oeil ceilings, rich carpeting in hallways with an Oriental rug–look center sec-tion, and many other interesting (and expensive-looking) decorative touches. The overall feel is of an old-world country club. The staircase in the main, two-deck-high foyer will remind you of something similar in a blockbuster hit about a certain ship where the stars, Kate Winslet and Leonardo DiCaprio, met on the staircase. Regular Renaissance Cruises passengers will probably be pleased with the fine taste with which her interiors have been designed and executed. The company's brochure is definitely understated.

The public rooms are basically spread over three decks. This is the first totally nonsmoking ship (there is no smoking anywhere, including cabins, dining room, public rooms, *or* on the open decks; whether the crew will be smoke-free remains to be seen).

The reception hall (lobby) features a staircase with intricate wrought iron railings. A large observation lounge, called the Sports Bar, is located high atop ship. This features a long bar with forward views (for the bartenders, that is), and a stack of distracting large-screen televisions all tuned to the same sports chan-nel (they remind me of looking into a television sales center); there's also an array of slot machines and bar counter-top electronic gaming machines.

There are plenty of bars aboard this ship, including one in each of the restaurant entrances. Perhaps the nicest of all bars and lounges can be found in the casino bar/lounge that is a beautiful room reminis-cent of London's grand hotels, which features an inviting marble fireplace (in fact there are *three* such fire-places aboard) and comfotable sofas and individual chairs.

The Library is a beautiful, grand room, designed in the Regency style, and features a fireplace, a high, indented, tromp l'oeil ceiling, and an excellent selection of books, as well as some very comfortable wing-back chairs with footstools, and sofas you could sleep on.

Renaissance Cruises provides a seamless cruise and tour package, geared specifically to North American passengers, at a price that is very hard to beat considering the destination-rich itineraries, together with pre- and postcruise land stays at high-quality hotels, and all transfers. At the end of the day, you should experience an excellent, hassle-free cruise vacation package aboard this or other ships in the R-class series. Renaissance Cruises also provides an excellent "vacation guarantee" called "Great Places Great Times" (this is also the name of the daily program on board) that is automatical-ly included with your cruise purchase.

Prices are kept low because the company sells direct to the public, and saves money in other ways, such as providing silk instead of fresh flowers throughout the ship. There may not be marble bathroom fittings, or caviar and other (more expensive) niceties, but the value for money is really excellent. There are no captain's cocktail parties or interdenominational church services, but there is plenty of entertain-ment if you want it, and high-quality hotels before and after your cruise, and all transfers, are included.

Dining staff gratuities are high, at $15.00 per day per person, and are pooled, due to the fact that you will be served by several different waiters in the four dining spots during the cruise (this means, however, that waiters don't get to know your likes, dislikes, and preferences). Also, 15 percent is added to all bar accounts (drink prices are moderate, while beer is high), and the company suggests another $5.00 per day for the cabin stewardess. Thus, for a five-day cruise, you should allow $100 per person, and for a ten-day cruise, $200 per person. *R One* and *R Two* feature cruises in the Mediterranean, *R Three* and *R Four* feature cruises from Tahiti to French Polynesia, *R Five* and *R Six* feature cruises in Europe.

Weak Points: There is no wraparound promenade deck outdoors (there is, however, a small jogging track around the perimeter of the swimming pool, and port and starboard side decks), and no wooden decks outdoors (instead, they are covered by Bollidt, a sand-colored rubberized material). The room service menu is extremely limited. Suggested gratuities are high (there is even a gratuities slot at the reception desk). Stairways, although carpeted, are tinny. In order to keep the prices low, the air routing to get to/from your ship is often not the most direct.

PHOTOGRAPHY

It is hard to find any situation more ideal for photography than a cruise. Your photographs enable you to share your memories with others at home. Here are some tips:

→ Use low-speed film in tropical areas such as the Caribbean or South Pacific (high-speed film is easily damaged by heat). Take plenty of film with you; standard sizes are available in the ship's shop, but the selection is limited. If you purchase film during a port visit, try to buy from an air-conditioned store, and check the expiration date.

→ Keep film cool, as the latent image on exposed film is fragile and easily affected by heat. There will be professional photographers on board who may develop film for you, for a fee (print film only).

→ When taking photographs in ports of call, respect the wishes of local inhabitants. Ask permission to photograph someone close-up. Most will smile and tell you to go ahead. But some people are superstitious or afraid of having their picture taken and will shy away from you. Do not press the point.

m/v R Two
★★★★ +
(M)

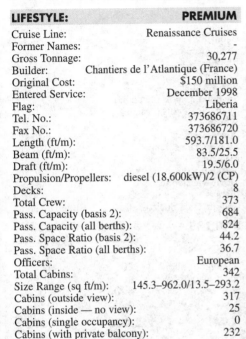

LIFESTYLE:	PREMIUM
Cruise Line:	Renaissance Cruises
Former Names:	-
Gross Tonnage:	30,277
Builder:	Chantiers de l'Atlantique (France)
Original Cost:	$150 million
Entered Service:	December 1998
Flag:	Liberia
Tel. No.:	373686711
Fax No.:	373686720
Length (ft/m):	593.7/181.0
Beam (ft/m):	83.5/25.5
Draft (ft/m):	19.5/6.0
Propulsion/Propellers:	diesel (18,600kW)/2 (CP)
Decks:	8
Total Crew:	373
Pass. Capacity (basis 2):	684
Pass. Capacity (all berths):	824
Pass. Space Ratio (basis 2):	44.2
Pass. Space Ratio (all berths):	36.7
Officers:	European
Total Cabins:	342
Size Range (sq ft/m):	145.3–962.0/13.5–293.2
Cabins (outside view):	317
Cabins (inside — no view):	25
Cabins (single occupancy):	0
Cabins (with private balcony):	232

Cabins (wheelchair accessible):	0
Cabin Current:	110 and 220 volts
Cabin TV:	Yes
Dining Rooms:	4
Elevators:	4
Casino:	Yes
Slot Machines:	Yes
Swimming Pools (outdoors):	1
Swimming Pools (inside):	0
Whirlpools:	2
Fitness Center:	Yes
Sauna/Steam Room:	No/Yes
Massage:	Yes
Self-Service Launderette:	Yes
Movie Theater/Seats:	No
Library:	Yes
Classification Society:	Bureau Veritas

RATINGS	POSSIBLE SCORE	SCORE ACHIEVED
Ship	500	423
Accommodation	200	164
Food	400	309
Service	400	303
Cruise	500	394
TOTAL	**2,000**	**1,593**

This ship, identical to sister ship *R One*, has been common-rated with it.

m/v R Three
★★★★ +
(M)

LIFESTYLE:		**PREMIUM**
Cruise Line:		Renaissance Cruises
Former Names:		-
Gross Tonnage:		30,277
Builder:	Chantiers de l'Atlantique (France)	
Original Cost:		$150 million
Entered Service:		August 1999
Flag:		Liberia
Tel. No.:		n/a
Fax No.:		n/a
Length (ft/m):		593.7/181.0
Beam (ft/m):		83.5/25.5
Draft (ft/m):		19.5/6.0
Propulsion/Propellers:	diesel (18,600kW)/2 (CP)	
Decks:		8
Total Crew:		373
Pass. Capacity (basis 2):		684
Pass. Capacity (all berths):		824
Pass. Space Ratio (basis 2):		44.2
Pass. Space Ratio (all berths):		36.7
Officers:		European
Total Cabins:		342
Size Range (sq ft/m):	145.3–962.0/13.5–293.2	
Cabins (outside view):		317
Cabins (inside — no view):		25
Cabins (single occupancy):		0
Cabins (with private balcony):		232
Cabins (wheelchair accessible):		0
Cabin Current:		110 and 220 volts
Cabin TV:		Yes
Dining Rooms:		4
Elevators:		4
Casino:		Yes
Slot Machines:		Yes
Swimming Pools (outdoors):		1
Swimming Pools (inside):		0
Whirlpools:		2
Fitness Center:		Yes
Sauna/Steam Room:		No/Yes
Massage:		Yes
Self-Service Launderette:		Yes
Movie Theater/Seats:		No
Library:		Yes
Classification Society:		Bureau Veritas

RATINGS	POSSIBLE SCORE	SCORE ACHIEVED
Ship	500	423
Accommodation	200	164
Food	400	309
Service	400	303
Cruise	500	394
TOTAL	**2,000**	**1,593**

This ship, virtually identical to sister ships *R One* and *R Two*, has been common-rated with them. Any changes will be made in the next edition of this book.

m/v R Four
★★★★ +
(M)

LIFESTYLE:	**PREMIUM**
Cruise Line:	Renaissance Cruises
Former Names:	-
Gross Tonnage:	30,277
Builder:	Chantiers de l'Atlantique (France)
Original Cost:	$150 million
Entered Service:	November 1999
Flag:	Liberia
Tel. No.:	n/a
Fax No.:	n/a
Length (ft/m):	593.7/181.0
Beam (ft/m):	83.5/25.5
Draft (ft/m):	19.5/6.0
Propulsion/Propellers:	diesel (18,600kW)/2 (CP)
Decks:	8
Total Crew:	373
Pass. Capacity (basis 2):	684
Pass. Capacity (all berths):	824
Pass. Space Ratio (basis 2):	44.2
Pass. Space Ratio (all berths):	36.7
Officers:	European
Total Cabins:	342
Size Range (sq ft/m):	145.3–962.0/13.5–293.2
Cabins (outside view):	317
Cabins (inside — no view):	25
Cabins (single occupancy):	0
Cabins (with private balcony):	232
Cabins (wheelchair accessible):	0
Cabin Current:	110 and 220 volts
Cabin TV:	Yes
Dining Rooms:	4
Elevators:	4
Casino:	Yes
Slot Machines:	Yes
Swimming Pools (outdoors):	1
Swimming Pools (inside):	0
Whirlpools:	2
Fitness Center:	Yes
Sauna/Steam Room:	No/Yes
Massage:	Yes
Self-Service Launderette:	Yes
Movie Theater/Seats:	No
Library:	Yes
Classification Society:	Bureau Veritas

RATINGS	POSSIBLE SCORE	SCORE ACHIEVED
Ship	500	423
Accommodation	200	164
Food	400	309
Service	400	303
Cruise	500	394
TOTAL	**2,000**	**1,593**

This ship, virtually identical to sister ships *R One, R Two,* and *R Three*, has been common-rated with them. Any changes will be made in the next edition of this book.

m/v R Five
★★★★ +
(M)

LIFESTYLE:	PREMIUM
Cruise Line:	Renaissance Cruises
Former Names:	-
Gross Tonnage:	30,277
Builder:	Chantiers de l'Atlantique (France)
Original Cost:	$150 million
Entered Service:	February 2000
Flag:	Liberia
Tel. No.:	n/a
Fax No.:	n/a
Length (ft/m):	593.7/181.0
Beam (ft/m):	83.5/25.5
Draft (ft/m):	19.5/6.0
Propulsion/Propellers:	diesel (18,600kW)/2 (CP)
Decks:	8
Total Crew:	373
Pass. Capacity (basis 2):	684
Pass. Capacity (all berths):	824
Pass. Space Ratio (basis 2):	44.2
Pass. Space Ratio (all berths):	36.7
Officers:	European
Total Cabins:	342
Size Range (sq ft/m):	145.3–962.0/13.5–293.2
Cabins (outside view):	317
Cabins (inside — no view):	25
Cabins (single occupancy):	0
Cabins (with private balcony):	232

Cabins (wheelchair accessible):	0
Cabin Current:	110 and 220 volts
Cabin TV:	Yes
Dining Rooms:	4
Elevators:	4
Casino:	Yes
Slot Machines:	Yes
Swimming Pools (outdoors):	1
Swimming Pools (inside):	0
Whirlpools:	2
Fitness Center:	Yes
Sauna/Steam Room:	No/Yes
Massage:	Yes
Self-Service Launderette:	Yes
Movie Theater/Seats:	No
Library:	Yes
Classification Society:	Bureau Veritas

RATINGS	POSSIBLE SCORE	SCORE ACHIEVED
Ship	500	423
Accommodation	200	164
Food	400	309
Service	400	303
Cruise	500	394
TOTAL	**2,000**	**1,593**

This ship, virtually identical to sister ships *R One, R Two, R Three,* and *R Four,* has been common-rated with them. Any changes will be made in the next edition of this book.

m/v R Six
★★★★ +
(M)

LIFESTYLE: **PREMIUM**

Cruise Line:	Renaissance Cruises
Former Names:	-
Gross Tonnage:	30,277
Builder:	Chantiers de l'Atlantique (France)
Original Cost:	$150 million
Entered Service:	May 2000
Flag:	Liberia
Tel. No.:	n/a
Fax No.:	n/a
Length (ft/m):	593.7/181.0
Beam (ft/m):	83.5/25.5
Draft (ft/m):	19.5/6.0
Propulsion/Propellers:	diesel (18,600kW)/2 (CP)
Decks:	8
Total Crew:	373
Pass. Capacity (basis 2):	684
Pass. Capacity (all berths):	824
Pass. Space Ratio (basis 2):	44.2
Pass. Space Ratio (all berths):	36.7
Officers:	European
Total Cabins:	342
Size Range (sq ft/m):	145.3–962.0/13.5–293.2
Cabins (outside view):	317
Cabins (inside — no view):	25
Cabins (single occupancy):	0
Cabins (with private balcony):	232

Cabins (wheelchair accessible):	0
Cabin Current:	110 and 220 volts
Cabin TV:	Yes
Dining Rooms:	4
Elevators:	4
Casino:	Yes
Slot Machines:	Yes
Swimming Pools (outdoors):	1
Swimming Pools (inside):	0
Whirlpools:	2
Fitness Center:	Yes
Sauna/Steam Room:	No/Yes
Massage:	Yes
Self-Service Launderette:	Yes
Movie Theater/Seats:	No
Library:	Yes
Classification Society:	Bureau Veritas

RATINGS	POSSIBLE SCORE	SCORE ACHIEVED
Ship	500	423
Accommodation	200	164
Food	400	309
Service	400	303
Cruise	500	394
TOTAL	**2,000**	**1,593**

This ship, virtually identical to sister ships *R One, R Two, R Three, R Four,* and *R Five*, has been common-rated with them. Any changes will be made in the next edition of this book.

s/s/c Radisson Diamond

★★★★ +

(S)

LIFESTYLE:	LUXURY
Cruise Line:	Radisson Seven Seas Cruises
Former Names:	-
Gross Tonnage:	20,295
Builder:	Rauma Yards (Finland)
Original Cost:	$125 million
Entered Service:	May 1992
Flag:	Bahamas
Tel. No.:	1307631
Fax No.:	1307645
Length (ft/m):	430.4/131.2
Beam (ft/m):	104.9/32.0
Draft (ft/m):	26.2/8.0
Propulsion/Propellers:	diesel (11,340kW)/2 nozzles
Decks:	6
Total Crew:	200
Pass. Capacity (basis 2):	354
Pass. Capacity (all berths):	354
Pass. Space Ratio (basis 2):	57.3
Pass. Space Ratio (all berths):	57.3
Officers:	Scandinavian/European
Total Cabins:	177
Size Range (sq ft/m):	220.0/20.5
Cabins (outside view):	177
Cabins (inside — no view):	0
Cabins (single occupancy):	0
Cabins (with private balcony):	123

Cabins (wheelchair accessible):	2
Cabin Current:	110 and 220 volts
Cabin TV:	Yes
Dining Rooms:	1 (+1 Grill Restaurant)
Elevators:	3
Casino:	Yes
Slot Machines:	Yes
Swimming Pools (outdoors):	1
Swimming Pools (inside):	0
Whirlpools:	1
Fitness Center:	Yes
Sauna/Steam Room:	Yes/Yes
Massage:	Yes
Self-Service Launderette:	No
Movie Theater/Seats:	No
Library:	Yes
Classification Society:	Det Norske Veritas

RATINGS	POSSIBLE SCORE	SCORE ACHIEVED
Ship	500	413
Accommodation	200	172
Food	400	334
Service	400	332
Cruise	500	389
TOTAL	**2,000**	**1,640**

Accommodation: Nicely designed, spacious, and well-equipped cabins all have outside views, and most have private balconies with outdoor lights. All are furnished in blonde woods, with marble bathroom vanities and a tiny bathtub. There are bay windows in 47 suites.

All cabins are of the same dimensions, with the exception of two VIP master suites with private balconies. Each cabin has an oversized window or floor-to-ceiling balcony windows/door. There is a spacious sitting area with sofa and chairs; a dressing table with hair dryer; minibar and refrigerator; telephone; color remote-control television with integral video player; twin beds that convert to a queen-size unit; two good, bright, adjustable reading lamps; a personal safe (somewhat hidden and awkward for older passengers to reach and operate); full-length mirror; and excellent drawer space. The closet space, however, is really minimal, adequate for short cruises but tight for two on a seven-night cruise, worse for longer cruises. The cabin bathrooms have really small tubs (they are really shower tubs).

Each cabin has a minibar that is stocked with beer and soft drinks; half-liter bottles of four liquors are provided. Bottled mineral water is provided.

Dining: The two-deck-high dining room is elegant, has a 270-degree view over the stern, and open seating, so you can dine with whomever you wish, when you wish. The cuisine quality and food presentation is European in style, and outstanding in quality, choice, and presentation. Also features health foods and dietary specials. The waitresses (there are no waiters) are really charming, supervised superbly by experienced Italian headwaiters. As far as wines go, although basic whites and reds are included for lunch and dinner, a separate wine list is available for those who appreciate better wines (at extra cost). Dining, in fact, is the vessel's strongest point.

The Grill is a 50-seat alternative Italian casual indoor/outdoor dining spot (there is no extra charge). Run like a real restaurant ashore (make your reservations early each day you want to eat there), this informal dining spot features superb homemade pasta dishes daily, has a fine menu, including cream sauces and exotic garnishes. Each day is different, and food is presented, in small portions, course by course. It

380

is lovingly prepared and exquisite to taste, although somewhat rich. Seating is at sturdy, practical glass-topped wooden tables for two, four, or six. Tableside dessert flambeaus are often featured. Dining in it is an experience, not just an alternative restaurant

Other Comments: This ship features an innovative design, based on the SWATH (Small Waterplane Area Twin Hull) technology. She is, thus, very stable when at sea (except, of course, in rough seas), with four stabilizing fins (two on the inner side of each pontoon), so that motion is really minimized when compared with conventional (monohull) vessels. The wide beam of this design also provides outstanding passenger space, although the public rooms are stacked vertically and are contained mostly on the inside of the ship, which is like a seagoing version of a Radisson hotel ashore.

The casino has gaming tables on one side of the passageway, slot machines on the other (good for serious game players who do not want the sound of slot machines to intrude).

A five-deck-high atrium has glass-enclosed elevators (which, together with the staircase, take up most of the space). There is also a little-used underwater viewing area (it actually consists of just two portholes). There is a good outdoor jogging track.

Has a well-stocked library and video center, and a sophisticated business center with facilities that are ideal for small groups and conventions. For groups and meetings, the high-tech audio and video conference facilities, and a high-tech security system that uses approximately 50 cameras to monitor just about everywhere, provide a good feeling of exclusivity.

There is also a retractable, free-floating water sports marina platform, but it is really only useful in dead calm sea conditions. There are jet-skis, and a water-ski boat.

<u>Weak Points</u>: The design means that many public rooms are inside, with little or no connection with the sea. Flowers, and more flowers, would help a lot. The ship has a maximum speed of 12.5 knots, which means it is fine for leisurely island cruising but is slow going on longer itineraries. The awkward one-way (contra-flow) interior staircase is frustrating. The spaciousness of the ship, while providing the flexibility of several individual public rooms, actually detracts from the overall flow. Also awkward is the multilevel entertainment room (show lounge). The health spa facilities are very good but cannot be reached by elevator. There are still some uncomfortable chairs in the main dining room. The meet-and-greet service is inconsistent and is the subject of passenger complaints.

This semisubmersible, twin-hulled cruise vessel, which some have said looks like a white-caped "Batman" from the stern, certainly has the most unusual and distinctive looks of any cruise ship, although its design has not been as successful as hoped. This ship will appeal to those seeking extremely high standards of service in sophisticated and personable, somewhat "hotel-style" surroundings, and unstructured daytime activities. One nice plus is the fact that all gratuities are included. The standard of onboard service is high, which helps to make up for the design and structural shortcomings of the vessel.

m/s Regal Empress
★★ +
(M)

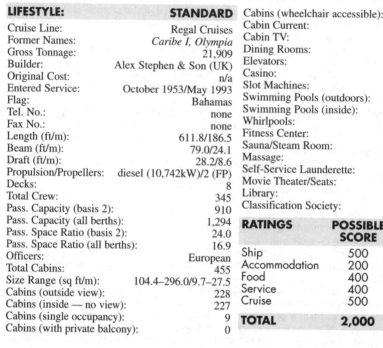

LIFESTYLE:	STANDARD
Cruise Line:	Regal Cruises
Former Names:	*Caribe I, Olympia*
Gross Tonnage:	21,909
Builder:	Alex Stephen & Son (UK)
Original Cost:	n/a
Entered Service:	October 1953/May 1993
Flag:	Bahamas
Tel. No.:	none
Fax No.:	none
Length (ft/m):	611.8/186.5
Beam (ft/m):	79.0/24.1
Draft (ft/m):	28.2/8.6
Propulsion/Propellers:	diesel (10,742kW)/2 (FP)
Decks:	8
Total Crew:	345
Pass. Capacity (basis 2):	910
Pass. Capacity (all berths):	1,294
Pass. Space Ratio (basis 2):	24.0
Pass. Space Ratio (all berths):	16.9
Officers:	European
Total Cabins:	455
Size Range (sq ft/m):	104.4–296.0/9.7–27.5
Cabins (outside view):	228
Cabins (inside — no view):	227
Cabins (single occupancy):	9
Cabins (with private balcony):	0
Cabins (wheelchair accessible):	1
Cabin Current:	110/220 volts
Cabin TV:	Yes
Dining Rooms:	1
Elevators:	3
Casino:	Yes
Slot Machines:	Yes
Swimming Pools (outdoors):	1
Swimming Pools (inside):	0
Whirlpools:	2
Fitness Center:	Yes
Sauna/Steam Room:	No/No
Massage:	Yes
Self-Service Launderette:	No
Movie Theater/Seats:	Yes/90
Library:	Yes
Classification Society:	Lloyd's Register

RATINGS	POSSIBLE SCORE	SCORE ACHIEVED
Ship	500	240
Accommodation	200	99
Food	400	201
Service	400	206
Cruise	500	216
TOTAL	**2,000**	**962**

Accommodation: There is a wide range of cabin sizes and configurations, in ten suite/cabin grades. Most are small, yet spacious enough, with good closet and reasonable drawer space, and heavy-duty fittings, although the decor is generally dark and dull. The largest cabins are four "penthouse suites" on Upper Deck, with views over the bow (when you stand up), and in 1997, several suites with private balconies were added.

Dining: This lovely old-world dining room is a step back in time to a more gracious era, with its original oil paintings on burnished wood paneling, ornate lighting fixtures and etched glass panels, and original murals depicting New York and Rio. There are two seatings. Most tables are for groups of six or more, with a few tables for four. Smoking and nonsmoking sections are provided on the starboard and port sides respectively. The food is plentiful and of a reasonably high standard considering the price, with the exception of the buffets, which are really basic and unimaginative.

Other Comments: This ship has a traditional ocean liner profile. There is a good amount of open deck space for sun worshippers, although this can become very crowded when the ship is full. Traditional liner features include polished teak decking and handrails.

The enclosed (air-conditioned) promenade deck is popular with strollers, and for those that like to sit and read.

Inside the ship you'll find plenty of real woods, heavy brass, and art deco detailing throughout many of her public rooms, with fine satin woods and brass featured on her interior staircases. There really are few public rooms except for a large casino, single-level show lounge (with slightly raised port and starboard sections), a nightclub/disco, and a piano lounge.

There is, however, a fine, old-fashioned library with untouched, original paneling, although the book selection is poor and out of date; the dog-eared paperbacks just do not look right; and no magazines are provided.

Features four- to ten-day Gulf of Mexico/Panama Canal cruises from Port Manatee (Florida) during the winter; a long cruise (over 50 days) around South America in October; and short cruises from New York during the summer. This ship provides a basic cruise experience in reasonably adequate surroundings, but remember that, although she underwent some much-needed refurbishment in 1997, she is an old ship and the service is perfunctory, at best.

Weak Points: Expect to be in a line for embarkation, disembarkation, and buffets. The ship is extremely cramped, with little space to move around when full, particularly on the short party cruises. The ship has an awkward layout, and many passageways do not extend for the length of the ship. Finally, the tipping glasses stationed around the ship are particularly insulting.

SHIPBOARD ETIQUETTE

Cruise lines want you to have a good vacation, but there are some rules to be observed.

↪ In public rooms, smoking and nonsmoking sections are available. In the dining room, however, cigar and pipe smoking are not permitted at all.

↪ If you take a video camera with you, be aware that you are not allowed to tape any of the professional entertainment shows and cabarets due to international copyright infringement regulations.

↪ It is all right to be casual when on vacation, but not to enter a ship's dining room in just a bathing suit. Bare feet, likewise, are not permitted. If you are uncomfortable eating with the typical ten-piece dining room cutlery setting, don't fret; some cruise lines now have etiquette classes to help you.

m/v Regal Princess
★★★★
(L)

LIFESTYLE:	PREMIUM
Cruise Line:	Princess Cruises
Former Names:	-
Gross Tonnage:	69,845
Builder:	Fincantieri Navali (Italy)
Original Cost:	$276.8 million
Entered Service:	August 1991
Flag:	Liberia
Tel. No.:	1245712
Fax No.:	1245712
Length (ft/m):	811.0/247.2
Beam (ft/m):	105.6/32.2
Draft (ft/m):	25.5/7.8
Propulsion/Propellers:	diesel (24,000kW)/2 (CP)
Decks:	12
Total Crew:	696
Pass. Capacity (basis 2):	1,590
Pass. Capacity (all berths):	1,910
Pass. Space Ratio (basis 2):	43.9
Pass. Space Ratio (all berths):	36.5
Officers:	Italian
Total Cabins:	795
Size Range (sq ft/m):	189.4–586.6/17.6–54.5
Cabins (outside view):	624
Cabins (inside — no view):	171
Cabins (single occupancy):	0
Cabins (with private balcony):	184

Cabins (wheelchair accessible):	10
Cabin Current:	110 and 220 volts
Cabin TV:	Yes
Dining Rooms:	1
Elevators:	9
Casino:	Yes
Slot Machines:	Yes
Swimming Pools (outdoors):	2
Swimming Pools (inside):	0
Whirlpools:	4
Fitness Center:	Yes
Sauna/Steam Room:	Yes/Yes
Massage:	Yes
Self-Service Launderette:	Yes
Movie Theater/Seats:	Yes/169
Library:	Yes
Classification Society:	Registro Navale Italiano

RATINGS	POSSIBLE SCORE	SCORE ACHIEVED
Ship	500	382
Accommodation	200	156
Food	400	271
Service	400	299
Cruise	500	401
TOTAL	**2,000**	**1,509**

For comments, see *Crown Princess*.

s/s Rembrandt
★★★ +
(L)

LIFESTYLE:	STANDARD
Cruise Line:	Premier Cruise Lines
Former Names:	*Rotterdam*
Gross Tonnage:	38,645
Builder:	Rotterdamsche Dry Dock (Holland)
Original Cost:	$30 million
Entered Service:	September 1959/December 1997
Flag:	Bahamas
Tel. No.:	630600610
Fax No.:	1302554
Length (ft/m):	748.6/228.20
Beam (ft/m):	94.1/28.71
Draft (ft/m):	29.6/9.04
Propulsion/Propellers:	steam turbine (28,700kW)/2 (FP)
Decks:	10
Total Crew:	550
Pass. Capacity (basis 2):	1,142
Pass. Capacity (all berths):	1,481
Pass. Space Ratio (basis 2):	33.8
Pass. Space Ratio (all berths):	26.0
Officers:	International
Total Cabins:	587
Size Range (sq ft/m):	113.0–339.2/10.5–34.3
Cabins (outside view):	312
Cabins (inside — no view):	275
Cabins (single occupancy):	32

Cabins (with private balcony):	0
Cabins (wheelchair accessible):	0 (ramps available)
Cabin Current:	110 volts
Cabin TV:	No
Dining Rooms:	2
Elevators:	8
Casino:	Yes
Slot Machines:	Yes
Swimming Pools (outdoors):	1
Swimming Pools (inside):	1
Whirlpools:	0
Fitness Center:	Yes
Sauna/Steam Room:	Yes/No
Massage:	Yes
Self-Service Launderette:	Yes
Movie Theater/Seats:	Yes/620
Library:	Yes
Classification Society:	Lloyd's Register

RATINGS	POSSIBLE SCORE	SCORE ACHIEVED
Ship	500	306
Accommodation	200	128
Food	400	262
Service	400	275
Cruise	500	303
TOTAL	**2,000**	**1,274**

Accommodation: There is a wide choice of cabin sizes and configurations (she was built before the days of modular cabins), but all of them are comfortable and come well equipped with solid wood cabinetry, solid fittings, and good quality furnishings, plenty of drawer space, and all cabins have illuminated closets. Some cabins have upper and lower berths rather than beds. There are plenty of cabins for single passengers, a welcome touch. All cabin bathrooms have exposed plumbing, however, a throwback to her former days as a transatlantic liner, but all have a personal toiletries cabinet, glass shelves, and just enough mirror facing.

There are also 12 deluxe suites (these even have a wall clock built into the vanity desk mirror front), and 24 suites. Some have large walk-in closets, while others have regular (illuminated) closets, vanity desks, and an abundance of drawers and other storage spaces, sleeping area and lounge with sofa, table, and chairs befitting a Miami Beach art deco hotel. Passengers in accommodation designated as suites receive amenity kits (if booked at brochure rates), champagne and chocolate truffles, late afternoon canapes, and fruit basket.

All cabins have good soundproofing. The cabin service menu consists of five items (available 24 hours).

Dining: There are two dining rooms, both of which are set low down, have high domed ceilings, neat wall artwork (with fish logo), and offer good basic fare, with reasonable banquet food and somewhat robotic, rushed service. For breakfast and lunch open seating is generally featured, and there are two seatings for dinner (both smoking and nonsmoking areas are provided, so nonsmokers should be aware that they may sit adjacent to smokers).

In the main dining room the food is attractively presented, but the meals are not memorable, and standards are still spotty. When the ship is in Europe, the vegetables have taste, when she is in South America, this is not quite the case. There is a rather limited selection of breads, cheese, and fruit. Self-service buffets are featured in the Lido Cafe, with seating both indoors and outdoors (but it is difficult to get away from smokers), while an outdoor grill provides the requisite hamburgers.

Other Comments: *Rembrandt* — such a fitting name for this sturdily built steamship and distinguished ocean liner! She has handsome, rounded lines, and a thick, royal blue, riveted hull (they don't build ships this way today). This grand dame is still lovely — and indeed she is well loved by her many followers. Gracious and graceful, she was well cared for by her previous owners, Holland America Line. She is being extremely well maintained (even improved) under her new owners, Premier Cruise Lines, who want, quite rightly, to bring back the utter *romance* of cruising by operating a collection of carefully maintained, former ocean liners. Has expansive open deck and sunbathing space, with real teakwood promenade decks outdoors and wooden deck lounge chairs (with good cushioned pads that make it a pleasure to relax on).

Inside the ship, there are numerous public rooms to play in, but the decor is somewhat a mismatch of color combinations and, at times, might seem a little dark. However, the acres of beautiful wood paneling and wood trim throughout provide a real solid ship feel (almost impossible to find aboard today's new ships), and she has a most interesting wrought iron staircase — a carryover from her former transatlantic days when she was first operated as a two-class ship. The dance floors feature lovely inlaid marquetry and parquet patterns, and her heavy-duty fittings and fixtures makes her a floating study in solidly crafted art deco workmanship. There is a decent (but now dated) collection of artwork throughout the ship.

The two-level Ritz Carlton lounge (complete with a gorgeous chandelier and wide, curved staircase) is still one of the most elegant art deco rooms afloat. There is a lovely theater, complete with a mezzanine balcony, in the old tradition (although the seats are not staggered). The one room not to be missed is the Ambassador Lounge, with its bordello-red and black chairs and pink spotted light fixtures — a fascinating place.

A cruise aboard this stately old ship fits comfortably — rather like a well-worn shoe — and the price is right. However, do remember that she is an old lady, and cannot compete with all the latest contemporary ships with their high-tech facilities (but then, it's the old-world charm of a well-proportioned ocean liner that passengers enjoy). She is, however, an extremely comfortable steamship.

She was acquired by Premier Cruise Lines in September 1997 from her former owners, Holland America Line, and operates seven-night Caribbean cruises the winter and seven-night Canada-New England cruises during the summer.

Choose this ship if you want to experience the thrill of sailing aboard a real (former) ocean liner, with high-ceilinged public rooms, expansive stairways, and wide promenade deck. All port charges are included.

<u>Weak Points</u>: The fireplace in the casino seems out of place (so does the casino). Has poor (low-budget) entertainment. Communication (between service staff and passengers) remains the single most important thing for Premier Cruise Lines to concentrate on — many of the crew speak or understand very little English.

m/s Renaissance Seven
★★★★
(S)

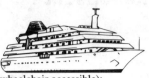

LIFESTYLE:	PREMIUM
Cruise Line:	Renaissance Cruises
Former Names:	-
Gross Tonnage:	4,280
Builder:	Nuovi Cantieri Apuania (Italy)
Original Cost:	$25 million
Entered Service:	December 1991
Flag:	Liberia
Tel. No.:	1151322
Fax No.:	1250146
Length (ft/m):	297.2/90.60
Beam (ft/m):	50.1/15.30
Draft (ft/m):	12.9/3.95
Propulsion/Propellers:	diesel (5,000kW)/2 (CP)
Decks:	5
Total Crew:	72
Pass. Capacity (basis 2):	114
Pass. Capacity (all berths):	114
Pass. Space Ratio (basis 2):	37.5
Pass. Space Ratio (all berths):	37.5
Officers:	Italian
Total Cabins:	57
Size Range (sq ft/m):	215.0–312.0/20.0–29.0
Cabins (outside view):	57
Cabins (inside — no view):	0
Cabins (single occupancy):	0
Cabins (with private balcony):	4

Cabins (wheelchair accessible):	0
Cabin Current:	110 volts
Cabin TV:	Yes
Dining Rooms:	1
Elevators:	1
Casino:	Yes
Slot Machines:	Yes
Swimming Pools (outdoors):	1
Swimming Pools (inside):	0
Whirlpools:	1
Fitness Center:	No
Sauna/Steam Room:	Yes/No
Massage:	Yes
Self-Service Launderette:	No
Movie Theater/Seats:	No
Library:	Yes
Classification Society:	Registro Navale Italiano

RATINGS	POSSIBLE SCORE	SCORE ACHIEVED
Ship	500	378
Accommodation	200	160
Food	400	283
Service	400	313
Cruise	500	372
TOTAL	**2,000**	**1,506**

Accommodation: The spacious cabins combine highly polished imitation rosewood paneling with lots of mirrors and hand-crafted Italian furniture, lighted walk-in closets, three-sided vanity mirrors, and just about everything you need, including a television, VCR unit, and refrigerator (pre-stocked when you book, but at extra cost). The bathrooms, however, are small; they have real teakwood floors and marble vanities, but no bathtubs.

Dining: The dining room (operates with open seating for all meals) is small and elegant, with tables for two, four, six, and eight. You simply sit where you like, with whom you like, and at what time you like. The meals are self-service, buffet-style cold foods for breakfast and lunch, with hot foods chosen from a table menu and served properly. The dining room operation works well. The food quality, choice, and presentation are all fairly decent, and close to California "lean cuisine," although there is little flair.

Other Comments: Contemporary mega-yacht looks and handsome styling, with twin flared funnels. Originally a series of eight ships, now only two are still in operation by Renaissance Cruises (*Renaissance Seven* is chartered to Raymond & Whitcomb of New York, and is named *Regina Renaissance* for the period of the charter). There is one teak promenade deck outdooors, and a reasonable amount of open deck and sunbathing space. The water sports facilities include an aft platform, sailfish, snorkel equipment, and Zodiacs.

Inside the ship, one finds an elegant interior design, with polished wood-finish everywhere. The main lounge, the focal point for all social activities, has six pillars that destroy sight lines to the small stage area. There is also a very small book and video library.

This vessel is very comfortable and totally inviting, and features destination-intensive cruising for the privileged passenger who appreciates the finer things in life and is prepared to pay accordingly. Although neither ship nor product delivery is anywhere near the standard of a Seabourn Cruise Line vessel, for example, this intimate ship can still provide a good cruise experience for a moderate sum of money.

m/s Renaissance Eight
★★★★
(S)

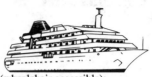

LIFESTYLE:	PREMIUM
Cruise Line:	Renaissance Cruises
Former Names:	-
Gross Tonnage:	4,280
Builder:	Nuovi Cantieri Apuania (Italy)
Original Cost:	$25 million each
Entered Service:	May 1992
Flag:	Liberia
Tel. No.:	1151375
Fax No.:	1250145
Length (ft/m):	297.2/90.60
Beam (ft/m):	50.1/15.30
Draft (ft/m):	12.9/3.95
Propulsion/Propellers:	diesel (5,000kW)/2 (CP)
Decks:	5
Total Crew:	72
Pass. Capacity (basis 2):	114
Pass. Capacity (all berths):	114
Pass. Space Ratio (basis 2):	37.5
Pass. Space Ratio (all berths):	37.5
Officers:	Italian
Total Cabins:	57
Size Range (sq ft/m): 215.0 — 312.0/20.0–29.0	
Cabins (outside view):	57
Cabins (inside — no view):	0
Cabins (single occupancy):	0
Cabins (with private balcony):	4

Cabins (wheelchair accessible):	0
Cabin Current:	110 volts
Cabin TV:	Yes
Dining Rooms:	1
Elevators:	1
Casino:	Yes
Slot Machines:	Yes
Swimming Pools (outdoors):	1
Swimming Pools (inside):	0
Whirlpools:	1
Fitness Center:	No
Sauna/Steam Room:	Yes/No
Massage:	Yes
Self-Service Launderette:	No
Movie Theater/Seats:	No
Library:	Yes
Classification Society:	Registro Navale Italiano

RATINGS	POSSIBLE SCORE	SCORE ACHIEVED
Ship	500	378
Accommodation	200	160
Food	400	283
Service	400	313
Cruise	500	372
TOTAL	**2,000**	**1,506**

For comments, see *Renaissance Seven*.

m/v Rhapsody
★★★
(M)

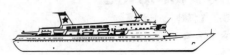

LIFESTYLE:	STANDARD
Cruise Line:	Mediterranean Shipping Cruises
Former Names:	*Cunard Princess, Cunard Conquest*
Gross Tonnage:	17,495
Builder:	Burmeister & Wein (Denmark)
Original Cost:	£12 million
Entered Service:	March 1977/May 1995
Flag:	Panama
Tel. No.:	1104111
Fax No.:	1104111
Length (ft/m):	541.0/164.9
Beam (ft/m):	76.1/23.2
Draft (ft/m):	19.0/5.82
Propulsion/Propellers:	diesel (15,670kW)/2 (CP)
Decks:	8
Total Crew:	350
Pass. Capacity (basis 2):	788
Pass. Capacity (all berths):	959
Pass. Space Ratio (basis 2):	22.2
Pass. Space Ratio (all berths):	18.1
Officers:	Italian
Total Cabins:	394
Size Range (sq ft/m):	87.1–264.8/8.1–24.6
Cabins (outside view):	267
Cabins (inside — no view):	127
Cabins (single occupancy):	0
Cabins (with private balcony):	0

Cabins (wheelchair accessible):	0
Cabin Current:	110 and 220 volts
Cabin TV:	suites only
Dining Rooms:	1
Elevators:	2
Casino:	Yes
Slot Machines:	Yes
Swimming Pools (outdoors):	1
Swimming Pools (inside):	0
Whirlpools:	2
Fitness Center:	Yes
Sauna/Steam Room:	Yes/No
Massage:	No
Self-Service Launderette:	No
Movie Theater/Seats:	Yes/135
Library:	Yes
Classification Society:	Lloyd's Register

RATINGS	POSSIBLE SCORE	SCORE ACHIEVED
Ship	500	323
Accommodation	200	121
Food	400	216
Service	400	238
Cruise	500	296
TOTAL	**2,000**	**1,194**

Accommodation: Although the cabins are small and compact, with somewhat tinny (noisy) metal fixtures and very thin walls that provide extremely poor cabin insulation, they are adequate for short cruises. The soft furnishings are pleasing, and the closet and drawer space is reasonable. The bathrooms are adequate, if a little tight, with little storage space for toiletries.

Dining: Features a pleasant, bubbly dining room that has sea views from large picture windows, but it is fairly noisy due to its open design. There are two seatings. The standard "banquet" food is reasonable and tailored mainly to Italian passengers, with typical Italian dishes including plenty of pasta (but sadly, there is no tableside cooking). The service is bubbly, cheerful, attentive, and comes with a smile, but lacks finesse. There is a limited selection of breads and fruits. The cabin service menu is very limited.

Other Comments: This ship is almost identical to her sister, the former *Cunard Countess*, with the same contemporary profile and good looks. She was acquired in 1995 by StarLauro Cruises (now known as Mediterranean Shipping Cruises) as a replacement for its *Achille Lauro*, which caught fire and sank in 1995. There is a good amount of open deck space for sun-worshippers.

There is a good selection of public rooms with attractive decor in light, bright colors, including an observation lounge above the bridge, overlooking the bow. Has an excellent indoor-outdoor entertainment night club and bar, which incorporates the occasional use of an aft open deck area. The show lounge is a single-level room with raised seating on its port and starboard sides (several pillars obstruct sight lines).

This ship will provide a very comfortable first cruise experience, featuring destination-intensive itineraries, in a pleasing, casual, but high density environment.

This ship is now marketed mostly to Europeans, and to Italian passengers in particular (who form about 60 percent of the passengers). While the ship still looks sharp following an extensive refit and refurbishment in 1997, the standard of food and service offered are disappointing.

<u>Weak Points</u>: There is no outdoor wraparound promenade deck outdoors. The cabins really are very small.

m/s Rhapsody of the Seas
★★★★
(L)

LIFESTYLE:	STANDARD
Cruise Line:	Royal Caribbean International
Former Names:	-
Gross Tonnage:	78,491
Builder:	Chantiers de l'Atlantique (France)
Original Cost:	$275 million
Entered Service:	May 1997
Flag:	Norway
Tel. No.:	325790011
Fax No.:	325790012
Length (ft/m):	915.3/279.0
Beam (ft/m):	105.6/32.2
Draft (ft/m):	24.9/7.6
Propulsion/Propellers:	diesel-electric (50,400kW)/2 (FP)
Decks:	11
Total Crew:	765
Pass. Capacity (basis 2):	2,000
Pass. Capacity (all berths):	2,435
Pass. Space Ratio (basis 2):	39.2
Pass. Space Ratio (all berths):	32.2
Officers:	International
Total Cabins:	1,000
Size Range (sq ft/m):	148.5–1,059.2/13.8–98.4
Cabins (outside view):	593
Cabins (inside — no view):	407
Cabins (single occupancy):	0

Cabins (with private balcony):	229
Cabins (wheelchair accessible):	14
Cabin Current:	110 and 220 volts
Cabin TV:	Yes
Dining Rooms:	1
Elevators:	9
Casino:	Yes
Slot Machines:	Yes
Swimming Pools (outdoors):	1
Swimming Pools (inside):	1 (inside/outside)
Whirlpools:	6
Fitness Center:	Yes
Sauna/Steam Room:	Yes/Yes
Massage:	Yes
Self-Service Launderette:	No
Movie Theater/Seats:	No
Library:	Yes
Classification Society:	Det Norske Veritas

RATINGS	POSSIBLE SCORE	SCORE ACHIEVED
Ship	500	439
Accommodation	200	169
Food	400	248
Service	400	298
Cruise	500	384
TOTAL	**2,000**	**1,538**

Accommodation: The standard cabins are of an adequate size, and have just enough functional facilities to make them comfortable for a one-week cruise, but longer might prove confining. The decor is bright and cheerful, although the ceilings are plain. Twin lower beds convert to queen-size beds, and there is a reasonable amount of closet and drawer space (there is little room to maneuver between the bed and desk/television unit). The bathrooms are functional, although the shower units themselves are small. The towels could be larger and thicker. In the passageways, upbeat artwork depicts musical themes, from classical to jazz and popular.

The ultimate accommodation aboard this ship is the Royal Suite, which resembles a Palm Beach apartment, complete with white baby grand (player) piano. The decor is simple and elegant, with pastel colors, and wood accented ceiling treatments.

Dining: The two-level main dining room (called Edelweiss) is attractive and works well, although the noise level can be high. There are two seatings. The quality and serving of meals aboard Royal Caribbean International ships has become very mechanized over the past few years. It can best be described as good, but rather basic, hotel banquet food, but, as is typical aboard so many ships today, there is little taste. While meats are of reasonable quality, the fish is not, and most vegetables taste the same. In other words, the meals are basically sound, but certainly not memorable. There is also a limited selection of breads and cheeses. There is a decent but fairly basic wine list, but the prices are high. The dining room features open seating for breakfast and lunch, while dinner is at 6:00pm (main seating) and 8:30pm (second seating).

The informal dining spots are well designed, with contemporary decor and colors, but the food is really basic fare and disappointing. The four-sided self-service buffet area is small for the number of passengers that use it. More money needs to be spent for better-quality ingredients. Each evening, buffets feature a different theme, something this company has been doing for more than 25 years — perhaps it's time for more creativity. One thing this company does once each cruise is to feature "Galley Buffet" whereby passengers go through a section of the galley picking up food for a midnight buffet.

Other Comments: This striking ship shares design features that make all Royal Caribbean International ships identifiable, including a Viking Crown Lounge, which is a terrific multilevel night spot (the music can be loud and overbearing, however, and so can the cigarette smoke around the bar). The Viking Crown Lounge (which is also the ship's disco) aboard this and sister ship *Vision of the Seas* is positioned just forward of the center of the ship. The funnel is located well aft — a departure from all other RCI ships to date which have the lounge positioned around, or at the base of, the funnel. The ship's stern is beautifully rounded. There is a reasonable amount of open-air walking space, although this can become cluttered with deck lounge chairs.

There is a wide range of interesting public rooms, lounges, and bars to play in, and the interiors have been cleverly designed to avoid congestion and aid passenger flow into revenue areas. Speaking of which, for those who enjoy gambling, the astrologically-themed casino is large and glitzy (although not as bold as aboard some of the company's other ships), again typical of most of the new large ships; a couple of pieces of "electrostatic" art in globe form provide fascinating relief.

There is, as one might expect, a large shopping area, although the merchandise is consistently tacky, and identical to that found in most American malls. The artwork throughout the ship is really upbeat and colorful, and has a musical theme: classical, jazz, popular, and rock 'n' roll. Much improved over previous new ships in the fleet is the theater, with more entrances, less bottlenecks; there are still pillars obstructing sight lines from many seats, however. Also improved are the facilities for children and teens.

This ship has good health spa facilities, set in a spacious environment on one of the uppermost decks. The decor here has Egypt as its theme, with pharaohs lining the pool.

Ship lovers will enjoy the chair fabric in the Shall We Dance lounge, with its large aft-facing windows, and the glass case-enclosed mechanical sculptures.

Royal Caribbean International provides a consistently good, highly programmed cruise vacation for those seeking to travel in a large ship, with a large number of other lively passengers. What, in particular, makes this ship feel warm and cozy are the use of fine, light wood surfaces throughout her public rooms, as well as the large array of potted plants everywhere.

<u>Weak Points</u>: The daily program is so full of the day's events, in small type size, that it is *extremely* difficult to read. The light colored carpeting used on the stairwells is impractical.

m/s Rotterdam
★★★★ +
(L)

LIFESTYLE:	PREMIUM
Cruise Line:	Holland America Line
Former Names:	-
Gross Tonnage:	59,652
Builder:	Fincantieri (Italy)
Original Cost:	$250 million
Entered Service:	December 1997
Flag:	The Netherlands
Tel. No.:	324616710
Fax No.:	324616713
Length (ft/m):	777.5/237.00
Beam (ft/m):	105.8/32.25
Draft (ft/m):	25.5/7.80
Propulsion/Propellers:	diesel-electric (37,500kW)/2 (CP)
Decks:	12
Total Crew:	593
Pass. Capacity (basis 2):	1,320
Pass. Capacity (all berths):	1,668
Pass. Space Ratio (basis 2):	45.1
Pass. Space Ratio (all berths):	35.7
Officers:	Dutch
Total Cabins:	660
Size Range (sq ft/m):	184.0-1,124.8/17.1-104.5
Cabins (outside view):	542
Cabins (inside — no view):	118
Cabins (single occupancy):	0

Cabins (with private balcony):	160
Cabins (wheelchair accessible):	20
Cabin Current:	110 and 220 volts
Cabin TV:	Yes
Dining Rooms:	2
Elevators:	12
Casino:	Yes
Slot Machines:	Yes
Swimming Pools (outdoors):	1
Swimming Pools (inside):	1 (magrodome cover)
Whirlpools:	2
Fitness Center:	Yes
Sauna/Steam Room:	Yes/Yes
Massage:	Yes
Self-Service Launderette:	Yes
Movie Theater/Seats:	Yes/235
Library:	Yes
Classification Society:	Lloyd's Register

RATINGS	POSSIBLE SCORE	SCORE ACHIEVED
Ship	500	446
Accommodation	200	175
Food	400	281
Service	400	271
Cruise	500	435
TOTAL	**2,000**	**1,608**

Accommodation: The accommodation is spread over five decks (a number of cabins have full or partially obstructed views). Interestingly, no cabin is more than 144 ft (44 m) from a stairway, which makes it easier to get from cabins to public rooms. All cabin doors feature a birds-eye maple look, and hallways feature framed fabric panels to make them warmer and less clinical.

All standard inside and outside cabins are tastefully furnished, and have twin beds that convert to a queen-size bed (space is tight for walking between beds and vanity unit). There is a decent amount of closet and drawer space, although this will prove tight for the longer voyages featured. The bathrooms, which are fully tiled, are disappointingly small (particularly for long cruises) and have small shower tubs, utilitarian personal toiletries cupboards, and exposed under-sink plumbing. There is no detailing to distinguish them from bathrooms aboard the *Statendam*-class ships, given that this is claimed by Holland America Line as the "flagship" of the fleet.

There are 36 full verandah suites (Navigation Deck), including four penthouse suites, which share a private Concierge Lounge with a concierge to handle such things as special dining arrangements, shore excursions, and special requests, although strangely there are no butlers for these suites, as aboard ships with similar facilities. Each suite has a separate steward's entrance and separate bedroom, dressing, and living areas. Suite passengers get personal stationery, complimentary laundry and ironing, cocktail hour hors d'oeuvres, and other goodies, as well as priority embarkation and disembarkation. The concierge lounge, with its latticework teak detailing and private library is accessible only by private key-card.

Handicapped passengers have 20 cabins to choose from, including two of the large "penthouse" suites (which include concierge services). However, there are different cabin configurations, and it is wise to check.

Dining: There is one principal, large two-level dining room (La Fontaine), with tables for four, six, or eight, similar to the *Statendam*-class ships (there are just nine tables for two). Open seating is featured for breakfast and lunch, with two seatings for dinner (with both smoking and nonsmoking sections on both upper and lower levels). Fine Rosenthal china and good cutlery is featured (although there are no fish knives).

Instead of the more formal dining room, the Lido Buffet is open for casual dinners on several nights each cruise (typically three nights on a seven-night cruise), in an open-seating arrangement. Tables are set with crisp linens, flatware, and stemware. A set menu is featured, and this includes a choice of four entrees.

The food is marginally better than that presently served aboard other Holland America Line ships, with better buffets and more attention to detail, although it does not come up to the standard of other ships in the premium segment of the industry. What is definitely *not* luxurious are the packets (not glass jars) of breakfast jam, marmalade and honey, and the long lines.

There is also an 88-seat alternative restaurant called Odyssey Italian, decorated in the manner of an opulent baroque Italian villa, and available to all passengers on a reservation basis. This alternative restaurant is a first on any Holland America Line ship (there's no extra charge). The room, whose basic color is black with gold accenting, is divided into three sections. The cuisines from the Perugia, Tuscany, and Umbria regions of Italy are featured, although the portions are very small.

Other Comments: She has been constructed to look like a slightly larger (longer and beamier), but certainly a much sleeker version of the *Statendam*-class ships, while retaining the graceful lines of the former *Rotterdam*, including a nicely-raked bow, as well as the familiar interior flow and design style. Also retained is the twin-funnel feature well recognized by former Holland America Line passengers, though somewhat streamlined. The new *Rotterdam* (the sixth Holland America Line ship to bear the name) is capable of 25 knots, which is useful for the longer distance itineraries she features.

The focal interior point is a three-deck-high atrium, in an oval, instead of circular, shape. The atrium's focal point is a huge "one-of-a-kind" clock, which includes an astrolabe, an astrological clock, and 14 other clocks in a structure that takes up three decks. Instead of just the two staircases aboard the *Statendam*-class ships, *Rotterdam* features three (better from the viewpoint of safety) and passenger accessibility. There is a magrodome-covered pool on the Lido Deck between the mast and the ship's twin funnels, as aboard the company's *Statendam*-class ships, which have only one large, very square funnel.

The interior public spaces also carry on the same layout and flow as found aboard the *Statendam*-class ships. The interior decor is best described as restrained, with much use of wood accenting. One room features a glass ceiling similar to that found aboard a former *Statendam*. As a whole, the decor of this ship is extremely refined, with much of the traditional ocean liner detailing so loved by frequent Holland America Line passengers. Additions are children's and teens' play areas, although these really are token gestures by a company that traditionally does not cater well to children. Popcorn is available at the Wajang Theatre for moviegoers, while adjacent is the popular Java Cafe. The casino, which is located in the middle of a major passenger flow, now features blackjack, roulette, poker, and dice tables alongside the requisite rows of slot machines.

The artwork consists of a collection of 17th-century Dutch and Japanese artifacts together with contemporary works specially created for the ship, although there seems little linkage between some of the items.

Holland America Line's new flagship replaced the former ship of the same name when she was retired in September 1997 — just in time for the start of the company's 125th anniversary in 1998. She is the most contemporary ship for Holland America Line, with lighter, brighter decor. She is an extremely comfortable ship in which to cruise, with some fine, elegant, and luxurious decorative features. However, these are marred by the poor quality of dining room food and service and the lack of understanding of what it takes to make a "luxury" cruise experience, despite what is touted in the company's brochures. Refreshingly, the company does not add an automatic 15 percent gratuity for beverage purchases.

The company does offer cappuccino and espresso coffees, and free ice cream during certain hours of the day aboard its ships, as well as hot hors d'oeuvres in all bars — something other major lines seem to have dropped, or charge extra for.

<u>Weak Points</u>: With one whole deck of suites (and a dedicated, private concierge lounge, and preferential passenger treatment), the company has in effect created a two-class ship. The charge ($1.00) to use the washing machines and dryers in the self-service launderette really is irritating and petty, particularly for suite passengers who pay high prices for long cruises. Communication (in English) with many of the staff, particularly in the dining room and buffet areas, can prove very frustrating! Nonsmokers should avoid this ship, as smokers are everywhere.

y/s Royal Clipper
(S)

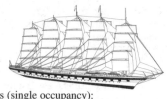

LIFESTYLE:	PREMIUM
Cruise Line:	Star Clippers
Former Names:	-
Gross Tonnage:	5,000
Builder:	De Merwede (Holland)
Original Cost:	$75 million
Entered Service:	Spring 2000
Flag:	Luxembourg
Tel. No.:	n/a
Fax No.:	n/a
Length (ft/m):	439.6/134.0
Beam (ft/m):	54.1/16.5
Draft (ft/m):	18.5/5.6
Type of Vessel:	sail-cruise (square rigger)
No. of Masts:	5
Sail Area (sq ft/sq m):	56,000/5,204.5
Main Propulsion:	42 sails
Propulsion/Propellers:	diesel (3,700kW)/1 (CP)
Decks:	5
Total Crew:	100
Pass. Capacity (basis 2):	224
Pass. Capacity (all berths):	246
Pass. Space Ratio (basis 2):	22.3
Pass. Space Ratio (all berths):	20.3
Officers:	International
Total Cabins:	112
Size Range (sq ft/m):	100.0–320.0/9.3–29.7
Cabins (outside view):	112
Cabins (inside — no view):	0

Cabins (single occupancy):	0
Cabins (with private balcony):	14
Cabins (wheelchair accessible):	0
Cabin Current:	110 and 220 volts
Cabin TV:	Yes
Dining Rooms:	1
Elevators:	0
Casino:	No
Slot Machines:	No
Swimming Pools (outdoors):	3
Whirlpools:	0
Fitness Center:	No
Sauna/Steam Room:	No/No
Massage:	Yes
Self-Service Launderette:	No
Library:	Yes
Classification Society:	Lloyd's Register

RATINGS	POSSIBLE SCORE	SCORE ACHIEVED
Ship	500	NYR
Accommodation	200	NYR
Food	400	NYR
Service	400	NYR
Cruise	500	NYR
TOTAL	**2,000**	**NYR**
Expected Score Range:		**1500-1700**

Accommodation: There are two owner's suites; these are to be the most lavish accommodation, while another 14 deck suites also promise luxurious appointments, plenty of space, a private balcony, and 24-hour butler service; all have Jacuzzi bathtubs.

All other standard cabins have twin beds that can convert into a queen-size bed, a television with movies, 24-hour news, radio, hairdryer, and satellite-linked telephone.

Dining: The dining room, which seats 250, is constructed on several connecting levels, and seats all passengers at a single seating under a three-deck-high atrium dome. One corner can be closed off for private parties.

Other Comments: Announced as the largest true sailing ship in the world, she is an extension of the company's two other (smaller) tall ships. *Royal Clipper*'s design is based on the only other five-masted sailing ship to be built — the 1902-built *Preussen*, and has the same dimensions (she is much larger than the famous *Cutty Sark*, for example). *Royal Clipper* is only the second five-masted fully-rigged sailing vessel ever to be constructed. Her masts reach as high as 197 ft (60.0 m) above the waterline, and with up to 42 sails, she will look magnificent when under full sail.

She was under construction for only a short time due to the fact that her hull was almost finished (at Gdansk shipyard, Poland) for another owner but became available to Star Clippers for completion and fitting out. The ship is instantly recognizable due to her geometric black and white hull markings. Power winches, as well as hand winches, are employed in her deck fittings, as well as a mix of horizontal furling for the squaresails and hydraulic power assist to roll the squaresails along the yardarm.

The sail handling system is such that she can be converted from a full rigger to a schooner in an incredibly short amount of time.

Inside, a three-deck-high midships atrium sits under one of the ship's three swimming pools, and funnels sunlight down through a piano lounge, a deck of cabins, and into the dining room. A forward observation lounge is a real plus, and is connected to the piano lounge via a central corridor. The Edwardian library/card room is decorated with a belle epoque fireplace. The female massage staff will be from Thailand.

The Captain Nemo Club is a lounge where passengers can observe fish and sea life when the ship is at anchor, through thick glass portholes (floodlit from underneath at night to attract the fish). Snorkeling gear is available at no cost, while scuba diving is available at an extra charge, and an aft platform will be used to access the shore tenders and for swimming.

This new spectacular tall ship operates seven-night and 14-day cruises in the Grenadines and Lower Windward Islands of the Caribbean during the winter (based on Barbados) and in the Mediterranean during the summer (based on Cannes). It is good to note that her officers navigate using both traditional (sextant) and contemporary methods (advanced electronic positioning system).

DID YOU KNOW...?

...that the first vessel built exclusively for cruising was Hamburg-Amerika Line's two-funnel yacht, the 4,409-tonne *Princessin Victoria Luise*? This luxury ship even included a private suite for the German Kaiser.

...that the first ship to be fitted with real stabilizers (not an autogyro device) was the Peninsular & Oriental Steam Navigation Company's 1949-built 24,215-tonne *Chusan*?

...that the first consecrated oceangoing Roman Catholic Chapel aboard a passenger ship was in Compagnie Generale Transatlantique's *Ile de France* of 1928?

m/v **Royal Princess**
★★★★ +
(L)

LIFESTYLE:	PREMIUM
Cruise Line:	Princess Cruises
Former Names:	-
Gross Tonnage:	44,348
Builder:	Wartsila (Finland)
Original Cost:	$165 million
Entered Service:	November 1984
Flag:	Great Britain
Tel. No.:	1440211
Fax No.:	1440215
Length (ft/m):	754.5/230.0
Beam (ft/m):	95.8/29.2
Draft (ft/m):	25.5/7.8
Propulsion/Propellers:	diesel (29,160kW)/2 (CP)
Decks:	9
Total Crew:	520
Pass. Capacity (basis 2):	1,200
Pass. Capacity (all berths):	1,275
Pass. Space Ratio (basis 2):	36.9
Pass. Space Ratio (all berths):	34.7
Officers:	British
Total Cabins:	600
Size Range (sq ft/m):	67.8–805.1/6.3–74.8
Cabins (outside view):	600
Cabins (inside — no view):	0
Cabins (single occupancy):	0
Cabins (with private balcony):	150

Cabins (wheelchair accessible):	4
Cabin Current:	110 and 220 volts
Cabin TV:	Yes
Dining Rooms:	1
Elevators:	6
Casino:	Yes
Slot Machines:	Yes
Swimming Pools (outdoors):	2 (+2 splash pools)
Swimming Pools (inside):	0
Whirlpools:	2
Fitness Center:	Yes
Sauna/Steam Room:	Yes/No
Massage:	Yes
Self-Service Launderette:	Yes
Movie Theater/Seats:	Yes/150
Library:	Yes
Classification Society:	Lloyd's Register

RATINGS	POSSIBLE SCORE	SCORE ACHIEVED
Ship	500	411
Accommodation	200	170
Food	400	273
Service	400	296
Cruise	500	401
TOTAL	**2,000**	**1,551**

Accommodation: The all-outside cabins (152 have private balconies and there are only four suite and cabin types) are well thought out, very comfortable, and well-appointed. The suites are extremely attractive, and feature excellent personal toiletry amenity kits.

All cabins have a full bathtub and shower, and three-sided mirrors. Bathrobes are provided for all passengers. Prompt, attentive room service is available 24 hours a day. Note that some cabins on Baja and Caribe decks have lifeboat-obstructed views. The cabin numbering system remains illogical, with numbers going through several hundred series on the same deck.

Dining: The elegant dining room (nonsmoking) is set low down, adjacent to the lobby. There are two seatings. The food and service are moderately good, although most food is really overcooked and the selection of vegetables is limited. The quality of fish is poor, with most covered by gravy-based sauces, and little or no garnish (the meat quality is good, however). There is always a pasta dish on the menu, and table captains are willing to make something special for you. The portions are generous, and presentation is improving, albeit slowly.

The in-cabin service menu is really basic and could include more items. The indoor-outdoor Lido Café was expanded dramatically in a refit not long ago and now features 24-hour food availability for casual dining, and better beverage stations that mean less lines.

Other Comments: This ship has handsome, contemporary outer styling, with a short, well-raked bow. Quality construction and materials were used throughout. Has an excellent amount of outdoor deck and sunbathing space, and traditional wraparound.

Well-designed, though slightly unconventional interior layout and passenger flow provides passenger cabins that are located above the public room decks. Features include large, beautifully appointed and spacious public rooms rather than the smaller, more intimate public rooms and lounges found aboard many ships today. There are spacious passageways and delightful, imposing staircases. Contemporary without being the least bit garish, the decor reflects the feeling of space, openness, and light.

The Horizon Lounge, set around the funnel base, has fine views, and makes for a peaceful environment during the day. This ship will provide a fine cruise experience in spacious, elegant surroundings, at the appropriate price, although attention to the small details of service finesse is often missing.

When this ship first debuted, she was a state-of-the-art vessel. It is amazing to see that now she is lagging behind the latest ships in several ways, although still a very fine ship, there is increasing competition in the marketplace.

<u>Weak Points</u>: The signs throughout the ship are adequate at best, and some of them are difficult to read.

DID YOU KNOW...?

...that in 1903 the British liner *Lucania* became the first ship to have wireless equipment, which enabled her to keep in touch with both sides of the Atlantic Ocean at the same time?

...that the first ship-to-shore wireless telegraphy took place on the American passenger ship *St. Paul*, in 1899?

...that the first twin-screw passenger ship was the Compagnie Generale Transatlantique's 3,200-tonne *Washington*, built in 1863 and converted in 1868?

...that the first floating eclipse expedition was led by US astronomer Ted Pedas in 1972, when 800 passengers sailed to a spectacular rendezvous with a total sun eclipse in the North Atlantic?

...that the first passenger ship to exceed 80,000-tonnes was the Compagnie Generale Transatlantique's *Normandie*, which measured at 82,799-tonnes in 1936?

...that the first gravity lifeboats were aboard the Compagnie Generale Transatlantique's *Ile de France* of 1928?

...that the official *lingua franca* of the maritime world is English?

m/v Royal Star
★★ +
(S)

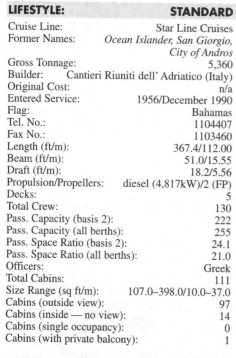

LIFESTYLE:	STANDARD
Cruise Line:	Star Line Cruises
Former Names:	*Ocean Islander, San Giorgio,*
	City of Andros
Gross Tonnage:	5,360
Builder:	Cantieri Riuniti dell' Adriatico (Italy)
Original Cost:	n/a
Entered Service:	1956/December 1990
Flag:	Bahamas
Tel. No.:	1104407
Fax No.:	1103460
Length (ft/m):	367.4/112.00
Beam (ft/m):	51.0/15.55
Draft (ft/m):	18.2/5.56
Propulsion/Propellers:	diesel (4,817kW)/2 (FP)
Decks:	5
Total Crew:	130
Pass. Capacity (basis 2):	222
Pass. Capacity (all berths):	255
Pass. Space Ratio (basis 2):	24.1
Pass. Space Ratio (all berths):	21.0
Officers:	Greek
Total Cabins:	111
Size Range (sq ft/m):	107.0–398.0/10.0–37.0
Cabins (outside view):	97
Cabins (inside — no view):	14
Cabins (single occupancy):	0
Cabins (with private balcony):	1

Cabins (wheelchair accessible):	0
Cabin Current:	110 and 220 volts
Cabin TV:	No
Dining Rooms:	1
Elevators:	1
Casino:	Yes
Slot Machines:	Yes
Swimming Pools (outdoors):	1
Swimming Pools (inside):	0
Whirlpools:	0
Fitness Center:	Yes
Sauna/Steam Room:	Yes/No
Massage:	Yes
Self-Service Launderette:	No
Movie Theater/Seats:	No
Library:	Yes
Classification Society:	American Bureau of Shipping

RATINGS	POSSIBLE SCORE	SCORE ACHIEVED
Ship	500	273
Accommodation	200	108
Food	400	213
Service	400	237
Cruise	500	249
TOTAL	**2,000**	**1,080**

Accommodation: The cabins, although not large, are pleasantly decorated with good-quality furnishings and ample closet and drawer space. The cabin bathrooms, however, are really tiny, although the suites have two bathrooms (and a hairdryer) and a refrigerator. There is a limited cabin service menu.

Dining: The Belvedere Restaurant is a charming dining room, with reasonably good service and an international cuisine, although the standards are variable. There are two seatings. Table wines are included with meals for lunch and dinner. A limited selection of breads, cheeses, and fruits. Choice of teas is poor.

Other Comments: The African Safari Club is a 32-year-old Swiss hotel and tour operator that specializes in land-based safaris and East African resort stays. The company, which has six hotels in Mombasa, has been operating this ship for several years (under its Star Line Crusies brand name) in conjunction with these land-based safaris. *Royal Star* is a charming little vessel (she was formerly operated by the now defunct Ocean Cruise Lines), with a well-balanced profile. There is an open bridge policy for all passengers while the ship is at sea (weather permitting). Has reasonable open deck space for sunbathing (but remember this operates for much of the year close to the equator, so the sun is *incredibly* strong).

This small vessel is well suited to cruising in sheltered areas. Moderately clean and tidy throughout, the ship provides a reasonably warm, friendly, relaxed and highly personable ambience, although service finesse is decidedly lacking. Has attractive contemporary interior decor, with lots of brass railings, and solid wood doors. Has a newly improved fitness center. Entertainment is very low-key, and the Filipino crew provides much of it.

Well-packaged and operated, with excellent itineraries, this little ship will provide a most enjoyable cruise and safari experience in very comfortable, small-ship surroundings, at an extremely realistic price (port taxes are included). The African Safari Club has its own DC10 aircraft to transport you from Frankfurt to Mombasa (check with your travel agent in case a visa is needed). The currency is the deutschmark.

Weak Points: Cleanliness leaves much to be desired, particularly in the "back of house" areas.

m/s Ryndam
★★★★
(L)

LIFESTYLE:	**PREMIUM**
Cruise Line:	Holland America Line
Former Names:	-
Gross Tonnage:	55,451
Builder:	Fincantieri (Italy)
Original Cost:	$215 million
Entered Service:	November 1994
Flag:	The Netherlands
Tel. No.:	624506613
Fax No.:	1306563
Length (ft/m):	719.3/219.3
Beam (ft/m):	101.0/30.8
Draft (ft/m):	24.6/7.5
Propulsion/Propellers:	diesel-electric (34,560kW)/2 (CP)
Decks:	10
Total Crew:	557
Pass. Capacity (basis 2):	1,266
Pass. Capacity (all berths):	1,627
Pass. Space Ratio (basis 2):	43.8
Pass. Space Ratio (all berths):	34.0
Officers:	British/Dutch
Total Cabins:	633
Size Range (sq ft/m):	186.2–1,124.8/17.3–104.5
Cabins (outside view):	502
Cabins (inside — no view):	131
Cabins (single occupancy):	0

Cabins (with private balcony):	150
Cabins (wheelchair accessible):	6
Cabin Current:	110 and 220 volts
Cabin TV:	Yes
Dining Rooms:	1
Elevators:	12
Casino:	Yes
Slot Machines:	Yes
Swimming Pools (outdoors):	1
Swimming Pools (inside):	1 (magrodome)
Whirlpools:	2
Fitness Center:	Yes
Sauna/Steam Room:	Yes/No
Massage:	Yes
Self-Service Launderette:	Yes
Movie Theater/Seats:	Yes/249
Library:	Yes
Classification Society:	Lloyd's Register

RATINGS	POSSIBLE SCORE	SCORE ACHIEVED
Ship	500	418
Accommodation	200	162
Food	400	281
Service	400	299
Cruise	500	388
TOTAL	**2,000**	**1,548**

This is one in a series of four ships of the same size and layout. For comments, see *Maasdam*.

m/s Saga Rose
★★★★
(M)

LIFESTYLE:		**PREMIUM**
Cruise Line:		Saga Shipping
Former Names:		*Gripsholm, Sagafjord*
Gross Tonnage:		24,474
Builder:	Forges et Chantiers de la Mediteranee	
		(France)
Original Cost:		$30 million
Entered Service:		October 1965/May 1997
Flag:		Bahamas
Tel. No.:		330826410
Fax No.:		330826411
Length (ft/m):		619.6/188.88
Beam (ft/m):		80.3/24.49
Draft (ft/m):		27.0/8.25
Propulsion/Propellers:	diesel (20,150kW)/2 (FP)	
Decks:		7
Total Crew:		350
Pass. Capacity (basis 2):		584
Pass. Capacity (all berths):		620
Pass. Space Ratio (basis 2):		41.9
Pass. Space Ratio (all berths):		39.4
Officers:		British
Total Cabins:		322
Size Range (sq ft/m):	96.8–387.5/9.0–36.0	
Cabins (outside view):		290
Cabins (inside — no view):		32
Cabins (single occupancy):		60

Cabins (with private balcony):	26
Cabins (wheelchair accessible):	8
Cabin Current:	110 volts
Cabin TV:	Yes
Dining Rooms:	1
Elevators:	4
Casino:	No
Slot Machines:	No
Swimming Pools (outdoors):	1
Swimming Pools (inside):	1
Whirlpools:	0
Fitness Center:	Yes
Sauna/Steam Room:	Yes/No
Massage:	Yes
Self-Service Launderette:	Yes
Movie Theater/Seats:	Yes/181
Library:	Yes
Classification Society:	Det Norske Veritas

RATINGS	POSSIBLE SCORE	SCORE ACHIEVED
Ship	500	376
Accommodation	200	157
Food	400	281
Service	400	282
Cruise	500	307
TOTAL	**2,000**	**1,403**

Accommodation: Has large, very spacious suites and cabins (in 18 categories), with superb appointments, all with excellent insulation, and all completely refurbished in 1997. There is also a large number of single cabins (excellent for the over-fifties traveler who enjoys privacy). There is a generous drawer, under-bed storage, and lighted closet space. The service provided by the cabin stewardesses is good. Soft 100 percent cotton bathrobes and towels are provided in all cabins.

Dining: The dining room is superb in the classic sense, and has a central ceiling that is two decks high, large ocean-view picture windows, and a horseshoe-shaped grand staircase. There is one seating at assigned tables, and the chinaware and flatware are of a high quality. Creative cuisine uses good-quality ingredients. The food is reasonably well presented, and garnishes are consistent with nouvelle cuisine, although the choice is limited. Pastries and dessert items are of a good standard, and there is a reasonable choice of cheese and fruit. Also features a fairly comprehensive wine list, with moderate prices. Generally good service in the style of a grand hotel from thoughtful and attentive waiters.

Other Comments: She is still one of the most beautifully proportioned ships afloat, with a sweeping profile and well placed buff-colored funnel amidships. Like an aging Bentley, she will never go out of style. Built for long-distance cruising, she has a very spacious interior, with high-ceilinged public rooms and tasteful decor (but there are too many low-back chairs).

Quiet as a fine watch, this classic ship provides a refined life at sea for the discriminating over-50 passenger. *Note*: Those under 50 are not allowed. Clean and graceful, with well-rounded lines, her grey hull contrasts against the large funnel. Built to a high standard, this ship has been well maintained and is operated with pride by her new owners.

Features fine quality furnishings and fittings, including hardwoods, brass, and stainless steel. In fact, it is difficult to find any plastic in her. There are wide promenade decks, as well a large, old-style cinema.

Her ballroom/main lounge is among the nicest afloat for real cocktail parties, with furniture that can be moved for almost any configuration, and a large wood dance floor.

Saga Rose fits like an old shoe — so comfortable that you do not want to discard it. It is made from the best materials, and fits well as soon as you "put it on." She attracts passengers that appreciate quality surroundings and decent service. Designed and created for long-distance cruising, the ship excels in quiet, refined living, featuring numerous nights at sea and extended itineraries in surroundings of high comfort, for those over 50. Her high repeat passenger base confirms that there is a place for a ship such as this. Indeed, a voyage aboard this ship should prove to be a most pleasurable travel experience.

This is classic cruising for her mainly British passengers (the ship is based at Dover and Southampton), under the banner of Saga Holiday International whose staff have a reputation for being attentive (note that the cabin voltage is 110 volts, so take adapters if you have any electrical appliances). She is a gracious old lady (now more than 30 years old), having seen some fine service throughout the world. All port taxes, insurance, and tips are included.

Weak Points: The food is still disappointing, and service levels need improvement. There are few balcony cabins.

R/M/S St. Helena
★★★ +
(S)

LIFESTYLE:	STANDARD
Cruise Line:	Curnow Shipping
Former Names:	-
Gross Tonnage:	6,767
Builder:	A&P Appledore (Scotland)
Original Cost:	£32 million
Entered Service:	October 1990
Flag:	England
Tel. No.:	1441730
Fax No.:	1441731
Length (ft/m):	344.4/105.0
Beam (ft/m):	62.9/19.2
Draft (ft/m):	19.6/6.0
Propulsion/Propellers:	diesel (6,534kW)/2 (CP)
Decks:	4
Total Crew:	53
Pass. Capacity (basis 2):	96
Pass. Capacity (all berths):	128
Pass. Space Ratio (basis 2):	70.4
Pass. Space Ratio (all berths):	52.8
Officers:	British/St. Helenian
Total Cabins:	49
Size Range (sq ft/m):	51.0–202.0/4.8–18.7
Cabins (outside view):	37
Cabins (inside — no view):	12
Cabins (single occupancy):	0
Cabins (with private balcony):	0
Cabins (wheelchair accessible):	1
Cabin Current:	220 volts
Cabin TV:	No
Dining Rooms:	1
Elevators:	1
Casino:	No
Slot Machines:	Yes (3)
Swimming Pools (outdoors):	1
Swimming Pools (inside):	0
Whirlpools:	0
Fitness Center:	No
Sauna/Steam Room:	No/No
Massage:	No
Self-Service Launderette:	Yes
Movie Theater/Seats:	No
Library:	Yes
Classification Society:	Lloyd's Register

RATINGS	POSSIBLE SCORE	SCORE ACHIEVED
Ship	500	289
Accommodation	200	132
Food	400	276
Service	400	281
Cruise	500	274
TOTAL	**2,000**	**1,252**

Accommodation: The accommodation is in two-, three-, or four-berth cabins (there are 11 grades), which are quite simply furnished, yet comfortable. There are nine cabins that do not have private facilities.

Dining: The dining room is totally nonsmoking. It has two seatings, which, on such a small ship, is rather disruptive. The food is very British, with hearty breakfasts and a relatively simple menu, attractively presented on fine china. Afternoon tea, complete with freshly baked cakes, is a must. If you want tea or coffee at any time, you can make it yourself in the steward's pantry, even in the middle of the night.

Other Comments: This is a fine little combination of contemporary working cargo-passenger ship that has all modern conveniences, including stabilizers and air-conditioning. Passengers can even take their pets. Operates just like a full-size cruise vessel, and has an "open bridge" policy. The swimming pool, however, is really a "dip" pool only, and is tiny.

Inside, the decor is tasteful and homey. There is a pleasant library/reading lounge (audio recordings and videos are also available). There is a complimentary self-service laundry facility.

The brochure states that landing at Ascension is at times "a hazardous process" due to slippery and steep wharf steps — now that's telling it like it is. The staff is warm, welcoming, eager to see you enjoying the journey, and delightful to sail with.

The ship operates a regular Cardiff–Tenerife–St. Helena–Ascension Island–Tristan Da Cunha–Cape Town line service, which is like a mini-cruise, or long voyage, with lots of days at sea. St. Helena was the final place of exile for Napoleon Bonaparte, and the island can only be reached by sea. There are, at present, six round-trip sailings a year. Occasionally, a special theme sailing is featured, such as one for ornithologists. And for those who have yet to meet Father Neptune when crossing the Equator, rest assured that you will get to meet him.

<u>Weak Points</u>: The plastic deck furniture spoils the outdoors (teak tables and chairs would be much better — and able to withstand the inclement weather sometimes incurred).

m/s Sapphire
★★★
(M)

LIFESTYLE:	STANDARD
Cruise Line:	Thomson Cruises
Former Names:	*Princesa Oceanica, Sea Prince,*
	Ocean Princess, Italia, Princess Italia
Gross Tonnage:	12,183
Builder:	Cantieri Navale Felszegi (Italy)
Original Cost:	n/a
Entered Service:	August 1967/April 1996
Flag:	Cyprus
Tel. No.:	1125326
Fax No.:	1125327
Length (ft/m):	491.7/149.8
Beam (ft/m):	70.9/21.5
Draft (ft/m):	21.6/6.6
Propulsion/Propellers:	diesel (11,050kW)/2 (CP)
Decks:	8
Total Crew:	250
Pass. Capacity (basis 2):	576
Pass. Capacity (all berths):	650
Pass. Space Ratio (basis 2):	22.5
Pass. Space Ratio (all berths):	18.7
Officers:	Greek
Total Cabins:	288
Size Range (sq ft/m):	75.3–226.0/7.0–21.0
Cabins (outside view):	149
Cabins (inside — no view):	139
Cabins (single occupancy):	6

Cabins (with private balcony):	0
Cabins (wheelchair accessible):	0
Cabin Current:	110 volts
Cabin TV:	No
Dining Rooms:	1
Elevators:	5
Casino:	Yes
Slot Machines:	Yes
Swimming Pools (outdoors):	1
Swimming Pools (inside):	0
Whirlpools:	0
Fitness Center:	No
Sauna/Steam Room:	No/No
Massage:	Yes
Self-Service Launderette:	No
Movie Theater/Seats:	Yes/170
Library:	Yes
Classification Society:	Registro Navale Italiano

RATINGS	POSSIBLE SCORE	SCORE ACHIEVED
Ship	500	306
Accommodation	200	137
Food	400	239
Service	400	257
Cruise	500	281
TOTAL	**2,000**	**1,220**

Accommodation: There are seven cabin grades, but you should note that *cabins are not assigned* until you arrive at the port of embarkation. The cabin closet and drawer space is very limited. Reasonable-sized cabins have pleasing, though plain decor, furnishings, and fittings. All have tiled bathrooms, but they are small. continental breakfast in your cabin will cost you about $7.50 (£4.50) per person extra (each time). There is also a 24-hour cabin service menu for snacks, all at extra cost.

Dining: The dining room is charming and has an art deco feel, a raised center ceiling, and lovely etched glass dividers, but the noise level is high from the waiter stations. There are two seatings. You'll find that service is reasonably attentive from a willing, friendly staff. There is a good general standard of international cuisine, although do remember that this is a low-cost cruise, and so you should not expect high-class cuisine.

For casual breakfast and luncheon, the Café de Paris (located indoors but looking out onto the pool deck) is the place (it also has a bar).

Other Comments: The ship's long, low, handsome lines and swept-back aft-placed funnel provide a very attractive profile for this small ship. There is a good amount of open deck and sunbathing space, but the heated pool outdoors is small.

Inside, fairly smart, contemporary interior decor is featured. A mix of attractive colors, together with much use of mirrored surfaces, add warmth in the public rooms. Some public rooms have a fairly low ceiling height. Harry's Bar is perhaps the most popular gathering place, although there are few seats (the gaming tables are adjacent). There is also a cinema with comfortable seating.

Cyprus-based Louis Cruise Lines purchased the ship in August 1995 and, following an extensive refurbishment, placed her into service in April 1996 on behalf of Thomson, the UK tour operator. This ship will take its mainly British passengers to some decent destinations in good, contemporary surroundings, and in a relaxed casual style (you will probably fly to/from the ship on Britannia Airways, a Thomson-owned company). The realistic, inexpensive price of this product is a real bonus, and gratuities are included.

403

m/v Seabourn Goddess I
★★★★★
(S)

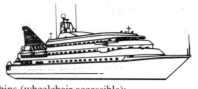

LIFESTYLE:	LUXURY
Cruise Line:	Seabourn Cruise Line
Former Names:	*Sea Goddess I*
Gross Tonnage:	4,260
Builder:	Wartsila (Finland)
Original Cost:	$34 million
Entered Service:	April 1984
Flag:	Norway
Tel. No.:	1454141/1454143
Fax No.:	1454142
Length (ft/m):	343.8/104.81
Beam (ft/m):	47.9/14.60
Draft (ft/m):	13.6/4.17
Propulsion/Propellers:	diesel (3,540kW)/2 (CP)
Decks:	5
Total Crew:	90
Pass. Capacity (basis 2):	116
Pass. Capacity (all berths):	116
Pass. Space Ratio (basis 2):	36.7
Pass. Space Ratio (all berths):	36.7
Officers:	British/Norwegian
Total Cabins:	58
Size Range (sq ft/m):	179.0–410.0/16.7–38.0
Cabins (outside view):	58
Cabins (inside — no view):	0
Cabins (single occupancy):	0
Cabins (with private balcony):	0
Cabins (wheelchair accessible):	0
Cabin Current:	110 and 220 volts
Cabin TV:	Yes
Dining Rooms:	1
Elevators:	1
Casino:	Yes
Slot Machines:	Yes
Swimming Pools (outdoors):	1
Swimming Pools (inside):	0
Whirlpools:	1
Fitness Center:	Yes
Sauna/Steam Room:	Yes/No
Massage:	Yes
Self-Service Launderette:	No
Movie Theater/Seats:	No
Library:	Yes
Classification Society:	Lloyd's Register

RATINGS	POSSIBLE SCORE	SCORE ACHIEVED
Ship	500	448
Accommodation	200	174
Food	400	372
Service	400	370
Cruise	500	435
TOTAL	**2,000**	**1,799**

Accommodation: The cabins are fully equipped all-outside "suites." Beds are positioned next to the window so that you can entertain in the living area without going past the sleeping area (as one must aboard the other small Seabourn Cruise Line and Silversea Cruises ships, for example). All cabinetry and furniture is of thick blonde wood, with beautifully rounded edges. A long vanity desk in the sleeping area has a large mirror above it (but no three-sided mirrors for women to see the back of their hair) and two small drawers for cosmetic items; there is also a brass clock located on one wall. A long desk in the lounge area has six drawers, plus a vertical cupboard unit that houses a sensible safe, refrigerator, and drinks cabinet. There is also a VCR unit.

The beds have thick cotton duvets, and non-allergenic pillows (and duvets) are also available. The bathrooms, which now urgently need updating, are very tight (particularly for those who are of larger than average build), and doors open inward, so space inside really is at a premium. There is a glass shelf for personal toiletry items while an under-sink drawer and cupboard provides space for larger items. Plush, thick 100 percent cotton bathrobes and towels are supplied.

For the ultimate accommodation aboard this ship, choose a double suite (there are eight of them), each with interconnecting doors. This will provide two bathrooms (his and hers), with one suite acting as a lounge/dining room, the other for use as a bedroom.

One drawback is the fact that the insulation between cabins is not as good as it could be, although rarely does this present problems, as most passengers aboard the Goddesses are generally extremely quiet, considerate types who are allergic to noise.

Dining: The dining salon is bright, warm, and inviting in its new primrose yellow decor. It is cozy, yet with plenty of space around each table for fine service, and the ship provides a floating culinary celebration in one (open) seating. Open seating means you can dine wherever, whenever, and with whomever you want. Course-by-course meals can also be served in your cabin.

Tables for two, four, six, or eight are immaculately laid with settings of real silver base plates, pristine white table linen, and fresh flowers (there are also fresh flowers in several wall sconces). Hutschenreuther, Villeroy and Boch, and Tiffany are the appointments. There is even a box of spare spectacles for menu reading in case you forget your own. You get leather-bound menus and supremely attentive, close-to-impeccable, personalized European service.

The Goddess experience really is all about dining, and is the height of culinary excellence at sea. Only the very freshest and finest quality ingredients are used in the best culinary artistry. Fine European service is provided.

The ship features exquisite, creative cuisine, with everything prepared individually to order. Special orders are welcomed, and flaming desserts are cooked at your table. You can also dine, course by course in your suite for any meals, at any time (you can also eat à la carte 24 hours a day if you wish). There is plenty of fine quality caviar, at any time of the day or night. And, thankfully, never a hint of baked Alaska!

Wines are included in the cruise fare for lunch and dinner. Real wine connoisseurs will appreciate the availability of an extra wine list (at extra cost). If you want to do something different with a loved one, you can also arrange to dine one evening on the open (but covered) deck, overlooking the swimming pool and stern — it is a magical, and very romantic setting.

There is also an informal outdoor Cafe, where excellent buffets are provided for breakfast and luncheon, and you never have to get, or carry, your food (the waiters will do that for you). Recently added teakwood tables and chairs add an additional (essential) air of luxury.

Other Comments: This is a small ship with an ultra-sleek profile and the ambience of a private club. She has been well maintained, although, at 15 years old, there are signs of wear and tear. The ship was refurbished in late 1997, when new teakwood deck furniture was added. At her stern is a small water sports platform; water ski boats, Windsurfers, jet skis, scuba, and snorkeling equipment are provided at no extra charge. However, the sea conditions have to be just right (minimal swell) for these items to be used, which, on average is once or twice in a seven-night cruise. You may also be allowed to swim off the stern platform.

Inside, there is a delightful feeling of unabashed but discreet sophistication. Elegant, chic public rooms and decor has flowers and potpourri everywhere. There is even a cute (meaning small) gymnasium and sauna, hidden around the funnel base. Oriental rugs can be found in the lobby. Fine quality furnishings and fabrics are used throughout, with marble and blonde wood accents.

Unadulterated indulgence and refined, unstructured and langorous private living at sea is the hallmark of life aboard this vessel. This is for the experienced, independent traveler who does not like cruise ships, and especially for those that do not like large ships, glitzy lounges, platoons of people, or kids running around. No one under the age of 16 is allowed aboard — without exception, a new rule brought into effect in 1998 to the cheers of many repeat passengers.

The Seabourn Goddesses are really the ultimate boutique ships — like having your own private island where hospitality and anticipation are art forms practiced to a very high level. The staff is delightful and accommodating ("no" is not in the staff's vocabulary); if there is anything special you want, you have only to ask, and the staff will be only too happy to oblige — in the style of the best European hotels.

The dress code is resort casual by day (one could almost live in one's bathrobe), dressy by night (gentlemen *must* wear jacket and tie to the dining room).

Port charges and insurance are not included. All gratuities are included. Life could hardly be better at sea — so, as many regular *Seabourn Goddess* passengers say, why bother with ports of call at all? Embarkation starts at 3:00pm, never before, in case you are eager to get aboard.

Weak Points: Although these were the first of the mega-yacht-style ships when they were built, no cabins have private balconies (they arrived just a couple of years later aboard other, newer ships). The company has sadly seen fit to decrease the standard of personal amenities supplied in the bathrooms and some other little special touches and details have disappeared lately, and such things are thus reflected in the scores. Drinks are no longer included (except for basic dinner wines), and this means that the product has changed somewhat. Those who have been regular *Sea Goddess* passengers in the past will not take lightly to the change, nor will they like having to sign pieces of paper for drinks.

m/v Seabourn Goddess II
★★★★★
(S)

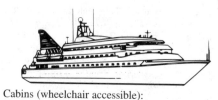

LIFESTYLE: **LUXURY**

Cruise Line:	Seabourn Cruise Line
Former Names:	*Sea Goddess II*
Gross Tonnage:	4,260
Builder:	Wartsila (Finland)
Original Cost:	$34 million
Entered Service:	May 1985
Flag:	Norway
Tel. No.:	1453752/623373710
Fax No.:	1453752
Length (ft/m):	343.8/104.81
Beam (ft/m):	47.9/14.60
Draft (ft/m):	13.6/4.17
Propulsion/Propellers:	diesel (3,540kW)/2 (CP)
Decks:	5
Total Crew:	90
Pass. Capacity (basis 2):	116
Pass. Capacity (all berths):	116
Pass. Space Ratio (basis 2):	36.7
Pass. Space Ratio (all berths):	36.7
Officers:	British/Norwegian
Total Cabins:	58
Size Range (sq ft/m):	179.0–410.0/16.7–38.0
Cabins (outside view):	58
Cabins (inside — no view):	0
Cabins (single occupancy):	1
Cabins (with private balcony):	0
Cabins (wheelchair accessible):	0
Cabin Current:	110 and 220 volts
Cabin TV:	Yes
Dining Rooms:	1
Elevators:	1
Casino:	Yes
Slot Machines:	Yes
Swimming Pools (outdoors):	1
Swimming Pools (inside):	0
Whirlpools:	1
Fitness Center:	Yes
Sauna/Steam Room:	Yes/No
Massage:	Yes
Self-Service Launderette:	No
Movie Theater/Seats:	No
Library:	Yes
Classification Society:	Lloyd's Register

RATINGS	POSSIBLE SCORE	SCORE ACHIEVED
Ship	500	448
Accommodation	200	174
Food	400	372
Service	400	370
Cruise	500	435
TOTAL	**2,000**	**1,799**

For comments, see *Seabourn Goddess I.*

m/s Seabourn Legend
★★★★★
(S)

LIFESTYLE:	**LUXURY**
Cruise Line:	Seabourn Cruise Line
Former Names:	*Queen Odyssey, Royal Viking Queen*
Gross Tonnage:	9,975
Builder:	Schichau Seebeckwerft (Germany)
Original Cost:	$87 million
Entered Service:	March 1992/July 1996
Flag:	Norway
Tel. No.:	1316175
Fax No.:	1316176
Length (ft/m):	439.9/134.10
Beam (ft/m):	62.9/19.20
Draft (ft/m):	16.7/5.10
Propulsion/Propellers:	diesel (7,280kW)/2 (CP)
Decks:	6
Total Crew:	150
Pass. Capacity (basis 2):	200
Pass. Capacity (all berths):	200
Pass. Space Ratio (basis 2):	49.8
Pass. Space Ratio (all berths):	49.8
Officers:	Norwegian
Total Cabins:	100
Size Range (sq ft/m):	277.0–590.0/25.7–54.8
Cabins (outside view):	100
Cabins (inside — no view):	0
Cabins (single occupancy):	0
Cabins (with private balcony):	6
Cabins (wheelchair accessible):	4
Cabin Current:	110 and 220 volts
Cabin TV:	Yes
Dining Rooms:	1
Elevators:	3
Casino:	Yes
Slot Machines:	Yes
Swimming Pools (outdoors):	1
Swimming Pools (inside):	0
Whirlpools:	3
Fitness Center:	Yes
Sauna/Steam Room:	Yes/Yes
Massage:	Yes
Self-Service Launderette:	Yes
Movie Theater/Seats:	No
Library:	Yes
Classification Society:	Det Norske Veritas

RATINGS	POSSIBLE SCORE	SCORE ACHIEVED
Ship	500	463
Accommodation	200	186
Food	400	352
Service	400	353
Cruise	500	442
TOTAL	**2,000**	**1,796**

Accommodation: All the suites are comfortably large and beautifully equipped with everything one could need (they are larger than those aboard the company's smaller Seabourn Goddesses, but the ship is also larger, and carries almost double the number of passengers). All suites feature a sleeping area and separate living area, large walk-in closet (illuminated automatically when you open the door), 100 percent thick cotton towels and plush terrycloth bathrobes, designer soaps, video player unit, personalized stationery, and leather ticket wallet (this arrives suitably boxed and nicely packaged before your cruise). Nonsmoking cabins are also available, as are course-by-course dinners (during restaurant dinner hours), and 24-hour room service. Menus for each dinner are delivered to your suite during the day.

For the ultimate in privacy the two Owner's suites (001/002), located forward on Deck 6 offer a superb and private living environment at sea. Each has a walk-in closet, second closet, one full bathroom, and a second room with toilet and washbasin (for guests). There is also a forward-facing balcony, complete with sun lounge chairs and wooden drinks table. These are secluded, and good for nude sunbathing. The living area has ample bookshelf space (included is a complete edition of Encyclopedia Britannica), large refrigerator and drinks cabinet, television, and VCR (plus a second television in the bedroom). All windows, as well as the door to the balcony, have manual blinds, and a complete blackout is possible in both bedroom and living room. On the Christmas cruise, each Owner's Suite has its own decorated and illuminated Christmas tree, a nice touch.

Dining: In-suite, course-by-course dining is available at any time. Elegant decor prevails in the formal dining room, which has a mixture of marble and carpeted floor. Seabourn's fine, extremely creative cuisine is artfully presented, with almost all items cooked to order. Open seating dining means you can dine when you want, with whomever you wish. The silverware (150 gram weight — the best available) is by Robbe & Berling.

The menu is not repeated, no matter how long the voyage. Special orders are available whenever you want them, and caviar is always available on request. Tableside flambeaus are presented, as are flaming desserts cooked at your table. There is always a good selection of exotic fruits and cheeses. Basic wines are included for lunch and dinner, but all others (the decent ones) are at extra cost. The wine list is quite extensive, with prices ranging from moderate to high; many of the wines come from the smaller, more exclusive vineyards. The European dining room staff is hand picked and provides excellent service.

In addition, breakfast (available until at least 11:00am — civilized enough for late-risers) and lunch buffets and informal alternative, casual candlelight dinners (except on formal nights) can be taken in the popular Veranda Cafe adjacent to the swimming pool.

Other Comments: This is a strikingly sleek ship with a handsome profile, almost identical in looks to *Seabourn Pride* and *Seabourn Spirit*, but built to an even higher standard, with streamline "decorator" bars located along the side of the upper superstructure. The ship features two fine mahogany water taxis for use as shore tenders. There is also an aft water sports platform and marina, which can be used in suitably calm warm-water areas. Water sports facilities include a small, enclosed "dip" pool, sea kayaks, snorkel equipment, windsurfers, water ski boat, and Zodiac inflatable boats.

Inside, there is a wide central passageway throughout the accommodation areas. The finest quality interior fixtures, fittings, and fabrics have been combined in her sumptuous public areas to present an outstanding, elegant decor, with warm color combinations (there is no glitz anywhere) and some fine artwork. Wonderful, 360-degree mural in the reception lobby (the ship's interior designer is painted into the mural). Relaxed by day, a more formal dress code applies at night.

This ship provides discerning passengers with an outstanding level of personal service and a superb, utterly civilized cruise experience. For a grand, small ship cruise experience in the finest surroundings, with only just over 100 other couples as neighbors, this ship is very difficult to beat. Note that drinks are no longer included in the cruise fare. Gratuities are no longer included, but are charged to your shipboard account at $10–$13 per day, depending on the accommodation grade chosen.

<u>Weak Points</u>: The plastic chairs on the open decks really are unacceptable for this type of ship and should be changed to teakwood. Sadly, there is no wraparound promenade deck outdoors, however, and there is little shade adjacent to the swimming pool.

m/s Seabourn Pride
★★★★★
(S)

LIFESTYLE:	**LUXURY**
Cruise Line:	Seabourn Cruise Line
Former Names:	-
Gross Tonnage:	9,975
Builder:	Seebeckwerft (Germany)
Original Cost:	$50 million
Entered Service:	December 1988
Flag:	Norway
Tel. No.:	1311351
Fax No.:	1311352
Length (ft/m):	439.9/134.10
Beam (ft/m):	62.9/19.20
Draft (ft/m):	16.8/5.15
Propulsion/Propellers:	diesel (5,355kW)/2 (CP)
Decks:	6
Total Crew:	150
Pass. Capacity (basis 2):	200
Pass. Capacity (all berths):	200
Pass. Space Ratio (basis 2):	49.8
Pass. Space Ratio (all berths):	49.8
Officers:	Norwegian
Total Cabins:	100
Size Range (sq ft/m):	277.0–575.0/25.7–53.4
Cabins (outside view):	100
Cabins (inside — no view):	0
Cabins (single occupancy):	0
Cabins (with private balcony):	6

Cabins (wheelchair accessible):	4
Cabin Current:	110 and 220 volts
Cabin TV:	Yes
Dining Rooms:	1
Elevators:	3
Casino:	Yes
Slot Machines:	Yes
Swimming Pools (outdoors):	1 (plus 1 aft marina-pool)
Swimming Pools (inside):	0
Whirlpools:	3
Fitness Center:	Yes
Sauna/Steam Room:	Yes/Yes
Massage:	Yes
Self-Service Launderette:	Yes
Movie Theater/Seats:	No
Library:	Yes
Classification Society:	Det Norske Veritas

RATINGS	POSSIBLE SCORE	SCORE ACHIEVED
Ship	500	462
Accommodation	200	186
Food	400	352
Service	400	353
Cruise	500	442
TOTAL	**2,000**	**1,795**

Accommodation: The all-outside cabins (called suites in brochure-speak) are comfortably large and beautifully equipped with everything, including refrigerator, personal safe, VCR unit, personalized stationery, and large walk-in illuminated closet with wooden hangers. Electric blackout blinds are provided for the large windows in addition to curtains. All cabinetry is made of blonde woods, with softly rounded edges, and cabin doors are neatly angled away from passageway (each pair of cabins also has a further door fronting on the passageway outside). The cabin ceilings are, however, quite plain.

The marble bathrooms feature two wash basins, a decent sized bathtub, plenty of storage areas, 100 percent thick cotton towels, plush terrycloth bathrobe, designer soaps, and a full range of personal bathroom amenities. Course-by-course in-cabin dining is available during dinner hours; there is also 24-hour room service.

For the ultimate in privacy the two Owner's Suites (001/002), located forward on Deck 6 offer a superbly private living environment. Each has a walk-in closet plus a second closet, one full bathroom, and a second room with toilet and washbasin (for guests), and butler service. There is also a forward-facing balcony, complete with sun lounge chairs and wooden drinks table. These are secluded, and good for nude sunbathing. The living area has ample bookshelf space (included is a complete edition of Encyclopedia Britannica), refrigerator and drinks cabinet, television and VCR (there is a second television in the bedroom), four-person dining table, and large circular glass coffee table. All windows, as well as the door, to the balcony have electric blinds, and a complete blackout is possible in both bedroom and living room. On the Christmas cruise, the Owner's Suites are decorated and illuminated with their own Christmas trees. However, the telephone system to call the butler is archaic and very awkward.

Dining: The part marble, part carpeted dining room features portholes and elegant decor but is not as warm and intimate as that found aboard the Seabourn Goddesses. The silverware (150 gram weight — the best available) is by Robbe & Berling.

409

Open seating dining means that you can dine when you want, with whom you wish. Course-by-course meals can also be served in your cabin.

Culinary excellence prevails, however, and both food quality and presentation are outstanding. The menus are extremely creative, and not repeated, even on long cruises. Special orders are welcome, and caviar is always available (on request). The service is close to impeccable, although with a full ship it can prove a little inconsistent at times.

Relaxed breakfast and lunch buffets, and candlelight dinners (except on formal nights) can be taken in the informal Veranda Cafe instead of the dining room.

Each day, red and white wines are provided in the dining room for lunch and dinner, and are included in the cruise fare. Any other wines you select from the wine list are at extra cost. The wine list is reasonably extensive, and prices range from moderate to high, with many wines coming from smaller, exclusive vineyards.

Other Comments: This luxuriously appointed cruise vessel has sleek exterior styling with a handsome profile with swept-back, rounded lines, and is an identical sister vessel to *Seabourn Spirit*. She also has two superb mahogany water taxis for shore visits.

There is an aft water sports platform and marina, which is used in suitably calm, warm-water areas. Water sports facilities include an aft platform, enclosed marina pool, banana boat, pedalos, scuba, sea kayaks, snorkel, Windsurfers, and water ski boat.

There is a wide central passageway throughout the accommodation areas. Inviting, sumptuous public areas have warm colors. Fine quality interior fixtures, fittings, and fabric combine to present an outstanding, elegant decor, color combinations, and artwork. For a small ship, there is wide range of public rooms from which to choose. These include a main lounge (small cabaret shows are featured); night club (this was expanded in 1999); an observation lounge with bar; large, deep armchairs; and a cigar smoking area complete with cabinet, cigar humidor, and small selection of good cigars (this was added in 1999). There is also a small business center, small meeting room, even a small casino with roulette and blackjack tables, and a cubbyhole with a few slot machines.

A small, but well equipped health spa/fitness center has sauna and steam rooms, and a separate exercise room, with videotapes for private, individual aerobics workouts.

Not for the budget-minded, this ship is for those desiring the utmost in supremely elegant, stylish, small-ship surroundings, but she is perhaps too small for long voyages in open waters. Presents an utterly civilized cruise vacation. Gratuities are not provided free any longer, but are charged automatically to your shipboard account, at $10–$13 per day, depending on the grade of accommodation chosen.

Weak Points: The deck lounge chairs are plastic (although light and easy to store, they are second class, and should be made of wood or stainless steel). There is no wraparound promenade deck outdoors. There are no seat cushions on the wooden chairs at the indoor/outdoor cafe. There is only one dryer in the self-service launderette.

m/s Seabourn Spirit
★★★★★
(S)

LIFESTYLE:	**LUXURY**
Cruise Line:	Seabourn Cruise Line
Former Names:	-
Gross Tonnage:	9,975
Builder:	Seebeckwerft (Germany)
Original Cost:	$50 million
Entered Service:	November 1989
Flag:	Norway
Tel. No.:	1310464
Fax No.:	1310527
Length (ft/m):	439.9/134.10
Beam (ft/m):	62.9/19.20
Draft (ft/m):	16.8/5.15
Propulsion/Propellers:	diesel (5,355kW)/2 (CP)
Decks:	6
Total Crew:	150
Pass. Capacity (basis 2):	200
Pass. Capacity (all berths):	200
Pass. Space Ratio (basis 2):	48.8
Pass. Space Ratio (all berths):	48.8
Officers:	Norwegian
Total Cabins:	100
Size Range (sq ft/m):	277.0–575.0/25.7–53.4
Cabins (outside view):	100
Cabins (inside — no view):	0
Cabins (single occupancy):	0
Cabins (with private balcony):	6

Cabins (wheelchair accessible):	4
Cabin Current:	110 and 220 volts
Cabin TV:	Yes
Dining Rooms:	1
Elevators:	3
Casino:	Yes
Slot Machines:	Yes
Swimming Pools (outdoors):	1 (plus aft marina-pool)
Swimming Pools (inside):	0
Whirlpools:	3
Fitness Center:	Yes
Sauna/Steam Room:	Yes/Yes
Massage:	Yes
Self-Service Launderette:	Yes
Movie Theater/Seats:	No
Library:	Yes
Classification Society:	Det Norske Veritas

RATINGS	POSSIBLE SCORE	SCORE ACHIEVED
Ship	500	462
Accommodation	200	186
Food	400	352
Service	400	353
Cruise	500	442
TOTAL	**2,000**	**1,795**

For comments, see *Seabourn Pride*.

m/s Seabourn Sun
★★★★★
(M)

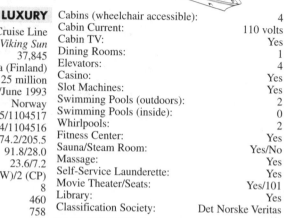

LIFESTYLE:	LUXURY
Cruise Line:	Seabourn Cruise Line
Former Names:	*Royal Viking Sun*
Gross Tonnage:	37,845
Builder:	Wartsila (Finland)
Original Cost:	$125 million
Entered Service:	December 1988/June 1993
Flag:	Norway
Tel. No.:	1104515/1104517
Fax No.:	1104514/1104516
Length (ft/m):	674.2/205.5
Beam (ft/m):	91.8/28.0
Draft (ft/m):	23.6/7.2
Propulsion/Propellers:	diesel (21,120kW)/2 (CP)
Decks:	8
Total Crew:	460
Pass. Capacity (basis 2):	758
Pass. Capacity (all berths):	814
Pass. Space Ratio (basis 2):	49.9
Pass. Space Ratio (all berths):	46.4
Officers:	European/Norwegian
Total Cabins:	380
Size Range (sq ft/m):	137.7–723.3/12.8–67.2
Cabins (outside view):	355
Cabins (inside — no view):	25
Cabins (single occupancy):	2
Cabins (with private balcony):	145

Cabins (wheelchair accessible):	4
Cabin Current:	110 volts
Cabin TV:	Yes
Dining Rooms:	1
Elevators:	4
Casino:	Yes
Slot Machines:	Yes
Swimming Pools (outdoors):	2
Swimming Pools (inside):	0
Whirlpools:	2
Fitness Center:	Yes
Sauna/Steam Room:	Yes/No
Massage:	Yes
Self-Service Launderette:	Yes
Movie Theater/Seats:	Yes/101
Library:	Yes
Classification Society:	Det Norske Veritas

RATINGS	POSSIBLE SCORE	SCORE ACHIEVED
Ship	500	427
Accommodation	200	178
Food	400	350
Service	400	349
Cruise	500	435
TOTAL	**2,000**	**1,739**

Accommodation: The Owner's Suite, at 723 sq ft (67.2 m^2), is one desirable living space. It is light and airy, and features two bathrooms, one of which has a large whirlpool bathtub with ocean views, and anodized gold bathroom fittings. The living room contains a large dining table and chairs, large sofas, and plenty of space to spread out.

Eighteen penthouse suites have large balconies and gracious butler service, two sofas, large bar/entertainment center (minibar-refrigerator, color television, VCR, and CD player); bathrooms have separate toilet, sink, and toiletries cabinets, connecting sliding door into the bathroom, large mirror, two toiletries cabinets, plenty of storage space, full bathtub, and anodized gold fittings. Each evening the butler brings different goodies — hot and cold hors d'oeuvres and other niceties. Free liquor and wines are provided in the penthouse suites.

If you choose one of the penthouses on Sky Deck, it might be best on the starboard side where they are located in a private hallway, while those on the port side (including the owner's suite) are positioned along a public hallway. All of the penthouse suites on Bridge Deck are positioned along private hallways.

Most of the other cabins (spread over five other decks) are of generous proportions and are well appointed, with just about everything you would need (including a VCR unit). Some 38 percent of all cabins have a private balcony. All cabins, however, have walk-in closets, lockable drawers, full-length mirrors, hairdryers, large fluffy cotton bathrobes, and ample cotton towels. A good mix of Scandinavian and Filipino stewardesses provide excellent, unobtrusive service. Four well-equipped, L-shaped cabins for the handicapped are well designed, fairly large, and feature special wheel-in bathrooms with shower facilities and closets. The only disappointment is with the rather plain cabin ceilings. All cabins underwent complete refurbishment in 1997.

Dining: Excellent cuisine and fine service are provided in a completely unhurried, caring atmosphere, with one seating dining and menus that are not repeated, no matter how long the voyage. Crystal glasses, fine quality plateware, and cutlery are provided. The food is creative and well presented, with good use of

412

color combinations and garnishes. There is an excellent, well-chosen wine list from distinguished vintners from around the world. Although the dining room wine list is extensive, the wine prices are very high. Mineral water, however, should be served for all meals in the dining room, instead of the standard chlorinated ship water provided.

There is also a good indoor-outdoor lido buffet area (Garden Cafe), with a fine variety and creative presentation (particularly the special themed buffets that are provided), as well as Venezia, a separate à la carte Italian restaurant that is an elegant alternative dining spot, with a great view. For those wanting a light dinner alternative in a casual setting, The Bistro is also available at night. Finally, if you want total privacy, you can also dine, course by course, in your suite or cabin.

Other Comments: This contemporary, well-designed ship has sleek, flowing lines, a sharply raked bow and a well-rounded profile, with lots of floor-to-ceiling glass. Seabourn acquired this ship in 1998.

The ship's tenders are thoughtfully air-conditioned and even have radar and a toilet. Wide teakwood decks provide excellent walking areas, including a wraparound promenade deck outdoors. Sadly, there is no way to get from the uppermost pool, which has a swim-up/sit-in bar, to the second pool, located adjacent to the small health spa and gymnasium, without first going inside the vessel (there always seem to be compromises when ships are designed and built).

Inside the ship there are two glass-walled elevators. Separate baggage elevators mean passengers do not have to wait for luggage. The interior layout is very spacious (it is ideal when a maximum of 600 passengers are aboard). Impressive public rooms and tasteful decor reign. Two handrails — one wooden, one chrome — are thoughtfully provided on all stairways, a thoughtful extra touch.

The Stella Polaris Lounge, the ship's forward observation lounge, is simply one of the most elegant lounges at sea. Pebble Beach is the name of the ship's own golf club, complete with wet bar and electronic golf simulator. The Dickens Library is well organized, although it is not large enough. Distinguished male guest hosts are provided on all cruises. The Oak Room features a marble fireplace, but sadly, it cannot be used due to United States Coast Guard regulations (the ship operates principally out of US ports); it would, however, make a fine library.

This fine vessel operates mainly long-distance cruises in great comfort (free shuttle buses are provided in almost all ports of call). There are two outdoor swimming pools. The gymnasium is good, although the sauna and massage treatment areas could be larger. An excellent lecture program presents subjects of cultural interest, while gentlemen "dance hosts" provide fine partners for ladies traveling alone.

Whether by intention or not, the ship has a two-class feeling, with passengers in "upstairs" penthouse suites and "A" grade staterooms gravitating to the somewhat quieter Stella Polaris lounge (particularly at night), while other passengers (the participants) go to the main entertainment deck.

This ship has a wide range of facilities, including a concierge, self-service launderettes (useful when on long voyages), excellent guest lecture program, 24-hour information office, and true 24-hour cabin service, for the discriminating passenger who demands the finest in spacious personal surroundings, food and service, regardless of price. Almost first class, this *Sun* is set to shine for a long time.

Committed to the pursuit of gracious living at sea, she is a fine grand floating hotel. The ship's direct competitors are *Crystal Harmony/Crystal Symphony* (arguably more elegant ships, with larger suites, but with two seatings for dinner) and the outstanding new *Europa* (principally for German-speaking passengers).

While *Seabourn Sun* is not perfect (the perfect ship has still not yet been delivered), the few design flaws that are evident (for example: poorly designed bar service counters; odd signs in elevators) are minor points. Even though the hardware is not perfect, the software (personnel and service) are generally very good.

A cruise aboard *Seabourn Sun* should prove to be an extremely civilized travel experience (although, as with any ship, the larger the cabin the better), with plenty of space, uncluttered surroundings, and no lines anywhere. Gratuities are extra, added to your shipboard account at $10–$13 per day, according to accommodation grade chosen. Perhaps the ship's best asset is her friendly and personable, mostly European crew.

Seabourn Sun acquired her new name in late 1999, and the ship was scheduled to undergo an extensive refurbishment. A new rating and full review will appear in the next edition of this guide, but you should expect the scores to be approximate to the present one.

Weak Points: The cabin ceilings are plain. All drinks should be, but are not, included. She is a very spacious ship, but is showing signs of wear and tear in some areas (particularly the accommodation passageways). The library is not large enough.

Note: Rated as *Royal Viking Sun*, prior to name change and refit.

s/s SeaBreeze
★★ +
(M)

LIFESTYLE:	STANDARD
Cruise Line:	Premier Cruise Lines
Former Names:	*Federico "C", Royale*
Gross Tonnage:	21,900
Builder:	Ansaldo Sestri-Ponente (Italy)
Original Cost:	n/a
Entered Service:	March 1958/March 1989
Flag:	Panama
Tel. No.:	1336354
Fax No.:	1336355
Length (ft/m):	605.6/184.61
Beam (ft/m):	78.9/24.06
Draft (ft/m):	29.0/8.84
Propulsion/Propellers:	steam turbine (21,350kW)/2 (FP)
Decks:	8
Total Crew:	400
Pass. Capacity (basis 2):	844
Pass. Capacity (all berths):	1,270
Pass. Space Ratio (basis 2):	25.9
Pass. Space Ratio (all berths):	17.2
Officers:	International
Total Cabins:	423
Size Range (sq ft/m):	64.5–258.3/6.0–24.0
Cabins (outside view):	247
Cabins (inside — no view):	176
Cabins (single occupancy):	2
Cabins (with private balcony):	0
Cabins (wheelchair accessible):	0
Cabin Current:	110 and 220 volts
Cabin TV:	No
Dining Rooms:	1
Elevators:	4
Casino:	Yes
Slot Machines:	Yes
Swimming Pools (outdoors):	1
Swimming Pools (inside):	0
Whirlpools:	3
Fitness Center:	Yes
Sauna/Steam Room:	No/No
Massage:	Yes
Self-Service Launderette:	No
Movie Theater/Seats:	Yes/110
Library:	Yes
Classification Society:	Lloyd's Register

RATINGS	POSSIBLE SCORE	SCORE ACHIEVED
Ship	500	252
Accommodation	200	111
Food	400	218
Service	400	235
Cruise	500	264
TOTAL	**2,000**	**1,080**

Accommodation: There is a wide variety of cabin sizes, with many different configurations to choose from. Many cabins can accommodate five, which is good for families with children. The drawer space is limited but closet space is good. *Note*: As these cruises provide a very casual atmosphere you will not need many clothes.

Dining: The dining room has a bright, cheerful decor, but it is noisy, and the tables are rather close together for serving comfort (however, there are several tables for two). There are two seatings. The dining room operation is well run, and the meals are attractively presented. The buffets are also colorful and well presented. Premier Cruise Lines provides birthday and other celebration cakes at no charge, unlike some lines.

Other Comments: This ship's classic 1950s ocean liner styling still looks moderately attractive. The open deck and sunbathing spaces aboard this high-density ship are very limited, and thus the ship feels crowded when full. There is, however, a wraparound promenade deck outdoors, good for walking. The ship has been well maintained, and still sparkles despite her age.

Inside, she has a rather awkward interior layout, which is vertical, rather than horizontal, with most public rooms located at the stern of the ship. This is a carryover from her former ocean liner days as a three-class ship, and this hinders passenger flow and makes it difficult to find one's way around at first. However, the public rooms are bright and cheerful, and tastefully decorated, although there are lots of mirrored and chromed surfaces. There is no real finesse, but the staff is very willing to please and is quite attentive.

This ship has plenty of life and atmosphere, is fairly comfortable, caters well to families, and remains a very good value for a first cruise experience, but she is getting old and perhaps should be retired soon. Having said that, she provides a feeling of the ships of yesteryear, and could be said to provide a more romantic setting than that found aboard some of the latest homogeneous ships. Premier Cruise Lines does a good job of providing a good all-round cruise experience at an attractive price.

Weak Points: The purser's desk staff needs to be sent to charm school; their unpleasantness in dealing with passengers is a constant source of complaints.

414

s/y Sea Cloud
★★★★ +
(S)

LIFESTYLE:	**LUXURY**	Cabins (inside — no view):	0
Cruise Line:	Sea Cloud Cruises	Cabins (single occupancy):	0
Former Names:	*Antaria, Patria, Angelita, Hussar*	Cabins (with private balcony):	0
Gross Tonnage:	2,532	Cabins (wheelchair accessible):	0
Builder:	Krupp Werft (Germany)	Cabin Current:	220 volts
Entered Service:	1931/1978 (restored)	Cabin TV:	No
Flag:	Malta	Dining Rooms:	1
Tel. No.:	1256105	Elevators:	0
Fax No.:	1256173	Casino:	No
Length (ft/m):	315.9/96.30	Slot Machines:	No
Beam (ft/m):	49.0/14.94	Swimming Pools (outdoors):	0
Draft (ft/m):	16.8/5.13	Whirlpools:	0
Type of Vessel:	barquentine	Fitness Center:	No
No. of Masts:	4 (17.7 meters)/(29 sails)	Sauna/Steam Room:	No/No
Sail Area (sq ft/sq m):	32,292/3,000	Massage:	No
Main Propulsion:	sail power	Self-Service Launderette:	No
Propulsion/Propellers:	diesel (4,476kW)/1 (FP)	Library:	Yes
Decks:	3	Classification Society:	Germanischer Lloyd
Total Crew:	60		
Pass. Capacity (basis 2):	68		
Pass. Capacity (all berths):	68		
Pass. Space Ratio (basis 2):	37.2		
Pass. Space Ratio (all berths):	37.2		
Officers:	American/European		
Total Cabins:	34		
Size Range (sq ft/m):	102.2–409.0/9.5–38.0		
Cabins (outside view):	34		

RATINGS	POSSIBLE SCORE	SCORE ACHIEVED
Ship	500	416
Accommodation	200	172
Food	400	339
Service	400	329
Cruise	500	417
TOTAL	**2,000**	**1,673**

Accommodation: All of the accommodation is very comfortable, but the two owner's suites (Cabins 1 and 2) are really opulent, and feature real, original Chippendale furniture, fine gilt detailing, a real fireplace, French canopy bed, and large Italian Carrara marble bathrooms. The Owner's Cabin (Number 1) is decorated in white throughout, and has a fireplace and Louis Phillippe chairs. Owner's Cabin Number 2 is completely paneled in rich woods, and retains the mahogany secretary used 60 years ago by Mr. Edward F. Hutton himself (Marjorie Post's husband).

Other cabins (both the original ones, and some newer additions) are all beautifully furnished (all were refurbished in 1993). There is a good amount of closet and drawer space and all cabins feature a personal safe and telephone. The cabin bathrooms, too, are quite luxurious, and equipped with really everything you will need, including bathrobes and hairdryer, and an assortment of personal toiletry items (there is also a 110 volt AC shaver socket in each bathroom). Note that there is no cabin food or beverage service.

Dining: The dining room, created from the original owner's living room/saloon, is located in the center of the vessel. It is exquisite and elegant in every detail (it also houses the ship's library), has beautiful wood paneled walls and a wood beam ceiling. There is ample space at each table, so there is never a crowded feeling, and dining is taken in one open seating, so you can sit and dine with whom you wish, where you wish. German chefs are in charge, and the cuisine is very international, with a good balance of "nouvelle cuisine" and regional dishes featured (depending on which region the ship is sailing in). Outstanding quality food and cuisine are featured throughout. Place settings for dinner (often by candlelight) are navy blue, white, and gold china.

European wines are usually provided for lunch and dinner. There is always excellent seafood and fish (this is always purchased fresh, locally, when available, as are most other ingredients). For breakfast and lunch, buffets are featured. These are really good, and beautifully presented, often outdoors on the Promenade Deck. Meals are announced by the ship's bell.

Other Comments: *Sea Cloud* is the oldest and most beautiful tall ship sailing, and the largest private yacht ever built (three times the size of Captain Cook's *Endeavour*), an authentic 1930s barkentine whose three masts are as high as a 20-story building (191.5 ft/58.3 m above the main deck). She was the largest private yacht ever built when constructed in 1931 by E. F. Hutton for his wife, Marjorie Merriweather Post (the American cereal heiress). Built as *Hussar*, for $1 million in the Krupp shipyard in Kiel, Germany, this steel-hulled yacht is immensely impressive when in port, but absolutely exhilarating when under full sail.

There is plenty of deck space, even under the vast expanse of white sail, and the promenade deck outdoors still has wonderful varnished sea chests. The decks themselves are made of irreplaceable mahogany. The original engine room (with diesel engines) is still in operation for the rare occasions when sail power cannot be used.

During World War II, the vessel saw action as a weather observation ship, under the code name *IX-99*. You can still see five chevrons on the bridge, one for each half-year of duty, serving as a reminder of those important years.

In addition to her retained and refurbished original suites and cabins, with their gorgeous wood paneling and antiques and dressers, some newer, smaller cabins were also added when a consortium of German yachtsmen purchased the ship. The owners spent $7.5 million refurbishing her. Many original oil paintings adorn her interior walls.

Her interiors exude warmth, and are finely handcrafted. There is much antique mahogany furniture, fine original oil paintings, gorgeous carved oak paneling, and burnished brass everywhere, as well as some finely detailed ceilings.

Sea Cloud is, without doubt, the ultimate, most romantic sailing ship afloat today. Although there are many imitations, there still is none better than this vintage vessel. She is still kept close to her original state when built. The ship operates under charter for much of the year, and sails in both the Caribbean and Mediterranean waters.

A cruise aboard *Sea Cloud* is, today, in four words, a truly exhilarating experience, and still much today as it was when she was first launched. She really is a special ship like no other, for the discerning few to relish the uncompromising comfort and elegance of a bygone era. Truly a stately home afloat, this ship remains one of the world's finest travel and holiday experiences, and a wonderful escape from the stress and strain of life ashore. Activities are few, and so relaxation is the key.

On the last night of the cruise, the sailor's choir sings seafaring songs for all. The US dollar is used as onboard currency. Gratuities are suggested at $10–$12 per person, per day.

The owning company which is German (it actually consists of a consortium of nine owners), also operates the new river vessel *River Cloud*, introduced in May 1996, for cruises on the Danube, Main, Mosel, and Rhine areas.

<u>Weak Points</u>: The interior staircase is steep, as they are aboard almost all sailing vessels. Remember that a sailing ship sails, and even a big sailing vessel such as this can heel to one side occasionally. Somehow the plastic chairs on deck just do not go with this ship's romantic, very exclusive image.

s/y Sea Cloud II
(S)

LIFESTYLE:	LUXURY
Cruise Line:	Sea Cloud Cruises
Former Names:	-
Gross Tonnage:	8,378
Builder:	Astilleros Gondan (Spain)
Original Cost:	DM50 million
Entered Service:	2000
Flag:	Malta
Tel. No.:	n/a
Fax No.:	n/a
Length (ft/m):	383.8/117.0
Beam (ft/m):	52.4/16.0
Draft (ft/m):	17.7/5.4
Type of Vessel:	barquentine
No. of Masts:	4/(24 sails)
Sail Area (sq ft/sq m):	32,292/3,000
Main Propulsion:	sail power
Propulsion/Propellers:	diesel (2,500kW)/1 (FP)
Decks:	4
Total Crew:	56
Pass. Capacity (basis 2):	96
Pass. Capacity (all berths):	96
Pass. Space Ratio (basis 2):	87.2
Pass. Space Ratio (all berths):	87.2
Officers:	German
Total Cabins:	48
Size Range (sq ft/m):	215.2-322.9/20.0-30.0

Cabins (outside view):	48
Cabins (inside — no view):	0
Cabins (single occupancy):	0
Cabins (with private balcony):	0
Cabins (wheelchair accessible):	0
Cabin Current:	110 and 220 volts
Cabin TV:	Yes
Dining Rooms:	1
Elevators:	0
Swimming Pools (outdoors):	0
Whirlpools:	0
Exercise Room:	Yes
Sauna/Steam Room:	Yes/No
Massage:	Yes
Self-Service Launderette:	No
Library:	Yes
Classification Society:	Germanischer Lloyd

RATINGS	POSSIBLE SCORE	SCORE ACHIEVED
Ship	500	NYR
Accommodation	200	NYR
Food	400	NYR
Service	400	NYR
Cruise	500	NYR
TOTAL	**2,000**	**NYR**
Expected Score Range:		**1600-1800**

Accommodation: All of the cabins have a private bathroom with shower and plenty of storage space for personal toiletries.

Dining: The one-seating dining room operates an open seating policy, so you can dine with whom you wish. It is decorated in light, modern maritime style, with wood and carpeted flooring, comfortable chairs with armrests, and circular light fixtures. The gold-rimmed plateware used for the captain's dinner has the ship's crest embedded in the white porcelain; it is extremely elegant (and very collectible).

Other Comments: This new three-masted tall ship has the look, ambience, and feel of a 1930s sailing vessel, and complements the company's beautiful 1931-built *Sea Cloud* in almost every way, including her external appearance. A small water sports platform is built into the aft quarter of the starboard side.

   Completely elegant in decor, but using modern materials to reproduce the period design intended, the interior designers have managed to continue the same beautiful traditional look and interior design of her sister ship, *Sea Cloud*. Design details and special decorative touches will make you feel at home instantly.

   The main lounge is elegance personified. At press time, the ship was scheduled to be operated under charter to various organizations, such as Raymond & Whitcomb (New York).

m/s Sea Princess
★★★★ +
(L)

LIFESTYLE:	**PREMIUM**	Cabins (with private balcony):	446
Cruise Line:	Princess Cruises	Cabins (wheelchair accessible):	20
Former Names:	-	Cabin Current:	110 and 220 volts
Gross Tonnage:	77,000	Cabin TV:	Yes
Builder:	Fincantieri (Italy)	Dining Rooms:	2 main/3 others
Original Cost:	$300 million	Elevators:	11
Entered Service:	December 1998	Casino:	Yes
Flag:	Liberia	Slot Machines:	Yes
Tel. No.:	363689510	Swimming Pools (outdoors):	3
Fax No.:	363689520	Swimming Pools (inside):	0
Length (ft/m):	856.2/261.00	Whirlpools:	5
Beam (ft/m):	105.8/32.25	Fitness Center:	Yes
Draft (ft/m):	26.0/7.95	Sauna/Steam Room:	Yes
Propulsion/Propellers:	diesel-electric	Massage:	Yes
	(46,080kW)/2 (FP)	Self-Service Launderette:	Yes
Decks:	10	Movie Theater/Seats:	Yes
Total Crew:	900	Library:	Yes
Pass. Capacity (basis 2):	1,950	Classification Society:	Registro Navale Italiano

RATINGS	POSSIBLE SCORE	SCORE ACHIEVED
Ship	500	442
Accommodation	200	168
Food	400	271
Service	400	299
Cruise	500	406
TOTAL	**2,000**	**1,586**

Pass. Capacity (all berths): 2,250
Pass. Space Ratio (basis 2): 39.4
Pass. Space Ratio (all berths): 34.2
Officers: Italian
Total Cabins: 1,050
Size Range (sq ft/m): 158.2–610.3/14.7–56.7
Cabins (outside view): 652
Cabins (inside — no view): 398
Cabins (single occupancy): 0

For comments, see *Dawn Princess*.

t/s/s Seawind Crown
★★★
(M)

LIFESTYLE:	STANDARD
Cruise Line:	Premier Cruise Lines
Former Names:	*Vasco da Gama,*
	Infante Dom Henrique
Gross Tonnage:	24,568
Builder:	Cockerill-Ougree (Belgium)
Original Cost:	n/a
Entered Service:	September 1961/October 1991
Flag:	Panama
Tel. No.:	1331251
Fax No.:	1331252
Length (ft/m):	641.6/195.59
Beam (ft/m):	84.4/25.73
Draft (ft/m):	26.9/8.20
Propulsion/Propellers:	steam turbine
	(16,180kW)/2 (FP)
Decks:	8
Total Crew:	362
Pass. Capacity (basis 2):	764
Pass. Capacity (all berths):	931
Pass. Space Ratio (basis 2):	33.4
Pass. Space Ratio (all berths):	26.3
Officers:	Greek
Total Cabins:	387
Size Range (sq ft/m):	118.4–559.7/11.0–52.0
Cabins (outside view):	266
Cabins (inside — no view):	121
Cabins (single occupancy):	6

Cabins (with private balcony):	2
Cabins (wheelchair accessible):	2
Cabin Current:	220 volts
Cabin TV:	Yes
Dining Rooms:	2
Elevators:	4
Casino:	Yes
Slot Machines:	Yes
Swimming Pools (outdoors):	2
Swimming Pools (inside):	0
Whirlpools:	0
Fitness Center:	Yes
Sauna/Steam Room:	Yes/No
Massage:	Yes
Self-Service Launderette:	No
Movie Theater/Seats:	Yes/208
Library:	Yes
Classification Society:	Lloyd's Register

RATINGS	POSSIBLE SCORE	SCORE ACHIEVED
Ship	500	289
Accommodation	200	128
Food	400	220
Service	400	231
Cruise	500	250
TOTAL	**2,000**	**1,118**

Accommodation: Has a wide assortment of cabins; some with queen-, double-, or twin beds, some with upper/lower berths. All cabins have excellent closet and drawer space, refrigerator, hairdryer, cotton bathrobes, and towels. The suites (they really are suites) are huge; occupants get nice little extras.

Dining: The two dining rooms are comfortable, and both food and service are good, considering the cruise fare charged. There are two seatings. Most tables are for four, six, or eight (there are few tables for two). Do remember that you get what you pay for, and the food budget is low. There is a limited selection of breads, cheeses, and fruits, and the dining room breakfast and lunch buffets are repetitive.

Other Comments: This former long-distance liner has been extensively refurbished. She has a handsome profile, classic lines, deep draft (keeps her stable), and is being well maintained. Has a long foredeck, rakish bow, and teak promenade decks (one outdoors, one covered).

Inside, she is a surprisingly spacious, classic cruise vessel. There is a mix of old-world elegance and contemporary features. A host of intimate public rooms feature tasteful decor and pastel tones, but generally, the eclectic decor has little color coordination. However, new original oil paintings grace her interiors, including some Guy Buffet dining scenes (as aboard the ships of Crystal Cruises).

There is a delightful chapel, and a well equipped hospital. Features lots of fine wood paneling and trim throughout her interiors, spacious foyers, and wide stairways so typical of the more classic ships. Has a good-size cinema, but the seats should be staggered for better viewing. Sports facilities include paddle-tennis and indoor squash court. Has a very poor library.

There is a multinational passenger mix on each cruise, but the principal nationalities are Brazilian and North American. The ship is now based year-round in Brazil.

Weak Points: The emergency drill is conducted in six languages. Nonsmokers be warned — smokers are everywhere. Has a steep gangway in main embarkation port. Announcements in several languages are irritating. Disorganized disembarkation.

419

m/s Seawing
★★★
(M)

LIFESTYLE: STANDARD

Cruise Line:	Airtours Sun Cruises
Former Names:	*Southward*
Gross Tonnage:	16,710
Builder: Cantieri Navale del Tirreno et Riuniti (Italy)	
Original Cost:	n/a
Entered Service:	November 1971/March 1995
Flag:	Bahamas
Tel. No.:	1104165
Fax No.:	1104165
Length (ft/m):	535.7/163.30
Beam (ft/m):	74.7/22.79
Draft (ft/m):	21.3/6.50
Propulsion/Propellers:	diesel (13,400kW)/2 (CP)
Decks:	7
Total Crew:	302
Pass. Capacity (basis 2):	784
Pass. Capacity (all berths):	904
Pass. Space Ratio (basis 2):	21.3
Pass. Space Ratio (all berths):	18.4
Officers:	International
Total Cabins:	392
Size Range (sq ft/m):	89.3–255.1/8.3–23.7
Cabins (outside view):	260
Cabins (inside — no view):	132
Cabins (single occupancy):	0
Cabins (with private balcony):	0

Cabins (wheelchair accessible):	0
Cabin Current:	110 volts
Cabin TV:	No
Dining Rooms:	1
Elevators:	4
Casino:	Yes
Slot Machines:	Yes
Swimming Pools (outdoors):	1
Swimming Pools (inside):	0
Whirlpools:	0
Fitness Center:	Yes
Sauna/Steam Room:	Yes/No
Massage:	Yes
Self-Service Launderette:	No
Movie Theater/Seats:	No
Library:	Yes
Classification Society:	Det Norske Veritas

RATINGS	POSSIBLE SCORE	SCORE ACHIEVED
Ship	500	269
Accommodation	200	111
Food	400	241
Service	400	248
Cruise	500	296
TOTAL	**2,000**	**1,165**

Accommodation: There are three cabin grades (Standard, Superior, and Deluxe) and five price categories. *Note*: Cabins are not assigned until you reach the ship at the embarkation port. Room service food items incur an extra charge. The ten Boat Deck deluxe cabins are reasonably spacious for the size of the vessel, although the two forward-facing units overlook the mooring deck, can prove noisy, and are much smaller than the other eight suites; they all come fairly well equipped, and have full bathtubs. All other cabins (both those with an outside "sea view" and those "inside" with no view) are very compact (dimensionally challenged), but basically clean and tidy, with adequate closet space for a one-week cruise.

Dining: The dining room is reasonably charming, with warm colors. There are two seatings. The food is adequate (for the price), but not memorable, so do not expect gourmet fare. Bread and fruit selections are poor. Service and ambience are both informal. There is an extra charge for room service menu items. The wine list is acceptable, and the prices are very reasonable.

Other Comments: This ship, which was formerly operated by Norwegian Cruise Line, was the first ship with which Airtours entered the cruise marketplace. She has a crisp, clean profile with rakish superstructure, dual funnels, and inboard lifeboats. The open deck and sunbathing space is rather limited, and the swimming pool is small.

Inside, there is a good selection of comfortable public rooms with bright, contemporary decor. Perhaps the favorite is the night club, set high atop the forward mast. Also has a balconied theater. The sight lines in the showroom are poor. Families with children will find lots to do.

Airtours provides good value for money with these cruises, designed for the young at heart. This ship provides all the right ingredients for an active, fun-filled short cruise vacation for sun loving couples and families at the right price, but the ship shows her age in places. This is basic, but reasonably sound, cruising for those wanting a no-frills vacation in pleasant surroundings, at a really modest price level. Onboard drinks prices are very reasonable.

Insurance is included (at an extra charge, unless you decline it). Formerly operated by Norwegian Cruise Line, the ship is now owned and operated by Airtours Sun Cruises and tailored specifically to the UK family cruise market (onboard currency is the pound sterling). Airtours also has its own fleet of aircraft, and this is one reason that the company is able to offer complete cruise-air-stay packages at such modest rates.

Weak Points: Do remember that this is a high-density ship, which means lines for buffets, embarkation, and disembarkation. There are too many repetitive (holiday-camp style) announcements. The ship can be rowdy at times when there are lots of children running around, particularly during holiday sailings. There is little professional entertainment, operating as it does with "blue coat" social staff/entertainers.

WHY IS A CRUISE VACATION SO POPULAR?

Well, over eight million people cannot be wrong (that's how many people took a cruise last year)! Cruising is popular today because it takes one away from the pressures and strains of contemporary life by offering an escape from reality. Cruise ships are really self-contained resorts, without the crime, which can take you to several destinations in the space of just a few days.

The sea has always been a source of adventure, excitement, romance, and wonder. It is beneficial and therapeutic, and, because you pay in advance, you know what you will spend on your vacation without any hidden surprises. There is no traffic (except when you go ashore in ports of call), and no pollution. The hassles of ordinary travel are almost eliminated in one pleasant little package. It's no wonder that 85 percent of passengers want to go again. And again. And again.

m/s Sensation
★★★ +
(L)

LIFESTYLE: **STANDARD**

Cruise Line:	Carnival Cruise Lines
Former Names:	-
Gross Tonnage:	70,367
Builder:	Kvaerner Masa-Yards (Finland)
Original Cost:	$300 million
Entered Service:	November 1993
Flag:	Panama
Tel. No.:	1341372
Fax No.:	n/a
Length (ft/m):	855.0/260.6
Beam (ft/m):	103.0/31.4
Draft (ft/m):	25.9/7.9
Propulsion/Propellers:	diesel-electric (42,240kW)/2 (CP)
Decks:	10
Total Crew:	920
Pass. Capacity (basis 2):	2,040
Pass. Capacity (all berths):	2,594
Pass. Space Ratio (basis 2):	34.4
Pass. Space Ratio (all berths):	26.7
Officers:	Italian
Total Cabins:	1,020
Size Range (sq ft/m):	173.2–409.7/16.0–38.0
Cabins (outside view):	618
Cabins (inside — no view):	402
Cabins (single occupancy):	0

Cabins (with private balcony):	54
Cabins (wheelchair accessible):	20
Cabin Current:	110 volts
Cabin TV:	Yes
Dining Rooms:	2
Elevators:	14
Casino:	Yes
Slot Machines:	Yes
Swimming Pools (outdoors):	3
Swimming Pools (inside):	0
Whirlpools:	6
Fitness Center:	Yes
Sauna/Steam Room:	Yes/Yes
Massage:	Yes
Self-Service Launderette:	Yes
Movie Theater/Seats:	No
Library:	Yes
Classification Society:	Lloyd's Register

RATINGS	POSSIBLE SCORE	SCORE ACHIEVED
Ship	500	395
Accommodation	200	151
Food	400	221
Service	400	270
Cruise	500	348
TOTAL	**2,000**	**1,385**

Accommodation: The standard cabins are of a decent size, and although plainly decorated, they have ample closet and drawer space for a one-week cruise. Remember to take shampoo and other toiletries (shower cap for ladies, for example), as the company provides only soap and ice water in cabins. There are 28 outside suites, all with better decor, nicer soft furnishings, and whirlpool tubs in their larger bathrooms.

Dining: There are two huge, noisy dining rooms (both nonsmoking) with the usual efficient, assertive service. Improved cuisine is still mediocre, and not Carnival's strong point. There are two seatings. Service is attentive, but completely programmed and inflexible. The wine list is reasonably good.

Other Comments: The ship features almost vibration-free service from diesel-electric propulsion system. Has a dramatic six-deck-high atrium, with cool marble and hot neon, topped by a large colored glass dome and featuring a spectacular artistic centerpiece. Features expansive open-deck areas and an excellent health spa with a large gymnasium and the latest high-tech muscle machines. There are public entertainment lounges, bars, and clubs galore, with something for everyone. Dazzling colors and design themes in handsome public rooms connected by wide indoor boulevards.

There is also a $1 million art collection, much of it bright and vocal. The library is a lovely room, but there are almost no books (Carnival thinks its passengers do not read). The Michelangelo Lounge is a creative thinker's delight, while Fingers Lounge is sheer sensory stimulation. Lavish but elegant multitiered showroom (there are 20 pillars to obstruct some sight lines) and high energy razzle-dazzle shows. Dramatic three-deck-high glass enclosed health spa. Banked jogging track. Gigantic casino has nonstop action. This ship will entertain you well. (See also comments for *Imagination* and other Carnival ships.) The ship now operates seven-night cruises year-round from the Port of Tampa, Florida, as from December 1998.

Weak Points: As in most Carnival ships, there is a sense of overwhelming sensory indulgence, like in a video game parlor. There are too many loud, repetitive announcements. The constant and aggressive hustling for drinks by bar waiters is irritating, as are drinks in plastic glasses.

m/s Seven Seas Navigator (S)

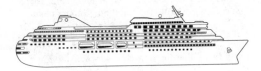

LIFESTYLE:	PREMIUM
Cruise Line:	Radisson Seven Seas Cruises
Former Names:	-
Gross Tonnage:	30,000
Builder:	T. Marriotti (Italy)
Original Cost:	$200 million
Entered Service:	August 1999
Flag:	Italy
Tel. No.:	n/a
Fax No.:	n/a
Length (ft/m):	559.7/170.6
Beam (ft/m):	71.5/21.8
Draft (ft/m):	21.3.0/6.5
Propulsion/Propellers:	diesel (13,000kW)/2 (CP)
Passenger Decks:	8
Total Crew:	325
Pass. Capacity (basis 2):	490
Pass. Capacity (all berths):	490
Pass. Space Ratio (basis 2):	61.2
Pass. Space Ratio (all berths):	56.6
Officers:	European/International
Total Cabins:	245
Size Range (sq ft/m):	301.3–1,173.3/28.0–109.0
Cabins (outside view):	245
Cabins (inside — no view):	0
Cabins (single occupancy):	0
Cabins (with private balcony):	196

Cabins (wheelchair accessible):	4
Cabin Current:	110 and 220 volts
Cabin TV:	Yes
Dining Rooms:	1 main, 1 alternative
Elevators:	5
Casino:	Yes
Slot Machines:	Yes
Swimming Pools (outdoors):	1
Swimming Pools (inside):	0
Whirlpools:	2
Fitness Center:	Yes
Sauna/Steam Room:	Yes/Yes
Massage:	Yes
Self-Service Launderette:	Yes
Movie Theater/Seats:	No
Library:	Yes
Classification Society:	Registro Navale Italiano

RATINGS	POSSIBLE SCORE	SCORE ACHIEVED
Ship	500	NYR
Accommodation	200	NYR
Food	400	NYR
Service	400	NYR
Cruise	500	NYR
TOTAL	**2,000**	**NYR**
Expected Score Range:		**1600-1800**

Accommodation: This is an all-suite ship (in 11 categories) with extremely large living spaces. Almost 90 percent of all suites feature a private balcony, with floor-to-ceiling sliding glass doors, while ten suites are interconnecting, and 38 suites have an extra bed for a third occupant. To give you an idea of size comparison, the smallest suite is more than twice the size of the smallest cabin aboard the world's largest cruise ship, Royal Caribbean International's *Voyager of the Seas*.

All grades of accommodation feature a walk-in closet, European king-sized bed or twin beds, wooden cabinetry with nicely rounded edges, plenty of drawer space, minibar-refrigerator, television/VCR player, personal safe, and other accoutrements of fine living at sea in the latest design format. The refrigerator is stocked with complimentary soft drinks and a bar set-up on embarkation. The marble-appointed bathroom has a full-size bathtub, as well as a separate shower enclosure, 100 percent cotton bathrobe, and hairdryer.

The largest living spaces are four master suites, both with forward-facing views (one pair have huge wraparound fore- and side balconies, while the second pair has side balconies). Each suite has a completely separate bedroom with dressing table; the living room features a full dining room table and chair for up to six persons, wet bar, counter, bar stools, large sofa, and several individual chairs, and an audio-visual console/entertainment center. Each suite has a main bathroom and a guest bathroom.

Four suites for the phyically challenged have private balconies, and are ideally located adjacent to the elevators (correcting a mistake made when the company's *Radisson Diamond* was constructed, when they were located as far from any elevators as they possibly could be).

Dining: There is one main dining room, with ocean-view picture windows and open seating dining, which means that you may be seated when and with whom you wish. Complimentary wines are served during dinner, and a connoisseur wine list is available for those who prefer to choose a vintage wine (at extra cost). The company also features "heart healthy" cuisine.

An alternative dining spot, Portofino Grill, features informal Italian dining for lunch, and for dinner (reservations required), authentic Northern Italian cuisine. For casual meals there is also an indoor/outdoor Grill.

You can also choose to dine in your cabin. There is a 24-hour room service menu; during dinner hours, you can choose from the full dining rooom menu.

Other Comments: This new ship was built by using a hull that was already constructed in St. Petersburg, Russia, as *Blue Sea*. The superstructure was incorporated into the hull in an Italian shipyard, with the result being that the new ship was delivered in record time. She is large enough to be stable over long stretches of water, and her passenger space ratio promises an outstanding amount of space for everyone.

The ship's interiors feature a mix of classical and contemporary Italian styling and decor throughout, with warm, soft colors, and fine, soft furnishings.

The Vista Lounge is the ship's forward-view observation lounge. At the opposite end of the ship is Galileo's, a large piano lounge with good views.

A Navigator's Lounge features warm mahogany and cherry wood paneling and large, comfortable, mid-back tub chairs. Menawhile, next door, cigars and cognac can be taken in the delightful Connoisseur's Club — a first for a Radisson Seven Seas Cruises vessel.

There is a two-deck-high show lounge, with reasonable sight lines from most seats (several pillars obstruct the views, particularly from some of the side balcony seats). The extensive library also features three computers with direct E-mail/Internet access (for a fee).

She will spend her inaugural season in the Mediterranean, but is designed for worldwide cruise itineraries. This new ship promises to be the most luxurious of all the ships in the Radisson Seven Seas cruises fleet. All gratuities are included. It is expected that this new vessel could well turn out to be a replacement for the pleasant, but now tired *Song of Flower*, which may well be sold.

Weak Points: There is no wraparound promenade deck outdoors, although there is a jogging track high atop the aft section of the ship around the funnel housing.

m/s Shota Rustaveli
★★
(M)

LIFESTYLE: **STANDARD**

Cruise Line:	Ukrainian Passenger Fleet
Former Names:	-
Gross Tonnage:	20,499
Builder:	VEB Mathias Thesen (Germany)
Original Cost:	n/a
Entered Service:	June 1968
Flag:	Ukraine
Tel. No.:	1400253
Fax No.:	1400253
Length (ft/m):	576.6/175.77
Beam (ft/m):	77.4/23.60
Draft (ft/m):	26.5/8.09
Propulsion/Propellers:	diesel (15,700kW)/2 (CP)
Decks:	8
Total Crew:	350
Pass. Capacity (basis 2):	493
Pass. Capacity (all berths):	602
Pass. Space Ratio (basis 2):	41.4
Pass. Space Ratio (all berths):	34.0
Officers:	Russian/Ukrainian
Total Cabins:	249
Size Range (sq ft/m):	n/a
Cabins (outside view):	244
Cabins (inside — no view):	5
Cabins (single occupancy):	0
Cabins (with private balcony):	0

Cabins (wheelchair accessible):	0
Cabin Current:	220 volts
Cabin TV:	No
Dining Rooms:	3
Elevators:	3
Casino:	No
Slot Machines:	No
Swimming Pools (outdoors):	2
Swimming Pools (inside):	0
Whirlpools:	0
Fitness Center:	Yes
Sauna/Steam Room:	Yes/No
Massage:	Yes
Self-Service Launderette:	Yes
Movie Theater/Seats:	Yes/130
Library:	Yes
Classification Society:	RS

RATINGS	POSSIBLE SCORE	SCORE ACHIEVED
Ship	500	184
Accommodation	200	85
Food	400	155
Service	400	196
Cruise	500	182
TOTAL	**2,000**	**802**

Accommodation: Apart from two De-Luxe grade cabins with private balconies, this ship has small but very comfortable outside cabins, with attractive wood accents, solid fixtures, and pleasing decor. Many portholes actually open, which is unusual in today's world of air-conditioned ships.

Dining: The dining room is reasonably comfortable. There are two seatings. With both French and Russian chefs, the food is acceptable (although it is quite stodgy), but there is little choice. Limited selection of breads and fruits. Free carafes of wine for lunch and dinner. Service is attentive but somewhat inflexible.

Other Comments: She has good-looking, well-built traditional styling, with an all-white profile, but the general ship maintenance is not good in some areas. Built as one of five sister ships, she has good teak wood decks and wraparound open promenade. There is a good amount of open deck space for sunbathing, with real wooden deck chairs.

Spacious interior with reasonably pleasing decor, although somewhat spartan and dated. The colors are a little somber, and the ceilings are plain. There is a good amount of wood paneling and trim used in accenting the decor. Decent inside swimming pool.

This ship was renovated in 1991, and is often chartered to European cruise-tour companies. European cruise staff cater well to principally French- and Italian-speaking passengers. Good for the passenger on a low budget who does not expect any degree of luxury or finesse.

<u>Weak Points</u>: This ship has a steep, narrow gangway in some ports. Do expect to stand in some lines for embarkation, disembarkation, buffets, and shore tenders. Unfortunately, the aroma inside the vessel is one of well-worn socks (very stale).

425

m/s Silver Cloud
★★★★★
(S)

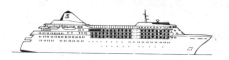

LIFESTYLE:	LUXURY
Cruise Line:	Silversea Cruises
Former Names:	-
Gross Tonnage:	16,927
Builder:	Visentini/Mariotti (Italy)
Original Cost:	$125 million
Entered Service:	April 1994
Flag:	Bahamas
Tel. No.:	1306601
Fax No.:	1306602
Length (ft/m):	514.4/155.8
Beam (ft/m):	70.62/21.4
Draft (ft/m):	17.3/5.3
Propulsion/Propellers:	diesel (11,700kW)/2 (CP)
Decks:	6
Total Crew:	198
Pass. Capacity (basis 2):	296
Pass. Capacity (all berths):	315
Pass. Space Ratio (basis 2):	57.1
Pass. Space Ratio (all berths):	53.7
Officers:	Italian
Total Cabins:	148
Size Range (sq ft/m):	240.0–1,314.0/22.2–122.0
Cabins (outside view):	148
Cabins (inside — no view):	0
Cabins (single occupancy):	0
Cabins (with private balcony):	110

Cabins (wheelchair accessible):	2
Cabin Current:	110 and 220 volts
Cabin TV:	Yes
Dining Rooms:	1 (+ 1 informal cafe)
Elevators:	4
Casino:	Yes
Slot Machines:	Yes
Swimming Pools (outdoors):	1
Swimming Pools (inside):	0
Whirlpools:	2
Fitness Center:	Yes
Sauna/Steam Room:	Yes/Yes
Massage:	Yes
Self-Service Launderette:	Yes
Movie Theater/Seats:	Yes/306
Library:	Yes
Classification Society:	Registro Navale Italiano

RATINGS	POSSIBLE SCORE	SCORE ACHIEVED
Ship	500	442
Accommodation	200	181
Food	400	344
Service	400	340
Cruise	500	422
TOTAL	**2,000**	**1,729**

Accommodation: The all-outside suites (75 percent of which have fine private teakwood balconies) have convertible queen-to-twin beds and are beautifully fitted out with just about everything one needs, including huge floor-to-ceiling windows, large walk-in closets, dressing table, writing desk, stocked minibar-refrigerator (no charge), and fresh flowers. Marble floor bathrooms have bathtub and plenty of towels. Personalized stationery, bathrobes, and good amenities kit in all cabins. The top suites also have CD players.

All cabins have televisions and video player (PAL, not VHS system). However, the walk-in closets do not actually provide much hanging space (particularly for such items as full-length dresses), and it would be better for the door to open outward instead of inward (the drawers themselves are poorly positioned). Although the cabin insulation above and below each cabin is good, the insulation between cabins is not (a privacy curtain installed between entry door and sleeping area would be most useful), and light from the passageway leaks into the cabin, making it hard to achieve a dark room.

Note that the cabins with balconies on the lowest deck can suffer from sticky salt spray when the ship is moving, so the balconies require lots of cleaning. Each evening, the stewardesses bring plates of canapes to your suite — just right for a light bite with cocktails.

Dining: The contemporary dining room has an attractive arched gazebo center and a wavy ceiling design as its focal point, and is set with fine Limoges china and well-balanced Christofle flatware. Meals are served in an open seating, which means you can eat when you like (within the given dining room opening times), and with whom you like. Meals can also be served, course-by-course, in your suite, although the balcony tables are rather low for dining outdoors. The dining is good throughout the ship, with a choice of formal and informal areas, although the cuisine and presentation doesn't quite match up to that of products such as the smaller Seabourn ships. Standard table wines are included for lunch and dinner, but there is also a "connoisseur list" of premium wines at extra charge. Oh, and the house champagne is Moet & Chandon.

An alternative Italian restaurant, called Cucina Italiana, is very popular for evening alternative dining. By day it acts as an informal cafe, but by night turns into a lovely intimate dining spot, complete with candlelight and print tablecloths.

The ship also provides 24-hour in-cabin dining service (full course-by-course dinners are available).

Other Comments: *Silver Cloud* and *Silver Wind* have handsome profiles, rather like small versions of *Crystal Harmony/Crystal Symphony,* or a larger version of the Seabourn ships. The size is just about ideal for highly personalized cruising in an elegant environment. The vertical cake-layer stacking of public rooms aft and the positioning of accommodation units forward ensures quiet cabins. Features an artificial grass-covered wraparound promenade deck outdoors, and a spacious swimming pool deck.

The spacious interior is well planned, and with elegant decor and fine quality soft furnishings, is accented by the gentle use of brass and fine woods and very creative ceilings throughout. The spa areas need improvement, and the tiled decor is bland and uninviting.

There is a useful business center as well as a CD-ROM and hardback book library, open 24 hours a day. There is an excellent two-level showroom with tiered seating, but the entertainment is disappointing and not as good as when the ship first debuted.

There is an excellent amount of space per passenger and there is no hint of a line anywhere in this unhurried envrironment. Excellent documentation is provided before your cruise, all of which comes in a high quality document wallet.

An elegant onboard ambience prevails, and there is no pressure, no hype, and an enthusiastic staff to pamper you, with a high ratio of Europeans. Insurance is extra (it *was* included when Silversea Cruises first started). Refreshingly, all drinks, gratuities, and port taxes *are* included, and, refreshingly, no further tipping anywhere on board is allowed. This ship is perhaps ideal for those who enjoy spacious surroundings, excellent food, and some entertainment. It would be difficult *not* to have a good cruise vacation aboard this ship, albeit at a fairly high price. Silversea Cruises has come a long way since its inception, and continues to refine its product. The company's many international passengers react well to the ambience, food, service, and the staff, most of whom go out of their way to please.

Few ships make it to a five-star rating today, but Silversea Cruises has earned an enviable reputation for high quality in a short space of time.

Weak Points: The officers should, but rarely do, host dining room tables. Some vibration is evident when bow thrusters or the anchors are used, particularly in the forwardmost cabins. The self-service launderette is poor and not large enough for longer cruises, when passengers like to be able to do their own small items. Sadly, crew facilities are minimal, and so keeping consistency is difficult, as high crew turnover is a fact of life.

m/s Silver Shadow
(S)

LIFESTYLE:	**LUXURY**
Cruise Line:	Silversea Cruises
Former Names:	-
Gross Tonnage:	25,000
Builder:	Visentini/Mariotti (Italy)
Original Cost:	$150 million
Entered Service:	Fall 2000
Flag:	Bahamas
Tel. No.:	n/a
Fax No.:	n/a
Length (ft/m):	597.1/182.0
Beam (ft/m):	81.8/24.8
Draft (ft/m):	19.6/6.0
Propulsion/Propellers:	diesel/2 (CP)
Decks:	11
Total Crew:	295
Pass. Capacity (basis 2):	388
Pass. Capacity (all berths):	400
Pass. Space Ratio (basis 2):	64.4
Pass. Space Ratio (all berths):	62.5
Officers:	Italian
Total Cabins:	194
Size Range (sq ft/m):	287.4–936.5/26.7–87
Cabins (outside view):	194
Cabins (inside — no view):	0
Cabins (single occupancy):	0
Cabins (with private balcony):	157

Cabins (wheelchair accessible):	2
Cabin Current:	110 and 220 volts
Cabin TV:	Yes
Dining Rooms:	1 main, 1 grill, 1 cafe
Elevators:	5
Casino:	Yes
Slot Machines:	Yes
Swimming Pools (outdoors):	1
Swimming Pools (inside):	0
Whirlpools:	2
Fitness Center:	Yes
Sauna/Steam Room:	Yes/Yes
Massage:	Yes
Self-Service Launderette:	Yes
Movie Theater/Seats:	No
Library:	Yes
Classification Society:	Registro Navale Italiano

RATINGS	POSSIBLE SCORE	SCORE ACHIEVED
Ship	500	NYR
Accommodation	200	NYR
Food	400	NYR
Service	400	NYR
Cruise	500	NYR
TOTAL	**2,000**	**NYR**
Expected Score Range:		**1700-1900**

Accommodation: There are two owners' suites, four grand suites, nine silver suites, 161 balcony suites, 20 vista suites (without balcony), and 2 handicapped suites.

The standard Veranda Suites are 360 sq ft (33.5 m^2). For comfort, Silversea-monogrammed Frette bed linens are provided in all cabins, as are soft down pillows, 100 percent cotton bathrobes, and a range of personal toiletry amenities.

Dining: The main dining room (The Restaurant) provides open seating dining in elegant surroundings, with Cristofle silverware.

A poolside Grill provides a casual alternative daytime dining spot. Dinner can also be served course-by-course in your own suite.

For even more informal dining, an informal Terrace Café is featured (this has proved popular aboard the company's first two ships, *Silver Cloud* and *Silver Wind*). In the evening this features regional Italian cuisine.

Other Comments: This new ship is the latest generation of vessels, slightly larger than the company's first two ships, *Silver Cloud* and *Silver Wind*, with a streamlined profile and sleek single funnel. The design of this new ship (a sister ship is also due to enter service in 2001) has evolved from the experience and success gained from the first pair.

In a first for Silversea Cruises, a cigar smoking lounge has been incorporated, as has a computer learning center.

Silversea Cruises features "all-inclusive" fares (they do not, however, include vintage wines, or massage, or other personal services), but they do include many things that are at extra cost compared to most other cruise lines in the industry. The passenger mix includes many nationalities, which actually makes for a more interesting experience, although the majority of passengers are North American.

m/v Silver Star
★★ +
(S)

LIFESTYLE:	STANDARD
Cruise Line:	Mano Cruises
Former Names:	*Royal Dream, Odessa Song, Bashkiriya*
Gross Tonnage:	5,092
Builder:	VEB Mathias-Thesen (Germany)
Original Cost:	n/a
Entered Service:	1964/1998
Flag:	Malta
Tel. No.:	1257176
Fax No.:	1257177
Length (ft/m):	400.5/122.1
Beam (ft/m):	52.4/16.0
Draft (ft/m):	18.3/5.59
Propulsion/Propellers:	diesel/2
Decks:	6
Total Crew:	130
Pass. Capacity (basis 2):	286
Pass. Capacity (all berths):	425
Pass. Space Ratio (basis 2):	17.8
Pass. Space Ratio (all berths):	11.9
Officers:	Ukrainian
Total Cabins:	157
Size Range (sq ft/m): 4.35x2.9/3.07x2.9 + 2.97x2.71	
Cabins (outside view):	124
Cabins (inside — no view):	23
Cabins (single occupancy):	0

Cabins (with private balcony):	0
Cabins (wheelchair accessible):	0
Cabin Current:	220 volts
Cabin TV:	No
Dining Rooms:	1
Elevators:	0
Casino:	Yes
Slot Machines:	Yes
Swimming Pools (outdoors):	1
Swimming Pools (inside):	0
Whirlpools:	0
Fitness Center:	No
Sauna/Steam Room:	Yes/No
Massage:	No
Self-Service Launderette:	No
Movie Theater/Seats:	No
Library:	Yes
Classification Society:	Hellenic Register

RATINGS	POSSIBLE SCORE	SCORE ACHIEVED
Ship	500	211
Accommodation	200	98
Food	400	248
Service	400	235
Cruise	500	265
TOTAL	**2,000**	**1,057**

Accommodation: The two suites, Silver Iris and Silver Jasmine, are the largest of the seven cabin grades, which is a lot for this small ship. They have a separate living room and bedroom, plus a bathroom with full-sized bathtub.

Other cabins are small and basic, yet reasonably comfortable, and the few inside cabins are fairly large. Most cabins have beds in an L-shaped configuration; some cabins have third and fourth upper berths, although the closet and drawer space is extremely limited when all are occupied; all have a private bathroom with shower (soap and shampoo are provided). The cabin insulation is poor, and drawer space is modest.

Dining: The dining room, which is set low down and has portholes, is decorated in typical Middle Eastern style. There are two seatings. The food is surprisingly good, with lots of fresh salads and vegetables, as well as good meats and local fish. There is certainly plenty of variety. Kosher food can also be supplied — for a surcharge, per passenger, per cruise.

Other Comments: This former Russian vessel has a large square funnel, and is now operated under a 15-year charter to Mano Cruises of Haifa, Israel. There is little outdoor walking space, although there is a decent amount of open deck and sunbathing space. The swimming pool is really just a "dip" pool, however, and the painted steel decks forward of the pool really should be covered with wood or other heat-absorbing materials.

There are two main public rooms. One is the main lounge/showroom, which has a bar on the port side adjacent to the entrance. The lounge seating is arranged around the circular wooden dance floor. The second room is the ship's disco at night. There is also a small room that is usually used for children.

Silver Star (nothing to do with Silversea Cruises) is an older vessel that has received the benefit of extensive refit and refurbishment work, and is now operating seven-night Mediterranean cruises almost exclusively for the local Israeli market. The ship itself is very basic, but the food provides a highlight.

Weak Points: This really is a high-density ship, with little space per person. There is a charge for use of the sauna.

m/s Silver Wind
★★★★★
(S)

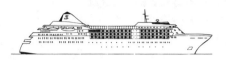

LIFESTYLE:	LUXURY
Cruise Line:	Silversea Cruises
Former Names:	-
Gross Tonnage:	16,927
Builder:	Visentini/Mariotti Italy)
Original Cost:	$125 million
Entered Service:	January 1995
Flag:	Italy
Tel. No.:	1152245
Fax No.:	1152250
Length (ft/m):	514.4/155.8
Beam (ft/m):	70.62/21.4
Draft (ft/m):	17.3/5.3
Propulsion/Propellers:	diesel (11,700kW)/2 (CP)
Decks:	6
Total Crew:	197
Pass. Capacity (basis 2):	296
Pass. Capacity (all berths):	315
Pass. Space Ratio (basis 2):	57.1
Pass. Space Ratio (all berths):	53.7
Officers:	Italian
Total Cabins:	148
Size Range (sq ft/m):	240.0–1,314.0/22.2–122.0
Cabins (outside view):	148
Cabins (inside — no view):	0
Cabins (single occupancy):	0
Cabins (with private balcony):	110

Cabins (wheelchair accessible):	2
Cabin Current:	110 and 220 volts
Cabin TV:	Yes
Dining Rooms:	1 (+ 1 informal cafe)
Elevators:	4
Casino:	Yes
Slot Machines:	Yes
Swimming Pools (outdoors):	1
Swimming Pools (inside):	0
Whirlpools:	2
Fitness Center:	Yes
Sauna/Steam Room:	Yes/Yes
Massage:	Yes
Self-Service Launderette:	Yes
Movie Theater/Seats:	Yes/306
Library:	Yes
Classification Society:	Registro Navale Italiano

RATINGS	POSSIBLE SCORE	SCORE ACHIEVED
Ship	500	442
Accommodation	200	181
Food	400	344
Service	400	340
Cruise	500	422
TOTAL	**2,000**	**1,729**

For comments, see *Silver Cloud.*

s/y Sir Francis Drake
★★
(S)

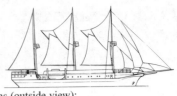

LIFESTYLE:	STANDARD
Cruise Line:	Tall Ship Adventures
Former Names:	*Godewind, Landkirchen*
Gross Tonnage:	450 DWT
Builder:	(Germany)
Original Cost:	n/a
Entered Service:	1917/1988
Flag:	Equatorial Guinea
Tel. No.:	n/a
Fax No.:	n/a
Length (ft/m):	162.4/49.5
Beam (ft/m):	22.9/7.0
Draft (ft/m):	9.1/2.8
Type of Vessel:	topsail schooner
No. of Masts:	3 (9 manually-furled sails)
Sail Area (sq ft/sq m):	1,968/600
Main Propulsion:	sail power
Propulsion/Propellers:	diesel/1 (FP)
Decks:	2
Total Crew:	14
Pass. Capacity (basis 2):	28
Pass. Capacity (all berths):	28
Pass. Space Ratio (basis 2):	16.0
Pass. Space Ratio (all berths):	16.0
Officers:	New Zealand
Total Cabins:	14
Size Range (sq ft/m):	80.0–120.0/7.4–11.1

Cabins (outside view):	14
Cabins (inside — no view):	0
Cabins (single occupancy):	0
Cabins (with private balcony):	0
Cabins (wheelchair accessible):	0
Cabin Current:	220 volts
Cabin TV:	No
Dining Rooms:	1
Casino:	No
Slot Machines:	No
Swimming Pools (outdoors):	0
Whirlpools:	0
Fitness Center:	No
Sauna/Steam Room:	No/No
Massage:	No
Self-Service Launderette:	No
Library:	No
Classification Society:	Germanischer Lloyd

RATINGS	POSSIBLE SCORE	SCORE ACHIEVED
Ship	500	212
Accommodation	200	74
Food	400	158
Service	400	186
Cruise	500	244
TOTAL	**2,000**	**874**

Accommodation: The cabins come in a variety of configurations, with a mixture of beds and upper berths (bunk beds) that are quite narrow but reasonably comfortable for a sailing vessel.

Dining: Charming dark-wood paneled dining room with wood-trimmed chairs and picture windows. Sit where you like and with whom you like in the single open seating. The cuisine is decidedly basic Americana fare, with fresh fish purchased locally. Although the chef will try to accommodate requests, vegetarians may find it tough going. The food quality is simple fare, and definitely nothing fancy, although most passengers seem happy with it.

Other Comments: This is an authentic topsail schooner, restored to her original condition, and well appointed. More than a windjammer, this tall ship is quite a treasure for those who do not want nor expect the service finesse offered aboard regular cruise ships. This ship should appeal to those who enjoy water sports, scuba diving, and snorkeling. Sunfish, water-skis, and a sea kayak are available for passenger use. There are some cozy chairs and wooden benches on deck.

Inside the vessel, there is much wood paneling, brass fittings, and solid furniture. Carries snorkeling equipment. Passengers can, and often do, participate in hoisting the sails, but otherwise, there is little to do but relax and let her crew help you totally unwind (there are no organized activities).

This is unhurried hands-on cruising in only moderately comfortable, but very basic surroundings, combined with plenty of beaches and water sports. It is an opportunity to sail aboard one of the last tall ships. The itineraries include the Virgin Islands and the Grenadines (itineraries do vary from cruise to cruise, depending on weather and other local conditions). The ship usually anchors at night in a sheltered bay, so you're rocked gently to sleep. Remember to pack very lightly (shorts and tee-shirts are really all you'll need). Tipping, at about $10 per person per day, is expected.

<u>Weak Points</u>: The ship has steep interior stairways, as aboard most true sailing vessels. The constant music on deck is irritating.

t/s/s Sky Princess
★★★★
(L)

LIFESTYLE:	PREMIUM
Cruise Line:	Princess Cruises
Former Names:	*Fairsky*
Gross Tonnage:	46,392
Builder:	C.N.I.M. (France)
Original Cost:	$156 million
Entered Service:	March 1984
Flag:	Liberia
Tel. No.:	1442264
Fax No.:	1442266
Length (ft/m):	788.6/240.39
Beam (ft/m):	91.3/27.84
Draft (ft/m):	26.7/8.15
Propulsion/Propellers:	steam turbine (21,700kW)/2 (CP)
Decks:	11
Total Crew:	550
Pass. Capacity (basis 2):	1,200
Pass. Capacity (all berths):	1,350
Pass. Space Ratio (basis 2):	38.6
Pass. Space Ratio (all berths):	34.3
Officers:	British
Total Cabins:	600
Size Range (sq ft/m):	1698.9- 519.9/15.7–48.3
Cabins (outside view):	385
Cabins (inside — no view):	215
Cabins (single occupancy):	0
Cabins (with private balcony):	10
Cabins (wheelchair accessible):	10
Cabin Current:	110 and 220 volts
Cabin TV:	Yes
Dining Rooms:	2
Elevators:	6
Casino:	Yes
Slot Machines:	Yes
Swimming Pools (outdoors):	3
Swimming Pools (inside):	0
Whirlpools:	1
Fitness Center:	Yes
Sauna/Steam Room:	Yes/No
Massage:	Yes
Self-Service Launderette:	Yes
Movie Theater/Seats:	Yes/283
Library:	Yes
Classification Society:	Lloyd's Register

RATINGS	POSSIBLE SCORE	SCORE ACHIEVED
Ship	500	386
Accommodation	200	161
Food	400	268
Service	400	298
Cruise	500	398
TOTAL	**2,000**	**1,511**

Accommodation: Features spacious and very comfortable, well-appointed cabins, with all the essentials and good-size rectangular showers. There are, however, many inside cabins. The cabin walls and ceilings are plain and unappealing. The large Lido Deck suites are very lovely units, and provide good living space. Many cabins have one or two upper berths, which make them extremely cramped when occupied, but they are useful for families with children. As in all Princess Cruises ships, cabin service is very good. A room service menu is available 24 hours a day.

Dining: The dining rooms are brightly lit and decor is pleasant, although there are no tables for two. There are two seatings. Pasta dishes, created by the head waiters, are good, but other food lacks quality, flair, and presentation. Service, while reasonably attentive, is somewhat impersonal and superficial.

The Veranda Cafe, a popular outdoor buffet area for breakfast and lunch, is poorly designed and always congested, although some improvements have been made recently. Has a popular pizzeria.

Other Comments: This well-designed contemporary vessel has a short, sharply raked bow, and swept-back funnel. She is the first cruise ship to have steam turbine machinery since Cunard's *Queen Elizabeth 2* debuted in 1969, which means that there is almost no vibration.

The layout is comfortable, and it is easy to find one's way around. The clean, bland, clinical, yet oddly tasteful minimalist interior decor lacks warmth. There is a fine array of public rooms, including expansive shops. Improved showroom, with good visibility from all seats. The Horizon Lounge, set atop the ship, is restful at night. Split casino configuration. Features decent health spa/fitness facilities.

This ship provides a well-balanced, pleasing cruise experience for the mature passenger, with plenty of space and little crowding. British officers and a European dining crew help to create a friendly ambience.

Weak Points: Sadly, there is no wraparound promenade deck outdoors, although there is a good enclosed promenade deck.

m/s Song of Flower
★★★★ +
(S)

LIFESTYLE:	**LUXURY**
Cruise Line:	Radisson Seven Seas Cruises
Former Names:	*Explorer Starship*
Gross Tonnage:	8,282
Builder:	KMV (Norway)/Lloyd Werft (Germany)
Original Cost:	n/a
Entered Service:	1986/February 1990
Flag:	Bahamas
Tel. No.:	1310152
Fax No.:	1310153
Length (ft/m):	407.4/124.2
Beam (ft/m):	52.4/16.0
Draft (ft/m):	16.0/4.9
Propulsion/Propellers:	diesel (5,500kW)/2 (CP)
Decks:	6
Total Crew:	144
Pass. Capacity (basis 2):	198
Pass. Capacity (all berths):	198
Pass. Space Ratio (basis 2):	41.8
Pass. Space Ratio (all berths):	41.8
Officers:	Norwegian
Total Cabins:	100
Size Range (sq ft/m):	183.0–398.0/17.0–37.0
Cabins (outside view):	100
Cabins (inside — no view):	0
Cabins (single occupancy):	0
Cabins (with private balcony):	10

Cabins (wheelchair accessible):	0
Cabin Current:	220 volts
Cabin TV:	Yes
Dining Rooms:	1
Elevators:	2
Casino:	Yes
Slot Machines:	Yes
Swimming Pools (outdoors):	1
Swimming Pools (inside):	0
Whirlpools:	1
Fitness Center:	Yes
Sauna/Steam Room:	Yes/No
Massage:	Yes
Self-Service Launderette:	No
Movie Theater/Seats:	No
Library:	Yes
Classification Society:	Det Norske Veritas

RATINGS	POSSIBLE SCORE	SCORE ACHIEVED
Ship	500	405
Accommodation	200	162
Food	400	342
Service	400	344
Cruise	500	398
TOTAL	**2,000**	**1,651**

Accommodation: There are ten elegant suites; ten cabins are strictly nonsmoking. All others are well equipped, complete with bathrobes and slippers, refrigerator, and VCR unit. All come with excellent closet and drawer space. Many have bathtubs, but they are tiny (shower tubs would be a better description). Disabled passengers should choose a cabin with a shower instead of a bath. Sadly, there are no in-cabin dining facilities for dinner. When compared with the Seabourn Goddesses, Seabourn, and Silversea ships, the cabins are somewhat lacking and plain.

Dining: The dining room is really most charming and has warm colors, a welcoming ambience, and one seating, with no assigned tables. Very creative food and presentation, with small portions attractively presented. All alcoholic and nonalcoholic beverages included with the exception of some premium wines. Outstanding personal service from a warm, highly personable, and attentive staff. There are also several tables for two. Hand-scripted menus look like those one would find in an English country hotel. A new addition is an Italian alternative dining spot, called A Taste of Italy created in what was formerly the casino.

Other Comments: This is an excellent small cruise ship (originally built as the ro-ro vessel *Begonia* in 1974 and fully converted in 1986), with tall, twin funnels that give a somewhat squat profile. If only the foredeck and bow could be a little longer it would provide a more sleek appearance! She has been well maintained and cared for and is very clean throughout, although her interiors are now looking quite tired. There is a good amount of sheltered open deck and sunbathing space. Water sports facilities include snorkel equipment.

Inside, the interior decor is warm, with many pastel colors used in the public rooms, passageways, and on the stairways. High-quality soft furnishings and fabrics have been used throughout, to good effect, making the ship very comfortable, though not luxurious, by any means. The health spa facility is very compact and short on space, but is reasonably adequate.

The well-tiered showroom is good, comfortable, and has good sight lines from almost all seats. Has a fine, warm, caring staff who really do try to anticipate your needs. Totally understated elegance and warm, informal lifestyle. This ship will provide a fine, destination-intensive, yet relaxing cruise experience, delivered with a good amount of style and panache. Gratuities are included, and no further tipping is allowed, although port charges are extra.

Weak Points: Announcements for the day's activities are completely unnecessary when everything is listed in the daily program. Vibration, particularly at the stern, and at some tables in the dining room, is a problem that continues to undermine the fine standard of hospitality experienced in the overall cruise product.

CRUISING FOR HONEYMOONERS

Cruising is popular as a honeymoon vacation. The advantages are obvious: you pack and unpack only once; it is a hassle-free and crime-free environment; and you get special attention, if you want it. It is also easy to budget in advance, as one price often includes airfare, cruise, food, entertainment, several destinations, shore excursions, and pre- and post-cruise hotel stays. Once you are married, some cruise lines often offer discounts to entice you to book a future (anniversary) cruise. Just think, no cooking meals, everything will be done for you. You can think of the crew as your very own service and kitchen staff.

Cruise lines offer a variety of honeymoon packages, just as hotels and resorts on land do. Although not all cruise lines provide all services, typically they might include:

→ Private captain's cocktail party for honeymooners.

→ Tables for two in the dining room.

→ Set of crystal champagne or wine glasses.

→ Honeymoon photograph with the captain, and photo album.

→ Complimentary champagne (imported or domestic) or wine.

→ Honeymoon cruise certificate.

→ Champagne and caviar for breakfast.

→ Flowers in your suite or cabin.

→ Complimentary cake.

→ Special T-shirts.

m/s Sovereign of the Seas
★★★ +
(L)

LIFESTYLE:	STANDARD
Cruise Line:	Royal Caribbean International
Former Names:	-
Gross Tonnage:	73,192
Builder:	Chantiers de l'Atlantique (France)
Original Cost:	$183.5 million
Entered Service:	January 1988
Flag:	Norway
Tel. No.:	1310711
Fax No.:	1310711
Length (ft/m):	879.9/268.2
Beam (ft/m):	105.9/32.3
Draft (ft/m):	24.9/7.6
Propulsion/Propellers:	diesel (21,844kW)/2 (CP)
Decks:	12
Total Crew:	840
Pass. Capacity (basis 2):	2,276
Pass. Capacity (all berths):	2,744
Pass. Space Ratio (basis 2):	32.1
Pass. Space Ratio (all berths):	26.6
Officers:	Norwegian
Total Cabins:	1,138
Size Range (sq ft/m):	118.4- 446.7/11.0–41.5
Cabins (outside view):	722
Cabins (inside — no view):	416
Cabins (single occupancy):	0
Cabins (with private balcony):	0

Cabins (wheelchair accessible):	6
Cabin Current:	110 volts
Cabin TV:	Yes
Dining Rooms:	2
Elevators:	13
Casino:	Yes
Slot Machines:	Yes
Swimming Pools (outdoors):	2
Swimming Pools (inside):	0
Whirlpools:	2
Fitness Center:	Yes
Sauna/Steam Room:	Yes/No
Massage:	Yes
Self-Service Launderette:	No
Movie Theater/Seats:	Yes-2/144 each
Library:	Yes
Classification Society:	Det Norske Veritas

RATINGS	POSSIBLE SCORE	SCORE ACHIEVED
Ship	500	381
Accommodation	200	141
Food	400	244
Service	400	286
Cruise	500	334
TOTAL	**2,000**	**1,386**

Accommodation: The twelve suites on Bridge Deck are reasonably large and nicely furnished. The standard (inside and outside) cabins are very small, however, although an arched window treatment and colorful soft furnishings give the illusion of more space. Almost all cabins have twin beds that convert to a double bed configuration, with moveable bedside tables. All of the standard cabins have very little closet and drawer space; pack only a minimal amount of clothing.

Dining: Two dining rooms provide well-presented food and service, but there are no tables for two. There are two seatings. The food varies but doesn't seem to have much taste. Poor breads, rolls, and fruit selection, but a good selection of light meals, and a vegetarian menu is available. There is an adequate wine list and prices. The staff is perhaps overly friendly for some tastes.

Other Comments: This is a handsome mega-ship with well-balanced profile and nicely rounded lines. Open deck space is adequate. A Viking Crown Lounge is built around the funnel and has superb views. Has a wide wraparound outdoors polished wood deck, and there is a basketball court for sports fans.

While the interior layout is awkward (being designed in a vertical stack, with most public rooms located aft, and accommodation located forward), the ship has an impressive array of spacious and elegant public rooms. A stunning five-deck-high Centrum lobby has cascading stairways and two glass-walled elevators. There is a good two-level showroom and a decent array of shops, albeit with lots of tacky merchandise. Casino gamers will find blackjack, craps, Caribbean stud poker, and roulette tables, plus an array of slot machines.

A good range of children's and teens' programs and counselors. The dress code is very casual.

This floating resort provides a well-tuned, yet very impersonal short cruise experience, for a lot of passengers. The ship was extensively refurbished in 1997, when some 220 new third and fourth berths were added to increase capacity to over 2,700, and the shopping area was increased. Also added were more seats in the dining rooms. Features three- and four-night cruises to the Bahamas year-round, from Miami.

Weak Points: There is congested passenger flow in some areas. There are too many announcements.

i/b Sovetskiy Soyuz
★★★ +
(S)

LIFESTYLE: **STANDARD**

Cruise Line: Murmansk Shipping/Quark Expeditions
Former Names: -
Gross Tonnage: 20,646
Builder: Baltic Shipyard, Murmansk (Russia)
Original Cost: $150 million
Entered Service: December 1989
Flag: Russia
Tel. No.:   1402512
Fax No.:   1401511
Length (ft/m):   492.1/150.0
Beam (ft/m):   98.4/30.0
Draft (ft/m):   36.0/11.0
Propulsion/Propellers: nuclear-powered
     turbo-electric (55,950kW)/3 (CP)
Decks: 4
Total Crew: 130
Pass. Capacity (basis 2):   100
Pass. Capacity (all berths):   100
Pass. Space Ratio (basis 2):   206.4
Pass. Space Ratio (all berths):   206.4
Officers: Russian/Ukrainian
Total Cabins: 50
Size Range (sq ft/m):   130.0–300.0/14.3–27.8
Cabins (outside view):   50
Cabins (inside — no view):   0
Cabins (single occupancy):   0
Cabins (with private balcony):   0

Cabins (wheelchair accessible):   0
Cabin Current: 220 volts
Cabin TV: Yes
Dining Rooms: 1
Elevators: 0
Casino: No
Slot Machines: No
Swimming Pools (inside):   1
Whirlpools: 0
Fitness Center: Yes
Sauna/Steam Room: Yes-2/No
Massage: No
Self-Service Launderette: Yes
Lecture/Film Room: Yes (seats 100)
Library: Yes
Zodiacs: 4
Helicopter Pad: 2 helicopters for passenger use
Classification Society: RS

RATINGS	POSSIBLE SCORE	SCORE ACHIEVED
Ship	500	319
Accommodation	200	135
Food	400	244
Service	400	250
Cruise	500	344
TOTAL	**2,000**	**1,292**

Accommodation: All of the cabins are generously sized (considering the type of specialized vessel this is), and all are outside, with private facilities, VCR, and refrigerator. There is, however, a limited amount of closet and drawer space in most cabins. The bathrooms are small and utilitarian, and you will need to take your own favorite toiletry items.

Dining: Has a nicely appointed dining room. There is one seating and tables are not assigned, so you can sit and dine where and with whom you please. When the ship is under charter to Quark Expeditions, the catering is provided by a Swedish company, and the cuisine is surprisingly hearty, with plenty of meat and potato dishes, but little fruit and cheese. Remember that these are not meant to be gourmet cruises, but the food is actually decent, and there is certainly plenty of it.

Other Comments: The ultimate in technology accompanies this special ship, one of a fleet of the world's most powerful ice breakers. Two helicopters are carried for reconnaissance and passenger sightseeing use (their use is included in the expedition cruise fare).

Rugged, unpretentious, yet surprisingly comfortable surroundings prevail inside. There are two lounges to choose from. A tiered lecture theater with stage is the setting for a team of biologists, scientists, geologists, and other lecturers. There is also a heated indoor pool. Attentive and friendly Russian service is provided. Passengers are also allowed on the bridge at all times.

Yamal is another (out of a series of six built between 1959 and 1993) of these incredible nuclear-powered icebreakers that is often under charter to expedition cruise companies. She really is an incredible vessel, with a three-inch thick reinforced bow for negotiating tough ice conditions (it really is noisy when ploughing through ice, of course). Carries enough fuel for four years without refueling! This is undoubtedly one of the most exciting, seat-of-your-pants expedition cruise experiences available today.

m/s Splendour of the Seas
★★★★
(L)

LIFESTYLE:	STANDARD
Cruise Line:	Royal Caribbean International
Former Names:	-
Gross Tonnage:	69,130
Builder:	Chantiers de l'Atlantique (France)
Original Cost:	$325 million
Entered Service:	March 1996
Flag:	Norway
Tel. No.:	1316155
Fax No.:	1316156
Length (ft/m):	867.0/264.20
Beam (ft/m):	105.0/32.00
Draft (ft/m):	23.9/7.3
Propulsion/Propellers:	diesel (40,200kW)/2 (CP)
Decks:	11
Total Crew:	720
Pass. Capacity (basis 2):	1,804
Pass. Capacity (all berths):	2,064
Pass. Space Ratio (basis 2):	38.3
Pass. Space Ratio (all berths):	33.4
Officers:	Norwegian
Total Cabins:	902
Size Range (sq ft/m):	137.7–1,147.4/12.8–106.6
Cabins (outside view):	575
Cabins (inside — no view):	327
Cabins (single occupancy):	0
Cabins (with private balcony):	231

Cabins (wheelchair accessible):	17
Cabin Current:	110 and 220 volts
Cabin TV:	Yes
Dining Rooms:	1
Elevators:	11
Casino:	Yes
Slot Machines:	Yes
Swimming Pools (outdoors):	1
Swimming Pools (inside):	indoor/outdoor with sliding roof
Whirlpools:	4
Fitness Center:	Yes
Sauna/Steam Room:	Yes/Yes
Massage:	Yes
Self-Service Launderette:	No
Movie Theater/Seats:	No
Library:	Yes
Classification Society:	Det Norske Veritas

RATINGS	POSSIBLE SCORE	SCORE ACHIEVED
Ship	500	432
Accommodation	200	169
Food	400	246
Service	400	289
Cruise	500	386
TOTAL	**2,000**	**1,522**

Accommodation: The 17 cabin categories really are far too many to deal with, but in this ship even the standard cabins are of a good size. All cabins have a sitting area, and beds that convert to double configuration, and there is ample closet and drawer space, although there is not much space around the bed (bathroom showers are disappointing). There are sadly no cabins for singles.

Dining: Dramatic 20-foot-high glass side walls in the large, two-deck-high dining room. There are two seatings. There is also a large indoor-outdoor cafe, and a good-size snack area, providing more informal dining choices. Menus presentation and food choices were much improved in the last couple of years. Full vegetarian menus. Consistently adequate food and service, with smartly dressed, attentive waiters.

Other Comments: This large ship has a nicely raked bow. With engines midships, vibration and noise are kept low, and the ship's maximum 24-knot speed means she is well equipped for long-distance itineraries. There is an expansive use of glass throughout the ship's uppermost decks, which provides passengers with some contact with the sea. Passengers who enjoy golf might find the (extra charge) 18-hole, 6,000-sq-ft (557.5 m²) miniature golf fun; the holes themselves are 155–230 sq ft (14.3–21.4 m²).

Inside, the decor is stunning, contemporary, and very colorful. There are two entertainment decks to play on. Excellent tiered and balconied two-deck-high show lounge has excellent sight lines and comfortable seats; several large-scale production shows are provided; and an orchestra pit can be raised or lowered as required. Dazzling casino (lots of mirrored surfaces and colored lights). A seven-deck-high atrium connects with the impressive Viking Crown Lounge via glass-walled elevators. The library is a fine facility, with over 2,000 books. A fine collection of artwork, with a common nautical/solar theme throughout.

See in-depth comments for sister ship *Legend of the Seas*. This is a well-integrated, fine-tuned, comfortable and well-liked product, for first-time passengers.

<u>Weak Points</u>: Constant music in public hallways and all open decks is difficult to get away from. There are too many announcements by too many untrained staff.

m/v Star Aquarius
★★★ +
(L)

LIFESTYLE:	STANDARD
Cruise Line:	Star Cruises
Former Names: *Langkapuri Star Aquarius, Athena*	
Gross Tonnage:	40,022
Builder:	Wartsila (Finland)
Original Cost:	SEK650 million
Entered Service:	April 1989/December 1993
Flag:	Panama
Tel. No.:	02011719543
Fax No.:	02011719514
Length (ft/m):	579.3/176.6
Beam (ft/m):	97.1/29.6
Draft (ft/m):	20.3/6.2
Propulsion/Propellers:	diesel (23,760kW)/2 (CP)
Decks:	12
Total Crew:	750
Pass. Capacity (basis 2):	1,530
Pass. Capacity (all berths):	1,900
Pass. Space Ratio (basis 2):	26.1
Pass. Space Ratio (all berths):	21.0
Officers:	Scandinavian
Total Cabins:	718
Size Range (sq ft/m):	67.8–145.3/6.3–13.5
Cabins (outside view):	303
Cabins (inside — no view):	415
Cabins (single occupancy):	42
Cabins (with private balcony):	0

Cabins (wheelchair accessible):	6
Cabin Current:	220 volts
Cabin TV:	Yes
Dining Rooms:	4 (+3 cafes)
Elevators:	5
Casino:	Yes
Slot Machines:	Yes
Swimming Pools (outdoors):	1
Swimming Pools (inside):	1
Whirlpools:	6
Fitness Center:	Yes
Sauna/Steam Room:	Yes/Yes
Massage:	Yes
Self-Service Launderette:	No
Movie Theater/Seats:	No
Library:	Yes
Classification Society:	Det Norske Veritas

RATINGS	POSSIBLE SCORE	SCORE ACHIEVED
Ship	500	323
Accommodation	200	130
Food	400	289
Service	400	305
Cruise	500	330
TOTAL	**2,000**	**1,377**

Accommodation: Except for some very large suites for top-paying passengers, the cabins are very small (the ship was originally built as a Baltic ferry), and come with just basic facilities (some are for families, with quad occupancy), and very little drawer space. The standard cabin bathrooms are very small.

The top suites, each of which is decorated in luxurious materials, feature two bathrooms, butler service, a private club meeting room, private sun deck, and spa.

Dining: With seven restaurants to choose from, there is a wide choice of cuisine and dining styles. The Ocean Palace is a Chinese restaurant (featuring Cantonese and Sichuan cuisine) — it features a Hong Kong chef and live fish tanks from which to select your seafood, as well as private dining rooms. Kamogawa Japanese restaurant includes a sushi bar and waitresses in kimonos, as well as private tatami rooms. Marco Polo (Italian) restaurant features candlelight dining. Spice Island buffet restaurant is for laksa, satay, and hawker delights. Mariner buffet has food to choose from large open-concept kitchen stalls, and children's buffet. Castaway Cafe features afternoon teas and coffees. Blue Lagoon offers fast-food snacks (open 24 hours a day) and noodles.

There are more choices for food and dining options aboard this ship than most other current cruise ships, and the choice is particularly good for families with children. *Note*: Your cruise fare includes only basic buffet meals — all other restaurants are à la carte, and fairly expensive.

Other Comments: This ex-Viking Line ferry was skillfully converted into a cruise vessel specifically for the Asian family market, with a reduction in berths to 1,900 (from 2,200). The ship sports a stunning deep-blue hull and a blue band around the funnel base. Scandinavian design is combined with a touch of the Orient. This ship even has a helipad. She features a large duty-free shopping center and supermarket, and there is an imperial casino for gambling VIPs, with a 13-feet-high, finely detailed ceiling, and regal decor (there is also a second casino for general passenger use). Has a karaoke lounge and eight private karaoke rooms.

Besides a general Universe Fitness and Health Bar (with juice bar and low-calorie items), there is also a superb health club for men (King Neptune), offering an extensive range of features and facilities, including a gymnasium, indoor pool and two whirlpools, plus all massage, steam, and sauna facilities.

There are 11 meeting rooms (all have audiovisual facilities), two conference auditoriums and a business center, with full secretarial support, computers, fax, telex, and copy machines. There are really good, extensive family facilities for children and teens, including a wide assortment of computers and video game machines in the huge children's entertainment and play center. Where this ship really scores is in its programming, with a wide range and variety of activities for the whole family, so its Asian passengers will never be bored. There is also free ice cream for kids.

However, such a high-density ship means very crowded public rooms, lots of noise, and long lines for shore visits, buffets, embarkation, and disembarkation. The amount of open deck space is rather limited (most Asians, however, spend little time in the sun).

Finally, with a low, very attractive ticket price, everything on board (including food, except for the buffet restaurant) costs extra, so a cruise for the family can end up being quite expensive. The ship does, however, offer a tremendous number of choices for the whole family, and the service and hospitality is good. The ship operates short cruises from Taiwan. All gratuities are included.

s/v **Star Clipper**
★★★★
(S)

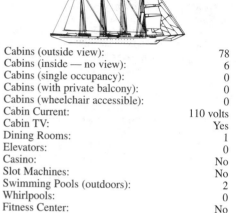

LIFESTYLE:	STANDARD
Cruise Line:	Star Clippers
Former Names:	-
Gross Tonnage:	3,025
Builder:	Scheepswerven van Langerbrugge (Belgium)
Original Cost:	$30 million
Entered Service:	May 1992
Flag:	Luxembourg
Tel. No.:	1253210
Fax No.:	1253206
Length (ft/m):	366.1/111.6
Beam (ft/m):	49.2/15.0
Draft (ft/m):	17.7/5.6
Type of Vessel:	barkentine schooner
No. of Masts:	4 (208 ft)
Sail Area (sq ft/sq m):	36,221/3,365/
	16 manually furled sails
Main Propulsion:	sail power
Propulsion/Propellers:	diesel (1,030kW)/1 (CP)
Decks:	4
Total Crew:	72
Pass. Capacity (basis 2):	168
Pass. Capacity (all berths):	180
Pass. Space Ratio (basis 2):	18.0
Pass. Space Ratio (all berths):	16.8
Officers:	European
Total Cabins:	84
Size Range (sq ft/m):	95.0–150.0/8.8–14.0

Cabins (outside view):	78
Cabins (inside — no view):	6
Cabins (single occupancy):	0
Cabins (with private balcony):	0
Cabins (wheelchair accessible):	0
Cabin Current:	110 volts
Cabin TV:	Yes
Dining Rooms:	1
Elevators:	0
Casino:	No
Slot Machines:	No
Swimming Pools (outdoors):	2
Whirlpools:	0
Fitness Center:	No
Sauna/Steam Room:	No/No
Massage:	No
Self-Service Launderette:	No
Library:	Yes
Classification Society:	Lloyd's Register

RATINGS	POSSIBLE SCORE	SCORE ACHIEVED
Ship	500	396
Accommodation	200	157
Food	400	288
Service	400	296
Cruise	500	393
TOTAL	**2,000**	**1,530**

Accommodation: Has well-equipped, comfortable, contemporary cabins that feature wood-trimmed cabinetry and wall-to-wall carpeting, two-channel audio, color television, lockable personal safe, and full-length mirrors. The bathrooms are compact units, feature gray marble tiling, toiletries cabinet, and some under-shelf storage space. The shower is a push-button affair, timed for a short shower (this can prove frustrating when trying to wash your hair, but is typical of vessels built as true sailing ships). There is no "lip" to prevent water from the shower from moving over the bathroom floor. The bed linen is of a mix of 50 percent cotton and 50 percent polyester. A few cabins have a third, upper pullman-style berth.

The deluxe cabins also feature a full-sized bathtub and mini-bar/refrigerator. Note that there is no cabin food or beverage service.

Dining: The dining room is quite attractive, and features lots of wood accenting and nautical decor. Buffet breakfasts and lunches are featured, together with a mix of buffet and à la carte dinners (generally a choice of two entrées). There is one seating. The seating arrangement (mostly with tables of six) makes it difficult for waiters to serve properly. However, it is in an open seating arrangement, so you can dine with whomever you wish, and this *is* supposed to be a casual experience. While cuisine aboard the Star Clippers is perhaps less than the advertised "gourmet" excellence (as far as presentation and choice are concerned), it is nevertheless fairly creative, and one has to take into account the tiny galley provided.

Perhaps fewer passenger cabins and more room in the galley would have enabled the chefs to provide a better dining experience than the present arrangement. There is a limited choice of bread rolls, pastry items, and fruits.

Tea and coffee should be, but is not, available 24 hours a day, particularly in view of the fact that there is no cabin food service at all. When it is available, paper cups are provided (real china would be better).

Other Comments: This is one of a pair of almost identical tall ships; it is a sailing vessel with cruise accommodation that evokes memories of the 19th-century clipper sailing ships. Accurate four-masted barkentine-

440

rigged vessel with graceful lines, a finely shaped hull and masts that are 19.3 m tall. Breathtaking when under full sail, she displays excellent sea manners. This working clipper ship relies on the wind about 80 percent of the time. A diesel engine is used as backup in emergencies, for generating electrical power, and for desalinating the approximately 40 tonnes of seawater each day for shipboard needs. The crew performs almost every task, including hoisting, trimming, winching, and repairing the sails.

Water sports facilities include a water ski boat, sunfish, scuba, and snorkel equipment, and eight Zodiac infatable craft. Sports directors provide basic dive instruction (for a fee).

The whole cruise experience evokes the feeling of sailing aboard some famous private yacht at the turn of the century. *Star Flyer* (sister to *Star Clipper*), the first clipper sailing ship to be built for 140 years, became the first commercial sailing vessel to cross the North Atlantic in 90 years

Some of the amenities of large modern cruise vessels are provided, such as air-conditioning, cashless cruising, occasional live music, a small shop, and a pool to "swim" in. Inside the vessel, classic Edwardian nautical decor throughout is clean, warm, intimate, and inviting. The paneled library has a fireplace, and chairs that are supremely comfortable. A cruise aboard her means no lines, no hassle, and "Sailing a Square Rigger" classes are a part of every cruise.

Each morning, passengers gather for "captain's story-time" — normally held on an open deck area adjacent to the bar — which, incidentally, has a fine collection of single malt whiskies. The captain also explains sailing maneuvers when changing the rigging or directing the ship as it sails into port, and notes the important events of the day. Passengers are encouraged to lend a hand, pulling on thick ropes to haul up the main sail. And they love it.

The vessel provides a carefree sailing cruise experience in a totally casual, unstructured setting at a modest price. Take minimal clothing: short-sleeved shirts and shorts for the men, shorts and tops for the ladies are the order of the day (and night). No jackets, ties, high-heeled shoes, cocktail dresses, or the slightest hint of formal wear. The deck crew consists of real sailors, brought up with yachts and tall ships — and most would not set foot aboard a cruise ship.

Star Clipper and *Star Flyer* promote total informality. They are really fine experiences, and highly recommended for even the most jaded cruisegoer. It is no exaggeration to say that to be aboard either *Star Clipper* or *Star Flyer* is to seem to have died and gone to yachtsman's heaven.

Weak Points: This ship is not for the physically impaired or children. The internal stairs are steep, as in most sailing vessels. The tipping system, where all tips are pooled (the suggested amount is $8 per passenger, per day), causes concern for many passengers.

s/v **Star Flyer**
★★★★
(S)

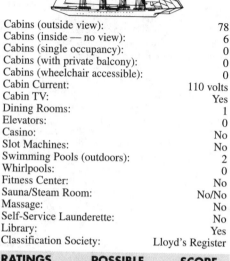

LIFESTYLE:	STANDARD
Cruise Line:	Star Clippers
Former Names:	-
Gross Tonnage:	3,025
Builder:	Scheepswerven van Langerbrugge (Belgium)
Original Cost:	$25 million
Entered Service:	July 1991
Flag:	Luxembourg
Tel. No.:	1546232
Fax No.:	1546231
Length (ft/m):	366.1/111.6
Beam (ft/m):	49.2/15.0
Draft (ft/m):	17.7/5.6
Type of Vessel:	barkentine schooner
No. of Masts:	4 (208 ft)
Sail Area (sq ft/sq m):	36,221/3,365/
	16 manually furled sails
Main Propulsion:	sail power
Propulsion/Propellers:	diesel (1,030kW)/1 (CP)
Decks:	4
Total Crew:	72
Pass. Capacity (basis 2):	168
Pass. Capacity (all berths):	180
Pass. Space Ratio (basis 2):	18.0
Pass. Space Ratio (all berths):	16.8
Officers:	European
Total Cabins:	84
Size Range (sq ft/m):	95.0–150.0/8.8–14.0

Cabins (outside view):	78
Cabins (inside — no view):	6
Cabins (single occupancy):	0
Cabins (with private balcony):	0
Cabins (wheelchair accessible):	0
Cabin Current:	110 volts
Cabin TV:	Yes
Dining Rooms:	1
Elevators:	0
Casino:	No
Slot Machines:	No
Swimming Pools (outdoors):	2
Whirlpools:	0
Fitness Center:	No
Sauna/Steam Room:	No/No
Massage:	No
Self-Service Launderette:	No
Library:	Yes
Classification Society:	Lloyd's Register

RATINGS	POSSIBLE SCORE	SCORE ACHIEVED
Ship	500	396
Accommodation	200	157
Food	400	288
Service	400	296
Cruise	500	393
TOTAL	**2,000**	**1,530**

For comments, see *Star Clipper*.

m/v Star Pisces
★★★ +
(L)

LIFESTYLE:	STANDARD
Cruise Line:	Star Cruises
Former Names:	*Kalypso*
Gross Tonnage:	40,012
Builder:	Wartsila (Finland)
Original Cost:	SEK650 million
Flag:	Panama
Tel. No.:	635286122
Fax No.:	635286111
Length (ft/m):	579.3/176.6
Beam (ft/m):	97.1/29.6
Draft (ft/m):	20.3/6.2
Propulsion/Propellers:	diesel (23,760kW)/2 (CP)
Decks:	12
Total Crew:	750
Pass. Capacity (basis 2):	1,530
Pass. Capacity (all berths):	2,000
Pass. Space Ratio (basis 2):	26.1
Pass. Space Ratio (all berths):	20.0
Officers:	Scandinavian
Total Cabins:	598
Size Range (sq ft/m):	67.8–145.3/6.3–13.5
Cabins (outside view):	258
Cabins (inside — no view):	340
Cabins (single occupancy):	0
Cabins (with private balcony):	0
Cabins (wheelchair accessible):	0

Cabin Current:	220 volts
Cabin TV:	Yes
Dining Rooms:	5 (+2 cafes)
Elevators:	5
Casino:	Yes
Slot Machines:	Yes
Swimming Pools (outdoors):	1
Swimming Pools (inside):	1
Whirlpools:	3
Fitness Center:	Yes
Sauna/Steam Room:	Yes/Yes
Massage:	Yes
Self-Service Launderette:	No
Movie Theater/Seats:	No
Library:	Yes
Classification Society:	Det Norske Veritas

RATINGS	POSSIBLE SCORE	SCORE ACHIEVED
Ship	500	323
Accommodation	200	130
Food	400	289
Service	400	305
Cruise	500	330
TOTAL	**2,000**	**1,377**

Accommodation: There are six grades of accommodation. Except for some large imperial suites, almost all cabins are *extremely* small, and come with just the basic facilities. Many cabins have third- and fourth-person upper berths which are good for families who don't mind tight quarters. The cabin insulation is poor, and the bathrooms are really tiny.

Dining: There are seven restaurants that together provide a wide choice of cuisine and dining styles. A Chinese restaurant has live fish tanks from which to select your fish and seafood. A Japanese restaurant includes a sushi bar, waitresses in kimonos, and private tatami rooms. An Italian restaurant features candlelight dining. A Spice Island buffet restaurant features items such as laksa, satay, and hawker delights. In addition, there are three other snack cafes. Your cruise fare includes only the basic buffet restaurants — all other restaurants are à la carte and expensive.

Other Comments: This ship is wide and squat-looking in the water, has a Scandinavian design combined with a touch of the Orient. The large blue funnel has a single, large yellow (gold) star as the company's logo. Although the outdoor deck and sunbathing space is limited, it is little used by its Asian passengers.

There is a helipad, a huge duty-free shopping center, and a supermarket. The Regal Casino (essentially for VIPs) is large and has a high, detailed ceiling. There is also a second casino for general use. Has a fine health club for men (with many "extra" services). There are many meeting rooms, conference auditoriums, and a business center. The facilities for children are extensive and include computers and educational rooms, play areas, and a huge video machine section. Free ice cream for kids. Excellent Asian hospitality and there are lots of activities for the whole family.

Skillfully converted into a cruise vessel for the Asian family market, this ship was based on Hong Kong for several years before being moved into her new cruise area. The ship offers short cruises, with lots of Asian hospitality, choice of dining venues and styles, an abundance of karaoke and gambling opportunities, all in a modern ship with colorful surroundings. The initial ticket price is extremely low, but almost everything on board costs extra.

The ship operates short cruises from Osaka, Japan, to Korea. All gratuities are included (see also comments for *Star Aquarius*).

Weak Points: This high-density ship means that many of the public rooms will be crowded. The open deck space is poor, although this is mostly unused by Asian passengers. The cabins (and bathrooms) really are *very* small.

FAMILY REUNIONS

A cruise can provide the ideal place for a family reunion. Here are some tips to take into account when planning one.

→ Let your travel agent do the planning and make all the arrangements (ask for group discount if the total in your group adds up to more than fifteen). Make sure that together you choose the right cruise line, for the right reasons.

→ Book twelve months in advance if possible, so that you can arrange cabins close to each other (remember to arrange for everyone to be at the same dinner seating, if the ship operates two seatings).

→ If anyone in the group has a birthday or anniversary, tell your travel agent to arrange a special cake (most cruise lines do not charge extra for this). Special private parties can also be arranged, although there will be an additional cost. If the group is not too large, you may be able to request to dine at the captain's table.

→ Arrange shore excursions as a group (in some ports, private arrangements may prove unbeatable).

→ Finally, get everything in writing (particularly cabin assignments and locations.

m/s Statendam
★★★★
(L)

LIFESTYLE:	**PREMIUM**	
Cruise Line:	Holland America Line	
Former Names:	-	
Gross Tonnage:	55,451	
Builder:	Fincantieri (Italy)	
Original Cost:	$215 million	
Entered Service:	January 1993	
Flag:	The Netherlands	
Tel. No.:	1302515	
Fax No.:	1302516	
Length (ft/m):	719.4/219.3	
Beam (ft/m):	101.0/30.8	
Draft (ft/m):	24.6/7.5	
Propulsion/Propellers:	diesel-electric (34,560kW)/2 (CP)	
Decks:	10	
Total Crew:	557	
Pass. Capacity (basis 2):	1,266	
Pass. Capacity (all berths):	1,627	
Pass. Space Ratio (basis 2):	43.8	
Pass. Space Ratio (all berths):	34.0	
Officers:	Dutch	
Total Cabins:	633	
Size Range (sq ft/m):	186.2–1,124.8/17.3–104.5	
Cabins (outside view):	502	
Cabins (inside — no view):	131	
Cabins (single occupancy):	0	

Cabins (with private balcony):	150
Cabins (wheelchair accessible):	6
Cabin Current:	110 and 220 volts
Cabin TV:	Yes
Dining Rooms:	1
Elevators:	12
Casino:	Yes
Slot Machines:	Yes
Swimming Pools (outdoors):	1
Swimming Pools (inside):	1 (magrodome)
Whirlpools:	2
Fitness Center:	Yes
Sauna/Steam Room:	Yes/No
Massage:	Yes
Self-Service Launderette:	Yes
Movie Theater/Seats:	Yes/249
Library:	Yes
Classification Society:	Lloyd's Register

RATINGS	POSSIBLE SCORE	SCORE ACHIEVED
Ship	500	418
Accommodation	200	162
Food	400	281
Service	400	299
Cruise	500	388
TOTAL	**2,000**	**1,548**

This is one in a series of four ships of almost identical size and layout. For comments, see *Maasdam*.

m/s Stella Oceanis
★★ +
(S)

LIFESTYLE:	STANDARD
Cruise Line:	Royal Olympic Cruises
Former Names:	*Aphrodite*
Gross Tonnage:	6,000
Builder:	Cantieri Riuniti dell' Adriatico (Italy)
Original Cost:	n/a
Entered Service:	1965/1967
Flag:	Greece
Tel. No.:	1130471
Fax No.:	1130471
Length (ft/m):	344.9/105.14
Beam (ft/m):	55.5/16.92
Draft (ft/m):	14.9/4.56
Propulsion/Propellers:	diesel (8,090kW)/1 (CP)
Decks:	6
Total Crew:	140
Pass. Capacity (basis 2):	300
Pass. Capacity (all berths):	369
Pass. Space Ratio (basis 2):	20.0
Pass. Space Ratio (all berths):	16.2
Officers:	Greek
Total Cabins:	159
Size Range (sq ft/m):	96.0–208.0/9.0–19.3
Cabins (outside view):	113
Cabins (inside — no view):	46
Cabins (single occupancy):	0
Cabins (with private balcony):	0

Cabins (wheelchair accessible):	0
Cabin Current:	220 volts
Cabin TV:	No
Dining Rooms:	1
Elevators:	1
Casino:	No
Slot Machines:	No
Swimming Pools (outdoors):	1
Swimming Pools (inside):	0
Whirlpools:	0
Fitness Center:	No
Sauna/Steam Room:	No/No
Massage:	No
Self-Service Launderette:	No
Movie Theater/Seats:	No
Library:	Yes
Classification Society:	Lloyd's Register

RATINGS	POSSIBLE SCORE	SCORE ACHIEVED
Ship	500	265
Accommodation	200	110
Food	400	218
Service	400	247
Cruise	500	239
TOTAL	**2,000**	**1,079**

Accommodation: The cabins (there are eight categories) are small and rather plain and have limited closet and drawer space, but those on the Lido and Stella Decks have interconnecting doors. Some cabins have a full bathtub, while others have a shower only. All cabins have private bathrooms, but there is little space for personal toiletries.

Dining: The dining room is tastefully decorated and reasonably charming, although the ceiling is plain. It is small and, therefore, has two seatings. Good food, but there is really little choice, although the salads are good. Dining room seating and table assignments are done by the maître d' upon embarkation.

Other Comments: She is a tidy-looking, well-maintained ship with clean, rounded lines. Outside on deck, there is only a limited amount of open deck and sunbathing space.

The number of public rooms is limited, but this is a small ship, and the rooms are all nicely decorated, although in dated 1970s style. Perhaps the most popular room is the Plaka Taverna, which is paneled in rich woods. An intimate, casual, and friendly atmosphere prevails. Has a narrow, steep gangway in some ports of call, as do many ships that are many years old.

This ship lacks the sophistication of some of the other ships in the fleet, but is nonetheless charming. Royal Olympic Cruises (a combination of the Greek companies Epirotiki Lines and Sun Line Cruises) provides a good destination-intensive cruise experience, made better by the charming, friendly officers and crew.

The dress code is casual throughout (no formal nights). Gratuities (suggested at $9 per person per day) are pooled among the crew.

s/s **Stella Solaris**
★★★
(M)

LIFESTYLE:	STANDARD
Cruise Line:	Royal Olympic Cruises
Former Names:	*Stella V, Camboge*
Gross Tonnage:	17,832
Builder: Ateliers et Chantiers de France (France)	
Original Cost:	n/a
Entered Service:	July 1953/June 1973
Flag:	Greece
Tel. No.:	1130226
Fax No.:	1130733
Length (ft/m):	545.1/166.15
Beam (ft/m):	72.4/22.08
Draft (ft/m):	25.8/7.88
Propulsion/Propellers:	steam turbine (17,900kW)/2 (FP)
Decks:	8
Total Crew:	320
Pass. Capacity (basis 2):	620
Pass. Capacity (all berths):	700
Pass. Space Ratio (basis 2):	28.7
Pass. Space Ratio (all berths):	25.4
Officers:	Greek
Total Cabins:	329
Size Range (sq ft/m):	96.8–226.0/9.0–21.0
Cabins (outside view):	250
Cabins (inside — no view):	79
Cabins (single occupancy):	0

Cabins (with private balcony):	0
Cabins (wheelchair accessible):	0
Cabin Current:	110 and 220 volts
Cabin TV:	Yes
Dining Rooms:	1
Elevators:	3
Casino:	Yes
Slot Machines:	Yes (in separate room)
Swimming Pools (outdoors):	1
Swimming Pools (inside):	0
Whirlpools:	0
Fitness Center:	Yes
Sauna/Steam Room:	No/Yes
Massage:	Yes
Self-Service Launderette:	No
Movie Theater/Seats:	Yes/275
Library:	Yes
Classification Society:	Lloyd's Register

RATINGS	POSSIBLE SCORE	SCORE ACHIEVED
Ship	500	329
Accommodation	200	136
Food	400	213
Service	400	248
Cruise	500	267
TOTAL	**2,000**	**1,193**

Accommodation: There are 11 cabin grades (166 suites and deluxe; 163 standard inside and outside cabins). The outside cabins can best de described as adequate (particularly those on Sapphire, Ruby, and Emerald Decks), although many have what amounts to almost a full bathtub (inside cabins have very small bathrooms, however). All bathrooms have mosaic tiled floors.

The cabin decor has been only slightly changed over the years, but presently features slightly brighter fabrics and colors than previously, although the old pegboard ceilings remain as a reminder that the ship was built in the fifties. Note that the insulation between cabins and between decks is *extremely* poor. The accommodation passageways are reasonably wide, however.

The suites on Boat Deck (all have names of Greek islands) overlook the promenade deck outdoors — a feature not found aboard many ships today — and many of them have windows that can be opened. However, those located in the aft third of the ship are subject to the irritating noise of deck lounge chairs being moved on the pool deck above. There is an abundance of closet and drawer space, a vanity unit, a television (cannot be seen from the bed, only in the lounge area), and a telephone. The bathrooms come with a decent-sized bathtub, small toiletries cabinet, and hairdryer. Bathrobes may be obtained upon request (suite passengers only).

Note that many cabins located on aft on Sapphire Deck and amidships on Emerald Deck are subject to throbbing engine noise. The towels are thin, although they are of 100 percent cotton. Personal amenities provided are soap, shampoo (doubles as bath foam), and body lotion.

A room service menu with limited items, such as sandwiches and cookies and beverages, is available 24 hours a day (better selection available 7:00am to 11:00pm).

Dining: The large, high-ceilinged dining room (totally nonsmoking) has tables for four or six (although when the ship is not full, tables for two can be arranged). The room's focal point is a huge mural in shades of bronze, copper, and gold that depicts scenes from Greek mythology. There are two seatings. Features a wide variety of food, with spa and vegetarian dishes on each lunch and dinner menu. However, the food

447

has very little taste. Open seating for breakfast and lunch (a breakfast buffet is set up in the dining room, but a regular breakfast men is also available). Dining room seating and table assignments are done by the maître d' upon embarkation.

The wine list is a mixture of a couple of good wines (but poor vintages) and a selection of reasonably priced wines, including many from Greece.

The old-world service from Greek dining room stewards adds to the experience, although it is not nearly as good as it was in former years, and is far too hurried.

Informal breakfast and lunch buffets are available in the Lido Cafe (inside) adjacent to the pool, although the room is very small. The selection really is very limited, as is the food display. Breakfast features too many tinned fruits and packaged items.

The ship makes its own potato chips, revered by repeat passengers, and available in all bars on many days.

Other Comments: This ship has a traditional ship profile, with a royal blue hull and a large, attractive funnel amidships. She was originally built to carry cargo and passengers to Indonesia during the war the French waged in that area in the fifties and was then successfully converted into a cruise vessel in the early seventies.

Although she is now one of the oldest cruise ships still in existence, she is reasonably clean and tidy, although maintenance is fighting a losing battle. There is an expansive amount of open deck space, and this includes a wraparound promenade deck outdoors. Much of the teakwood decking and caulking are now well worn, but the well-polished railings are good. Has an attractive figure-eight pool and sunbathing area. The mostly Greek staff is friendly, and some of them have been with the company for many years.

Inside, the public rooms have good quality, solid furniture and fixtures, although everything has that well-worn look (sagging seats, broken springs). Sadly, there is no forward observation lounge, although there is a feeling of space and old-world grace. The elevators are large and can even accommodate wheelchairs (although access to most of the ship is awful).

There are also plenty of public restrooms, although, for some reason, many seem to be permanently locked. The fresh flowers that were formerly everywhere, are now sadly missing. The show lounge, which is combined with a bar (which itself is home to three blackjack tables) is large, with old-style chairs and banquette seating; all the shows feature cabaret-style entertainers. A health spa added a few years ago provides some much-needed facilities, although the $10 per-person charge to use the steam room (incorrectly called a Turkish Bath) is irritating.

This ship is for the much older passenger who seeks a relaxed, unhurried, and old-world cruise experience in decent, though very tired, surroundings, at reasonable cost, with reasonably friendly service, but without the hype of the more contemporary ships.

Features well-planned, interesting itineraries. There are always a number of lecturers aboard for each cruise, as well as one or two gentlemen dance "hosts." Gratuities ("suggested" at $9 per person, per day) are given to the Chief Steward, then pooled and shared among the crew.

<u>Weak Points</u>: This ship really is very tired and worn (and needs considerable financial investment to improve her interiors), and so are many of the crew, who seem to have lost the art of hospitality (unless they know you well). Gone is the grace of yesteryear. The seats in the cinema are not staggered — hence sight lines are poor. Port information literature is very limited for those who want to go ashore independently. The in-cabin audio channels are not available at night. There is no enforcement of smoking and nonsmoking areas. Vibration at the stern is irritating.

m/s Sunbird
★★★ +
(L)

LIFESTYLE:	STANDARD
Cruise Line:	Airtours Sun Cruises
Former Names:	*Song of America*
Gross Tonnage:	37,584
Builder:	Wartsila (Finland)
Original Cost:	$140 million
Entered Service:	December 1982/May 1999
Flag:	Bahamas
Tel. No.:	7323353225
Fax No.:	7323353223
Length (ft/m):	705.0/214.88
Beam (ft/m):	93.1/28.40
Draft (ft/m):	22.3/6.80
Propulsion/Propellers:	diesel (16,480kW)/2 (CP)
Decks:	11
Total Crew:	540
Pass. Capacity (basis 2):	1,432
Pass. Capacity (all berths):	1,595
Pass. Space Ratio (basis 2):	26.2
Pass. Space Ratio (all berths):	23.5
Officers:	International
Total Cabins:	716
Size Range (sq ft/m):	118.4–425.1/11.0 — 39.5
Cabins (outside view):	420
Cabins (inside — no view):	296
Cabins (single occupancy):	0
Cabins (with private balcony):	0

Cabins (wheelchair accessible):	0
Cabin Current:	110 volts
Cabin TV:	Yes
Dining Rooms:	1
Elevators:	7
Casino:	Yes
Slot Machines:	Yes
Swimming Pools (outdoors):	2
Swimming Pools (inside):	0
Whirlpools:	0
Fitness Center:	Yes
Sauna/Steam Room:	Yes/No
Massage:	Yes
Self-Service Launderette:	No
Movie Theater/Seats:	No
Library:	Yes
Classification Society:	Det Norske Veritas

RATINGS	POSSIBLE SCORE	SCORE ACHIEVED
Ship	500	329
Accommodation	200	120
Food	400	241
Service	400	259
Cruise	500	326
TOTAL	**2,000**	**1,275**

Accommodation: Accommodation is provided in just four grades (Standard, Superior, Promenade, and Deluxe) and six types, making it an easy matter to select your cabin. Most cabins are of a similar size (which is very small when compared to today's newer ships) and the insulation between them is rather poor. The cabins also have mediocre closets and very little storage space, yet somehow everyone seems to manage (the ship was built originally for Caribbean cruising). However, they really are adequate for a one-week cruise, as you will need only a small selection of mainly casual clothes (and shoes can always go under the bed, as will luggage, if it's not too fat). In the bathrooms, although they are rather cheerful, space is tight, with shower curtains that you will end up dancing with.

You can be more "exclusive" if you book one of the new deluxe suites — you will gain additional space and better, more personalized service. The additional space includes a lounge area with a coffee table and two chairs, a vanity desk, more drawers, more storage space, and a separate sleeping area that can be curtained off. Occupants also get a private balcony, private butler service, video player, and bathrobes. You will also be able to eat in your suite from the full dining room menu for breakfast, lunch, and dinner.

Do note that the cabin voltage is 110 volts, so British passengers (the majority) will need to take a US-style adapter for any electrical appliances such as a hairdryer. Note that although cabin grades are chosen when you book your cruise, the actual cabins are not assigned until you arrive at the ship. The accommodation deck hallways are also quite narrow.

Dining: The Dining Room is a large room and consists of a central (main) section and two long, narrow wings on both port and starboard sides, with large, ocean-view windows. However, the low ceiling creates a high level of ambient noise. There are two seatings. There are tables for four to eight (but, sadly, there are no tables for two). The service is average in this efficiently run dining room operation. The food is of a generally decent quality and the portions are quite substantial, although the menus are standard and deviation is difficult. Bottled water is offered (pushed), but there is an extra cost for it; the ship's own drinking water (for which there is no charge) is not provided unless requested.

For casual, self-serve breakfasts and lunches, the Veranda Cafe is the alternate choice, although the tables and seats outdoors are of white plastic.

Other Comments: This is the largest ship in the four-ship Airtours fleet. She is a smart-looking, contemporary ship with nicely rounded lines, a sharply raked bow, and a single funnel. When the ship first debuted, it was christened (named) by opera singer Beverly Sills for Royal Caribbean International, the ship's former owners (*Carousel* and *Sundream* were also purchased from the same company), although in the case of *Sunbird*, the lounge that wraps around the funnel housing was not removed. It is a fine place from which to observe the world around and below you.

The ship was acquired by the UK-based Airtours Cruises in 1999. There is a decent amount of open deck and sunbathing space (but it certainly will be crowded when the ship is full, which is most of the time), and nicely polished wooden decks and rails.

Inside, there is a good array of public rooms, mostly with musical-themed decor. The main public rooms are located just one deck up from the dining room, in a convenient horizontal layout. These include the principal show lounge, casino, and night club. There is also a small conference center for meetings and group business.

When Airtours first started in cruising, its ships were effective under the control of an outside management company. Now, however, all Airtours ships and personnel are under direct Airtours ownership and management, which means a more consistent product.

The addition of *Sunbird*, Airtours' third ship, provides more choice for all, but particularly for the many repeat passengers that Airtours Sun cruises has quickly acquired. This ship should prove to be a good choice if you are a first-time passenger seeking a well-rounded, destination-intensive cruise at a *very modest* price. The pre- and post-cruise land stays are also well organized. Airtours provides a consistent, well-tuned, and well-packaged fun product, in comfortable surroundings, and it should prove to be a good vacation that is particularly suited to couples and families with children. Airtours also has its own fleet of aircraft, and this is one reason that the company is able to offer complete cruise-air-stay packages at such low rates.

Weak Points: Like the other ships in the fleet, the space per passenger is tight when the ship is full (which is most of the time). There are too many irritating announcements and low-quality entertainment. The cabin televisions are extremely small.

m/s Sundream
★★★
(L)

LIFESTYLE:	STANDARD
Cruise Line:	Airtours Sun Cruises
Former Names:	*Song of Norway*
Gross Tonnage:	22,945
Builder:	Wartsila (Finland)
Original Cost:	$13.5 million
Entered Service:	November 1970/May 1997
Flag:	Bahamas
Tel. No.:	1310562
Fax No.:	1310562
Length (ft/m):	637.5/194.32
Beam (ft/m):	78.8/24.03
Draft (ft/m):	21.9/6.70
Propulsion/Propellers:	diesel (13,400kW)/2 (CP)
Decks:	8
Total Crew:	423
Pass. Capacity (basis 2):	1,076
Pass. Capacity (all berths):	1,257
Pass. Space Ratio (basis 2):	21.3
Pass. Space Ratio (all berths):	18.2
Officers:	International
Total Cabins:	538
Size Range (sq ft/m):	118.4–265.8/11.0–24.7
Cabins (outside view):	346
Cabins (inside — no view):	192
Cabins (single occupancy):	0
Cabins (with private balcony):	0

Cabins (wheelchair accessible):	0
Cabin Current:	110 volts
Cabin TV:	No
Dining Rooms:	1
Elevators:	4
Casino:	Yes
Slot Machines:	Yes
Swimming Pools (outdoors):	1
Swimming Pools (inside):	0
Whirlpools:	0
Fitness Center:	Yes
Sauna/Steam Room:	No/No
Massage:	No
Self-Service Launderette:	No
Movie Theater/Seats:	No
Library:	Yes
Classification Society:	Det Norske Veritas

RATINGS	POSSIBLE SCORE	SCORE ACHIEVED
Ship	500	310
Accommodation	200	115
Food	400	236
Service	400	253
Cruise	500	312
TOTAL	**2,000**	**1,226**

Accommodation: The cabins are provided in just four grades (Standard, Superior, Promenade, and Deluxe) and six types, making it an easy matter to select your accommodation. Most cabins are of a similar size (small by today's standards) and the insulation between them is rather poor. The cabins also have mediocre closets and very little storage space, yet somehow everyone seems to manage (the ship was built originally for Caribbean cruising). However, they really are adequate for a one-week cruise, as you will need only casual clothes, and, with these destination-intensive cruises, you really will not need many clothes anyway (shoes can always go under the bed). The largest cabins are named after famous explorers of the world.

The best advice is therefore to take only casual clothing and only the things you really need. Do note that cabin voltage is 110 volts, so British passengers will need to take adapters for electrical appliances such as a hairdryer. Note that although cabin grades are chosen when you book your cruise, the actual cabins are not assigned until you arrive at the ship. The accommodation deck hallways are also quite narrow.

Dining: The large King and I dining room is reasonably attractive, but noisy. There are two seatings. It is a good operation, but the food, while consistent in quality and presentation, is not memorable. The service, by friendly Filipino waiters and wine waiters, is generally adequate. There is an adequate, but limited, wine list, and the wines are almost all very young.

Other Comments: This smart ship, built originally for many years by Royal Caribbean International (then Royal Caribbean Cruise Line), has sleek modern lines, with a sharply-raked bow, and a single blue funnel, aft of which is a large amount of open deck space for sports. Has a polished wraparound wooden deck outdoors. There is a reasonable amount of open deck space, but it does get crowded when the ship is full (which is almost always), particularly around the small swimming pool.

Inside the ship, the layout is quite logical, which makes it easy to find one's way around. The decor is based on themed Broadway musicals, with fairly bright, crisp, clean colors. The passageways are not wide, but they do contain lots of artwork and wood trim. In fact, there is an abundance of artwork throughout this ship. There are several lounges and bars to choose from, most of which are located on one deck.

She is the sister ship to *Carousel* and was stretched in 1978 when she was operated by Royal Caribbean International. Airtours is now partly owned by Carnival Corporation, who also own Carnival Cruise Lines (and others). *Sundream*, which commenced operations for Airtours Sun Cruises (one of Britain's Big Three tour companies) in May 1997, caters efficiently to novice passengers with well-programmed flair, and provides an activity-filled cruise product in comfortable, but fairly busy surroundings, at very modest cruise rates for its mainly British and Canadian passengers. Features seven-night Caribbean (winter) and seven-night Mediterranean (summer) cruises. Airtours also has its own fleet of aircraft, and this is one reason that the company is able to offer complete cruise-air-stay packages at such modest rates.

Weak Points: There are many announcements. Many seats in the My Fair Lady show lounge have poor sight lines obstructed by several pillars. The cruise staff remind one of holiday camp "blue coats" with their well-meaning participation activities.

m/s Sun Princess
★★★★ +
(L)

LIFESTYLE:	PREMIUM
Cruise Line:	Princess Cruises
Former Names:	-
Gross Tonnage:	77,000
Builder:	Fincantieri (Italy)
Original Cost:	$300 million
Entered Service:	December 1995
Flag:	Liberia
Tel. No.:	1260136/363633451
Fax No.:	1260137/363633420
Length (ft/m):	856.2/261.00
Beam (ft/m):	105.8/32.25
Draft (ft/m):	26.0/7.95
Propulsion/Propellers:	diesel-electric (28,000kW)/2 (FP)
Decks:	10
Total Crew:	900
Pass. Capacity (basis 2):	1,950
Pass. Capacity (all berths):	2,250
Pass. Space Ratio (basis 2):	39.4
Pass. Space Ratio (all berths):	34.2
Officers:	Italian
Total Cabins:	975
Size Range (sq ft/m):	134.5–753.4/12.5–70.0
Cabins (outside view):	603
Cabins (inside — no view):	372
Cabins (single occupancy):	0

Cabins (with private balcony):	410
Cabins (wheelchair accessible):	19
Cabin Current:	110 and 220 volts
Cabin TV:	Yes
Dining Rooms:	2 main/3 others
Elevators:	11
Casino:	Yes
Slot Machines:	Yes
Swimming Pools (outdoors):	4
Swimming Pools (inside):	0
Whirlpools:	5
Fitness Center:	Yes
Sauna/Steam Room:	Yes/Yes
Massage:	Yes
Self-Service Launderette:	Yes
Movie Theater/Seats:	No
Library:	Yes
Classification Society:	Registro Navale Italiano

RATINGS	POSSIBLE SCORE	SCORE ACHIEVED
Ship	500	442
Accommodation	200	168
Food	400	271
Service	400	299
Cruise	500	406
TOTAL	**2,000**	**1,586**

For comments, see *Dawn Princess.*

m/s SuperStar Europe
(M)

LIFESTYLE:	**PREMIUM**
Cruise Line:	Star Cruises
Former Names:	*Europa*
Gross Tonnage:	37,012
Builder:	Bremer Vulkan (Germany)
Original Cost:	$120 million
Entered Service:	January 1982
Flag:	Bahamas
Tel. No.:	1320211/1320213
Fax No.:	1320212
Length (ft/m):	654.9/199.63
Beam (ft/m):	93.8/28.60
Draft (ft/m):	27.6/8.42
Propulsion/Propellers:	diesel (21,270kW)/2 (FP)
Passenger Decks:	10
Total Crew:	300
Pass. Capacity (basis 2):	600
Pass. Capacity (all berths):	1,000
Pass. Space Ratio (basis 2):	61.6
Pass. Space Ratio (all berths):	37.0
Officers:	Scandinavian
Total Cabins:	316
Size Range (sq ft/m):	150.6–419.8/14.0–39.0
Cabins (outside view):	260
Cabins (inside — no view):	56
Cabins (single occupancy):	32
Cabins (with private balcony):	0

Cabins (wheelchair accessible):	1
Cabin Current:	110 and 220 volts
Cabin TV:	Yes
Dining Rooms:	1
Elevators:	4
Casino:	Yes
Slot Machines:	Yes
Swimming Pools (outdoors):	2 (1 magrodome)
Swimming Pools (inside):	1 (fresh water)
Whirlpools:	0
Fitness Center:	Yes
Sauna/Steam Room:	Yes/No
Massage:	Yes
Self-Service Launderette:	Yes
Movie Theater/Seats:	No
Library:	Yes
Classification Society:	Germanischer Lloyd

RATINGS	POSSIBLE SCORE	SCORE ACHIEVED
Ship	500	NYR
Accommodation	200	NYR
Food	400	NYR
Service	400	NYR
Cruise	500	NYR
TOTAL	**2,000**	**NYR**
Expected Score Range:		**1,500-1,700**

Accommodation: All of the original cabins aboard this ship are very spacious, and all were refurbished in 1995 and refreshed in 1999. All feature illuminated closets, dark wood cabinetry with rounded edges, several full-length mirrors, color television and VCR player, a minibar/refrigerator, a personal safe, a hairdryer, and excellent cabin insulation.

The bathrooms have deep bathtubs (cabins without bathtub have a large shower enclosure), a three-head shower unit, two deep sinks, large toiletries cabinet, and handsome-sized amenities, although the bath towels are a little small. Unlike newer ships, there are no cabins with private balconies.

During a refit in 1999 (when Star Cruises acquired the ship) eight suites were added (these were formerly officers' cabins).

Dining: The dining room is large, with ocean-view windows on two sides and a good amount of space around each table. There are two seatings for meals. There is also a large, extremely varied cold table for all meals.

The cuisine is based on a standard seven-day menu cycle, with a wide variety of Asian foods provided.

Other Comments: Originally constructed for Hapag-Lloyd, she was the flagship of the German cruise industry for many years before the company ordered a replacement that came into service in September 1999. The ship's new owners, Star Cruises, purchased the ship in April 1998 and leased her back to Hapag Lloyd until July 1999, when she went into drydock to have many changes made to her exterior and interiors.

Exterior changes include a new sponson stern — added in order to comply with the newest stability regulations. She is a well-designed handsome contemporary ship that presents a well-balanced profile. There is an excellent amount of outdoor deck and sunbathing space, although the former FKK (nude sunbathing) deck has been dispensed with.

The ship was originally constructed with a wide range of good-size public rooms, most of them with high ceilings that promoted an even greater sense of spaciousness. Dark, restful colors were applied in many public rooms and cabins and subtle, hidden lighting was used throughout, particularly on the stairways. The indoor swimming pool is larger than most outdoor pools aboard new, much larger ships, with adjacent sauna, fitness/exercise center, and beauty salon.

Star Cruises has made some changes to some public rooms and open areas, while leaving others alone. A casino has been added — located in what was formerly the cinema, with a spiral stairway down to a slot machine room. There is also a small private gambling club, and, naturally for the Asian market, karaoke rooms. Eight suites have been added, and most cabins can now accommodate one or two additional persons, which means her original spacious feel has been greatly eroded in order to cater more to families with children. A children's playroom has replaced the former flower shop.

When operated by her former owners, it was the food, service, and quiet, refined ambience that her many repeat passengers enjoyed. However, the standards of service and hospitality had decreased substantially during her last year under Hapag-Lloyd — due, in part, to ever increasing union problems under the German flag.

Under Star Cruises, the ship now has European officers and mostly Asian service staff. Good service and hospitality are provided in what is a much more informal, relaxed setting, with a more casual dress code (in reality, there is no dress code, particularly for Asian passengers).

Cruises are of seven days in duration, and the ship sails year-round from Laem Chabang (the port for Pattaya, Thailand), her new homeport. This makes it possible for passengers to combine their cruise with a resort stay in Thailand. Note that international passengers flying into Bangkok will face a three- to four-hour journey to the port from the airport.

Weak Points: There are no balcony cabins. There is no wraparound promenade deck outdoors (there are, however, half-length port and starboard promenades).

m/s SuperStar Gemini
★★★ +
(M)

LIFESTYLE:	STANDARD
Cruise Line:	Star Cruises
Former Names:	*Crown Jewel*
Gross Tonnage:	19,046
Builder:	Union Navale de Levante (Spain)
Original Cost:	$100 million
Entered Service:	August 1992/July 1995
Flag:	Panama
Tel. No.:	1336652/97028549
Fax No.:	1336637/1336642
Length (ft/m):	537.4/163.81
Beam (ft/m):	73.8/22.50
Draft (ft/m):	17.7/5.40
Propulsion/Propellers:	diesel (13,200kW)/2 (CP)
Decks:	9
Total Crew:	470
Pass. Capacity (basis 2):	820
Pass. Capacity (all berths):	900
Pass. Space Ratio (basis 2):	23.2
Pass. Space Ratio (all berths):	21.1
Officers:	Scandinavian
Total Cabins:	404
Size Range (sq ft/m):	139.9–349.8/13.0 — 32.5
Cabins (outside view):	281
Cabins (inside — no view):	123
Cabins (single occupancy):	0
Cabins (with private balcony):	10

Cabins (wheelchair accessible):	4
Cabin Current:	110 and 220 volts
Cabin TV:	Yes
Dining Rooms:	1
Elevators:	4
Casino:	Yes
Slot Machines:	Yes
Swimming Pools (outdoors):	1
Swimming Pools (inside):	0
Whirlpools:	3 (2 outside/1 inside)
Fitness Center:	Yes
Sauna/Steam Room:	Yes/Yes
Massage:	Yes
Self-Service Launderette:	No
Movie Theater/Seats:	No
Library:	Yes
Classification Society:	Det Norske Veritas

RATINGS	POSSIBLE SCORE	SCORE ACHIEVED
Ship	500	360
Accommodation	200	148
Food	400	275
Service	400	283
Cruise	500	332
TOTAL	**2,000**	**1,398**

Accommodation: The standard (inside and outside) and deluxe grade cabins are small but nicely furnished, and most feature broad picture windows (note that some deluxe cabins on Deck 6 have lifeboat-obstructed views). They are practical and comfortable, with wood-trimmed accents and multicolored soft furnishings, but there is *very* little drawer space (in fact there is almost none), and the closet space is also quite tight. The bathrooms are decent for the size of the ship, and each features two small toiletries cabinets, although the shower cubicle is small. However, note the cabin soundproofing is very poor; the 100 percent cotton towels are thin; there is little room for luggage, so take only what is really necessary (casual clothing only, no formal attire needed — even the captain's gala dinner night asks for "smart casual" attire).

The Executive Suites (eight have a private balcony, although the partitions are not of the floor-to-ceiling type — so you can hear your neighbors clearly — or smell their smoke) and Junior Suites (these are really little larger than standard and deluxe cabins, but with more closet space) are nicely furnished. The sleeping area can be curtained off from the living area. A tea/coffee making set, and laser disc player are provided (only in the Executive Suites).

Bathrobes, slippers and toiletry amenities are provided in all cabins, as well as a small color television, a telephone, and bottled water.

Note: No cabins have a bathtub. Hairdryers are not supplied for any cabin category, so take your own if you need to use one. Also, there is no room service for such items as coffee or tea, nor is there a menu for snacks. The cabin numbering system and signage is confusing.

Dining: The attractive Ocean Palace dining room is located aft and has large picture windows on three sides (although the accenting in the center of the ceiling makes the room appear round). There are two seatings. It is not open for dinner each night, but is dependent on the itinerary.

The ambience is good, but there are few tables for two (most tables are for four, six, or eight). Features international cuisine with an Oriental touch, and there is open seating for all meals, except for dinner on the single "formal" night. On the six-day cruise, one night includes a barbecue outside on the pool deck (the main dining room is closed on this night). The wine list itself is reasonable, but the wines are all young and prices are high (the cost of wines and spirits in Southeast Asia is high due to high import duties), and champagne is incredibly expensive.

There is also an informal cafe, called Mariner's Buffet (a pork-free eatery). Breakfast here always includes some Southeastast Asian dishes such as Nasi Lemak and Fried Noodles, as well as western favorites. Lunch and dinner are also provided in this eatery. Australian passengers will appreciate the ample supply of Vegemite.

There is a good selection of beer, including some regional varieties, and some draft lager.

Other Comments: *SuperStar Gemini* is a handsome mid-sized cruise ship with smart exterior styling (the largest cruise vessel ever built in Spain). There is a wraparound promenade deck outdoors.

Although the fit and finish was originally poor, Star Cruises has made the ship's interiors much warmer and more colorful. Inside, the ship has a traditional layout that provides reasonable horizontal passenger flow, although the passageways are narrow. There are picture windows in almost all of the public rooms that connect passengers with the sea and the outside light. There is a fair amount of open deck and sunbathing space, including a neat area high atop the ship in front of a glass windbreak area — lovely for those balmy evenings outdoors — away from the crowds inside. Cushioned pads are provided for the deck lounge chairs.

Other features include a five-deck-high glass-walled atrium, and there is a karaoke/disco lounge. Has attractive decor, with upbeat art deco color combinations and splashy, colorful soft furnishings. The artwork is fairly plain and simple and could be improved. The fitness center/spa area is decent but quite cramped.

Communication at the Reception Desk can be frustrating — the staff has little finesse, although they are improving.

This very informal ship caters specifically to Australian, European (mainly British and German), as well as local Singaporean passengers (all announcements are in English). The ship presently operates seven-day cruises, from Singapore. The dress code is — well, there really isn't any — it's totally casual.

All in all, the company provides really good value for money cruising in a homely ship that is bright, contemporary, and very informal, although the staff is young, fresh, and needs far more training and experience in hospitality and flexibility. Gratuities are included and no further tipping is allowed. With a better-trained staff, the extra points could well put her just over into the four-star category. All in all, however, you should have an enjoyable, fun voyage for a destination-intensive week, with acceptable, but not memorable food and service.

Weak Points: The staff is poorly trained, and there is a high turnover. There are too many announcements. Music plays constantly in public spaces, hallways, and on open decks, making a relaxing cruise experience impossible.

m/s SuperStar Leo
★★★★ +
(L)

LIFESTYLE:	STANDARD
Cruise Line:	Star Cruises
Former Names:	-
Gross Tonnage:	76,800
Builder:	Meyer Werft (Germany)
Original Cost:	$350 million
Entered Service:	October 1998
Flag:	Panama
Tel. No.:	63526110/63526120/63526130
Fax No.:	335256125
Length (ft/m):	879.2/268.0
Beam (ft/m):	105.6/32.2
Draft (ft/m):	25.9/7.9
Propulsion/Propellers:	2 diesels (50,400kW)/2 (CP)
Decks:	10
Total Crew:	1,300
Pass. Capacity (basis 2):	1,974
Pass. Capacity (all berths):	2,800
Pass. Space Ratio (basis 2):	38.9
Pass. Space Ratio (all berths):	27.4
Officers:	Scandinavian
Total Cabins:	1,385
Size Range (sq ft/m):	150.6–638.3/14.0–59.3
Cabins (outside view):	608
Cabins (inside — no view):	379
Cabins (single occupancy):	0
Cabins (with private balcony):	391

Cabins (wheelchair accessible):	4
Cabin Current:	240 volts
Cabin TV:	Yes
Dining Rooms:	6
Elevators:	9
Casino:	Yes
Slot Machines:	Yes
Swimming Pools (outdoors):	2
Swimming Pools (inside):	0
Whirlpools:	4
Fitness Center:	Yes
Sauna/Steam Room:	Yes/Yes
Massage:	Yes
Self-Service Launderette:	No
Movie Theater/Seats:	Yes/973
Library:	Yes
Classification Society:	Det Norske Veritas

RATINGS	POSSIBLE SCORE	SCORE ACHIEVED
Ship	500	434
Accommodation	200	161
Food	400	338
Service	400	322
Cruise	500	417
TOTAL	**2,000**	**1,672**

Accommodation: Three whole decks of cabins feature private balconies, while two-thirds of all cabins have an outside view. Both the standard outside-view and inside (no-view) cabins really are small, although the bathrooms have a good-size shower stall (all cabins have extra berths for a third/fourth person). All cabins feature a personal safe, 100 percent cotton towels and 100 percent cotton European duvets. Bathrooms include personal toiletry items.

Choose one of the six largest suites (named Hong Kong, Malaysia, Shanghai, Singapore, Thailand, and Tokyo) and you'll have an excellent amount of private living space, with separate lounge and bedroom. Each suite has a large en-suite bathroom that is part of the bedroom and open to it, rather like the latest trend in land-based, high-cost interior architect-designed bathrooms. They feature kidney bean-shaped Jacuzzi bathtub (in the Singapore and Malaysia suites bathtubs have ocean views and a window that actually opens), two sinks, and separate shower enclosure and separate toilet. The artwork is exotic (possibly erotic) and wood-paneled walls. The Singapore and Hong Kong suites and the Malaysia and Thai suites can be combined to form a double suite (good for families with children and maid).

Choose one of the 12 Zodiac suites (each is named after a sign of the Zodiac) and you will get the second largest accommodation aboard the ship. Each suite has a separate lounge, bedroom, and bathroom and an interconnecting door to an ocean-view cabin with private balcony (good for families). All cabinetry features richly lacquered woods, large (stocked) wet bar with refrigerator, dining table (with a top that flips over to reveal a card table) and four chairs, a sofa and drink table. The bedroom is small but features a queen-size bed; there is a good amount of drawer space, although the closet space is rather tight (it contains two personal safes). The bathroom, with gorgeous mosaic tiled floor, is a good size and features a large Jacuzzi tub and separate shower stall, both with set next to ocean-view windows, as well as a separate toilet.

Dining: There is certainly plenty of choice when it comes to fine dining and informal food outlets, with a total of eight places to eat (all are nonsmoking). Four are included in the price of your cruises: Windows on the World is the equivalent of the main dining room. It seats 632 in two seatings, is two decks high at the aftmost section, and has huge cathedral-style windows set in three sections that overlook the ship's stern and wake. There are no waiter stations adjacent to the tables; they are tucked neatly away in side wings, thus avoiding the high noise levels normally found in large dining rooms. Blue Lagoon is a small, casual street café with about 24 seats, featuring noodle dishes, fried rice, and other Southeast Asian cuisine (adjacent is a karaoke street bar called The Bund). Raffles Café is a large self-serve buffet restaurant with indoor/outdoor seating for 400, and, as you might expect, pseudo-Raffles Hotel-like decor, with rattan chairs, overhead fans, and wood paneling. Garden Room Restaurant has 268 seats and features Chinese cuisine.

Three others are à la carte restaurants: Taipan is a Chinese Reastaurant, with traditional Hong Kong-themed decor and items like dim sum made from fresh, not frozen, ingredients (there are also two small private dining rooms). Shogun is a Japanese restaurant and sushi bar, for sashimi, sushi, and tempura. A section can be closed off to make the Samurai Room, with 22 seats, while a traditional tatami room has seats for eight. There's also a teppanyaki grill, with ten seats, where the chef cooks in front of you. Maxim's, a small à la carte restaurant with ocean-view windows, features fine dining in the classic French style.

In the atrium lobby there is a casual patisserie serving several types of coffees, teas, cakes, and pastries (at extra cost).

Other Comments: *SuperStar Leo* is the first new ship ordered specifically for the Asian market, now joined by sister ship *SuperStar Virgo*. Both have the distinctive red/blue funnel with gold star logo. There is a wraparound promenade deck outdoors, good for strolling. Passengers can actually stand right at the bow of this ship, with arms spread in an eagle-like position, just like the stars in the film *Titanic*. Just imagine the photographs, although for the best ones, like in in the film, you'll need to bring a helicopter! Just in case you do, there is a landing pad for helicopters.

Inside, there are two indoor boulevards (as in Carnival Cruise Lines' *Fantasy*-class ships) and a beautiful, six-deck-high central atrium lobby, with three glass-walled elevators and ample space to peruse the shops and cafes that line its inner sanctum. Indeed, the lobby is modeled after the lobby of the Hyatt Hotel in Hong Kong, with no clutter from the usual run of desks found aboard other cruise ships; instead, there is only the reception desk — no desk for shore excursions or for banking.

The interior design theme revolves around art, architecture, history, and literature. The ship has a mix of both eastern and western design and decor details, and public room names have been chosen to appeal to a mixture of Australian, European, and Asian passengers. Three stairways are each carpeted in a different color, which helps new cruise passengers find their way around easily.

The main show lounge (Moulin Rouge, with 973 seats) is two decks high (there is a separate balcony level is reserved for "club" members only), with almost no support columns to obstruct the sight lines, and a revolving stage for Broadway-style reviews. Shows that have included live tigers have given way to lavish production shows (one of which is a topless dancer "girlie" show at extra charge). The show lounge also turns into a large-screen cinema, with superb surround sound.

. A 450-seat room atop the ship is an observation lounge during the day and a night club at night, with live music. From it, a spiral stairway takes you down to a navigation bridge viewing area, where you can see the captain and bridge officers at work.

There is a business center (complete with 167-seat conference center, good for small groups) and writing room, as well as private mahjong and karaoke rooms, and a smoking room, for those who enjoy cigars and cognac. There is, of course, a shopping plaza set around the second level of the lobby.

Sports facilities include a jogging track, golf driving range, and basketball and tennis courts, as well as four levels of sunbathing decks. Health devotees will enjoy Caesar's (Cleopatra's for women) and the Nero Fitness Center, with facilities and services to pamper you (all at extra charge — even for use of the sauna and steam rooms), including Thai massage outdoors on deck.

Families with children should note that teens have their own huge video arcade, while children get to play in a wet 'n' wild aft pool (complete with pirate ship and caves) and two whirlpool tubs. Plus there's all the fun and facilities of Charlie's child-care center (open 24 hours a day), which includes a painting room, computer learning center, and small cinema. There's even a room full of cots for toddlers to use for sleepovers, and even the toilets are at a special low height. Over 15,069 sq ft (1,400 m^2) is devoted to children's facilities — all tucked well away from adult recreation areas.

Star Cruises has established a Southeast Asian (including Australia) region cruise audience for its diverse fleet of ships. *SuperStar Leo* and sister ship *SuperStar Virgo* are the first pair of newbuilds for this growing company, with more ships on order (the next pair of ships, slightly larger, is named the *Libra*-class).

Originally positioned in Singapore, *SuperStar Leo* is now based on Hong Kong for the active local market and is certainly the most stunning and luxurious of any of the ships sailing year-round from this busy Asian spot, operating short cruises to China and Vietnam.

459

The dress code is casual — very casual (no jacket and tie needed), and the ship operates under a "no-tipping" policy. While the initial cruise fare seems very reasonable, the extra costs and charges can soon mount up if you want to indulge in more than the basics. For priority check-in, disembarkation, generally better service, and accommodation, book "Balcony Class" rather than "Non-Balcony-Class." Passengers from the local Hong Kong area will cruise aboard this ship principally to gamble, and so a low priority is placed on entertainment.

<u>Weak Points</u>: The "balcony class" cabins have extremely narrow balconies. While the ship is stunning and offers a wide choice of dining venues, keeping consistency of product delivery depends on the quality of the service staff.

Exercizing on the Sports Deck of Star Cruises' **SuperStar Leo.**

m/s SuperStar Virgo
★★★★
(L)

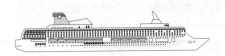

LIFESTYLE:	STANDARD
Cruise Line:	Star Cruises
Former Names:	-
Gross Tonnage:	76,800
Builder:	Meyer Werft (Germany)
Original Cost:	$350 million
Entered Service:	September 1999
Flag:	Panama
Tel. No.:	n/a
Fax No.:	n/a
Length (ft/m):	879.2/268.0
Beam (ft/m):	105.6/32.2
Draft (ft/m):	25.9/7.9
Propulsion/Propellers:	diesel (50,400kW)/2 (CP)
Decks:	10
Total Crew:	1,300
Pass. Capacity (basis 2):	1,974
Pass. Capacity (all berths):	2,800
Pass. Space Ratio (basis 2):	38.9
Pass. Space Ratio (all berths):	27.4
Officers:	Scandinavian
Total Cabins:	1,385
Size Range (sq ft/m):	150.6–638.3/14.0–59.3
Cabins (outside view):	608
Cabins (inside — no view):	379
Cabins (single occupancy):	0
Cabins (with private balcony):	391

Cabins (wheelchair accessible):	4
Cabin Current:	240 volts
Cabin TV:	Yes
Dining Rooms:	6
Elevators:	9
Casino:	Yes
Slot Machines:	Yes
Swimming Pools (outdoors):	2
Swimming Pools (inside):	0
Whirlpools:	4
Fitness Center:	Yes
Sauna/Steam Room:	Yes/Yes
Massage:	Yes
Self-Service Launderette:	No
Movie Theater/Seats:	No
Library:	Yes
Classification Society:	Det Norske Veritas

RATINGS	POSSIBLE SCORE	SCORE ACHIEVED
Ship	500	434
Accommodation	200	161
Food	400	338
Service	400	322
Cruise	500	417
TOTAL	**2,000**	**1,672**

For general comments, see *SuperStar Leo*. *SuperStar Virgo* is based in Singapore and operates Monday–Friday and Friday–Monday cruises. There is a targeted mix of 60 percent international (mainly Australian, British, German) and 40 percent local passengers on the Monday–Friday cruise and mostly Singaporean passengers (lots of families with children, who are allowed to roam around the ship uncontrolled) on the Friday–Monday cruise. There are lots of activities and entertainment and a lot of young passengers. Having these two distinct markets makes it difficult to rate the ship, and so, after sailing on both cruises, the resultant score is an average for both types of cruise and audience.

The names of the four dining spots included in the cruise fare have different names from those aboard *SuperStar Leo*. They are Bella Vista (Italian), Noble House (Chinese), The Pavilion Room, and Mediterranean Buffet (Asian/western foods).

The à la carte restaurants are Palazzo (Italian), The Taj (Indian/Vegetarian), and Samurai (Japanese), with two Teppanyaki grill rooms.

With so many dining choices (most at extra cost) it really depends on how much you are prepared to pay as to what your final cruise experience will be like. For priority check-in, disembarkation, and generally better service, book "Balcony Class" rather than "Non-Balcony-Class" accommodation.

The decor aboard *SuperStar Virgo* is much more European in design, taste, and color combinations than sister ship *SuperStar Leo*, and the layout has been changed and improved (for a slightly different market). The lobby, for example, has become an Italian piazza, with a stunning trompe l'oeil ceiling.

The dress code is casual — very casual (no jacket and tie needed), and the ship operates under a "no-tipping" policy. While the initial cruise fare seems very reasonable, the extra costs and charges can soon mount up if you want to indulge in more than the basics.

SuperStar Virgo operates two- and three-night cruises from Singapore to Malaysia and Thailand on two itineraries (summer and winter). All gratuities are included.

m/s Switzerland
★★★
(S)

LIFESTYLE:	STANDARD
Cruise Line:	Leisure Cruises
Former Names:	*Daphne, Therisos Express,*
	Port Sydney
Gross Tonnage:	15,739
Builder:	Swan, Hunter (UK)
Original Cost:	n/a
Entered Service:	March 1955/July 1975/April 1997
Flag:	Liberia
Tel. No.:	1243127/663601714
Fax No.:	66361715
Length (ft/m):	532.7/162.39
Beam (ft/m):	70.2/21.42
Draft (ft/m):	28.4/8.66
Propulsion/Propellers:	diesel (9,850kW)/2 (FP)
Decks:	7
Total Crew:	210
Pass. Capacity (basis 2):	422
Pass. Capacity (all berths):	486
Pass. Space Ratio (basis 2):	37.2
Pass. Space Ratio (all berths):	32.3
Officers:	International
Total Cabins:	211
Size Range (sq ft/m):	150.0–398.2/14.0–37.0
Cabins (outside view):	189
Cabins (inside — no view):	22
Cabins (single occupancy):	0

Cabins (with private balcony):	6
Cabins (wheelchair accessible):	0
Cabin Current:	220 volts
Cabin TV:	Yes
Dining Rooms:	1
Elevators:	2
Casino:	Yes
Slot Machines:	Yes
Swimming Pools (outdoors):	1
Swimming Pools (inside):	0
Whirlpools:	4
Fitness Center:	Yes
Sauna/Steam Room:	Yes/Yes
Massage:	Yes
Self-Service Launderette:	No
Movie Theater/Seats:	No
Library:	Yes
Classification Society:	Registro Navale Italiano

RATINGS	POSSIBLE SCORE	SCORE ACHIEVED
Ship	500	316
Accommodation	200	122
Food	400	241
Service	400	275
Cruise	500	291
TOTAL	**2,000**	**1,245**

Accommodation: This ship has some very spacious forward-facing suites (incorrectly called penthouses) as well as the more standard cabins. All have good solid fittings and heavy-duty doors. There really is plenty of closet and drawer space. The cabin insulation is not good. The cabin bathrooms are of a generous size and fitted out well, but there is no pull-out clothes line (needed for long cruises), and walls are plain. There is no room service.

The penthouse suites have a completely separate bedroom and living room, plus a balcony (passengers are brought complimentary cocktails on days at sea and have a butler service). A minibar-refrigerator is provided, but all items are at extra cost. Bathrobes and a good range of toiletry amenities are provided.

Dining: The dining room is reasonably charming and has an uncluttered seating arrangement, with several tables for two located by large picture windows (other tables are for four, six, or eight). There is a single, unhurried seating with assigned tables.

Features friendly, attentive service by Russian and Ukrainian staff. The food is not very creatively presented, but is of a good general standard, provided by a respected Swiss maritime catering company. Dinners consist of a selection of only one or two appetizers and entrees, but there is normally a good choice of cheeses. At all meals (except formal days) a salad buffet table, complete with cheese selection, is provided for lunch and dinner, although the salad selection is similar every day. Breakfast buffet is also provided in the dining room. There is also a separate informal cafe (Neptune Bar) for breakfast and lunch buffets. There is also a neat wine bar (Piazzo Vino) with a decent selection.

Other Comments: This ship (originally built for Port Line and converted into a cruise ship at a cost of $37 million in 1975) has expansive outdoor decks and plenty of sunbathing space. She was refitted and completely refurbished in early 1997 for her present owners. There is no forward-looking observation lounge and no wraparound promenade deck outdoors.

Features bright, contemporary decor in the public rooms. Has a large, fine theater, which is especially good for meetings and groups. Other public rooms have fairly high ceilings.

The ship is almost identical in outward appearance to sister ship *Princess Danae*. Originally constructed as a general cargo vessel, she was rebuilt as a cruise ship and operated for many years for Carras Cruises as *Daphne*, then by Costa Cruises, also as *Daphne*. Now owned and operated by the Swiss-based Leisure Cruises, she is a very comfortable vessel. There is much emphasis on health and fitness, with a wellness program that includes Ayurvedic treatments in the Aqua Vitalis spa and yoga and tai chi as part of the exercise program.

The use of mobile phones aboard ship is not permitted — this is good. This ship maintains an air of intimacy, has a fine range of public rooms, and should represent good value when cruising on her itineraries. The currency on board is the Swiss Franc. A 15 percent gratuity is added to all bar bills, and other gratuities are not included in the fare. Operated by Leisure Cruises, the ship is chartered at various times of the year by other organizations.

t/s Symphony
★★ +
(M)

LIFESTYLE: STANDARD

Cruise Line:	Mediterranean Shipping Cruises
Former Names:	*EnricoCosta, Enrico "C", Provence*
Gross Tonnage:	16,495
Builder:	Swan, Hunter (UK)
Original Cost:	n/a
Entered Service:	March 1951/1995
Flag:	Panama
Tel. No.:	1150561
Fax No.:	1150561
Length (ft/m):	579.0/176.49
Beam (ft/m):	73.1/22.31
Draft (ft/m):	24.6/7.52
Propulsion/Propellers:	diesel (11,768kW)/2 (FP)
Decks:	7
Total Crew:	330
Pass. Capacity (basis 2):	632
Pass. Capacity (all berths):	845
Pass. Space Ratio (basis 2):	26.0
Pass. Space Ratio (all berths):	19.5
Officers:	Italian
Total Cabins:	316
Size Range (sq ft/m):	86.1–216.3/8.0–20.1
Cabins (outside view):	159
Cabins (inside — no view):	157
Cabins (single occupancy):	0
Cabins (with private balcony):	0

Cabins (wheelchair accessible):	0
Cabin Current:	220 volts (DC)
Cabin TV:	No
Dining Rooms:	1
Elevators:	2
Casino:	Yes
Slot Machines:	Yes
Swimming Pools (outdoors):	3
Swimming Pools (inside):	0
Whirlpools:	0
Fitness Center:	No
Sauna/Steam Room:	No/No
Massage:	No
Self-Service Launderette:	No
Movie Theater/Seats:	Yes/102
Library:	No
Classification Society:	Registro Navale Italiano

RATINGS	POSSIBLE SCORE	SCORE ACHIEVED
Ship	500	243
Accommodation	200	110
Food	400	214
Service	400	235
Cruise	500	267
TOTAL	**2,000**	**1,069**

Accommodation: There are a wide variety of cabin sizes and configurations to choose from. Most of the cabins are compact but comfortable units, with tasteful pastel decor and soft furnishings to match. They have real chrome locks and keys — a throwback to her former life as an ocean liner. The accommodation passageways have wooden handrails, but inconsistent lighting quality.

Dining: The dining room is comfortable, though very noisy, but does have wooden porthole surrounds. The painted pegboard ceiling in many areas looks old and shabby and should be replaced. There are two seatings. There is good, bubbly Italian service and food, with good pasta, but other dishes lack quality and have poor presentation and consistency.

Other Comments: Has traditional ocean liner styling and a well balancd profile, preserved from her former life as a cargo-passenger liner. Has a large, single funnel. This solidly built vessel received an extensive refurbishment in 1996. She has a deep draft, and so she is reasonably stable at sea. Although there are fairly decent open deck promenade areas, there is no wraparound promenade deck.

Inside, a great amount of fine old wood paneling and brass trim throughout the ship adds some warmth and old-world elegance often lacking in many of the new breed of glitzy ships. The newer facilities added during various refurbishments are fine while others have been much upgraded. The public rooms feature what is best described as "Belle Epoque" decor and are rather smart and welcoming, but they are cerainly crowded when full.

This ship caters primarily to budget-minded European passengers looking for a Mediterranean cruise without the trimmings and carries principally Italian passengers (at least 60 percent). It offers a basic, no-frills cruise experience.

Weak Points: The ship does not have stabilizers. The ceilings are very plain and uninteresting. The entertainment is loud and of very poor quality. There are too many loud, unnecessary, and repetitious announcements.

m/s Taras Shevchenko
★ +
(M)

LIFESTYLE:	STANDARD
Cruise Line:	Ukrainian Passenger Fleet
Former Names:	-
Gross Tonnage:	20,027
Builder:	VEB Mathias Thesen (Germany)
Original Cost:	n/a
Entered Service:	April 1967/1994
Flag:	Ukraine
Tel. No.:	1400266
Fax No.:	1400266
Length (ft/m):	577.4/176.00
Beam (ft/m):	77.4/23.60
Draft (ft/m):	26.7/8.16
Propulsion/Propellers:	diesel (15,700kW)/2 (CP)
Decks:	8
Total Crew:	370
Pass. Capacity (basis 2):	574
Pass. Capacity (all berths):	712
Pass. Space Ratio (basis 2):	34.8
Pass. Space Ratio (all berths):	28.1
Officers:	Ukrainian
Total Cabins:	287
Size Range (sq ft/m):	n/a
Cabins (outside view):	287
Cabins (inside — no view):	0
Cabins (single occupancy):	0
Cabins (with private balcony):	0

Cabins (wheelchair accessible):	0
Cabin Current:	220 volts
Cabin TV:	No
Dining Rooms:	3
Elevators:	3
Casino:	Yes
Slot Machines:	Yes
Swimming Pools (outdoors):	2
Swimming Pools (inside):	1
Whirlpools:	1
Fitness Center:	Yes
Sauna/Steam Room:	Yes/No
Massage:	No
Self-Service Launderette:	Yes
Movie Theater/Seats:	Yes/130
Library:	Yes
Classification Society:	RS

RATINGS	POSSIBLE SCORE	SCORE ACHIEVED
Ship	500	184
Accommodation	200	85
Food	400	151
Service	400	185
Cruise	500	177
TOTAL	**2,000**	**782**

Accommodation: This ship has all-outside cabins that are moderately comfortable, although the storage space for luggage is limited and drawer space is really minimal. Each cabin has private facilities, although there is little space for personal toiletry items, and some of the plumbing is exposed and badly maintained.

There are ten suites, which, for the size of the ship, are very spacious and rather tastefully appointed, with plenty of closet and drawer space and large bathrooms.

Dining: The dining room is functional, nothing more, and the decor needs to be upgraded. There is one seating, with assigned tables. The food is extremely basic, yet seemingly adequate for the ship's clientele, but there is little menu choice. The dining room service is provided by nonsmiling, untrained Ukrainian waitresses. There is a poor selection of bread rolls, cheeses, and fruits, and almost nothing in the way of bar snacks.

Other Comments: *Taras Shevchenko* is a solidly constructed vessel with nicely rounded lines and a classic profile, with an all-white, ice-hardened hull. Decent amount of open deck and sunbathing space. Complete wraparound promenade deck outdoors, but there are no cushioned pads for the deck chairs, and the decks are well worn.

Inside, the ship, which has a number of public rooms, has very plain decor. The layout is disjointed and signage is poor. The ceilings in public areas are also plain and boring. Some refurbishment has upgraded the vessel somewhat and added more color. There is a spacious music salon.

This ship simply is not up to western standards. The ship was renovated in 1988 and now needs further significant refurbishing. The ship provides a very basic cruise experience at a modest rate, for a mostly French and Italian clientele. There is absolutely no finesse in either service or hospitality.

Weak Points: A musty (old potatoes) kind of odor permeates throughout the ship. The (fixed) gangway is narrow and can be steep in many ports. There is a lot of exposed plumbing — in cabin bathrooms and public restrooms, much is patched and in really poor condition. In fact, time seems to have passed this ship by.

t/t/s Topaz
★★ +
(L)

LIFESTYLE: **STANDARD**

Cruise Line:	Thomson Cruises
Former Names:	*Olympic, FiestaMarina, Carnivale, Empress of Britain, Queen Anna Maria*
Gross Tonnage:	31,500
Builder:	Fairfield Shipbuilding (UK)
Original Cost:	£7.5 million
Entered Service:	April 1956/1994
Flag:	Panama
Tel. No.:	1132333
Fax No.:	1132334
Length (ft/m):	640.0/195.08
Beam (ft/m):	87.0/26.51
Draft (ft/m):	29.0/8.84
Propulsion/Propellers:	steam turbine (22,400kW)/2 (FP)
Decks:	9
Total Crew:	550
Pass. Capacity (basis 2):	1,050
Pass. Capacity (all berths):	1,386
Pass. Space Ratio (basis 2):	30.0
Pass. Space Ratio (all berths):	22.7
Officers:	Greek
Total Cabins:	528
Size Range (sq ft/m):	100.7–301.3/9.36–28.0
Cabins (outside view):	228
Cabins (inside — no view):	300
Cabins (single occupancy):	6
Cabins (with private balcony):	0
Cabins (wheelchair accessible):	0
Cabin Current:	110 volts
Cabin TV:	Yes
Dining Rooms:	3
Elevators:	4
Casino:	Yes
Slot Machines:	Yes
Swimming Pools (outdoors):	2
Swimming Pools (inside):	1
Whirlpools:	1
Fitness Center:	Yes
Sauna/Steam Room:	No/No
Massage:	Yes
Self-Service Launderette:	No (has ironing room)
Movie Theater/Seats:	No
Library:	No
Classification Society:	Lloyd's Register

RATINGS	POSSIBLE SCORE	SCORE ACHIEVED
Ship	500	262
Accommodation	200	114
Food	400	218
Service	400	236
Cruise	500	266
TOTAL	**2,000**	**1,096**

Accommodation: There is a wide range of cabins and many different configurations (a carryover from her former days as a transatlantic liner), although they are assigned in only three categories: superior outside, standard outside, and standard inside. Most of them are actually quite small, although many come with rich wood furniture, and all of them have been redecorated at some stage. Many of the cabins have third and fourth berths — good for families with children. She is an old ship, however, and the cabin bathrooms are small, even in the five "suites." The smallest cabins are very small (particularly the bathrooms). The cabins are not assigned until the day of embarkation, so you cannot choose when you book, except for the grade of cabin you pay for.

Dining: The dining room is large, but crowded, and noisy, although it has been pleasingly redecorated. There are two seatings. The food, be aware, is certainly not for gourmets — rather being quantity instead of quality. Dining room seating and table assignments are done by the maître d' upon embarkation.

The 24-hour informal eatery (Yacht Club) is a fine piece of design, but, in practice, it is an awful operation.

Other Comments: This solidly built former ocean liner has a large funnel amidships and the "sheer" of a classic 1950s ship that has had many lives. The ship has also been through a number of refurbishments over the years (she is now over 40 years old, but has been well maintained), and spent a great deal of her former life operated by Carnival Cruise Lines. All of the lifeboats are of the open-air type and could well be updated. Teak outdoor and glass-enclosed indoor promenade decks encircle the ship.

Inside the ship, the colors are bright and stimulating, and the public rooms have jazzy decor, but it's so nice to see several public rooms with high ceilings. The casino is large for a ship that is catering principally to Europeans. Some delightful original woods and polished brass can be found throughout her public spaces, a large whirlpool has been added, and there is a colorful tiled outdoor deck.

This ship is presently under charter to Thomson Cruises, a British company that provides good basic cruise vacation in a very casual setting. This could be the right ship for a first cruise, at a very modest price, to some fascinating destinations. Do remember, however, that she *is* an old lady, and does not have the latest high-tech facilities and features.

Topaz also features Thomson's first foray into "all-inclusive" pricing, whereby all drinks, including beer and basic wines (and gratuities), are included in the cruise fare (very good for families with children, who need constant soft drinks). However, you'll pay extra for drinks from the "premium brands" list, as well as champagne. Note that shore excursions, laundry/cleaning, and purchases from the ship's shops are *not* included in the "all-inclusive" price (neither are alcoholic drinks after 2:00am).

Weak Points: The announcements and constant background music are irritating. Expect some lines (queues) for embarkation, disembarkation, buffets, and shore excursions.

SHIP TALK

Helm: the apparatus for steering a ship.

House Flag: the flag denoting the company to which a ship belongs.

Hull: the frame and body of the ship exclusive of masts or superstructure.

Leeward: the side that is sheltered from the wind.

Manifest: a list of the ship's passengers, crew, and cargo.

Nautical Mile: one sixtieth of a degree of the circumference of the earth.

Pilot: a person licensed to navigate ships into or out of a harbor or through difficult waters, and to advise the captain on handling the ship during these procedures.

Pitch: the rise and fall of a ship's bow that may occur when the ship is under way.

Port: the left side of a ship when facing forward.

Quay: berth, dock, or pier.

Rudder: a finlike device astern and below the waterline, for steering the vessel.

Screw: a ship's propeller.

Stabilizer: a gyroscopically operated retractable "fin" extending from either or both sides of the ship below the waterline to provide a more stable ride.

Starboard: the right side of the ship when facing forward.

Stern: the aftmost part of the ship that is opposite the bow.

Tender: a smaller vessel, often a lifeboat, which is used to transport passengers between the ship and shore when the vessel is at anchor.

Wake: the track of agitated water left behind a ship when in motion.

Waterline: the line along the side of a ship's hull corresponding to the water surface

Windward: the side toward which the wind blows.

Yaw: the erratic deviation from the ship's set course, usually caused by a heavy sea.

m/t/s Triton
★★ +
(M)

LIFESTYLE:	STANDARD
Cruise Line:	Royal Olympic Cruises
Former Names:	*Cunard Adventurer, Sunward II*
Gross Tonnage:	14,155
Builder:	Rotterdamsche Dry Dock (Holland)
Original Cost:	n/a
Entered Service:	October 1971/May 1992
Flag:	Greece
Tel. No.:	1131266
Fax No.:	1131266
Length (ft/m):	491.1/149.70
Beam (ft/m):	70.5/21.50
Draft (ft/m):	19.22/5.86
Propulsion/Propellers:	diesel (19,860kW)/2 (CP)
Decks:	7
Total Crew:	265
Pass. Capacity (basis 2):	756
Pass. Capacity (all berths):	945
Pass. Space Ratio (basis 2):	18.7
Pass. Space Ratio (all berths):	14.9
Officers:	Greek
Total Cabins:	378
Size Range (sq ft/m):	118.4–131.3/11.0–12.2
Cabins (outside view):	236
Cabins (inside — no view):	142
Cabins (single occupancy):	0
Cabins (with private balcony):	0

Cabins (wheelchair accessible):	0
Cabin Current:	110 and 220 volts
Cabin TV:	No
Dining Rooms:	1
Elevators:	2
Casino:	Yes
Slot Machines:	Yes
Swimming Pools (outdoors):	1
Swimming Pools (inside):	0
Whirlpools:	0
Fitness Center:	Yes
Sauna/Steam Room:	Yes/No
Massage:	Yes
Self-Service Launderette:	No
Movie Theater/Seats:	Yes/96
Library:	No
Classification Society:	Lloyd's Register

RATINGS	POSSIBLE SCORE	SCORE ACHIEVED
Ship	500	278
Accommodation	200	96
Food	400	205
Service	400	226
Cruise	500	242
TOTAL	**2,000**	**1,047**

Accommodation: Features cabins in eight grades, most of which are small (narrow) and basic. The closet and drawer space (the drawers are rather tinny) is minimal, and cabin soundproofing is very poor. There are 32 cabins (in the two highest grades) with a bathtub/shower, otherwise the cabin bathrooms have very small shower units, and little space for personal toiletry items (however, the ship operates short cruises, so you won't need to take much).

Dining: While the dining room is reasonably attractive and has contemporary colors and ambience, it is also very noisy. There are two seatings for dinner on most nights (open seating for the first night of the cruise), and open seating for breakfast and lunch. The cuisine is continental, which means much use of oils and salt. The choice is reasonable, but the presentation is spotty and inconsistent. Limited choice of bread rolls and fruits. The Greek dining room staff provides service that can be best described as selectively friendly, but it is hurried. Dining room seating and table assignments are done by the maître d' upon embarkation.

Casual breakfast and lunch (with limited choices) can also be taken outside on deck adjacent to the swimming pool, or in the main lounge when the weather is inclement.

Other Comments: This ship, originally built for Cunard/Overseas National Airways for informal cruises, has a reasonably handsome profile, a deep clipper bow, and twin funnels. The ship has been fairly well maintained, although she is now showing her age. There is a wraparound painted steel outdoors promenade deck of sorts, as well as a decent amount of open deck space for sunbathing, and a small kidney-shaped swimming pool, although space is extremely tight when the ship is full (which is most of the time). Much of the open space outdoors is covered by canvas awnings, much appreciated by many passengers as a shelter from the intensity of the summer sun.

Inside, a good general layout and passenger flow makes it easy to find your way around in a short time. There is a good choice of public rooms, most of which are dressed in cheerful, warm colors. However, the decor and artwork is eclectic, some of it left over from the ship's former days with Norwegian Cruise Line and Cunard, while the deck names are Greek. Has a good night club with forward observation views.

The show lounge is a single level room, with sight lines obstructed by six pillars and the fact that there is no sloping floor, so only those passengers seated in the first few rows can see below waist level. There is no library (although there is a token gesture of two unkempt bookcases with a few old paperbacks).

On one of the upper decks, a dance floor is provided outdoors, with a bar by the name of Jailhouse Rock — good for lively nights under the summer stars (but not used early and late in the season when the weather is cooler).

These destination-intensive itineraries (typically from April to November) are excellent for those who want to see many places in a short time (there are two ports of call on most days), but, be warned, they are *extremely* busy, particularly on the first day (there are no days at sea). In other words, these three- and four-night cruises are not for relaxing, but are for sightseeing.

Triton is a decent down-home ship for short cruises around the Greek islands and Mediterranean. The dress code is very casual throughout (there are no formal nights), so leave your coats and ties and long dresses at home, as you simply do not need them. Gratuities (suggested at $8 per person, per day) are pooled among the crew on the last day.

Forget about such things as chocolates on your pillow and the other niceties associated with cruising aboard other cruise lines. This one will get you around the Greek islands in low-budget surroundings, with food that is more quantity than quality and service that is mostly indifferent. *Note*: with two sets of passengers each week it is hard to provide friendly contact.

Weak Points: This really is a high-density ship with crowded public areas. Expect lines for buffets and shore excursions. There are too many announcements for tours, in many languages, when in ports of call. The nature of the Greek island cruises means that crew contracts are seasonal, and, at the end of the season (end of October/beginning of November) most crew members are tired and clearly want to go home — and it shows — to the detriment of the product.

m/s Tropicale
★★★
(L)

LIFESTYLE:	STANDARD
Cruise Line:	Carnival Cruise Lines
Former Names:	-
Gross Tonnage:	36,674
Builder:	Aalborg Vaerft (Denmark)
Original Cost:	$100 million
Entered Service:	January 1982
Flag:	Liberia
Tel. No.:	1240561
Fax No.:	n/a
Length (ft/m):	671.7/204.76
Beam (ft/m):	86.7/26.45
Draft (ft/m):	23.3/7.11
Propulsion/Propellers:	diesel (19,566kW)/2 (CP)
Decks:	10
Total Crew:	550
Pass. Capacity (basis 2):	1,022
Pass. Capacity (all berths):	1,400
Pass. Space Ratio (basis 2):	35.8
Pass. Space Ratio (all berths):	26.1
Officers:	Italian
Total Cabins:	511
Size Range (sq ft/m):	180.0–350.0/16.7–32.5
Cabins (outside view):	324
Cabins (inside — no view):	187
Cabins (single occupancy):	0
Cabins (with private balcony):	12

Cabins (wheelchair accessible):	11
Cabin Current:	110 volts
Cabin TV:	Yes
Dining Rooms:	1
Elevators:	8
Casino:	Yes
Slot Machines:	Yes
Swimming Pools (outdoors):	3
Swimming Pools (inside):	0
Whirlpools:	0
Fitness Center:	Yes
Sauna/Steam Room:	Yes/No
Massage:	Yes
Self-Service Launderette:	Yes
Movie Theater/Seats:	No
Library:	Yes
Classification Society:	Lloyd's Register

RATINGS	POSSIBLE SCORE	SCORE ACHIEVED
Ship	500	314
Accommodation	200	121
Food	400	217
Service	400	268
Cruise	500	319
TOTAL	**2,000**	**1,239**

Accommodation: Most of the inside and outside cabins are of the standard cookie-cutter variety, with little imaginative decor and just enough closet and drawer space for passengers to manage for a week.

Dining: The dining room is located on a lower deck. It is colorful, cheerful, brightly lit, but *very* noisy and cramped, and there are no tables for two. There are two seatings. The cuisine is reasonably adequate fare, with emphasis on quantity but not quality (it looks better than it tastes). Service is very hurried and without finesse, but it is reasonably cheerful. The buffets are nothing special. The wine list is decent, although there are no wine waiters.

Other Comments: This ship, the first newbuild for Carnival Cruise Lines, has a fairly distinctive contemporary look, with a single large, wing-tipped funnel in Carnival's red, white, and blue colors.

The interior design is well laid-out, and the ship has good passenger flow. The public rooms are decorated in stimulating colors throughout, wich are designed to make everyone excited and thus head for the casino, where the action is always lively. This is the only ship in the present fleet that has a movie theater.

Tropicale is a good ship for families with children, as the company goes out of its way to entertain young cruisers as well as their parents.

When the ship was built and introduced, it heralded the new-look for Carnival Cruise Lines. Now, however, the ship looks decidedly dated, the young disco-crowd "fun ship" theme having worn thin when compared with the newer, larger ships in the fleet (and other ships). This is *not* a luxury cruise product, nor does it pretend to be. But you will have fun, and there are plenty of almost round-the-clock gambling opportunities.

<u>Weak Points</u>: Dated decor, fittings and colors. Low-quality cabinetry. Noise and music everywhere.

s/s Universe Explorer
★★★
(M)

LIFESTYLE:	STANDARD
Cruise Line:	World Explorer Cruises
Former Names:	*Enchanted Seas, Queen of*
Bermuda, Canada Star, Liberte, Island Sun,	
Volendam, Monarch Sun, Brasil	
Gross Tonnage:	22,162
Builder:	Ingalls Shipbuilding (USA)
Original Cost:	$26 million
Entered Service:	September 1958/November 1990
Flag:	Panama
Tel. No.:	1131605
Fax No.:	1331605
Length (ft/m):	617.4/188.2
Beam (ft/m):	84.3/25.7
Draft (ft/m):	27.2/8.3
Propulsion/Propellers:	steam turbine
	(19,000kW)/2 (FP)
Decks:	8
Total Crew:	365
Pass. Capacity (basis 2):	737
Pass. Capacity (all berths):	894
Pass. Space Ratio (basis 2):	30.0
Pass. Space Ratio (all berths):	24.7
Officers:	European
Total Cabins:	371
Size Range (sq ft/m):	103.3–292.7/9.6–27.2
Cabins (outside view):	291
Cabins (inside — no view):	80

Cabins (single occupancy):	5
Cabins (with private balcony):	0
Cabins (wheelchair accessible):	0
Cabin Current:	110 volts
Cabin TV:	Yes
Dining Rooms:	1
Elevators:	3
Casino:	No
Slot Machines:	No
Swimming Pools (outdoors):	1
Swimming Pools (inside):	0
Whirlpools:	0
Fitness Center:	Yes
Sauna/Steam Room:	No/No
Massage:	Yes
Self-Service Launderette:	No
Movie Theater/Seats:	Yes/167
Library:	Yes
Classification Society:	American Bureau of Shipping

RATINGS	POSSIBLE SCORE	SCORE ACHIEVED
Ship	500	279
Accommodation	200	111
Food	400	226
Service	400	258
Cruise	500	285
TOTAL	**2,000**	**1,159**

Accommodation: The cabins, of which there are many different sizes and configurations, are mostly of quite generous proportions for a ship of this size, with heavy-duty furniture and fittings and a good amount of closet and drawer space. The bathrooms are, however, quite old fashioned and a bit utilitarian.

Dining: The dining room is rather charming and warm and has large windows that provide plenty of light and a nice ambience. There are two seatings. The menu choice is somewhat limited and quite basic, but service is attentive and comes with a smile, even if it is without finesse. There is only a moderate selection of bread rolls, cheeses (mostly of the standard supermarket processed kind), and fruits.

Other Comments: This ship has a classic, compact 1960s traditional ocean liner profile that is quite low and rather squat. She was originally ordered and sailed for the long-defunct Moore-McCormack Lines, and has had a long list of operators and name changes, and has undergone an extensive amount of refurbishment over the years. Has nicely finished teak decks outdoors. Being an older ship, there are spacious promenade areas for walking outdoors, as well as plenty of sheltered and open sunbathing space.

Inside, the public rooms are moderately spacious and well appointed. Almost all have high ceilings, pleasing, but dated decor and colors that do not jar the senses. The showroom is good but cannot compare with those on larger, more modern ships, and the sight lines are poor. Although there is a large casino, it has been turned into a large library while the ship is operated by World Explorer Cruises.

This ship will provide a reasonably enjoyable cruise experience in comfortable surroundings reminiscent of old-world style. Now under long-term charter to World Explorer Cruises.

Where the ship scores well is in her program of lecturers and educational features for passengers who want to learn more about their cruise surroundings than found aboard the more regular cruise vessels. The ship offers a mixture of 14-night Alaska cruises in the summer, with cruises to the Western Caribbean and Yucatan Peninsula in the winter, as well as an annual around-the-world cruise under the "Semester at Sea" banner for school children.

m/s Veendam
★★★★
(L)

LIFESTYLE:	**PREMIUM**
Cruise Line:	Holland America Line
Former Names:	-
Gross Tonnage:	55,451
Builder:	Fincantieri (Italy)
Original Cost:	$215 million
Entered Service:	May 1996
Flag:	Bahamas
Tel. No.:	330943511
Fax No.:	330943512
Length (ft/m):	719.3/219.3
Beam (ft/m):	101.0/30.8
Draft (ft/m):	24.6/7.5
Propulsion/Propellers:	diesel-electric (34,560kW)/2 (CP)
Decks:	10
Total Crew:	561
Pass. Capacity (basis 2):	1,266
Pass. Capacity (all berths):	1,627
Pass. Space Ratio (basis 2):	43.8
Pass. Space Ratio (all berths):	34.0
Officers:	British/Dutch
Total Cabins:	633
Size Range (sq ft/m):	186.2–1,124.8/17.3–104.5
Cabins (outside view):	502
Cabins (inside — no view):	131
Cabins (single occupancy):	0
Cabins (with private balcony):	150
Cabins (wheelchair accessible):	6
Cabin Current:	110 and 220 volts
Cabin TV:	Yes
Dining Rooms:	1
Elevators:	12
Casino:	Yes
Slot Machines:	Yes
Swimming Pools (outdoors):	1
Swimming Pools (inside):	1 (magrodome)
Whirlpools:	2
Fitness Center:	Yes
Sauna/Steam Room:	Yes/No
Massage:	Yes
Self-Service Launderette:	Yes
Movie Theater/Seats:	Yes/249
Library:	Yes
Classification Society:	Lloyd's Register

RATINGS	POSSIBLE SCORE	SCORE ACHIEVED
Ship	500	417
Accommodation	200	162
Food	400	282
Service	400	300
Cruise	500	387
TOTAL	**2,000**	**1,548**

This is one in a series of four ships of almost identical size and layout. For comments, see *Maasdam*.

m/v Victoria
★★★ +
(M)

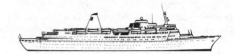

LIFESTYLE:	PREMIUM
Cruise Line:	P&O Cruises
Former Names:	*Sea Princess, Kungsholm*
Gross Tonnage:	27,670
Builder:	John Brown & Co. (UK)
Original Cost:	$22 million
Entered Service:	April 1966/February 1979
Flag:	Great Britain
Tel. No.:	1440320
Fax No.:	1440320
Length (ft/m):	660.2/201.23
Beam (ft/m):	87.1/26.57
Draft (ft/m):	28.0/8.56
Propulsion/Propellers:	diesel (18,800kW)/2 (CP)
Decks:	7
Total Crew:	417
Pass. Capacity (basis 2):	744
Pass. Capacity (all berths):	778
Pass. Space Ratio (basis 2):	37.1
Pass. Space Ratio (all berths):	35.5
Officers:	British
Total Cabins:	379
Size Range (sq ft/m):	137.7–466.0/12.8–43.3
Cabins (outside view):	291
Cabins (inside — no view):	88
Cabins (single occupancy):	14
Cabins (with private balcony):	0
Cabins (wheelchair accessible):	10
Cabin Current:	220 volts
Cabin TV:	Yes (higher grade cabins only)
Dining Rooms:	1
Elevators:	4
Casino:	Yes
Slot Machines:	Yes
Swimming Pools (outdoors):	2
Swimming Pools (inside):	1
Whirlpools:	1
Fitness Center:	Yes
Sauna/Steam Room:	Yes/No
Massage:	Yes
Self-Service Launderette:	Yes
Movie Theater/Seats:	Yes/289
Library:	Yes
Classification Society:	Lloyd's Register

RATINGS	POSSIBLE SCORE	SCORE ACHIEVED
Ship	500	371
Accommodation	200	148
Food	400	272
Service	400	265
Cruise	500	339
TOTAL	**2,000**	**1,395**

Accommodation: There is a wide range of cabins to choose from, including six suites. Most cabins have a decent amount of space, and many of them feature fine wood-paneled walls. Most have been nicely refurbished over the years. In the latest refurbishment, all new soft furnishings were changed, televisions replaced, and bathrooms revamped.

Most cabins have excellent closet and drawer space and fine wood-paneled walls. Generous-sized bathrooms have solid fixtures and storage space for toiletries. Some cabins have upper and lower berths. The bathroom towels are small, however.

Dining: The tiered European-style dining room is fairly elegant, with old-world traditions and charm, and display of 18th-century Chinese porcelain (has some nice etched glass panels with nautical themes). There are tables for two, four, six, and eight (more tables for two were added during the 1997 refurbishment). There are two seatings. Good general food and selection that is tailored for British tastes and excellent service from the Goanese staff. Buffets are very basic and disappointing in both display and food quality, as is the selection of breads and fruits. The wine list, also, is very limited.

The casual outdoor Lido Buffet was remodeled in the last refit, and now is less congested owing to a redesign of the area, more temperature-controlled display space and better serving lines. However, the plastic chairs at the Lido buffet should at least have cushions.

Other Comments: This is a solidly built ex-ocean liner (originally built for the now-defunct Swedish America Line) that has flowing, rounded lines and a well-balanced profile, with that "sheer" that makes her look like a "real" ship. She has been nicely refurbished and well maintained (and arguably improved) since becoming a P&O Cruises ship in the late 1970s. The open deck and sunbathing space is good.

Inside, there are numerous spacious public rooms trimmed with fine woods and with fine furnishings and fabrics. One nice feature is an indoor (sea water) swimming pool, together with the usual associated saunas and gymnasium.

There is a decent variety of entertainment aboard the ships of P&O Cruises, as well as a good program of special theme cruises. Antiques, The Archers, art appreciation, classical music, comedy, cricket, gardening, jazz, motoring, popular fiction, Scottish dance, sequence dancing were among the themes in 1999 (check with your travel agent to see what is available at the time you want to take your cruise).

This ship will provide an enjoyable, very traditional, and conservative British cruise experience, but with 30 years afloat she does look a little worn in places, although she underwent a $9-million refurbishment in late 1997. Port taxes and insurance are included for British passengers.

DID YOU KNOW...?

...that the first "en suite" rooms (with private bathroom in cabin) were on board Cunard Line's *Campania* of 1893?

...that the first liner to offer private terraces with their first class suites was *Normandie* in 1935?

...that the first single berth cabins built as such were aboard Cunard Line's *Campania* of 1893?

...that the first ships to feature private balconies were a trio of ships built for the Compagnie des Messageries Maritimes, France? They were the 13,520-tonne *Cambodge*, *Laos*, and *Vietnam*, built in 1953.

...that the first ship to be fitted with interior plumbing was the 6,283-tonne *Normandie*, of 1883?

...that the first ship to be fitted with an internal electric lighting system was aboard the Inman liner *City of Berlin* in 1879?

...that cruising today is not the same as it was in the nineteenth century? On the first cruise ships there was little entertainment, and passengers had to clean their own cabins! Orders enforced on all ships sailing from Great Britain in 1849, for example, instructed all passengers to be in their beds by 10:00pm!

m/s Viking Serenade
★★★ +
(L)

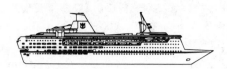

LIFESTYLE:	STANDARD
Cruise Line:	Royal Caribbean International
Former Names:	*Stardancer, Scandinavia*
Gross Tonnage:	40,132
Builder:	Dubigeon-Normandie (France)
Original Cost:	$100 million
Entered Service:	October 1982/June 1991
Flag:	Liberia
Tel. No.:	1104204
Fax No.:	1103132
Length (ft/m):	623.0/189.89
Beam (ft/m):	88.6/27.01
Draft (ft/m):	23.9/7.3
Propulsion/Propellers:	diesel (19,800kW)/2 (CP)
Decks:	11
Total Crew:	612
Pass. Capacity (basis 2):	1,512
Pass. Capacity (all berths):	1,863
Pass. Space Ratio (basis 2):	26.5
Pass. Space Ratio (all berths):	21.5
Officers:	International
Total Cabins:	756
Size Range (sq ft/m):	143.1–398.2/13.3–37.0
Cabins (outside view):	478
Cabins (inside — no view):	278
Cabins (single occupancy):	0
Cabins (with private balcony):	5
Cabins (wheelchair accessible):	4
Cabin Current:	110 volts
Cabin TV:	Yes
Dining Rooms:	2
Elevators:	5
Casino:	Yes
Slot Machines:	Yes
Swimming Pools (outdoors):	1 (magrodome)
Swimming Pools (inside):	0
Whirlpools:	0
Fitness Center:	Yes
Sauna/Steam Room:	Yes/No
Massage:	Yes
Self-Service Launderette:	No
Movie Theater/Seats:	No
Library:	No
Classification Society:	Det Norske Veritas

RATINGS	POSSIBLE SCORE	SCORE ACHIEVED
Ship	500	339
Accommodation	200	127
Food	400	241
Service	400	284
Cruise	500	350
TOTAL	**2,000**	**1,341**

Accommodation: The tiny, dimensionally challenged cabins are reasonably well appointed and have a moderate amount of closet space for short cruises. There are too many inside cabins, and drawer space is poor. The cabin bathrooms are tiny, so you should expect to dance with the shower curtain, particularly if you have a larger-than-average–size body.

Dining: The two large dining rooms are reasonably attractive and well laid out (romantic passengers should note that there are no tables for two, however). There are two seatings. The cuisine is typical of standard hotel banquet food, perfectly portioned, with rather robotic presentation. Poor salads, bread rolls, and fruits, but what is really disappointing is the fact that there is so little taste in the food.

Other Comments: This ship has a good amount of open deck and sunbathing space, and there is a magrodome-covered pool for use in inclement weather.

Inside, there is a wide array of public rooms and facilities, including a conference center and the Viking Crown Lounge cantilevered around the funnel. Public rooms have contemporary decor, tasteful colors, and good quality furnishings. Fine health spa facilities. Attentive service from Caribbean staff. This ship should provide a decent short cruise experience for families with children.

The ship underwent a $75-million reconstruction in 1991. Provides a well-programmed cruise experience in upbeat surroundings. Has operated from Los Angeles to Mexico for several years.

<u>Weak Points:</u> There are too many loud, irritating announcements and background music almost everywhere. Passenger participation events tend to be very juvenile. The cabins are tiny and the ship always feels crowded.

m/s Vision of the Seas
★★★★
(L)

LIFESTYLE: **STANDARD**

Cruise Line:	Royal Caribbean International
Former Names:	-
Gross Tonnage:	78,491
Builder:	Chantiers de l'Atlantique (France)
Original Cost:	$275 million
Entered Service:	May 1998
Flag:	Liberia
Tel. No.:	363671111/363671211
Fax No.:	363676120/373676220
Length (ft/m):	915.3/279.0
Beam (ft/m):	105.6/32.2
Draft (ft/m):	24.9/7.6
Propulsion/Propellers:	diesel-electric (50,400kW)2 (FP)
Decks:	11
Total Crew:	660
Pass. Capacity (basis 2):	2,000
Pass. Capacity (all berths):	2,435
Pass. Space Ratio (basis 2):	39.2
Pass. Space Ratio (all berths):	32.2
Officers:	International
Total Cabins:	1,000
Size Range (sq ft/m):	148.5–1,059.2/13.8–98.4
Cabins (outside view):	593
Cabins (inside — no view):	407
Cabins (single occupancy):	0
Cabins (with private balcony):	229
Cabins (wheelchair accessible):	14
Cabin Current:	110 and 220 volts
Cabin TV:	Yes
Dining Rooms:	1
Elevators:	9
Casino:	Yes
Slot Machines:	Yes
Swimming Pools (outdoors):	1
Swimming Pools (inside):	1 (inside/outside)
Whirlpools:	6
Fitness Center:	Yes
Sauna/Steam Room:	Yes/Yes
Massage:	Yes
Self-Service Launderette:	No
Movie Theater/Seats:	No
Library:	Yes
Classification Society:	Det Norske Veritas

RATINGS	POSSIBLE SCORE	SCORE ACHIEVED
Ship	500	440
Accommodation	200	169
Food	400	252
Service	400	302
Cruise	500	384
TOTAL	**2,000**	**1,547**

Accommodation: The accommodation ranges from large suites, each of which has its own private balcony, to standard inside and outside cabins. All are reasonably tastefully furnished and come equipped with all the necessary amenities needed for a one-week cruise. The company provides colorful soft furnishings that make one's home away from home look like the inside of a modern Scandinavian hotel — minimalist, yet colorful.

Choose a "C" grade suite if you want spacious accommodation that includes a separate (curtained off) sleeping area, a good-size outside balcony (with part, not full, partition), lounge with sofa, two chairs and coffee table, three closets, plenty of drawer and storage space, television, and video player. The bathroom is large and features a full-size bathtub, integral shower, and two washbasins/two toiletries cabinets.

All of the other standard inside and outside cabins have colorful soft furnishings, twin beds that convert to queen-size, a sofa, a coffee table, and a vanity desk unit with drawers and cupboards. A color television sits on swivel base so that it can be seen from both bed and sitting area (sofa). The bathroom is very small and has a toilet, shower cubicle, and sink, but there is no cabinet for personal toiletries.

Dining: The dining room is set on two levels, with large ocean-view picture windows on two sides (rectangular windows on the upper level, large circular windows on the lower level) and a large connecting stairway and is nonsmoking. There are two seatings. RCI's standard of dining room food and service has always been consistent in presentation, although the food generally has little taste, the result of controlled food costs as well as the use of many mixes and pre-prepared items. While most passengers seem to enjoy it, it has become very standard, nonmemorable fare, and really needs more attention and creativity. Vegetarian dishes are available for lunch and dinner. The wine list features only standard wines — none of any decent vintage.

The Windjammer Café is the ship's informal dining spot and offers more choice for for those who enjoy casual meals, in a contemporary setting, with attractive colors and decor, and large ocean-view windows that provide plenty of light. However, only the basics are available at the beverage stations.

Other Comments: This striking ship, sixth in the *Vision*-class of vessels, shares design features that make all Royal Caribbean International ships identifiable, including a Viking Crown Lounge (which is also the ship's disco). Aboard this ship (and sister ship *Rhapsody of the Seas*, which debuted in 1998) the Viking Crown Lounge is located just forward of the center of the ship, with the funnel located well aft — a departure from all other RCI ships to date. The ship's stern is beautifully rounded. There is a reasonable amount of open-air walking space, although this can become cluttered with deck lounge chairs (which do not have cushioned pads).

Inside, the ship provides the latest incarnation of RCI's interpretation of a floating contemporary hotel and presents the nicest mix of colors and decor of any of the *Vision*-class ships, with lots of warm beige and pink tones (particularly in the expansive atrium).

The artwork (which cost $6 million) is plentiful, colorful, and very creative (much seems to have been inspired by that aboard *Galaxy*, which belongs to sister company Celebrity Cruises), with more previously blank wall space covered with interesting artworks of differing shapes and sizes. Most noticeable is the extensive use of glass (two beautiful glass sculptures stand out — one in the atrium at the entrance to a Champagne Bar, one on the upper level of the Viking Crown Lounge). There are plenty of public rooms, bars, and lounges to play in, as well as a large, well-lit casino.

The spa, with its solarium and indoor/outdoor dome-covered pool, Inca- and Mayan-theme decor, sauna/steam rooms and gymnasium, provides a haven for the health-conscious and fitness buff (although there is a pizza bar forward of the pool area); there is a lovely "Mayan Serpent" sculpture in the solarium.

The Viking Crown Lounge is a multi-level night spot (the music can be loud and overbearing, however, and so can cigarette smoke around the bar — one of few places where smokers can light up). Perhaps the best atmosphere can be found in the nautical-theme Schooner Bar. The Library features an excellent array of hardback books, as well as a neat wooden sculpture of something that looks like the Tin Man (from *The Wizard of Oz*).

The entertainment throughout is upbeat (in fact, it is difficult to get away from music and noise), but is typical of the kind of resort hotel found ashore in Las Vegas. There is even background music in all corridors and elevators, and constant music outdoors on the pool deck. If you want a quiet relaxing vacation, this is the wrong ship. If you enjoy big-city life with a fine array of sounds and entertainment around you, this could be just right.

<u>Weak Points</u>: The staff is only mildly accommodating, and only a small percentage say hello when passing you in the corridors (this included the officers). In other words, the hospitality factor is below average. The elevators talk to you ("going up/going down" is informative, but monotonous, although the illuminated picture displays of decks is good).

m/s **Vistamar**
★★★ +
(S)

LIFESTYLE:	STANDARD
Cruise Line:	plantours & Partner
Former Names:	-
Gross Tonnage:	7,478
Builder:	Union Navale de Levante (Spain)
Original Cost:	$45 million
Entered Service:	September 1989
Flag:	Panama
Tel. No.:	1332275
Fax No.:	1332275
Length (ft/m):	396.9/121.0
Beam (ft/m):	55.1/16.82
Draft (ft/m):	14.9/4.55
Propulsion/Propellers:	diesel (3,900kW)/2 (CP)
Decks:	6
Total Crew:	110
Pass. Capacity (basis 2):	299
Pass. Capacity (all berths):	320
Pass. Space Ratio (basis 2):	25.0
Pass. Space Ratio (all berths):	23.3
Officers:	Spanish
Total Cabins:	152
Size Range (sq ft/m):	129.1–150.6/12.0–14.0
Cabins (outside view):	126
Cabins (inside–no view):	24
Cabins (single occupancy):	5
Cabins (with private balcony):	11

Cabins (wheelchair accessible):	0
Cabin Current:	220 volts
Cabin TV:	Yes
Dining Rooms:	1
Elevators:	3
Casino:	No
Slot Machines:	No
Swimming Pools (outdoors):	1
Swimming Pools (inside):	0
Whirlpools:	0
Fitness Center:	Yes
Sauna/Steam Room:	Yes/No
Massage:	Yes
Self-Service Launderette:	No
Movie Theater/Seats:	No
Library:	Yes
Classification Society:	Det Norske Veritas

RATINGS	POSSIBLE SCORE	SCORE ACHIEVED
Ship	500	311
Accommodation	200	129
Food	400	247
Service	400	271
Cruise	500	304
TOTAL	**2,000**	**1,262**

Accommodation: The passenger accommodation areas are located forward, while public rooms are positioned aft, which means there is a minimal amount of noise in the cabins. There are ten cabin grades, but just two different sizes: suites with private balcony and queen-size bed; and outside-view or inside (no-view) cabins for two, three, or four persons. The cabins are moderately comfortable, although the bathrooms are *extremely* small and tight, and both closet and drawer space are limited. Cabins have twin beds with wooden headboard, a small vanity/writing desk, a color television, climate-control, and a telephone. Most of the cabinetry is made with a wood finish.

The suites have a small, narrow private balcony outdoors. They also have a more spacious bathroom, with a bathtub and integral shower. The living area is also larger and comes with a sofa, a coffee table, a vanity/writing desk, and a larger color television.

Dining: The Andalucia Restaurant is quite warm and inviting, with contemporary colors and decor, and large picture windows. The room's focal point is a model of a sailing vessel with an emerald green hull (about the same color as the fabrics on the dining room chairs). There is one seating, with assigned tables for four, six, or eight (there are no tables for two, and window-side tables are for six). The food is reasonably basic but adequate, with a typical choice of three entrees for dinner, but the selection of breads, cheeses, and fruits is small, and the overall cuisine really is rather basic, as is the wine list.

Other Comments: This ship has a small, fairly smart contemporary, but rather squat ship profile. The ship has an "open-bridge" policy, so you can join the captain and other navigation officers at almost any time. There is a good open observation deck at the forwardmost part of the ship — atop the navigation bridge — but other open deck and sunbathing space is extremely limited. The tiny outdoor pool has a large splash surround.

The interior layout has all the public rooms located aft, in a "cake-layer" stacking, with a single, central staircase that takes up most of the space in the three-deck-high atrium. Features include wood trimmed interior decor, which is attractive and warm, although the mirrored metallic ceilings are somewhat irritating.

There is a rather jazzy night club/disco, with acres of glass, set around the base of the funnel. A four-deck-high atrium with a "sky dome" has a glass-walled elevator and a wraparound staircase. The library has very comfortable high wing-back chairs, but not many books. One nice feature is the many green plants that are placed throught the ship to help to make the interiors look less clinical, and warmer.

This ship is under charter to plantours & Partner for German-speaking passengers, since 1991, and the product is aimed at the inexpensive standard market. Tipping is recommended at DM10–12 per person, per day (the onboard currency is the deutschmark).

<u>Weak Points</u>: The tiny "dip" swimming pool is virtually useless. The ship's operation is rather sloppy. There is no walking track or wraparound promenade deck outdoors. The fit, finish, and maintenance of this ship are all quite poor and well below the standard expected. The deck lounge chairs do not have cushioned pads.

GOING P.O.S.H.

This colloquialism for "grand" or "first rate" has its origin in the days of ocean steamship travel between England and India. Wealthy passengers would, at some considerable cost, book round-trip passage as "Port Outward, Starboard Home." They would thus secure a cabin on the cooler side of the ship while crossing the unbearably hot Indian Ocean under the sun. Abbreviated as P.O.S.H., the expression soon came to be applied to first-class passengers who could afford that luxury. (*Brewers Dictionary of Phrase & Fable*, Cassell Ltd.).

However, the reality is that the monsoon winds that blow in and out of the Asian area shift between winter and summer, so that the sheltered side of a ship would change according to the season. Further, in looking at deck plans of ships of the period, most cabins were located *centrally*, with indoor promenades or corridors along each side, so the actual definition of the origin of P.O.S.H. could be said to be taken as artistic license.

m/s Volendam
(L)

LIFESTYLE:	PREMIUM
Cruise Line:	Holland America Line
Former Names:	-
Gross Tonnage:	63,000
Builder:	Fincantieri (Italy)
Original Cost:	$300 million
Entered Service:	July 1999
Flag:	The Netherlands
Tel. No.:	n/a
Fax No.:	n/a
Length (ft/m):	781.0/238.0
Beam (ft/m):	105.8/32.25
Draft (ft/m):	25.5/7.80
Propulsion/Propellers:	diesel-electric (37,500kW)/2 (CP)
Decks:	10
Total Crew:	561
Pass. Capacity (basis 2):	1,440
Pass. Capacity (all berths):	1,440
Pass. Space Ratio (basis 2):	43.7
Pass. Space Ratio (all berths):	43.7
Officers:	Dutch
Total Cabins:	720
Size Range (sq ft/m):	151.0–1172.0/14.04–108.9
Cabins (outside view):	581
Cabins (inside — no view):	139
Cabins (single occupancy):	0
Cabins (with private balcony):	197
Cabins (wheelchair accessible):	23
Cabin Current:	110 volts
Cabin TV:	Yes
Dining Rooms:	1 main (+1 alternative)
Elevators:	16
Casino:	Yes
Slot Machines:	Yes
Swimming Pools (outdoors):	2
Swimming Pools (inside):	1 (magrodome cover)
Whirlpools:	2
Fitness Center:	Yes
Sauna/Steam Room:	Yes/Yes
Massage:	Yes
Self-Service Launderette:	Yes
Movie Theater/Seats:	Yes/205
Library:	Yes
Classification Society:	Lloyds Register

RATINGS	POSSIBLE SCORE	SCORE ACHIEVED
Ship	500	NYR
Accommodation	200	NYR
Food	400	NYR
Service	400	NYR
Cruise	500	NYR
TOTAL	**2,000**	**NYR**
Expected Score Range:		**1500-1700**

Accommodation: The range of accommodation is similar to that found aboard the similarly sized *Rotterdam*. There is one penthouse suite and 28 suites, while the rest comprise a mix of outside-view and inside (no-view) cabins. However, there are many more balcony cabins (called "minisuites") aboard this ship than aboard the slightly smaller *Statendam*-class ships (*Maasdam, Ryndam, Statendam, Veendam*).

With the exception of one penthouse suite, located forward on the starboard side, the bathrooms in the other suites are a little disappointing — not as spacious or opulent as expected.

Dining: There is one main restaurant and one alternative dining spot (for dinner). The main restaurant is quite a grand room, spread over two decks, with ocean views on three sides with a grand staircase to connect the upper and lower levels. There are two seatings for dinner and open seating for breakfast and lunch.

An alternative, casual-dress restaurant seats 88, and there is no charge, although reservations are required. It is created in the style of a California artists' bistro and provides Italian cuisine (this features a set menu together with nightly specials). Passengers have more choice and an occasional change of venue (anyone booking suite-grade accommodation gets priority reservations).

In addition, there is the Lido Buffet, a casual, self-serve café that has proven popular aboard all Holland America Line ships for breakfast and lunch, as well as an outdoor grill for those who enjoy hamburgers, hot dogs, and other grilled fast-food items. The Lido Buffet is also open for casual dinners on several nights each cruise (typically three nights on a seven-night cruise), in an open-seating arrangement. Tables are set with crisp linens, flatware, and stemware. A set menu is featured, and this includes a choice of four entrees.

Other Comments: This is the third ship of the same name for Holland America Line, and the first of the evolving generation afte the *Statendam*-class ships. The name is derived from the fishing village of the same name, located north of Amsterdam, Holland. Her hull is dark blue, in keeping with all Holland

America Line ships. Although similar in size to the line's flagship *Rotterdam*, this ship has a single funnel, not unlike those found aboard the company's much smaller *Nieuw Amsterdam* and *Noordam*.

Having been built to approximately the same size as the company's newest *Rotterdam*, the same layout and public rooms have been incorporated into her interiors. This carries on the same flow and comfortable feeling so passengers will immediately feel at home aboard almost any ship in the Holland America Line fleet.

The principal design theme for the ship's interiors is flowers. The interior focal point is a crystal sculpture, located in the three-deck-high atrium, by one of Italy's leading contemporary glass artists, Luciano Vistosi. The health spa facilities include more treatment rooms (each has shower and toilet).

In the casino bar, also known as the ship's sports bar, a cinematic theme presents visions of Hollywood, and includes a collection of costumes, props, photos, and posters of movies and the stars who made them.

At the Lido Deck swimming pool, leaping dolphins are the focal point, but in a different design to that seen aboard the *Statendam*-class ships. The pool itself is also one deck higher than the *S*-class ships, with the positive result that you can now have direct access between the aft and midships pools aboard this ship (not so aboard the *S*-class ships).

This ship is perhaps best for older passengers who seek safe, pleasant surroundings and food that is not too adventurous. Holland America Line provides cappuccino and espresso coffees and free ice cream during certain hours of the day aboard its ships, as well as hot hors d'oeuvres in all bars — something other major lines seem to have dropped, or charge extra for. Also, the line does not add an automatic 15 percent for beverage purchases, unlike many others.

This ship operates seven- to 13-day cruises in the Caribbean during her inaugural season. Sister ship *Amsterdam* follows in late 2000 (there was, however, no more space to include her in this edition of the book).

m/s Voyager of the Seas
(L)

LIFESTYLE:	STANDARD
Cruise Line:	Royal Caribbean International
Former Names:	-
Gross Tonnage:	142,000
Builder:	Kvaerner Masa-Yards (Finland)
Original Cost:	$500 million
Entered Service:	November 1999
Flag:	Liberia
Tel. No.:	n/a
Fax No.:	n/a
Length (ft/m):	1,020.9/311.2
Beam (ft/m):	157.4/48.0
Draft (ft/m):	28.8/8.8
Propulsion/Propellers:	diesel-electric (42,000kW)/ 3 pods (2 azimuthing/1 fixed)
Decks:	14
Total Crew:	1,176
Pass. Capacity (basis 2):	3,114
Pass. Capacity (all berths):	3,838
Pass. Space Ratio (basis 2):	45.6
Pass. Space Ratio (all berths):	36.9
Officers:	Scandinavian
Total Cabins:	1,557
Size Range (sq ft/m):	150.6–1,146.0/14.0 — 106.5
Cabins (outside view):	939
Cabins (inside — no view):	618
Cabins (single occupancy):	0
Cabins (with private balcony):	757

Cabins (wheelchair accessible):	26
Cabin Current:	110 volts
Cabin TV:	Yes
Dining Rooms:	5 + 4 cafes
Elevators:	14 (6 glass-enclosed)
Casino:	Yes
Slot Machines:	Yes
Swimming Pools (outdoors):	3
Swimming Pools (inside):	0
Whirlpools:	6
Fitness Center:	Yes
Sauna/Steam Room:	Yes/Yes
Massage:	Yes
Self-Service Launderette:	No
Movie Theater/Seats:	No
Library:	Yes
Classification Society:	Det Norske Veritas

RATINGS	POSSIBLE SCORE	SCORE ACHIEVED
Ship	500	NYR
Accommodation	200	NYR
Food	400	NYR
Service	400	NYR
Cruise	500	NYR
TOTAL	**2,000**	**NYR**
Expected Score Range:		**1,500-1,700**

Accommodation: There is a big range of 22 cabin categories from which to choose, in four major groupings: Premium ocean-view suites and cabins, Promenade-view (inside) cabins, ocean-view cabins, and interior (no-view) cabins. Note that many cabins are of a similar size — good for incentives and large groups — and 300 have interconnecting doors — good for families.

Many of the inside cabins have bay windows that look *into* an atrium — a cruise industry first (but a copy of those aboard the Baltic ferries *Silja Europa* and *Silja Serenade* with inside cabins that look into a shopping plaza). Regardless of what cabin grade you choose, all (except for the Royal Suite and Owner's Suite) feature twin beds that convert to a queen-size unit, television, radio, telephone, personal safe, vanity unit, hairdryer, and private bathroom.

The largest accommodation includes luxuriously appointed penthouse suites (whose passengers have to share the rest of the ship with everyone else, except for their own exclusive private concierge club). The largest of these is the Royal Suite, which is positioned on the port side of the ship. It features a king-sized bed in a separate bedroom, living room with queen-size sofa bed, baby grand piano, refrigerator/wet bar, dining table, entertainment center, and large bathroom.

The slightly smaller, but still highly desirable, Owner's Suites (there are ten of them, all located in the center of the ship, on both port and starboard sides) and the Royal Family suites (four of them) all feature similar items. However, the four Royal Family suites, which have two bedrooms (including one with third/fourth upper pullman berths) are located at the stern of the ship and have magnificent views over the ship's wash.

Dining: The main dining room is extremely large and is set on three levels (each has an operatic name and theme: Carmen, La Boheme, and Magic Flute, all of which are connected by a dramatic three-deck-high staircase). The dining room is totally nonsmoking, and there are two seatings

The cuisine in the main dining room is similar in nature to that offered aboard the company's present ships. In other words, we are talking about mass banquet catering that offers standard fare comparable to that found in American family-style restaurants ashore. Such items as caviar (once a standard menu item) incur a hefty extra charge.

Alternative dining options for casual and informal meals at all hours (according to company releases) include: Cafe Promenade, for continental breakfast, all-day pizzas, and specialty coffees; Windjammer Café, for casual buffet-style breakfast, lunch, and light dinner (except for the last night of the cruise); Island Grill, for casual dinner (no reservations necessary) featuring a grill and open kitchen; Portofino, an "upscale" Euro-Italian restaurant, for dinner (reservations required); SeaSide Diner, a retro-1950s all-day, all-night eatery featuring jukebox hits and indoor-outdoor seating; and Sprinkles, for round-the-clock ice cream and yogurt.

Other Comments: *Voyager of the Seas* is a stunning floating resort (one of three such vessels being built for the company, the others being *Explorer of the Seas* and *Adventurer of the Seas*, set to debut in 2000 and 2001, respectively). The exterior design is not unlike an enlarged version of the company's *Vision*-class ships. She is the largest cruise vessel in the world in terms of tonnage measurement (although, to keep things in perspective, she is not quite as long as the ss *Norway*).

With her large proportions, she provides more facilities and options and caters to more passengers than any other Royal Caribbean International ship has in the past, and yet the ship manages to have a healthy passenger space ratio (the amount of space per passenger). She is simply too large to go through the Panama Canal, thus limiting her itineraries almost exclusively to the Caribbean, or as a floating island resort.

The ship's propulsion is derived from three pod units, with 14-megawatt motors (two outboard units and one fixed at the centerline) instead of conventional rudders and propellers in the latest configuration of high-tech propulsion systems.

At certain times, passengers can stand right at the bow of this ship, arms spread in an "eagle-like" position, just like the stars in the film *Titanic*. Just imagine the photographs, although for the best ones, like in the film, you'll need to bring a helicopter! Those seeking a view of the navigation bridge will be able to see what's happening from a special spot above the bridge.

Embarkation and disembarkation take place through two stations/access points in a new passenger terminal in Miami. These are are designed to minimize the inevitable lines at the start and end of the cruise (that's over 1,500 people for each access point). Once inside the ship, *you'll need good walking shoes*, particularly when you need to go from one end to the other — it really is quite a long way.

The Royal Promenade is the length of two football fields, with two internal lobbies (atria) that are up to 11 decks high. Restaurants, shops, and entertainment locations front this winding street and inside "with-view" cabins look into it.

The casino is naturally large. Casino gaming includes blackjack, Caribbean stud poker, roulette (including the world's largest interactive roulette wheel and activated by a roulette ball tower that is four decks high), and craps.

For the more sporting, youthful passengers, there is a rock-climbing wall — located outdoors at the base of the mast — fun when you're 200 feet (70 meters) above the ocean — an in-line skating track, a dive-and-snorkel shop, a full-size basketball court, and nine-hole golf driving range. A 15,000-sq ft (1,393.5 m^2) health spa includes a large aerobics room, a fitness center (with the usual stairmasters, treadmills, stationary bikes, weight machines, and free weights), treatment rooms, men's and women's sauna/steam rooms, with another 10,000 sq ft (929 m^2) featuring a relaxing Solarium.

The 1,350-seat show lounge is five decks high. It features hydraulic pit and stage areas and is decorated in the style of the La Scala opera house in Milan. A second show lounge (Studio B) comes complete with telescopic seating for a mere 900, and the latest in broadcast facilities. A number of slim pillars obstruct clear-view arena stage sight lines, however. Underneath the arena floor is a regulation-size ice-skating rink, featuring *real* ice. At press time, prices were thought to be $5 per session, including skate rental, or $3 if you take your own skates.

If ice-skating in the Caribbean doesn't appeal to you, more sedate, but no less important facilities include a stunning two-deck library (the first aboard any ship), and a whopping $12 million has been spent on permanent artwork. Drinking places include a neat Aquarium Bar, complete with 50 tonnes of glass and water in four large aquariums (whose combined value is over $1 million). Other drinking places include the small and intimate Champagne Bar, Crown & Anchor Pub, and a Connaoisseur Club for cigars and cognacs. Meanwhile, jazz lovers might appreciate High Notes, an intimate room for cool music, or the Schooner Bar piano lounge. Golfers might enjoy the 19th Hole, a golf bar.

There is a large television studio, located adjacent to rooms that can be used for trade show exhibit space. Lovers could tie the knot in a wedding chapel in the sky, called the Skylight Chapel (it's located on the upper level of the Viking Crown Lounge). Water lovers can enjoy a long water slide featured at one of the aft outdoor pools; all of the swimming pools provide a resort-like environment, with the latest in high-tech everything.

Royal Caribbean International has, since its inception, always been an innovater in the cruise industry, and will probably remain so with this new vessel, the first of three such ships to be placed into service by the company. *Voyager of the Seas* operates seven-night cruises from Miami to Labadee (a private island), Ocho Rios, and Cozumel.

In terms of sheer size, this ship outdoes every other ship in the cruise industry, but in terms of personal service, it's more like the reverse, although the company tries hard to provide a good standard of highly programmed service from its hotel staff. This is impersonal city life at sea, millennium-style. Welcome to the real, fake world of highly programmed resort living. But if you dare to go outside, you might even be able to see the sea — now there's a novelty!

Weak Points: As the largest ship in the world, be aware that if you meet someone somewhere, and want to meet them again you'll need to make an appointment for this really is a large American-style floating resort city for the lively of heart and foot.

PLIMSOLL MARK

The safety of ships at sea and all those aboard owe much to the nineteenth-century social reformer, Samuel Plimsoll, a member of the British parliament concerned about the frequent loss of ships due to overloading. In those days, some shipowners would load their vessels down to the gunwales to squeeze every ounce of revenue out of them. They gambled on good weather, good fortune, and good seamanship to bring them safely into port. Consequently, many ships went to the bottom of the sea — the result of their buoyancy being seriously impaired by overloading.

Plimsoll helped to enact legislation that came to be known as the Merchant Shipping Act of 1875. This required shipowners to mark their vessels with a circular disc 12 inches (30.5 centimeters) long bisected by a line 18 inches (45.7 centimeters) long, as a measure of their maximum draft; that is, the depth to which a ship's hull could be safely immersed at sea. The Merchant Shipping Act of 1890 went even further, and required the Plimsoll mark (or line) to be positioned on the sides of vessels in accordance with tables drawn up by competent authorities.

The Plimsoll mark is now found on the ships of every nation. The Plimsoll mark indicates three different depths: the depth to which a vessel can be loaded in fresh water, which is less buoyant than salt water; the depth in summer, when seas are generally calmer; and the depth in winter, when seas are much rougher.

m/s Westerdam
★★★★
(L)

LIFESTYLE:	PREMIUM
Cruise Line:	Holland America Line
Former Names:	*Homeric*
Gross Tonnage:	53,872
Builder:	Meyer Werft (Germany)
Original Cost:	$150 million
Entered Service:	May 1986/November 1988
Flag:	Netherlands
Tel. No.:	1302534
Fax No.:	1302532
Length (ft/m):	797.9/243.23
Beam (ft/m):	95.1/29.00
Draft (ft/m):	23.6/7.20
Propulsion/Propellers:	diesel (23,830kW)/2 (CP)
Decks:	9
Total Crew:	612
Pass. Capacity (basis 2):	1,494
Pass. Capacity (all berths):	1,773
Pass. Space Ratio (basis 2):	36.0
Pass. Space Ratio (all berths):	30.3
Officers:	Dutch
Total Cabins:	747
Size Range (sq ft/m):	129.1–425.1/12.0–39.5
Cabins (outside view):	495
Cabins (inside — no view):	252
Cabins (single occupancy):	0
Cabins (with private balcony):	0

Cabins (wheelchair accessible):	4
Cabin Current:	110 volts
Cabin TV:	Yes
Dining Rooms:	1
Elevators:	7
Casino:	Yes
Slot Machines:	Yes
Swimming Pools (outdoors):	2 (1 with magrodome)
Swimming Pools (inside):	0
Whirlpools:	2
Fitness Center:	Yes
Sauna/Steam Room:	Yes/No
Massage:	Yes
Self-Service Launderette:	Yes-5
Movie Theater/Seats:	Yes/237
Library:	Yes
Classification Society:	Lloyd's Register

RATINGS	POSSIBLE SCORE	SCORE ACHIEVED
Ship	500	388
Accommodation	200	152
Food	400	282
Service	400	290
Cruise	500	368
TOTAL	**2,000**	**1,480**

Accommodation: The cabins are generously proportioned, well appointed, and equipped with almost everything, including ample closet, drawer, and storage space and good-size bathrooms (towels are scratchy and small). There are, however, far too many inside cabins, and the cabin insulation is rather poor.

Dining: The dining room has a raised central dome, and the portholes are highlighted at night by lighting. There are two seatings for dinner, and a single seating for breakfast and lunch. The food, while attractive, is rather tasteless. The selection of cheeses and fresh fruits is disappointing. The service is reasonable, but communication can prove frustrating sometimes. The Verandah Cafe and Lido Cafe serve breakfast and lunch in self-serve buffet style, but the long lines and crowded environment are not enjoyable.

Other Comments: This, the second-largest passenger ship in the Holland America fleet, underwent an $84-million "chop and stretch" operation in 1990 after being purchased by Holland America Line. Indeed, you can tell where the midsection was inserted due to the fact that the windows are larger than the fore and aft sections. The ship has good teak outside decks and a wraparound promenade deck with real wooden deck lounge chairs. Good amount of deck space for sunbathing. The magrodome-covered swimming pool deck is, however, too small for the number of passengers. There is some noticeable vibration in some areas.

The ship has elegant, functional, and restful interior decor. The public rooms are decorated in pastel tones. Has good passenger flow, but the layout is awkward to learn at first. Good quality furnishings and fabrics are used throughout. The expanded health and fitness center is an improvement.

She is a well-run, modern ship that provides a satisfactory cruise experience, generally for the older passenger, but increasingly for families with kids. The product has some nice extras, like chocolates and classical music at night in the Explorer's Lounge, hot hors d'oeuvres at cocktail times, and good dance music. The line does not add an automatic 15 percent for beverage purchases, unlike many other cruise lines.

Weak Points: The entertainment is mediocre, even though better production shows are now presented. A $1.50 charge for the washing machines in the self-service launderettes is petty.

m/v Wilderness Adventurer

★★
(S)

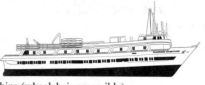

LIFESTYLE:	STANDARD
Cruise Line:	Glacier Bay Cruises and Tours
Former Names:	*Caribbean Prince*
Gross Tonnage:	89.5
Builder:	Blount Shipyards (USA)
Original Cost:	$6 million
Entered Service:	1983/1997
Flag:	USA
Tel. No.:	n/a
Fax No.:	n/a
Length (ft/m):	156.6/47.7
Beam (ft/m):	38.0/11.0
Draft (ft/m):	6.5/1.8
Propulsion/Propellers:	diesel (1,472kW)/1 (FP)
Decks:	3
Total Crew:	20
Pass. Capacity (basis 2):	68
Pass. Capacity (all berths):	76
Pass. Space Ratio (basis 2):	1.1
Pass. Space Ratio (all berths):	1.0
Officers:	American
Total Cabins:	34
Size Range (sq ft/m):	n/a
Cabins (outside view):	30
Cabins (inside — no view):	4
Cabins (single occupancy):	0
Cabins (with private balcony):	0
Cabins (wheelchair accessible):	0
Cabin Current:	110 volts
Cabin TV:	No
Dining Rooms:	1
Elevators:	0
Casino:	0
Slot Machines:	0
Swimming Pools (outdoors):	0
Swimming Pools (inside):	0
Whirlpools:	0
Fitness Center:	0
Sauna/Steam Room:	No/No
Massage:	No
Self-Service Launderette:	No
Movie Theater/Seats:	No
Library:	Yes
Classification Society:	American Bureau of Shipping

RATINGS	POSSIBLE SCORE	SCORE ACHIEVED
Ship	500	181
Accommodation	200	83
Food	400	204
Service	400	214
Cruise	500	257
TOTAL	**2,000**	**939**

Accommodation: The cabins (there are only three types to choose from, one on each of three decks) really are spartan, ultra-tiny, no-frills units that are just about adequate if you are not used to or do not want anything better. While 14 cabins have a double bed, all others have two lower beds, and eight also have an upper (pullman) berth. Each cabin has its own private bathroom, although these really are miniscule. There is no room service for food or snack items.

Dining: The dining room is a room that has minimal decor, but the open seating policy means that you can dine with whomever you wish, in a single seating. The cuisine is decidedly plain and simple Americana fare, as is the cutlery (no fish knifes are used, for example), it is rather tasty. This is due to the fact that the ingredients are all fresh. If you want wine or other drinks, you must bring your own.

Other Comments: This vessel, originally built for the American Canadian Caribbean Line, is good for real in-depth, up-close cruising along the coastline of Alaska. One bonus is the fact that at the bow of the vessel, a "bow gangway" comes into its own for landing passengers. The ship is also equipped with a unique, retractable wheelhouse for passenger under low bridges on island waterways and also has a platform for those who want to swim off the stern. A fleet of two-person kayaks is carried for up-close, in-your-face personal exploration of the Alaska shoreline. Water sports facilities include a glass-bottom boat/sunfish sailboat.

The dress code is absolutely casual (not even a jacket for men is needed, and no ties, please). There is an ample supply of snorkeling gear aboard the vessel, so there is really no need to take your own. However, do make sure you take comfortable walking shoes, as well as photographic materials for wildlife spotting. All tips are pooled by all staff, using the amounts recommended in the cruise line's brochure of $8–$12 per passenger, per day, which is high for the services offered.

<u>Weak Points</u>: There is an almost constant throbbing from the diesel engines/generator. Remember that there is no doctor on board, and so anyone with medical problems should really not consider this vessel.

m/v Wilderness Discoverer
★★
(S)

LIFESTYLE:	STANDARD
Cruise Line:	Glacier Bay Cruises and Tours
Former Names:	*Mayan Prince*
Gross Tonnage:	95
Builder:	Blount Industries (USA)
Original Cost:	$7.5 million
Entered Service:	June 1992/1998
Flag:	USA
Tel. No.:	n/a
Fax No.:	n/a
Length (ft/m):	169.0/51.5
Beam (ft/m):	38.0/11.5
Draft (ft/m):	6.7/2.0
Propulsion/Propellers:	diesel (1,472kW)/1 (FP)
Decks:	3
Total Crew:	22
Pass. Capacity (basis 2):	84
Pass. Capacity (all berths):	88
Pass. Space Ratio (basis 2):	7.9
Pass. Space Ratio (all berths):	7.4
Officers:	American
Total Cabins:	42
Size Range (sq ft/m):	70.0–80.0/6.5–7.4
Cabins (outside view):	37
Cabins (inside — no view):	5
Cabins (single occupancy):	0
Cabins (with private balcony):	0

Cabins (wheelchair accessible):	0
Cabin Current:	110 volts
Cabin TV:	No
Dining Rooms:	1
Elevators:	0
Casino:	0
Slot Machines:	0
Swimming Pools (outdoors):	0
Swimming Pools (inside):	0
Whirlpools:	0
Fitness Center:	No
Sauna/Steam Room:	No/No
Massage:	No
Self-Service Launderette:	No
Movie Theater/Seats:	No
Library:	Yes
Classification Society:	American Bureau of Shipping

RATINGS	POSSIBLE SCORE	SCORE ACHIEVED
Ship	500	181
Accommodation	200	83
Food	400	204
Service	400	214
Cruise	500	257
TOTAL	**2,000**	**939**

Accommodation: There are four cabin grades spread over three decks, and all are dimentionally challenged, so take only the most minimal amount of clothing and personal effects you possible can. There are six cabins on the lowest deck that do not have a window, and they are *really tiny*. While seven cabins have a double bed, all others have two lower beds, and several also have an upper (pullman) berth. There is no room service for food or snack items or beverages. The air-conditioning consists of recirculated air. Each cabin has its own private bathroom, although these really are miniscule.

Dining: The dining room is mildly attractive and has a single, open-seating policy. There is a "bring-your-own-bottle" policy aboard this ship, whether you want wine with dinner, or, indeed, any alcoholic beverages at all. The food is reasonably sound Americana fare, with good presentation and decent creativity.

Other Comments: This vessel, originally built for the US East Coast-based American Canadian Caribbean Line, is small and squat, has a shallow draft, and is designed specifically for in-depth coastal cruising. There is even a glass-bottom boat/sunfish sailboat.

A cruise aboard her is for those who really enjoy the camaraderie of others, there is little service, and no entertainment. Indeed, unless you go to your cabin, there is no getting away from other passengers. Take only very casual clothing, as the attire is strictly non-dressy.

The ship is also equipped with a unique, retractable wheelhouse for passage under low bridges on island waterway itineraries, and there is a small platform for those who want to swim off the stern.

The vessel was acquired in early 1998 by the Tlingit Indian-owned company and presently operates five-night roundtrip Alaskan cruises from Juneau to Haines, Skagway, Sitka, Glacier Bay, and Tracy Arm during the summer, and Baja, California, cruises during the winter. The cruises are *very* expensive (particularly when compared with other ships operating in the same areas), and are for those who want to be up close to nature and wildlife in a small environment. Gratuities are expected, at about $8 per person, per day.

m/y/s Wind Song
★★★★
(S)

LIFESTYLE:	PREMIUM
Cruise Line:	Windstar Cruises
Former Names:	-
Gross Tonnage:	5,350
Builder:	Ateliers et Chantiers du Havre (France)
Original Cost:	$34.2 million
Entered Service:	July 1987
Flag:	Bahamas
Tel. No.:	1103120
Fax No.:	1103123
Length (ft/m):	439.6/134.0
Beam (ft/m):	51.8/15.8
Draft (ft/m):	13.4/4.1
Type of Vessel:	computer-controlled sail-cruiser
No. of Masts:	4/6 self-furling sails
Sail Area (sq ft/sq m):	21,489/1,996.4
Main Propulsion:	a) engines/b) sails
Propulsion/Propellers:	diesel-electric (1,400kW)/1 (CP)
Decks:	7
Total Crew:	91
Pass. Capacity (basis 2):	148
Pass. Capacity (all berths):	159
Pass. Space Ratio (basis 2):	36.1
Pass. Space Ratio (all berths):	33.6
Officers:	British
Total Cabins:	74
Size Range (sq ft/m):	185.0–220.0/17.0–20.5

Cabins (outside view):	74
Cabins (inside — no view):	0
Cabins (single occupancy):	Yes — available
Cabins (with private balcony):	0
Cabins (wheelchair accessible):	0
Cabin Current:	110 volts
Cabin TV:	Yes
Dining Rooms:	3
Casino:	Yes
Slot Machines:	Yes
Swimming Pools (outdoors):	1 (dip pool)
Whirlpools:	1
Fitness Center:	Yes
Sauna/Steam Room:	Yes/No
Massage:	Yes
Self-Service Launderette:	No
Library:	Yes
Classification Society:	Bureau Veritas

RATINGS	POSSIBLE SCORE	SCORE ACHIEVED
Ship	500	398
Accommodation	200	166
Food	400	296
Service	400	301
Cruise	500	387
TOTAL	**2,000**	**1,548**

Accommodation: The cabins are all outside, one-price units (except for one owner's suite) and come completely equipped with everything you really need. Most have two portholes with deadlights (steel covers that provide a complete blackout at night). There is even a CD player (there is a small selection aboard ship, so it may be a good idea to take your own best-loved CDs), as well as a minibar-refrigerator (all drinks are at extra cost), a television, a VCR, and 24-hour room service with a limited menu. The decor is a pleasant mix of rich woods, natural fabrics, colorful soft furnishings, and hi-tech yacht-style amenities. When watching a movie in your cabin, you can also order popcorn to be delivered.

The bathrooms are a neat figure-eight shape and, although a little tight, are well-equipped, efficiently designed units, complete with a teakwood floor. Each has an excellent shower (no cabin bathrooms have bathtubs) and two toiletries cabinets with plenty of space. Bathrobes, of 100 percent cotton, are provided, and so are fragrant soap, shampoo, body lotion, shower cap, and mouthwash.

Dining: There is one rather chic and elegant dining room, with ocean views from large, picture windows. Features nouvelle cuisine, which is creative and attractively presented (including some signature dishes created by Joachim Splichal), and almost up to the standard of the small luxury ships. A single (open) seating means you dine when you want and with whom you wish.

When the company first started, European waiters provided service with practiced European finesse. However, those waiters have been replaced by Indonesians, whose communication skills at times can prove frustrating, although the service is pleasant enough. The selection of breads, cheeses, and fruits could be better.

There is a big push to sell wines, although the prices are extremely high, as they are for most alcoholic drinks (even bottled water is the highest in the industry, at $7.00 per liter bottle).

In addition, there is often casual dinner on the open deck under the stars, with grilled seafood and steaks. At the bars, hot and cold hors d'oeuvres appear at cocktail times.

Other Comments: This is a long, sleek-looking craft that is part yacht — part cruise ship, with four giant masts that tower 169.5 ft (51.66 m) above the deck (they are actually 204 ft, or 62.1 m, high), and fitted with computer-controlled sails; the masts, sails, and rigging alone cost $5 million. One of three identical vessels (a fourth, *Wind Saga*, was never built). When the masts for *Wind Star* (first of the three original Windstar vessels) were lowered into position, a US silver dollar, dated 1889, was placed under mast number two (the main mast).

There is little open deck space when the ship is full, due to the amount of complex sail machinery. There is a tiny dip pool. At the stern is a small water sports platform for those who enjoy all the goodies the ship offers (but only when at anchor, and only in really calm sea conditions). Water sports facilities include a banana boat, kayaks, sunfish sailboats, Windsurfers, water-ski boat, scuba and snorkel equipment, and four Zodiacs. You will be asked to sign a waiver if you wish to use the water sports equipment.

Features a finely crafted interior with pleasing, blonde woods, together with soft, complementary colors and decor that is chic, even elegant, but a little cold. Note that the main lounge aboard *Wind Star* is of a different design than *Wind Song* and *Wind Spirit*.

No scheduled activities help to make this a real relaxing, unregimented "get-away-from-it-all" vacation. The Windstar ships will cruise you in extremely comfortable surroundings that are bordering on contemporary luxury, yet in an unstructured environment.

Windstar Cruises ships provide a very relaxing, virtually unstructured cruise experience that is just right for seven idyllic nights in sheltered areas (but can be disturbing when a Windstar vessel is in small ports with several huge cruise ships). Ideal for couples who do not like large ships. This ship provides a delightful way to unwind in a stress-free environment. The dress code is casual (no jackets and ties required), even for dinner (the brochure states casual elegance). There are no formal nights or theme nights.

Wind Song sails seven-night Costa Rica cruises year-round. *Wind Spirit* sails Caribbean and Mediterranean itineraries. *Wind Star* sails seven-night Caribbean (from Barbados); and ten- and 11-day Southeast Asia cruises (from Singapore) starting December 1998.

You will probably be under sail for under 40 percent of the time (conditions and cruise area winds permitting). Gratuities are "not required" by the friendly, smiling staff, according to the brochure, but passengers find they are always accepted. Finally, this is cruising with no worries, no hassles, and no wanna go back home!

Weak Points: Be prepared for the "whine" of the vessel's generators, which are needed to run the air-conditioning and lighting systems 24 hours a day. That means you will also hear it at night in your cabin (any cabin), and takes most passengers a day or two to get used to. The swimming pool is a tiny "dip" pool. Beverage prices are high. The library is small, and needs more hardback fiction. The staff members, though friendly, are casual and a little sloppy in the finer points of service at times.

m/y/s Wind Spirit
★★★★
(S)

LIFESTYLE:	PREMIUM
Cruise Line:	Windstar Cruises
Former Names:	-
Gross Tonnage:	5,350
Builder: Ateliers et Chantiers du Havre (France)	
Original Cost:	$34.2 million
Entered Service:	April 1988
Flag:	Bahamas
Tel. No.:	1104434
Fax No.:	1103224
Length (ft/m):	439.6/134.0
Beam (ft/m):	51.8/15.8
Draft (ft/m):	13.4/4.1
Type of Vessel:	computer-controlled sail-cruiser
No. of Masts:	4/6 self-furling sails
Sail Area (sq ft/sq m):	21,489/1,996.4
Main Propulsion:	a) engines/b) sails
Propulsion/Propellers:	diesel-electric (1,400kW)/1 (CP)
Decks:	5
Total Crew:	88
Pass. Capacity (basis 2):	148
Pass. Capacity (all berths):	159
Pass. Space Ratio (basis 2):	36.1
Pass. Space Ratio (all berths):	33.6
Officers:	European
Total Cabins:	74
Size Range (sq ft/m):	182.9–220.6/17.0–22.5

For comments, see *Wind Song*.

Cabins (outside view):	74
Cabins (inside — no view):	0
Cabins (single occupancy):	0
Cabins (with private balcony):	0
Cabins (wheelchair accessible):	0
Cabin Current:	110 volts
Cabin TV:	Yes
Dining Rooms:	1 (+ 1 informal cafe)
Casino:	Yes
Slot Machines:	Yes
Swimming Pools (outdoors):	1 (dip pool)
Whirlpools:	1
Fitness Center:	Yes
Sauna/Steam Room:	Yes/No
Massage:	Yes
Self-Service Launderette:	No
Library:	Yes
Classification Society:	Bureau Veritas

RATINGS	POSSIBLE SCORE	SCORE ACHIEVED
Ship	500	398
Accommodation	200	166
Food	400	296
Service	400	301
Cruise	500	387
TOTAL	**2,000**	**1,548**

n/y/s Wind Star
★★★★
S)

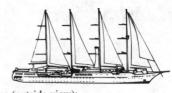

IFESTYLE:	PREMIUM
ruise Line:	Windstar Cruises
ormer Names:	-
jross Tonnage:	5,350
3uilder:	Ateliers et Chantiers du Havre (France)
Original Cost:	$34.2 million
Entered Service:	December 1986
'lag:	Bahamas
el. No.:	1104266
ax No.:	1103210
ength (ft/m):	439.6/134.0
3eam (ft/m):	51.8/15.8
Draft (ft/m):	13.4/4.1
ype of Vessel:	computer-controlled sail-cruiser
No. of Masts:	4/6 self-furling sails
ail Area (sq ft/sq m):	21,489/1,996.4
Main Propulsion:	a) engines/b) sails
ropulsion/Propellers:	diesel-electric (1,400kW)/1 (CP)
Decks:	5
otal Crew:	88
ass. Capacity (basis 2):	148
ass. Capacity (all berths):	168
ass. Space Ratio (basis 2):	36.1
ass. Space Ratio (all berths):	33.6
Officers:	European
otal Cabins:	74
Size Range (sq ft/m):	182.9–220.6/17.0–22.5

Cabins (outside view):	74
Cabins (inside — no view):	0
Cabins (single occupancy):	0
Cabins (with private balcony):	0
Cabins (wheelchair accessible):	0
Cabin Current:	110 volts
Cabin TV:	Yes
Dining Rooms:	1 (+ 1 informal cafe)
Casino:	Yes
Slot Machines:	Yes
Swimming Pools (outdoors):	1 (dip pool)
Whirlpools:	1
Fitness Center:	Yes
Sauna/Steam Room:	Yes/No
Massage:	Yes
Self-Service Launderette:	No
Library:	Yes
Classification Society:	Bureau Veritas

RATINGS	POSSIBLE SCORE	SCORE ACHIEVED
Ship	500	398
Accommodation	200	166
Food	400	296
Service	400	301
Cruise	500	387
TOTAL	**2,000**	**1,548**

For comments, see *Wind Song*.

Water sports facilities include an aft marina platform, kayaks, Windsurfers (2), Sunfish sailboats (2), water-ski boat, scuba, and snorkeling equipment, and Zodiacs (4).

m/y/s Wind Surf
★★★★ +
(S)

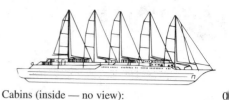

LIFESTYLE: PREMIUM

Cruise Line:	Windstar Cruises
Former Names:	*Club Med I*
Gross Tonnage:	14,745
Builder:	Ateliers et Chantiers du Havre (France)
Original Cost:	$140 million
Entered Service:	February 1990/May 1998
Flag:	Bahamas
Tel. No.:	1103120
Fax No.:	1103123
Length (ft/m):	617/185.1
Beam (ft/m):	65.6/20.0
Draft (ft/m):	16.4/5.0
Type of Vessel:	high-tech sail-cruiser
No. of Masts:	5/7 computer-controlled sails
Sail Area (sq ft/sq m):	26,910/2,500
Main Propulsion:	a) engines/b) sails
Propulsion/Propellers:	diesel (9,120kW)/2 (CP)
Decks:	8
Total Crew:	163
Pass. Capacity (basis 2):	312
Pass. Capacity (all berths):	312
Pass. Space Ratio (basis 2):	47.2
Pass. Space Ratio (all berths):	47.2
Officers:	European
Total Cabins:	156
Size Range (sq ft/m):	188.0–375.6/57.3–114.5
Cabins (outside view):	156

Cabins (inside — no view):	0
Cabins (single occupancy):	0
Cabins (with private balcony):	0
Cabins (wheelchair accessible):	0
Cabin Current:	110 and 220 volts
Cabin TV:	Yes
Dining Rooms:	(+ 1 informal cafe)
Elevators:	2
Casino:	Yes
Slot Machines:	Yes
Swimming Pools (outdoors):	2
Whirlpools:	2
Fitness Center:	Yes
Sauna/Steam Room:	Yes/No
Massage:	Yes
Self-Service Launderette:	No
Library:	Yes
Classification Society:	Bureau Veritas

RATINGS	POSSIBLE SCORE	SCORE ACHIEVED
Ship	500	424
Accommodation	200	166
Food	400	299
Service	400	293
Cruise	500	395
TOTAL	**2,000**	**1,577**

Accommodation: All of the standard cabins are very nicely equipped, have crisp and inviting decor, and feature a minibar-refrigerator, 24-hour room service, a safe, a TV, plenty of storage space, bathrobes, hairdryers, and two portholes. There are six 4-person cabins; 35 doubles are fitted with an extra Pullman berth, and several cabins have an interconnecting door (good for families).

Some 31 new suites (double the size of the former standard cabins) were added to Deck 3 during an extensive refit in 1998, resulting in a decrease of passenger capacity from that of the ship's former owners (Club Mediterranee). All except one of the new suites features two bathrooms and a separate living/dining area and bedroom (you can even have in-suite massage).

Dining: The Restaurant (with 272 seats) has tables for two, four, or six, and a single (open) seating is featured for all meals, so you can sit with whom you wish, when you like. The ship provides a mixture of California and continental cuisine. Signature dishes created by master chefs Joachim Splichal and Jeanne Jones are featured daily.

Apart from the main dining room, there is also the Veranda Bistro, with its open terrace for informal (buffet) meals, including dinner (it really is lovely to be outside, eating an informal meal on a balmy night).

Other Comments: One of a pair of the world's largest sail-cruisers is part cruise ship, part yacht. She is a larger, grander sister to the original three Windstar vessels. Five huge masts of 164.0 ft/50.0 m provide seven sails with a total surface area of 26,881 sq ft (2,497 m^2). No human hands touch the sails, as everything is handled electronically by computer control from the bridge.

Features a large, hydraulic water sports platform at the stern, and extensive water sports facilities that include 12 Windsurfers, 3 sailboats, 2 water-ski boats, 20 single scuba tanks, snorkels, fins and masks, and four motorized watersport boats (for water-skiing, etc), all at no extra charge.

The principal new facility aboard this ship is a totally new, expanded health spa, with some excellent facilities and treatment rooms, and a staff of 12 (there are special spa packages that can be pre-booked through your travel agent), and a good fitness center. The ship also has small meeting rooms.

This vessel should be superb for the more upscale active singles and couples who might like the informality found aboard this vessel.

This ship was acquired by Windstar Cruises in March 1998. Her passenger capacity was reduced from 386 to 312, and 31 new larger suites were created from former smaller (standard) cabins.

She now features cruises from Barbados (November through March) and from Nice (May through October). However, note that the European itineraries are really port-intensive, which means you sail each night and are in port each day. With such itineraries, there seems little point to having the sails. More balanced itineraries would be much better (on three out of four Caribbean itineraries there is one day at sea).

This ship has become a larger, more upscale partner for the three original Windstar Cruises vessels presently operating (*Wind Song, Wind Spirit, Wind Star*). All gratuities and port taxes are included in the brochure price (no additional gratuities are expected), which itself is considerably higher than those of the three smaller vessels in the fleet.

m/s World Discoverer
★★★★
(S)

LIFESTYLE:	STANDARD
Cruise Line:	Society Expeditions
Former Names:	*Bewa Discoverer*
Gross Tonnage:	3,724
Builder:	Schichau Unterweser (Germany)
Original Cost:	n/a
Entered Service:	1974
Flag:	Liberia
Tel. No.:	1242744
Fax No.:	1242744
Length (ft/m):	287.1/87.51
Beam (ft/m):	49.6/15.12
Draft (ft/m):	14.6/4.46
Propulsion/Propellers:	diesel (3,530kW)/1 (CP)
Decks:	7
Total Crew:	75
Pass. Capacity (basis 2):	137
Pass. Capacity (all berths):	137
Pass. Space Ratio (basis 2):	27.1
Pass. Space Ratio (all berths):	27.1
Officers:	European
Total Cabins:	71
Size Range (sq ft/m):	89.0–218.0/8.2–20.2
Cabins (outside view):	71
Cabins (inside — no view):	0
Cabins (single occupancy):	5
Cabins (with private balcony):	0
Cabins (wheelchair accessible):	0

Cabin Current:	220 volts
Cabin TV:	No
Dining Rooms:	1
Elevators:	1
Casino:	No
Slot Machines:	No
Swimming Pools (outdoors):	1
Swimming Pools (inside):	0
Whirlpools:	0
Fitness Center:	No
Sauna/Steam Room:	No/No
Massage:	No
Self-Service Launderette:	No
Lecture Room/Theater:	Yes
Library:	Yes
Zodiacs:	Yes
Helicopter Pad:	No
Classification Society:	American Bureau of Shipping

RATINGS	POSSIBLE SCORE	SCORE ACHIEVED
Ship	500	356
Accommodation	200	153
Food	400	295
Service	400	301
Cruise	500	369
TOTAL	**2,000**	**1,474**

Accommodation: The cabins are of good proportions given the size of the ship; they are reasonably comfortable and very tastefully furnished. The cabin closet space is rather limited, however, and the bathrooms are small, with little space for toiletry items.

Dining: The dining room is very attractive and quite cozy (there are even a few tables for two). There is a single (open) seating, so you dine when you want, with whom you wish. Big picture windows and comfortable chairs make for an elegant setting. Features excellent cuisine and service, although it relies heavily on dairy products. Limited selection of breads and fruits.

Other Comments: This sophisticated, small, but very comfortable vessel was built expressly for expedition and adventure cruises and has a well-proportioned profile with a contemporary, swept-back funnel. Features an ice-hardened hull, is extremely maneuverable, and is well maintained. The ship is well equipped for in-depth expedition cruising in comfort. Water sports facilities include scuba diving and snorkeling equipment, fishing, water-ski boat, and equipment for Windsurfing.

Inside the ship, the decor is rather elegant, with warm colors and fine soft fabrics throughout. Naturalists and expert lecturers and nature specialists escort every expedition. She is one of the nicest of the expedition cruise vessels of this type in service today. The passenger gangway is rather narrow and steep, however.

This ship provides a fine setting for expedition cruising to some of the most remote destinations in the world. It is expensive, but well worth it for discerning, well-traveled passengers yearning for a sense of adventure and for those who enjoy learning about the world around us and its fascinating peoples.

m/s World Renaissance
★★ +
(M)

LIFESTYLE:	STANDARD
Cruise Line:	Royal Olympic Cruises
Former Names:	*Awani Dream, World Renaissance, Renaissance, Homeric Renaissance*
Gross Tonnage:	11,724
Builder:	Chantiers de l'Atlantique (France)
Original Cost:	n/a
Entered Service:	May 1966/January 1996
Flag:	Greece
Tel. No.:	1130440
Fax No.:	1130440
Length (ft/m):	492.1/150.02
Beam (ft/m):	69.0/21.06
Draft (ft/m):	22.9/7.00
Propulsion/Propellers:	diesel (10,060kW)/2 (FP)
Decks:	8
Total Crew:	204
Pass. Capacity (basis 2):	457
Pass. Capacity (all berths):	599
Pass. Space Ratio (basis 2):	25.6
Pass. Space Ratio (all berths):	19.5
Officers:	Greek
Total Cabins:	242
Size Range (sq ft/m):	110–270/10.2–25.0
Cabins (outside view):	178
Cabins (inside — no view):	63
Cabins (single occupancy):	1
Cabins (with private balcony):	0

Cabins (wheelchair accessible):	0
Cabin Current:	110 volts
Cabin TV:	No
Dining Rooms:	1
Elevators:	1
Casino:	Yes
Slot Machines:	Yes
Swimming Pools (outdoors):	2
Swimming Pools (inside):	0
Whirlpools:	0
Fitness Center:	Yes
Sauna/Steam Room:	Yes/No
Massage:	Yes
Self-Service Launderette:	No
Movie Theater/Seats:	Yes/110
Library:	Yes
Classification Society:	Lloyd's Register

RATINGS	POSSIBLE SCORE	SCORE ACHIEVED
Ship	500	244
Accommodation	200	105
Food	400	238
Service	400	243
Cruise	500	266
TOTAL	**2,000**	**1,096**

Accommodation: Some of the cabins have some fine wood paneling. They are homey and reasonably spacious, though certainly not luxurious. The cabin bathrooms are tiled, but are very small, and there is little space for toiletries.

Dining: The dining room is reasonably pleasant, although there are no tables for two. The tables are close together, and there are two seatings. The cuisine is now predominantly Indonesian, with plenty of spicy foods. There is thus a limited selection of breads, pastry, fruit, and cheeses. The service is very basic and there is really no finesse.

Other Comments: This ship has traditional 1960s styling and profile topped by a slender funnel. She was operated for many years by Epirotiki Lines (now part of Royal Olympic Cruises), and is now back with ROC after a short sojourn in Indonesia with Awani Dream Cruises, who ceased operations in late 1997. She has a pencil-slim funnel and white superstructure atop a royal blue hull.

The ship has a generous amount of open deck and sunbathing space for its size. The interior layout, however, is disjointed and awkward, and signage could be better.

Inside the ship, the decor can be said to be both "colonial" and "eclectic," with some touches that still remind one of her original days as a French ship. Although the main lounge is comfortable, there are few other public rooms, and therefore the ship always feels busy (crowded). The library, as a room, is a restful place to relax. Has a friendly Greek staff and good basic service, although there is little refinement.

Weak Points: The ship has a steep passenger gangway in most ports of call. There is no wraparound promenade deck outdoors, and there are no cushioned pads for the deck lounge chairs.

s/y Yankee Clipper
(S)

LIFESTYLE	STANDARD
Cruise Line:	Windjammer Barefoot Cruises
Former Names:	*Pioneer, Cressida*
Gross Tonnage:	327
Builder:	Krupp, Germany
Entered Service:	1927/1965
Flag:	Equitorial Guinea
Tel. No.:	n/a
Fax No.:	n/a
Length (ft/m):	197.0/60.0
Beam (ft/m):	30.0/9.1
Draft (ft/m):	17.0/5.1
Type of Vessel:	schooner
No. of Masts:	3
Sail Area (sq ft/sq m):	8,000/743.2
Main Propulsion:	sail power
Propulsion/Propellers:	diesel/1 (FP)
Decks:	3
Total Crew:	24
Pass. Capacity (basis 2):	64
Pass. Capacity (all berths):	64
Pass. Space Ratio (basis 2):	5.1
Pass. Space Ratio (all berths):	5.1
Officers:	International
Total Cabins:	32
Size Range (sq ft/m):	65–86/6.0–7.9
Cabins (outside view):	32
Cabins (inside — no view):	0
Cabins (single occupancy):	0
Cabins (with private balcony):	0
Cabins (wheelchair accessible):	0
Cabin Current:	110 volts
Cabin TV:	No
Dining Rooms:	1
Elevators:	0
Casino:	0
Slot Machines:	0
Swimming Pools (outdoors):	0
Whirlpools:	0
Fitness Center:	No
Sauna/Steam Room:	No/No
Massage:	No
Self-Service Launderette:	No
Library:	Yes
Classification Society:	none

RATINGS	POSSIBLE SCORE	SCORE ACHIEVED
Ship	500	NYR
Accommodation	200	NYR
Food	400	NYR
Service	400	NYR
Cruise	500	NYR
TOTAL	**2,000**	**NYR**
Expected Score Range:		**900-1100**

She was built as one of the only armor-plated privated yachts in the world. Confiscated during World War II as a war prize, she was later acquired by the Vanderbilts. She joined the Windjammer Barefoot Cruises fleet in 1965. Sails from Grenada. For other comments regarding Windjammer Barefoot Cruises, see *Flying Cloud.*

m/v Yorktown Clipper
★★★ +
(S)

LIFESTYLE:	STANDARD		Cabins (wheelchair accessible):	0
Cruise Line:	Clipper Cruise Line		Cabin Current:	110 volts
Former Names:	-		Cabin TV:	No
Gross Tonnage:	2,354		Dining Rooms:	1
Builder:	First Coast Shipbuilding (USA)		Elevators:	0
Original Cost:	$12 million		Casino:	No
Entered Service:	April 1988		Slot Machines:	No
Flag:	USA		Swimming Pools (outdoors):	0
Tel. No.:	n/a		Swimming Pools (inside):	0
Fax No.:	n/a		Whirlpools:	0
Length (ft/m):	257.0/78.30		Fitness Center:	No
Beam (ft/m):	43.0/13.10		Sauna/Steam Room:	No/No
Draft (ft/m):	8.0/2.43		Massage:	No
Propulsion/Propellers:	diesel (1,044kW)/2 (FP)		Self-Service Launderette:	No
Decks:	4		Movie Theater/Seats:	No
Total Crew:	40		Library:	Yes
Pass. Capacity (basis 2):	138		Classification Society: American Bureau of Shipping	
Pass. Capacity (all berths):	138			
Pass. Space Ratio (basis 2):	17.0			
Pass. Space Ratio (all berths):	17.0			
Officers:	American			
Total Cabins:	69			
Size Range (sq ft/m):	121.0–138.0/11.2–12.8			
Cabins (outside view):	69			
Cabins (inside — no view):	0			
Cabins (single occupancy):	0			
Cabins (with private balcony):	0			

RATINGS	POSSIBLE SCORE	SCORE ACHIEVED
Ship	500	295
Accommodation	200	121
Food	400	277
Service	400	265
Cruise	500	309
TOTAL	**2,000**	**1,267**

Accommodation: The all-outside cabins are really quite small, but, with lots of wood-accented trim and restful colors, they are reasonably comfortable and tastefully furnished. The bathrooms, likewise, are small, with little space for toiletry items (but a night-light is provided, so you don't have to turn on bright lights in the middle of the night — a thoughtful touch). There is no room service for food and beverage items, as found aboard larger ships.

Dining: The dining room is warm and fairly inviting and has large picture windows, although there are no tables for two. There is one open seating, so you dine with whom you wish. The service is provided by a young, all-American, midwestern team that smiles a lot and is quite friendly. The finesse associated with European service is simply not to be found, however. The food, however, is of a good quality, and made from locally purchased fresh ingredients. There is little menu choice, but the food provided is nicely presented. There is an adequate but very limited selection of breads and fruits.

Other Comments: This small vessel was built specifically to operate coastal and inland waterway cruises. She has a shallow draft and good maneuverability and has been well maintained since new. There is a teak wood outdoor sun deck. Inflatable rubber Zodiac craft are used for for close-in shore excursions.

Inside, there is a glass-walled observation lounge. This ship offers a decidedly "Americana" experience for those seeking to learn more about the coastal ports around the US during the summer months, while Caribbean cruises are featured during the winter months.

A casual, completely nonregimented lifestyle is featured aboard, and this can best be compared to a small, congenial country club without any of the pretentiousness, and a good antidote to cruising aboard large ships. There are no mindless activities or corny games and no entertainment as such, except for an occasional movie after dinner (the dining room converts to a movie screening room after dinner). There are, however, always one or two lecturers aboard each sailing, which highlights the learning experience that is an essential part of cruising with Clipper Cruise Lines.

497

This really should not be compared with big-ship ocean cruising. The price, however, is high for wha you get when compared to many other ships, and airfare is extra. A nonsmoking policy throughout all inte rior areas was put into effect December 1996.

Weak Points: She really is a high-density ship, with only two public rooms: a dining room and a lounge. High engine and generator noises are quite irritating when the ship is underway and need getting used to (not so noticeable for those who may be hard of hearing).

SHOPPING

→ Many cruise lines that operate in Alaska, the Bahamas, the Caribbean, and Mexican Riviera openly engage a company that provides the services of a "shopping lecturer." The shopping lecturer promotes selected shops, goods, and services heavily, fully authorized by the cruise line (which receives a commission from the same). This relieves the cruise director of any responsibilities, together with any question about his involvement, credibility, and financial remuneration.

→ Shopping maps, with "selected" stores highlighted, are placed in your cabin. Often, they come with a "guarantee" such as: "Shop with confidence at each of the recommended stores. Each merchant listed on this map has been carefully selected on the basis of quality, fair dealing, and value. These merchants have given Cruise Line X a guarantee of satisfaction valid for thirty (30) days after purchase, excluding passenger negligence and buyers' regret, and have paid a promotional fee for inclusion as a guaranteed store."

→ Know in advance just what you are looking for, especially if your time is limited. But if time is no problem, browsing can be fun.

→ When shopping time is included in shore excursions, be wary of stores recommended by tour guides; the guides are likely to be receiving commissions from the merchants.

→ Shop around and compare prices before you buy. Good shopping hints and recommendations are often given in the port lecture at the start of your cruise.

→ When shopping for local handicrafts, make sure they have indeed been made locally.

→ Be wary of "bargain-priced" name brands as they may well be counterfeit and of dubious quality. For watches, check the guarantee. Some shopping information may be available in information literature about the port and this should be available at the ship's shore excursion office.

→ Remember that the ship's shops are also duty free, and, for the most part, competitive in price. The shops on board are closed while in port, however, due to international customs regulations.

m/s Zaandam
(L)

LIFESTYLE:	PREMIUM
Cruise Line:	Holland America Line
Former Names:	-
Gross Tonnage:	63,000
Builder:	Fincantieri (Italy)
Original Cost:	$300 million
Entered Service:	March 2000
Flag:	The Netherlands
Tel. No.:	n/a
Fax No.:	n/a
Length (ft/m):	777.5/237.00
Beam (ft/m):	105.8/32.25
Draft (ft/m):	25.5/7.80
Propulsion/Propellers:	diesel-electric (37,500kW)/2 (CP)
Decks:	10
Total Crew:	561
Pass. Capacity (basis 2):	1,440
Pass. Capacity (all berths):	1,440
Pass. Space Ratio (basis 2):	43.7
Pass. Space Ratio (all berths):	43.7
Officers:	Dutch
Total Cabins:	720
Size Range (sq ft/m):	151.0–1172.0/14.04–108.9
Cabins (outside view):	581
Cabins (inside — no view):	139
Cabins (single occupancy):	0
Cabins (with private balcony):	197

Cabins (wheelchair accessible):	23
Cabin Current:	110 volts
Cabin TV:	Yes
Dining Rooms:	1 main (+1 alternative)
Elevators:	16
Casino:	Yes
Slot Machines:	Yes
Swimming Pools (outdoors):	2
Swimming Pools (inside):	1 (magrodome cover)
Whirlpools:	2
Fitness Center:	Yes
Sauna/Steam Room:	Yes/Yes
Massage:	Yes
Self-Service Launderette:	Yes
Movie Theater/Seats:	Yes/205
Library:	Yes
Classification Society:	Lloyds Register

RATINGS	POSSIBLE SCORE	SCORE ACHIEVED
Ship	500	NYR
Accommodation	200	NYR
Food	400	NYR
Service	400	NYR
Cruise	500	NYR
TOTAL	**2,000**	**NYR**
Expected Score Range:		**1500-1700**

For comments, see *Volendam*.

m/v Zenith
★★★★ +
(L)

LIFESTYLE:	PREMIUM
Cruise Line:	Celebrity Cruises
Former Names:	-
Gross Tonnage:	47,255
Builder:	Meyer Werft (Germany)
Original Cost:	$210 million
Entered Service:	April 1992
Flag:	Liberia
Tel. No.:	1245564
Fax No.:	1245567
Length (ft/m):	681.0/207.59
Beam (ft/m):	95.1/29.00
Draft (ft/m):	23.6/7.20
Propulsion/Propellers:	diesel (19,960kW)/2 (CP)
Decks:	9
Total Crew:	670
Pass. Capacity (basis 2):	1,374
Pass. Capacity (all berths):	1,796
Pass. Space Ratio (basis 2):	34.3
Pass. Space Ratio (all berths):	26.3
Officers:	Greek
Total Cabins:	687
Size Range (sq ft/m):	172.2–500.5/16.0–46.50
Cabins (outside view):	541
Cabins (inside — no view):	146
Cabins (single occupancy):	0
Cabins (with private balcony):	0

Cabins (wheelchair accessible):	4
Cabin Current:	110 volts
Cabin TV:	Yes
Dining Rooms:	1
Elevators:	7
Casino:	Yes
Slot Machines:	Yes
Swimming Pools (outdoors):	2
Swimming Pools (inside):	0
Whirlpools:	3
Fitness Center:	Yes
Sauna/Steam Room:	Yes/No
Massage:	Yes
Self-Service Launderette:	No
Movie Theater/Seats:	Yes/850
Library:	Yes
Classification Society:	Lloyd's Register

RATINGS	POSSIBLE SCORE	SCORE ACHIEVED
Ship	500	417
Accommodation	200	161
Food	400	317
Service	400	323
Cruise	500	413
TOTAL	**2,000**	**1,631**

Accommodation: The suites on Deck 10 are very tastefully furnished, although they are not as large as the suites aboard the company's three larger vessels, *Century, Galaxy,* and *Mercury.* They do, however, have excellent bathrooms and come with butler service. All accommodation designated as suites have duvets on the beds instead of sheets and blankets.

The standard-sized inside and outside cabins are reasonably well insulated and have a good amount of closet and drawer space. They are nicely appointed and spacious enough for seven-night cruises, being much larger than cabins aboard the ships of sister company Royal Caribbean International, for example.

The bathrooms are very practical and well laid-out, with large shower areas, and various toiletries are provided (soap, shampoo/conditioner, body lotion, and shower cap). Note that most outside cabins on Bermuda Deck have lifeboat-obstructed views. The cabin soundproofing is fair to very good, depending on the location.

Dining: The large dining room, which features a raised section in its center, has several tables for two, as well as for four, six, or eight (in banquettes), although the chairs do not have armrests. There are two seatings. The cuisine, its presentation, and service are really very good. There is a separate menu for vegetarians and children.

For informal meals, the Windsurf Cafe features good buffets for breakfast (including an omelet station) and luncheon (including a pasta station). At peak times, however, the buffets (port side for smokers, starboard side for nonsmokers), is simply too small. At night, the dining area changes into an alternative dining spot for passengers who want good food, but in a more casual setting than the main restaurant, with items such as grilled salmon, steaks, and rotisserie chicken, as well as specialties that change frequently.

The Grill, located outdoor adjacent to (but aft of) the Windsurf Café, serves typical fast-food items. And for those who cannot live without them, freshly baked pizzas (in a box) can be delivered in an insulated pouch to your cabin.

Other Comments: This ship has a smart, contemporary profile with a powerful thrust owing to her blue paint striping along the sides, separating the hull from the superstructure, like her sister, *Horizon*, which is two years older.

Inside, there is a similar interior layout and elegant but decor that most find a little warmer and an enlarged and enhanced forward observation lounge with a larger dance floor.

The principal deck that houses many of the public entertainment rooms features a double-width indoor promenade. The feeling is one of uncluttered surroundings. Intelligent, well-chosen artworks are provided throughout. An art deco-style hotel-like lobby (reminiscent of hotels in Miami Beach) has a two-deck-high ceiling and a spacious feel to it. Soothing pastel colors and high-quality soft furnishings have been used throughout this ship. There is a good-size library.

There is also an excellent show lounge (with better shows than *Horizon*), with main and balcony levels, and good sight lines from almost all seats (however, the railing in the balcony level does impede viewing). Has a good (seasonal) program for children and teenagers, with specially trained youth counselors. There is a large, elegantly appointed casino with its own bar, while outside is a satellite-linked BankAtlantic ATM machine (there is a $5 access charge) in case you didn't bring enough cash.

A refurbishment in mid-1999 added a Michael's Club cigar smoking lounge in what was an underused discotheque, as well as an enlarged library, and small business center. Also added is a popular martini bar, a room dedicated to the display of art (for art auctions), and an expanded health spa that now includes a rasul treatment room and an enlarged beauty salon with ocean-view windows.

This ship will provide you with a well-packaged cruise vacation in elegant, calming surroundings, with finely presented food in a formal dining room setting, and service by a well-trained service staff which includes a large percentage of Europeans. Almost all passengers feel that the company exceeds their expectations from a seven-night cruise experience.

<u>Weak Points</u>: The doors to the public restrooms and the outdoor decks are rather heavy. The public restrooms are still clinical and need some "softening" treatment. There are cushioned pads for poolside deck lounge chairs only, but not for chairs on other outside decks. The food on the room service menu is very basic. Unlike the company's larger *Century*, *Galaxy*, and *Mercury*, there is no AquaSpa thalassotherapy pool.

"Gray Market" ships are so called due to the fact that they do not run on regularly scheduled itineraries other than those ships which operate one-, two-, and three-night "cruises" for the principal benefit of casino players whose local laws prohibit them from casino gaming on land. Other ships operate under charter to companies and private individuals, typically on overnight and other short cruises.

m/s Hong Kong Dragon Star (S)

Cruise Line:	Topnew Cruises	Beam (ft/m):	55.7/17.00
Ship Base:	Hong Kong	Draft (ft/m):	14.4/4.40
Former Names:	*Columbus Caravelle,*	Propulsion/Propellers:	diesel (6,000kW)/2 (CP)
Ernest Hemingway, Sally Caravelle, Delfin Caravelle		Passenger Decks:	5
Gross Tonnage:	7,560	Total Crew:	120
Builder:	Rauma Yards (Finland)	Pass. Capacity (basis 2):	250
Built:	1990	Pass. Space Ratio (basis 2):	29.0
Length (ft/m):	381.8/116.40		

Comments: The smart-looking ship presently caters to Hong Kong's resident population, a fairly sophisticated local market that enjoys overnight gambling jamboree cruises. Twin swept-back outboard funnels highlight the smart exterior design of this small cruise ship, which has an ice-hardened hull and a shallow draft. She was originally built for the now defunct Finnish company, Delfin Cruises.

The ship's contemporary interior design features pleasing colors and complementary fabrics. There is an attractive winter garden area, an observation bar, outdoor observation decks, and good facilities for lecturers or group meetings.

m/s Leisure World (S)

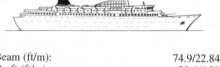

Cruise Line:	New Century Cruise Lines	Beam (ft/m):	74.9/22.84
Ship Base:	Singapore	Draft (ft/m):	20.6/6.29
Former Names:	*Fantasy World, Asean World,*	Propulsion/Propellers:	diesel (12,950kW)/2 (CP)
	Shangri-La World, Skyward	Passenger Decks:	8
Gross Tonnage:	16,254	Total Crew:	250
Builder:	Seebeckwerft (Germany)	Pass. Capacity (basis 2):	730
Built:	1969	Pass. Space Ratio (basis 2):	22.2
Length (ft/m):	525.3/160.13		

Comments: This ship operates inconveniently just off Singapore (actually Batam in Malaysia and occasionally from Singapore itself) in international waters for overnight gambling jamborees. The ship is reached by fast ferry from Singapore.

She is a mildly attractive, but rather dated seventies-looking ship with a distinctive daytime sun lounge set high and forward around the ship's mast and features plenty of light. The ship's interiors features light, airy decor in clean, crisp colors. There is a pleasant show lounge, although the ceiling height is low. There is a good karaoke lounge for those inevitable, but popular, sing-alongs. The casino is fairly extensive, and the action is constant and noisy.

Being a very high-density ship means crowded public areas, lots of noise, and lines for buffets and elevators. Despite what company brochures and advertising claim, this is not a luxury liner, by any stretch of the imagination. It attracts many gamblers, who like the fast-paced action. Weekend cruises attract many families. The ship is adequate for short cruises for active passengers wanting comfortable, friendly and casual surroundings.

m/s **Megastar Aries**
(S)

Cruise Line:	Star Cruises	Draft (ft/m):	10.9/3.3
Ship Base:	Singapore	Propulsion/Propellers:	diesel (3,356kW)/2 (CP)
Former Names:	*Aurora I, Lady-D, Lady Diana*	Passenger Decks:	4
Gross Tonnage:	3,300	Officers:	Scandinavian
Builder:	Flender Werft (Germany)	Total Crew:	59
Built:	1992	Pass. Capacity (basis 2):	80
Length (ft/m):	269.6/82.2	Pass. Space Ratio (basis 2):	41.2
Beam (ft/m):	45.9/14.0		

Comments: This ship was built originally for the defunct Windsor Line. Presently operated by Star Cruises for private charters, together with sister ship *MegaStar Taurus*.

Although she operates principally in sheltered areas, being small, she does roll in strong seas, however. Although there is no wrap-around promenade deck outdoors, there are teakwood decks for strolling and real wooden "steamer" chairs. The swimming pool, located forward of the mast on the uppermost deck, is tiny, however, as it is really a "dip" pool. There is a cute wooden bar on the port side of the ship's funnel, added when Star Cruises took over the vessel.

Inside, public room space is limited, but there is a warm friendly ambience. Wood-accented trim and fine soft furnishings, plush chairs and sofas, and fresh flowers are everywhere. There is a library and a separate karaoke room. This is strictly a private club at sea, for VIPs.

Rather like having the privileges of a private yacht, without the burden of ownership. This ship is ideal for small corporate charters and for high-roller gamblers and operates year-round only on short cruises, based on Port Klang (Malaysia) and Singapore.

m/s **MegaStar Taurus**
(S)

Cruise Line:	Star Cruises	Draft (ft/m):	10.9/3.3
Ship Base:	Singapore	Propulsion/Propellers:	diesel (3,356kW)/2 (CP)
Former Names:	*Aurora II, Lady Sarah*	Passenger Decks:	4
Gross Tonnage:	3,300	Officers:	Scandinavian
Builder:	Flender Werft (Germany)	Total Crew:	59
Built:	1992	Pass. Capacity (basis 2):	80
Length (ft/m):	269.6/82.2	Pass. Space Ratio (basis 2):	41.2
Beam (ft/m):	45.9/14.0		

Comments: This ship was built originally for the defunct Windsor Line. Presently operated by Star Cruises for private charters, together with sister ship *MegaStar Aries*.

She operates principally in sheltered areas, but being small, she does roll in strong seas. Although there is no wraparound promenade deck outdoors, there are teakwood decks for strolling and real wooden "steamer" chairs. The swimming pool, located forward of the mast on the uppermost deck, is tiny, however, as it is really a "dip" pool. There is a cute wooden bar on the port side of the ship's funnel, added when Star Cruises took over the vessel. Inside, public room space is limited, but there is a warm friendly ambience. Wood-accented trim and fine soft furnishings, plush chairs and sofas, and fresh flowers are everywhere. There is a library and a separate room for karaoke sing-a-longs. This is strictly a private club at sea, for those that want to celebrate a special event and for VIPs.

Rather like having the privileges of a private yacht, without the burden of ownership. This ship is ideal for small corporate charters and for high-roller gamblers and operates year-round only on short cruises, based on Port Klang (Malaysia) and Singapore.

m/s Neptune
(S)

Cruise Line:	Ki Development Corp	Beam (ft/m):	67.6/20.62
Ship Base:	Hong Kong	Draft (ft/m):	17.7/5.40
Former Names:	*Walrus, Nautican, Crown Monarch*	Propulsion/Propellers:	diesel (13,680kW)/2 (CP)
Gross Tonnage:	15,271	Passenger Decks:	5
Builder:	Union Navale de Levante (Spain)	Total Crew:	215
Built:	1990	Pass. Capacity (basis 2):	510
Length (ft/m):	494.4/150.72	Pass. Space Ratio (basis 2):	29.9

Comments: This ship presently operates short cruises from Hong Kong and caters to a local market that includes gamblers and nightlife lovers.

She is a moderately handsome, highly maneuverable small ship with a swept back funnel and a profile that is quite well balanced. There is a reasonably good amount of open deck and sunbathing space. The lifeboats are well located to avoid obstructed views.

The interior is well designed and there is a good layout and passenger flow. There are numerous public rooms to choose from, all tastefully decorated in contemporary colors.

This ship, presently operates from Hong Kong on what are known locally as "gray market" cruises under a three-year charter to the Ki Development Corporation; various local tour operators and travel agencies sell the short cruises. The ship provides local passengers with a reasonably good short cruise experience in pleasant, comfortable, and contemporary surroundings, at a modest price.

ms Oriental Pearl
(S)

Cruise Line:	Oriental Pearl Entertainment	Beam (ft/m):	65.9/20.10
Ship Base:	Hong Kong	Draft (ft/m):	19.0/5.80
Former Names:	*Costa Playa/Pearl/*	Propulsion/Propellers:	diesel (12,060kW)/2 (CP)
	Ocean Pearl/Pearl of Scandinavia/Finnstar	Passenger Decks:	9
Gross Tonnage:	12,475	Total Crew:	232
Builder:	Wartsila (Finland)	Pass. Capacity (basis 2):	489
Built:	1967	Pass. Space Ratio (basis 2):	25.5
Length (ft/m):	517.4/157.7		

Comments: Originally built as a ferry, but reconstructed in 1988 as a cruise vessel, she now operates overnight cruises for gambling jamborees for the local Hong Kong market. After sailing for many years in Southeast Asia, the ship then spent a couple of years in the Caribbean before being permanently based in Hong Kong.

Her interiors include reasonably tasteful decor that features many earth tones, with splashes of color added. There is also some interesting artwork. Some nicely refinished woods give much warmth. However, the layout is awkward, with several dead-end passageways. Indonesian and Filipino hotel staff provide personal service with a smile, although standards have declined. There are too many irritating announcements.

However, there is too much use of reflective, mirror-polished ceilings that are distracting. The seats in the small "screening room" cinema, which has a small, but wide screen, are not staggered, and so the sight lines are not good.

m/s Sun Viva
(S)

Cruise Line:	Sun Cruises	Beam (ft/m):	50.1/15.30
Ship Base:	Singapore	Draft (ft/m):	13.2/4.05
Former Names:	*Renaissance Five*	Propulsion/Propellers:	diesel (5,000kW)/2 (CP)
Gross Tonnage:	4,200	Passenger Decks:	5
Builder:	Nuovi Cantieri Apuania (Italy)	Total Crew:	72
Built:	1991	Pass. Capacity (basis 2):	114
Length (ft/m):	297.2/90.60	Pass. Space Ratio (basis 2):	36.8

Comments: The ship has contemporary mega-yacht looks and handsome styling with twin flared funnels. Sun Cruises also operates sister ship *Sun Viva II* (ex-*Renaissance Five*). The navigation bridge is a well-rounded half-moon design. Originally one of four identical vessels, she is now available for short cruise charters.

There is one promenade deck outdoors, and a reasonable amount of open deck and sunbathing space. All of the deck furniture (tables, chairs) are made of teak, and the deck lounge chairs have thick cushioned pads. There is a teak water sports platform at the stern of the ship.

Inside the ship, there is an elegant interior design. The main lounge, the focal point for all social activities, has six pillars that destroy sight lines to the small stage area. There is also a very small book and video library.

This ship is very comfortable and totally inviting, presently used for charters and short cruises for gambling high-rollers who like their ships to be small and exclusive.

m/s Sun Viva II
(S)

Cruise Line:	Sun Cruises	Draft (ft/m):	13.7/4.20
Ship Base:	Singapore	Beam (ft/m):	50.1/15.30
Former Names:	*Renaissance Six*	Propulsion/Propellers:	diesel (5,000kW)/2 (CP)
Gross Tonnage:	4,200	Passenger Decks:	5
Builder:	Nuovi Cantieri Apuania (Italy)	Total Crew:	72
Built:	1991	Pass. Capacity (basis 2):	114
Length (ft/m):	297.2/90.60	Pass. Space Ratio (basis 2):	36.8

Comments: The ship has contemporary mega-yacht looks and handsome styling with twin flared funnels. The navigation bridge is a well-rounded half-moon design. Originally one of four identical vessels, she is now available for short cruise charters, together with sister ship *Sun Viva*.

There is one promenade deck outdoors and a reasonable amount of open deck and sunbathing space. All of the deck furniture (tables, chairs) are made of teak, and the deck lounge chairs have thick cushioned pads. There is a teak water sports platform at the stern of the ship.

Inside the ship, there is an elegant interior design. The main lounge, the focal point for all social activities, has six pillars that destroy sight lines to the small stage area. There is also a very small book and video library.

This ship is very comfortable and totally inviting, presently used for charters and short cruises for gambling high-rollers who like their ships to be small and exclusive.

ms The Mercury
(S)

Cruise Line:	Universal Cruises	Beam (ft/m):	50.1/15.30
Ship Base:	Singapore	Draft (ft/m):	11.9/3.65
Former Names:	*Renaissance I*	Propulsion/Propellers:	diesel (3,514kW)/2 (CP)
Gross Tonnage:	3,990	Passenger Decks:	5
Builder:	Cantieri Navale Ferrari (Italy)	Total Crew:	72
Built:	1989	Pass. Capacity (basis 2):	100
Length (ft/m):	289.6/88.30	Pass. Space Ratio (basis 2):	39.9

Comments: This small ship, together with sister ship *The Neptune* (ex-*Renaissance II*), has contemporary mega-yacht looks and a reasonably handsome profile. She is being operated from Singapore strictly for charters and private functions.

Exquisite all-outside suites combine gorgeous, highly polished imitation rosewood paneling with lots of mirrors, handcrafted Italian furniture, and a wet bar (pre-stocked when you book, at extra cost). Has wooden outside promenade deck. Features refined and attractive interior decor. The accommodation is located forward, with public rooms aft.

However, the tiny "dip" pool is not a swimming pool. The open deck and sunning space is quite cramped. Plastic woods instead of real woods are used everywhere (looks too perfect). Space for luggage is tight, and there is not really enough drawer space. Bathrooms are very compact and none have bathtubs.

ms The Neptune
(S)

Cruise Line:	Universal Cruises	Beam (ft/m):	50.1/15.30
Ship Base:	Singapore	Draft (ft/m):	11.9/3.65
Former Names:	*Renaissance II*	Propulsion/Propellers:	diesel (3,514kW)/2 (CP)
Gross Tonnage:	3,990	Passenger Decks:	5
Builder:	Cantieri Navale Ferrari (Italy)	Total Crew:	72
Built:	1990	Pass. Capacity (basis 2):	100
Length (ft/m):	289.6/88.30	Pass. Space Ratio (basis 2):	39.9

Comments: This small ship, together with sister ship *The Mercury* (ex-*Renaissance I*), has contemporary mega-yacht looks and a reasonably handsome profile. She is being operated from Singapore strictly for charters and private functions.

Exquisite all-outside suites combine gorgeous, highly polished imitation rosewood paneling with lots of mirrors, handcrafted Italian furniture, and a wet bar (pre-stocked when you book, at extra cost). Has wooden outside promenade deck. Features refined and attractive interior decor. The accommodation is located forward, with public rooms aft.

However, the tiny "dip" pool is not a swimming pool. The open deck and sunning space is quite cramped. Plastic woods instead of real woods are used everywhere (looks too perfect). Space for luggage is tight, and there is not really enough drawer space. Bathrooms are very compact and none have bathtubs.

THE CRUISE INDUSTRY: MILESTONES (1960–1999)

1960

Passenger shipping directories listed more than 30 companies operating transatlantic voyages for the better part of each year. Many ships were laid up from 1960 to 1970, and most were sold for a fraction of their value (or building cost). Most passenger lines simply went out of business or tried to survive by mixing transatlantic crossings with voyages south in search of the sun, which proved difficult for those without sufficient air-conditioning systems.

Britannic, the last passenger ship to wear the White Star Line colors, was withdrawn from service and sent to Inverkeithing, Scotland, to be scrapped.

1961

Charalambos A. Keusseouglou, who began his career at Home Lines (the immigrant passenger carrier), founded Sun Line.

1962

Compagnie Generale Transatlantique's ss *France*, at 1,035 feet, the world's longest passenger ship ever built, entered service between Le Havre and New York despite growing competition from the airlines.

1963

Cunard Line's RMS *Queen Elizabeth* made an experimental cruise from New York to the West Indies, with great success. This led to her being fitted with full air conditioning in a 1965–66 refit and more extensive cruising activities.

Home Lines ceased regularly scheduled transatlantic services.

1965

P&O obtained the remaining shares of the Orient Steam Navigation Company. Orient Line was absorbed into the P&O Group (the name P&O-Orient Line disappeared forever). The new company became known as the Peninsular & Oriental Steam Navigation Company.

Stanley B. McDonald founded Princess Cruises.

Sitmar Cruises commenced cruise operations from Sydney, Australia.

American President Lines ceased passenger-carrying operations.

1966

Soviet transatlantic service was reopened with the Black Sea Shipping Company's *Aleksandr Pushkin* inaugurating service between Montreal and Leningrad (now St. Petersburg) for the first time since 1949.

The Norwegian company, Klosters Reederei, formed a partnership with Miami businessman Ted Arison to market Caribbean cruises from Miami. Kloster provided the ship and Arison provided the passengers.

Sanford Chobol founded Commodore Cruise Line, with a single ship, *Boheme* (presently *Freewinds*).

1967

Cunard announced the withdrawal of the transatlantic liners *Queen Mary* and *Queen Elizabeth*. *Queen Mary* was withdrawn from service on September 26 after completing 1,001 transatlantic crossings. She was sold to the City of Long Beach, California — she left Southampton on October 31, 1967, and has been in Long Beach ever since.

1968

American Export Lines ceased its transatlantic passenger service.

Cunard's *Queen Elizabeth* (at 83,673 grt, then the world's largest ever passenger ship) was withdrawn from service in October. She had steamed a total of 3,472,672 miles and carried a total of 2,311,324 passengers (1,500,000 peacetime passengers and 811,324 wartime passengers) during her career. She was sold to a Ft. Lauderdale consortium, "Queens, Inc.," which quickly failed. She was then sold to the Hong Kong-based shipping tycoon, C.Y. Tung, in September, 1970, who had the ship towed from Southampton via Cape Horn to Hong Kong on February 10, 1971. The ship then underwent an extensive refit and was renamed *Seawise University*.

Cunard Line ceased regularly scheduled transatlantic service to Canada.

Zim Lines ceased transatlantic passenger service.

Cunard Line refused delivery of *Queen Elizabeth 2* from her builder, John Brown, in December, because of unacceptable turbine vibration levels. Repairs led to a five-month delay to her maiden transatlantic crossing.

Boise Cascade purchased Princess Cruises from its founder, Stanley B. McDonald, who re-purchased the line two years later.

1969

Lars-Eric Lindblad's *Lindblad Explorer*, expressly designed for close-in expedition cruising, was launched.

Royal Caribbean Cruise Line was founded January 31 by a consortium of Norwegian shipping companies, Gotaas-Larsen (an American-owned company), I.M. Skaugen, and Anders Wilhelmsen, and incorporated as Royal Caribbean Cruise Line A/S in Oslo. Edwin Stephan, who provided the initial concept and wisdom, was made president and set up the Miami marketing arm of the company, which, at the end of 1968, ordered two new sister ships for delivery in 1970 and 1971.

The liner *United States* was laid up in November following a strike against the ship by the militant seamen's union, and the fact that the US government no longer wanted to subsidize the loss-making ship (which cost $118.8 million between 1955 and 1969). She was subsequently laid up for 23 years beginning November 7, 1969, until sold to Marmara Marine, Inc., on April 27, 1992.

1970

Royal Viking Line was founded by a consortium of three partners (Bergen Line, A.F. Klaveness, and Nordenfjeldske) who each contributed one ship (*Royal Viking Sea*, *Royal Viking Sky*, and *Royal Viking Star*).

Germany's Norddeutscher Lloyd and Hapag (Hamburg American Line) merged on September 1. They chose the new name of Hapag-Lloyd.

1971

Cunard Line was sold to Trafalgar House Investments.

508

Holland America Line ceased transatlantic passenger service.

Canadian Pacific ceased passenger-carrying operations.

1972

American President Lines ceased passenger operations.

Ted Arison founded Carnival Cruise Lines, following a disagreement with Knut Kloster when both worked for Kloster's Norwegian Cruise Lines. After unsuccessfully trying to purchase Cunard's *Carmania* and *Franconia*, he learned of the availability of the *Empress of Canada*. Carnival was funded and operated as a subsidiary of the Boston-based American International Travel Service, Inc. (AITS), and commenced with just one ship, *Mardi Gras* (ex-*Empress of Canada*). After a poor start (the ship ran aground on its first voyage – ships from other companies named a drink after her called "Mardi Gras on the Rocks") the company went from strength to strength. Under Arison's aggressive direction it has become the biggest success story of the contemporary cruise industry, which it has helped shape.

1973

Holland America Line withdrew sister ships *Veendam* and *Volendam* and laid them up owing to competition from other ships combined with high operating costs, a fall in the value of the US dollar, and a dramatic rise in fuel costs. The ships were chartered to Monarch Cruise Lines in 1976 (*Veendam* became *Monarch Star*, *Volendam* became *Monarch Sun*). The Dutch-flag ships were re-registered in Panama and staffed by a multinational crew.

Sitmar Cruises began operations from Sydney, Australia, with a single ship, *Fairstar* (a converted troop carrier formerly operated by Bibby Line).

Deutsche Atlantik Line suspended operations, following financial difficulty. The company's *Hanseatic* (in service for only four years) was laid up at Hamburg. In December, a possible sale of the ship to Ryutsu Kaiun KK of Japan for $25 million failed. She was instead sold to Robin International Corporation, New York, acting as buyers for the Black Sea Shipping Company of Odessa. Renamed *Maksim Gorkiy* the ship is still in service for Phoenix Seereisen of Germany.

1974

P&O purchased Princess Cruises from its founder, Stanley B. McDonald.

Sitmar Line ceased scheduled line voyages and concentrated on cruising activities.

In July, the Compagnie Generale Transatlantique announced that after only 12 years of service, the ss *France* was to be withdrawn from service on October 25. She was losing money and was being subsidized by the French government to the tune of $12 million a year. As the ship was about to berth in Le Havre on September 12, angry French trade unionists took over the ship from its officers and anchored her in the entrance channel, in protest to the impending loss of jobs. Passengers disembarked by tender. The ship was able to dock on October 9 and was laid up.

The Port Authority of New York and New Jersey opened its new Passenger Ship Terminal in November. It included six berths at three piers (formerly Piers 88, 90, and 92) and cost $35 million.

The Union Castle Steamship Company ceased operations as a passenger line.

Royal Cruise Lines' first ship, *Golden Odyssey*, purpose-built to accommodate the equivalent passenger load of a Boeing 747 aircraft (425 passengers), was introduced. Founded by Pericles S. Panagopoulos in 1971, the company attracted a loyal US West Coast following, gained mainly through direct marketing methods.

509

1975

Island Princess and *Pacific Princess* (Princess Cruises) become the "stars" in the American television show *The Love Boat*.

Greek Line, Shaw Savill, and Swedish America Line all ceased passenger operations. Carnival Cruise Lines purchased the former Greek Line ship *Queen Anna Maria* for $3.2 million.

1976

The Italian Line and Lloyd Triestino ceased transatlantic passenger operations.

1977

World Explorer Cruises was founded and entered the cruise industry with a single ship, *Universe*.

Princess Grace of Monaco christened *Cunard Princess* at the Passenger Ship Terminal in March, the first time a passenger ship christening had taken place in the Port of New York.

Union-Castle/Safmarine, the South Africa-based shipping company, ceased passenger operations when its last vessel, S.A. *Vaal*, was sold to Carnival Cruise Lines in April.

Holland America Line absorbed the operation of Monarch Cruise Lines Inc. Its two ships were handed back to Holland America Line in January 1978.

1978

Richard Hadley founded United States Cruises. He paid $5 million for the liner *United States*.

After sailing on an unsuccessful June 30 cruise from New York for new owners Venture Cruise Lines (also called America Cruise Lines), *America* (ex-*Australis*) was arrested for debt and auctioned on August 28. Her previous owners, the Chandris Group, re-purchased the ship and renamed her *Italis*.

1979

American Hawaii Cruises was formed. Jimmy Carter, then president of the US, signed a bill re-documenting *Independence* under the US flag. The new company began cruise operations on June 21, 1980, with *Independence*, joined by sister ship *Constitution* in 1982.

Lindblad Special Expeditions was founded by Sven-Olof Lindblad (son of Lars-Eric Lindblad) to provide expedition cruise vacations to seldom-visited destinations.

Society Expeditions was formed by a group of German investors under the direction of sole stockholder T. C. Schwartz, expressly to manage and operate adventure/expedition cruises by the purpose-built *World Discoverer*.

In June, the liner ss *France* was purchased by Lauritz Kloster. The ship was rebuilt at Bremerhaven for Caribbean cruises by Lloyd Werft. She was renamed *Norway* and transferred to Norwegian Caribbean Lines in September 1984.

President Jimmy Carter spent a week aboard the river steamboat *Delta Queen*, whose life began on Scotland's Clydeside in 1926. The steamboat is now on the US National Register of Historic Places.

1980

Sea Goddess Cruises was founded by Helge Naarstad. *Sea Goddess I*, the first of two identical ships, was delivered four years later, in 1984.

Royal Caribbean Cruise Line's *Song of Norway* and *Nordic Prince* were lengthened at the Wartsila shipyard in Helsinki between March and June.

Denmark's United Steamship Company (DFDS) founded Scandinavian World Cruises to operate one-day cruises from Miami (the company subsequently became SeaEscape).

The International Organization of Masters, Mates and Pilots formed a joint venture company with Aloha Pacific Cruises and purchased *Monterey* (the last US flag ship to qualify under the Jones Act to operate between American ports) for intended cruise service in Tahiti. The purchase was completed in 1981 (the union poured $5.7 million into the ship, for upkeep alone, between 1981 and 1986).

After a planned merger with Royal Viking Line failed in May, Norwegian America Cruises (formerly Norwegian America Line) was formed to manage *Sagafjord* and *Vistafjord*.

1981

Transatlantic service provided by Soviet-registered ships was discontinued due to the US government embargo.

Astor Cruises was formed in the UK and began operations with a single new ship, *Astor*.

Royal Viking Star was lengthened in the A. G. Weser shipyard in Bremerhaven, Germany. Sister ships *Sky* and *Sea* were lengthened by the same shipyard (in 1982 and 1983, respectively).

1982

The British government chartered *Queen Elizabeth 2* (Cunard Line) for use as a troop carrier for the famous Ghurka Regiment, among others, during the Falklands War between Argentina and Britain, at $225,000 per day. The ship eluded an Argentinean submarine sent to destroy her, due to the submarine's ineffectiveness in the icebergs close to the Falklands, and the speed of *QE2*. The government also chartered P&O Cruises' *Canberra* for use as a troopship (sailed from Southampton April 9, returned to Southampton July 11, went back to passenger service in September), as well as B&I Line's *Uganda* (for use as a hospital ship). All three ships performed well.

Lindblad Travel, the company founded by Lars-Eric Lindblad in 1969, sold its *Lindblad Explorer* and the rights to the Lindblad name to Salen-Lindblad Cruising.

1983

Holland America Line ceased operating New York–Bermuda cruises. The company moved its headquarters from New York to Seattle.

Ocean Cruise Lines was founded by Gerry Herrod, as an offshoot of Travellers, Europe's largest tour operator for Americans abroad.

P&O appointed Jeffrey Sterling as chairman in order to fend off an unwanted takeover bid by Trafalgar House Investments, owners of Cunard Line.

Premier Cruise Lines was co-founded by Bruce Nierenburg and Bjornar Hermansen, both former executives of Norwegian Cruise Lines.

B&I's *Uganda* was chartered by the British Ministry of Defense in January for two years for service between Ascension and the Falkland Islands. This ended passenger service for the British and India Steam Navigation Company (B&I).

Cunard's parent company, Trafalgar House, purchased Norwegian America Cruises (NAC) in May, together with *Sagafjord* and *Vistafjord*.

Salen-Lindblad Cruising's *Lindblad Explorer* became the first passenger ship to successfully navigate the Northwest Passage (in September), sailing 4,790 miles from Saint John's, Newfoundland, to Point Barrow, Alaska. The 41-day cruise, which started on August 20, finished in Yokohama, Japan on September 29. When the ship reached Point Barrow, the champagne flowed and beards were shaved off (the crew had all vowed not to shave until that point). Lars Wikander provided the idea and planning expertise.

1984

Sundance Cruises was founded by Stanley B. McDonald with a single ship, *Sundancer*.

Carnival Cruise Line launched a $10 million television advertising campaign, the largest ever seen in the cruise industry. Two different 30-second spots were aired a total of 133 times in the US.

An American investment group headed by J. H. Whitney & Company signed an agreement in principle in May to purchase Royal Viking Line and its three ships for $240 million. The sale did not go through. Instead, Royal Viking Line was purchased by Kloster Cruise Limited, Oslo.

Delta Steamship Lines ceased passenger-carrying operations. Its four ships (*Santa Magdalena*, *Santa Maria*, *Santa Mariana*, and *Santa Mercedes*) were sold.

Regency Cruises was founded by Anastassios Kiriakidis, Fred Mayer, and William Schanz. The company completed its initial public stock offering in June and commenced operations with a single ship, *Regent Sea*, in November.

Windstar Sail Cruises was founded in December by Karl Andren and Jacob Stolt-Nielsen to build and operate a fleet of three sail-cruise ships originally designed by Kai Levander, then of Wartsila Shipyard in Helsinki, Finland. Andren intended to re-launch the age of commercial sail.

Dolphin Cruise Line was founded by Peter Bulgarides and Paris Katsoufis (but actually owned by Ulysses Shipping, Piraeus).

Premier Cruise Lines, owned by the Greyhound-Dial Corporation, entered the cruise industry with its first ship.

1985

The Chandris Group of Companies acquired Fantasy Cruises from GoGo Tours. Fantasy Cruises became known as Chandris Fantasy Cruises in the US and Chandris Cruises in the UK.

The first sailing ship designed for crewing by physically challenged passengers was launched at Wivenhoe, Essex, on October 15. The sts *Lord Nelson* is owned by the Jubilee Sailing Trust, whose patron, His Royal Highness Prince Andrew, officially named the vessel at Southampton, England, on May 9, 1986.

1986

Signet Cruise Line was founded in Norway by an investment group headed by Atle Brynestad. Owing to a lawsuit brought by an American who claimed the right to the name Signet, the company changed its name to Seabourn Cruise Line. Its first ship, *Seabourn Pride*, would enter service in December 1988, one cruise later than the planned maiden voyage, which was canceled due to a major storm front encountered during the transatlantic delivery voyage.

Eastern Cruise Lines, Western Cruise Lines, and Sundance Cruises merged to become Admiral Cruises.

Diamond Cruise Ltd. was founded in Helsinki, Finland, by Captain Offe Nyblin and his partner Christian Aspegren. They were to take delivery of *Radisson Diamond*, a semi-submersible twin-hulled vessel.

Cunard acquired Sea Goddess Cruises, together with *Sea Goddess I* and *Sea Goddess II*, through a complex financial and management package negotiated with Norske Cruise A/S, whose 138 shareholders provided the funding for the construction and introduction of the new luxury yacht-ship concept.

1987

Carnival Cruise Lines made its first public stock offering.

Cunard's *QE2* was converted from steam turbine to diesel-electric power. It was the largest ever conversion in maritime history.

Society Expeditions was purchased by German businessman Heiko Klein, chairman of Discoverer Reederei, the company that owns the vessels marketed and operated by Society Expeditions.

Kockums, the Swedish shipyard, ceased shipbuilding operations following the delivery of twin cruise ships for Carnival Cruise Lines, *Celebration* (1987) and *Jubilee* (1986).

Bahama Cruise Line became Bermuda Star Line.

Ocean Cruise Lines merged with Pearl Cruises.

Princess Cruises replaced almost 500 unionized British hotel and catering staff aboard its five ships.

The United States Public Health Service (USPH) resumed ship inspections January 1 after being halted in May 1986 due to public interest and cooperation of the cruise lines.

Holland America Line acquired a 50 percent share in Windstar Sail Cruises (now Windstar Cruises) in March.

Norwegian Caribbean Lines changed its name and logo (though not its initials: NCL) to Norwegian Cruise Line.

1988

Commodore Cruise Lines sold its *Boheme* to the Church of Scientology. The ship was renamed *Freewinds*.

Crystal Cruises was formed as a wholly-owned division of Nippon Yusen Kaisha (NYK) of Japan, the world's largest shipping company. The company's first ship, *Crystal Harmony*, was to enter service in July 1990.

The three owning partners of Royal Caribbean Cruise Line (Gotaas-Larsen, I. M. Skaugen, and Anders Wilhelmsen) decided, in March, to merge RCCL with the Gataas-Larsen–dominated Admiral Cruises (the Swedish company Axel Johnson group and the Finnish EFFOA group held 49 percent). Named Royal Admiral Cruises (later to become Royal Caribbean Cruises), the new group was owned 36 percent by Gotaas-Larsen and 28 percent each by Skaugen and Wilhelmsen, while Johnson/EFFOA held the remaining 8 percent of stock.

Home Lines ceased operations in April. Its *Atlantic* (1984) and *Homeric* (1986) were purchased by Holland America Line. *Atlantic* was subsequently placed under long-term charter to Premier Cruise Lines (now Premier Cruise Lines).

Effjohn International purchased Bermuda Star Line in May for $17 million. Included in the deal were *Bermuda Star*, *Queen of Bermuda*, and *Veracruz I*. The company was renamed BSL Cruises, Inc.

Sitmar Cruises (Societa Italiana Trasporti Marittimi), founded in 1938 by Alexandre Vlasov, was purchased by Princess Cruises (part of the P&O Group) for $210 million. The two companies merged their North American operations.

Carnival Cruise Lines' negotiations with Gotaas-Larsen to purchase its Royal Caribbean Cruise Line share for $260 million emerged in August, following RCCL's administration move from Oslo to Miami. At first, I. M. Skaugen and Wilhelmsen tried to pre-empt the Carnival offer. Later, Skaugen accepted a similar offer from Carnival Corporation. Wilhelmsen, the remaining partner in RCCL (28 percent), found the financing to pre-empt the Carnival offer of $567 million by going 50/50 with the Hyatt Hotel group of companies, owned by the Pritzker family of Chicago. The new joint owners paid the agreed amount five days before the deadline date of October 5.

Holland America Line completed the purchase of Windstar Sail Cruises. Carnival Cruise Lines acquired Holland America Line in November, including its land-based hotel/transport operations and Windstar Cruises, for $625 million, plus liabilities that pushed the purchase price effectively to $900 million.

1989

The Chandris Group of Companies announced the creation of Celebrity Cruises, which ordered two new cruise ships, to be named *Horizon* and *Zenith*, from the Meyer Werft shipyard in Papenburg, Germany. The company also announced plans for the conversion of *Galileo* into *Meridian* at the Lloyd Werft shipyard in Bremerhaven, Germany.

Ocean Quest International was formed to provide seven-day cruises for scuba diving enthusiasts and entered the industry with a single ship, *Ocean Spirit* (ex-*Sunward*). The venture later failed after a diver died in the ship's hyperbaric decompression chamber.

Meyer Werft, Papenburg, Germany, became the first shipyard to conduct a "chop and stretch" operation on a major cruise vessel in drydock (all other ships being previously lengthened while afloat), when *Westerdam* (ex-*Homeric*) was lengthened in the same covered building shed, alongside *Horizon*, then under construction for Celebrity Cruises.

Renaissance Cruises was formed by Fearnley & Eger (a 120-year-old Oslo-based shipping concern) to build and market eight small premium cruise vessels. *Renaissance I – Renaissance VIII*, entered service between 1989 and 1992.

Showa Line entered the cruise passenger market in Japan for the first time in 60 years with the introduction of its new *Oceanic Grace*.

Mitsui OSK Line entered the cruise market in Japan for the first time in 50 years with its 23,340-grt, 600-passenger *Fuji Maru* which was especially built for the charter and incentive market for Japanese companies.

The Panama Canal is 75 years old. The canal, cutting a 75-mile swath through the isthmus of Panama, which joins the North and South American continents, is the only place in the world where it is possible to cruise over the Continental Divide.

Lars-Eric Lindblad's Lindblad Travel company went into bankruptcy.

Aloha Pacific Cruises went into bankruptcy just six months after start-up. The company's single ship, *Monterey*, was put up for sale.

Wartsila Industries, Helsinki, Finland, one of the most famous and prestigious builders of cruise ships, collapsed in a tangle of financial problems. It was reorganized as Masa-Yards (presently owned by Kvaerner of Norway).

1990

Starlite Cruises (part of the Piraeus-based Lelakis Group) was formed to provide ships for one-day and seven-day cruises.

Ocean Cruise Lines was purchased by Croisieres Paquet, itself owned by the French giant Accor leisure company.

Japan Cruise Line entered the cruise market in Japan with its new 21,906-grt, 606-passenger *Orient Venus* for charters and incentive cruises for Japanese companies.

Two intimate 68-passenger cruise vessels, *Lady Diana* and *Lady Sarah*, were refused delivery in March by the newly formed Windsor Line, owned by a Greek anthropologist. The line was wound up and the two ships were later sold.

On March 15, Aloha Pacific Cruises' *Monterey* was put up for auction by the Connecticut Bank & Trust Company. It was purchased by the Mediterranean Shipping Company, which chartered it to StarLauro Cruises.

Chandris Cruises introduced its new Celebrity Cruises in April with the debut of the reconstructed *Meridian* and the brand new *Horizon*.

Delfin Cruises, established one year earlier with two small ships for cruise service in the Baltic Sea, ceased operations.

At the start of the Persian Gulf War, the US government chartered *Cunard Princess* for six months for use as a rest and relaxation center for US service personnel in the Persian Gulf. The ship was docked in Bahrain for the $31 million charter.

1991

Carnival Cruise Lines acquired a 25 percent stake in Seabourn Cruise Line.

When the Soviet Union was dissolved, its cruise fleet was converted into four constituent parts: Baltic Shipping Company (Russia), Black Sea Shipping Company (Ukraine), Estonian Shipping Company (Estonia), Far East Shipping Company (Russia).

In March, Fearnley & Eger, owner of Renaissance Cruises, sought voluntary liquidation and protection from its creditors under Chapter 11 of the US Bankruptcy Code. Renaissance Cruises was sold to a new investors, consisting of the Cameli Group, controlled by Sebastiano Cameli (Italy), and Luxury Liners, Ltd., a holding company involving Norwegian shipowner Jorgen Jahre (controlled by Edward B. Rudner in the US).

In April, Carnival Cruise Lines announced it would buy Premier Cruise Lines, but later backed out of the $220 million deal with the Dial Corporation after Carnival inspected Premier's books and insisted on paying less for the company following a dispute over Premier's short-term earnings potential.

Effjohn International purchased Crown Cruise Line together with the rights to operate its fleet of small ships.

Seawind Cruise Line commenced cruise operations with a single ship, *Seawind Crown* (ex-*Vasco da Gama*), following a 70/30 percent interest purchase in the company by Swedish concern Nordisk and Arcalia Shipping, of Lisbon.

Nippon Yusen Kaisha (NYK) purchased Salen Lindblad Cruising.

Nippon Yusen Kaisha (NYK) Cruises introduced *Asuka*, the first cruise vessel specifically designed for Japanese individual cruise passengers.

New York-based Overseas Shipholding Group agreed to lend Kloster Cruise $175 million in exchange for a 50 percent stake in the company. The offer was withdrawn after OSG reviewed Kloster's financial structure and profitability.

1992

Society Expeditions ceased operations. Its *Society Explorer* and *World Discoverer* were put up for sale. The company also refused to take delivery of the brand new *Society Adventurer* (presently *Hanseatic*), built at the Rauma Shipyards, Finland.

Costa Cruise Lines introduced its new Euro-Luxe cruise concept with the debut of *CostaClassica*.

Admiral Cruises ceased operations. Its two vessels, *Azure Seas* and *Emerald Seas,* were sold to other interests (Dolphin Cruise Line and SunFest Cruises, respectively), for a total of $3.9 million.

Some 16 cruise ships were chartered as accommodation vessels in Barcelona for the 1992 Olympic Games (July 24–August 9), due to lack of hotel space in the city. The ships provided about 44,000 bed nights for the games.

Hurricane Andrew hit the south Miami area; several hundred cruise line executives and employees were among the homeless. Carnival Cruise Lines deployed *Mardi Gras* for use as an accommodation ship to provide living quarters for 600 staff members affected by the hurricane.

The Chandris Group of Companies and Overseas Shipholding Group (OSG) signed an agreement in Paris on October 21 to form a joint venture company called Celebrity Cruise Lines, Inc. Chandris supplied three Celebrity Cruises and three Fantasy Cruises ships; OSG supplied $220 million cash in funding. Chandris held a 51 percent interest.

Chargeurs and Accor, the French property and leisure industries group that own Paquet Cruises and Ocean Cruise Lines, purchased a 23 percent stake in Costa Crociere, the parent company of Costa Cruises, through a rights issue worth 80 billion lire ($60 million). The agreement signaled the first cross-border venture in Europe. The buy-in by the French company reduced the Costa family's stake in Costa Crociere from 40 percent to 31 percent.

1993

In January, Carnival Cruise Lines formed Fiesta Marina Cruises specifically for the Spanish-speaking Latin American market. The company's single ship, *FiestaMarina* (ex-*Carnivale*), commenced operations October 22 from San Juan. Everything aboard ship was in Spanish. It was unsuccessful. The company ceased operations in September 1994.

Cunard and Effjohn announced a joint venture, good for ten years, and formed Cunard Crown Cruises.

Bruce Nierenberg founded American Family Cruises to cater to American families, with a plan to use two Costa ships (*CostaRiviera* and *EugenioCosta*). *CostaRiviera* was converted into *American Adventure*.

In May, Rainbow Cruises purchased all the stock of Regency Cruises. Both companies were merged under the name Regency Cruises.

American Hawaii Cruises' secured lenders forced the line into involuntary bankruptcy in federal court in Honolulu. The company was later purchased by the Delta Queen Steamboat Company.

George Poulides founded Festival Cruises. The company re-acquired *The Azur* (now renamed *Azur*) following an eight-year charter to Chandris Fantasy Cruises.

SeaQuest Cruises ceased operations. *Frontier Spirit* was returned to its Japanese owners and was chartered to Germany's Hanseatic Tours, renamed *Bremen*.

Kloster Cruise Limited signed a letter of intent to sell Royal Cruise Line and Royal Viking Line to ASA Investors, Inc., a consortium of 60 chief executives and former chief executives of US companies. The purchase price of $565 million (less $60 million for advance bookings) was to include Royal Cruise Line's *Crown Odyssey, Royal Odyssey,* and *Star Odyssey*

(*Golden Odyssey was* sold separately and not included), and Royal Viking Line's *Royal Viking Queen* and *Royal Viking Sun.* This equaled $505 million for a total of 3,887 beds, or $129,920 per bed. The deal was to be completed in the spring of 1994, but fell through, the investment group concluding there was not sufficient profit potential.

1994

Delta Queen Steamboat Company changed its corporate name to American Classic Voyages Company. The company owns American Hawaii Cruises and the Delta Queen Steamboat Company.

Trafalgar House, Cunard's parent company, signed an agreement to purchase the rights to the name Royal Viking Line, together with *Royal Viking Sun,* for $170 million. *Royal Viking Queen* (not part of the agreement) went to Royal Cruise Line, and renamed *Queen Odyssey* (presently *Seabourn Legend*), on January 1, 1995.

American Family Cruises ceased operations in September. The company's single ship, *American Adventure*, was returned to the Costa Cruises fleet, to be renamed *CostaRiviera*.

Cycladic Cruises, based in Greece, ceased operations. Its two vessels were subsequently sold to other companies.

Radisson Diamond Cruises and Seven Seas Cruise Line merged to become Radisson Seven Seas Cruises.

Star Cruises was founded by parent company Genting Berhad and commenced operations with two ships, *Star Aquarius* and *Star Pisces.*

1995

British company Airtours purchased *Southward* from Norwegian Cruise Line and *Nordic Prince* from Royal Caribbean Cruises in late 1994, and, after refits, commenced operations in March 1995.

Commodore Cruise Line was sold to International Cruise Finance, Ltd.

Regency Cruises ceased operations abruptly at the end of October. Several vessels were impounded and subsequently put up for auction.

1996

Royal Venture Cruise Line commenced operations in March with a single ship, *Sun Venture* (ex-*Ukraine*), but ceased operations abruptly. The company restarted as Royal Seas Cruise Line, using the same ship, renamed *Royal Seas.* It too failed almost immediately.

Kloster Cruise (parent company of Norwegian Cruise Line and Royal Cruise Line) announced the closure of its Royal Cruise Line division. *Crown Odyssey* and *Royal Odyssey* went to Norwegian Cruise Line as *Norwegian Crown* and *Norwegian Star*, respectively. *Queen Odyssey* went to Seabourn Cruise Line as *Seabourn Legend. Star Odyssey* was sold to Fred Olsen Cruise Lines to become *Black Watch.*

Baltic Line ceased cruise operations.

Sunshine Cruise Lines ceased operations. The company's *Baltica* was acquired by Arcalia Shipping (now renamed *Princess Danae*).

Carnival Corporation, parent company of Carnival Cruise Lines; Holland America Line; Seabourn Cruise Line; and Windstar Cruises purchased a 29.6 percent share in Airtours Plc, for approximately $310 million.

Cunard (together with parent company Trafalgar House) was purchased by Kvaerner.

517

1997

Carnival Corporation, jointly with Airtours, purchased the shares of Costa Cruises for $300 million. The deal was completed in June. Costa Cruises remains a wholly-owned subsidiary of Carnival Corporation.

Germany's AquaMarin Cruises ceased cruise operations. Its single ship, *Astor*, was chartered to Transocean Tours, for ten years.

Carnival Corporation purchased the sail-cruise vessel *Club Med I*. The ship was renamed *Wind Surf* and added to the three ships in the Windstar Cruises fleet.

Majesty Cruise Line ceased operations. Its single ship, *Crown Majesty*, was traded to Norwegian Cruise Line for $110 million.

Showa Line sold its only ship, *Oceanic Grace*, to Spice Island Cruises and ceased cruise operations (the ship's name is presently *Clipper Odyssey*).

Celebrity Cruises was purchased by Royal Caribbean International for $1.3 billion, the largest deal in the cruise industry. Celebrity Cruises continues to operate as a separate brand.

Miami-based Cruise Holdings Ltd. purchased three cruise companies — Dolphin Cruise Lines, Premier Cruise Lines, Seawind Cruise Line — then promptly merged them into one company: Premier Cruise Lines. The company also purchased the former Holland America Line ship *Rotterdam* (now *Rembrandt*).

Arkona Reisen's *Aida* was purchased by Norwegian Cruise Line, who promptly leased the ship back to the German company.

Hapag-Lloyd Seetouristik's *Europa* was sold to Star Cruises, but leased back to Hapag-Lloyd until mid-1999, when a new Europa entered service.

Star Cruises purchased *Europa* (ex-Hapag-Lloyd Seetouristik), to be renamed *SuperStar Europe*, for $75 million, and *Sun Viking* (ex-Royal Caribbean International), presently named *Hyundai Bongnae*, for $30 million.

P&O Cruises' *Canberra* was withdrawn from service and sent to Pakistan for scrap. During her career, the ship carried 6, 500 troops to the South Atlantic in the 1982 Falkland Islands war and held 3,200 Argentine prisoners of war aboard the ship.

CTC Cruises (UK) ceased operations. The company's chartered vessel, *Kareliya*, was put up for auction after being arrested in Haifa.

Awani Dream Cruises ceased operations. The company's two ships (*Awani Dream* and *Awani Dream II*) were purchased by Royal Olympic Cruises.

1998

Costa Cruises celebrated its 50th year of cruise operations.

Holland America Line celebrated its 125th year of passenger operations.

Australia repealed its cabotage laws, allowing international cruise ships to dock and operate from Australian ports without restrictions.

Hebridean Island Cruises was sold to Altnamara Shipping and Gallic Shipping, a joint venture company.

Cunard was sold for $500 million by owning company Kvaerner to a consortium that includes Carnival Corporation as majority shareholder together with a group led by Christiana Markets of Norway. Cunard and Seabourn Cruise Line continue to operate as separate brands under the umbrella name of Cunard Line.

Royal Caribbean International sold its *Song of America* for $95 million to Airtours Sun Cruises, who now operate the vessel, renamed *Sunbird.*

Ivaran Lines, operator of the hybrid container-cruise vessel *Americana,* was sold to Canadian Pacific Ships.

Orient Lines, together with its single ship *Marco Polo,* was purchased by Norwegian Cruise Line for $54 million ($8 million in cash plus shares).

A new company, Norwegian Capricorn Line, began operations from Sydney, Australia, with one ship in a joint venture with Norwegian Cruise Line.

1999

Crown Cruise Line was reintroduced as an upscale division of Commodore Cruise Line.

The United States Maritime Administration (MarAd) approved a loan guarantee for more than $1 billion that will fund the creation of two new larger cruise ships to be built in the US for American Classic Voyages, parent company of American Hawaii Cruises.

Ivaran Lines ceased cruise operations aboard its *Americana.*

OCEANGOING CRUISE SHIPS TO DEBUT: 2000–2003

CRUISE LINE	NAME OF SHIP	TONNES	COST
2000			
Carnival Cruise Lines	Carnival Victory	101,353	$440 million
Celebrity Cruises	Millennium	85,000	$350 million
Costa Cruises	CostaAtlantica	82,000	$390 million
Holland America Line	Amsterdam	63,000	$300 million
Holland America Line	Zaandam	63,000	$300 million
P&O Cruises	Aurora	76,000	$320 million
Princess Cruises	Ocean Princess	77,000	$300 million
Renaissance Cruises	R Five	30,200	$168.5 million
Renaissance Cruises	R Six	30,200	$168.5 million
Renaissance Cruises	R Seven	30,200	$168.5 million
Royal Caribbean International	Explorer of the Seas	142,000	$500 million
Royal Olympic Cruises	Olympic Voyager	25,000	$165 million
Star Clippers	Royal Clipper	5,000	$75 million
Sea Cloud Cruises	Sea Cloud II	3,000	DM50 million
Silversea Cruises	Silver Shadow	25,000	$150 million
2001			
Carnival Cruise Lines	Carnival Spirit	84,000	$375 million
Carnival Cruise Lines	tba	84,000	$375 million
Celebrity Cruises	tba	85,000	$350 million
Celebrity Cruises	tba	85,000	$350 million
Festival Cruises	tba	47,900	$250 million
Princess Cruises	tba	109,000	$425 million
Princess Cruises	tba	109,000	$425 million
Radisson Seven Seas Cruises	Seven Seas Mariner	46,000	$280 million
Renaissance Cruises	R Eight	30,200	$168.5 million
ResidenSea	The World of ResidenSea (*)	40,000	$280 million
Royal Caribbean International	Radiance of the Seas	85,000	$350 million
Royal Olympic Cruises	tba	25,000	$165 million
Silversea Cruises	Silver Mirage	25,000	$150 million
Star Cruises	SuperStar Libra	91,000	$400 million
2002			
American Classic Cruises	Queen of the Americas	72,000	$440 million
Carnival Cruise Lines	tba	84,000	$375 million
Carnival Cruise Lines	Carnival Conquest	101,353	$450 million
Celebrity Cruises	tba	85,000	$350 million
Festival Cruises	tba	47,900	$250 million
Radisson Seven Seas Cruises	tba	46,000	$280 million
Royal Caribbean International	Adventure of the Seas	142,000	$500 million
Royal Caribbean International	Brilliance of the Seas	85,000	$350 million
Star Cruises	SuperStar Scorpio	91,000	$400 million
2003			
American Classic Cruises	tba	72,000	$440 million
Carnival Cruise Lines	Carnival Glory	101,353	$450 million
Celebrity Cruises	tba	85,000	$350 million

NOTES:

This chart shows ships under firm contract. It is given in alphabetical order according to cruise line.
"Delivery/debut dates may be brought forward or put back, therefore precise months are not listed."
tba = to be announced
"* = letter of intent, not firm contract (at press time)"

LENGTH (feet)	LENGTH (meters)	PASSENGERS (lower bed capacity)	BUILDER
882.6	269	2,642	Fincantieri (Italy)
964.5	294	1,950	Chantiers de l'Atlantique (France)
957	291.7	2,100	Kvaerner Masa-Yards (Finland)
777.5	237	1,380	Fincantieri (Italy)
777.5	237	1,440	Fincantieri (Italy)
885.8	270	1,800	Meyer Werft (Germany)
856.2	261	1,950	Fincantieri (Italy)
593.7	181	684	Chantiers de l'Atlantique (France)
593.7	181	684	Chantiers de l'Atlantique (France)
593.7	181	684	Chantiers de l'Atlantique (France)
1019.7	311	3,114	Kvaerner Masa-Yards (Finland)
590.5	180	800	Blohm & Voss (Germany)
439.6	134	228	Blohm & Voss (Germany)
383.8	117	96	Astilleros Gondan (Spain)
597.1	182	396	Marriotti/Visentini (Italy)
957	291.7	2,100	Kvaerner Masa-Yards (Finland)
957	291.7	2,100	Kvaerner Masa-Yards (Finland)
964.5	294	1,950	Chantiers de l'Atlantique (France)
964.5	294	1,950	Chantiers de l'Atlantique (France)
708.6	216	1,250	Chantiers de l'Atlantique (France)
935	285	2,600	Fincantieri (Italy)
935	285	2,600	Fincantieri (Italy)
713	217.3	720	Chantiers de l'Atlantique (France)
593.7	181	684	Chantiers de l'Atlantique (France)
629.9	192	400	Apuania (Italy)
962.9	263.5	2,100	Meyer Werft (Germany)
590.5	180	800	Blohm & Voss (Germany)
597.1	182	396	Marriotti/Visentini (Italy)
964.9	294.13	2,400	Chantiers de l'Atlantique (France)
840	256	1,900	Ingalls Shipbuilding (USA)
957	291.7	2,100	Kvaerner Masa-Yards (Finland)
882.6	269	2,642	Fincantieri (Italy)
964.5	294	1,950	Chantiers de l'Atlantique (France)
708.6	216	1,250	Chantiers de l'Atlantique (France)
708.6	216	720	Chantiers de l'Atlantique (France)
1019.7	311	3,114	Kvaerner Masa-Yards (Finland)
962.9	263.5	2,100	Meyer Werft (Germany)
964.9	294.13	2,400	Chantiers de l'Atlantique (France)
840	256	1,900	Ingalls Shipbuilding (USA)
882.6	269	2,642	Fincantieri (Italy)
964.5	294	1,950	Chantiers de l'Atlantique (France)

521

INDEX TO SHIPS' RATINGS

SMALL SHIPS (LESS THAN 500 PASSENGERS)
82 Ships/72 Rated

Ship	Score	Rating
Seabourn Goddess I	1799	5
Seabourn Goddess II	1799	5
Seabourn Legend	1796	5
Seabourn Pride	1795	5
Seabourn Spirit	1795	5
Hanseatic	1740	5
Silver Cloud	1729	5
Silver Wind	1729	5
Hebridean Princess	1699	4+
Clipper Odyssey	1678	4+
Sea Cloud	1673	4+
Song of Flower	1651	4+
Paul Gauguin	1645	4+
Radisson Diamond	1640	4+
Clelia II	1613	4+
Le Levant	1609	4+
Minerva	1594	4+
Wind Surf	1577	4+
Wind Song	1548	4
Wind Spirit	1548	4
Wind Star	1548	4
Club Med 2	1546	4
Le Ponant	1540	4
Star Clipper	1530	4
Star Flyer	1530	4
Renaissance Seven	1506	4
Renaissance Eight	1506	4
World Discoverer	1474	4
Bremen	1461	4
Nippon Maru	1441	4
Orient Venus	1405	4
Fuji Maru	1397	3+
Columbus	1383	3+
Galapagos Explorer II	1365	3+
Sovetskiy Soyuz	1292	3+
Kapitan Khlebnikov	1287	3+
Delphin	1279	3+
Yorktown Clipper	1267	3+
Nantucket Clipper	1265	3+
Caledonian Star	1263	3+
Monet	1263	3+
Vistamar	1262	3+
St. Helena	1252	3+

Ship	Score	Rating
Switzerland	1245	3
Polaris	1210	3
Clipper Adventurer	1175	3
Black Prince	1144	3
Astra II	1134	3
Funchal	1097	2+
Explorer	1095	2+
Grande Caribe	1095	2+
Grande Mariner	1095	2+
Odysseus	1091	2+
Niagara Prince	1087	2+
Royal Star	1080	2+
Stella Oceanis	1079	2+
Enchanted Capri	1074	2+
Silver Star	1057	2+
Kristina Regina	1052	2+
Galapagos Discovery	1042	2+
Princesa Amorosa	991	2+
Don Juan	947	2
Professor Khromov	947	2
Wilderness Discoverer	939	2
Wilderness Adventurer	939	2
Orpheus	914	2
Jason	909	2
Dalmacija	895	2
Sir Francis Drake	874	2
Arcadia (Golden Sun Cruises)	724	1+
Atalante	711	1+
Ambasador I	705	1+
Europa	NYR	NYR
Flying Cloud	NYR	NYR
Legacy	NYR	NYR
Mandalay	NYR	NYR
Polynesia	NYR	NYR
Royal Clipper	NYR	NYR
Sea Cloud II	NYR	NYR
Seven Seas Navigator	NYR	NYR
Silver Shadow	NYR	NYR
Yankee Clipper	NYR	NYR

MID-SIZE SHIPS (500–1,000 PASSENGERS)

66 Ships/63 Rated

Ship	Score	Rating
Crystal Symphony	1769	5
Crystal Harmony	1761	5
Seabourn Sun	1739	5
Caronia	1690	4+
Asuka	1681	4+
Pacific Venus	1669	4+
R One	1593	4+
R Two	1593	4+
R Three	1593	4+
R Four	1593	4+
R Five	1593	4+
R Six	1593	4+
Astor	1547	4
Arkona	1532	4
Marco Polo	1523	4
Hyundai Kumgang	1498	4
Norwegian Star	1427	4
Black Watch	1420	4
Saga Rose	1403	4
SuperStar Gemini	1398	3+
Victoria	1395	3+
Maxim Gorkiy	1385	3+
Crown Dynasty	1381	3+
Pacific Princess	1370	3+
Hyundai Pungak	1366	3+
Flamenco	1292	3+
Ocean Majesty	1274	3+
Albatros	1253	3+
Hyundai Bongnae	1245	3
Olympic Countess	1240	3
Sapphire	1220	3
CostaAllegra	1210	3
CostaMarina	1209	3
Azur	1198	3
Bolero	1197	3
Rhapsody	1194	3
Stella Solaris	1193	3
Emerald	1177	3
Seawing	1165	3
Universe Explorer	1159	3
CostaRiviera	1152	3
Enchanted Isle	1134	3
Seawind Crown	1118	3

Ship	Score	Rating
Ausonia	1109	3
Italia Prima	1103	3
Princess Danae	1101	3
World Renaissance	1096	2+
OceanBreeze	1095	2+
Independence	1092	2+
Monterey	1087	2+
SeaBreeze	1080	2+
Symphony	1069	2+
Aegean I	1062	2+
Triton	1047	2+
Fair Princess	1034	2+
Apollon	997	2+
Regal Empress	962	2+
Mermoz	946	2
Dolphin IV	942	2
Princesa Victoria	937	2
Olvia	842	2
Shota Rustaveli	802	2
Taras Shevchenko	782	1+
Ocean Explorer I	NYR	NYR
Olympic Voyager	NYR	NYR
SuperStar Europe	NYR	NYR

LARGE SHIPS (OVER 1,000 PASSENGERS)

85 Ships/75 Rated

Ship	Score	Rating
Queen Elizabeth 2 (Grill Class)	1785	5
Galaxy	1697	4+
Mercury	1697	4+
Century	1696	4+
SuperStar Leo	1672	4+
SuperStar Virgo	1672	4+
Queen Elizabeth 2 (Caronia Class)	1647	4+
Grand Princess	1637	4+
Oriana	1637	4+
Zenith	1631	4+
Horizon	1618	4+
Rotterdam	1608	4+
Dawn Princess	1586	4+
Ocean Princess	1586	4+
Sea Princess	1586	4+
Sun Princess	1586	4+
Disney Magic	1553	4+
Disney Wonder	1553	4+
Royal Princess	1551	4+
Aida	1548	4
Maasdam	1548	4
Ryndam	1548	4
Statendam	1548	4
Veendam	1548	4
Vision of the Seas	1547	4
Rhapsody of the Seas	1538	4
Enchantment of the Seas	1535	4
Grandeur of the Seas	1533	4
Legend of the Seas	1528	4
Splendour of the Seas	1522	4
Sky Princess	1511	4
Crown Princess	1509	4
Regal Princess	1509	4
Nieuw Amsterdam	1498	4
Noordam	1498	4
Westerdam	1480	4
Carnival Destiny	1455	4
Arcadia (P & O Cruises)	1436	4
Norwegian Crown	1434	4
Norwegian Dream	1432	4
Norwegian Wind	1432	4
CostaVictoria	1406	4
Queen Elizabeth 2	1398	3+

Ship	Score	Rating
(Mauretania Class)		
Majesty of the Seas	1394	3+
Monarch of the Seas	1394	3+
Norwegian Sea	1392	3+
Norway	1393	3+
Paradise	1390	3+
Elation	1387	3+
Sovereign of the Seas	1386	3+
Ecstasy	1385	3+
Fantasy	1385	3+
Fascination	1385	3+
Imagination	1385	3+
Inspiration	1385	3+
Sensation	1385	3+
Norwegian Majesty	1378	3+
Star Aquarius	1377	3+
Star Pisces	1377	3+
CostaRomantica	1369	3+
CostaClassica	1368	3+
Nordic Empress	1355	3+
Viking Serenade	1341	3+
Celebration	1318	3+
Holiday	1318	3+
Jubilee	1318	3+
Rembrandt	1274	3+
Sunbird	1275	3+
Melody	1259	3+
Tropicale	1239	3
Carousel	1226	3
Sundream	1226	3
Topaz	1096	2+
Oceanic	1093	2+
IslandBreeze	1087	2+
Aurora	NYR	NYR
Carnival Triumph	NYR	NYR
Carnival Victory	NYR	NYR
CostaAtlantica	NYR	NYR
Millennium	NYR	NYR
Mistral	NYR	NYR
Norwegian Sky	NYR	NYR
Volendam	NYR	NYR
Voyager of the Seas	NYR	NYR
Zaandam	NYR	NYR

CRUISE LINE ADDRESSES

MAJOR CRUISE LINE HEAD OFFICE ADDRESSES

NORTH AMERICA

Abercrombie & Kent
1520 Kensington Road
Oak Brook, IL 60523-2141
USA
web site: www.aandktours.com

Alaska's Glacier Bay Tours and Cruises
Glacier Bay Park Concessions, Inc.
520 Pike Street, Suite 1400
Seattle, WA 98101
USA
web site: www.glacierbaytours.com

Alaska Sightseeing/Cruise West
4th & Battery Building, Suite 700
Seattle, WA 98121
USA
web site: www.cruisewest.com

American Canadian Caribbean Line
461 Water Street
Warren, RI 02885
USA
web site: www.accl-smallships.com

American Hawaii Cruises
1380 Port of New Orleans Place
New Orleans, LA 70130-1890
USA
web site: www.cruisehawaii.com

Bergen Line
405 Park Avenue
New York, NY 10022
USA
web site: www.bergenline.com

Cape Canaveral Cruise Line
7099 North Atlantic Avenue
Cape Canaveral, FL 32920
USA

Carnival Cruise Lines
3655 NW 87 Avenue
Miami, FL 33178-2428
USA
web site: www.carnival.com

Celebrity Cruises
1050 Port Boulevard
Miami, FL 33124
USA
web site: www.celebrity-cruises.com

528

Classical Cruises/Travel Dynamics
132 East 70 Street
New York, NY 10021
USA
web site: www.classicalcruises.com

Clipper Cruise Line
7711 Bonhomme Avenue
St. Louis, MO 63105
USA
web site: www.clippercruise.com

Club Mediterranee, SA
75 Valencia Ave.
Coral Gables, FL 33134
USA
web site: www.clubmed.com

Commodore Cruise Line
4000 Hollywood Blvd, Suite 385 South
Hollywood, FL 33021
USA
web site: www.commodorecruise.com

Costa Cruises
World Trade Center
80 SW 8 Street, 27th Floor
Miami, FL 33130-3097
USA
web site: www.costacruises.com

Crystal Cruises
2049 Century Park East
Suite 1400
Los Angeles, CA 90067
USA
web site: www.crystalcruises.com

Cunard Line
6100 Blue Lagoon Drive, Suite 400
Miami, FL 33126
USA
web site: www.cunardline.com

Delta Queen Steamboat Company
30 Robin Street Wharf
New Orleans, LA 70130
USA
web site: www.deltaqueen.com

Disney Cruise Line
210 Celebration Place, Suite 400
Celebration, FL 33747-4600
USA
web site: www.disney.com/DisneyCruise

Eurocruises (Delphin Seereisen GmbH, Fred Olsen Cruise Lines, Kristina Cruises)
303 West 13th Street
New York, NY 10014
USA

First European Cruises
95 Madison Avenue, Suite 1203
New York, NY 10016
USA

Holland America Line
300 Elliott Avenue West
Seattle, WA 98119
USA
web site: www.hollandamerica.com

Lindblad Special Expeditions
720 Fifth Avenue, Suite 605
New York, NY 10019
USA
web site: www.expeditions.com

Marine Expeditions
890 Young Street, 3rd Floor
Toronto, Ontario
CANADA M4W 3P4

Mediterranean Shipping Cruises
420 5th Avenue
New York, NY 10018
USA

Norwegian Cruise Line
7665 Corporate Center Drive
Miami, FL 33126
USA
web site: www.ncl.com

Orient Lines
1510 SE 17th Street
Ft. Lauderdale, FL 33316
USA
web site: www.orientlines.com

Premier Cruise Lines
400 Challenger Road
Port Canaveral, FL 32920
USA
web site: www.premiercruises.com

Princess Cruises
10100 Santa Monica Blvd, #1800
Los Angeles, CA 90067-4189
USA
web site: www.princesscruises.com

Quark Expeditions
980 Post Road
Darien, CT 06820
USA
web site:
www.quark-expeditions.com

Radisson Seven Seas Cruises
600 Corporate Drive, Suite 410
Ft. Lauderdale, FL 33180
USA
web site: www.rssc.com

Raymond & Whitcomb
400 Madison Avenue
New York, NY 10017
USA

Regal Cruises
300 Regal Cruises Way
Palmetto, FL 34220
USA
web site: www.regalcruises.com

Renaissance Cruises
1800 Eller Drive, Suite 300
Ft. Lauderdale, FL 33335-0307
USA
web site:
www.renaissancecruises.com

Royal Caribbean International
1050 Caribbean Way
Miami, FL 33132-2096
USA
web site: www.royalcaribbean.com

Royal Olympic Cruises
One Rockefeller Plaza
New York, NY 10020
USA
web site:
www.royalolympiccruises.com

Seabourn Cruise Line
6100 Blue Lagoon Drive
Suite 400
Miami, FL 33126
USA
web site: www.seabourn.com

Silversea Cruises
110 E. Broward Boulevard
Suite 300
Ft. Lauderdale, FL 33301
USA
web site: www.silversea.com

Society Expeditions, Inc.
2001 Western Ave., Suite 300
Seattle, WA 98121
USA
web site:
www.societyexpeditions.com

Star Clippers
4101 Salzedo Avenue
Coral Gables, FL 33146
USA
web site: www.star-clippers.com

Tall Ship Adventures
1010 South Joliet Street, Suite 200
Aurora, CO 80012
USA
web site: www.asource.com/tallship

Temptress Adventure Cruises
1600 N.W. Le Jeune Road
Suite 301
Miami, FL 33126
USA
web site:
www.temptresscruises.com

Voyager Cruise Line
520 Pike Street, Suite 1400
Seattle, WA 98101
USA

Windjammer Barefoot Cruises
1759 Bay Road
Miami Beach, FL 33119
USA
web site: www.windjammer.com

Windstar Cruises
300 Elliott Avenue West
Seattle, WA 98119
USA
web site:
www.windstarcruises.com

World Cruise Company
890 Young Street, 3rd Floor
Toronto, Ontario
CANADA M4W 3P4
web site: www.worldcruiseco.com

World Explorer Cruises
555 Montgomery Avenue
San Francisco, CA 94111
USA
web site: www.wecruise.com

REST OF THE WORLD

Airtours Sun Cruises
Wavell House
Holcombe Road
Helmshore, Rossendale
Lancashire BB4 4NB
UK

Arkona Reisen
Am Seehafen 1
Siemenstrasse 90
63203 New Isenberg
GERMANY

Compagnie Les Isles des Ponant Cruises
60 Boulebard Marchal Juin
44100 Nantes
FRANCE

Costa Crociere
Via Gabriele D'Annunzio, 2/80
16121 Genoa
ITALY
web site: www.costacruises.com

Croatia Cruise Lines
Riva 16
51000 Rijeka
CROATIA
web site:
www.globalquesttravel.com

Croisieres Paquet
5 rue Gabriel Faure
06046 Nice - Cedex 1
FRANCE

Delphin Seereisen GmbH
Blumenstrasse 20
63004 Offenbach/Main
GERMANY

Direct Cruises
182 Upper Richmond Road
Putney
London SW15 2SH
ENGLAND

Discoverer Reederei GmbH
Marcusallee 9
28359 Bremen
GERMANY

Festival Cruises
99 Akti Miouli
GR 185 38, Piraeus
GREECE

Fred Olsen Cruise Lines
Fred Olsen House
White House Road
Ipswich
Suffolk 1P1 5LL
ENGLAND

Golden Sea Cruises
Filonos 64
Piraeus 185 35
GREECE

Golden Sun Cruises
16 Voukourestiou Street
10671 Athens
GREECE
web site:
www.goldensuncruises.com

Hapag-Lloyd Seetouristik
Ballindamm 25
D-20095 Hamburg
GERMANY
web site: www.hapag-lloyd.com

Hebridean Island Cruises Ltd
Acorn Park
Skipton
North Yorkshire BD23 2UE
ENGLAND

Jahn Reisen GmbH
Eisenheimerstrasse 61
8000 Munich 21
GERMANY

Klein Tours
Avenue Shyris 1000
Quito
ECUADOR
web site:
ecuador@kleintours.com.ec

Kristina Cruises
Korkeavuorenkatu 2
Kotka
FINLAND

Leisure Cruises
P.O. Box 1312
CH-8640 Rapperswil
SWITZERLAND

Louis Cruise Lines
54-58 Evangoros Avenue (P.O. Box
1306)
Nicosia
CYPRUS

Mitsui OSK (Passenger Line) Ltd
Syosen Mitsui Building
1-1 Taramonon 2-Chome
Minato-ku
Tokyo 105
JAPAN

NYK Line (Nippon Yusen Kaisha)
CPO Box 1250
Tokyo 100-91
JAPAN
web site: www.asukacruise.co.jp

Neckermann Seereisen
Hochhaus am Beseler Platz
6000 Frankfurt am Main 1
GERMANY

New Paradise Cruises
P.O. Box 50157
3601 Limassol
CYPRUS

P&O Cruises
77 New Oxford Street
London WC1A 1PP
ENGLAND
web site: www.pocruises.com

P&O Holidays
P.O. Box 5287
Sydney 2001
New South Wales
AUSTRALIA

Phoenix Seereisen
Kolnstrasse 80
53111 Bonn
GERMANY

Plantours
Obern Street 69
Bremen 28195
GERMANY

St. Helena Shipping
The Shipyard
Porthleven
Cornwall TR13 9JA
ENGLAND

SAGA Cruises (Saga Shipping)
Folkestone
Kent
ENGLAND

Sea Cloud Cruises
Ballindamm 17
D-200095 Hamburg
GERMANY
web site: www.seacloud.com

Seetours International GmbH
Seilerstrasse 23
60313 Frankfurt
GERMANY

Spice Island Cruises
Jalan Padang Galak No. 25
Sanur, Denpasar 80228
(PO Box 3581)
Bali
INDONESIA

Star Cruises
Star Cruises Terminal
Pulau Indah
PO Box No. 288
42009 Pelabuhan Klang
Selangor Darul Ehsan
MALAYSIA
web site: www.starcruises.com.my

Star Line Cruises
P.O. Box 81443
Mombasa
KENYA

Sun Cruises
304 Orchard Road
#05-0-2 Lucky Plaza
238863
SINGAPORE

Swan Hellenic Cruises
77 New Oxford Street
London WC1A 1PP
ENGLAND
web site: www.swan-hellenic.co.uk

Thomson Cruises
Greater London House
Hampstead Road
London NW1 7SD
ENGLAND
web site:
www.thomson-holidays.com

Transocean Tours
Postfach 10 09 07
28009 Bremen
GERMANY

Transtours
49 avenue de l'Opera
75002 Paris
FRANCE

Venus Cruise
13-F Osaka Ekimae No. 2
1-2-2 1300 Umeda
Osaka 530
JAPAN

Other Cruise Line Web Addresses

Canodros	www.canodros.com
Captain Cook Cruises	www.captcookcrus.com.au
Cruceros Australis	www.australis.com
Eurocruises	www.eurocruises.com
KD River Cruises of Europe	www.rivercruises.com
Victoria Cruises	www.victoriacruises.com

SHIP AND CRUISE LINE INDEX

A

Abercrombie & Kent 10, 115, 121, 123, 142, 193, 240, 528

Aegean I 67, 130, 144, 525

Aida 20-21, 51-52, 67, 101, 146-148, 335, 518, 526

Airtours (Sun Cruises) 10, 14, 67, 78, 142-144, 186-187, 420-421, 449-452, 505, 517-519, 523, 529-530

Alaska Sightseeing/Cruise West 10, 115, 142, 528

Albatros 67, 130, 149, 524

Ambasador I 67, 151, 523

American Canadian Caribbean Line 10, 115, 142, 259-260, 319, 486-487, 528

American Hawaii Cruises 10, 72, 78, 142, 278, 510, 516-517, 519, 528

Apollon 67, 152, 525

Arcadia (Golden Sun Cruises) 67, 75, 143-144, 154, 523, 529

Arcadia (P&O Cruises) 35, 67, 72, 75, 78, 130, 132, 142, 155-156, 166, 352-353, 473-474, 511, 518, 520, 526, 530

Arcalia Shipping 10, 142, 366, 515, 517/Classic International Cruises 10, 142, 251, 366

Arkona 10, 20, 52, 67, 142, 146-147, 157-159, 335, 518, 524, 529

Arkona Touristik 10, 146, 157

Astor 67, 130, 157, 159, 511, 518, 524

Astra II 67, 161-162, 523

Asuka 67, 130, 163, 515, 524

Atalante 67, 165, 523

Aurora 20, 55, 67, 75, 115, 166-167, 503, 520, 527, 529

Ausonia 67, 168, 525

Azur 67, 170, 175, 313, 516, 524

B

Black Prince 67, 173, 523

Black Sea Shipping Company 234, 507, 509, 515

Black Watch 27, 67, 174, 517, 524

Bolero 67, 175-176, 313, 524

Bremen 67, 101, 123, 177-178, 369, 516, 522, 529-530

C

Caledonian Star 67, 179, 522

Canodros 10, 255, 530

Cape Canaveral Cruise Line 10, 142, 528

Carnival Cruise Lines 3, 10, 20-21, 27, 33-34, 51, 63, 69, 72, 75, 78, 132, 142, 152, 180-183, 186, 188-189, 229-230, 242-243, 270, 277, 280, 283, 287, 359, 422, 452, 459, 466, 470, 509-510, 513-517, 520, 528

Carnival Destiny 20, 36, 43, 62, 67, 180, 182-183, 526

Carnival Triumph 20, 43, 67, 182, 527

Carnival Victory 67, 183, 520, 527

Caronia 67, 184-185, 368-371, 524, 526

Carousel 27, 67, 75, 186, 450, 452, 527

Celebration 19, 67, 69, 188, 404, 414, 513, 527-528

Celebrity Cruises 10, 33-35, 66, 72, 78, 142, 190-191, 257-258, 272-273, 306-307, 309, 313, 477, 500, 514-516, 518, 520, 528

Century 20-21, 33, 42-43, 66-67, 100, 190-191, 258, 273, 306-307, 309, 500-502, 526

Classic International Cruises 10, 142, 251, 366

Classical Cruises 10, 142, 293-294, 528

Clelia II 67, 192, 522

Clipper Adventurer 67, 194, 523

Clipper Cruise Line 10, 115, 142, 194-196, 318, 497, 528

Clipper Odyssey 67, 196, 518, 522

Club Med 2 67, 124, 197, 522

Club Med Cruises 10, 197

Columbus 67, 115, 125, 132, 198-199, 266, 502, 522

Commodore Cruise Line 10, 142, 211, 234-235, 507, 517, 519, 528

Compagnie des Isles du Ponant 10, 142, 293, 295

CostaAllegra 67, 200-201, 205, 524

CostaAtlantica 67, 202, 520, 527

CostaClassica 17, 43, 67, 203, 207-208, 210, 516, 527

Costa Cruises 5, 10, 33-34, 89, 142, 200, 202-203, 205-210, 366, 463, 516-518, 520, 528

531

DEAR PASSENGER,

You are most welcome to send me your observations concerning any recent cruises taken. Please complete the following basic information when sending comments (both positive and negative) concerning your recent cruise experience. The best Pet Peeves may be incorporated in the next edition of this book.

Although I cannot acknowledge receipt of this comment form, due to my non-stop travel schedule, I do thank you for your input, and for purchasing this book.

Cruise Date _____

Ship Name_____

Cruise Line _____

Suite/Cabin Number _____

Dining Room Seating:

_____(Open) _____(First)_____(Second)

Your Comments _____

_____

_____

Your Pet Peeves

(1) _____

_____

(2) _____

_____

(3) _____

_____

Please send to the address below:

Mr Douglas Ward
Berlitz Guide to Cruising
Canada House
1 Carrick Way
New Milton
Hampshire BH25 6UD
ENGLAND